The Insider's Guide to

THE SAT*

KARL WEBER

Author of nearly 20 books offering frank and impartial test-preparation advice

www.petersons.com

PETERSON'S
THOMSON LEARNING™

Australia • Canada • Mexico • Singapore • Spain • United Kingdom • United States

PETERSON'S
THOMSON LEARNING

About Peterson's

Founded in 1966, Peterson's, a division of Thomson Learning, is the nation's largest and most respected provider of lifelong learning online resources, software, reference guides, and books. The Education Supersite℠ at petersons.com—the Web's most heavily traveled education resource—has searchable databases and interactive tools for contacting U.S.-accredited institutions and programs. CollegeQuest℠ (CollegeQuest.com) offers a complete solution for every step of the college decision-making process. GradAdvantage™ (GradAdvantage.org), developed with Educational Testing Service, is the only electronic admissions service capable of sending official graduate test score reports with a candidate's online application. Peterson's serves more than 55 million education consumers annually.

Thomson Learning is among the world's leading providers of lifelong learning, serving the needs of individuals, learning institutions, and corporations with products and services for both traditional classrooms and for online learning. For more information about the products and services offered by Thomson Learning, please visit www.thomsonlearning.com. Headquartered in Stamford, Connecticut, with offices worldwide, Thomson Learning is part of The Thomson Corporation (www.thomson.com), a leading e-information and solutions company in the business, professional, and education marketplaces. The Corporation's common shares are listed on the Toronto and London stock exchanges.

For more information, contact Peterson's, 2000 Lenox Drive, Lawrenceville, NJ 08648; 800-338-3282; or find us on the World Wide Web at: www.petersons.com/about

ISBN 0-7689-0594-X

Printed in Canada

10 9 8 7 6 5 4 3 2 02 01

Acknowledgments

The *Insider's Guide to the SAT Assessment* has been a team effort. I've been fortunate enough to have the assistance of a very talented group of educators and writers who skillfully crafted significant portions of the manuscript, drawing on both their considerable knowledge and notable literary skills to complement my abilities beautifully. In particular, I wish to acknowledge and thank:

Dr. Harold D. Shane
Peter Lanzer
Nancy J. Brandwein
Robert A. Kaplan
Laura A. Weber
Mary-Jo D. Weber

Naturally, any errors or inadequacies that the book may contain are mine alone.

I also want to thank Bob Schaeffer of FairTest and John Nelson and Andrea Wilson of Kaplan Educational Centers for their helpful responses to my many inquiries. Thanks, too, to Karen Reinisch, Stephanie Hammett, and Bob Sehlinger.

And my gratitude especially, and always, to Mary-Jo Weber, my wife, whose love makes it all worthwhile.

Karl Weber
Chappaqua, New York

About the Author

Karl Weber has been helping students prepare for the SAT and other standardized exams for twenty years. He was a teacher, writer, and editor for Stanley H. Kaplan Educational Centers and later designed and taught the verbal test-preparation programs at Mathworks, a school in New York City. Weber is featured on a popular series of test-preparation videos published by Video Aided Instruction, a producer of educational materials located in Roslyn Heights, New York.

Weber is also well known in the publishing industry as an editor, literary agent, and book developer. He was the editor of two of the best investment books of all time, as selected in 1997 by *Worth* magazine, and also worked with former president Jimmy Carter on two best-selling books about the Christian religion, *Living Faith* and *Sources of Strength.* He lives with Mary-Jo Weber, his wife of 25 years, in Chappaqua, New York.

SAT Schedule for 2000–2001

SAT I and SAT II subject exams will be given on six Saturdays during the 2000–2001 school year. Current dates, according to the Educational Testing Service (ETS) are: October 14, November 4, and December 2, 2000; and January 27, May 5, and June 2, 2001. In addition, the SAT I only will be given on March 31 (in the United States and its possessions only).

Note that you must register approximately five weeks in advance of your preferred test date. ETS's late registration option gives you as few as four additional days in which to register, and there's an extra charge (currently $15) for that service. Sign up early and don't risk missing out.

Also note: If you are considering taking the SAT I more than once in order to maximize your scores, we recommend you choose the October, January, or May exams. Reason: Only these exams are included in ETS's "Question and Answer" service, which allows you to see your test after you've taken it. This service can be ordered when you register for the test, for an additional fee of $10.00. It's a crucial tool for improving your scores the second time around.

See Chapters 11 and 12 in this book for more information on how to plan your testing schedule for the greatest benefit to you.

Contents

Why "*Insider's*"?
The *Insider's Guide* Declaration of Independence xiii

Introduction
How This Guide Was Researched and Written xvii

Part I First Things First **1**

Chapter 1 An Insider's Look at the SAT **2**
Instructions 2
The Insider's SAT Diagnostic Test Answer Sheet 3
The Insider's SAT Diagnostic Test 5
Answer Key 28
Scoring Guide 29
Score Conversion Table 31
Explanatory Answers 33

Chapter 2 Making Your Plan **42**
How to Get Where You Want to Go 42
The Insider's Route to Top Scores 42
Making the Most of the Time You Have 45
Just the Facts 49

Part II Getting Inside the SAT **51**

Chapter 3 Finding Your Way Around the SAT **52**
The Official Description 52
The Insider's Report 55
Making the Test Work for You 58
Just the Facts 64

Chapter 4 Analogies **65**
The Test Capsule 65
The Official Description 66
The Insider's Report:
Strategies That Really Work 67
The Insider's Report: The Best Tips 71
The Insider's Report:
The Most Important Warnings 73
Just the Facts 74
Practice, Practice, Practice: Analogy Exercises 75
Answer Key 86
Explanatory Answers 86

Chapter 5 Sentence Completions **93**
The Test Capsule 93
The Official Description 94
The Insider's Report: Strategies That Really Work... 95
The Insider's Report: The Best Tips 101
The Insider's Report:
The Most Important Warnings 102
Just the Facts 104
Practice, Practice, Practice:
Sentence Completion Exercises 105
Answer Key 121
Explanatory Answers 121

Chapter 6 Critical Reading **129**
The Test Capsule 129
The Official Description 130
The Insider's Report: Strategies That Really Work... 131
The Insider's Report: The Best Tips 137
The Insider's Report:
The Most Important Warnings 139
Just the Facts 141
Practice, Practice, Practice:
Critical Reading Exercises 142
Answer Key 170
Explanatory Answers 170

Chapter 7 Multiple-Choice Math **177**
The Test Capsule 177
The Official Description 178
The Insider's Report: Strategies That Really Work... 179
The Insider's Report: The Best Tips 183
The Insider's Report:
The Most Important Warnings 190
Just the Facts 192
Practice, Practice, Practice:
Multiple-Choice Math Exercises 193
Answer Key 215
Explanatory Answers 216

Chapter 8 Quantitative Comparisons **231**
The Test Capsule 231
The Official Description 232
The Insider's Report: Strategies That Really Work... 233
The Insider's Report: The Best Tips 239
The Insider's Report: The Most Important Warnings 240
Just the Facts 243
Practice, Practice, Practice: Quantitative Comparison Exercises 244
Answer Key 276
Explanatory Answers 277

Chapter 9 Math Grid-Ins **291**
The Test Capsule 291
The Official Description 292
The Insider's Report: Strategies That Really Work... 294
The Insider's Report: The Best Tips 296
The Insider's Report: The Most Important Warnings 297
Just the Facts 298
Practice, Practice, Practice: Math Grid-In Exercises . 299
Answer Key 317
Explanatory Answers 323

Part III The Insider's SAT **335**

Chapter 10 The Insider's SAT Sample Test **336**
Instructions 336
The Insider's SAT Sample Test Answer Sheet 337
The Insider's SAT Sample Test 339
Answer Key 376
Scoring Guide 377
Score Conversion Table 379
Explanatory Answers 381

Part IV Making It Official **399**

Chapter 11 Scheduling and Taking the Test **400**
Deciding When to Take the SAT 400
Registering for the Exam 401
The Insider's Report: Know Your Options 402
When Test Time Comes 405
Just the Facts 407

Chapter 12 Understanding Your Scores 408
Your SAT Score Report 408
How Colleges Interpret SAT Scores 411
The Insider's Report: Know Your Options 412
Just the Facts 418

Chapter 13 The Insider's Tip Sheet 419
Overall Strategies for the SAT 419
Verbal Strategies 420
Math Strategies 421

Part V Appendices **423**

Appendix A The Insider's SAT Word List 425

Appendix B The Insider's SAT Math Review 461

Appendix C The Insider's Stress-Buster's Guide 507

Appendix D College Admissions Calendar and Checklist 515

Appendix E College Application Log 521

Appendix F State Student Financial Aid Offices 525

Appendix G Financial Aid Glossary 533

The *Insider's Guide* Declaration of Independence

The SAT has become one of the crucial hurdles in the lives of most Americans. Your performance on the SAT plays a major role in determining whether or not you'll be able to attend the college of your choice.

Taking the test is also a major rite of passage for American teenagers. Every year, close to two million students (along with their parents, friends, and families) invest countless days and nights in the anxiety-, hope-, and fear-inducing rituals centered on the exam: cramming beforehand, sweating through the four-hour testing ordeal, nervously comparing notes afterward, and checking the mailbox daily looking for that oh-so-slow-in-coming envelope containing the fateful scores. It all feels nerve-wracking and more than a little unfair.

To survive the process—and to make it work for you—you need help.

YOU CAN'T DEPEND ON THE TEST-MAKERS

Unfortunately, it seems that almost everyone involved in the standardized testing industry (and make no mistake, it *is* an industry—a big one) has some kind of ax to grind.

The test-makers themselves—the College Board, which sponsors the SAT program, and the Educational Testing Service, which writes and administers the test—have a huge vested interest in the survival and credibility of their exam. Both the College Board and ETS are not-for-profit organizations. That doesn't make them immune to the pressures felt by every organization in a competitive industry. They make their living by producing the SAT for use by colleges as part of the student admission process. The fine salaries and nice offices enjoyed by the executives at the College Board and ETS are dependent on having college admission officers, and the general public, continue to believe that the SAT is a useful, accurate, and basically fair tool for measuring student abilities. If that belief were to vanish, colleges would stop asking students to take the SAT, and the people who work for the College Board and ETS would have to find new jobs.

Therefore, everything the test-makers say publicly about the SAT must serve the purpose of bolstering public confidence in the accuracy and fairness of the exam. That is why, for decades, the test-makers strenuously claimed that it was impossible to improve your SAT scores significantly by preparing beforehand. They feared that, if it became generally recognized that SAT scores could be improved through study programs, the perceived fairness of the SAT program might ultimately crumble.

In recent years, under pressure from students, parents, public advocacy groups, and politicians, the test-makers have changed their stance to some degree. For the first time, they have made some actual past exams publicly available (they used to be kept strictly secret). They stopped calling it the "Scholastic *Aptitude* Test," which implies that the exam measures some unchanging, innate ability. And they admitted—however grudgingly—that study and preparation could improve SAT scores significantly. (Not missing a beat, they also began publishing and selling their own SAT preparation materials.)

Nonetheless, concerns about image and credibility still constrain the test-makers. They must be careful to avoid any suggestion that the SAT, or any part of the SAT, can be successfully negotiated by mastering a handful of relatively simple techniques. If students can score higher on the SAT by using a few easy-to-learn "tricks," then the exam begins to appear more like a gimmick than a serious educational tool. From the test-makers' point of view, that would never do.

Thus, the test-makers have a vested interest in stressing how difficult, time-consuming, and intellectually challenging it is to prepare for the SAT. They want desperately to bolster the image of the SAT as an "unbeatable" exam. It's understandable. In their shoes, most of us would feel—and behave—the same.

Don't misunderstand. We don't consider the College Board or ETS crass, unprofessional, or venal. They are highly competent specialists in test design and administration, and undoubtedly they sincerely believe in the value of their work. But the nature of that work makes it impossible for them to offer you the kind of disinterested, unbiased, and completely honest advice you need about the best and easiest ways to prepare for the SAT.

TEST-PREP SCHOOLS HAVE THEIR OWN AGENDA

What about the other sources of test-taking advice and information? Aren't they immune to these biases?

Yes, but most of them have their own biases. For example, over the last two decades, several nationwide chains of test-preparation schools have sprung up. They offer classroom courses, supplemented with printed and electronic study material, to help students prepare for the SAT and other exams. Some of these have become big businesses in their own right, owned by or affiliated with major media conglomerates. You can buy books and software bearing the names of these schools and containing some of the techniques and strategies taught in their classroom programs.

Naturally, like any business people, the executives who manage these schools are interested in keeping profits high. To do this, they must funnel as many students as possible through their classroom programs. Given a choice, they'd much rather have you buy one of their ambitious, multi-week courses than a book or even a piece of software. (The profit on a book that costs $15 to $20 can't begin to compare with the profit on an $800 course.) Thus, they must view their books primarily as promotional vehicles for their schools. They hope that some of the students who buy their books will be sufficiently impressed—and perhaps sufficiently intimidated—to sign up for a class.

In their case, the vested interest lies in making the SAT appear scary enough to drive you into an $800 classroom program—and in making the test-taking strategies and techniques you need to learn appear complicated and arcane enough to demand weeks of work with a teacher or tutor.

Again, don't misunderstand. Some test-preparation schools offer fine programs. (In Chapter 2, we'll give you some pointers about how to evaluate them and decide whether a classroom course is a good choice for you.) And some of the books and software they produce can be quite helpful in preparing for an exam. But, just as with the test-makers themselves, we think the inherent self-interest in how the test-prep schools do business inevitably colors the kind of advice they give you and the kinds of preparation they recommend.

OUR PLEDGE

We have no such bias. We have no vested interest in the reputation or image of the SAT, and we are not selling classroom courses for any exam. Our only concern is to offer you the most efficient, accurate, and useful guidance for earning your highest possible score on the SAT. If a particular type of math question can be solved without performing any calculations, or a certain kind of analogy question can be answered even if you don't recognize some of the words, or some parts of a reading passage can be safely ignored, we're free to say so, thus letting you focus your time and energy in more effective ways—and earn a higher score in the process.

That's why we proudly bear the banner of the *Insider's Guides*. Authorized and controlled by no one, we serve only one master: you, our reader. Thanks for making the *Insider's Guide* part of your preparation program for the ACT. We hope you'll enjoy using it to boost your test scores and help you gain admission to the college of your dreams.

How This Guide Was Researched and Written

The authors of this book are specialists in test-preparation, teaching, and the writing of educational materials. We've followed the development of the SAT for twenty years, tracking and analyzing the changes in the kinds of questions used and the skills tested. We've also worked with students (and teachers) in various settings, helping them to develop the test-taking abilities and self-confidence needed to do well on the exam. (We've even prepared children of our own for the SAT.)

Based on these years of experience, we've developed a keen awareness of what the SAT is like and what techniques the test-makers use to measure the strengths and weaknesses of individual students. Equally important, we've developed a strong sense as to what kinds of test-taking strategies most students find really beneficial and which ones, frankly, are more complicated or confusing than helpful. This expertise has helped to shape both the contents and the style of this guide.

The individual chapters are each based on extensive analysis of actual SAT exams. Take, for example, "The Insider's SAT Word List." Rather than simply create a vocabulary list based on instinct or on the recommendations of high school English teachers, we started by compiling a list of all vocabulary words actually tested on recent SAT exams, including difficult words used in answer choices, vocabulary questions related to reading passages, and sentence completion and analogy questions. We then selected the words that turned up most frequently on the exam, eliminating some that would have made the list only through the quirk of appearing in a particular reading passage and are unlikely to recur any time soon.

To increase the value of the list as a learning tool, we then added not only clear, accurate definitions and sample sentences illustrating the meanings of the words, but also word root explanations—we call them Word Origins—that will help you to connect these words to others that have appeared on the SAT. This will make it easy for you to learn two, three, or four new words rather than one at a time. The result, we believe, is the most up-to-date, complete, and truly useful SAT vocabulary list currently available. And we've applied a similar approach to every topic on the exam.

Special Features

1. The Insider's SAT Word List
2. The Insider's SAT Math Review
3. The Insider's Stress-Buster's Guide
4. College Admissions Calendar and Checklist
5. College Application Log
6. State Student Financial Aid Offices
7. Financial Aid Glossary

Part I

First Things First

Chapter 1

An Insider's Look at the SAT

INSTRUCTIONS

The following Insider's SAT Diagnostic Test will provide you with your first look at the format, contents, and difficulty levels of the SAT. It will also allow you to diagnose your strengths and weaknesses and help you focus on the skills and test areas where you have the greatest opportunity to boost your SAT score.

This test is about half the length of the real SAT. Take it under true testing conditions. Complete the entire test in a single sitting. Eliminate distractions (TV, music) and clear away notes and reference materials.

Time each section of the test separately with a stopwatch or kitchen timer, or have someone else time you. If you run out of time before answering all the questions, stop and draw a line under the last question you finished. Then go on to the next test section. When you are done, score yourself based only on the questions you finished in the allotted time. Later, for practice purposes, you should answer the questions you were unable to complete in time.

Enter your responses on the answer sheets provided on pages 3 and 4. The answer key, explanatory answers, and information about interpreting your test results appear at the end of the test, beginning on page 28.

The Insider's SAT Diagnostic Test Answer Sheet

Section 1

1. A B C D	7. A B C D	13. A B C D	19. A B C D	25. A B C D
2. A B C D	8. A B C D	14. A B C D	20. A B C D	26. A B C D
3. A B C D	9. A B C D	15. A B C D	21. A B C D	27. A B C D
4. A B C D	10. A B C D	16. A B C D	22. A B C D	28. A B C D
5. A B C D	11. A B C D	17. A B C D	23. A B C D	29. A B C D
6. A B C D	12. A B C D	18. A B C D	24. A B C D	30. A B C D

Section 2

1. A B C D	3. A B C D	5. A B C D	7. A B C D	9. A B C D
2. A B C D	4. A B C D	6. A B C D	8. A B C D	10. A B C D

Section 3

1. A B C D	4. A B C D	7. A B C D	10. A B C D	12. A B C D
2. A B C D	5. A B C D	8. A B C D	11. A B C D	13. A B C D
3. A B C D	6. A B C D	9. A B C D		

Section 4

1. A B C D	4. A B C D	7. A B C D	10. A B C D	13. A B C D
2. A B C D	5. A B C D	8. A B C D	11. A B C D	14. A B C D
3. A B C D	6. A B C D	9. A B C D	12. A B C D	15. A B C D

16.

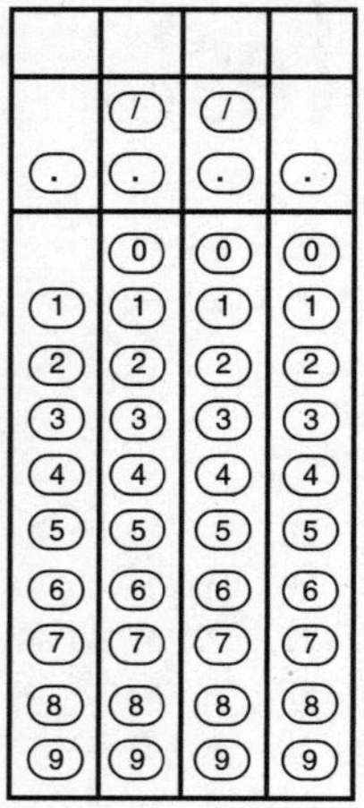

17.

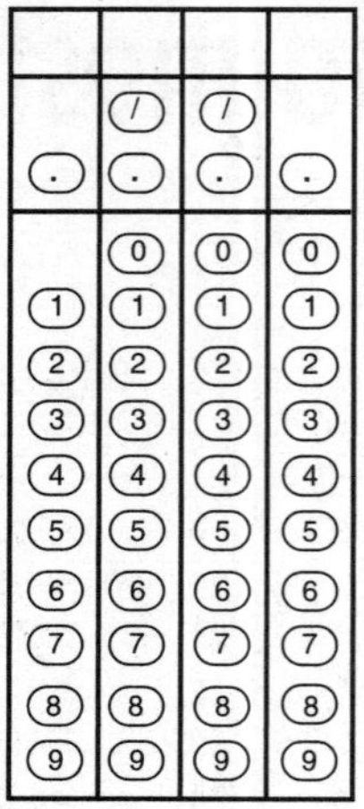

18.

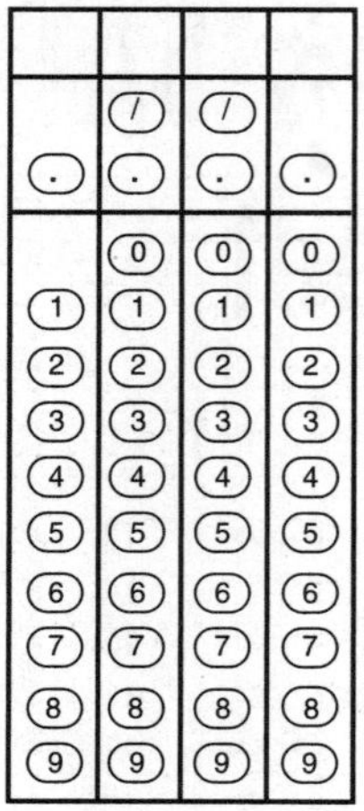

19.

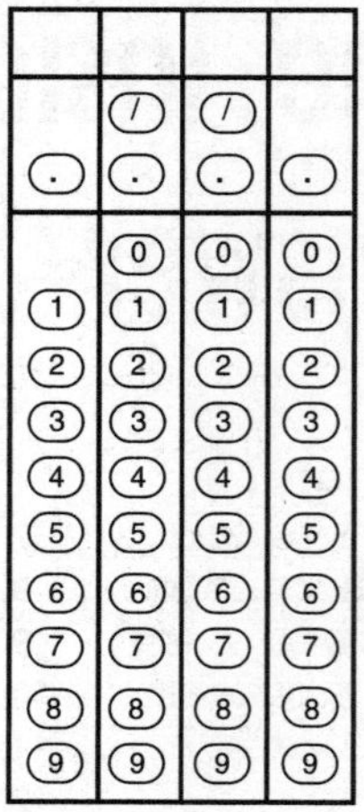

20.

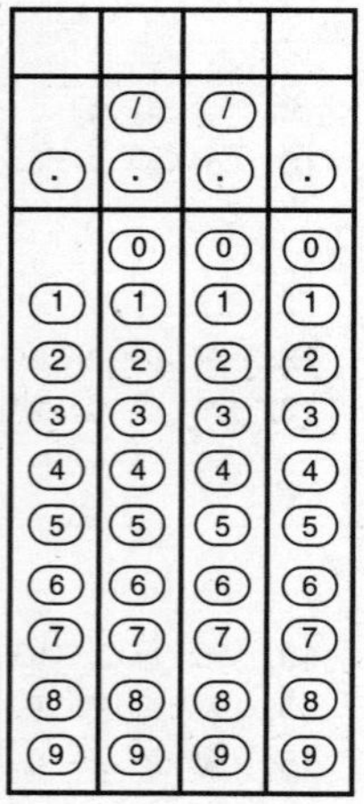

21.

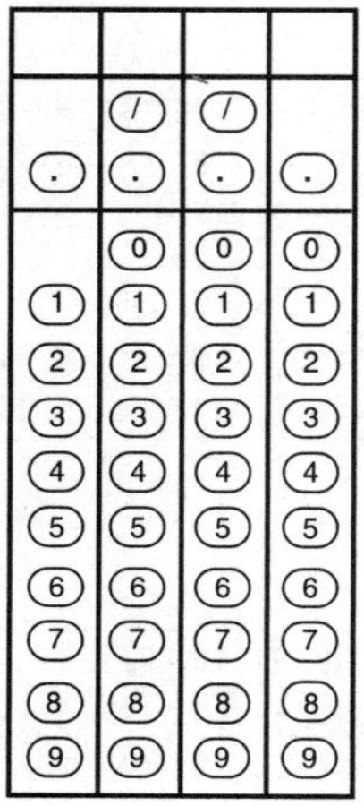

22.

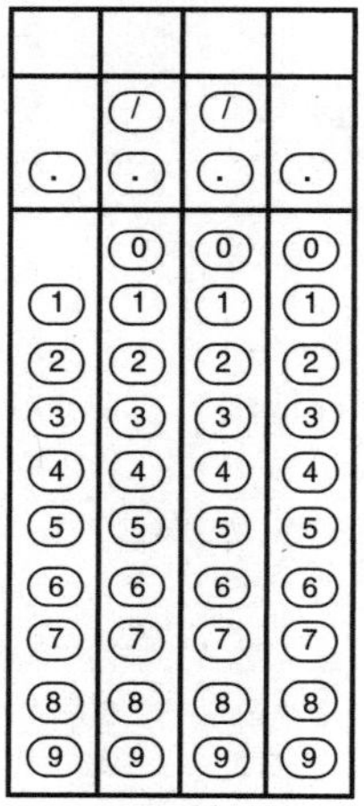

23.

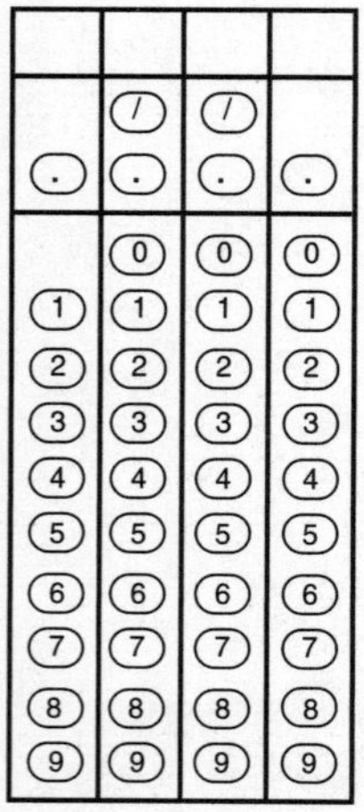

24.

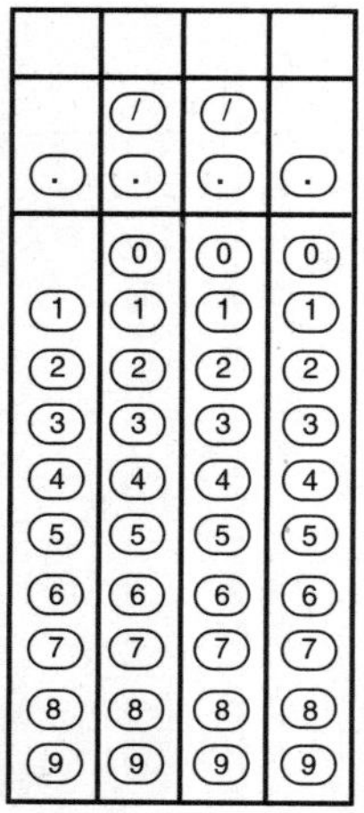

25.

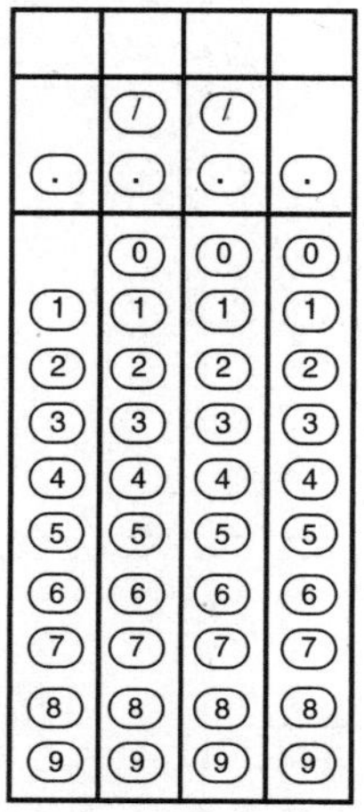

SECTION 1

30 Questions

Time—30 Minutes

For each question in this section, select the best answer from among the choices given and fill in the corresponding oval on the answer sheet.

Each sentence below has one or two blanks, each blank indicating that something has been omitted. Beneath the sentence are five words or sets of words labeled (A) through (E). Choose the word or set of words that, when inserted in the sentence, *best* fits the meaning of the sentence as a whole.

Example:

Medieval kingdoms did not become constitutional republics overnight; on the contrary, the change was ________.

(A) unpopular
(B) unexpected
(C) advantageous
(D) sufficient
(E) gradual

(A) (B) (C) (D) ●

1. The ________ public image of the football player made some interviewers quake at the thought of meeting him, but his amicable personality ________ their fears.

(A) hostile..substantiated
(B) tenacious..mitigated
(C) belligerent..vindicated
(D) truculent..mollified
(E) pugnacious..exacerbated

2. Today it is hard to believe that there remains any ________ region on earth, as the advent of television has made it possible to travel to virtually every corner of the globe from our living rooms.

(A) unexplored
(B) fertile
(C) uninhabited
(D) undeveloped
(E) unspoiled

GO ON TO THE NEXT PAGE

3. Harold went back to school to escape the _______ of his job, which consisted of nothing but endless, _______ paperwork.
   (A) pressure..boring
   (B) rigor..intimidating
   (C) tedium..mindless
   (D) onerousness..fascinating
   (E) oppressiveness..ever-changing

4. Plastic surgeons worked diligently to _______ the damage caused by the car accident, but unfortunately their years of training and experience proved _______.
   (A) eradicate..exorbitant
   (B) counteract..effective
   (C) enhance..futile
   (D) mend..fruitless
   (E) improve..inviolable

5. Carpenter's attempt to smear her opponent with false accusations of adultery was _______, and when her duplicity was discovered, many voters were understandably _______.
   (A) contemptible..bemused
   (B) despicable..appalled
   (C) disreputable..ambivalent
   (D) ingenious..jubilant
   (E) exemplary..disgusted

6. The flooding of the river banks, _______ occurrence in this lush region of South America, always causes _______, for if the event is mistimed, all of the community's life-sustaining crops may be destroyed.
   (A) a perennial..rejoicing
   (B) an unprecedented..turmoil
   (C) an annual..apprehension
   (D) a constant..fear
   (E) a novel..consternation

7. Many students were _______ to learn the university had decided to cut back on funding dedicated to scholarships, and their _______ was visible in the protests they staged during the week following the announcement.
   (A) dubious..ambivalence
   (B) embittered..candor
   (C) euphoric..jubilation
   (D) chagrined..anger
   (E) incensed..support

8. The belief that humans are not the only intelligent life-form in the universe is _______, as is evidenced by the _______ of stories about UFO sightings and alien abductions.
   (A) common..proliferation
   (B) increasing..scarcity
   (C) widespread..plausibility
   (D) preposterous..diversity
   (E) verifiable..suppression

9. The so-called Zapatistas in Mexico celebrated the fourth anniversary of their uprising this week, but the celebration was _______ due to _______, which have led many members of the movement to feel that they may never fully achieve their political and social goals.
   (A) morose..victories
   (B) divisive..quarrels
   (C) subdued..setbacks
   (D) jubilant..accomplishments
   (E) premature..obstacles

Directions: Each question below consists of a related pair of words or phrases, followed by five pairs of words or phrases labeled (A) through (E). Select the pair that *best* expresses a relationship similar to that expressed in the original pair.

Example:

CRUMB : BREAD ::

(A) ounce : unit
(B) splinter : wood
(C) water : bucket
(D) twine : rope
(E) cream : butter

(A) ● (C) (D) (E)

10. PROGRAM : BROADCAST ::
(A) crime : investigate
(B) opera : compose
(C) lecture : attend
(D) news : confirm
(E) book : publish

11. BARGE : VESSEL ::
(A) truck : vehicle
(B) yacht : rowboat
(C) bicycle : wheel
(D) caboose : train
(E) sailboat : liner

12. PRINT : VISIBLE ::
(A) meaning : plausible
(B) form : tangible
(C) reality : understandable
(D) speech : audible
(E) message : transcribable

13. VAT : STORE ::
(A) warehouse : put
(B) pool : swim
(C) pipe : convey
(D) bin : gather
(E) tub : fill

14. OMNIPOTENCE : POWER ::
(A) omnivorousness : life
(B) panacea : illness
(C) omniscience : knowledge
(D) holocaust : fire
(E) omnipresence : proximity

15. ADVOCATE : ARGUE ::
(A) arbiter : judge
(B) orator : defend
(C) accuser : deny
(D) actor : personify
(E) debater : shout

GO ON TO THE NEXT PAGE

Directions: Each passage below is followed by questions based on its content. Answer the questions on the basis of what is *stated* or *implied* in the passage and in any introductory material that may be provided.

Questions 16–20 are based on the following passage.

Beginning in the 1880s, a school of painters called the Impressionists introduced a significant new style to European and American art. The passage that follows explains some of the philosophical implications of the Impressionists' artistic achievements.

Line The Impressionist painters expressly disavowed any interest in philosophy, yet their new approach to art had far-reaching philosophical implications. For the view of matter that the Impressionists assumed differed profoundly from the view that had previously prevailed among artists. This view helped to unify the artistic works created in the new style.

The ancient Greeks had conceived of the world in concrete terms, even endowing abstract qualities with bodies. This Greek view of matter persisted, so far as painting was concerned, into the nineteenth century. The Impressionists, on the other hand, viewed light, not matter, as the ultimate visual reality. The philosopher Taine expressed the Impressionist view of things when he said, "The chief 'person' in a picture is the light in which everything is bathed."

In Impressionist painting, solid bodies became mere reflectors of light, and distinctions between one object and another became arbitrary conventions; for by light all things were welded together. The treatment of both color and outline was transformed as well. Color, formerly considered a property inherent in an object, was seen to be merely the result of vibrations of light on the object's colorless surface. And outline, whose function had formerly been to indicate the limits of objects, now marked instead merely the boundary between units of pattern, which often merged into one another.

The Impressionist world was composed not of separate objects but of many surfaces on which light struck and was reflected with varying intensity to the eye through the atmosphere, which modified it. It was this process that produced the mosaic of colors that formed an Impressionist canvas. "Light becomes the sole subject of the picture," writes Mauclair. "The interest of the object upon which it plays is secondary. Painting thus conceived becomes a purely optic art." From this profoundly revolutionary form of art, then, all ideas—religious, moral, psychological—were excluded, and so were all emotions except certain aesthetic ones. The people, places, and things depicted in an Impressionist picture do not tell a story or convey any special meaning; they are, instead, merely parts of a pattern of light drawn from nature and captured on canvas by the artist.

16. According to the passage, the Impressionist painters differed from the ancient Greeks in that they
    (A) considered color to be a property inherent in objects
    (B) regarded art primarily as a medium for expressing moral and aesthetic ideas
    (C) treated the objects depicted in a painting as isolated, rather than united in a single pattern
    (D) were unconcerned with the psychological aspects of artistic expression
    (E) treated light, rather than matter, as the ultimate reality

17. According to the passage, an Impressionist painting is best considered
    (A) a harmonious arrangement of solid physical masses
    (B) a pattern of lights of varying intensities
    (C) a mosaic of outlines representing the edges of objects
    (D) an analysis of the properties of differing geometric forms
    (E) an experimental combination of several types of space

18. The word "conceived" in line 11 most nearly means
    (A) believed
    (B) produced
    (C) considered
    (D) depicted
    (E) concocted

19. It can be inferred from the passage that the Impressionist approach to painting was
    (A) highly objective
    (B) politically motivated
    (C) profoundly religious
    (D) classically oriented
    (E) ultimately conservative

20. It can be inferred from the passage that an Impressionist painter would be most likely to agree with which of the following statements?
    (A) A picture is significant primarily as a symbol of the artist's mental state.
    (B) The highest purpose of art is to teach philosophical truths.
    (C) The quality of a picture has nothing to do with the nature of the objects it depicts.
    (D) An artist should strive to recreate on canvas the inner nature of objects from real life.
    (E) The Impressionist way of painting is a natural development from previous approaches to art.

GO ON TO THE NEXT PAGE

Question 21–30 are based on the following passage.

Community cancer clusters are localized patterns of excessive cancer occurrence. The following passage discusses the difficulties involved in identifying common causes for community cancer clusters.

Community cancer clusters are viewed quite differently by citizen activists than by epidemiologists. Environmentalists and concerned local residents, for instance, might immediately suspect environmental radiation as the culprit when a high incidence of cancer cases occurs near a nuclear facility. Epidemiologists, in contrast, would be more likely to say that the incidences were "inconclusive" or the result of pure chance. And when a breast cancer survivor, Lorraine Pace, mapped twenty breast cancer cases occurring in her West Islip, Long Island, community, her rudimentary research efforts were guided more by hope—that a specific environmental agent could be correlated with the cancers—than by scientific method.

When epidimiologists study clusters of cancer cases and other noncontagious conditions such as birth defects or miscarriage, they take several variables into account, such as background rate (the number of people affected in the general population), cluster size, and specificity (any notable characteristics of the individual affected in each case). If a cluster is both large and specific, it is easier for epidemiologists to assign blame. Not only must each variable be considered on its own, but it must also be combined with others. Lung cancer is very common in the general population. Yet when a huge number of cases turned up among World War II shipbuilders who had all worked with asbestos, the size of the cluster and the fact that the men had had similar occupational asbestos exposures enabled epidemiologists to assign blame to the fibrous mineral.

Furthermore, even if a cluster seems too small to be analyzed conclusively, it may still yield important data if the background rate of the condition is low enough. This was the case when a certain vaginal cancer turned up almost simultaneously in a half-dozen young women. While six would seem to be too small a cluster for meaningful study, the cancer had been reported only once or twice before in the entire medical literature. Researchers eventually found that the mothers of all the afflicted women had taken the drug diethystilbestrol (DES) while pregnant.

Although several known carcinogens have been discovered through these kinds of occupational or medical clusters, only one community cancer cluster has ever been traced to an environmental cause. Health officials often discount a community's suspicion of a common environmental cause because citizens tend to include cases that were diagnosed before the afflicted individuals moved into the neighborhood. Add to this the problem of cancer's latency. Unlike an infectious disease like cholera, which is cased by a recent exposure to food or water contaminated with the cholera bacterium, cancer may have its roots in an exposure that occurred ten to twenty years earlier. Citizens also conduct what one epidemiologist calls "epidemiologic gerrymandering,"—finding cancer cases, drawing a boundary around them, and then mapping this as a cluster.

Do all these caveats mean that the hard work of Lorraine Pace and other community activists is for nought? Not necessarily. Together with many other reports of breast cancer clusters on Long Island, the West Islip situation highlighted by Pace has helped epidemiologists lay the groundwork for a well-designed scientific study.

21. The "hope" mentioned in line 23 refers specifically to Pace's desire to
   (A) help reduce the incidence of breast cancer in future generations
   (B) improve her chances of surviving breast cancer
   (C) determine the culprit responsible for her own breast cancer case
   (D) refute the dismissive statements of epidemiologists concerning her research efforts
   (E) identify a particular cause for the breast cancer cases in West Islip

22. The case of the World War II shipbuilders with lung cancer (lines 41–47) is an example of
   (A) an occupational cluster
   (B) a medical cluster
   (C) a radiation cluster
   (D) an environmental cluster
   (E) an inconclusive cluster

23. The case of six young women with vaginal cancer (lines 52–62) is an example of a cluster that has
   (A) a high background rate and is fairly specific
   (B) a low background rate and is fairly specific
   (C) a high background rate and small size
   (D) a low background rate and inconclusive cluster size
   (E) a low background rate and is nonspecific

24. The passage suggests that the fact that "only one community cancer cluster has ever been traced to an environmental cause" (lines 66–68) is most likely due to the
   (A) methodological difficulties in analyzing community cancer clusters
   (B) general absence of carcinogenic agents from most communities
   (C) reluctance of epidemiologists to investigate environmental factors in cancer
   (D) lack of credibility of citizen activists in claiming to have identified cancer agents
   (E) effectiveness of regulations restricting the use of carcinogens in residential areas

25. The word "discount" (line 68) most nearly means
   (A) exacerbate
   (B) doubt
   (C) ridicule
   (D) provoke
   (E) heed

26. In lines 68–73 ("Health officials . . . into the neighborhood"), the author suggests that activists may mistakenly consider a particular incidence of cancer as part of a community cluster despite the fact that
   (A) the affected individual never worked with any carcinogenic material
   (B) the cancer was actually caused by a long-ago exposure
   (C) a high background rate suggests a purely random incidence
   (D) the size of the cluster is too small to be meaningful
   (E) the cancer actually arose in a different geographic location

GO ON TO THE NEXT PAGE

27. The reference to cancer's "latency" in line 74 refers to the tendency of cancer to
    (A) be linked to several underlying causes
    (B) exist in a dormant or hidden form
    (C) spread through the body at a surprisingly rapid rate
    (D) pass through phases of apparent cure and recurrence
    (E) be masked by other, unrelated illnesses

28. The "epidemiological gerrymandering" that the author describes in line 82 is most closely analogous to
    (A) a toddler declaring that all the toys in one area of the school playground are now his property
    (B) a school principal redistributing students in two classrooms so that each classroom has the same number of gifted students
    (C) a politician drawing election district boundaries so as to give one political party control of a majority of districts
    (D) a nurse erasing information on a patient's chart and substituting false data
    (E) a cartographer mistakenly redrawing the border between two counties so as to make the smaller county appear larger

29. The word "caveats" (line 86) refers to the
    (A) refusals by epidemiologists to examine the work of Pace and other activists
    (B) incidence of "gerrymandering" by citizens concerned about cancer
    (C) potential flaws in amateur studies of cancer clusters
    (D) warnings by activists concerning environmental dangers in their communities
    (E) tendencies of activists to assume environmental causes for cancer

30. The author suggests that the work of concerned citizens who map cancer clusters
    (A) has proven the existence of several environmental causes of cancer
    (B) generally takes into account such variables as the background rate of the disease
    (C) frequently involves the manipulation of data in order to strengthen a case
    (D) has sometimes paved the way for further studies by trained epidemiologists
    (E) is normally of little or no value to the scientific community

STOP End of Section 1. If you have any time left, go over your work in this section only. Do not work in any other section of the test.

SECTION 2

10 Questions

Time—15 Minutes

Directions: In this section solve each problem, using any available space on the page for scratchwork. Then decide which is the best of the choices given and fill in the corresponding oval on the answer sheet.

Notes:

1. The use of a calculator is permitted. All numbers used are real numbers.
2. Figures that accompany problems in this test are intended to provide information useful in solving the problems. They are drawn as accurately as possible EXCEPT when it is stated in a specific problem that the figure is not drawn to scale. All figures lie in a plane unless otherwise indicated.

Reference Information

Circle:

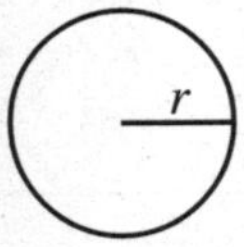

$C = 2\pi r$
$A = \pi r^2$

Rectangle:

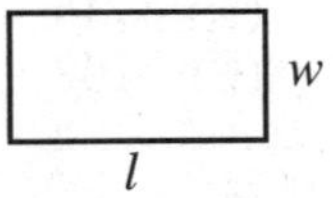

$A = lw$

Triangle:

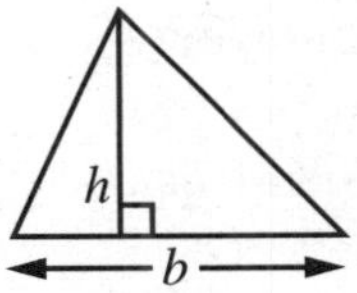

$A = \frac{1}{2}bh$

Rectangle Solid:

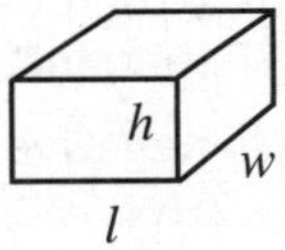

$V = lwh$

Cylinder:

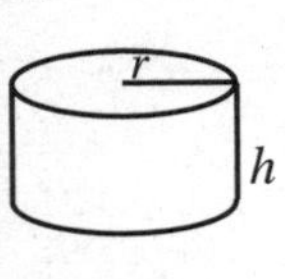

$V = \pi r^2 h$

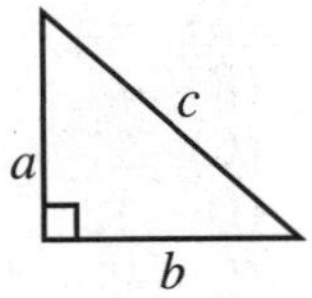

$a^2+b^2 = c^2$

Special Right Triangles

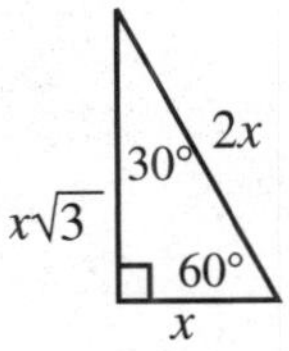

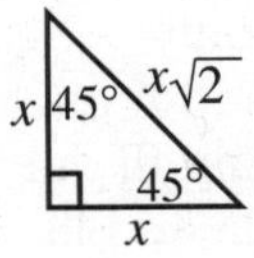

The number of degrees of an arc in a circle is 360.
The measure in degrees of a straight angle is 180.
The sum of the measures in degrees of the angles of a triangle is 180.

GO ON TO THE NEXT PAGE

1. Morton earns 20% more than Caroline, and Caroline earns $\frac{2}{3}$ of what Sasha earns. What percent of Sasha's earnings is Morton's?
   (A) 80%
   (B) 90%
   (C) 100%
   (D) 120%
   (E) 167%

2. If $y - 9 = 3 - y$, then $y =$
   (A) 12
   (B) 9
   (C) 6
   (D) 3
   (E) −6

3. If $\frac{RST}{K^2}$ is a positive number and R is negative, which of the following CANNOT be true?
   I. K is negative and S and T are negative.
   II. K and S are negative and T is positive.
   III. S and T are positive.

   (A) I only
   (B) II only
   (C) I and II only
   (D) I and III only
   (E) I, II, and III

4. The ratio of broken to unbroken eggs in a box of a dozen could be any of the following EXCEPT
   (A) 1:1
   (B) 1:2
   (C) 1:3
   (D) 1:5
   (E) 1:6

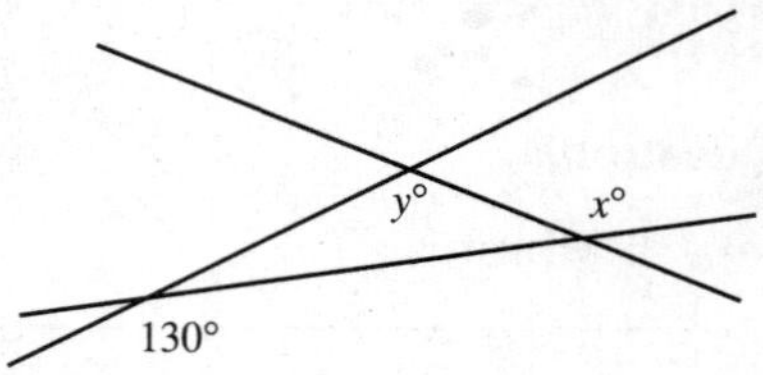

5. In the figure above, what is the relationship between x and y?
   (A) $x + y = 130$
   (B) $x + y = 50$
   (C) $y = 50 - x$
   (D) $x = y - 50$
   (E) $y = x - 50$

6. A rectangle has one side with a length of 12 and a diagonal with a length of 20. What is the area of the rectangle?
   (A) 60
   (B) 72
   (C) 96
   (D) 144
   (E) 192

7. Maria has 77¢ in a combination of pennies, nickels, and dimes. If she has two more dimes than she has nickels, what is the least number of pennies that she can possibly have?
   (A) 42
   (B) 27
   (C) 17
   (D) 12
   (E) 2

8. A car that averages m miles per gallon of gas in city traffic gets 25% better mileage on the highway. In terms of m, how many gallons of gas will it use if driven for 100 miles in city traffic and 200 miles on the highway?

(A) $150m$

(B) $\frac{260}{m}$

(C) $\frac{350}{m}$

(D) $\frac{300}{2.25m}$

(E) $\frac{420}{m}$

9. In the set of positive integers less than 100, how many are NOT evenly divisible by either 3 or 4?

(A) 25
(B) 42
(C) 48
(D) 50
(E) 58

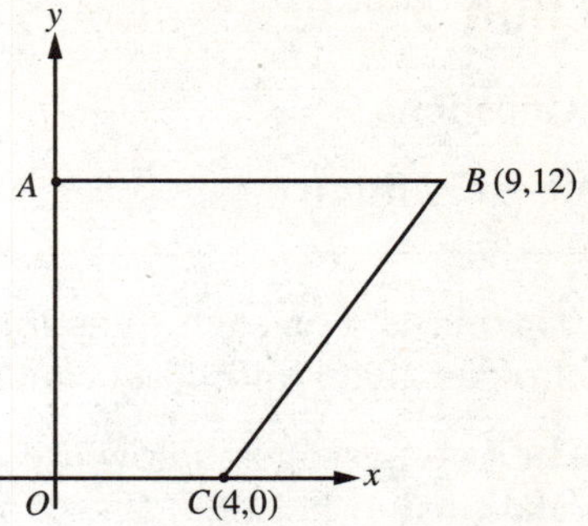

10. In the figure above, $AB \parallel OC$. What is the perimeter of the quadrilateral $ABCO$?

(A) 38
(B) 40
(C) 44
(D) 46
(E) 48

STOP End of Section 2. If you have any time left, go over your work in this section only. Do not work in any other section of the test.

SECTION 3

13 Questions

Time—15 Minutes

Directions: For each question in this section, select the best answer from among the choices given and fill in the corresponding oval on the answer sheet.

The two passages below are followed by questions based on their content and on the relationship between the two passages. Answer the questions on the basis of what is *stated* or *implied* in the passages and in any introductory material that may be provided.

Question 1–13 are based on the following passages.

These two passages consider the influence of the frontier on the development of the American character. The first passage is from Democracy in America *(1835) by Frenchman Alexis de Tocqueville, one of the most astute observers to visit America during the period of Western expansion. The second passage is from a speech given by Frederick Jackson Turner before the American Historical Association in 1893. Turner was a young historian at the University of Wisconsin who was among the first to make Americans aware of the significance of their pioneer past.*

Passage 1

It would be difficult to describe the avidity with which the American frontiersman rushes forward to secure the immense booty which fortune offers. In the pursuit, he fearlessly braves the arrow of the Indian and the diseases of the forest; he is unimpressed by the silence of the woods; the approach of beasts of prey does not disturb him, for he is goaded onwards by a passion stronger than the love of life. Before him lies a boundless continent, and he urges onwards as if time pressed, and he was afraid of finding no room for his exertions.

Fifty years have scarcely elapsed since Ohio was founded; the greater part of its inhabitants were not born within its confines; its capital has been built only thirty years, and its territory is still covered by an immense extent of uncultivated fields. Yet already the population of Ohio is proceeding westward, and most of the settlers who descend to the fertile prairies of Illinois are citizens of Ohio.

These men left their first country to improve their condition. They quit their second to ameliorate it still more. Fortune awaits them everywhere, but not happiness. The desire for prosperity has become an ardent and restless passion in their minds, which grows by what it feeds on. They early broke the ties which bound them to their natal earth, and they have contracted no fresh ones on their way. Emigration was at first necessary to them; it soon becomes a sort of game of chance, which they pursue for the emotions it excites as much as for the gain it procures.

In Europe, we tend to look upon a restless disposition, an unbounded desire of riches, and an excessive love of independence as propensities very dangerous to society. Yet these are the very elements which insure a long and peaceful future to the republics of America.

Without these unquiet passions, the population would collect in certain spots and would soon experience wants like those of the Old World, which it is difficult to satisfy. Such is the present good fortune of the New World that the vices of its inhabitants are scarcely less favorable to society than their virtues. These circumstances exercise a great influence on the estimation in which human actions are held in the two hemispheres. What we should call cupidity, the Americans frequently term a laudable industry, and they blame as faintheartedness what we consider to be the virtue of moderate desires.

Passage 2

Line The American frontier is sharply distinguished from the European frontier—a fortified boundary line running through dense populations. The most significant thing about the American frontier is that it lies at the hither edge of free land.

In studying the settlement of America, we have to observe how European life entered the continent and how America modified and developed that life and reacted on Europe. Our early history is the study of European seeds developing in an American environment. Too exclusive attention has been paid by institutional students to the European origins, too little to the American factors.

The frontier is the line of most rapid and effective Americanization. The wilderness masters the colonist. It finds him a European in dress, industries, tools, modes of travel, and thought. It takes him from the railroad car and puts him in the birch canoe. It strips off the garments of civilization and arrays him in the hunting shirt and the moccasin. It puts him in the log cabin of the Cherokee and Iroquois and runs a Native American-style palisade around him. In short, at the frontier the environment is at first too strong for the man. He must accept the conditions which it furnishes, or perish.

Little by little he transforms the wilderness, but the outcome is not the old Europe, not simply the development of European seeds. The fact is that here is a new product that is American. At first, the frontier was the Atlantic coast. It was the frontier of Europe in a very real sense. Moving westward, the frontier became more and more American. Each frontier leaves its traces behind it, and when it becomes a settled area the region still partakes of the frontier characteristics. Thus the advance of the frontier has meant a steady movement away from the influence of Europe, a steady growth of independence on American lines. Hence, to study this advance, the people who grew up under these conditions, and the political, economic and social results of it, is to study the really American part of our history.

1. The author of Passage 1 implies that the contrast between those qualities esteemed by Americans and by Europeans is a contrast between all of the following EXCEPT

(A) freedom and dependence
(B) restlessness and rootedness
(C) craving and contentment
(D) bravery and cowardice
(E) passion and restraint

2. In line 29, "ameliorate" most nearly means

(A) ramify
(B) refine
(C) advance
(D) alleviate
(E) pursue

GO ON TO THE NEXT PAGE

3. The comment in Passage 1, "Fortune awaits them everywhere, but not happiness" (lines 30–31), implies that most Americans
   (A) will eventually find they preferred the old life they've abandoned
   (B) are unlikely to achieve the material prosperity they seek
   (C) prefer the pursuit of happiness to that of affluence
   (D) are too restless ever to find complete satisfaction in life
   (E) will soon discover the emptiness of mere wealth

4. In describing emigration as "a sort of game of chance" (lines 38–39), the author of Passage 1 implies that Americans find it enjoyable to
   (A) compete for wealth in a new territory
   (B) discover new lands, new peoples, and unknown creatures
   (C) test their strength against the forces of nature
   (D) enjoy the political and religious freedoms a new land offers
   (E) carve out a new civilization according to their own values

5. Passage 1 implies that "a restless disposition, an unbounded desire of riches, and an excessive love of independence" (lines 42–45) are qualities that
   (A) were formerly, but are no longer, exhibited in the Old World
   (B) are generally admirable, whether exhibited by Europeans or Americans
   (C) will prove in time to be injurious to American society
   (D) are a boon to the New World but would be deleterious in the Old World
   (E) are responsible for such wealth as is enjoyed in both the Old and New Worlds

6. According to Passage 1, the restlessness of Americans is beneficial to their society primarily because it will encourage them to
   (A) work especially hard
   (B) make new discoveries in science and technology
   (C) resist the dangers of tyranny and conformity
   (D) avoid forming political and social cliques
   (E) settle across the entire continent

7. The author of Passage 2 implies that the American frontier is generally unfortified because
   (A) it does not separate two hostile peoples
   (B) frontier-dwelling Americans are a friendly race
   (C) it mirrors economic rather than social divisions
   (D) the Native American peoples have been thoroughly subdued
   (E) Americans have abandoned the warlike ways of Europe

8. The author of Passage 2 uses the word "Americanization" (line 18) most nearly to mean
   (A) the transformation of the wilderness by European settlers
   (B) the adoption by colonists of non-European ways of living
   (C) the westward movement of European settlers across the continent
   (D) the gradual destruction of Native American culture
   (E) the creation of new social institutions along the frontier

9. As used in Passage 2, the phrase "on American lines" (lines 48–49) most nearly means
   (A) among disparate American groups
   (B) along state and national boundaries
   (C) in a uniquely American fashion
   (D) among descendants of the original American settlers
   (E) at the edge of the American frontier

10. To study what the author of Passage 2 considers "the really American part of our history" (lines 53–54), a student might examine all of the following EXCEPT
   (A) business ventures in early nineteenth-century Ohio
   (B) the founding of colonial-era communities on the Eastern seaboard
   (C) life in frontier settlements west of the Mississippi
   (D) Native American methods for hunting game and cultivating fields
   (E) the lifestyle of settlers in a Montana mining town in the 1890s

11. Where the author of Passage 2 remarks, "The wilderness masters the colonist" (lines 18–19), the author of Passage 1 might be more likely to say
   (A) the wilderness captivates the colonist
   (B) the colonist ignores the wilderness
   (C) the colonist exploits the wilderness
   (D) the wilderness destroys the colonist
   (E) the colonist luxuriates in the wilderness

GO ON TO THE NEXT PAGE

12. Both passages are concerned with the ways in which westward expansion
    (A) have changed the ways in which Americans relate to one another
    (B) have been misunderstood by students of American history
    (C) have diminished the influence of Europe on American institutions
    (D) hav caused Americans to cut their ties to prior homelands
    (E) have affected the development of the American character

13. Which of the following statements best expresses the most significant difference between Passage 1 and Passage 2?
    (A) Passage 1 emphasizes the inner motivations of the Western settlers; Passage 2 emphasizes how they were affected by circumstance.
    (B) Passage 1 emphasizes the vices of the American settlers; Passage 2 emphasizes their virtues.
    (C) Passage 1 describes the differences between Americans and Europeans; Passage 2 describes their similarities.
    (D) Passage 1 describes the opportunities the Western settlers sought; Passage 2 describes the dangers they faced.
    (E) Passage 1 explores the future of the American republic; Passage 2 attempts to reinterpret its past.

STOP End of Section 3. If you have any time left, go over your work in this section only. Do not work in any other section of the test.

SECTION 4

25 Questions

Time—30 Minutes

Directions: This section contains two types of questions. You have 30 minutes to complete both types. You may use any available space for scratchwork.

Notes:

1. The use of a calculator is permitted. All numbers used are real numbers.
2. Figures that accompany problems in this test are intended to provide information useful in solving the problems. They are drawn as accurately as possible EXCEPT when it is stated in a specific problem that the figure is not drawn to scale. All figures lie in a plane unless otherwise indicated.

Directions for Quantitative Comparison Questions

Questions 1–15 each consist of two quantities in boxes, one in Column A and one in Column B. You are to compare the two quantities and on the answer sheet fill in oval A if the quantity in Column A is greater; B if the quantity in Column B is greater; C if the two quantities are equal; D if the relationship cannot be determined from the information given.

E RESPONSES WILL NOT BE SCORED.

Notes:

1. In some questions, information is given about one or both of the quantities to be compared. In such cases, the given information is centered above the two columns and is not boxed.
2. In a given question, a symbol that appears in both columns represents the same thing in Column A as it does in Column B.
3. Letters such as x, n, and k stand for real numbers.

Examples

	Column A	Column B
E1	5^2	20

Answer: ● Ⓑ Ⓒ Ⓓ Ⓔ

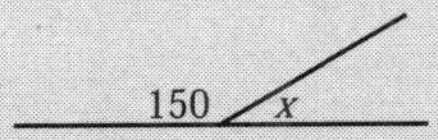

	Column A	Column B
E2	x	30

Answer: Ⓐ Ⓑ ● Ⓓ Ⓔ

r and s are integers

	Column A	Column B
E3	$r + 1$	$s - 1$

Answer: Ⓐ Ⓑ Ⓒ ● Ⓔ

	Column A	Column B
1.	$\frac{3}{7} + \frac{1}{5}$	$\frac{1}{3}$

$N > 1$

	Column A	Column B
2.	30% of N	10% of $3N$

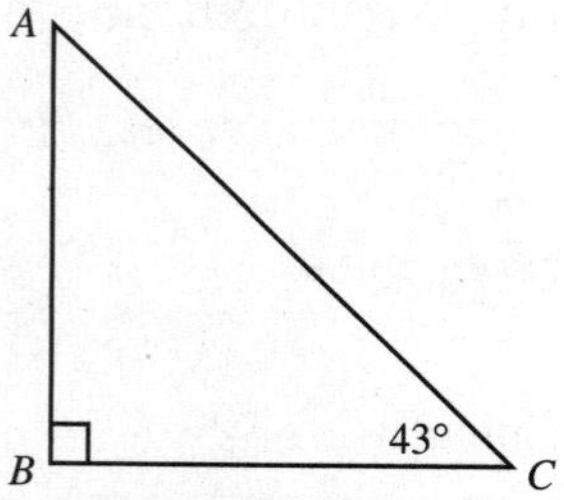

ABC is a right triangle.

	Column A	Column B
3.	AB	BC

$x = \frac{1}{3}$

$y = \frac{-2}{5}$

	Column A	Column B
4.	xy	$\frac{x}{y}$

	Column A	Column B
5.	$\frac{9}{\sqrt{3}}$	$3\sqrt{3}$

$1 < n < 3$

	Column A	Column B
6.	n^3	$3n$

Column A	Column B

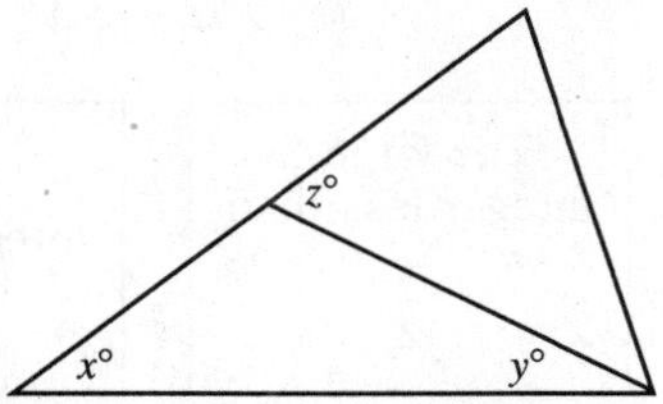

7. | $x + y$ | z |
|---|---|

k is a positive integer

8. | The remainder when $7k + 2$ is divided by 7. | The remainder when $7k + 2$ is divided by 14. |
|---|---|

Column A	Column B

a is chosen from $A = \{-1, 2, 3\}$
b is chosen from $B = \{-4, 5, 8\}$

9. | The smallest possible value of $\frac{a}{b}$ | -1 |
|---|---|

10. | The mean minus the mode of 1, 2, 2, 3, 3, 3, 3, 4, and 6 | The mean minus the median of 1, 2, 2, 3, 3, 3, 3, 4, and 6 |
|---|---|

An urn contains 10 balls numbered 1, 2, . . . , 10.
A ball is selected at random.

11. | The probability of drawing a number that is either even or a perfect square. | 0.6 |
|---|---|

GO ON TO THE NEXT PAGE

	Column A	Column B
12.	$\frac{x}{3} + \frac{y}{2}$	The average of x and y

$$\begin{array}{r} CD \\ -DC \\ \hline B7 \end{array}$$

B, C, and D are digits

	Column A	Column B
13.	$C - D$	4

$2 < x < 4$

	Column A	Column B
14.	The largest integer less than $\frac{x}{2}$	The largest integer less than $x - 3$

$x > y > 0$

	Column A	Column B
15.	$(x - y)^2$	$x^2 - y^2$

Directions for Student-Produced Response Questions

Each of the remaining 10 questions requires you to solve the problem and enter your answer by marking the ovals in the special grid, as shown in the examples below.

Answer: $\frac{7}{12}$ or 7/12 Answer: 2.5

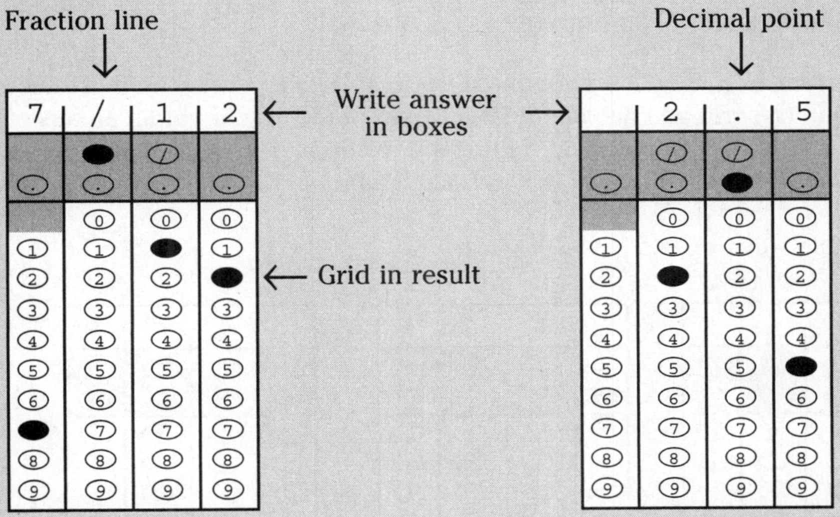

Answer: 201
Either position is correct.

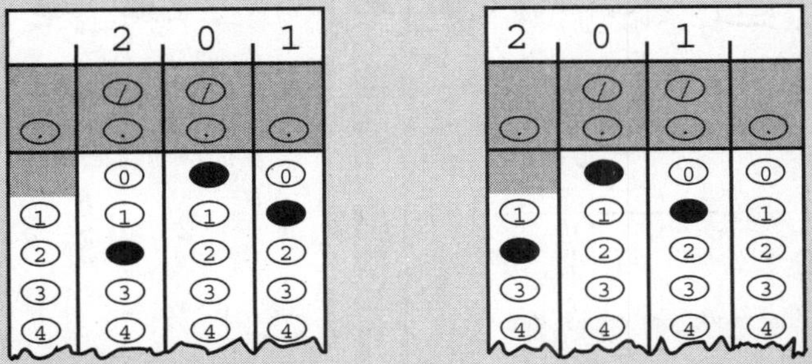

Note: You may start your answers in any column, space permitting. Columns not needed should be left blank.

- Mark no more than one oval in any column.
- Because the answer sheet will be machine-scored, you will receive credit only if the ovals are filled in correctly.
- Although not required, it is suggested that you write your answer in the boxes at the top of the columns to help you fill in the ovals accurately.

- Some problems may have more than one correct answer. In such cases, grid only one answer.
- No question has a negative answer.
- Mixed numbers such as $2\frac{1}{2}$ must be gridded as 2.5 or 5/2. If 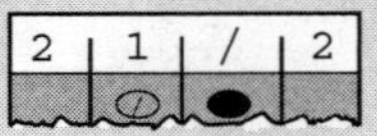

is gridded, it will be interpreted as $\frac{21}{2}$, not $2\frac{1}{2}$.
- *Decimal accuracy:* If you obtain a decimal answer, enter the most accurate value the grid will accommodate. For example, if you obtain an answer such as 0.6666 . . . , you should record the result as .666 or .667. Less accurate values such as .66 or .67 are not acceptable.

Acceptable ways to grid $\frac{2}{3} = .6666$

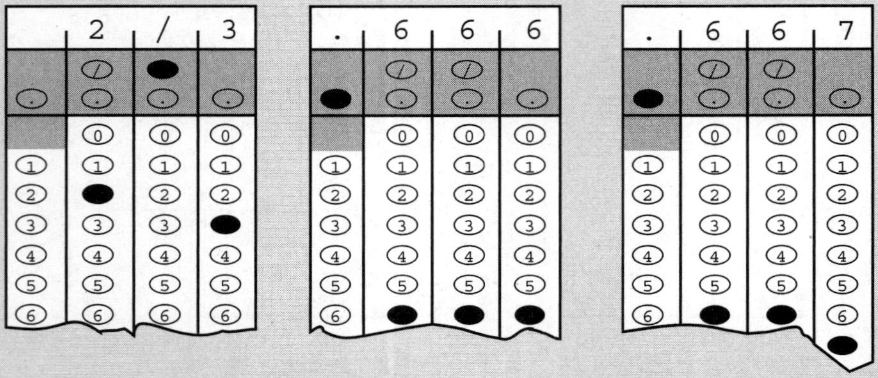

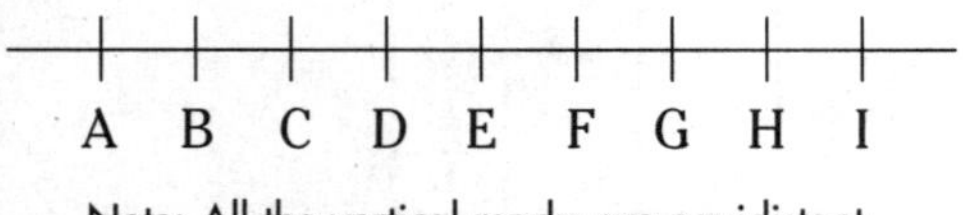

Note: All the vertical marks are equidistant.

16. On the number line above, if the coordinate of A is 3.72 and the coordinate of F is 3.82, what is the coordinate of H?

17. If $\frac{12}{a} = 2$ and $\frac{b}{3} = 3$, then $\frac{b+3}{2+a} =$

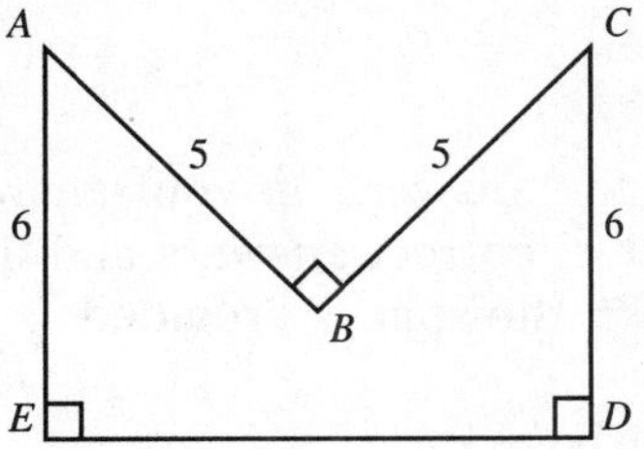

18. If the perimeter of *ABCDE* is 30, what is its area?

19. If $(x - 3)^2 = (x + 7)^2$, then $x^2 =$

20. Group A consists of three men having an average age of 40. Group B consists of five men having an average age of 44. One man leaves Group B and joins Group A. As a result, both groups now have the same average age. How old was the man who moved?

21. What is the area of a triangle with vertices at (−1,5), (3,5), and (3,−3)?

Age	Number
35–44	95
45–54	73
25–34	x
15–24	y
55–64	32

22. 300 people attended an art exhibit. Divided by age groups, the numbers present in order from greatest to smallest number are shown in the table above. If no two age groups had the same number of people attending, what is the maximum possible difference between x and y?

23. A 12-ounce bottle of milk that is 5% butterfat by volume is mixed with an 8-ounce bottle of milk that is 3% butterfat by volume. What percent of the resulting mixture is butterfat?

24. A group of nine pirates divided up a chest of gold coins. The captain took $\frac{1}{3}$ of the coins. The mate took $\frac{1}{4}$ of the remaining coins, and each of the seven crew members got 3 coins. How many coins were there originally?

25. ★(N)★ $= \frac{N}{2}$ if N is even, and ★(N)★ $= 3N + 1$ if N is odd. What is the value of ★(★(5)★)★?

STOP End of Section 4. If you have any time left, go over your work in this section only. Do not work in any other section of the test.

Answer Key

Compare the answers below with the answers on your answer sheets. For each section, fill in the number of correct answers and the number of incorrect answers (if indicated) in the spaces provided.

Verbal

Section 1 — Five-Choice Questions

1. D	11. A	21. E
2. A	12. D	22. A
3. C	13. C	23. B
4. D	14. C	24. A
5. B	15. A	25. B
6. C	16. E	26. E
7. D	17. B	27. B
8. A	18. C	28. C
9. C	19. A	29. C
10. E	20. C	30. D

Section 3 — Five-Choice Questions

1. D	8. B
2. C	9. C
3. D	10. D
4. A	11. C
5. D	12. E
6. E	13. A
7. A	

Mathematical

Section 2 — Five-Choice Questions

1. A	6. C
2. C	7. D
3. D	8. B
4. E	9. D
5. E	10. A

Section 4 — Four-Choice Questions

1. A	9. A
2. C	10. C
3. B	11. A
4. A	12. D
5. C	13. B
6. D	14. A
7. C	15. B
8. D	

Student-Produced Response Questions

16. 3.86
17. 1.5
18. 35.5
19. 4
20. 50
21. 16
22. 34
23. 4.2
24. 42
25. 8

Scoring Guide

COMPUTING YOUR VERBAL SCALED SCORE

Step 1. Count the number of correct answers you chose for the questions in Sections 1 and 3. Write the total here: ________

Step 2. Count the number of incorrect answers you chose for the questions in Sections 1 and 3. (Do not count questions you omitted.) Write the total here: ________

Step 3. Divide the total from Step 2 by 4. (The result may include a fraction.) Write the result here: ________

Step 4. Subtract the result from Step 3 from the total in Step 1. Write the result here: ________

Step 5. Round off the result from Step 4 to the nearest whole number. Round a number ending in $\frac{1}{2}$ *down*; for example, $28\frac{1}{2}$ rounds to 28. Write the result here: ________ This is your Verbal Raw Score.

Step 6. Look up your Verbal Raw Score on the Score Conversion Table (pages 31–32). Find the corresponding Verbal Scaled Score and write it here: ________

COMPUTING YOUR MATHEMATICAL SCALED SCORE

Step 1. Count the number of correct answers you chose for the questions in Sections 2 and 4. Write the total here: ________

Step 2. Count the number of incorrect answers you chose for the questions in Section 2. (Do not count questions you omitted.) Write the total here: ________

Step 3. Count the number of incorrect answers you chose for questions 1–15 in Section 4. (Do not count questions you omitted.) Write the total here: ________

Step 4. Divide the total from Step 2 by 4. (The result may include a fraction.) Write the result here: ________

Step 5. Divide the total from Step 3 by 3. (The result may include a fraction.) Write the result here: ________

Step 6. Add the totals from Steps 4 and 5. Write the result here: ________

Step 7. Subtract the result from Step 6 from the total in Step 1. Write the result here: ________

Step 8. Round off the result from Step 4 to the nearest whole number. Round a number ending in $\frac{1}{2}$ *down*; for example, $28\frac{1}{2}$ rounds to 28. Write the result here: _________ This is your Mathematical Raw Score.

Step 9. Look up your Mathematical Raw Score on the Score Conversion Table (pages 31–32). Find the corresponding Mathematical Scaled Score and write it here: _________

Score Conversion Table

Insider's SAT Diagnostic Text

Raw Score	Verbal Scaled Score	Mathematical Scaled Score
43	800	
42	780	
41	770	
40	760	
39	750	
38	730	
37	710	
36	700	
35	680	800
34	660	780
33	650	750
32	640	730
31	630	700
30	610	680
29	600	660
28	590	650
27	580	630
26	570	610
25	560	600
24	550	590
23	540	580
22	530	570
21	520	560
20	510	550
19	500	530
18	490	520
17	480	510
16	470	500
15	460	480
14	450	470
13	440	460
12	430	450
11	410	430
10	400	420
9	390	410

Raw Score	Verbal Scaled Score	Mathematical Scaled Score
8	380	400
7	360	380
6	350	360
5	340	350
4	320	330
3	300	310
2	270	300
1	240	250
0 or less	200	200

Explanatory Answers

SECTION 1

1. **The correct answer is (D).** The word "but" tells you that the two halves of the sentence contrast with one another. In choice (D), "truculent" fits the idea of "interviewers quaking," and "mollified" makes sense in combination with "his amicable personality."

2. **The correct answer is (A).** "Unexplored" fits the ideas in the sentence without adding any new ones. The sentence emphasizes the fact that almost every corner of the globe is easy to visit and see.

3. **The correct answer is (C).** The words "tedium" and "mindless" both fit each other and make sense in the context, which tells us that Harold was eager to "escape" his job.

4. **The correct answer is (D).** The word "but" alerts us to the fact that a contrast exists between the two halves of the sentence. "Mend" makes sense as a description of what the surgeons would try to do, and the word "fruitless" fits the contrast we expect.

5. **The correct answer is (B).** Here, the two halves of the sentence make similar or parallel points. Choice (B) makes sense because the word meanings are consistent: if what Carpenter did was "despicable," it makes sense that voters would be "appalled."

6. **The correct answer is (C).** The second half of the sentence shows that the flooding can be dangerous; hence, "apprehension" is a logical reaction. The word "always" tells us that the flooding is a frequent event; hence, "annual" makes sense as a description.

7. **The correct answer is (D).** We're looking for words that would describe how students might be expected to react to a reduction in scholarship funding. "Chagrined" and "anger" make sense in this context and also match one another appropriately.

8. **The correct answer is (A).** The phrase "as is evidenced" shows that what is stated in the second half of the sentence must help demonstrate or illustrate what is stated in the first half of the sentence. If UFO sightings are experiencing a "proliferation," then it would be logical to say that the belief in alien life-forms is "common."

9. **The correct answer is (C).** The second half of the sentence tells us that the movement "may never fully achieve [its] goals." Thus, "setbacks" makes sense for the second blank. Given the fact that the movement is facing setbacks, it is logical that its anniversary celebration should be "subdued."

10. **The correct answer is (E).** To *broadcast* a *program* is to disseminate it or make it publicly available; in the same way, to *publish* a *book* is to disseminate it or make it publicly available.

11. **The correct answer is (A).** A *barge* is a particular type of *vessel,* one dedicated to carrying cargo. A *truck* is a particular type of *vehicle,* also used to carry cargo.

12. **The correct answer is (D).** To be useful and to convey a meaning clearly, *print* must be *visible.* In the same way, *speech* must be *audible* if anyone is to understand it.

13. **The correct answer is (C).** A *vat* is used specifically to *store* liquids; a *pipe* is used to *convey* (that is, to carry or transport) liquids. Choice (D) is wrong because a bin isn't used to gather anything; a person may gather things and put them in a bin, but that's not quite the same thing.

14. **The correct answer is (C).** *Omnipotence* means the quality of being *all-powerful* (that is, able to do anything—like God or perhaps Bill Gates). *Omniscience* means the quality of being *all-knowing* (able to know anything). Omnipresence, choice (E), means the quality of being everywhere; proximity is the wrong word for the second part of the relationship, since it means "nearness," not "presence."

15. **The correct answer is (A).** An *advocate* is someone who *argues* (a lawyer, for instance); an *arbiter* is someone who *judges* (a judge or a sports referee, for instance). None of the other answer choices have an equally clear-cut relationship.

16. **The correct answer is (E).** The second paragraph of the passage expresses this idea: see the third sentence in particular ("The Impressionists, on the other hand, viewed light, not matter, as the ultimate visual reality").

17. **The correct answer is (B).** The third and fourth paragraphs make this point clear, especially the first sentence of the fourth paragraph, which refers to "light . . . reflected with varying intensity to the eye."

18. **The correct answer is (C).** In this context, the word "conceived" refers to a particular idea or theory about painting which the Impressionists had. Thus, it describes what they "considered" the art of painting to be.

19. **The correct answer is (A).** This summarizes the last paragraph, which explains how the Impressionists excluded all ideas and most emotions from their art. If virtually all human feelings and thoughts are eliminated, the result is an extreme objectivity.

20. **The correct answer is (C).** Again, the last paragraph is the key. It tells us that the Impressionists were not interested in the "meaning" of the things they painted—only in the pattern of light they created. Hence, the nature of the objects depicted is irrelevant.

21. **The correct answer is (E).** Refer back to the sentence in which the word "hope" appears. It says that Pace wanted to "correlate" something in the environment with the incidence of cancer, which is the same idea paraphrased in choice (E).

22. **The correct answer is (A).** Since the workers were all exposed to asbestos on the job, it seems clear that their cancers were an example of an occupational cluster.

23. **The correct answer is (B).** The story told in the third paragraph involves a "low background rate" because the number of people in the general population who suffer from this kind of cancer is very small; it is a "fairly specific" cluster (according to the definition given in the second paragraph) because of the notable characteristic shared by all the victims—all had taken DES while pregnant.

24. **The correct answer is (A).** Paragraph four, from which this observation is taken, is devoted to describing the difficulties experts have in gathering and interpreting information about cancer clusters with suspected environmental causes.

25. **The correct answer is (B).** We're told that health officials "discount" local suspicions because of the imprecision with which community members gather data. In other words, the officials are dubious about these suspicions.

26. **The correct answer is (E).** As the sentence says, "citizens tend to include cases that were diagnosed before the afflicted individuals moved into the neighborhood."

27. **The correct answer is (B).** Read the sentence *after* the one in which the word "latency" is used; it explains exactly what is meant by this concept.

28. **The correct answer is (C).** The "gerrymandering" described in the passage involves community activists drawing boundaries to fit their preconceived ideas or wishes, just as a politician does when he draws an election district boundary to produce a particular electoral result.

29. **The correct answer is (C).** The sentence in which the word "caveats" appears refers back to the previous paragraph, which describes the doubts the experts have about the work amateurs do in studying cancer clusters.

30. **The correct answer is (D).** This restates the idea found in the very last sentence of the passage.

SECTION 2

1. **The correct answer is (A).** Let M, C, and S be the earnings of the three people. M is 20% more than C, which means $M = 1.2C$. $C = \frac{2}{3}S$. Therefore, $M = (1.2)\frac{2}{3}S = 0.8S$. That is, M is 80% of S.

2. **The correct answer is (C).** Adding $y + 9$ to both sides of the equation:

$$\begin{array}{r} y - 9 = 3 - y \\ \underline{y + 9 = y + 9} \\ 2y = 12 \end{array}$$

Dividing by 2 yields $y = 6$.

3. **The correct answer is (D).** K^2 cannot be negative, so this possibility can be ignored. Since R is negative, the only way the fraction can be positive is if exactly one of S or T is negative. This corresponds only to case II. However, the question asks for those cases that are *not* possible: that is, cases I and III, which is choice (D).

4. **The correct answer is (E).** One dozen, of course, is 12. Letting the number of broken eggs be k, then, the ratio 1:2 leads to $k + 2k = 12$, or $k = 4$. So 1:2 is a possible ratio. Try the same with each of the answer choices, and you'll find that only the case 1:6, which yields $k + 6k = 12$, has no integer solution. The number of unbroken eggs must be a whole number, so (E) is the only impossible ratio given.

5. **The correct answer is (E).** The three angles in the triangle are 50°, y°, and 180° − x°. These must total 180°. Thus, $50 + y + 180 - x = 180$, which leads to $50 + y = x$, or $y = x - 50$.

6. **The correct answer is (C).** Since the diagonal and the sides form a right triangle, we can call the unknown side x and use the Pythagorean Theorem to get $x^2 + 12^2 = 20^2$; $x^2 = 256$; $x = 16$. Or we can recognize that 12:20 is a multiple of 3:5, so the other leg must be the appropriate multiple of 4, namely, 16. The area, then, is $\frac{1}{2}(12)(16) = 96$.

7. **The correct answer is (D).** Using P, N, and D to stand for pennies, nickels, and dimes, we have:

$$P + 5N + 10D = 77$$

Since $D = N + 2$, this gives us:

$$P + 5N + 10(N + 2) = 77$$
$$P + 15N + 20 = 77$$
$$P + 15N = 57$$

which means that $(57 - P)$ must be a positive number divisible by 15. The choices for $(57 - P)$ are 15, 30, or 45, which give us $P = 42$, 27, or 12. The least of these is 12.

8. **The correct answer is (B).** The total mileage is given by (miles per gallon) × (number of gallons). Letting m = miles per gallon in the city, then $1.25m$ gives us the miles per gallon on the highway. Thus, we have:

$$100 = mg_c \text{ and } 200 = 1.25mg_h$$

Thus, $g_c = \frac{100}{m}$, and $g_h = \frac{200}{1.25m} = \frac{160}{m}$.

So the sum is $\frac{100}{m} + \frac{160}{m} = \frac{260}{m}$

9. **The correct answer is (D).** Of all the positive integers less than 100, 33 are divisible by 3 (99 ÷ 3). Only 24 are divisible by 4 (99 ÷ 4, ignoring the remainder). Of the total of 57, we have counted the 8 numbers divisible by 12 twice. Hence, the number of digits divisible by 3 or 4 is 57 − 8 = 49. The number not divisible by either is 99 − 49 = 50.

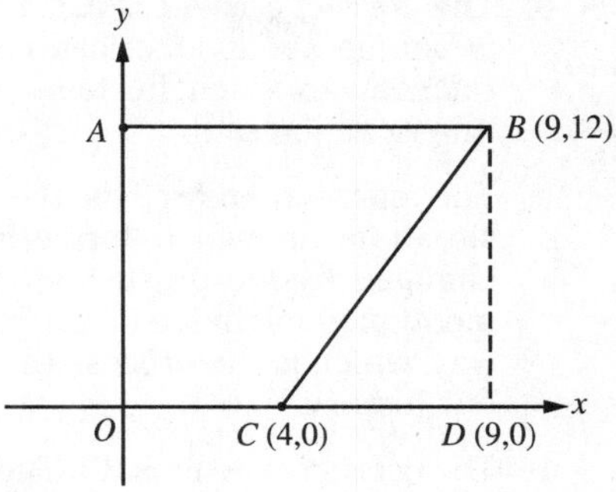

10. **The correct answer is (A).** Dropping a vertical line from B to D (9,0) on the x-axis creates a right triangle with side $CD = 5$ and side $BD = 12$ (see the figure above). Therefore, $BC = 13$. Consequently, $OA = 12$, $AB = 9$, $BC = 13$, and $CO = 4$. The perimeter is $12 + 9 + 13 + 4 = 38$.

SECTION 3

1. **The correct answer is (D).** All of the other contrasts listed can be found in one form or another in the last paragraph of Passage 1, but nowhere does the author imply that Europeans are "cowards."
2. **The correct answer is (C).** From the context, you can see that "ameliorate" is being used as a virtual synonym for "improve" (as found in the previous sentence).
3. **The correct answer is (D).** Look at the sentence *after* the one quoted; it explains that the passionate "desire for prosperity" felt by Americans is "restless" and unquenchable.
4. **The correct answer is (A).** The author is discussing here the love Americans have for trying their luck in a new territory to see whether riches await them there.
5. **The correct answer is (D).** The first three sentences of the last paragraph of Passage 1 explain this point: Restlessness and passion for wealth would cause dangerous problems in Europe, yet these same feelings "insure a long and peaceful future" to America.
6. **The correct answer is (E).** Read the third sentence of the last paragraph. Without restlessness, it says, America's population "would collect in certain spots," which would cause trouble. The implication is that the restlessness will have the fortunate effect of driving Americans to spread out across the whole country instead.
7. **The correct answer is (A).** This answer is implied in the first sentence of the passage. The European frontier is fortified because it separates "dense populations" which need to be kept apart rather than populated country from "free land."
8. **The correct answer is (B).** The various details about the frontier way of life that are mentioned in the third paragraph of Passage 2 define what the author means by "Americanization."

9. **The correct answer is (C).** The last paragraph of Passage 2 discusses what is unique about American culture. That uniqueness is what the author is referring to when he talks about "a steady growth of independence on American lines."

10. **The correct answer is (D).** All of the other answer choices describe situations in which formerly European people were being shaped and changed by life on the moving American frontier. The Native Americans mentioned in choice (D), however, didn't need to be "Americanized" in this way, which is the process the author considers "the really American part of our history."

11. **The correct answer is (C).** The author of Passage 1 focuses on how Americans want to use the wilderness as a source of wealth; hence, choice (C).

12. **The correct answer is (E).** Both authors are mainly interested in how the character of the typical American has been affected by life on a frontier of one kind or another.

13. **The correct answer is (A).** Passage 1 focuses on the "restlessness" and "passion" which drives Americans to keep moving west, while Passage 2 emphasizes the ways in which the frontier changes Americans.

SECTION 4

1. **The correct answer is (A).** The sum in column A is $\frac{22}{35}$, which is considerably larger than $\frac{1}{3}$.

2. 30% of $N = (0.3)N$; 10% of $3N = (0.1)(3N) = (0.3)N$.

3. Angle A is 47°, and we know that the side opposite the larger angle is always the larger side. Hence $BC > AB$.

4. $xy = \frac{1}{3} \times \frac{-2}{5} = \frac{-2}{15}$, and $\frac{x}{y} = \frac{1}{3} \times \frac{5}{-2} = \frac{5}{-6}$ or $-\frac{5}{6}$. For negative numbers, the one with the smaller absolute value is the larger number. Hence, Column A is larger.

5. **The correct answer is (C).** Rationalizing the denominator, $\frac{9}{\sqrt{3}} = \frac{9}{\sqrt{3}} \times \frac{\sqrt{3}}{\sqrt{3}} = \frac{9\sqrt{3}}{\sqrt{3}} = 3\sqrt{3}$. Thus, the quantities are equal.

6. **The correct answer is (D).** Try different values of n. You'll find that, for n near 1, such as $n = 1.1$, $n^3 < 3n$, but for n near 3, like 2.9, $n^3 > 3n$. So you can't tell which is greater. (Actually, $n^3 = 3n$ at $n = \sqrt[3]{3}$ which equals around 1.44.)

7. **The correct answer is (C).** The missing angle in the triangle is $180° - z°$, the supplement of $z°$. Hence, $x + y = z$.

8. **The correct answer is (D).** The quantity in column A is always 2. The quantity in column B is also 2 when k is even, but it is 9 when k is odd. Try $k = 3$ or 5, for example. Since two answers are possible, the correct choice is (D).

9. **The correct answer is (A).** The smallest value of the fraction will arise when it is negative. So you must pick a positive number from one set and a negative number from the other. If you choose to let $a = -1$, then the smallest negative number (largest absolute value) you can get is when $b = 5$, for which $\frac{a}{b} = -\frac{1}{5}$. If you choose $b = -4$, the smallest negative number you can get is for $a = 3$, for which $\frac{a}{b} = -\frac{3}{4}$. Both possibilities are larger than -1.

10. **The correct answer is (C).** The mean, mode, and median are all 3. Therefore, both quantities are 0.

11. **The correct answer is (A).** There are 5 even numbers plus two odd perfect squares (1 and 9). Hence the probability is $7 \div 10 = 0.7$, which is greater than 0.6.

12. **The correct answer is (D).** The average of x and y is $\frac{x+y}{2} = \frac{x}{2} + \frac{y}{2}$. Hence, we need only compare $\frac{x}{2}$ to $\frac{x}{3}$. Since x could be zero, positive, or negative, we do not know which is larger or whether they are equal.

13. **The correct answer is (B).** The top number equals $10C + D$. The lower one equals $10D + C$. The difference is $9C - 9D = 9(C - D)$, which is divisible by 9. (In fact, whenever you transpose the digits of a number and take the difference, the result must be divisible by 9.) The only two-digit number divisible by 9 that ends in 7 is 27. Hence, $B = 2$, and $C - D$ is either 2 or 3, depending upon whether or not there is a "carry." In either case, it is less than 4. Actually, since $C - D = 3$, D is less than C. Then $(D + 1) - C$ leaves 7, and the only possibility is $CD = 85$ and $DC = 58$.

14. **The correct answer is (A).** Dividing the given triple inequality by 2 yields $1 < \frac{x}{2} < 2$. Hence, the largest integer less than $\frac{x}{2}$ must be 1. Subtracting 3 from all parts of the given inequality yields $-1 < (x - 3) < 1$. Hence, the largest integer less than $(x - 3)$ could be 0 or -1, both of which are less than 1.

15. **The correct answer is (B).** Factoring both quantities, we try to solve:

$$(x - y)(x - y) > (x - y)(x + y)$$

Since $x > y$, $(x - y) > 0$. So divide by this quantity to get:

$$(x - y) > (x + y).$$

But since x and y are both positive, exactly the reverse is true! That is, $(x - y) < (x + y)$. Therefore, Column B is larger.

16. There are five spaces between A and F. Hence, the tick marks must be in units of 0.02. Hence $G = 3.84$ and $H = 3.86$.

17. From what's given, $a = 6$ and $b = 9$. Thus, $\frac{(9 + 3)}{(2 + 6)} = \frac{12}{8} = 1.5$. Note: any fraction or decimal of equivalent value would be considered correct.

18. Since the total perimeter is 30, $DE = 8$. Connecting A to C forms a rectangle $ACDE$ with area $6 \times 8 = 48$. The right triangle ABC has area $\frac{1}{2}(5)(5) = 12.5$. Subtracting this area from that of the rectangle leaves $48 - 12.5 = 35.5$.

19. $A^2 = B^2$ implies that $A = B$ or $A = -B$. Thus, from the given equation:

$$x - 3 = x + 7,$$

which is impossible, or:

$$\begin{aligned} x - 3 &= -(x + 7) \\ x - 3 &= -x - 7 \\ 2x &= -4 \\ x &= -2 \\ x^2 &= 4 \end{aligned}$$

Alternatively, you could expand the square of $x - 3$ and $x + 7$ to get the same result.

20. The total of the ages of the men originally in group A must be 120 (3×40.) Let x be the age of the man who leaves group B. The new total is $(120 + x)$. The total of the ages of the men originally in group B must be 220 (5×44.) The new total is $(220 - x)$. Since both groups now have 4 men and the same average, the totals must be the same, that is:

$$\begin{aligned} 120 + x &= 220 - x \\ 2x &= 100 \\ x &= 50 \end{aligned}$$

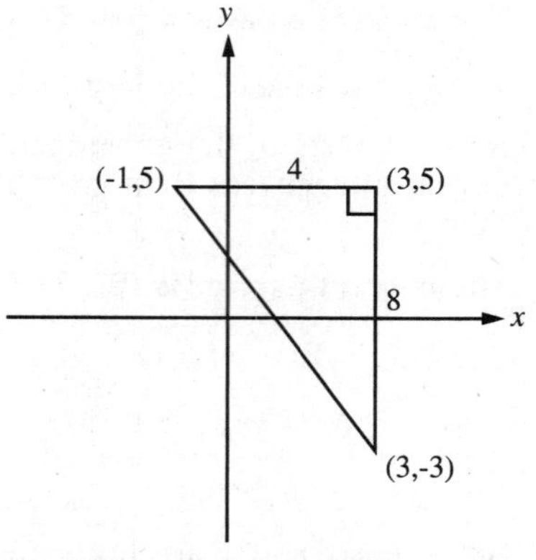

21. Sketch the triangle on the xy-plane, as shown in the figure above. You can see that it is a right triangle with one leg 4 and the other 8. The area, therefore, is $\frac{1}{2}(4)(8) = 16$.

22. Knowing that the total is 300 and $95 + 73 + 32 = 200$, $x + y = 100$. Since y must be at least 33, the greatest difference is 34 when $y = 33$ and $x = 67$.

23. 5% of 12 is $(.05)(12) = 0.6$, and 3% of 8 is $(.03)(8) = 0.24$. Therefore, we have a total of 0.84 oz. of butterfat in 20 oz. of liquid. $0.84 \div 20 = 0.042 = 4.2\%$.

24. Let C be the number of coins. The captain took $\frac{1}{3}C$, leaving $\frac{2}{3}C$. The mate took $\frac{1}{4}$ of this amount or $\frac{1}{4} \times \frac{2}{3}C = \frac{1}{6}C$, leaving $\frac{2}{3}C - \frac{1}{6}C = \frac{1}{2}C$. Since each of the 7 crewmen got 3 coins, $\frac{1}{2}C = 21$, and $C = 42$.

25. Since 5 is an odd number, $\bigstar(5)\bigstar = 3(5) + 1 = 16$. Since 16 is even, $\bigstar(\bigstar(5)\bigstar)\bigstar = \bigstar(16)\bigstar = \frac{16}{2} = 8$.

Chapter 2

Making Your Plan

Get the Scoop On . . .

- The three levels of SAT skills and how you can improve all three
- How to develop a personalized study plan focused on your current skill levels and needs
- How to tailor your study plan to the amount of time you have to prepare

HOW TO GET WHERE YOU WANT TO GO

As you decide to which colleges you intend to apply, your personal SAT goals should be based largely on the credentials needed to win admission to the college(s) of your choice.

Now we come to the heart of this book. How can you make sure that your SAT scores will be a help rather than a hindrance to you when you apply to colleges? What steps can you take to close the gap that may exist between your current levels of SAT skills and the ones you'll need to earn your highest possible score?

The rest of this book will help you answer those questions.

THE INSIDER'S ROUTE TO TOP SCORES

There are three levels of skill that can help boost your SAT scores. Each requires a different kind of preparation. Most important, each requires a different time frame to be completely developed. If you want to reach your full potential on the SAT, you'll want to devote time and energy to all three levels of skill.

Here's how the three levels work.

Level One—Testwiseness (30 to 100 points)

This first level of test-taking skill is the low-hanging fruit of test-preparation—skills that are relatively quick and simple to learn and that can rapidly boost your total SAT score from 30 to 100 points.

Level One includes such skills as:

- Familiarity with the format, structure, and question types found on the exam
- Understanding of the *guessing penalty* and how to manage it
- Ability to budget your time wisely as you work through each section of the exam
- Awareness of the *ladder of difficulty* and how to climb it

Level One skills are specific to the SAT. A student who'd never seen an SAT exam before and had done no preparatory reading about the test would lack these skills and therefore would lose points through sheer ignorance of the game.

Fortunately, Level One skills are easy to learn. Many students pick up some of them just by taking an SAT exam. That's why, as the test-makers admit, most students increase their scores by 30 to 50 points whenever they take the exam a second time, even if they do no studying between the two tests.

If your preparation for the SAT is condensed into just a couple of weeks, you'll need to focus especially on Level One skills. Chapters 1 through 3 and 10 through 12 in this book are particularly focused on Level One.

Level Two—Topic Strategies (50 to 200 points)

FYI

Some of the terms and topics in this explanation may not be familiar to you. Don't worry—you'll learn much more about them in Chapter 3.

Skills at this level are a bit more complex. They generally take longer to learn but have a correspondingly greater payoff. If you work to improve your Level Two skills (as well as your Level One skills), you can expect to boost your overall SAT score by anywhere from 50 to 200 points.

Level Two includes such skills as:

- Knowing how to interpret the relationships between words on analogy questions
- Ability to recognize the logical connections between parts of a sentence or a reading passage
- Awareness of how and when to use rounding off and *guesstimating* when working on math problems
- Understanding of the technique of *plugging in numbers* in quantitative comparison questions

Level Two skills relate specifically to particular question types on the SAT. However, they involve intellectual abilities that can be used in other contexts as well. For instance, if you're good at seeing the logical connections between parts of a reading passage, this will help you not only on the SAT but whenever you do any difficult reading—in a high school textbook, for example.

You've probably developed some Level Two skills already, both in school and out. However, you probably aren't aware of how to apply these skills directly to answering SAT questions. Since these skills are somewhat complex (and because there are many of them), it'll take you a while to master them. But the rewards can be great.

If you have four weeks or more to prepare for the SAT, you'll have enough time to delve fairly deeply into Level Two skills. Chapters 4 through 9 of this book explain them in detail.

Level Three—Broad-Based Verbal and Math Abilities (100 to 400 points)

These are the most general skills, and they take the longest time to fully develop. In a sense, Level Three skills are the ones the test-makers originally intended the SAT to focus on, and certainly your performance on the test will be heavily affected by your Level Three skills. If you devote significant time and effort to improving your Level Three skills (along with levels One and Two), you can aim for an increase of your overal SAT score of from 100 to 400 points.

Level Three includes such skills as:

- Knowledge of the meanings and correct usage of a large number of difficult English words
- Ability to read and understand complex passages dealing with challenging topics from science, the humanities, the social sciences, and literature
- Familiarity with the basic facts, principles, and procedures of arithmetic, algebra, and geometry
- Ability to quickly recognize numerical relationships and to manipulate them accurately and creatively

Level Three skills clearly go well beyond the requirements of the SAT exam. In fact, you've probably been learning and practicing skills like these in every high school class you've ever taken (well, maybe not gym).

You'll continue to develop and improve your Level Three skills in many ways between now and when you take the SAT: through your ongoing high school coursework; through challenging reading that you may do for school or any other purpose; and through the intellectual exercise you get whenever you take a test, including sample SAT exams you use as part of your test-prep program.

The more time you have between now and the exam, the greater your chances of improving your Level Three skills. In this book, Appendixes

A and B specifically address these skills by offering you help in building your word knowledge and sharpening your understanding of mathematics.

In addition, you'll find that you are using and practicing your Level Three skills every time you work on an exercise or sample test from any chapter in this book. Just as regular, disciplined exercise improves your overall muscle tone and strengthens your heart, *mental workouts* are the key to strengthening your Level Three skills.

MAKING THE MOST OF THE TIME YOU HAVE

As with almost any form of learning, preparing for the SAT is an investment of time. The more you have, the better your chances of boosting your score significantly. Next, we'll walk you through three different study plans, each tailored to a specific amount of preparation time. Find the plan that fits your circumstances, and adapt it to your needs.

If You Have Two Weeks to Prepare

Obviously, if you plan to take the SAT in two weeks or less and are just beginning your preparation program, your time is at a premium. You'll have to make the most of every available hour between now and the day of the test. As much as you can, cut back or eliminate nonessential activities over the next two weeks (sports, movies, after-school jobs) and focus your energies on the exam.

You can still develop a plan that will make a significant difference in your test scores by relying heavily on Level One skills, but you need to make it your highest priority, starting today. The outline shown in Table 2.1 will help.

If You Have Four to Six Weeks to Prepare

With a month or more to get ready for the SAT, you can make some major improvements in your test-taking skills. You can delve rather deeply into Level Two skills as well as mastering all the key Level One skills. It'll take some discipline and some hard work, of course. Try to cut back on nonessential activities between now and the day of the exam, and set aside significant blocks of time (evenings, weekends) for reading, study, and practice. If you do this, following the steps we suggest in Table 2.2, you'll boost your score.

If You Have Three Months or More to Prepare

Congratulations! Through astute planning, admirable self-discipline, or sheer good luck, you've positioned yourself so that you have ample time

Table 2.1
Your Two-Week Plan—The Steps to Take

1. If you haven't already, take the SAT Diagnostic Test (Chapter 1). Set aside 90 minutes and take the exam under true test conditions. Then grade your performance using the Scoring Guide beginning on page 29.
2. Based on the results of your SAT Diagnostic Test, identify the *two* question types on which you need the greatest improvement.
3. Turn to Part II of this book and read Chapter 3, Finding Your Way Around the SAT. It will give you an overview of the real SAT and a number of important hints about test-taking strategy that will help boost your scores.
4. Then find the two chapters from Chapters 4 through 9 that cover the two question types you identified in Step 2. Study those chapters, and try your hand on at least two of the practice exercises in each one. If you achieve an above-average or excellent score on both practice exercises, move on. Otherwise, reread the chapter and do as many additional practice exercises as you can.
5. Turn to Appendix B, The SAT Math Review. This part of the book covers the fifty math topics most frequently tested on the SAT. Take 15 minutes to skim this appendix, pencil in hand. Circle the number of any topic you find new or unfamiliar. Then set aside an afternoon or evening to read those topics in detail.
6. If you have time, read the chapters in Part II that you haven't already read.
7. Sometime in the week before the SAT, set aside 3 hours. Take the SAT (Chapter 10) under true test conditions. Then grade your performance using the Scoring Guide beginning on page 377.
8. Compare your performance on the SAT with your performance on the SAT Diagnostic Test. Is there any one question type where your performance still lags? If you have time, read or reread the chapter in Part II that covers that question type.
9. Two days before the SAT, read Chapter 11 and follow its advice about how to approach the weekend of the exam.
10. After taking the SAT, read Chapter 12.

to prepare thoroughly for one of the most important challenges of your academic life. With three months or more to prepare, you can improve all three levels of your SAT skills and give yourself an excellent chance of achieving or surpassing your score goals.

Take advantage of your foresight by pacing yourself intelligently. Set aside time every week to pursue your test-prep program, preferably in

Table 2.2
Your Four- to Six-Week Plan—The Steps to Take

1. If you haven't already, take the SAT Diagnostic Test (Chapter 1). Set aside 90 minutes and take the exam under true test conditions. Then grade your performance using the Scoring Guide beginning on page 29.
2. Based on the results of your SAT Diagnostic Test, identify the four question types on which you need the greatest improvement.
3. Turn to Part II of this book and read Chapter 3, Finding Your Way Around the SAT. It will give you an overview of the real SAT and a number of important hints about test-taking strategy that will help boost your scores.
4. As soon as possible, begin to set aside 15 minutes each day to study Appendix A, The SAT Word List. Plan to read the definitions and explanations of fifteen words from the word list each day. At this rate, you'll have been exposed to every word on the list within five weeks.
5. Now, find the four chapters from Chapters 4 through 9 that cover the four question types you identified in Step 2. Over the next two weeks, study those chapters, and try your hand on at least two of the practice exercises in each chapter. If you achieve an above-average or excellent score on both practice exercises, move on. Otherwise, reread the chapter and do as many additional practice exercises as you can.
6. Next, turn to Appendix B, The SAT Math Review. This part of the book covers the 50 math topics most frequently tested on the SAT. Over the next week, read this appendix thoroughly. With a pencil, circle the number of any topic you find difficult or confusing. Between now and the date of the exam, review the circled topics from time to time.
7. If you have time, read the chapters in Part II that you haven't already read.
8. Sometime in the week before the SAT, set aside 3 hours. Take the SAT (Chapter 10) under true test conditions. Then, grade your performance using the Scoring Guide beginning on page 377.
9. Compare your performance on the SAT with your performance on the SAT Diagnostic Test. Is there any one question type where your performance still lags? If you have time, read or reread the chapter in Part II that covers that question type.
10. Two days before the SAT, read Chapter 11 and follow its advice about how to approach the weekend of the exam.
11. After taking the SAT, read Chapter 12.

Table 2.3
Your Three-Month Plan—The Steps to Take

1. If you haven't already, take the SAT Diagnostic Test (Chapter 1). Set aside 90 minutes and take the exam under true test conditions. Then grade your performance using the Scoring Guide beginning on page 29.
2. Based on the results of your SAT Diagnostic Test, rank the six question types in order of priority from the one on which you need the greatest improvement to the one in which you currently perform the best.
3. Turn to Part II of this book and read Chapter 3, Finding Your Way Around the SAT. It will give you an overview of the real SAT and a number of important hints about test-taking strategy that will help boost your scores.
4. As soon as possible, begin to set aside 15 minutes each day to study Appendix A, The SAT Word List. Plan to read the definitions and explanations of fifteen words from the word list each day. At this rate, you'll have been exposed to every word on the list within five weeks. As suggested in the appendix, also start your own vocabulary notebook and add to it frequently.
5. Now, read Chapters 4 through 9 in the priority sequence you identified in Step 2. Also try your hand on at least two of the practice exercises in each chapter. If you achieve an above-average or excellent score on both practice exercises, move on. Otherwise, reread the chapter and do as many additional practice exercises as you can.
6. Next, turn to Appendix B, The SAT Math Review. This part of the book covers the fifty Math topics most frequently tested on the SAT. Over the next week, read this appendix thoroughly. With a pencil, circle the number of any topic you find difficult or confusing. Between now and the date of the exam, review the circled topics from time to time.
7. Sometime in the week before the SAT, set aside 3 hours. Take the SAT (Chapter 10) under true test conditions. Then, grade your performance using the Scoring Guide beginning on page 377.
8. Compare your performance on the SAT with your performance on the SAT Diagnostic Test. Is there any one question type where your performance still lags? If you have time, reread the chapter in Part II that covers that question type.
9. Two days before the SAT, read Chapter 11 and follow its advice about how to approach the weekend of the exam.
10. After taking the SAT, read Chapter 12.

major chunks—2 or 3 hours at a time on an evening or a weekday. An extended study program spread out over twelve weeks or more will boost your score more than an intensive, high-pressure program with the same number of study hours crammed into fewer weeks.

The steps in Table 2.3 will guide you through the planning process.

Once you've sketched your plan, turn to Chapter 3. There you'll begin developing your Level One skills by learning what to expect on the real SAT and some of the best test-taking strategies for every part of the exam.

JUST THE FACTS

- Level One skills involve Testwiseness and can be developed quickly.
- Level Two skills involve Topic Strategies and take more time to develop.
- Level Three skills involve Broad-Based Verbal and Math Abilities and take the longest time to develop.
- Skills at all three levels can help boost your SAT scores.
- Depending on your schedule, your personal study program can delve more or less deeply into all three kinds of skills.

Part II

Getting Inside the SAT

Chapter 3

Finding Your Way Around the SAT

Get the Scoop On . . .

- What to expect when you take the SAT
- Why you *don't* have to answer every question
- How to make the most of every minute
- How guessing can improve your score

THE OFFICIAL DESCRIPTION

FYI

If something weird comes up on your SAT, don't let it boggle you. It's just the test-makers playing tricks with your mind. As we'll explain later, any truly weird questions probably won't count in your test score.

How the Test Is Organized

The SAT is a 3-hour test made up of seven separately-timed sections. (Actually, you'll be in the testing room for 4 hours or more on exam day. You'll spend 3 hours answering questions and 1 to $1\frac{1}{2}$ hours filling out forms, listening to instructions, resting briefly between sections, and so on.) Five of the sections last 30 minutes each; the other two last 15 minutes.

The SAT questions are divided into two broad categories—Verbal and Mathematical. There are three specific types of Verbal questions: analogies, sentence completions, and critical reading. There are also three types of Math questions: multiple-choice problems, quantitative comparisons, and grid-in problems. (You'll find a chapter in this book for each of these six question types, filled with test-taking strategies and practice questions.)

Your SAT will include three Verbal sections, two of them 30 minutes long and one 15 minutes long. It will also include three Math sections, two of them 30 minutes long and one 15 minutes long. And there will be an additional 30-minute section containing either Verbal or Math questions. This is referred to as the equating section. We'll explain its significance and purpose later.

Three important notes about the structure and contents of the SAT:

- **The sections may appear in any order.** Most often, the two 15-minute sections come last, numbered in the test booklet as Sections 6 and 7. The other five sections, each 30 minutes long, may appear in any order: for example, your SAT could start with a

Verbal section or a Math section, and the equating section could appear anywhere in the sequence. Verbal and Math sections often alternate but they needn't always.

- **Several forms of the test are given at any time.** The test-makers refer to different editions of the SAT as forms. Each form has a different batch of questions (also called items). On any given test day, several forms are used, not only across the country but even within the same test room. The person sitting next to you may be working on a completely different exam. Among other benefits to the test-makers, this discourages cheating! So don't be alarmed if you notice that your neighbor is working on a Verbal section while you're working on a Math section—it's no mistake.

FYI

Remember, these seven sections—including the equating section—may appear in any order *on your SAT.*

- **The test-makers may change the test format if they wish.** Don't assume that your SAT will precisely follow the format outlined here. Although variations are rare, they do happen; and from time to time, the test-makers experiment with new formats and new types of questions.
- The Map of the SAT (Table 3.1) gives a more detailed listing of the types and quantities of questions you'll probably encounter on the exam.

Table 3.1
Map of the SAT

Verbal Sections	Math Sections
TYPE A—30 Minutes 9 sentence completions 6 analogies 15 critical reading questions (based on two passages)	**TYPE A—30 Minutes** 25 multiple-choice problems
30 TOTAL QUESTIONS	25 TOTAL QUESTIONS
TYPE B—30 Minutes 10 sentence completions 13 analogies 12 critical reading questions (based on one passage)	**TYPE B—30 Minutes** 15 quantitative comparisons 10 grid-in problems
35 TOTAL QUESTIONS	25 TOTAL QUESTIONS
TYPE C—15 Minutes 13 critical reading questions (based on one pair of linked passages)	**TYPE C—15 Minutes** 10 multiple-choice problems
13 TOTAL QUESTIONS	10 TOTAL QUESTIONS
Verbal Total—78 Questions	***Math Total—60 Questions***
	The Equating Section 30 minutes—Verbal or Math questions

How You Mark Your Answers

Most of the questions on the SAT are multiple-choice questions. You'll usually have five answers to choose from, labeled (A) through (E). One type of Math question, quantitative comparisons, has just four answer choices, (A) through (D). Once you pick the best answer, you'll mark your choice on the separate answer sheet by using a pencil to darken the appropriate oval next to the number for that question. This produces an answer sheet that can be scored quickly, accurately, and cheaply by a machine.

> **FYI**
>
> *In March 1999, Judge Ronald L. Buckwalter ruled that the use of an SAT cutoff score of 820 (combined math and verbal) for sports eligibility by the NCAA was not justified and had an improper "disparate impact" on minority student-athletes. If you're a student-athlete, check with the colleges to which you plan to apply for any recent developments.*

One of the Math sections includes ten questions, called grid-in problems, for which no answer choices are given. You have to figure out your own answers for these questions. Then you'll mark your answers on a special grid which provides both space for writing in the numbers that make up your answer (for example, 156) and matching ovals to be darkened in (in this case, ovals for the digits 1, 5, and 6). Fitting your answers to grid-in problems into the special grid is an art in itself. We'll explain it in detail in the appropriate chapter later in this book.

How the Test Is Scored

There are several steps involved in taking your SAT answer sheet, covered with blackened ovals, and turning it into two 3-digit numbers that will be your answer to the age-old, nosy question—Whadjaget?

First, for each of the test areas—Verbal and Mathematical—your *raw score* is calculated. Your raw score is determined by taking the number of questions you answer correctly and subtracting from it a fraction of the number of questions for which you choose a wrong answer. (Exception: for grid-in problems, nothing is subtracted for wrong answers.) The fraction to be subtracted is for all five-answer multiple-choice questions; it is for the quantitative comparisons, which have just four answer choices. If you leave a question blank, you subtract nothing.

> **FYI**
>
> *Subtracting a fraction for each wrong multiple-choice answer is what people sometimes call the guessing penalty. It takes away any likely score increase based on purely random guessing. (As we'll discuss, this does not mean that you shouldn't guess. You should guess! Later, we'll show you why and how.)*

The raw score is rounded to the nearest whole number and then converted into a *scaled score*. You'll receive both a Verbal and a Mathematical scaled score. These are the 3-digit scores most people are thinking of when they talk about SAT scores. The lowest possible scaled score, for both Verbal and Math areas is 200; the highest is 800.

The system of converting a raw score into a scaled score varies slightly from one test to another, since the test forms vary slightly in difficulty. If you get a slightly harder SAT, the score conversion table for your exam will be a little easier—you'll be able to get a couple more questions wrong while still earning the same scaled score. The test-makers have an elaborate system based on statistical theories for figuring out exactly how much they need to compensate for slightly harder or easier test forms. The idea is to make any given score—say, a 580 Verbal—represent the same level of difficulty no matter when or where the test is given.

The test-makers point out (quite properly) that the scaled scores are only approximately accurate in the following sense—if you took the SAT a hundred times (how's that for a fun idea?), the scores you'd earn would obviously vary. On a good day, you might earn a Math score of (let's say) 630. On a bad day, you might score 580. But your 100 scores should supposedly cluster around some central number which represents your true ability. Maybe in your case it's around 600.

Now, of course, it's impractical to expect anyone to take the SAT 100 times. So the SAT people have to be satisfied with a single score that they consider an approximation of your true score. Statistical theory suggests that, for the SAT, your scaled score is probably within about 30 points of your true score. Therefore, strictly speaking, if you earn a score of 600 on the Math portion of the SAT, you should think of it as representing a range of about 30 points either way—that is, from 570 to 630. And if your best friend scores 590, does that mean you are better at math than she is? Maybe, maybe not. The SAT isn't a precise enough measuring tool to say for sure.

Finally, you'll also be given *percentile scores* in each test area. These are based on a comparison of your performance to that of two groups of college-bound seniors: those in your home state, and those from the entire nation. The percentile score shows what percentage of these students scored lower than you. If you have a Math percentile score of 62 in the state column, for example, that means that 62 percent of the students in your state scored lower than you. (The remaining 38 percent scored the same, or higher.) Obviously, the higher your percentile scores, the better.

Average SAT scaled scores are just around 500 for both the Verbal and Math sections. What is a good SAT score? It all depends. It depends on what colleges you hope to be admitted to; it depends on how many students you are competing against for admission and how high their scores are; it depends on your other credentials and how heavily you want the SAT to weigh in the admission decision. We'll discuss the deeper meanings of SAT scores—and how they may change your life—in further detail later in this book.

THE INSIDER'S REPORT

Some Questions Don't Count

We've already mentioned what the test-makers call the equating section. This is a 30-minute test section containing questions that will not count on your score. Why is this section used? How should you deal with it as a test-taker?

First, the purpose—as we've explained, the test-makers are eager to make the scoring of the SAT fair to you no matter when or where you take the exam. This means compensating for the fact that some forms of the test are, inevitably, a little harder or a little easier than others. One way the test-makers deal with this is by asking groups of students from various test dates and locations to answer some of the same questions. By comparing how well Groups A and B do with these questions, they can estimate the average skill levels of the two groups. Then, by comparing how Groups A and B do on the rest of their exams—where the questions are totally different—they can estimate which exam is harder than the other, and by how much. We're oversimplifying slightly, but in basic terms, this is how equating works; it's a statistical process intended to equalize scores across two or more forms of the exam.

As of October 1998, over 280 colleges and universities in the U.S. had made scores on the SAT (or ACT) optional for admission, according to FairTest in Cambridge, Massachusetts. This is an increase from 192 in 1994. However, the vast majority of North American colleges—nearly 2,000 in all—still require either SAT or ACT scores from all applicants.

The equating section on every test is used partly for this purpose. It's also used to test newly-written questions before they are given to students for real. Seeing how students perform on the new questions lets the test-makers decide whether the questions are too hard, too easy, too confusing, not confusing enough, etc.

You can think of the equating section as a kind of experiment. The test-makers are testing future test questions in the best way available—by using you as their laboratory rats. (Another appealing concept, eh?) And since the questions are purely for experimental purposes, they don't count on your score. Whether you get them all right or all wrong doesn't matter—your SAT scores won't be affected.

It would be nice if you knew which test section was the equating section. Then you could take a little nap during that 30-minute interval. However, the equating section isn't marked in any way. You can see why: if the rats know it's an experiment, they don't take it seriously, and it ruins the test results! Some people claim they can recognize equating sections, and maybe they can; but we wouldn't recommend that you count on doing so. Since you can't use the 30 minutes to work on other sections, you might as well do your best on all the questions anyway.

There's just one thing to remember about the equating section: Anything on your SAT that is truly weird probably will not count on your score. The test-makers sometimes experiment with new and bizarre types of questions. "Maybe it would be fun to test logic," they say—or grammar, or the ability to read bus schedules. Long before new question types are included for real on the exam, they are tested by the test-makers on students like you. Most never show up on the real exam. But while they are being tested, they strike terror into the hearts of unsuspecting test-takers who (correctly) observe, "I never saw questions like this before!"

Table 3.2
Sample Score Conversion Table—Verbal

Raw Score	Percentage Right	Scaled Score
78	100	800
70	90	750
65	83	700
60	77	650
52	67	600
44	56	550

If your SAT includes a section with weird questions unlike anything you read about in this book, don't let it scare you. It is (almost certainly) an equating section that will not count in your final SAT scores.

You Don't Need to Answer Every Question

The score conversion formula for every SAT is a little different—but notice how high you can score if you answer just 65 to 75 percent of the questions right!

There are many differences between a standardized test like the SAT and the classroom tests you're used to taking. Here's a crucial one—to do well on a classroom test, you need to answer correctly 80 to 90 percent of the questions, or more. Not on the SAT. You can earn a high score on the SAT by answering two thirds to three quarters of the questions right.

Think about that. On a classroom test, if you get 66 to 75 percent of the questions right, you'll earn a grade of D or (at best) C. On the SAT, the same percentage of correct answers yields a grade that's the equivalent of B+! The Sample Score Conversion Tables (Tables 3.2 and 3.3) give a few details.

This fact about standardized tests has several important implications for you:

- **You don't have to answer every question.** In truth, most students omit some questions on each test section. And that's perfectly okay. Even if you leave two or three questions blank on each

Table 3.3
Sample Score Conversion Table—Math

Raw Score	Percentage Right	Scaled Score
60	100	800
56	93	750
53	88	700
48	80	650
42	70	600
35	58	550

section, you can still score well into the 700s (provided you perform well on the questions you do answer, of course).

- **Getting a handful of questions wrong is not fatal.** If you run into a series of tough questions—five questions based on a reading passage that you find very hard to understand, for example—don't despair. Give an educated guess for each of the tough questions—get a couple of them right—and then move on. You can still earn a high overall score, as long as you don't let the few killer questions get you down.
- **Almost everyone gets some questions wrong.** It's a deliberate feature of the SAT. Here's why—on a classroom test, if everyone scores 95 percent, the teacher is usually delighted; it means he has done a great job of teaching. But if everyone scored 700 on the SAT, the test-makers would be depressed. Their job is to create a test that yields a broad range of scores. They want a few 700s, a few 300s, and a nice sampling of 400s, 500s, and 600s in between. This proves that they are differentiating among students—sorting the sheep from the goats, and both from the donkeys, cows, and emus—that is what they are paid to do.

To accomplish this, they write questions that vary greatly in difficulty: a few very hard, a few very easy, and many others scattered along the range in between. So when you take the SAT, expect each section to include a few questions you find very, very difficult. Answer them as best as you can and move on. Almost no one gets every question right.

FYI

Be careful not to get bogged down on a few very hard questions. The time you spend wrestling one tough problem into submission could be spent answering three easy questions—and getting three times as much credit.

Every Question Is Worth the Same Amount

Some of the questions will be very hard. You may find that it takes you 2 or 3 minutes to solve some of the math problems—an eternity on the SAT. Others will be shockingly easy. The answer may jump out at you as soon as you see the question and you may spend 15 seconds or less on the item. The easy questions are worth just as much as the hard ones. The test-makers only look at how many questions you answer right; they couldn't care less which ones they are.

MAKING THE TEST WORK FOR YOU

Budget Your Time

The SAT isn't a speed test. Most students find they have time to answer all, or nearly all, of the questions in each section. But you'll have no time to waste. If you aren't efficient in the use of your precious 30 (or 15) minutes, you may find yourself having to leave blank some questions you could surely have answered—and losing some valuable points. Here are the best methods for making sure you don't run out of time before you run out of questions.

Overview each section before you begin your work. When the proctor says, "Begin work on Section 1," don't immediately begin answering questions. Take the first 30 seconds to overview the entire section. Leaf through the test booklet to check the format, contents, and length of the section. How many questions are there? How many reading passages? How many problems of the type you hate (or like) the most? Overviewing the section will prevent you from having the unpleasant surprise of turning what you thought was the last page of the section to discover one more set of questions—just as the proctor says, "Put down your pencil."

Tackle first the question types you find easiest. Having overviewed the section, you'll know before you begin work what question types appear in the section and in what order. Now consider this—you don't have to work through the questions in the order they're printed. Instead, pick the question type you find easiest, fastest, and even (if possible) the most fun. Start with that batch of questions, no matter where it appears.

FYI

Reset your watch to noon as each section begins. This makes it easy to tell at a glance how many minutes remain.

This has several benefits. It will allow you to quickly rack up a bunch of easy points at the very start of the test period. It will help you to develop a good rhythm and a sense of confidence for the rest of the section. And it eliminates the possibility of running out of time just as you begin work on the questions you find easiest. (If you *must* run out of time—and with practice there's no reason why you should—better to omit several questions you find very hard and of which you'd probably get only a couple right, rather than several easy questions that represent sure points for you.)

Skip and mark the hardest questions so you can try them later. Since every question on the SAT is worth the same amount, it's crucial not to get bogged down on a few very tough questions. (Every section has them.) Instead, once you've discovered that a particular question is a very hard one—a math problem requiring complicated figuring, for example—stop working on it. Put an X mark in the margin of your test booklet next to the question number, and move on.

If you have time at the end of the section, you can double back and tackle the three or four toughest questions you'd skipped and marked before. This will ensure that you get to all of the easier questions in the section, accumulating almost certain points toward your score. And it may help you in another way—sometimes, when you return to a question several minutes after skipping it, the right answer which eluded you before seems obvious. Why does this happen? No one knows for sure. Maybe your unconscious mind ponders the question while you consciously think about other items. But this effect does occur, and you should take advantage of it.

Practice timing along with test-taking skills. Between now and the day of the SAT, whenever you work on practice exercises or sample tests, follow the time restrictions given. Set up a kitchen timer while you work, or ask your Mom or your brother to act as a proctor. Not only will this give you practice in working under time pressure, but it also allows you to develop an inner clock keyed to the timing of the real SAT.

Scale the Difficulty Ladder

FYI

Remember: if you start work on a question other than question 1, be sure to mark your answers in the right spaces on your answer sheet.

In each section, you'll be given questions in batches. For example, a Verbal section usually contains a batch of sentence completions followed by a batch of analogies and then a batch of reading comprehension questions. In general, the questions within each batch are arranged from easiest to hardest. (The only exception is reading comprehension questions, which are usually arranged roughly in order of the contents of the reading passage.) So, for example, in a batch of thirteen analogies, the first three or four are likely to be quite easy, the last three or four are likely to be quite hard, and the ones in between are likely to be, well, in between.

Now, your idea of what is easy or difficult may not be same as that of the average student. It's possible that a particular question that appears at the start of a batch may strike you as hard, while a question at the end may strike you as easy. But, in general, you'll find the questions getting harder as you work your way through any given batch. We call this the ladder of difficulty. It affects your approach to the exam in several ways.

- **Be prepared to skip and mark items near the end of a batch.** Obviously, since the hardest questions usually appear near the end of a batch, you'd be more inclined to skip and mark the last question or two in a batch than the first question or two.
- **Expect trickier answer choices near the end of a batch.** You're more likely to encounter subtle wrong answers ("distractors," as the test-makers call them) at the top of the difficulty ladder than at the bottom. So read all the answer choices especially carefully near the end of the batch, and be on guard for tricks. This is where they're likely to appear.
- **Don't be suspicious of easy questions near the start of a batch.** Sometimes test-takers outsmart themselves. Encountering a shockingly easy question, they say, "Hmm! This looks too easy. It must be a trap! Instead of picking the obvious answer (B), I'll pick answer (D), which is probably correct in some convoluted, complicated

way. That'll show them!" The trouble is the obvious answer may just be the correct one. Remember, the SAT is specifically designed to include some very easy questions, along with some very hard ones. A few items should appear surprisingly simple. One clue is where the questions appears in the batch. If an obvious question is the first, second, or third item in the batch, then it probably is obvious. If it appears at the end of the batch, be suspicious—it may be a trap.

Never Read the Directions

When you watch a TV show, have you ever noticed how you know that it's time for a commerical without even looking at a clock? Through your years of TV watching, you've developed an inner clock that's finely tuned to the rhythms of TV. In the same way, practicing the timing of the real SAT will make it easy for you to sense, as you work, when you need to move a little faster or when you have plenty of time and can afford to cruise.

One piece of test-taking advice dispensed by old-fashioned teachers (and some current books, alas!) is, "Always read the directions carefully before you start work—preferably twice." The trouble with this advice is that, on the SAT, the precious minutes allotted for each test section include the time for reading the directions. So if you spend 3 minutes studying the directions, that's 3 minutes less you have to answer the questions.

The truth is that the test directions don't change from one exam to the next (unless the test-makers are trying out some weird new question type, as explained above—in which case the questions won't count in your score anyway). So get to know the directions and the best strategies for answering the questions thoroughly before the day of the exam. Then, when you take the test, all you need to do is to verify the question type ("Oh, here's a batch of quantitative comparisons") and immediately begin work.

Using the Answer Sheet

As we've explained, you'll mark your answers on an answer sheet that is separate from the question booklet. How you use the answer sheet does matter. Follow the directions provided by the test-makers: fill in the oval for the answer you want completely and erase all stray marks, lest you confuse the stupid machine that the test-makers have hired to grade your exam. Here are some important additional tips:

- **Check your location on the answer sheet every five items.** Get into the habit of making sure that you are filling in the right answer in the right location at least once every five questions. This will preclude your discovering, as you complete a section, that you've mismarked the answers for the last twenty questions (ouch!).

- **Be extra careful when you skip questions.** It's easy to forget to leave a blank space on the answer sheet when you skip a question. Make a point of remembering.

- **Practice using sample answer sheets.** Most study books (including this one) with practice tests include answer sheets with ovals like those used on the real exam. Don't ignore them. Use them when you take practice tests. Filling in the real sheet on the day of the SAT will be second nature to you—and one less thing you have to worry about.

- **If you do goof up . . . and discover that you have mismarked the last five or ten answer spaces, don't panic!** Raise your hand and get the attention of the proctor. Explain what happened and ask for 5 minutes after the section is over with your answer sheet only, so you can (calmly and carefully) correct the misplaced answer choices. She will probably say "Yes."

When Crunch Time Comes

Practice this system before test day, and be prepared to use it if you find yourself running short of time.

Occasionally, despite having practiced and used the best time-budgeting techniques, you might find yourself running out of time before you run out of questions in a section. If that happens, don't get upset. Instead, spend the last 5 minutes extracting the most possible points from the remaining questions. How? By following the procedure described below—The 5-Minute Drill (Table 3.4).

Guessing Will Improve Your Score

Having heard of the guessing penalty, many students think they will hurt their scores by guessing. Wrong! Here's how the guessing penalty really works and why it usually pays to guess.

As we explained before, you'll lose a fraction of a point from your raw score for every question you answer wrong. Suppose there were twenty Verbal questions that you had absolutely no clue about—any of the five answers had an equal chance of being right. If you were to guess at random on each of these questions, on average you would get one in five right (since there are five answers to choose from). So out of 20 questions, you'd likely get four right. (In reality, you might be lucky and get five or six right, or unlucky and get two or three right; but on average, you'd expect to get four.) That would add four points to your raw score.

However, you'd have answered sixteen of the twenty questions wrong. The guessing penalty subtracts $\frac{1}{4}$ of a point for every wrong answer. Since $\frac{1}{4}$ times 16 equals 4, you'd lose four points for the sixteen wrong answers. This would exactly offset the gain of four points on the correct answers, leaving you with a net of zero—no gain, no loss. That's how the guessing penalty is supposed to work.

Table 3.4
The 5-Minute Drill

1. When you notice that 5 minutes remain to work on the section, answer the question you are looking at promptly.
2. Then overview the remaining questions in the section by glancing through them quickly.
3. Decide which of the remaining questions look quickest and easiest. Read and answer them promptly, guessing if necessary.
4. If a reading passage remains, take about 30 seconds to skim through it, looking only for the main idea and the author's overall point of view. Then, glance at the questions that follow the passage and answer whichever ones you have a hunch about. The vocabulary items will probably be fastest—start with those.
5. If a batch of Math problems, sentence completions, or analogies remains, glance at them and pick three to five to answer—probably near the start of the batch. Focus on items with vocabulary you know or math topics you are comfortable with.
6. Guess freely. On every item where you feel there is a particular answer that sounds wrong, guess at random from among the other answers. If you have a good feeling about a particular answer choice, pick it and move on.
7. Don't bother marking answers for questions that you have no time to look at or think about. Because of the guessing penalty, you're unlikely either to lose or gain points by completely random guessing.

But (and it's a big but) it only works this way if your guessing is absolutely random. If you have even an inkling, a hunch, a notion, a feeling about a question, you will probably gain points by guessing. Here's why.

Take the same batch of twenty questions. Suppose that instead of being totally clueless, you were able to eliminate just one answer choice from each question as being almost certainly incorrect—leaving four equal possibilities to choose from. Obviously, your chance of guessing right on any question would increase from one in five to one in four. On average, you'd be likely to answer five questions correctly out of the twenty, rather than four. And even after subtracting $\frac{1}{4}$ point for each wrong answer, you'd come out ahead:

$$5 - \left(15 \times \frac{1}{4}\right) = 5 - 3\frac{3}{4} = 1\frac{1}{4} \text{ raw points net gain}$$

Maybe $1\frac{1}{4}$ extra raw points doesn't sound like much. But depending on where you are in the scoring range, it can amount to ten, twenty, or even thirty points on the 200–800 scale! Thus, it's possible that educated guessing—even by eliminating only one wrong answer—can change, for example, a 580 to a 600. That's a big difference.

The truth is that, when you aren't sure of the answer for a question, you rarely have to make a totally random guess. You will almost always have at least some information you can use to improve your odds of guessing right. On a math problem, for example, you might follow a hunch that tells you that the answer is (say) less than 20, so answer (A), (B), or (C) is probably correct. Or on a verbal problem, you might sense that the answer should probably sound more negative than positive, thus eliminating answers (B) and (E). You get the idea. Any time you have even a clue as to what the right answer is—or is not—it pays to guess.

So don't let the words "guessing penalty" intimidate you. Go ahead and guess. You'll gain points by doing it.

JUST THE FACTS

- Preview the test section before you start work and budget your time accordingly.
- Remember that every question is worth the same amount—don't sweat the hardest ones.
- Expect questions to get tougher as you work through a batch.
- Use the 5-Minute Drill if you're running out of time.
- Don't be afraid to guess.

Chapter 4

Analogies

Get the Scoop On . . .

- Proven strategies for acing analogies
- The nine top analogy types used on the SAT
- How to guess the meaning of analogy words you don't know
- The most common analogy traps and how to avoid them

THE TEST CAPSULE

What's the Big Idea?

You'll be given a pair of words (the stem pair) that have a certain logical relationship to one another. You have to pick the pair of words from five answer choices that has the same logical relationship.

How Many?

Your SAT will probably have a total of nineteen analogies. In one Verbal section, you can expect six analogies out of thirty total questions; in another Verbal section, expect fourteen analogies out of thirty-five total questions.

How Much Do They Count?

Analogies are nineteen out of seventy-eight total Verbal questions. They count as 24 percent of your overall verbal score.

How Much Time Should They Take?

You need to answer analogies at a rate of better than 1 per minute. Aim to finish a batch of six analogies in 4 minutes, and a batch of thirteen analogies in 9 minutes.

What's the Best Strategy?

Build a bridge—a sentence that defines the logical relationship between the two words in the question stem. Then test the bridge with each pair of words in the five answer choices. Only one will work!

What's the Worst Pitfall?

Picking an answer because the words it contains are similar on the surface to those in the question stem. (Maybe both the stem words and the answer words have to do with cooking, for instance.) Ignore surface similarities and look deeper to find the most similar logical relationship.

THE OFFICIAL DESCRIPTION

What They Are

Analogies test your ability to recognize the relationships between pairs of words. You'll be given a pair of words in capital letters (the stem pair) that have a particular relationship to one another. You'll then be given five additional pairs of words labeled (A), (B), (C), (D), and (E) (the answer choices). Your job is to select that answer choice with a pair of words whose relationship is similar to the relationship between the words in the stem pair.

Where They Are

In the typical SAT, you'll have three Verbal sections. Two will be 30 minutes long, and one will be 15 minutes long. Each of the 30-minute sections will include a batch of analogies, which generally appear in the middle of the section, after a batch of sentence completions and before a batch of reading comprehension questions. Reminder—the test-makers claim the right to change the format at any time! However, the typical format we just described is what you're most likely to encounter.

What They Measure

Specialized knowledge and classroom learning aren't tested by analogies. The words used are all general vocabulary words that a well-rounded high school junior should know.

To answer an analogy correctly, you need to know the meaning of the words in the stem pair and in the answer choices. You also need to understand the logical relationships between words, and at times these can be subtle. So analogies measure both your vocabulary knowledge and your understanding of logical relationships among ideas.

The Directions

> **Directions:** Each question below consists of a related pair of words or phrases, followed by five pairs of words or phrases labeled (A) through (E). Select the pair that *best* expresses a relationship similar to that expressed in the original pair.

Example

CRUMB : BREAD : :

(A) ounce : unit
(B) splinter : wood
(C) water : bucket
(D) twine : rope
(E) cream : butter

The correct answer is choice (B).

THE INSIDER'S REPORT—STRATEGIES THAT REALLY WORK

Build a Bridge

A bridge is a short sentence that contains both words in the stem pair and shows how they are related. Let's call the two words in the stem pair "X" and "Y." A typical bridge would define X in terms of Y. So, for the sample question from the directions above, the bridge might say, "A CRUMB is a very small piece that falls off or breaks off a piece of BREAD." Notice how this sentence explains the relationship between the two words. It also defines CRUMB (tells what a crumb is) in terms of BREAD. A lovely bridge! (No wonder—it's the test-makers' own example.)

Here are a couple of other examples. Suppose the stem pair was "OPERA : MUSIC." (By the way, you would read this aloud, "opera is to music.") The bridge might say, "An OPERA is a long, elaborate, classical work of MUSIC." If the stem pair was "SURGEON : SCALPEL," the bridge might be, "A SURGEON is a professional who uses a SCALPEL." Get the idea?

Plug in the Answer Choices

FYI

A strong bridge explicitly defines the relationship between the two words in the stem pair. By building a bridge, you force yourself to explain (to yourself) exactly how the two words logically fit together—the first step to solving any analogy question.

After you've created a bridge, turn to the answer choices. One by one, try to plug in the words from the answer choices into the same sentence. If your bridge is a strong one, only one pair of words will make sense.

Try this with the five answer choices for the sample question above. Only the words in choice (B) fit comfortably into the bridge: "A SPLINTER is a very small piece that falls off or breaks off of a piece of WOOD." Think about the others. Is an OUNCE a very small piece of a UNIT, choice (A)? No; an ounce is a kind of unit—a unit of weight. Is WATER a very small piece of a BUCKET, choice (C)? No; water might be carried in a bucket. The same with the other answers. So choice (B) is correct. (By the way, you would read the stem pair and the correct answer this way: "CRUMB is to BREAD as SPLINTER is to WOOD.")

Example

What if our stem pair is OPERA : MUSIC?

Which of these five answer choices fits the same bridge?

(A) novel : artistry
(B) painting : landscape
(C) oboe : instrument
(D) epic : poetry
(E) microphone : recording

The correct answer is (D), because only that word pair fits into the same bridge: "An EPIC is a long, elaborate, classical work of POETRY."

Get Narrow as Needed

FYI

Think of analogies as resembling proportions in math. A proportion like $\frac{2}{3} = \frac{4}{6}$ also describes analogous logical relationships among things. Do you see the similarity?

Sometimes the differences among the answer choices will be subtle—so subtle that the first bridge you've built won't eliminate the wrong answers. In this case, two or more answer choices may fit the bridge.

Example

SURGEON : SCALPEL : :

(A) judge : gavel
(B) painter : canvas
(C) executive : computer
(D) farmer : fertilizer
(E) carpenter : saw

If you built the bridge, "A SURGEON is a professional who uses a SCALPEL" and then tried plugging each of the answer pairs (A) through (E), you'd be dismayed to find that all five answer pairs could fit the bridge! A judge uses a gavel (the hammer used to pound on the bench); a painter uses a canvas; an executive uses a computer; a farmer uses fertilizer; and a carpenter uses a saw. Based on this bridge, all five answer choices could be considered correct! Now what?

Solution—narrow your bridge. Add details to the sentence to make it more specific.

In this case, you might narrow the bridge in this way: "A SURGEON is a professional who uses a SCALPEL as a tool for cutting." Now plug in the answer choices. Only one fits the new, narrower bridge: choice (E). That's the correct answer.

Of course, picking the correct answer depends on your narrowing the bridge correctly. You could concoct a misleading bridge that included details that pointed to a different answer. For example, you could say, "A SURGEON is a professional who wears a protective smock while using a SCALPEL." With that bridge, choice (B) is arguably correct, since artists, like surgeons, do often wear protective smocks. (The robe a judge wears isn't "protective," so choice (A) doesn't work. And the people in the other choices don't wear smocks at all.) Does this mean that choice (B) is just as good as choice (E)?

No. In fact, if you think about it, you probably find choice (B), and the bridge we made up that points to it, a little silly. The smock that a surgeon (or an artist) wears isn't central to his or her work and it certainly has little to do with the use of the scalpel. The first narrow bridge we created—the one that refers to the scalpel as a cutting tool—seems more sensible. It defines exactly what the scalpel does in the hands of the surgeon, which is similar to what the saw does in the hands of the carpenter.

The point is that it takes a bit of judgment to build the right bridge. You want to focus on the central, basic nature of the relationship between the two words—not on side issues that are irrelevant (like the surgeon's smock). It's a little subjective, yes. But nine times out of ten, devising the right bridge will strike you as a matter of common sense.

In fact, in the example we've been looking at, you may have been able to see the similarity between SURGEON : SCALPEL and carpenter : saw even without consciously building the new, narrow bridge. That's fine. But as you prepare for the test, practice your bridge-building technique. It will give you crucial help on the handful of really tough analogies that your test will contain.

Look for the Test-Makers' Favorite Relationships

They write test questions by the hundred, week in and week out. Like anyone else, they eventually start to repeat themselves. (Ever notice how the third album by your favorite rock band sounds a lot like their first and second albums—only less interesting?) But this is a good thing for you, the test-taker. It means that analogies fall into repeated patterns that you can practice and learn. If you know and understand the test-makers' favorite analogy relationships, you'll quickly pounce on them if they pop up on your exam.

FYI

If the correct answer for an analogy "jumps out at you" without the bridge-building step, great—go for it! But the more you practice bridge-building before *the test, the faster your instincts will supply answers on SAT day.*

Here are the top nine analogy relationships we've found on past and current SATs. (If any of the examples that follow contain words you're not sure about, you know what to do—grab your dictionary!)

Part : Whole
In this kind of analogy, one word names something that is part of what's named by the other word—usually a specific kind of part. Here are a couple of examples:

LID : POT : : roof : house

MOVEMENT : SYMPHONY : : scene : play

Opposites
Here, the two words in the pair are opposite or opposed in meaning. Examples:

NAIVE : SOPHISTICATED : : untutored : educated

WATER : DROUGHT : : food : famine

Actor : Action
This kind of analogy links a person or thing with what they commonly do. Examples:

COUNTERFEITER : FAKE : : blackmailer : extort

DETERGENT : CLEAN : : bleach : whiten

Actor : Acted Upon
The word pair includes a person or thing and another person or thing that is commonly acted upon or affected by the first. Examples:

TEACHER : CLASS : : orator : audience

NET : FISH : : trap : game

Action : Acted Upon
Here, an action is paired with the person or thing that commonly receives or is affected by the action. Examples:

ALPHABETIZE : FILES : : catalog : books

RAZE : BUILDING : : fell : tree

Action : Emotion
One of the words describes an action, the other an emotion with which it is commonly associated. Examples:

LOSS : MOURN : : triumph : celebrate

TREMBLE : FEAR : : shiver : cold

Thing : Description
This kind of word-pair includes one word that names a person or thing, another that describes it. Examples:

MISER : STINGY : : spendthrift : wasteful

GLADE : SHADY : : clearing : open

Description : Quality
Here, an adjective that describes a particular quality is paired with a noun that names the quality. Examples:

LIFELIKE : VIVIDNESS : : truthful : honesty

ARROGANT : PRIDE : : modest : humility

Differing Connotations
In this kind of analogy, two words are linked that have similar meanings but different feelings, moods, or nuances—in other words, different connotations. Examples:

CAR : JALOPY : : house : shanty

HIGH : SHRILL : : bright : blinding

Not every analogy on your exam will fit into one of these nine categories, but three quarters of them will. Those that don't will embody miscellaneous relationships of their own, like these examples:

MUSICIAN : CONCERT : : poet : reading

Here, a type of artist is paired with an event at which he or she might perform.

BOTANY : PLANT : : astronomy : star

A field of science is paired with a typical object that is studied in that field.

GAUNTLET : HAND : : helmet : head

A gauntlet is an armored glove worn, of course, on the hand. A helmet is an armored hat worn on the head.

THE INSIDER'S REPORT: THE BEST TIPS

Use the Analogy Structure to Guess Words You Don't Know

On some analogies, you may encounter words whose meaning you aren't sure of. Don't worry. You can use the analogy structure to help you guess the meaning of the unknown words. First, realize that all the word pairs contain words that are the same parts of speech. For example, if the stem pair contains a noun and a verb, like this:

TYRANT : OPPRESS

then each of the other word pairs will also contain a noun and a verb, in that order. So in any analogy with an unknown word, by looking at any of the other word pairs, you can tell whether the unknown word is a noun, verb, adjective, or any other part of speech—which in itself can be helpful in guessing its meaning.

Next, try using what you know about analogy relationships—and the words in the question that you *do* understand—to make a smart guess as to the meaning of the unknown word.

Example

ETYMOLOGY : WORD : :

(A) etiology : disease
(B) history : event
(C) literature : author
(D) microscopy : microbe
(E) psychology : insanity

(We've deliberately included some difficult, specialized words in this analogy, to illustrate a point; actually, a word like *etiology* is unlikely to be used in an analogy on the real SAT.) You may or may not know what ETYMOLOGY means in the stem pair, but you can tell by glancing at the other word pairs that it must be a noun, since the first word in every pair is a noun. And you can probably guess, from the way the word looks, that it refers to a study or science of some kind. (Words that end in *-ology*, like *biology* and *anthropology*, usually do.)

More students hurt themselves on the SAT by shunning the "obvious" than by taking it for granted. Don't be shy about guessing at word relationships! The test-makers are predictable, and the obvious connection is usually the right one.

Now, ETYMOLOGY is paired with WORD. From what you know of analogy relationships, you obviously know that ETYMOLOGY has something to do with a word or words. Given that fact, what's a possible meaning of ETYMOLOGY? Your first guess is likely to be that ETYMOLOGY is "the science or study of words." As it happens, that's not quite correct; but never mind. This guess is probably close enough to enable you to eliminate choices (B), (C), and (E) as clearly wrong. History can't be defined as "the science of events"; it's the study of the past, including events, people, forces, trends, and so on. Literature isn't "the science of authors"; it's what authors produce, namely books and other writings. And psychology isn't "the science of insanity"; it studies the mind and human behavior, including both sane and insane subjects. So by sheer guesswork—and a modicum of word-sense—you can narrow your choices to two, giving you great odds for guessing, even if you have little or no idea what *etiology* and *microscopy* mean.

The correct answer, by the way, is choice (A). ETYMOLOGY is actually the study of word origins—where words come from. Similarly, *etiology* is the study of the origins of disease—where particular illnesses come from. So the analogy is close. (Microscopy has nothing to do with the origin of microbes, if you're wondering.)

Not every obscure word in an analogy may be positioned quite so well for guessing. But many will be. Don't let one or more unknown words in a question alarm you; work from what you do know to make reasonable guesses as to the meaning of the new words, and don't be afraid to base your choice on these guesses.

FYI

If your bridge leaves two or three possible answers, try working backward from each of the live possibilities. Look at each word pair, build a bridge that defines their relationship, and then try to plug the stem pair into that bridge. It'll probably work with only one of the answer pairs—and that, of course, is the correct answer

Don't Fear the Flip-Flop

The logical relationship in the stem pair will run a certain way; the relationships in the answer choices will run the same way. For example, suppose you face this stem pair:

PROLIFIC : CREATOR

The relationship here is "Description : Thing," and it might be summarized by the bridge, "A PROLIFIC CREATOR is one that produces a lot (of offspring, ideas, artworks, or whatever)." Your job would be to find the answer choice with the same "Description : Thing" relationship, preferably using words that fit nicely into the same bridge. Choosing the right answer, as you've already seen, may at times be subtle, even tricky. But one kind of trick you *don't* have to worry about is the flip-flop. The test-makers do *not* try to trick you by giving you a correct word pair in reverse order, like this:

SOURCE : ABUNDANT

As we said before, on the SAT, you'll find that all the choices match the stem pair in their parts of speech. Similarly, you'll find that relationship reversals are not used to try to trick you. So don't worry about flip-flops—they don't turn up on the SAT.

When All Else Fails . . .

Sometimes—it should be rare—you won't be able to find the one best answer for an analogy question. Remember, the questions get harder as you move through a batch; so in a batch of thirten analogies, you're likely to find the last three or four to be quite hard. And you may encounter words whose meaning you don't know, and can't guess, even using the clues provided by the analogy structure. When this happens, work by elimination. Build the best bridge you can and plug in the answer choices. Eliminate any answer pairs that don't seem to fit, and guess from among the remaining answers.

Occasionally you may find that you've eliminated all the answers you understand, leaving only an answer that contains words you don't know. Don't be afraid—choose it!

THE INSIDER'S REPORT: THE MOST IMPORTANT WARNINGS

Ignore the Topics of the Word Pairs

FYI

Remember the wise advice of the great detective Sherlock Holmes: "When we have eliminated the impossible, what remains, however improbable, *must be the truth." Sherlock would have aced the SAT!*

It's easy to go wrong by focusing on the surface meanings of the words in the word pairs rather than on their underlying relationship.

Example

WING : FEATHER : :

(A) turtle : shell
(B) eagle : talon
(C) fish : fin
(D) wall : shingle
(E) bird : flight

The words in the stem pair refer to parts of a bird, of course. A hasty glance at the answer choices shows that four of them also refer to animals of one kind or another, and two choices (B) and (E), refer specifically to birds. So you might be tempted to pick one of these answers, misled by the surface similarity.

Don't! The correct answer is choice (D). A well-thought-out bridge will tell you why. The relationship between the words in the stem pair might be described this way: "The WING of a bird is covered by many small, overlapping segments, each called a FEATHER." Only choice (D) fits the same bridge: "The WALL of a house is [or may be] covered by many small, overlapping segments, each called a SHINGLE." Can you picture

FYI

Test-makers call wrong answers "distractors." You can see why. The wrong answers are deliberately designed to "distract" the unwary test-taker from the correct answer—which, on its surface, may appear far-fetched. Don't focus on the surface. Go deeper, focusing on the logical relationship between the words. That's what counts.

the similarity? No such similarity exists when you picture the turtle and its shell, the eagle and its talon (or claw), or any of the other items named in the choices.

Be Prepared to Jump from the Concrete to the Abstract

The test-makers sometimes like to make you connect a pair of words that are concrete (related to the physical world) with a pair that are abstract—related to the world of ideas. Practice recognizing such analogies. Here are a couple of examples:

SPARK : FIRE : : inspiration : invention

SPARK and FIRE are concrete, physical things; a SPARK is a small thing that helps to create a larger, more powerful force, a FIRE. *Inspiration* and *invention* are abstract ideas that have much the same relationship.

RETRACE : PATH : : reiterate : argument

When you RETRACE a PATH, you are walking over the same steps you took before, in a physical sense. When you *reiterate* an *argument*, you are repeating the same ideas you stated before, in an abstract sense.

JUST THE FACTS

- You need to answer analogies quickly—faster than one per minute. Practice makes it possible.
- Building a bridge that defines the analogy relationship is the basic, proven strategy.
- Look for the test-makers' nine favorite relationships—they come up again and again.
- When unfamiliar words are used, guess at their meanings based on familiar analogy relationships.
- Be ready for analogies that compare concrete relationships to abstract ones.

PRACTICE, PRACTICE, PRACTICE: ANALOGY EXERCISES

Instructions

The following exercises will give you a chance to practice the skills and strategies you've just learned for tackling analogy questions. As with all practice exercises, work under true testing conditions. Complete each exercise in a single sitting. Eliminate distractions (TV, music) and clear away notes and reference materials. Time yourself with a stopwatch or kitchen timer, or have someone else time you. If you run out of time before answering all the questions, stop and draw a line under the last question you finished. Then go ahead and tackle the remaining questions. When you are done, score yourself based only on the questions you finished in the allotted time.

Circle the letter of the correct response. In addition, any time your answer is a guess—any time you enter a response about which you are not certain—circle the number of that question. After you've completed the exercises, count the number of circled items and the number of these items that you answered correctly. Then divide the number of correct answers by the number of circled items. The result is your Guessing Quotient (G.Q.). If your G.Q. is higher than .20, you will probably boost your overall score by guessing on the real SAT.

Understanding Your Scores

0–3 correct: A poor performance. Study this chapter again, and start spending time each day studying the Insider's SAT Word List (Appendix A).

4–6 correct: A below-average score. Study this chapter again; especially make sure that you understand the nine most common analogy relationships used on the SAT.

7–9 correct: An average score. You may want to study this chapter again. Also be sure you are managing your time wisely (as explained in Chapter 3) and avoiding errors due to haste or carelessness.

10–12 correct: An above-average score. Depending on your personal target score and your strength on other verbal question types, you may or may not want to devote additional time to analogy study.

13–15 correct: An excellent score. You are probably ready to perform well on SAT analogy items.

EXERCISE 1

15 Questions

Time—10 Minutes

Directions: Each question below consists of a related pair of words or phrases, followed by five pairs of words or phrases labeled (A) through (E). Select the pair that *best* expresses a relationship similar to that expressed in the original pair.

1. PROTECT : HELMET : :
   (A) fit : cap
   (B) adorn : headdress
   (C) attract : wig
   (D) wear : armor
   (E) doff : hat

2. LETTER : ALPHABET : :
   (A) note : scale
   (B) word : poem
   (C) drop : water
   (D) hue : palette
   (E) symbol : code

3. FLORIST : BOUQUET : :
   (A) painter : easel
   (B) haberdasher : wardrobe
   (C) chef : dinner
   (D) gardener : bed
   (E) author : royalty

4. GENERAL : ADMIRAL : :
   (A) squadron : platoon
   (B) commander : follower
   (C) soldier : sailor
   (D) captain : officer
   (E) leader : manager

5. DELUGE : TRICKLE : :
   (A) flood : abundance
   (B) upheaval : serenity
   (C) downpour : drizzle
   (D) tornado : hurricane
   (E) wealth : plenty

6. TRAITOR : ALLEGIANCE : :
   (A) musician : harmony
   (B) opponent : friendship
   (C) thief : imprisonment
   (D) spy : espionage
   (E) adulterer : fidelity

7. RUDDER : SHIP : :
   (A) steering wheel : automobile
   (B) aileron : plane
   (C) wing : eagle
   (D) engine : locomotive
   (E) scale : fish

8. ACHE : ANALGESIC : :
   (A) fever : influenza
   (B) sleep : sedative
   (C) sensation : anesthetic
   (D) pleasure : narcotic
   (E) loneliness : nostalgia

9. AD LIB : REHEARSAL : :
   (A) random : foresight
   (B) accidental : preparation
   (C) unnecessary : intention
   (D) improvised : logic
   (E) aleatory : plan

10. SUPPRESS : REACTION : :
    (A) enlarge : photograph
    (B) stifle : sneeze
    (C) release : prisoner
    (D) foresee : accident
    (E) defy : command

11. OVERTURE : CODA : :
    (A) symphony : movement
    (B) preface : afterword
    (C) introduction : foreword
    (D) prologue : intermission
    (E) kickoff : touchdown

12. PROSCENIUM : CURTAIN : :
    (A) fence : gate
    (B) house : facade
    (C) movie : screen
    (D) doorway : lintel
    (E) window : shade

13. PAINT : DAUB : :
    (A) sculpt : carve
    (B) pluck : strum
    (C) sing : caterwaul
    (D) versify : compose
    (E) dance : perform

14. BEWILDERMENT : FLUMMOXED : :
    (A) ease : abashed
    (B) perplexity : nonplussed
    (C) originality : altered
    (D) equanimity : embarrassed
    (E) fear : undaunted

15. APPOINTMENT : TRYST : :
    (A) song : serenade
    (B) meeting : conference
    (C) arrangement : commitment
    (D) letter : note
    (E) engagement : betrothal

EXERCISE 2

15 Questions

Time—10 Minutes

Directions: Each question below consists of a related pair of words or phrases, followed by five pairs of words or phrases labeled (A) through (E). Select the pair that *best* expresses a relationship similar to that expressed in the original pair.

1. FOOT : ANKLE : :
   (A) arm : elbow
   (B) hand : wrist
   (C) finger : toe
   (D) knee : joint
   (E) head : neck

2. ACTOR : SCRIPT : :
   (A) architect : design
   (B) painter : mural
   (C) musician : score
   (D) judge : brief
   (E) student : textbook

3. LIBRARY : SHELF : :
   (A) grocery : food
   (B) bookstore : book
   (C) museum : case
   (D) auditorium : seat
   (E) office : desk

4. CHAUFFEUR : DRIVE : :
   (A) pilot : propel
   (B) painter : refurbish
   (C) engineer : tinker
   (D) captain : launch
   (E) mechanic : repair

5. PLAIN : ORNATE : :
   (A) austere : luxurious
   (B) simple : logical
   (C) obvious : unconcealed
   (D) embellished : beautiful
   (E) garish : gaudy

6. INGEST : GORGE : :
   (A) devour : envelop
   (B) swallow : engulf
   (C) grasp : seize
   (D) imbibe : guzzle
   (E) respire : breathe

7. ROADBLOCK : TRAVEL : :
   (A) detour : route
   (B) impediment : progress
   (C) filibuster : legislature
   (D) arrest : criminal
   (E) illness: physician

8. LACE : SHOE : :
   (A) cuff : trouser
   (B) drawstring : hood
   (C) zipper : pouch
   (D) clasp : brooch
   (E) brim : hat

9. FERVENT : ZEALOT : :
   (A) savory : epicure
   (B) foreign : xenophobe
   (C) lustful : lecher
   (D) charismatic : politician
   (E) patriotic : citizen

10. FIREARM : MUSKET : :
   (A) vessel : galleon
   (B) domicile : apartment
   (C) tool : pliers
   (D) vehicle : sled
   (E) appliance : dishwasher

11. SALVAGE : WRECK : :
    (A) bury : treasure
    (B) paint : antique
    (C) sink : vessel
    (D) retrieve : property
    (E) excavate : ruin

12. TEMPERAMENTAL : STOLID : :
    (A) moody : brusque
    (B) hostile : sedate
    (C) vivacious : lively
    (D) mercurial : impassive
    (E) intellectual : thoughtful

13. ENIGMA : MYSTIFIED : :
    (A) problem : apathetic
    (B) deception : misinterpreted
    (C) mistake : worried
    (D) dilemma : undecided
    (E) threat : irritated

14. SALT : BRINE : :
    (A) flavor : broth
    (B) seasoning : meal
    (C) thyme : herb
    (D) pepper : meat
    (E) sugar : syrup

15. ETHIC : NICETY : :
    (A) preference : whim
    (B) morality : scruple
    (C) creed : belief
    (D) dogma : teaching
    (E) doubt : misgiving

EXERCISE 3

15 Questions

Time—10 Minutes

Directions: Each question below consists of a related pair of words or phrases, followed by five pairs of words or phrases labeled (A) through (E). Select the pair that *best* expresses a relationship similar to that expressed in the original pair.

1. STEEPLE : CHURCH : :
   (A) mast : schooner
   (B) pillar : edifice
   (C) summit : mountain
   (D) altar : chapel
   (E) statue : pedestal

2. GONG : HAMMER : :
   (A) organ : pedal
   (B) oboe : reed
   (C) cymbal : sound
   (D) piano : key
   (E) drum : drumstick

3. CURE : MEDICATION : :
   (A) diagnose : drug
   (B) poison : antidote
   (C) treat : examination
   (D) prevent : vaccination
   (E) relieve : physician

4. STIFFNESS : RIGID : :
   (A) tangibility : rough
   (B) malleability : pliant
   (C) brittleness : soft
   (D) solidity : fluid
   (E) transparency : bright

5. HAIR : LOCK : :
   (A) species : specimen
   (B) quarry : ore
   (C) fabric : swatch
   (D) hand : thumb
   (E) branch : limb

6. SKINFLINT : MISERLINESS : :
   (A) philanthropist : wealth
   (B) spendthrift : wastefulness
   (C) pauper : indigence
   (D) investor : shrewdness
   (E) tightwad : generosity

7. JAM : BROADCAST : :
   (A) drown out : speech
   (B) misquote : statement
   (C) distort : image
   (D) paint over : damage
   (E) reroute : traffic

8. GRACEFUL : DANCER : :
   (A) powerful : athlete
   (B) stentorian : orator
   (C) harmonious : musician
   (D) vocal : singer
   (E) dexterous : juggler

9. RECRUIT : SOLDIER : :
   (A) elect : officer
   (B) appoint : committee
   (C) attract : audience
   (D) enroll : member
   (E) deploy : troop

10. GLAD : EUPHORIC : :
    (A) grateful : appreciative
    (B) unhappy : miserable
    (C) mournful : joyous
    (D) depressed : downcast
    (E) pleased : gratified

11. VINDICTIVE : FORGIVE : :
    (A) jealous : embrace
    (B) scornful : revile
    (C) eager : pause
    (D) insatiable : gratify
    (E) unyielding : compromise

12. POACHER : GAME : :
    (A) embezzler : bank
    (B) trespasser : privacy
    (C) burglar : window
    (D) arsonist : fire
    (E) plagiarist : text

13. QUARRY : MARBLE : :
    (A) mine : coal
    (B) ocean : tuna
    (C) silo : grain
    (D) well : gusher
    (E) reservoir : water

14. TYRO : EXPERIENCE : :
    (A) apprentice : mastery
    (B) elder : wisdom
    (C) journeyman : proficiency
    (D) rookie : talent
    (E) ingenue : charm

15. CATACLYSM : UPHEAVAL : :
    (A) colossus : statue
    (B) avalanche : earthquake
    (C) oppression : rebellion
    (D) disaster : calamity
    (E) casualty : war

EXERCISE 4

15 Questions

Time—10 Minutes

Directions: Each question below consists of a related pair of words or phrases, followed by five pairs of words or phrases labeled (A) through (E). Select the pair that *best* expresses a relationship similar to that expressed in the original pair.

1. PATH : HIGHWAY : :
   (A) yard : alley
   (B) vein : artery
   (C) branch : tree
   (D) walkway : ramp
   (E) brook : river

2. HOPELESS : DESPAIR : :
   (A) listless : enervation
   (B) careless : melancholy
   (C) tireless : fatigue
   (D) heedless : solemnity
   (E) feckless : gaiety

3. GRAIN : SAND : :
   (A) leaf : forest
   (B) stone : mountain
   (C) bird : aviary
   (D) knife : cutlery
   (E) drop : water

4. PIPES : PLUMBER : :
   (A) houses : carpenter
   (B) brushes : painter
   (C) seeds : farmer
   (D) tools : gardener
   (E) wiring : electrician

5. WHIRLPOOL : WATER : :
   (A) explosion : noise
   (B) tornado : air
   (C) hurricane : wind
   (D) vortex : movement
   (E) orbit : satellite

6. BIRD : NEST : :
   (A) salmon: lake
   (B) beaver : lodge
   (C) canary : cage
   (D) raccoon : forest
   (E) eagle : mountainside

7. FILTER : PURIFY : :
   (A) screen : project
   (B) drain : empty
   (C) sieve : sift
   (D) grate : pulverize
   (E) net : envelop

8. HAND : WATCH : :
   (A) mercury : thermometer
   (B) length : yardstick
   (C) needle : gauge
   (D) dial : radio
   (E) blade : sword

9. PLAUSIBLE : EXPLANATION : :
   (A) gullible : deception
   (B) watertight : alibi
   (C) attractive : proposal
   (D) defensible : theory
   (E) unlikely : coincidence

10. CAST : ACTOR : :
   (A) drama : protagonist
   (B) statue : sculptor
   (C) script : author
   (D) orchestra : musician
   (E) score : composer

11. IMMACULATE : STAIN : :
(A) colorless : hue
(B) eternal : change
(C) hermetic : seal
(D) formless : edge
(E) impervious : touch

12. HARBINGER : AFTERMATH : :
(A) precursor : ancestor
(B) omen : fulfillment
(C) genesis : progency
(D) forebear : descendant
(E) prediction : accuracy

13. SATIATE : DESIRE : :
(A) bite : hunger
(B) quench : thirst
(C) relax : tension
(D) appease : hostility
(E) suppress : longing

14. DELAY : DILATORY : :
(A) punctuality : punctilious
(B) threat : menacing
(C) authority : officious
(D) sleep : soporific
(E) activity : quiescent

15. KEEP : IMPREGNABLE : :
(A) message : indecipherable
(B) compartment : sealed
(C) code : unbreakable
(D) warrior : invincible
(E) safe : massive

EXERCISE 5

15 Questions

Time—10 Minutes

Directions: Each question below consists of a related pair of words or phrases, followed by five pairs of words or phrases labeled (A) through (E). Select the pair that *best* expresses a relationship similar to that expressed in the original pair.

1. WINDMILL : BREEZE : :
   (A) pinwheel : rotation
   (B) pump : well
   (C) dynamo : energy
   (D) water wheel : current
   (E) plow : oxen

2. PILOT : NAVIGATE : :
   (A) fireman : ignite
   (B) oarsman : propel
   (C) captain : commandeer
   (D) midshipman : obey
   (E) helmsman : dock

3. SHIVER : COLD : :
   (A) swelter : aridity
   (B) pant : anxiety
   (C) tremble : uncertainty
   (D) fan : heat
   (E) droop : fatigue

4. CLEAT : TURF : :
   (A) sock : carpet
   (B) galosh : puddle
   (C) sandal : footprint
   (D) spike : sand
   (E) boot : heel

5. SPECTRUM : COLOR : :
   (A) prism : hue
   (B) wave : frequency
   (C) form : shape
   (D) scale : tone
   (E) texture : sensation

6. WEAK : POWER : :
   (A) modest : eloquence
   (B) tired : endurance
   (C) craven : courage
   (D) frail : fragility
   (E) careless : intelligence

7. PATTERN : GARMENT : :
   (A) blueprint : structure
   (B) fashion : dress
   (C) design : execution
   (D) mentor : student
   (E) shape : sculpture

8. SKEPTICAL : DOUBT : :
   (A) indecisive : resolution
   (B) hesitant : disbelief
   (C) oblivious : euphoria
   (D) inquisitive : suspicion
   (E) sure : certainty

9. CURMUDGEONLY : GROUCH : :
   (A) irascible : philanthropist
   (B) whimsical : gallant
   (C) egotistical : altruist
   (D) criminal : trickster
   (E) maudlin : sentimentalist

10. RESIGNATION : SIGH : :
    (A) hope : wish
    (B) faith : pray
    (C) surprise : gasp
    (D) terror : fear
    (E) despair : plunge

11. BRIEF : LEGAL : :
    (A) spreadsheet : financial
    (B) review : theatrical
    (C) letter : administrative
    (D) formula : mathematical
    (E) journal : daily

12. IMPREGNABLE : ASSAULT : :
    (A) invincible : control
    (B) independent : conquest
    (C) inimitable : modification
    (D) immutable : alteration
    (E) intractable : destruction

13. LION : PRIDE : :
    (A) bird : vanity
    (B) cow : pasture
    (C) animal : zoo
    (D) fish : school
    (E) dog : kennel

14. ALLOY : METAL : :
    (A) aluminum : copper
    (B) compound : element
    (C) oxygen : gas
    (D) pair : individual
    (E) amalgam : silver

15. CAVE : SPELUNKER : :
    (A) trail : climber
    (B) ocean : diver
    (C) forest : woodcutter
    (D) wilderness : settler
    (E) moon : astronaut

Answer Key

Exercise 1	Exercise 2	Exercise 3	Exercise 4	Exercise 5
1. B	1. B	1. C	1. E	1. D
2. A	2. C	2. E	2. A	2. B
3. C	3. C	3. D	3. E	3. E
4. C	4. E	4. B	4. E	4. B
5. C	5. A	5. C	5. B	5. D
6. E	6. D	6. B	6. B	6. C
7. B	7. B	7. A	7. C	7. A
8. C	8. B	8. E	8. C	8. E
9. E	9. C	9. D	9. D	9. E
10. B	10. A	10. B	10. D	10. C
11. B	11. E	11. E	11. A	11. A
12. E	12. D	12. E	12. D	12. D
13. C	13. D	13. A	13. B	13. D
14. B	14. E	14. A	14. B	14. B
15. A	15. B	15. D	15. C	15. B

Explanatory Answers

EXERCISE 1

1. **The correct answer is (B).** The purpose of a *helmet* is to protect your *head*; the purpose of a *headdress* is to *adorn* (to decorate or beautify) your head.

2. **The correct answer is (A).** A *letter* is one of the items that is arranged in a particular sequence to form something called the *alphabet*. Similarly, a *note* is one of the items arranged in a sequence to form a musical *scale*.

3. **The correct answer is (C).** A *bouquet* is one of the standard or customary things produced by the craftsperson known as a *florist*. In the same way, a *dinner* is one of the customary things produced by a *chef*.

4. **The correct answer is (C).** Whereas a *general* is a military leader of soldiers who operate mainly on land, an *admiral* is a military leader whose troops operate mainly on the sea. Similarly, a *soldier* is based mainly on land, while a *sailor* is based mainly on the sea.

5. **The correct answer is (C).** A *deluge* is a huge flow of water, while a *trickle* is a tiny one. In the same way, a *downpour* is a huge and forceful rain, while a *drizzle* is a tiny one.

6. **The correct answer is (E).** A *traitor* is someone who betrays his *allegiance* (usually to his country); an *adulterer* is someone who betrays his *fidelity* (to a spouse).

7. **The correct answer is (B).** The *rudder* of a ship is a moving device that sticks into the medium through which the *ship* travels (the water) and helps to guide its movement. Likewise, the *aileron* on the wing of a *plane* sticks into the medium through which the plane travels (the air) and helps to guide its movement.

8. **The correct answer is (C).** An *ache* can be reduced or removed by means of an *analgesic* (a pain medication). Similarly, a *sensation* can be reduced or removed by means of an *anesthetic,* which dulls the nerves.

9. **The correct answer is (E).** Something that is *ad lib* (like a theatrical performance) is done without *rehearsal*—it's improvised. Something that is *aleatory* (meaning driven by chance like the toss of a pair of dice) is done without a *plan.*

10. **The correct answer is (B).** To *suppress* one's *reaction* is to deliberately hide it or to prevent it from being expressed. In the same way, to *stifle* a *sneeze* is to hold it in and prevent it from exploding.

11. **The correct answer is (B).** An *overture* is the opening movement or section of a musical piece; a *coda* is a concluding section to a musical piece. Similarly, the *preface* to a book comes at the start, while an *afterword* comes at the very end.

12. **The correct answer is (E).** A *proscenium* is the opening at the front of a stage, which is covered or concealed by a *curtain; a window* is the opening in the side of a house, which is covered or concealed by a *shade.*

13. **The correct answer is (C).** To *daub* is to *paint* in a haphazard way, showing little care or talent for the art of painting. Similarly, to *caterwaul* is to *sing* without care or talent, the way a cat in a back alley howls at the moon.

14. **The correct answer is (B).** A person who is *flummoxed* is overwhelmed by *bewilderment;* a person who is *nonplussed* is overwhelmed by *perplexity* (or confusion).

15. **The correct answer is (A).** A *tryst* is a special kind of *appointment*—one made between lovers, often in secret. A *serenade* is a special kind of *song*—one sung by a lover to his beloved, sometimes also in secret.

EXERCISE 2

1. **The correct answer is (B).** The *ankle* is the joint just above the *foot,* on which the foot rotates and moves; the *wrist* is in a similar relationship to the *hand.*

2. **The correct answer is (C).** An *actor's* performance is guided by a *script,* which is a written account of her part in the play. Similarly, a *musician's* performance is guided by the *score,* which is the written music she follows when playing a piece.

3. **The correct answer is (C).** Items in a *library* are stored and displayed on one of many *shelves;* items in a *museum* are stored and displayed in one of many *cases.*

4. **The correct answer is (E).** The job of a *chauffeur* is to *drive* a car; the job of a *mechanic* is to *repair* a car.

5. **The correct answer is (A).** Something that is *plain* is the opposite of *ornate*—the former means simple, the latter means fancy. Similarly, *austere* and *luxurious* are opposites; something that is *austere* is plain and severe, something *luxurious* is rich and comfortable.

6. **The correct answer is (D).** To *gorge* oneself is to eat, or *ingest,* without restraint (think of Thanksgiving dinner). To *guzzle* is to drink, or *imbibe,* without restraint.

7. **The correct answer is (B).** A *roadblock* stops *travel* from taking place (at least along that particular path); an *impediment* is an obstacle that prevents *progress* from being made.

8. **The correct answer is (B).** A *lace* is a string that is pulled and tied to hold a *shoe* in place. In the same way, a *drawstring* is pulled and tied to hold a *hood* in place.

9. **The correct answer is (C).** A *zealot* is a person who is *fervent*—deeply passionate about his beliefs. A *lecher* is someone who is *lustful*—full of unrestrained sexual desire.

10. **The correct answer is (A).** A *musket* is a particular kind of *firearm*—an old-fashioned one dating back to the seventeenth or eighteenth centuries. (Pictures of the Pilgrims often show them carrying muskets.) Similarly, a *galleon* is an old-fashioned kind of *vessel,* a ship that was used by explorers and merchants in the seventeenth and eighteenth centuries.

11. **The correct answer is (E).** To *salvage* a *wreck* is to explore it (by diving) and remove valuable or historic items from it for sale or safekeeping. In the same way, to *excavate* a *ruin* is to explore it (by digging) and remove valuable or historic items from it for sale or safekeeping.

12. **The correct answer is (D).** *Temperamental* and *stolid* describe opposite qualities; a *temperamental* person is filled with moods that rapidly change and that he expresses freely, while a *stolid* person has few moods and keeps his feelings mostly to himself. *Mercurial* and *impassive* have much the same relationship; a *mercurial* person is flighty and changeable, while an *impassive* person rarely changes his demeanor.

13. **The correct answer is (D).** An *enigma* (a difficult puzzle) is likely to leave you feeling *mystified;* a *dilemma* (a difficult choice) is likely to leave you feeling *undecided.*

14. **The correct answer is (E).** *Brine* is water saturated with *salt* (like ocean water, or the water pickles are cured in); *syrup* is water saturated with *sugar* (for use in making drinks or some kinds of sweets).

15. **The correct answer is (B).** An *ethic* is an important personal value, while a *nicety* is a minor one—a fine point that most people are willing to overlook from time to time. Similarly, *morality* refers to one's major beliefs, while a *scruple* is a small moral concern.

EXERCISE 3

1. **The correct answer is (C).** A *steeple* is the very highest part of a *church;* a *summit* is the very highest part of a *mountain.*
2. **The correct answer is (E).** A *gong* is played by being struck with a *hammer;* a *drum* is played by being struck with a *drumstick.*
3. **The correct answer is (D).** A *medication* is given (usually by a doctor), in hopes that it will *cure* some disease or condition. In the same way, a *vaccination* is given in hopes that it will *prevent* some disease from ever occurring.
4. **The correct answer is (B).** *Stiffness* is the quality of being *rigid* (difficult or impossible to bend). *Malleability* is the quality of being *pliant* (very easy to bend).
5. **The correct answer is (C).** A *lock* is a small piece of one's *hair,* which is often kept as a souvenir or remembrance of someone special. A *swatch* is a small piece of *fabric* usually used as a sample by a tailor or designer.
6. **The correct answer is (B).** A *skinflint* is a person who exhibits *miserliness* (stinginess) in the way he handles money. Similarly, a *spendthrift* exhibits *wastefulness* in the way he handles money.
7. **The correct answer is (A).** To *jam* a (radio or TV) *broadcast* is to block it or prevent it from being heard, usually by drowning out the signal with electronic noise. Likewise, to *drown out* a *speech* is to prevent it from being heard by making noise.
8. **The correct answer is (E).** When a *dancer* is skillful, he performs in a way that is *graceful;* when a *juggler* is skillful, we might call him *dexterous* (quick and sure-handed).
9. **The correct answer is (D).** To *recruit* a *soldier* is to convince someone to sign up for military service. Similarly, to *enroll* a *member* is to convince someone to join a club, a school, or other organization.
10. **The correct answer is (B).** To be *euphoric* is to feel extremely *glad;* to be *miserable* is to feel extremely *unhappy.*
11. **The correct answer is (E).** A *vindictive* (vengeful) person is unwilling to *forgive*—instead, she seeks revenge. Likewise, an *unyielding* person is unwilling to *compromise*—instead, she insists upon having her own way.
12. **The correct answer is (E).** A *poacher* is someone who illegally catches someone else's *game* (wild animals) for his own use; a *plagiarist* is someone who illegally steals someone else's *text* (writing) and passes it off as his own.
13. **The correct answer is (A).** A *quarry* is a hole in the ground from which stone of various kinds, including *marble,* is extracted for use by builders or sculptors. A *mine* is a hole in the ground from which ores and metals, including *coal,* are extracted for use in industry.
14. **The correct answer is (A).** A *tyro* is a complete beginner at something, a person with virtually no *experience.* Similarly, an *apprentice* is someone who is learning a new art or craft, a person with no *mastery* of the skill he wants to practice.
15. **The correct answer is (D).** A *cataclysm* is a particularly intense, severe, and overwhelming *upheaval;* a *disaster* is a particularly intense, severe, and overwhelming *calamity.*

EXERCISE 4

1. **The correct answer is (E).** A *path* is a little road (often so small that only one person can use it at a time), while a *highway* is a large road with room for thousands. A *brook* and a *river* have a similar size relationship.
2. **The correct answer is (A).** *Despair* is the state of feeling *hopeless*; *enervation* (complete lack of energy) is the state of feeling *listless.*
3. **The correct answer is (E).** A *grain* is a single, tiny piece of *sand;* one normally finds thousands or millions of grains of sand together (as at the beach). Similarly, a *drop* is a single, tiny bit of *water,* and one normally finds millions of drops of water together (as in a stream or lake).
4. **The correct answer is (E).** A *plumber* can often be found installing, fixing, or working with *pipes* in a house; an *electrician* can often be found doing the same kinds of things with the *wiring* in a house.
5. **The correct answer is (B).** A *whirlpool* is a violent, rapidly rotating spiral of *water* that can seize or drag anything in its path (a ship, for instance); a *tornado* is a similarly violent and powerful rotating column of *air,* which can be equally dangerous.
6. **The correct answer is (B).** A *bird* builds and lives in a *nest;* a *beaver* builds and lives in a *lodge.* The other answer choices refer to places where animals may live, but none of those creatures build the homes mentioned.
7. **The correct answer is (C).** The purpose of a *filter* is to *purify* what flows through it, which may be air, water, or some other substance. Similarly, the purpose of a *sieve* is to *sift* what flows through it, which may be flour, sand, or some other granular substance.
8. **The correct answer is (C).** The *hand* of a *watch* is the pointer, which indicates the time and is what one looks at when using the watch; the *needle* of the *gauge* (a car's gasoline gauge, for instance) plays the same role. The mercury in a thermometer is a little different; more than just a pointer, it is the substance that expands or contracts as temperature changes and therefore is the controlling mechanism of the entire device.
9. **The correct answer is (D).** An *explanation* that is *plausible* is one that is possible or believable—it may or may not be true, but at least it doesn't fly in the face of logic. Similarly, a *theory* that is *defensible* is one that knowledgeable people can advocate.
10. **The correct answer is (D).** An *actor* is one member of a *cast,* which is the group of people who participate in a theatrical performance. In the same way, a *musician* is one member of an *orchestra,* the group that puts on a musical concert.
11. **The correct answer is (A).** Something *immaculate* is very clean, completely without a *stain;* something *colorless* is completely without a *hue.*
12. **The correct answer is (D).** The two words here have a time relationship—a *harbinger* comes before an event and helps to foretell or predict it (crocuses are harbingers of spring), while the *aftermath* is what follows an event and bears its traces. In the same way, a *forebear* is an ancestor, one who comes before a certain person or time; a *descendant* follows or comes after.

13. **The correct answer is (B).** To *satiate* is to completely satisfy a *desire*; to *quench* is to completely satisfy a *thirst*.

14. **The correct answer is (B).** Someone who is *dilatory* makes a habit of *delay;* someone who is *menacing* frequently makes *threats*.

15. **The correct answer is (C).** A *keep* is the central stronghold of a castle; a valuable one would be *impregnable,* nearly impossible to break into. Similarly, a valuable *code* is one that is *unbreakable,* nearly impossible to decipher.

EXERCISE 5

1. **The correct answer is (D).** A *windmill* is a simple machine that generates energy when it is moved by the *breeze;* a *water wheel* is a simple machine that generates energy when it is moved by a *current* of water.

2. **The correct answer is (B).** The job of a *pilot* is to *navigate* (a ship or plane); the job of an *oarsman* is to *propel* (that is, to power) a boat.

3. **The correct answer is (E).** When you *shiver,* your body is expressing the fact that it is suffering from excessive *cold;* when you *droop,* your body is suffering from *fatigue*.

4. **The correct answer is (B).** A *cleat* is a special kind of footwear designed especially for use on *turf* (a grassy field); a *galosh* is a special kind of footwear for walking through a *puddle*.

5. **The correct answer is (D).** The *spectrum* is made up of a series of *colors* arranged in a particular pattern; a musical *scale* is made up of a series of *tones* that are also arranged in a fixed pattern.

6. **The correct answer is (C).** To be *weak* is to be lacking in *power;* to be *craven* is to be lacking in *courage*.

7. **The correct answer is (A).** A *pattern* is a drawing that is used as a guide by a tailor or seamstress when making a *garment*. A *blueprint* is a drawing that is used as a guide by a builder when making a *structure*.

8. **The correct answer is (E).** To be *skeptical* is to feel and to express *doubt* about the truth of something; to be *sure* is to feel and express *certainty*.

9. **The correct answer is (E).** A *grouch* is someone who is *curmudgeonly* (that is, argumentative, gloomy, and sarcastic); a *sentimentalist* is someone who is *maudlin* (excessively soft-hearted).

10. **The correct answer is (C).** A *sigh* is a particular kind of breath that often expresses the emotion of *resignation* (acceptance of what can't be helped). A *gasp* is a particular kind of breath that often expresses the emotion of *surprise*.

11. **The correct answer is (A).** A *brief* is a *legal* document (prepared by an attorney for use in connection with a court case); a *spreadsheet* is a *financial* document (prepared by an accountant for use in business).

12. **The correct answer is (D).** To be *impregnable* is to be able to withstand almost any kind of *assault;* to be *immutable* is to be unchangeable, and therefore able to turn away virtually any kind of *alteration*.

13. **The correct answer is (D).** A group of *lions* is a *pride;* a group of *fish* is a *school.*

14. **The correct answer is (B).** An *alloy* is a chemical mixture or blend of several *metals;* a *compound* is a chemical mixture or blend of several *elements.*

15. **The correct answer is (B).** A *spelunker* is a person who travels through and explores *caves* for fun, adventure, or for scientific reasons; a *diver* travels through and explores the *ocean* for similar reasons.

Chapter 5

Sentence Completions

Get the Scoop On . . .

- Proven strategies for mastering sentence completions
- The five kinds of sentence connections that unlock most sentence completions
- How signpost words can help you anticipate the missing words
- How you can choose the right answer even when you don't understand the sentence

THE TEST CAPSULE

What's the Big Idea?

You'll be given a sentence from which one or two words or phrases have been left out. You have to pick the words or phrases from five answer choices that best complete the sentence.

How Many?

Your SAT will probably have a total of nineteen sentence completions. In one Verbal section, you can expect nine sentence completions out of thirty total questions; in another Verbal section, expect ten sentence completions out of thirty-five total questions.

How Much Do They Count?

Sentence completions are nineteen out of seventy eight total Verbal questions. They count as 24 percent of your overall Verbal score.

How Much Time Should They Take?

You need to answer sentence completions at a rate of 1 per minute. Aim to finish a batch of nine sentence completions in 9 minutes, and to finish a batch of ten sentence completions in 10 minutes.

What's the Best Strategy?

Learn to recognize key words that show how the parts of the sentence are connected. Once you understand this connection, you can guess the meaning of the missing word or words.

What's the Worst Pitfall?

Picking an answer just because the words make sense when you plug them into the sentence. To some degree, *all the answers will make sense.* The best answer will not only make sense, but will also complete the meaning of the rest of the sentence without adding any *new* ideas.

THE OFFICIAL DESCRIPTION

Sentence completions are written to be self-contained. That is, each expresses a complete idea which you can understand without any outside information. Some of the words used in the sentences and in the answer choices are challenging, but they are general vocabulary words that a well-rounded high school student should know.

What They Are

Sentence completions are a kind of critical reading question. In this case, the items you'll be reading are quite short—single sentences that are just around ten to twenty-five words long. Each sentence will contain one or two blanks, which stand for words or phrases that have been left out. You'll then be given five words or phrases, or five pairs of words or phrases, labeled (A), (B), (C), (D), and (E) (the answer choices). Your job is to pick the word or phrase, or the pair of words or phrases, that fit best into the blanks.

Where They Are

In the typical SAT, you'll have three Verbal sections. Two will be 30 minutes long; one will be 15 minutes long. Each of the 30-minute sections will include a batch of sentence completions, which generally appear at the start of the section. Reminder—the test-makers claim the right to change the format at any time! However, the typical format we just described is what you're most likely to encounter.

What They Measure

To answer a sentence completion correctly, you need to understand the main idea of the sentence as well as its logical structure—that is, how the parts of the sentence are connected. You also need to know the meanings of the words in the answer choices. Sentence completions measure both your reading ability and your vocabulary knowledge.

The Directions

> **Directions:** Each sentence below has one or two blanks, each blank indicating that something has been omitted. Beneath the sentence are five words or sets of words labeled (A) through (E). Choose the word or set of words that, when inserted in the sentence, *best* fits the meaning of the sentence as a whole.

Example

Medieval kingdoms did not become constitutional republics overnight; on the contrary, the change was _______.

(A) unpopular
(B) unexpected
(C) advantageous
(D) sufficient
(E) gradual

The correct answer is (E).

THE INSIDER'S REPORT: STRATEGIES THAT REALLY WORK

Make Connections

Maybe you don't usually think about sentences as having parts, but they do. Most sentences contain not only a collection of words but also a number of *ideas*, which are connected to one another in various ways. When you understand how these ideas are connected, you can say that you really understand the sentence.

Look at the sample sentence completion above. You can probably see that it is made up of two main parts. (The semicolon (;) in the middle helps make this obvious—that's where the two parts divide.) Now, how are the two parts connected? How do the ideas in the two parts fit together? The first part talks about a certain historical event—the change of some governments from kingdoms to constitutional republics. It says that this event did not happen overnight. The second part talks about the same event, referring to it as "the change." It says something about that event which we can't be sure of until we've chosen an answer, because the crucial word—the last word in the sentence—has been omitted.

But by thinking about the words that *do* appear, we can see the connection between the two parts of the sentence. Both parts talk about "the change." The first part tells us something about what the change was *not* (namely, it was *not* a change that happened overnight). The second part will tell us something about what the change was. Do you see the difference?

The two parts of the sentence, then, talk about the same topic—this historical change—but they approach the topic differently. You might say that the first half expresses the idea negatively, but the second half expresses it positively. (As we'll discuss later, this is one common type of connection found in sentence completions.) Once you see this, you can easily guess the meaning of the missing word. If the change was *not* an overnight change, then what kind of change was it? The word we want should describe the *opposite* of "overnight"; it should mean something like *slow, long-drawn-out, lengthy.* The only answer choice close to this in meaning is (E), gradual—so that's the correct answer.

As you see, it's possible to figure out the connections between the parts of a sentence even when some of the words are actually missing. And once you recognize the connections, you can guess the words that are needed to complete the structure of the sentence.

Look for the Test-Makers' Favorite Connections

As in every part of the SAT, the test-makers often get repetitive with sentence completions. They start to follow similar patterns—patterns that are commonly found in sentences anyway, which involve particular types of connections among sentence parts. If you develop a feeling for these common connections, you'll spot them easily on the exam.

Here are the test-makers' five favorite kinds of sentence connections.

Contrast

Quite often, one part of the sentence contains an idea that is in contrast to, opposed to, or different from an idea in another part of the sentence. The sample sentence we looked at, dealing with the change of medieval kingdoms into constitutional republics, is an example—the idea of "overnight change" in the first part of the sentence is opposed to the idea of "gradual change" in the second part. Here's another example:

> Unlike Wordsworth, who wrote his best poetry during ________, Yeats wrote some of his finest poems when he was over seventy years old.
>
> (A) illness
> (B) war
> (C) youth
> (D) marriage
> (E) convalescence

You don't need to know anything about Wordsworth or Yeats to answer this question. You just need to recognize that the first part of the sentence tells you something about Wordsworth, which contrasts with what the second part tells you about Yeats. Since the second part says that Yeats wrote his best poetry when he was old ("over seventy years old"), then Wordsworth must have written his best poetry when he was young. The only answer choice that says so is choice (C).

Similarity

In this kind of sentence, one part of the sentence describes something that is similar to something described in another part of the sentence. Here's an example:

> Just as musicians in the 1970s were amazed by the powers of the electronic synthesizer, so musicians in the time of Bach ________ the organ, the technical wonder of its day.
>
> (A) railed against
> (B) marveled at
> (C) were troubled by
> (D) strove to master
> (E) practiced on

In this sentence, the words "Just as . . . so" tell you that the first part of the sentence and the second part of the sentence are describing two situations that are similar. The point is that musicians reacted to the organ in Bach's time the same way musicians reacted to the synthesizer in the 1970s. The sentence says that musicians in the 1970s "were amazed by" the synthesizer, so the words to fill in the blank should say something similar about the reaction to the organ. Only choice (B), "marveled at," says that, so it's the correct answer.

Example

In a sentence with this kind of organization, one part of the sentence states an idea, and another part gives an example of that idea. Look at this sentence:

> Biologists have often gained special insights by examining the life forms that develop in ________ regions, as illustrated by Darwin's studies of evolution among the finches on certain ________ Pacific islands.
>
> (A) arid..lush
> (B) harsh..tropical
> (C) typical..unusual
> (D) crowded..deserted
> (E) isolated..remote

You can tell by the words "as illustrated by" that the second part of this sentence gives an example of the idea presented in the first part of the sentence. What is that idea? It's a little hard to tell, because those darn test-makers have left out one of the crucial words. But you can see that the author is talking about how biologists have learned a lot by studying living things in some particular kind of location ("________ regions"). Then, in the second part of the sentence, she cites Darwin's work "on certain ________ Pacific islands" as an example. If Darwin's work is an example of the idea from the first part of the sentence, then the missing words in both parts should say more or less the same thing. (Otherwise, Darwin's work wouldn't illustrate or explain the idea.) So the "regions" being discussed in both parts of the sentence have to be similar.

Having figured this out, look at the five answer choices. Only choice (E) works. "Isolated" and "remote" mean approximately the same thing. In the other answer choices, the two words either have no clear relationship with one another or are almost opposite in meaning. None of them would fit the Example connection that we find in this sentence.

Restatement

In this kind of sentence, one part of the sentence restates or repeats (in different words) what is said in another part of the sentence. (Sometimes writers will do this to make a new or complicated idea a little clearer.) Here's an example:

Public attitudes toward business _______ are deeply _______; most people resent intrusive government rules, yet they expect government to prevent businesses from defrauding, endangering, or exploiting the public.

(A) ethics..cynical
(B) investment..divided
(C) practices..emotional
(D) regulation..ambiguous
(E) leaders..hostile

In this sentence, the second part that follows the semicolon (;)—is complete, with no missing words. It describes in some detail the public's attitude toward government rules in business. As you can see, the attitude described is pretty confused. On one hand, people don't like having the government involved in their lives ("intrusive government rules"). On the other hand, people expect the government to stop businesses from doing bad things—which is impossible, of course, unless the government *is* somewhat intrusive. It's a self-contradictory attitude, obviously (but sometimes people are like that).

Now, the first part of the sentence sums up this attitude in a few words—two of which are missing. Your job is to pick words to insert that will make this first part sum up, describe, or restate what the second part of the sentence says. You might begin by looking at the second word in each answer choice. We're looking for an adjective that describes the public attitude accurately. Choices (B) and (D) work best: "divided" and "ambiguous" both convey the idea that the public wants two things that don't go together very well. So we can more or less eliminate choices (A), (C), and (E), since the second word in each of those choices doesn't describe the public attitude nearly so well.

What about the first word to be inserted? We want a word that will complete the phrase, "Public attitudes toward business _______." So the missing word should accurately describe what the second part of the sentence describes. Of the choices we're given, choice (D) fits best: the attitudes described have to do with "business regulation," rules laid down for business by the government. Two other choices, "ethics" and "practices," work all right in the first blank space, but we've already eliminated those answer choices (A) and (C) because the second word in each is a poor fit. Therefore, the best answer is choice (D). When the two words are plugged into the sentence, the first part accurately restates the point made in more detail in the second part.

Cause and Effect

In this kind of sentence, one part describes something that causes, produces, or influences what's described in another part. Here's an example:

Because of the power and recognition that go with public office, incumbent politicians have enormous _______ when waging election campaigns against outside challengers.

(A) difficulties
(B) expenses
(C) advantages
(D) budgets
(E) concerns

FYI

Some sentences will have combi nations of two (or even more) kinds of connections. For example, the sentence about politics drew a contrast between "incumbent politicians" and "outside challeng-ers." So you could say that this sentence has both a Contrast connection and a Cause and Effect connection. Both connections help you to understand the meaning of the sentence.

The first part of this sentence describes something—the "power and recognition" of being in government—that causes or influences what's described in the second part. To fully understand the sentence, it helps to know that an "incumbent politician" is one who is already in office; but even if the word "incumbent" isn't already part of your vocabulary, you might be able to figure out its meaning from the rest of the sentence. "Incumbent politicians" are depicted here as running against "outside challengers." So to be "incumbent" is to be an "insider."

Logically, what effects would be caused by the "power and recognition" of public office? Would power and recognition make it easier to run for reelection, or harder? Easier, of course. The best answer is choice (C); the natural effect of the cause described in the first part of the sentence is "advantages" for the incumbent. The closest wrong answer is probably choice (D); but "enormous budgets" wouldn't necessarily be a logical effect of having "power and recognition," would they? A candidate with a lot of power and recognition could perhaps spend as much, or as little, as he would like.

Naturally, not every sentence correction on your SAT will have one of these five kinds of connections—but most of them will.

Clue in to Signpost Words that Mark the Connections

FYI

Think of signpost words as being like the "Yield," "Dangerous Curve," and "One Way" signs you look for when driving. They direct you as you read, making it obvious where you—and the sentence—are headed.

It will help you to recognize the common connections used in sentence completions if you learn to notice certain key words that the test-makers habitually use to mark them.

Here are examples of the signpost words to watch for.

Contrast

In the Contrast sentence about Wordsworth and Yeats (page 96), the key word is *Unlike*. By using that word to introduce part of the sentence, the author is deliberately signaling to you, "A Contrast is coming!" Here are some other signpost words that are used to signal Contrast connections:

although	nevertheless
but	nonetheless
by contrast	on the other hand
despite	whereas
however	yet

FYI

Sentence completion sentences are often long, complex, and confusing. Signpost words can save you. If you notice the signpost words and understand the connections they mark, you'll understand how the parts of the sentence fit together—even if you know nothing about the topic of the sentence.

Similarity

The sample Similarity sentence about the synthesizer and the organ (page 96) used the linked words "Just as . . . so" to signal the Similarity. Here are some other words and phrases that work as Similarity signposts:

as . . . as	
in the same way	resembles
like	same
likewise	similarly

Example

The sample sentence about Darwin's finches (page 97) used the signpost words "as illustrated by" to make it obvious that an Example was being given. Here are some other signpost words that can play the same role.

as in the case of	
for example	specifically
for instance	such as

Restatement

Our example of this kind of connection—the sentence about business regulation (page 98) didn't contain a signpost word. However, it did contain a different kind of telltale mark: the semicolon (;) that divided the sentence into two parts. A semicolon often indicates that what follows the mark is a restatement of what precedes it. The same is also true of the colon (:). Watch for these two punctuation marks. Think of them as signpost signs—wordless warnings that Restatement may be taking place nearby.

Also look for these words and phrases that often mark Restatement connections.

in fact	namely
in other words	so to speak
in short	that is

Cause and Effect

The signpost words *Because of* appeared at the start of our sample Cause and Effect sentence (the one about politics on page 99). Here are some typical signpost words that mark this kind of connection.

as a result	
causes	produces
consequently	results in
due to	therefore
leads to	thus

Notice that signpost words are often short, seemingly unimportant words. They don't contain much obvious information. Yet they are, in a sense, the most important words in any sentence!

Check Your Answer by Plugging in the Missing Word(s)

Once you've picked an answer choice, read the sentence with the word or words you've chosen inserted in the blank spaces. The sentence will make grammatical sense; all the answers are designed that way. The deeper question is whether or not the sentence sounds logical, consistent, and complete. The connections among the parts should be clear and correct. If signpost words promise a Contrast between two parts of the sentence, then those two parts should obviously contrast with one another. The same rule applies to other kinds of connections. If a certain type of connection is signaled by one or more signpost words, but not carried out in the words you've plugged in, then you've picked the wrong answer. Try again!

THE INSIDER'S REPORT: THE BEST TIPS

Read Any Tough Words as "Yadda Yadda Yadda"

We said something before that's worth repeating; if you notice the signpost words and understand the connections they mark, you'll understand how the parts of the sentence fit together—*even if you know nothing about the topic of the sentence.* Now we'll go one step further. If you understand how the parts of the sentence fit together, you can usually pick the right answer—*even if you don't understand a lot of the sentence.*

If you don't believe us, think back to our very first sample sentence:

> Medieval kingdoms did not become constitutional republics overnight; on the contrary, the change was ________.

You'll recall that the correct answer is "gradual." Now, what do you know about medieval European history, the transition from monarchies to republican government, the development and evolution of the concept of a national constitution, etc. etc.? Maybe a lot, probably only a little. It doesn't matter. For all you care, the sentence could read like this:

> *Yadda yadda yadda* did not become *yadda yadda yadda* overnight; on the contrary, the change was ________.

Who cares what the *yadda yadda yaddas* stand for? They could be anything: two styles of architecture, two scientific theories, a caterpillar and a butterfly, anything. The other words in the sentence (especially the signpost words) tell you all you need to know to pick the right answer.

Therefore, don't worry if the sentences contain words you don't understand or deal with unfamiliar topics. Substitute *yadda yadda yadda* for the tough ideas and focus on the words that connect those ideas. In most cases, you'll still be able to answer correctly.

Anticipate the Answer with Your Eyes Shut

As we discussed the various sample questions in this chapter, you may have noticed that we examined the sentences in detail before ever discussing the answer choices. We did that on purpose. When you take the SAT, you shouldn't even look at the answer choices until you've read the sentence carefully, looked for the connections among the parts of the sentence (using signpost words as clues), and then tried to guess the missing word or words—or at least what the missing words mean. We call this anticipating the answer with your eyes shut.

Why bother with this guessing game? Because, four of the five answer choices are *wrong.* They are distractors, designed specifically to draw your attention away from the correct answer. And they'll do just that if you give them half a chance. If you read the question and jump right down to the answer choices, you'll find choice (A) pretty plausible—after all, the test-makers are good at writing plausible answers. But choice (B) is even a little better. And what about choice (C)? It means something totally different than either choice (A) or (B), but it seems to fit the sentence, doesn't it? Then again, what *was* it that the original sentence said? Better read it over . . . . By now, a minute and a half has passed, and you're more confused than when you started.

Instead, after studying the sentence, guess the meaning of the missing word or words. Then *scan* the answers, looking simply for one that means the same as your guess. Chances are, it will jump out at you. Guessing first will keep you focused and keep the distractors at bay.

Work by Elimination

As with any question type, some items will be harder than others. The last three questions in any batch are likely to be the hardest. If you can't find an obvious answer—perhaps because you don't understand all of the words in the answer choices—eliminate answers that are clearly wrong, or that you have a strong hunch are wrong. Then, guess from what remains. If you can eliminate at least one wrong answer, it always pays to guess.

THE INSIDER'S REPORT: THE MOST IMPORTANT WARNINGS

Be Consistent!

It's crucial to look for an answer whose meaning is *consistent* with the rest of the sentence. Distractors are marked, sometimes subtly, by words whose meanings don't quite carry out the plan marked out by the rest of the sentence (especially by the signpost words). Here's an example:

In addition to being statesmen, Jefferson and Franklin were noted for their ______ interests, as exemplified by Jefferson's writings on the botany of Virginia and Franklin's experiments with electricity.

(A) varied
(B) literary
(C) artistic
(D) scientific
(E) multifarious

FYI

Most SAT sentence completions—about two thirds—have two blanks rather than one. This provides another way of working by elimination. Sometimes you can guess the meaning of one blank, but not the other. Good! Scan the answer choices, looking only for the word you've guessed. Eliminate the answers that don't include it (or a near-synonym). Then guess from what remains.

It so happens that Jefferson and Franklin had incredibly diverse interests and accomplishments, and if you are aware of this you may be tempted to choose answer (A) or (E), either of which would be factually true. Choices (B) and (C) could be defended on the ground of historical accuracy, too. But choice (D) is correct simply because it's the only answer that is completely consistent with the rest of the sentence. The second part of the sentence, beginning with the words "as exemplified by," gives two examples of Jefferson's and Franklin's interests—and both have to do with science. (The sentence illustrates the Example connection.) Thus, choice (D), scientific, is the best choice.

So the right answer to a sentence completion isn't just factually accurate, nor does it just fit logically and grammatically into the sentence. All five answers will do that. The best answer also ties in closely with the main idea of the rest of the sentence. That's what we call being consistent.

Don't Get Creative!

The flip side of being consistent is *not* to introduce any new ideas into the sentence. SAT sentences aren't terribly artistic or even necessarily interesting. They're more like very efficient little machines; precisely crafted to perform one function, with no unnecessary parts. Some distractors will be perfectly plausible words that fit the sentence and are wrong only because they introduce new ideas that aren't strictly necessary to complete the thought. An example:

Several of the mountaineers, ______ by the ______ of the icy slopes, lost their way and had to be led to safety by one of the guides.

(A) awe-struck..grandeur
(B) frightened..loneliness
(C) overcome..frigidity
(D) unnerved..slipperiness
(E) dazzled..brightness

As always, all five answer choices fit the sentence grammatically. What's more, all five are logically plausible. The icy slopes of a high mountain are quite likely to be grand, lonely, frigid, slippery, and bright, just as the answer choices state, and the reactions named ("awe-struck," "frightened," "overcome," etc.) are also plausible. The trouble with four of the answers is that they're just *too creative.* They tell us something about the mountain experience that the rest of the sentence doesn't say or imply. In short, they introduce new ideas. The correct answer is choice (E) because the rest of the sentence talks about how the mountaineers "lost their way and had to be led to safety." So this is a sentence primarily about getting lost. We want to fit words into the blanks that relate closely to the idea of getting lost, and choice (E) does that; it explains that the mountaineers got lost because the brightness of the icy slopes temporarily blinded ("dazzled") them. It completes the idea given in the rest of the sentence without adding anything new.

That's the sort of answer the test-makers like—straightforward, consistent, a little dull, and perfectly correct.

JUST THE FACTS

- The key to most sentence completions is recognizing how the parts of the sentence are connected.
- Get to know the signpost words that mark the five most common sentence connections.
- Try to anticipate the answer before looking at the choices.
- Check your answer by plugging it into the sentence.
- Look for answers that are consistent with the rest of the sentence and don't add new information.

PRACTICE, PRACTICE, PRACTICE: SENTENCE COMPLETION EXERCISES

Instructions

The following exercises will give you a chance to practice the skills and strategies you've just learned for tackling sentence completions. As with all practice exercises, work under true testing conditions. Complete each exercise in a single sitting. Eliminate distractions (TV, music) and clear away notes and reference materials. Time yourself with a stopwatch or kitchen timer, or have someone else time you. If you run out of time before answering all the questions, stop and draw a line under the last question you finished. Then go ahead and tackle the remaining questions. When you are done, score yourself based only on the questions you finished in the allotted time.

Circle the letter of the correct response. In addition, any time your answer is a guess—any time you enter a response about which you are not certain—circle the number of that question. After you've completed the exercises, count the number of circled items and the number of these items that you answered correctly. Then divide the number of correct answers by the number of circled items. The result is your Guessing Quotient (G.Q.). If your G.Q. is higher than .20, you will probably boost your overall score by guessing on the real SAT.

Understanding Your Scores

0–3 correct: A poor performance. Study this chapter again, as well as Chapter 6 on Critical Reading (since sentence completions and reading comprehension are closely related).

4–6 correct: A below-average score. Study this chapter again; especially make sure that you understand the five most common sentence connections used on the SAT.

7–9 correct: An average score. You may want to study this chapter again. Also, be sure you are managing your time wisely (as explained in Chapter 3) and avoiding errors due to haste or carelessness.

10–12 correct: An above-average score. Depending on your personal target score and your strength on other verbal question types, you may or may not want to devote additional time to sentence completion study.

13–15 correct: An excellent score. You are probably ready to perform well on SAT sentence completion items.

EXERCISE 1

15 Questions

Time—15 Minutes

Directions: Each sentence below has one or two blanks, each blank indicating that something has been omitted. Beneath the sentence are five words or sets of words labeled (A) through (E). Choose the word or set of words that, when inserted in the sentence, *best* fits the meaning of the sentence as a whole.

1. Friends of the theater have long decried the _______ of the New York drama critics, whose reviews can determine the fate of a play in a single night.
   (A) insensitivity
   (B) provinciality
   (C) intelligence
   (D) power
   (E) inaccuracy

2. The _______ manner in which the teacher candidate addressed the school board was a key factor in his rejection; the school board members agreed that enthusiasm is an essential quality in a teacher.
   (A) pretentious
   (B) solicitous
   (C) superficial
   (D) perfunctory
   (E) combative

3. His _______ writing style made it difficult to follow his thought processes—no surprise to his colleagues, who were familiar with his _______ manner of speech.
   (A) precise..arcane
   (B) laborious..tedious
   (C) trite..flippant
   (D) convoluted..circumlocutory
   (E) ambiguous..affected

4. The giant squid is still _______ marine biologists, as it has never been seen alive, making it impossible to study in its natural habitat.
   (A) fascinating to
   (B) enigmatic to
   (C) dangerous to
   (D) exploited by
   (E) famous among

5. Advertising can increase sales of a _______ product, but it cannot create demand for a bad one; consumers may buy a _______ item because of advertising—but only once.
   (A) good..new
   (B) reliable..costly
   (C) useful..valuable
   (D) needless..single
   (E) well-made..badly made

6. Like Truman, who was never considered a major national figure until Roosevelt's death made him president, Ford attained national prominence only after _______ thrust him into the presidency.
   (A) personal ambition
   (B) outside circumstances
   (C) popular acclaim
   (D) political intrigue
   (E) public demand

7. Thus far predictions that global _______ would lead to mass starvation have proven false; however, in the years to come, population _______ may yet prove to be one of the world's greatest problems.
   (A) pollution..expansion
   (B) overcrowding..growth
   (C) poverty..density
   (D) deforestation..control
   (E) warfare..stabilization

8. Representative Bunker's speech at the town meeting was quite _______, as it appeared to _______ the religious beliefs held by many members of the community.
   (A) cogent..attack
   (B) tactless..defend
   (C) inflammatory..ridicule
   (D) enthralling..denigrate
   (E) devious..belittle

9. The idea of children's literature _______ in the late eighteenth century, when educators first decided that children needed special _______ of their own.
   (A) emerged..books
   (B) changed..reading
   (C) grew..treatment
   (D) developed..training
   (E) receded..teaching

10. In some of the poorest neighborhoods of New York City, community gardens are springing up as _______ the filth and desolation of their urban surroundings.
   (A) an affirmation of
   (B) a validation of
   (C) a reaction to
   (D) an amplification of
   (E) a celebration of

11. The neighborhood group's rendering of the proposed office complex _______ the _______ of the project: as they appeared on the drawing, the proposed office buildings appeared to dwarf the rest of the downtown area.
   (A) minimized..grandiosity
   (B) accentuated..beauty
   (C) underscored..vastness
   (D) trivialized..enormity
   (E) revealed..immensity

12. Twentieth-century Japan faced the question of how to _______ the best of modern civilization without losing the benefits of Japan's _______ way of life.
   (A) reject..ancient
   (B) adopt..outmoded
   (C) assimilate..traditional
   (D) incorporate..contemporary
   (E) reshape..historic

13. The proposal to forbid the use of indoor furniture on front porches has divided the town along _______ lines; the affluent feel the old couches are eyesores, while those who cannot afford new outdoor furniture are _______ about what they feel is an attempt to restrict their lifestyle.
   (A) political..nonplussed
   (B) aesthetic..dismayed
   (C) class..pleased
   (D) racial..angry
   (E) socioeconomic..incensed

14. In his *Politics*, Aristotle characterizes Plato's support of collectivism as _______ and _______ the unity of the city; not only would it be difficult to institute and enforce, but the absence of private property would lead to bickering among the citizens.
(A) commendable. .deleterious to
(B) controversial. .essential to
(C) impractical. .detrimental to
(D) divisive. .indifferent toward
(E) unattainable. .supportive of

15. The bright coloration of American coot chicks is an anomaly; although colorful plumage is usually _______ to newborn birds because it may attract predators, among this species it appears to be _______, because parents are more likely to notice and care for brightly-colored offspring.
(A) pernicious. .fatal
(B) dangerous. .unnecessary
(C) deleterious. .favorable
(D) beneficial. .advantageous
(E) detrimental. .helpful

EXERCISE 2

15 Questions

Time—15 Minutes

Directions: Each sentence below has one or two blanks, each blank indicating that something has been omitted. Beneath the sentence are five words or sets of words labeled (A) through (E). Choose the word or set of words that, when inserted in the sentence, *best* fits the meaning of the sentence as a whole.

1. Mary's _______ personality made it difficult for her classmates to accept her, whereas June ingratiated herself with her sweetness and modesty.
   (A) gregarious
   (B) sociable
   (C) pretentious
   (D) cloying
   (E) winning

2. The myths of any tribe serve to explain and embody their _______; by examining a people's favorite _______, one can determine the things they most deeply cherish.
   (A) origins..legends
   (B) religion..pastimes
   (C) beliefs..occupations
   (D) history..rituals
   (E) values..stories

3. Although Paul and Philip grew up a few blocks apart and had virtually the same educational background, their adult lives took _______ paths.
   (A) parallel
   (B) divergent
   (C) improbable
   (D) intriguing
   (E) coinciding

4. The structure of social life among gibbons is _______ that of humans; they live in _______ groups consisting of a pair and their offspring, and may associate with other similar groups but spend the majority of their time with their nuclear family.
   (A) related to..nomadic
   (B) unlike..diurnal
   (C) parallel to..gargantuan
   (D) similar to..monogamous
   (E) identical to..nocturnal

5. Whereas privately owned delivery companies can _______ services that are unprofitable, the U.S. Postal Services, because it is _______, must serve the entire country.
   (A) increase..nationwide
   (B) concentrate..a monopoly
   (C) eliminate..government- sponsored
   (D) reduce..non-profit-making
   (E) provide..federally subsidized

6. Because frogs have no hair, scales, or feathers to _______ their paper-thin skin, they are _______ changes in the quality of the air and water in their environment.

(A) cover..invigorated by
(B) conceal..unaffected by
(C) warm..chilled by
(D) protect..hypersensitive to
(E) adorn..responsive to

7. As the war dragged on, with increased casualties and few signs of _______, morale among the soldiers _______.

(A) victory..stabilized
(B) progress..plummeted
(C) concern..collapsed
(D) hope..improved
(E) dismay..dwindled

8. Amelia Earhart's hope of being the first woman to fly around the globe was _______ when she disappeared in the middle of her _______ journey.

(A) thwarted..ill-fated
(B) realized..triumphant
(C) fulfilled..historic
(D) controversial..hazardous
(E) postponed..famous

9. The fact that the President's illness had been _______ was not uncovered for several months; when he suddenly and unexpectedly fell ill again, the doctors realized that his previous malady had not been a simple case of influenza.

(A) misdiagnosed
(B) remedied
(C) contagious
(D) deleterious
(E) inconsequential

10. Just as the advent of television failed to _______ the demand for motion pictures, so cable television and the older broadcast television seem likely to _______ for years to come.

(A) eliminate..coexist
(B) diminish..reciprocate
(C) alter . .decline
(D) increase . .expand
(E) affect..develop

11. Although the community was usually considered a safe haven for _______, some who expressed beliefs contrary to those of the majority were _______.

(A) dissenters..applauded
(B) free speech..disgruntled
(C) democracy..disagreed with
(D) freedom..necessary
(E) individuality..persecuted

12. The circadian rhythms of some breeds of hamsters are so _______ that, regardless of their surroundings, they _______ function according to the same 24-hour cycle.

(A) irregular..sometimes
(B) precise..unfalteringly
(C) anomalous..regularly
(D) unusual..continuously
(E) predictable..rarely

13. In classical literature, love was depicted not as an ennobling passion but as an unfortunate _______ that disabled the judgment, almost a kind of _______.

(A) condition..virtue
(B) sickness..retribution
(C) emotion..crime
(D) malady..insanity
(E) occurrence..insecurity

14. The birth of septuplets this year has led to a wave of newspaper articles presenting _______ accounts of the medical problems associated with multiple births, _______ the joyful stories about the septuplets which at first dominated the press.

(A) morose..minimizing
(B) perfunctory..reinforcing
(C) sobering..counterbalancing
(D) empathetic..obscuring
(E) grim..substantiating

15. The _______ of the human brain is extraordinary, as illustrated by the fact that, when an infant becomes blind, regions of the cerebral cortex that usually contribute to sight are taken over by another sensory system, as if to _______ the use of every region of the cortex.

(A) complexity..reduce
(B) versatility..prevent
(C) rigidity..regulate
(D) durability..simplify
(E) adaptability..maximize

EXERCISE 3

15 Questions

Time—15 Minutes

Directions: Each sentence below has one or two blanks, each blank indicating that something has been omitted. Beneath the sentence are five words or sets of words labeled (A) through (E). Choose the word or set of words that, when inserted in the sentence, *best* fits the meaning of the sentence as a whole.

1. Unlike the American worker, who expects to work for several different firms during his or her career, until recently the Japanese worker regarded employment as _______ commitment.

   (A) a lifetime
   (B) a significant
   (C) a bilateral
   (D) an economic
   (E) a moral

2. Andre's gift for music seemed to be _______; both his mother and grandfather before him had been famed concert pianists.

   (A) simulated
   (B) innate
   (C) accidental
   (D) inexplicable
   (E) prodigious

3. The many obvious lapses in the author's research make it _______ to accept the _______ of his conclusions.

   (A) easy..accuracy
   (B) impossible..meaning
   (C) attractive..logic
   (D) questionable..structure
   (E) difficult..validity

4. Her wildlife movies unflinchingly capture the _______ of the animal kingdom; predators stalking their prey, singling out the weak, young, and very old as easy kills, and the cold-blooded killing that is a necessity of life in the wild.

   (A) brutality
   (B) romance
   (C) color
   (D) mystery
   (E) grandeur

5. Although the Internet was originally created to facilitate scientific research and emergency communication, today most people consider it _______ enterprise, offering services marketed as sources of information and entertainment.

   (A) a commercial
   (B) a private
   (C) an obsolete
   (D) an insidious
   (E) an institutional

6. The qualities expected of a professional musician seem _______, for she must be studious, disciplined, and technically impeccable while bringing passion and _______ to each performance.

   (A) ambiguous..capriciousness
   (B) ephemeral..impulsiveness
   (C) paradoxical..spontaneity
   (D) varied..virtuosity
   (E) impossible..emotion

7. Homer is considered by many the _______ of the Western literary tradition; the work of poets, playwrights, and writers for many subsequent centuries drew upon themes and structures _______ his epic poems.

   (A) originator..divergent from
   (B) progenitor..derived from
   (C) forefather..leading to
   (D) pariah..based upon
   (E) catalyst..described in

8. Although he had been a _______ child, Roosevelt went on to become one of our nation's most _______ presidents, both mentally and physically.

   (A) precocious..able
   (B) sickly..vigorous
   (C) healthy..stalwart
   (D) typical..competent
   (E) feeble..unusual

9. Considering today's high divorce rate and the growing number of single-parent households, it is _______ to learn that the majority of Americans still accept the _______ belief in the importance of an intact nuclear family.

   (A) surprising..traditional
   (B) encouraging..obsolete
   (C) curious..unpopular
   (D) illuminating..controversial
   (E) astonishing..superficial

10. The apparent discovery of _______ on Europa, one of Jupiter's moons, has led to speculation that there may be _______ there, on the assumption that water and life are linked elsewhere as they are on Earth.

   (A) oxygen..vegetation
   (B) craters..toxins
   (C) an atmosphere..precipitation
   (D) ice..rivers
   (E) an ocean..life

11. The _______ the popular music scene by artists with a _______ amount of musical talent has led many to conclude that success in music has less to do with creativity than with image and advertising.

   (A) appearance on..disproportionate
   (B) control of..vast
   (C) rejection of..minuscule
   (D) domination of..minimal
   (E) exploitation of..noticeable

12. Some kinds of technological advances are easy to _______; television, space flight, and robots were _______ concepts decades before they became realities.
    (A) understand..scientific
    (B) achieve..little-known
    (C) foresee..familiar
    (D) denounce..theoretical
    (E) predict..unimaginable

13. Along with hunting and pollution, the _______ of eucalyptus trees, the koala's prime habitat and food source, is one of many _______ to the species.
    (A) delicacy..rivals
    (B) nurturance..dangers
    (C) razing..threats
    (D) leveling..advantages
    (E) life span..perils

14. As a result of increased _______ the connection between nutrition and health, many Americans are planning their _______ more carefully than in the past.
    (A) concern over..diets
    (B) awareness of..exercise
    (C) ignorance of..meals
    (D) publicity about..lives
    (E) controversy concerning..careers

15. As the whale shark plows through a dense clump of the small fish on which it feeds, its stomach is _______ the food, causing a _______ clearly visible to any observer.
    (A) glutted with..discomfort
    (B) processing..digestion
    (C) engulfing..sensation
    (D) distended with..swelling
    (E) gorged with..predation

EXERCISE 4

15 Questions

Time—15 Minutes

Directions: Each sentence below has one or two blanks, each blank indicating that something has been omitted. Beneath the sentence are five words or sets of words labeled (A) through (E). Choose the word or set of words that, when inserted in the sentence, *best* fits the meaning of the sentence as a whole.

1. The ________ of the judges was ensured by giving each contestant a code number by which he or she was identified.

   (A) impartiality
   (B) confusion
   (C) authority
   (D) accuracy
   (E) preparation

2. The doctor's ________ gave the patient new hope; now that someone had finally identified his illness, he was optimistic that a cure could be found.

   (A) examination
   (B) prescription
   (C) treatment
   (D) diagnosis
   (E) hypothesis

3. The ________ and ________ lifestyle of certain types of primates is widely divergent from the habits of most other primate species, who are active during the day and who form societies based on interrelationships that are quite complex.

   (A) sedentary..omnivorous
   (B) inactive..monogamous
   (C) nomadic..lonely
   (D) nocturnal..solitary
   (E) diurnal..gregarious

4. The marshes of Cape Cod, with their varied and plentiful plant and animal life, are of special interest to the ________.

   (A) geographer
   (B) painter
   (C) naturalist
   (D) vacationer
   (E) developer

5. The plan for a new shopping mall has come as an unpleasant surprise to many local residents, who ________ their small, quiet community and ________ the increased traffic and noise that the mall is likely to bring.

   (A) appreciate..anticipate
   (B) venerate..appreciate
   (C) enjoy..trivialize
   (D) deplore..recognize
   (E) cherish..dread

6. George Orwell began his career as a writer of party propaganda, and even after he turned to fiction, his work continued to serve many of the same ________ ends.

   (A) satirical
   (B) aesthetic
   (C) political
   (D) personal
   (E) religious

7. The biography depicts the well-known actress as ________ and ruthless, ________ the already widespread belief that she attained stardom through a series of unpalatable maneuvers.

(A) scheming..questioning
(B) charismatic..fostering
(C) power-mad..verifying
(D) vindictive..injuring
(E) cruel..challenging

8. Some consider animal experimentation inhumane while others defend it, but this ________ method of testing medicines continues because the benefits to human life are generally considered to ________ the harm done to animals.

(A) antiquated..imbalance
(B) misunderstood..mitigate
(C) inappropriate..exacerbate
(D) controversial..outweigh
(E) powerful..underscore

9. Because of the vulnerability of Japanese cities to ________, officials there have developed extensive safety plans for dealing with natural disasters.

(A) terrorism
(B) overcrowding
(C) civil disorder
(D) invasion
(E) earthquakes

10. Although William Shakespeare of Stratford-on-Avon is generally ________ to have created some of the most brilliant plays in the English language, some scholars are ________ about his authorial credentials.

(A) believed..dubious
(B) thought..biased
(C) predicted..unsure
(D) said..convinced
(E) known..certain

11. At the time of its construction, the gymnasium was highly ________; the students and faculty for whom it was planned were ________, but the community members who faced losing their neighborhood park were outraged.

(A) controversial..gratified
(B) warranted..skeptical
(C) fortuitous..euphoric
(D) unnecessary..impartial
(E) desirable..numerous

12. Even a ________ and apparently ________ invention may depend on an inexplicable stroke of genius, as suggested by the fact that some great civilizations never developed the wheel.

(A) vital..essential
(B) simple..obvious
(C) profound..brilliant
(D) primitive..ancient
(E) complex..obscure

13. The fact that many public accommodations, such as movie theaters and shopping malls, are inaccessible to wheelchairs is often ________, just as the loss of revenues to the proprietors of these businesses is ________.
    (A) deleterious..minimal
    (B) unnoticed..ignored
    (C) intentional..unwitting
    (D) protested..unseen
    (E) obvious..suppressed

14. Researchers have concluded that many of the ________ connections between cells in the brain are formed during the first three months after birth, suggesting that postnatal stimulation may have a ________ effect on an infant's development.
    (A) temporary..lasting
    (B) necessary..negative
    (C) trivial..pervasive
    (D) essential..profound
    (E) vital..minimal

15. Artists benefit from corporate support of the arts, but when they receive such support, they must also ________ some degree of corporate ________.
    (A) consider..responsibility
    (B) forfeit..freedom
    (C) accept..control
    (D) condone..generosity
    (E) reject..power

EXERCISE 5

15 Questions

Time—15 Minutes

Directions: Each sentence below has one or two blanks, each blank indicating that something has been omitted. Beneath the sentence are five words or sets of words labeled (A) through (E). Choose the word or set of words that, when inserted in the sentence, *best* fits the meaning of the sentence as a whole.

1. As a possible presidential contender, the governor found herself subject to intense public ________; every speech she made was widely reported on television and in newspapers.

   (A) attack
   (B) adulation
   (C) manipulation
   (D) criticism
   (E) scrutiny

2. Although many of the board members were ________ about the impending deal, others were ________ the benefits it would bring to the company.

   (A) euphoric..confident of
   (B) chagrined..unsure about
   (C) pleased..disturbed by
   (D) optimistic..dubious about
   (E) angry..skeptical of

3. The cause of the altercation remains ________; although the two men are neighbors, the police have been unable to find a link between them that might explain their mutual ________.

   (A) speculative..ambivalence
   (B) controversial..affection
   (C) secret..attraction
   (D) unknown..animosity
   (E) obvious..animus

4. Although Mark Twain and Garrison Keillor are both humorists from the American Midwest, their themes, styles, and attitudes are basically ________.

   (A) comic
   (B) different
   (C) timeless
   (D) unremarkable
   (E) identical

5. General dislike of the CEO was ________ in the ________ comments made at the board meeting.

   (A) implied..ambivalent
   (B) obvious..glowing
   (C) apparent..impartial
   (D) absent..contemptuous
   (E) noticeable..concise

6. Just as Mozart's music broke new ground in the world of classicism, so Beethoven's work also ________ the unspoken rules of the classical period and ________ changes that eventually led to a new style called romanticism.

   (A) obeyed..implemented
   (B) overturned..initiated
   (C) conformed to . .supported
   (D) evaded..resisted
   (E) eradicated..avoided

7. The members of any profession naturally seek to defend and protect one another; police officers, for instance, testify for one another in court, and doctors rarely _______ one another's medical decisions.

   (A) examine
   (B) criticize
   (C) applaud
   (D) explain
   (E) review

8. As the global acreage of rain forest becomes more and more _______, the _______ among its inhabitants becomes ever more intense.

   (A) polluted..communication
   (B) inadequate..distance
   (C) scarce..competition
   (D) deficient..collaboration
   (E) overpopulated..mating

9. The candidate _______ many of the causes that her opponent supports, leading some to question the necessity for her candidacy.

   (A) espouses
   (B) ignores
   (C) opposes
   (D) questions
   (E) derides

10. The _______ that computers are _______ educational tools has led many parents to believe that children don't need to be monitored when using the computer, as they do when watching TV or seeing a movie.

   (A) belief..malicious
   (B) hypothesis..powerful
   (C) misrepresentation..modern
   (D) misconception..benign
   (E) myth..dangerous

11. The remarkable fact that many inventions had their birth as toys suggests that people philosophize more freely when they know that their _______ leads to no _______ results.

   (A) cogitation..trivial
   (B) persistence..satisfactory
   (C) speculation..weighty
   (D) creativity..measurable
   (E) conjecture..inconsequential

12. As the cost of living rises and wages _______, it becomes more _______ for young adults entering the work force to support themselves, forcing greater numbers of adults between the ages of 25 and 34 to live with their parents.

   (A) vary..affordable
   (B) decline..advantageous
   (C) fall..prudent
   (D) increase..unusual
   (E) stagnate..difficult

13. Just as her older sister's _______ academic record had enabled her to attend a prestigious university, Martha was also _______ in hopes of securing admission to Columbia University.

   (A) impeccable..studious
   (B) perfect..presumptuous
   (C) modest..diligent
   (D) exemplary..optimistic
   (E) unparalleled..hard-working

14. Although the techniques used to monitor the active volcano were _______ and evacuation procedures were started _______, many of the island's inhabitants were killed by the eruption because they refused to leave their homes when urged by the foreign scientists.
    (A) useless..belatedly
    (B) comprehensive..gradually
    (C) effective..promptly
    (D) disruptive..immediately
    (E) exemplary..slowly

15. Personality is rooted as deeply in the need for _______, or at least personal interaction, as _______ well-being is rooted in chemical needs.
    (A) love..physical
    (B) hope..biological
    (C) affection..social
    (D) self-respect..bodily
    (E) companionship..natural

Answer Key

Exercise 1	Exercise 2	Exercise 3	Exercise 4	Exercise 5
1. D	1. C	1. A	1. A	1. E
2. D	2. E	2. B	2. D	2. D
3. D	3. B	3. E	3. D	3. D
4. B	4. D	4. A	4. C	4. B
5. E	5. C	5. A	5. E	5. A
6. B	6. D	6. C	6. C	6. B
7. B	7. B	7. B	7. C	7. B
8. C	8. A	8. B	8. D	8. C
9. A	9. A	9. A	9. E	9. A
10. C	10. A	10. E	10. A	10. D
11. C	11. E	11. D	11. A	11. C
12. C	12. B	12. C	12. B	12. E
13. E	13. D	13. C	13. B	13. A
14. C	14. C	14. A	14. D	14. D
15. E	15. E	15. D	15. C	15. A

Explanatory Answers

EXERCISE 1

1. **The correct answer is (D).** The missing word must fit the description of the critics given in the second half of the sentence. If they can determine the fate of a play in a single night, then clearly they have a lot of power.

2. **The correct answer is (D).** Remember that a semicolon (;) often indicates that the two halves of the sentence restate or paraphrase the same idea. The second half of this sentence tells us that the members of the school board wanted enthusiasm in a teacher candidate. Therefore, the word that describes the candidate they rejected should mean the opposite of enthusiastic. Perfunctory fits the bill.

3. **The correct answer is (D).** Since both blanks here describe something similar—the way this unnamed person communicates—the two words should be near-synonyms. And the words *difficult to follow his thought processes* make it clear that both missing words should mean "hard to understand, unnecessarily complicated."

4. **The correct answer is (B).** This sentence has a cause-and-effect relationship, as indicated by the word "as." If the squid has never been seen alive, one could logically conclude that it would be enigmatic.

5. **The correct answer is (E).** Both halves of the sentence make much the same point—people will buy good products but not bad ones. Only the words in choice (E) fit this idea.

6. **The correct answer is (B).** Obviously, the structure of this sentence is similarity. We want a phrase to fit in the blank that will match the description of how both Truman and Ford attained prominence. You don't need to know history; just realize that Ford's case must have resembled Truman's, in which pure accident (or outside circumstances) made him president.

7. **The correct answer is (B).** The word *however* tells you that the two halves of the sentence contrast with one another. The first half says that predictions of mass starvation have proven false; the second half says that, in the future, (something) may yet prove to be one of the world's greatest problems. Thus, the contrast involves the idea that a problem that doesn't exist now may come to exist in the future; the same problem is being discussed in the both parts of the sentence. Choice (B), makes sense because global overcrowding and population growth describe the same problem.

8. **The correct answer is (C).** The word *as* shows that the first half of the sentence describes the effect and the second half the cause. Choice (C) is right because the two words it contains work well together as a cause/effect pair—a speech that ridicules others would indeed be inflammatory.

9. **The correct answer is (A).** If it wasn't until the late eighteenth century that educators decided children needed books of their own, then that must have been when the idea of children's literature emerged; choice (A).

10. **The correct answer is (C).** Only reaction makes sense as a description of the relationship between a garden and surroundings that are full of filth and desolation.

11. **The correct answer is (C).** The second half of the sentence shows that vastness is the dominant quality of the proposed office complex.

12. **The correct answer is (C).** The sentence describes something that twentieth-century Japan wanted to achieve. Therefore, it must be referring to a desirable combination of the best of the old and the new. Choice (C) makes sense because it refers to assimilating (absorbing) what is good in modern life while retaining what is traditional. A negative word like *outmoded* Choice (B) wouldn't fit this context.

13. **The correct answer is (E).** Because the second half of the sentence contrasts the affluent with those who cannot afford new outdoor furniture, we can see that the first blank should be filled with a word referring to class or economic differences. This narrows the possibilities to choices (C) and (E). Choice (C) doesn't work because an attempt to restrict someone's lifestyle wouldn't logically make them feel pleased.

14. **The correct answer is (C).** The two words in this answer choice nicely paraphrase the two points made later in the sentence: impractical = difficult to institute, and detrimental to . . . unity = lead[ing] to bickering.

15. **The correct answer is (E).** The words *anomaly* and *although* suggest that the second half of the sentence is built around a contrast between the role colorful plumage usually plays among birds and the role it actually plays in this particular species. Thus, the two words must be nearly opposite in meaning, as the two words in choice (E) are.

EXERCISE 2

1. **The correct answer is (C).** The word *Whereas* shows that the sentence describes a contrast between Mary and June. Therefore, we want a word whose meaning is strongly opposed to sweetness and modesty. Pretentious works well in that role.
2. **The correct answer is (E).** The two parts of this sentence paraphrase the same idea. Therefore, the first blank should correspond to the idea of the things they most deeply cherish in the second half of the sentence, while the second blank should correspond to myths. Values and stories both work.
3. **The correct answer is (B).** The word *Although* tells you to look for a contrast of some kind—something that is surprising or that apparently contradicts another idea in the sentence. It does seem surprising that two men with so many similarities should have divergent (i.e., widely different) lives.
4. **The correct answer is (D).** The description of gibbon life in this sentence suggests a monogamous family base, which in turn is roughly parallel to the dominant structure of human social life.
5. **The correct answer is (C).** *Whereas* alerts you to look for a contrast in the sentence. We then read that the U.S. Postal Service must serve the entire country; the first blank, to convey the needed contrast, must suggest that private companies can eliminate services they don't want to provide.
6. **The correct answer is (D).** If frogs are lacking in structures to protect their skin, it would make sense that they would be hypersensitive to their environments.
7. **The correct answer is (B).** Clearly, the second blank must contain a word meaning something like fell; so only choices (B), (C), and (E) qualify. Of these, choices (C) and (E) can be eliminated because, in both, the first word brings in a new idea that isn't required or justified by the rest of the sentence.
8. **The correct answer is (A).** If she disappeared during the journey, then clearly her hope of flying around the globe was thwarted (choice A). Ill-fated is the logical word to use to describe a trip that ends this way (worse than losing your luggage).
9. **The correct answer is (A).** Looking only at the first half of the sentence, any of the five answer choices could work; however, the second half of the sentence makes it clear that the president's doctors had made a mistake in interpreting his symptoms, a situation described only by the word misdiagnosed.
10. **The correct answer is (A).** The words *Just as . . . so* make it clear that parallel situations are being described in the two halves of the sentence. Only the words in choice (A) logically establish the expected similarity.
11. **The correct answer is (E).** The contrast between the two halves of the sentence is signaled by the word *Although.* Choice (E) makes sense because the contradiction between a safe haven for individuality and the fact that those who disagree were sometimes persecuted is clear and sharp.

12. **The correct answer is (B).** You don't need to know the slightly arcane word "circadian" to understand the sentence. Even without that word, you can tell that these hamsters are behaving in a very regular fashion, since they function according to the same 24-hour cycle. Thus, their rhythms are certainly precise.

13. **The correct answer is (D).** If love was thought to disable the judgment (to confuse one's brains), then clearly the word insanity is an apt description.

14. **The correct answer is (C).** The word we want for the second blank must suggest how the articles about medical problems related to the joyful stories that first appeared. Only counterbalancing really makes sense.

15. **The correct answer is (E).** The phenomenon described in the sentence, in which parts of the brain change their function, clearly illustrates the adaptability of the brain.

EXERCISE 3

1. **The correct answer is (A).** The word *Unlike* of course shows us that the two halves of the sentence will contrast with one another. The idea of a lifetime commitment nicely contrasts with the idea of changing jobs several times.

2. **The correct answer is (B).** If musical talent runs in Andre's family, then it would be logical to consider his gift inborn, inherited, or innate.

3. **The correct answer is (E).** A simple cause and effect relationship is required here; if the research contains many obvious lapses, then accepting its conclusions would certainly be difficult.

4. **The correct answer is (A).** All we need here is a word that summarizes the tone of the second half of the sentence. A word like violence, bloodthirstiness, or brutality will work.

5. **The correct answer is (A).** If the Internet today offers services that are marketed, then it is clearly a commercial (that is, for-profit) enterprise.

6. **The correct answer is (C).** We can see that the sentence is suggesting contradictory or opposing qualities that a musician has, since "discipline" and "passion" are usually thought of as very different. The first blank, "paradoxical," captures this sense of contradiction, while the second blank, "spontaneity," fits nicely with "passion" and contrasts appropriately with "disciplined."

7. **The correct answer is (B).** Obviously, the sentence is discussing the effect Homer had on later writers. Therefore, "progenitor" makes sense for the first blank, and "derived from" logically fits the relationship of the later work to that of Homer.

8. **The correct answer is (B).** The word *Although* tells us to look for two words that are contradictory or opposite in meaning. *Sickly* and *vigorous* fill the bill nicely.

9. **The correct answer is (A).** Second blank first—since the nuclear family is being contrasted to today's marital trends, it's clear that the nuclear family is being discussed as something out of the past. Thus, a word like *traditional* or possible *obsolete*, choice (B) is needed. Choice (A) is the better answer because the sentence clearly suggests that the belief in the nuclear family is surprising, whereas the idea that it is encouraging drags in a value judgment unsupported by the rest of the paragraph.

10. **The correct answer is (E).** The second half of the sentence tells us that water and life are being linked; hence, "an ocean" and "life" make sense for the first half of the sentence.

11. **The correct answer is (D).** If the author believes that image and advertising are more important than creativity, then the artists he is discussing must have little talent, or, as the second word in choice (D) puts it, minimal talent.

12. **The correct answer is (C).** The fact that television and the other advances named were concepts long before they were realities suggests that they were easy to *foresee*.

13. **The correct answer is (C).** We can tell that the second blank must be a word like *dangers* or *threats,* since it is describing some phenomenon that resembles "hunting and pollution." Then, it's easy to see that the first blank must refer to the *razing* (destruction) of the koala's habitat and food.

14. **The correct answer is (A).** Since the sentence is discussing *nutrition,* we can see that the second blank must refer to food. And if Americans are planning their diets more carefully, then what must have increased is their *concern over* nutrition.

15. **The correct answer is (D).** The two blanks must be filled with words that go together logically and that, in combination, describe something that would be clearly visible to any observer. Only a swelling of the stomach would be visible in this way.

EXERCISE 4

1. **The correct answer is (A).** The use of a code number to keep the contestants' identities secret is clearly designed to maintain the judges' impartiality.

2. **The correct answer is (D).** The two halves of the sentence make the same point. Thus, the blank should be filled with a word that corresponds to the idea of identifying his illness—diagnosis.

3. **The correct answer is (D).** We want words here that suggest a contrast to the second half of the sentence, as indicated by the phrase "widely divergent from." Choice (D) works because *noctural* opposes active during the day, and *solitary* opposes the idea of interrelationships that are quite complex.

4. **The correct answer is (C).** All of the answers are inherently plausible, but only the *naturalist* would automatically be interested in varied and plentiful plant and animal life. Remember, don't bring in any new ideas that aren't strictly required by the rest of the sentence.

5. **The correct answer is (E).** The words *unpleasant surprise* make it clear that the residents don't want the mall. Therefore, the first blank should contain a positive word to describe their feelings about the community as it now exists, while the second blank should contain a negative word to describe how they feel about the increased traffic and noise they expect.

6. **The correct answer is (C).** We want a word that goes naturally with the idea of party propaganda. While such writing may be satirical or personal or even religious, we can only say for sure that it must be political.

7. **The correct answer is (C).** The first blank must match up with ruthless, while the second blank must describe how the image in the biography fits with the already widespread belief about the actress. Clearly, it will verify what people already believe.

8. **The correct answer is (D).** The word for the first blank, controversial, summarizes the point made in the first nine words of the sentence; the word for the second blank logically explains why animal experimentation continues.

9. **The correct answer is (E).** The missing word must describe a kind of natural disaster, since that is what the sentence describes.

10. **The correct answer is (A).** To complete the expected contrast (signaled by the word Although), we need a word like dubious or unsure for the second blank. Choice (C) is wrong because *predicted* makes no sense with reference to a past event.

11. **The correct answer is (A).** The word *but* shows that the reaction of the students and faculty was different from that of the community members (hence, gratified), and the word *controversial* describes the fact that the two groups had such opposite opinions.

12. **The correct answer is (B).** The word *Even* tells us that the kind of invention being described here is one that we normally wouldn't assume would depend on an inexplicable stroke of genius. To create the maximum amount of contrast, we want the words *simple* and *obvious,* which do in fact make sense as descriptions of the wheel.

13. **The correct answer is (B).** We can tell that the two parts of the sentence describe similar occurrences because of the words *just as* in the middle of the sentence. We want words for the two blanks that are similar in meaning, which *unnoticed* and *ignored* certainly are.

14. **The correct answer is (D).** The words *suggesting that* show that the two halves of the sentence have a cause-and-effect relationship; what's in the first half suggests what's in the second half. The two nearly-synonymous words *essential* and *profound* carry out the expected relationship.

15. **The correct answer is (C).** It's logical to conclude that, if artists are supported by corporations, they will also be influenced by those corporations.

EXERCISE 5

1. **The correct answer is (E).** All of the answer choices are plausible, but only *scrutiny* describes the governor's experience as described in the sentence without bringing in any new ideas.

2. **The correct answer is (D).** These two words carry out the required contrast between the reactions of the two groups of board members. Choice (C) is wrong because it makes no sense to imagine the board members being disturbed by the benefits the deal would produce.

3. **The correct answer is (D).** If police have been unable to find an explanation, then the cause remains unknown; since an altercation (an argument) is being discussed, the relationship between the two men must have involved some kind of animosity.

4. **The correct answer is (B).** Since the word *Although* tells us to look for a contrast between the two halves of the sentence, we can see that the blank must be filled with a word that mentions differences between the two writers rather than another similarity.

5. **The correct answer is (A).** The two words to be inserted here must suggest a logical relationship between the comments made and the attitude the board members felt. Only the words in choice (A) make sense; *ambivalent* comments might well *imply* negative feelings about the head of the company.

6. **The correct answer is (B).** The words *Just as . . . so* tell us that Beethoven, like Mozart, was a musical revolutionary. Therefore, to say that he *overturned* the rules and *initiated* changes makes good sense.

7. **The correct answer is (B).** We need a word that makes the behavior of the doctors parallel to the behavior of the police officers, since the two are given as examples of the same general principle.

8. **The correct answer is (C).** The missing words must logically suggest a cause-and-effect relationship. If room in the rain forests is becoming more *scarce,* then it's logical that *competition* among its inhabitants would increase.

9. **The correct answer is (A).** If some question the necessity for her candidacy, then her political positions must seem insignificant or pointless in some way. This would only be true if her positions are just the same as those of her opponent; that could make it seem silly for her to oppose him.

10. **The correct answer is (D).** We want words that suggest a feeling about computers that would lead parents to let their children use the devices without being watched. Only choice (D) works, because only *benign* is sufficiently positive to suggest that idea.

11. **The correct answer is (C).** To fit the idea of inventions originating as toys, we want the second blank to suggest results that are *not* serious or important—the opposite of what we think about toys. Hence, *weighty.*

12. **The correct answer is (E).** If more young adults are being forced to live with their parents, then their economic condition must be generally bad. To fit this notion, it makes sense to speak about wages stagnating (that is, failing to increase) and self-support being difficult.

13. **The correct answer is (A).** To attend a prestigious university would obviously require a good academic record, so the first word must be one that means something like excellent. And for the second blank, the word we want should relate to what's needed to achieve such a record; studious is the choice that makes the most sense.

14. **The correct answer is (D).** Clearly, the fact that the inhabitants were killed by the eruption contradicts the description needed of the monitoring and evacuation procedures (the word *Although* tells us this). Only the words in choice (D) create the necessary degree of contrast.

15. **The correct answer is (A).** The first blank should contain an idea that fits the concept of personal interaction; the second blank should contain a word that describes the kind of well-being that would have a chemical basis. Only *love* and *physical* fit both requirements.

Chapter 6

Critical Reading

Get the Scoop On . . .

- How the three-stage reading method can help you master the passages and get more questions right
- How to separate main ideas from supporting details when you read
- How to recognize the vital connections among ideas in the passages
- Why you should read with pencil in hand, and how marking up the passage can earn you extra points
- The kinds of deceptive wrong answers the test-makers love to use—and how to avoid them

THE TEST CAPSULE

What's the Big Idea?

In critical reading, you'll be given a passage to read. It may be a fictional or true-to-life narrative or memoir, or a non-fiction discussion of a topic from science, social studies, or the humanities. Then, you will have to answer a group of questions about the passage, testing how well you've understood its content.

How Many?

Your SAT will probably have a total of thirty-eight critical reading questions. They'll make up fifteen of the thirty items in one 30-minute Verbal section, twelve of the thirty-five items in another 30-minute Verbal section, and all thirteen items in a 15-minute Verbal section.

How Much Do They Count?

Critical reading questions are thirty-eight out of seventy-eight total verbal questions. They count as 49 percent of your overall verbal score.

How Much Time Should They Take?

You should spend about 1 minute per question on any group of reading passages. For example, when you tackle a set of two passages with a total of fifteen questions, plan to spend 15 minutes on the entire set. Expect to spend about half of that time on reading, the other half on answering the questions.

What's the Best Strategy?

Use the *three-stage method* when reading passages—previewing, reading, reviewing. With this approach, you'll gather much more information from the passage than with conventional one-step reading, and you'll be able to answer the questions that follow faster and more correctly.

What's the Worst Pitfall?

Choosing answers merely because they sound familiar or are factually true. The answers you pick must not only be plausible and true but must also relate directly to the question and be drawn from the most relevant portion of the passage.

THE OFFICIAL DESCRIPTION

What They Are

Critical reading on the SAT involves two steps. The first step is reading a prose passage, usually between 400 and 800 words long, which may be any of a variety of literary forms and deal with almost any subject. The second step is answering a group of five to twelve questions dealing with the content, form, and style of the passage. In one variation found on every SAT, two passages are presented that are linked by a common subject or theme. Each of the thirteen questions that follow deals with either one of the passages or with both passages together.

Where They Are

In the typical SAT, you'll have three Verbal sections. Two will be 30 minutes long, and one will be 15 minutes long. In one 30-minute section, you'll find fifteen critical reading questions; in the others, you'll find twelve critical reading questions. In both of these cases, the critical reading questions will probably follow a batch of sentence completions and a batch of analogies. The 15-minute Verbal section will consist of a "double passage" reading set with thirteen items. Reminder: the test-makers claim the right to change the format at any time! However, the typical format we just described is what you're most likely to encounter.

What They Measure

Critical reading is designed to measure your ability to handle the varied kinds of sophisticated, complex, and subtle reading that college students are called upon to do. In order to answer the questions, it's not enough to understand the basic facts presented in the passage; you also need to notice the more elusive *implications* in the passage (ideas that are suggested rather than directly stated) as well as the form, structure, and style of the passage (how the author has chosen to present ideas).

What They Cover

Critical reading passages consist of edited excerpts from a wide range of materials—scholarly or popular non-fiction books about almost any subject; articles from magazines, newspapers, or journals; personal accounts and memoirs; "opinion pieces" like speeches, and fictional narratives or stories. To date, the test-makers have not chosen passages of either poetry or drama for use in SAT critical reading.

The Directions

> **Directions:** The passage below is followed by questions based on its content. Answer the questions on the basis of what is *stated* or *implied* in the passage and in any introductory material that may be provided.

THE INSIDER'S REPORT: STRATEGIES THAT REALLY WORK

Preview, Read, Review

Critical reading on the SAT poses a unique time-management problem. Unlike the other question types, critical reading requires you to spend a large chunk of time doing something *before* you look at the questions—reading the passage itself. Under the circumstances, with time pressure a real concern for most students, it's easy to get impatient. The temptation to rush through the passage in your haste to start filling in answers may be very great.

Don't do it! Unless you invest some time in getting to know the passage well, your chances of answering most of the questions right are pretty slim. In fact, we'll go further. We'll recommend that you spend more time reading the passages than you normally would. Whereas most people ordinarily read anything once and once only, we suggest that you read or scan each passage on the SAT *three* times before answering a single question.

We have good reasons for this recommendation. The three-stage reading method is a proven technique used by skilled readers as the best way of getting the most possible information out of anything in writing. Paradoxically, you'll find—we can virtually guarantee it—that if you practice the three-stage method, you'll soon find that you're gathering more information out of what you read more quickly than ever before.

Here's how the three-stage method works.

Preview

First, preview the passage in one of two ways. You can skim its contents by letting your eyes quickly scroll down the page, picking up as much information as you can. Or you can read selected sentences from the passage. Specifically, the *first* sentence of each paragraph in the passage and the *last* sentence of the entire passage. Either of these methods works well; we suggest you experiment with both and choose the one you prefer.

What's the point of previewing? It's to give you some idea of what the passage is about and, generally, how it is organized, *before* you actually read it. Think about it—when you know, in general, what a teacher will be teaching, don't you find it easier to understand and absorb the lesson? (Educational researchers have proven it's true.) The same idea applies here—if you know generally what the passage is about before reading it, you'll understand it better.

Don't spend long on previewing. On the average SAT reading passage, this stage should take about 30 seconds. Practice with a watch until you get a feel for it.

FYI

If previewing quickly is a problem for you, try this: Sweep your index finger in a single, steady motion down the passage, taking about thirty seconds to scan the whole thing. Let your eyes follow your traveling finger as a guide. This will force you to keep moving as you preview rather than getting stuck with reading a sentence or paragraph that catches your attention.

Read

Having previewed the passage, go ahead and read it through, more or less in the conventional way. (We'll be suggesting some special reading techniques for this stage in a moment, but for now, just think of stage two as the familiar reading process you've always done.)

Review

The third stage involves scanning the passage one more time, reminding yourself of its main ideas, most important details, and overall structure. Like previewing, this should be a fast process—spend no more than 30 seconds to review an average SAT passage.

Why bother with reviewing? There are three main reasons. First, by the time you finish reading a complex, subtle, or confusing SAT passage, you may find that you don't really remember how the passage began. Reviewing refreshes your memory for the structure of the entire passage, making it easier for you to hold it in mind as a unit.

Second, reviewing can help you to understand the earlier parts of the passage better than you did when you first read them. Quite often, a point made in the first or second paragraph isn't fully explained until the third or fourth paragraph. Reviewing the whole thing ties together loose ends that otherwise might have remained slightly confusing.

Third, reviewing helps you remember which topics are discussed in which parts of the passage. This will make it easier when you need a specific detail to answer a question. Rather than scanning the whole passage, you'll probably be able to quickly zero in on the right paragraph.

Here's how the timing of the three-stage method works. Let's say the reading passage is 750 words long (toward the high end for SAT passages). The average student reads about 250 words per minute. So the three stages would take a total of 4 minutes:

Stage 1	Previewing	$\frac{1}{2}$ minute
Stage 2	Reading	3 minutes
Stage 3	Reviewing	$\frac{1}{2}$ minute
Total Time:		4 minutes

You'd spend about the same amount of time on the questions that follow the passage, making a total of 8 minutes for the passage and questions. On the exam, you'll find that this kind of timing works well and will leave you with ample time for the other verbal questions in the section.

Focus on Big Ideas, Not Little Details

FYI

The birth and death dates given for John Dalton in the passage are a classic example of insignificant details. Don't *waste energy trying to remember those dates. In the unlikely event there's a question about them, you can find them in a flash.*

Almost everything you read—on the SAT or elsewhere—can be broken down into two kinds of information—*main ideas* and *supporting details.* It's important to distinguish between the two when reading for the exam. The main ideas are worth focusing on; the supporting details are usually not.

How can you recognize the main ideas in a passage? There are several clues to look for.

- Main ideas tend to be broad and general; supporting details tend to be narrow and specific.
- Often, each paragraph of a passage is centered on a single main idea that is explicitly stated somewhere in the paragraph.
- The main idea often appears first or last in the paragraph; supporting details usually appear in the middle of the paragraph.

Consider the following example—a paragraph excerpted from an actual SAT reading passage.

> The myth of the infallible scientist evaporates when one thinks about the number of great ideas in science whose originators were

> correct in general but wrong in detail. The English physicist John Dalton (1766–1844) gets credit for modern atomic theory, but his mathematical formulas for calculating atomic weights were incorrect. The Polish astronomer Copernicus, who corrected Ptolemy's ancient concept of an Earth-centered universe, nevertheless was mistaken in the particulars of the planets' orbits.

There are three sentences in this paragraph. Of the three, which expresses a broad, general idea rather than a narrow, specific detail? The answer: the first sentence. It makes a general point—that scientists, even great ones, are not infallible. The second and third sentences give details to support and explain this idea—the second sentence describes the example of John Dalton, and the third sentence adds the example of Copernicus. Both are interesting and help to clarify the overall theme, but neither is as important as the first sentence, which states the author's main point.

Narrative passages can also be broken down into main ideas and supporting details. Here's another real SAT example.

> Nothing could be more generous, more joyous, than these natural meadows in summer. The flash and ripple and glimmer of the tall sunflowers, the chirp and gurgle of red-winged blackbirds swaying on the willow, the meadowlarks piping from grassy bogs, the peep of the prairie chick and the wailing call of plover on the flowery green slopes of the uplands made it all an ecstatic world to me. It was a wide world with a big, big sky that gave alluring hints of the still more glorious unknown wilderness beyond.

Which sentence here states the author's main idea? Again, it's the first sentence (although in this case the last sentence repeats and reinforces it). The long, very detailed second sentence is just a mass of specific images (sunflowers, blackbirds, or meadowlarks) to support the author's point that "these natural meadows" gave him a feeling of wildness and joy.

In both of these paragraphs, the details are interesting; they certainly add to the experience of reading the passage, and they help make the author's point vivid and understandable. But the details are of secondary importance. Don't spend a lot of time struggling to understand the details of a passage if they are tricky, and certainly don't try to memorize them. Instead, read them quickly, and make a mental note of where they are in case a question is asked about them. It probably won't happen.

Look for the Connections Among the Parts of the Passage

Think of a reading passage as a structure of ideas. Most passages are devoted to conveying a number of ideas that are connected to one another in some way. If you understand these ideas and the connections among them, you truly understand the passage as a whole.

The SAT is not about speed-reading. *If you can read at an average rate of 250 words per minute, as most high school students do, you'll have plenty of time for the passages on the exam. If you're not sure of your current reading speed, test yourself with a sample SAT passage and a watch. Just count the words and divide by the number of minutes spent to determine your rate.*

Quite often, the structure of ideas will be made very explicit, even obvious. Consider, for example, a reading passage containing five paragraphs that begin with the following five sentences.

1. Historians have long debated the reasons for the defeat of the Confederacy in the American Civil War.
2. For decades, the dominant theory held that the North's victory was due primarily to the superior economic resources available to the Union armies.
3. A second school of historians pointed instead to the geographic advantages enjoyed by the Northern generals.
4. In recent years, however, more and more historians have begun to claim that, contrary to traditional Southern belief, the Northern generalship was consistently superior.
5. In the end, perhaps the most likely explanation of the Northern victory is that it was caused by a combination of several factors.

Simply by reading these five sentences you can get a very good idea of the content and structure of the whole passage. The passage deals with the issue of why the North won the Civil War. Its structure is clear-cut. Paragraph (1) sets forth the question to be discussed. Paragraphs (2), (3), and (4) each suggest a different answer to the question. Paragraph (5) concludes the passage by suggesting a possible resolution of the disagreement.

Why is it helpful to recognize the logical structure of a reading passage? It helps you in several ways.

- It makes it easy to see the main ideas of the passage. In this case, the main ideas are the three separate theories that are presented and discussed.
- It tells you the *purpose* of the supporting details—even when you don't know what those details are. In this passage, for example, we've looked at only the first sentence of paragraph (2). Nonetheless, we can easily imagine what kind of supporting details will be given in the rest of the paragraph. The missing sentences will probably give examples of the superior economic resources enjoyed by the North (coal mines, factories, or railroad lines, for instance).
- If, in reading the complete passage, the actual details turn out to be complex or tricky, that would be okay. We'd still understand

the purpose and basic thrust even if the fine points were elusive. In most cases, that would be enough to answer any questions.

- The logical structure *organizes* all the information in the passage, making it easy to locate any detail that may be asked about. In this passage, if a question focuses on some detail related to the third of the three theories (Northern generalship), you'll be able to find the relevant paragraph quickly.
- The structure explains how the main ideas are related to one another. In this case, the main ideas are three different, conflicting explanations of the same historical event. One or more questions are likely to focus on the relationships among these ideas—for example, how they differ from one another, and why the earlier theories have been superseded by later ones.

SAT passages don't always boast such clear-cut, logical structures, but a structure of some kind is usually present. With practice, you can learn to recognize it.

Table 6.1 will help—it lists several of the most common types of logical structures found in SAT reading passages. Either alone or in combination, these structures underlie many of the passages you'll encounter on the exam. Practice looking for them whenever you read.

Mark Up the Passage as You Read

When tackling critical reading on the SAT, read with your pencil in hand. Use it to mark key points and logical connections as you find them, by underlining, circling, or starring them in the margin.

Table 6.1
Types of Logical Structures Often Used in SAT Reading Passages

1. Several theories or approaches to a single question or topic (often one theory or approach per paragraph)
2. One theory or idea illustrated with several detailed examples or illustrations (often one example or illustration per paragraph)
3. One theory or idea supported by several arguments (often one argument per paragraph)
4. Pro-and-con arguments presented on both sides of a single issue.
5. A comparison or contrast between two events, ideas, phenomena, or people
6. A cause-and-effect sequence showing how one event led to another (presented either in chronological order or via "flashback," with later events named *before* the earlier ones)

This will help you in two ways: the physical act of underlining particular words and phrases will strengthen your memory of the ideas you've highlighted, and the marks themselves will make it easier to find key parts of the passage if you need to locate them later.

Here are some specific suggestions about what to look for and mark as you read:

- **Look for the main idea of the passage as a whole.** This is one sentence that summarizes the central theme of the passage. Most passages contain such a sentence. It often appears near the beginning of the passage, to introduce the key idea; in other cases, it appears near the end, as a kind of summary or conclusion. When you find it, circle it.
- **Look for the main idea of each paragraph.** Remember the idea of the "topic sentence?" Your English teacher may have taught you to include one in every paragraph you write. SAT paragraphs often contain such a sentence that summarizes the central point of the paragraph. When you find one, underline it.
- **Look for the logical structure of the passage, and use numbers, symbols, or words to annotate it.** For example, if a passage is organized as a pro-and-con presentation of arguments on both sides of an issue, label each argument with the word "pro" or "con" in the margin. If a passage presents a series of historical events that show how one led to the next, circle the date of each event where it appears in the passage, and number the events in sequence in the margin—1, 2, 3, and so on.

As you practice, you'll find that you quickly develop your own system of signs and symbols. That's fine; no one has to understand your scratches but you, and you only need to understand them for the eight to ten minutes you'll be working on a given passage.

Practice marking up reading passages each time you work on critical reading between now and the day of the test.

The *process* of marking the passage is as important as the marks themselves. It encourages an active approach to reading as opposed to a passive one. Using this as part of the three-stage reading method will help you delve more deeply into the meaning of a passage than you ever did with conventional ways of reading.

THE INSIDER'S REPORT: THE BEST TIPS

Start with the Passage You Like Best

In some Verbal sections, you'll have two separate reading passages to work on. They're likely to be quite different in subject, style, and tone. Glance at both and decide which one appears more interesting or just easier. Tackle that passage first, even if it comes later in the test section. By doing this, you'll probably maximize your total score.

Preview the Question Stems

FYI

Marking up the passage helps you in the review stage of the three-stage reading method. To review the passage, just look back at the key words, phrases, and sentences you've marked.

Remember, the question stem is the part of the question that precedes the answer choices. "The author of the passage includes the details concerning Picasso's father primarily in order to emphasize . . ." would be an example of a question stem.

By previewing the stems, some students feel they get an advance look at the main themes of the passage and the details the test-makers plan to focus on. Other students, however, find this strategy more time-consuming than useful. Our recommendation is to try this technique a couple of times and decide whether you find it helpful. If you do, use it.

Double Passages: Compare as You Go

Every standard SAT exam includes one 15-minute Verbal section consisting of two closely linked reading passages that share a topic or theme. We call this the *double passage*. Of the thirteen questions that typically follow the double passage, eight to ten will deal with one or another of the passages, while three to five will ask you to compare, contrast, or connect them in some way.

Various logical relationships are possible between the two passages.

- **The two passages may be opposed.** The two authors may present differing sides of a certain debate or argument. It's likely that they will agree on certain basic premises, and they may even share particular goals or values; however, their differences will be more significant, and the passages will focus on these rather than on any shared beliefs.

FYI

If you do preview the question stems, remember these two important don'ts. (1) Don't try to memorize the question stems—it's too much to keep in mind. (2) Don't preview the answer choices. Remember, 80% of those choices are wrong.

- **The two passages may be in agreement.** The authors may be basically supportive of one another's ideas, opinions, or observations. Nonetheless, the passages will, of course, exhibit differences; the authors' personal backgrounds may be very different, leading them to emphasize varying elements of the topic or to have subtle points of disagreement. Look for these differences as well as the more obvious agreements.
- **The two passages may be complementary.** They may present diverse aspects of or approaches to a particular topic or idea, or they may consider two different topics that are related somehow. For example, one of the first double passages released by ETS consisted of a passage about silent movies paired with a passage about the art of mime. Here, the two topics under discussion were not the same, although they were related: each passage dealt with (1) a particular performing art (2) in which a story is acted out (3) without the use of words or sounds. These three connections were used as the basis for a comparison of the two passages.

The questions that follow the double passage will ask you to compare the two passages and the points of view they express, usually focusing on both their similarities and their differences. So as you read the double passage, look for points of agreement and disagreement between the authors, as well as places where the same idea is referred to using different words or terminology. When you find such connections, mark them; this will make it easier to refer to them when answering the questions. Draw lines between the passages (right across the page) or use matching symbols in the margins to mark places where the authors address the same points or related ideas. These will probably be sources for the questions to follow.

Refer to the Passage

When answering critical reading questions, refer to the passage as often as you need to. Most questions will focus on a particular paragraph or sentence of the passage. Many of the questions will contain explicit references to specific line numbers in the passage; others will simply mention particular details and expect you to locate them.

When this happens, you'll usually need to look back at the passage to answer the question correctly. Don't try to answer from memory. Quite often the wrong answer choices will be subtly wrong; only a careful review of the specific detail being asked about will enable you to see which answer is correct and why the others are not.

THE INSIDER'S REPORT: THE MOST IMPORTANT WARNINGS

Don't Pick the First Choice that Sounds Good

On all verbal questions, there are degrees of right and wrong. (By contrast, on math questions, correctness is much more black and white: if the right answer to a math problem is 16, then the answer 13 isn't "partially right" or "arguably right"—it's just plain wrong.)

The "grayness" of verbal answer choices is especially noticeable on critical reading questions. The test-makers are highly skilled at crafting wrong answer choices (distractors) that are plausible and attractive. So if you begin reading the answers to a critical reading question and find that choice (A) sounds good, don't just select it. Read on. Choice (C) may sound even better, and choice (E) may be best of all. Always read all five answers to a critical reading item before making your choice.

FYI

Some students have been taught that certain words or phrases mark wrong answers to critical reading questions. For instance, some teachers say that answer choices with words like "all," "every," "always," "none," and "never" are usually wrong. This is false.

Don't Pick an Answer Just Because It Sounds Familiar

One popular method used in crafting distractors is to draw the information for wrong answers from the passage itself. This makes for distractors that are especially tempting because they sound (and are) familiar. Your reaction may be, "Oh, yes, it says that right here in paragraph 2. This must be the right answer."

Such reasoning may be flawed. The correct answer for the particular question may be found in paragraph 4, and paragraph 2 may simply be irrelevant. Don't fall for this.

The best way to avoid this trap is to refer back to the portion of the passage being asked about before you pick an answer. Make sure the answer you choose comes from there, not from some other part of the passage.

Don't Pick an Answer Just Because It's True

Most of the passages you'll read on the SAT will be about topics you know only a little about. That's okay. The test-makers don't expect you to have any background knowledge, and none is needed to answer the questions.

Occasionally, however, you may encounter a passage on a topic you're familiar with. It may even be a topic you personally are fascinated by. This can be helpful—reading about something you like and care about is fun, and you'll probably find the passage easy to understand.

However, this situation can also be dangerous. The danger lies in bringing your own outside knowledge and opinions to the questions. You may be tempted to pick an answer choice because you happen to know it's true, or because you personally agree with it. Those aren't good reasons. The correct answer must be based specifically on the information in the passage, and it must reflect accurately the opinions and ideas expressed there—even if you happen to disagree with them.

So set aside your own knowledge and beliefs when reading a passage on a topic you care about. Pick answers based solely on what you find in the passage—not on anything else you happen to know.

Vocabulary Questions: Focus on the Passage

Virtually every SAT critical reading set will include one or more questions about the vocabulary used in the passage. Always answer these questions by looking back at the sentence referred to (it will generally be cited by line number). You need to pick the right answer based on how the word is used in that sentence, not based on your general sense of the word's meaning.

The words tested in this way won't necessarily look hard. On recent SATs, vocabulary questions have been based on such words as "impress," "camp," "living," "pursuit," and "proved." In one sense, these are easy words—most grade-school kids know and use them. But they are tricky in that each can have several meanings. For example, consider these sentences containing the word *impress*:

> Tony was eager to impress the college admissions officer with his intelligence and charm.
>
> During the early 1800s, officers of the British Navy would sometimes impress American citizens into serving as sailors on British ships.
>
> The king's scribe used a metal seal to impress the hot wax with the royal coat of arms.

In the first sentence, *impress* means to "attract the favorable notice of." In the second sentence, it means "coerce." In the third sentence, it means "stamp." The three meanings are vaguely related because the general idea of "pressing" or "marking" is involved in all three, but they're nonetheless quite different.

The lesson is clear—always refer back to the word's context in the passage. Only by doing so can you pick the meaning the test-makers are looking for.

JUST THE FACTS

- Use the three-stage method of previewing, reading, and reviewing to get the most out of every passage on the SAT.
- As you read, look for the main ideas in the passage and the connections among them.
- Read with pencil in hand and mark up key ideas in the passage as you find them.
- Learn the most common types of wrong answers used by the test-makers and how to avoid choosing them.

PRACTICE, PRACTICE, PRACTICE: CRITICAL READING EXERCISES

Instructions

The following exercises will give you a chance to practice the skills and strategies you've just learned for tackling critical reading questions. As with all practice exercises, work under true testing conditions. Complete each exercise in a single sitting. Eliminate distractions (TV, music) and clear away notes and reference materials. Time yourself with a stopwatch or kitchen timer, or have someone else time you. If you run out of time before answering all the questions, stop and draw a line under the last question you finished. Then go ahead and tackle the remaining questions. When you are done, score yourself based only on the questions you finished in the allotted time.

Circle the letter of the correct response. In addition, any time your answer is a guess—any time you enter a response about which you are not certain—circle the number of that question. After you've completed the exercises, count the number of circled items and the number of these items that you answered correctly. Then, divide the number of correct answers by the number of circled items. The result is your Guessing Quotient (G.Q.). If your G.Q. is higher than .20, you will probably boost your overall score by guessing on the real SAT.

Understanding Your Scores

0–3 correct: A poor performance. Study this chapter again and (if you haven't already) begin spending time each day in building your vocabulary using the SAT Word List in Appendix A.

4–6 correct: A below-average score. Study this chapter again, focusing especially on the skills and strategies you've found newest and most challenging.

7–9 correct: An average score. You may want to study this chapter again. Also, be sure you are managing your time wisely (as explained in Chapter 3) and avoiding errors due to haste or carelessness.

10–12 correct: An above-average score. Depending on your personal target score and your strength on other verbal question types, you may or may not want to devote additional time to critical reading.

13–15 correct: An excellent score. You are probably ready to perform well on SAT critical reading questions.

EXERCISE 1

15 Questions

Time—15 Minutes

Directions: Each passage below is followed by questions based on its content. Answer the questions on the basis of what is *stated* or *implied* in the passage and in any introductory material that may be provided.

Questions 1–8 are based on the following passage.

In this passage, excerpted from his autobiography published in 1845, Frederick Douglass, a black ex-slave, discusses life on a southern plantation as he experienced it prior to the American Civil War.

The men and women slaves received, as their monthly allowance of food, eight pounds of pork, or its equivalent in fish, and one bushel of corn meal. Their yearly clothing consisted of two coarse linen shirts; one pair of linen trousers, like the shirts; one jacket; one pair of trousers for winter, made of coarse "negro" cloth; one pair of stockings, and one pair of shoes; the whole of which could not have cost more than seven dollars. The allowance of the slave children was given to their mothers, or the old women having the care of them. The children unable to work in the field had neither shoes, stockings, jackets, nor trousers given to them; their clothing consisted of two coarse linen shirts per year. When these failed them, they went naked until the next allowance-day.

Children from seven to ten years old, of both sexes, almost naked, might be seen at all seasons of the year.

There were no beds given the slaves, unless one coarse blanket be considered such, and none but the men and women had these. This, however, is not considered a very great privation. They find less difficulty from the want of beds than from the want of time to sleep; for when their day's work in the field is done, the most of them having their washing, mending, and cooking to do, and having few or none of the ordinary facilities for doing either of these, very many of their sleeping hours are consumed in preparing for the field the coming day.

And when this is done, old and young, male and female, married and single, drop down side by side, on one common bed—the cold, damp floor—each covering himself or herself with their miserable blankets; and here they sleep till they are summoned to the field by the driver's horn.

At that sound, all must rise and be off to the field. There must be no halting; every one must be at his or her post; and woe betide them who hear not this morning summons to the field; for if they are not awakened by the sense of hearing, they are by the sense of feeling: no age nor sex finds any favor. Mr. Severe, the overseer, used to stand by the door of the quarter, armed with a large hickory stick and heavy cowskin, ready to whip any one who was so unfortunate as not to hear, or, from any other cause, was prevented from being ready to start for the field at the sound of the horn.

Mr. Severe was rightly named: he was a cruel man. I have seen him whip a woman, causing the blood to run half an hour at the time; and this, too, in the midst of her crying children, pleading for their mother's release. He seemed to take pleasure in manifesting his fiendish barbarity. Adding to his cruelty, he was a profane swearer. It was enough to chill the blood and stiffen the hair of an ordinary man to hear him talk. Scarce a sentence escaped him but was commenced or concluded by some horrid oath.

The field was the place to witness his cruelty and profanity. His presence made it the field of both blood and blasphemy. From the rising till the going down of the sun, he was cursing, raving, cutting, and slashing among the slaves of the field in the most frightful manner. However, his career was short. He died very soon after I went to Colonel Lloyd's; and he died as he lived, uttering, with his dying groans, bitter curses and horrid oaths. His death was regarded by the slaves as the result of a merciful providence.

Mr. Severe's place was filled by a Mr. Hopkins. He was a very different man. He was less cruel, less profane, and made less noise than Mr. Severe. His course was characterized by no extraordinary demonstrations of cruelty. He whipped, but seemed to take no pleasure in it. He was called by the slaves a good overseer.

1. The primary purpose of the passage is to
   - (A) outline the economic system by which a slave plantation was run
   - (B) denounce the cruelty with which slave children were treated
   - (C) explain why slaves were unable to improve their lot by their own efforts
   - (D) expose the inherent injustice of slavery as a social institution
   - (E) describe some of the living conditions to which slaves were subjected

2. The passage implies that slave children were considered by their owners to be
   - (A) property of considerable economic value
   - (B) creatures to be nurtured for their future usefulness
   - (C) of little value until they were old enough to work
   - (D) useful primarily as helpers to their parents
   - (E) more important than their parents

3. As used in line 28, the word "privation" most nearly means
   - (A) lack
   - (B) expense
   - (C) injustice
   - (D) solitude
   - (E) grievance

4. The passage implies that the slaves had little opportunity to sleep in part because
   - (A) their masters forced them to work in the fields until late at night
   - (B) they were wakened by the overseer well before dawn
   - (C) they had virtually no equipment for tending to their personal needs
   - (D) as one group of slaves was sleeping another was on its way to work
   - (E) the noise and confusion of the slaves' quarters made rest impossible

5. It can be inferred from the passage that Douglass considered the overseer, Mr. Severe, to be "rightly named" for all the following reasons EXCEPT that he
   (A) constantly swore at the slaves he managed
   (B) instilled the fear of God in his charges
   (C) took pleasure in meting out punishment
   (D) was particularly harsh in his treatment of the slaves
   (E) frightened the slaves by his actions and demeanor

6. As used in line 88, the phrase "a merciful providence" most nearly means a
   (A) natural tendency
   (B) harsh fate
   (C) divine intervention
   (D) just retribution
   (E) stroke of good luck

7. The author implies that the slaves were not greatly concerned about the lack of beds because they
   (A) were accustomed to sleeping on the floor
   (B) had little time to sleep
   (C) preferred sleeping with only a blanket
   (D) needed the warmth provided by sharing one sleeping space
   (E) were not accustomed to sleeping in beds

8. The passage could provide a historian with information concerning all of the following aspects of life in America prior to the Civil War EXCEPT the
   (A) status of many black Americans
   (B) extent of slavery in the United States
   (C) beliefs and behaviors of some slaveholders
   (D) attitudes of slaves toward their masters
   (E) economic system that existed under slavery

Questions 9–15 are based on the following passage.

A number of surprising difficulties are faced by physicists and industrial engineers in their attempts to understand and control the behavior of granular matter, such as sand, seeds, and powders.

For years, the contents of a child's sandbox have confounded some of the nation's top physicists. Sand and other granular materials such as powders, seeds, nuts, soil, and detergent behave in ways that seem to undermine natural laws and cost industries ranging from pharmaceuticals to agribusiness and mining billions of dollars.

Just shaking a can of mixed nuts can show you how problematic granular material can be. The nuts don't "mix"; they "unmix" and sort themselves out, with the larger Brazil nuts on top and the smaller peanuts on the bottom. In this activity and others, granular matter's behavior apparently goes counter to the second law of thermodynamics, which states that entropy, or disorder, tends to increase in any natural system.

Mimicking the mixed-nut conundrum with a jar containing many small beads and one large bead, one group of physicists claimed that vibrations causing the beads to percolate open up small gaps rather than larger ones. Thus, when a Brazil nut becomes slightly airborne, the peanuts rush in underneath and gradually nudge it to the top. Another group of physicists color-coded layers of beads to track their circulation in the container and achieved a different result. Vibrations, they found, drive the beads in circles up the center and down the sides of the container. Yet downward currents, similar to convection currents in air or water, are too narrow to accommodate the larger bead, stranding it on top.

One industrial engineer who has studied the problem says that both the "percolation" and "convection current" theories can be right, depending upon the material, and that percolation is the major factor with nuts. Given the inability of scientists to come up with a single equation explaining unmixing, you can see why industrial engineers who must manage granular materials go a little, well, "nuts." Take pharmaceuticals, for instance. There may be six types of powders with different-sized grains in a single medicine tablet. Mixing them at some speeds might sort them, while mixing at other speeds will make them thoroughly amalgamated. One aspirin company still relies on an experienced employee wearing a latex glove who pinches some powder in the giant mixing drum to see if it "feels right."

Granular material at rest can be equally frustrating to physicists and engineers. Take a tall cylinder of sand. Unlike a liquid, in which pressure exerted at the bottom increases in direct proportion to the liquid's height, pressure at the base of the sand cylinder doesn't increase indefinitely. Instead it reaches a maximum value and stays there. This quality allows sand to trickle at a nearly constant rate through the narrow opening separating the two glass bulbs of an hourglass, thus measuring the passage of time.

Physicists have also found that forces are not distributed evenly throughout granular material. It is this characteristic that may account for the frequent rupturing of silos in which grain is stored. In a silo, for instance, the column's weight is carried from grain to grain along jagged chains. As a result, the container's walls carry more of the weight than its base, and the force is significantly larger at some points of contact than at others.

Coming up with equations to explain, much less, predict, the distribution of these force chains is extremely difficult. Again, using beads, physicists developed a simple theoretical model in which they assume that a given bead transmits the load it bears unequally and randomly onto the three beads on which it rests. While the model agrees well with experimental results, it doesn't take into account all of the mechanisms of force transmission between grains of sand or wheat.

In the struggle to understand granular materials, sand-studying physicists have at least one thing in their favor. Unlike particle physicists who must secure billions of dollars in government funding for the building of supercolliders in which to accelerate and view infinitesimal particles, they can conduct experiments using such low-cost, low-tech materials such as sand, beads, marbles, and seeds. It is hoped that more low-tech experiments and computer simulations will lead to equations that explain the unwieldy stuff and reduce some of the wastage, guesswork, and accidents that occur in the various industries that handle it.

9. Which of the following titles most accurately describes the above passage?

(A) New Theories About the Physical Properties of Sand

(B) The Behavior of Granular Matter in Motion and at Rest

(C) The Percolation Theory Versus the Convection Current Theory of Unmixing

(D) Theoretical and Practical Problems in Handling Granular Matter

(E) How Physicists Are Helping to Solve Industrial Riddles

10. The percolation theory of unmixing is best illustrated by which of the following examples?
    (A) Larger rocks rising to the surface in a garden after a period of frost
    (B) Currents of small beads blocking the upward movement of large beads in a shaken container
    (C) Contents settling in a bag of potato chips so that the package appears less full after handling
    (D) Large nuts blocking the upward movement of small nuts in a shaken container
    (E) A can of multi-sized beads sorting into layers of large and small beads upon shaking

11. In saying that the percolation and convection current theories may both be right (lines 45–48), the industrial engineer means that
    (A) neither theory is supported by an adequate mathematical basis
    (B) both theories are still unproven, since they have not been tested on a variety of material
    (C) though the theories have different names, they describe the same physical mechanisms
    (D) the mechanism causing unmixing varies depending upon the type of granular material
    (E) both mechanisms are involved in all instances of unmixing

12. As used in line 27, the word "conundrum" most nearly means
    (A) hypothesis
    (B) experiment
    (C) enigma
    (D) paradox
    (E) phenomenon

13. Which of the following appears to be the best solution for combating the "unmixing" problem faced by pharmaceutical manufacturers that must prepare large quantities of powders?
    (A) To craft powders so that all the grains have similar sizes and shapes
    (B) To craft powders in which every grain weighs the same amount
    (C) To mix all the powders together at the same speed
    (D) To hire only engineers who have years of experience in powder mixing
    (E) To analyze and control the pattern of force chains in a vat of powder

14. The passage implies that, if the top bulb of an hourglass were filled with water instead of sand, the pressure pushing the water through the opening would
(A) increase as water trickles through the opening
(B) decrease as water trickles through the opening
(C) remain constant as water trickles through the opening
(D) be directed at the walls of the container rather than the base
(E) make the water trickle down in drops rather than a stream

15. In lines 105–115, the author implies that physicists studying granular material
(A) are grappling with issues that are less complicated than those confronting particle physicists
(B) are fortunate in having available a selection of relatively easy means of crafting experiments
(C) are less likely to receive government funding than are particle physicists
(D) are likely to soon develop a complete predictive model for the behavior of granular material
(E) know less about grains of sand than particle physicists know about infinitesimal forms of matter

EXERCISE 2

15 Questions

Time—15 Minutes

Directions: Each passage below is followed by questions based on its content. Answer the questions on the basis of what is *stated* or *implied* in the passage and in any introductory material that may be provided.

Questions 1–6 are based on the following passage.

Today, the theory of "continental drift," which supposes that the earth's great land masses have moved over time, is a basic premise accepted by most geologists. However, this was not always so, as discussed in the passage that follows.

Although Alfred Wegener was not the first scientist to propose the idea that the continents have moved, his 1912 outline of the hypothesis was the first detailed description of the concept and the first to offer a respectable mass of supporting evidence for it. It is appropriate, then, that the theory of continental drift was most widely known as "Wegener's hypothesis" during the more than fifty years of debate that preceded its ultimate acceptance by most earth scientists.

In brief, Wegener's hypothesis stated that, in the late Paleozoic era, all of the present-day continents were part of a single giant land mass, Pangaea, that occupied almost half of the earth's surface. About 40 million years ago, Pangaea began to break into fragments that slowly moved apart, ultimately forming the various continents we know today.

Wegener supported his argument with data drawn from geology, paleontology, zoology, climatology, and other fields. So impressive was his array of evidence that his hypothesis could not be ignored. However, until the 1960s, most scientists were reluctant to accept Wegener's ideas. There are several reasons why this was so.

First, although Wegener showed that continental movement was consistent with much of the geological and other evidence—for example, the apparent family relationships among forms of plants and animals now separated by vast expanses of ocean, once geographically united on the hypothetical pangaea—he failed to suggest any causal mechanism for continental drift sufficiently powerful and plausible to be convincing.

Second, while the period during which Wegener's theory was propounded and debated saw rapid developments in many branches of geology and an explosion of new knowledge about the nature of the earth and the forces at work in its formation, little of this evidence seemed to support Wegener. For example, data drawn from the new science of seismology, including experimental studies of the behavior of rocks under high pressure, suggested that the earth has far too much internal strength and rigidity to allow continents to "drift" across its surface. Measurements of the earth's gravitational field made by some of the early scientific satellites offered further evidence in support of this view as late as the early 1960s.

Third, and perhaps most significant, Wegener's theory seemed to challenge one of the most deeply-held philosophical bases of geology—the doctrine of uniformitarianism, which states that earth history must always be explained by the operation of essentially unchanging, continuous forces. Belief in the intervention of unexplained, sporadic, and massive shaping events—known as catastrophism—was considered beyond the pale by mainstream geologists.

Wegener was not, strictly speaking, a catastrophist—he did not suggest that some massive cataclysm had triggered the breakup of Pangaea—but his theory did imply a dramatic change in the face of the earth occurring relatively late in geologic history. Such a belief, viewed as tainted with catastrophism, was abhorrent to most geologists throughout the first half of this century.

1. According to the passage, Wegener believed that Pangaea
   (A) was destroyed in a massive cataclysm occurring about 40 million years ago
   (B) consisted of several large land areas separated by vast expanses of ocean
   (C) was ultimately submerged by rising oceans at the end of the Paleozoic era
   (D) has gradually drifted from its original location into its current position
   (E) contained in a single land mass the basic material of all the continents that exist today

2. It can be inferred from the passage that, by the end of the Paleozoic era,
   (A) early human beings existed on earth
   (B) many forms of plant and animal life existed on earth
   (C) the land mass of Pangaea no longer existed
   (D) a series of unexplained catastrophes had changed the face of the earth
   (E) most of today's land forms had taken their current shape

3. The passage provides information to answer which of the following questions?
   I. What geological forces caused the breakup of Pangaea?
   II. What evidence discovered in the 1960s lent support to Wegener's hypothesis?
   III. When did Wegener's hypothesis win acceptance by most earth scientists?

   (A) I only
   (B) II only
   (C) III only
   (D) I and III only
   (E) II and III only

4. The passage implies that the most significant reason for the opposition to Wegener's hypothesis on the part of many scientists was its
   (A) indirect challenge to a fundamental premise of geology
   (B) lack of supporting evidence from fields other than geology
   (C) impossibility of being tested by experimental means
   (D) conflict with data drawn from the fossil record
   (E) failure to provide a comprehensive framework for earth history

5. The author refers to the scientific information gathered by satellites in order to suggest the
   (A) philosophical changes that ultimately led to the acceptance of Wegener's hypothesis
   (B) dramatic advances in earth science during the 1960s
   (C) differing directions taken by various earth scientists in the decades following Wegener
   (D) nature of some of the evidence that appeared to refute Wegener
   (E) need for experimental demonstration before any new geological theory can be accepted

6. As used in line 86, the word "dramatic" most nearly means
   (A) exciting
   (B) violent
   (C) inexplicable
   (D) large-scale
   (E) rapid

Questions 7–15 are based on the following passage.

Many people living today appear to be nostalgic for the Victorian period of the nineteenth century—a time none of them actually remember. In this passage, a historian considers this phenomenon.

"The past is a foreign country: they do things differently there," wrote L. P. Hartley in his novel *The Go-Between*. As with a foreign country, he seems to suggest there is a romance about the past; we think of it as a time and place where things were not only different but, somehow, better. Hartley was a Briton writing of late Victorian England, but even in America we tend to think of those days—the years just before the turn of the twentieth century—as a time when life was slower, easier, and generally more pleasant.

Exactly why do we think of what Mark Twain labeled the "Gilded Age" as being such a time? None of us, of course, who live in the last quarter of the twentieth century, can remember those days. Our grandparents might have remembered traces of them—a world without central heating, indoor plumbing, talking pictures, or radio. Our parents will recall the days before air conditioning, television, and jet planes. Even we can easily remember when there were no CD players, personal computers, fax machines, or portable telephones.

While all this technology was intended to make—and has made—our lives easier and more enjoyable, many of us still look back at the turn of the century through a haze of nostalgia. Perhaps it's because we've begun to feel overwhelmed by all our machines and long for what we think of as a simpler time. Perhaps it's images of glowing coal stoves, the gentle aura of gaslight, the sound of a horse and buggy on the pavement, the simple pleasures of the "good old summertime," that make that era seem so appealing. Hence the cult popularity of a novel like Jack Finney's *Time and Again*, with its magical evocation of New York in the 1880s, or the universal sensation of well-being felt by both adults and children when they stroll the Victorian-style Main Street of a Disney theme park.

But was that world really as idyllic as we think? Although in our imaginations we see the "Gilded Age" as a more genteel time, the reality was less pleasant. In many respects, things were really not as good as we imagine they were in "the good old days."

Take, for example, those glowing coal stoves. Although they provided relatively little heat, coal-burning stoves were all too powerful at using up the oxygen in a room and replacing it with enough soot and dust to make a house almost uninhabitable. By the 1880s, those who could afford \$2,000 to \$4,000—a very considerable sum for the day—might install central heating, but early radiators, though cleaner, filled their homes with the constant noises of "water hammer" and hissing.

Then there were those horses in the street. We think nostalgically of the days before automobiles befouled our air, but horses and buggies produced a different kind of pollution. At the turn of the century in New York City, for example, there were 150,000 horses, each of which dropped between twenty and twenty-five pounds of manure every day, which was then spread around by the buggies' wheels. The stench was overwhelming, and there was so much manure in the streets that some observers voiced fears that America's cities would disappear like ancient Pompeii—but buried under something other than volcanic ash.

Even worse, perhaps, were those "good old summertimes." There was, of course, no air conditioning, and in the cities, at least, summers were hotter than they are today, because lower buildings did not protect the streets from the sun as much as today's skyscrapers. Contemporary clothing, too, added to the problem—heavy suits, long underwear, vests for men, and voluminous dresses with multiple undergarments and girdles for women. And the heat waves were not just unpleasant, they could be deadly—during the summer of 1896, 3,000 people and 2,000 horses died of the heat in New York City alone.

Much worse could be cited—the condition of the poor, the status of women and children, the state of medical science; the list is almost endless. While it's probably true that the pace of life was slower and, at least in that respect, perhaps more congenial to human sensibilities a hundred years ago, the truth is that the "good old days" really weren't so good after all.

7. The attitude of the author of this passage toward life a century ago might best be described as
   (A) nostalgic
   (B) pessimistic
   (C) realistic
   (D) sentimental
   (E) cynical

8. The author discusses the differences between life in Victorian times and today primarily in terms of
   (A) social structure
   (B) politics
   (C) technology
   (D) human rights
   (E) economics

9. The reference to the "haze of nostalgia" (line 38) through which most people view Victorian times suggests that their understanding of the era is
   (A) distorted by emotion
   (B) based mainly on books and movies
   (C) fundamentally accurate
   (D) overly influenced by contemporary values
   (E) derived from family recollections

10. The author mentions the use of Victorian style in the design of a theme park (lines 52–53) primarily to emphasize the
    (A) inaccuracy of modern depictions of Victorian life
    (B) timeless quality of Victorian-style art and architecture
    (C) role of the media in fostering a distorted image of the Victorian era
    (D) general sense of well-being enjoyed by those living in the Victorian period
    (E) popular appeal of images derived from Victorian times

11. As used in line 54, the word "idyllic" most nearly means
    (A) poetic
    (B) untroubled
    (C) primitive
    (D) rural
    (E) exciting

12. The author of the passage suggests that people are nostalgic about the Victorian era because they believe all the following EXCEPT
    (A) the pace of life was slower in the past
    (B) modern technology has made life more complicated
    (C) the past is more romantic than the present
    (D) there is something exotic about the past
    (E) people were more in touch with nature in the past

13. As used in line 69, the word "considerable" most nearly means
    (A) surprising
    (B) excessive
    (C) noteworthy
    (D) expensive
    (E) provocative

14. It can be inferred from the passage that all the following were true of life at the turn of the century EXCEPT
    (A) the status of women was lower
    (B) people's lives were affected more by the weather
    (C) medicine was in a more primitive state
    (D) the poor suffered even more than they do today
    (E) people were generally happier

15. It can be inferred from the passage that the author believes technology has made our lives all of the following EXCEPT
    (A) less uncomfortable
    (B) more confusing
    (C) more pleasant
    (D) faster-paced
    (E) less fulfilling

EXERCISE 3

15 Questions

Time—15 Minutes

Directions: Each passage below is followed by questions based on its content. Answer the questions on the basis of what is *stated* or *implied* in the passage and in any introductory material that may be provided.

Questions 1–4 are based on the following passage.

This is an excerpt from a profile of Toni Morrison, the African-American novelist who was awarded the Nobel Prize for Literature in 1993.

With the ascendance of Toni Morrison's literary star, it has become commonplace for critics to deracialize her by saying that Morrison is not just a "black woman writer," that she has moved beyond the limiting confines of race and gender to larger "universal" issues. Yet Morrison, a Nobel laureate with six highly acclaimed novels, bristles at having to choose between being a writer or a black woman writer and willingly accepts critical classification as the latter.

To call her simply a writer denies the key roles that Morrison's African-American roots and her black female perspective have played in her work. For instance, many of Morrison's characters treat their dreams as "real," are nonplussed by visitations from dead ancestors, and generally experience intimate connections with beings whose existence isn't empirically verifiable. While critics might see Morrison's use of the supernatural as purely a literary device, Morrison herself explains, "That's simply the way the world was for me and the black people I knew."

Just as her work has given voice to this little-remarked facet of African-American culture, it has affirmed the unique vantage point of the black woman. "I really feel the range of emotion and perception I have had access to as a black person and a female person are greater than that of people who are neither," says Morrison. "My world did not shrink because I was a black female writer. It just got bigger."

1. The author of the passage is chiefly concerned with
   (A) explaining Morrison's own viewpoint on the role of her race and gender in her novels
   (B) assessing the significance of the black female perspective in the modern American novel
   (C) acknowledging Morrison's success in giving voice to unknown aspects of the African-American experience
   (D) presenting a counter-argument to critics who seek to "deracialize" Morrison
   (E) explaining why being a writer and being a black female writer are distinct critical classifications

2. Morrison's use of the supernatural in her novels is mentioned by the author in order to explain
   (A) why some critics categorize her as a "writer" but not a "black woman writer"
   (B) the distinction between drawing from one's personal experience and using a literary device
   (C) the enormous critical acclaim Morrison's novels have received
   (D) one way in which Morrison's novels are rooted in her experience as an African-American woman
   (E) one of the universal themes that is woven throughout Morrison's novels

3. The author suggests that critics who seek to deny Morrison's racial and gender identity are motivated by a desire to
   (A) emphasize the broad human interest of the themes she writes about
   (B) explain the popular and commercial success her work has achieved
   (C) ignore the contributions of African-American writers to modern culture
   (D) downplay the role of the supernatural in her work
   (E) disparage her writing for its parochialism and narrowness

4. The passage suggests that the author would be most likely to agree with which of the following statements?
   (A) The intelligent critic often has a more profound understanding of art than the artist himself.
   (B) The true artist transcends her origins by transforming the personal into the universal.
   (C) For African Americans, the psychological importance of race will always outweigh that of gender.
   (D) The differences among human cultures are trivial by comparison with what they have in common.
   (E) The most universal art is often that which is most deeply rooted in a particular culture.

Questions 5–15 are based on the contents of the two passages below and the relationship between the two passages.

When the supposedly "unsinkable" ship R.M.S. Titanic, *enroute to New York, struck an iceberg and sank on the night of April 14, 1912, it sent shock waves around the world that continue to reverberate today. In these passages, taken from the transcripts of the U.S. Senate investigation of the disaster, two passengers recount their escapes from the sinking liner.*

Passage 1

Emily B. Ryerson, First-Class Passenger. At the time of the collision, I was awake and heard the engines stop, but felt no jar. My husband was asleep, so I rang and asked the steward what was the matter. He said, "There is a talk of an iceberg, ma'am, and they have stopped, not to run into it." I told him to keep me informed if there were any orders.

It was bitterly cold, so I put on a warm wrapper and looked out the window and saw the stars shining and a calm sea, but heard no noise. It was 12 o'clock. After about 10 minutes, I went out in the corridor and saw far off people hurrying on deck. A passenger ran by and called out "Put on your life belts and come up on the boat deck." I said, "Where did you get these orders?" He said, "From the captain." I went back then and told Miss Bowen and my daughter, who were in the next room, to dress immediately, roused my husband and the two younger children . . . and then remembered my maid.

By this time my husband was fully dressed, and we could hear the noise of feet tramping on the deck overhead. He was quite calm and cheerful and helped me put the life belts on the children and on my maid. I was paralyzed with fear of not all getting on deck together in time, as there were seven of us. My husband cautioned us all to keep together, and we went up to A deck, where we found quite a group of people we knew. Everyone had on a life belt, and they were very quiet and self-possessed.

We stood there for quite a long time—fully half an hour, I should say. Then we were ordered to the boat deck. My chief thought and that of everyone else was, I know, not to make a fuss and to do as we were told. My husband joked with some of the women he knew, and I heard him say, "Don't you hear the band playing?" I begged him to let me stay with him, but he said, "You must obey orders. When they say, 'Women and children to the boats,' you must go when your turn comes. I'll stay with John Thayer. We will be all right."

All this time we could hear the rockets going up—signals of distress. Again, we were ordered down to A deck. We saw people getting into boats, but we waited our turn. My boy, Jack, was with me. An officer at the window said, "That boy can't go." My husband stepped forward and said, "Of course, that boy goes with his mother; he is only 13." So they let him pass. I turned and kissed my husband, and as we left he and the other men I knew were all standing there together very quietly. The decks were lighted, and as you went through the window it was as if you stepped out into the dark.

The order was given to pull away, then they rowed off. Then suddenly, when we still seemed very near, I turned to see the great ship take a plunge toward the bow, the two forward funnels seemed to lean, and then she seemed to break in half as if cut with a knife, and as the bow went under the lights went out.

Passage 2

Daniel Buckley, Steerage Passenger. This night of the wreck, I was sleeping in my room on the *Titanic*, in the steerage. There were three other boys from the same place sleeping in the same room with me.

I heard some terrible noise and I jumped out on the floor, and the first thing I knew my feet were getting wet; the water was just coming in slightly. I told the other fellows to get up, that there was something wrong and that the water was coming in. They only laughed at me. One of them says—"Get back into bed. You are not in Ireland now."

I got on my clothes as quick as I could, and the three other fellows got out. The room was very small, so I got out, to give them room to dress themselves.

Two sailors came along, and they were shouting: "All up on deck! Unless you want to get drowned."

When I heard this, I went for the deck as quick as I could. When I got up on the deck I saw everyone having those life belts on except only myself; so I got sorry and said I would go back again where I was sleeping and get one, because there was one there for each person.

I went back again, and just as I was going down the last flight of stairs the water was up four steps, and dashing up, I did not go back into the room, because I could not. I got back on the deck again, and just as I got back there, I was looking around to see if I could get any of those life belts, and I met a first-class passenger, and he had two.

He gave me one, and fixed it on me.

Then the lifeboats were preparing. There were five lifeboats sent out. I was in the sixth. I was holding the ropes all the time, helping to let down the five lifeboats that went down first, as well as I could.

When the sixth lifeboat was prepared, there was a big crowd of men standing on the deck. When they jumped, I said I would go too. I went into the boat. Then two officers came along and said all of the men should come out. And they brought a lot of steerage passengers with them; and they were mixed, every way, ladies and gentlemen. And they said all the men should get out and let the ladies in. The men that were in the boat at first fought and would not get out, but the officers drew their revolvers, and fired shots over our heads, and then the men got out.

I was crying. There was a woman in the boat, and she had thrown her shawl over me, and she told me to stay in there. I believe she was Mrs. Astor. Then they did not see me. When the boat was ready, we were lowered down into the water and rowed away out from the steamer. We were only 15 minutes out when she sank. I saw the lights just going out as she went down. It made a terrible noise, like thunder.

5. The upper-class status of the narrator of the first passage can be inferred from all of the following EXCEPT the
   - (A) fact that she had a maid
   - (B) way she was addressed by the steward
   - (C) fact that her family occupied several cabins
   - (D) fact that her husband sent her ahead into a lifeboat
   - (E) fact that the officer deferred to her husband's judgment concerning their son

6. The words of the steward who first advised the narrator of Passage 1 about a problem with the ship (lines 6–8) suggest that he believed that the *Titanic* had been
   - (A) severely damaged and would sink
   - (B) severely damaged but would survive
   - (C) slightly damaged and would be late in arriving in New York
   - (D) slightly damaged but would arrive in New York on schedule
   - (E) not damaged at all

7. As used in line 38, the word "self-possessed" most nearly means
   - (A) in control of one's emotions
   - (B) anxious about one's own safety
   - (C) ready to obey orders
   - (D) holding all one's personal belongings
   - (E) eager to take action

8. It can be inferred that all of the following are true about the husband of the narrator of Passage 1 EXCEPT
   - (A) he made every effort to allay his wife's fears
   - (B) he tried to ensure that his son would survive
   - (C) he recognized that he would probably not survive
   - (D) he behaved as he thought was expected of him
   - (E) he assumed that he would follow his wife on another boat

9. The lower-class status of the narrator of Passage 2 can be inferred from the fact that he
   (A) shared a small cabin with several other men
   (B) awoke to find his cabin already awash with water
   (C) was unable to return to his cabin for a lifebelt
   (D) knew that a lifebelt was provided for each passenger
   (E) was ultimately able to escape with his life

10. It can be inferred that the seamen who first advised the narrator of Passage 2 about a problem with the ship believed that the *Titanic* had been
    (A) severely damaged and would sink
    (B) severely damaged but would survive
    (C) slightly damaged and would be late in arriving in New York
    (D) slightly damaged but would arrive in New York on schedule
    (E) not damaged at all

11. As used in line 28 of the second passage, the word "sorry" most nearly means
    (A) unfortunate
    (B) remorseful
    (C) regretful
    (D) ashamed
    (E) pathetic

12. The behavior of the first-class passenger with two lifebelts (lines 40–41) most clearly exemplifies
    (A) the persistence of class prejudices
    (B) individual generosity in a time of crisis
    (C) the element of luck in survival
    (D) how friendship can develop in unlikely circumstances
    (E) the role of social status in determining one's fate

13. Passage 2 implies that the men who gave up their places in the lifeboats to women (lines 61–62) were motivated primarily by
    (A) their hope that the ship might somehow remain afloat
    (B) their fear of personal embarrassment and disgrace
    (C) their belief that this was the moral thing to do
    (D) the threats of the ship's officers
    (E) their hope that they could swim to safety using their lifebelts

14. It can be inferred that the woman in the lifeboat hid the narrator of Passage 2 under her shawl because
    (A) she had previously met him on the ship
    (B) she could see he was very frightened
    (C) she did not think her husband would survive
    (D) she wanted someone to take care of her
    (E) she was herself very frightened

15. The experiences of the two narrators differed in all of the following respects EXCEPT the
    (A) relative ease with which they got off the ship
    (B) nature of their relationship to their traveling companions
    (C) way their traveling companions reacted to their alarms
    (D) style of their accommodations on the ship
    (E) general vantage point from which they observed the ships' sinking

EXERCISE 4

15 Questions

Time—15 Minutes

Directions: Each passage below is followed by questions based on its content. Answer the questions on the basis of what is *stated* or *implied* in the passage and in any introductory material that may be provided.

Questions 1–10 are based on the following passage.

This is an excerpt from an account of the creation of one of the world's best-known fictional characters, the detective Sherlock Holmes.

On July 1, 1882, a brief notice appeared in the *Portsmouth* (England) *Evening News*. It read simply, "Dr. Doyle begs to notify that he has removed to 1, Bush Villas, Elm Grove, next to the Bush Hotel." So was announced the newly-formed medical practice of a 23-year-old graduate of Edinburgh University—Arthur Conan Doyle. But the town of Southsea, the Portsmouth suburb in which Doyle had opened his office, already had several well-established physicians, and while he waited for patients, the young Dr. Doyle found himself with a great deal of time on his hands.

To fill it, he began writing—short stories, historical novels, whatever would keep him busy and, hopefully, bring additional funds into his sparsely-filled coffers. By the beginning of 1886, his practice had grown to the point of providing him with a respectable if not munificent income, and he had managed to have a few pieces published. Although literary success still eluded him, he had developed an idea for a new book, a detective story, and in March he began writing the tale that would give birth to one of literature's most enduring figures.

Although he was familiar with and impressed by the fictional detectives created by Edgar Allan Poe, Emile Gaboriau, and Wilkie Collins, Doyle believed he could create a different kind of detective, one for whom detection was a science rather than an art. As a model, he used one of his medical school professors, Dr. Joseph Bell. As Bell's assistant, Doyle had seen how, by exercising his powers of observation and deduction and asking a few questions, Bell had been able not only to diagnose his patients' complaints but also to accurately determine their professions and backgrounds. A detective who applied similar intellectual powers to the solving of criminal mysteries could be a compelling figure, Doyle felt.

At first titled *A Tangled Skein*, the story was to be told by his detective's companion, a Dr. Ormand Sacker, and the detective himself was to be named Sherrinford Holmes. But by April, 1886, when Doyle finished the manuscript, the title had become *A Study in Scarlet*, the narrator Dr. John H. Watson, and the detective Mr. Sherlock Holmes.

A tale of revenge, in which Holmes is able to determine that two Mormons visiting England from Utah have been killed by Jefferson Hope, an American working as a London hansom cab driver, *A Study in Scarlet* was rejected by several publishers before being accepted that fall for publication by Ward, Lock & Company as part of *Beeton's Christmas Annual* in 1887. Although the author asked to be paid a royalty based on sale of the book, his publisher offered instead only a flat fee of £25 for the copyright (the equivalent of approximately $50.00 today). Doyle reluctantly accepted.

A handful of reviewers commented kindly on the story, but the reading public as a whole was unimpressed. Ward, Lock published *A Study in Scarlet* in book form the following year, while the disappointed author returned to his historical novels, with which he had finally achieved some modest success. Fictional detection, Doyle thought, was behind him. In August, 1889, however, he was approached by the editor of the American *Lippincott's Monthly Magazine*, published in Philadelphia and London, to write another Sherlock Holmes story.

Although he had little interest in continuing Holmes's adventures, Doyle was still in need of money and accepted the offer.

Published in *Lippincott's* in February, 1890, and in book form later that year, *The Sign of the Four* chronicled Holmes's investigation of the murder of Bartholomew Sholto and his search for Jonathan Small and a treasure stolen by British soldiers in India. It too, however, met with little enthusiasm from the public. In the meantime, however, Doyle's other small literary successes had enabled him to move to London, where he became a consulting physician. Fortunately, even this new London practice did not keep him very busy, leaving him time to concentrate on his writing.

In April, 1891, he submitted a short Sherlock Holmes story, "A Scandal in Bohemia," to a new magazine called *The Strand*. It was with the publication of this story, and the series of Holmes tales which followed, that the public finally took an interest in Dr. Doyle's detective, enabling him to give up his practice and turn to writing full-time. Despite his own continuing lack of enthusiasm for his protagonist—he considered the Holmes stories insignificant compared to his "serious" historical novels—spurred by the public clamor for more Sherlock Holmes, Doyle eventually wrote fifty-six short stories and four novels in the series, and in the process created what may be the best-known character in all of English literature.

1. According to the passage, Arthur Conan Doyle began writing for all the following reasons EXCEPT
   (A) his medical practice did not keep him very busy
   (B) he needed additional income
   (C) he was not interested in practicing medicine
   (D) he was fond of literary fiction
   (E) he was interested in pursuing an author's career

2. As used in line 40, the word "deduction" most nearly means
   (A) decreasing
   (B) discounting
   (C) reducing
   (D) reasoning
   (E) subtracting

3. It can be inferred from the passage that Sherlock Holmes differed from previous fictional detectives in that
   (A) he focused his detective skills on the solving of crimes
   (B) he conducted his investigations on a scientific basis
   (C) he used his own background in medicine as a source of detective methods
   (D) his cases were chronicled by a companion rather than by the detective himself
   (E) his exploits were based on the experiences of a real individual

4. In line 47, "compelling" most nearly means
   (A) forceful
   (B) inescapable
   (C) believable
   (D) fascinating
   (E) insistent

5. In can be inferred from the passage that the first two Sherlock Holmes tales were similar in all the following respects EXCEPT
   (A) both were based on historical events
   (B) both involve non-British characters or locales
   (C) both were originally published in periodicals rather than as books
   (D) neither received a strong initial reception from the public
   (E) both were written more for financial than literary reasons

6. The author implies that Doyle's move to London was primarily triggered by
   (A) Doyle's desire to move in literary circles
   (B) the popularity of the Sherlock Holmes stories
   (C) the failure of his medical practice in Southsea
   (D) an increase in Doyle's income from writing
   (E) a growing demand for Doyle's medical services

7. The author uses the word "Fortunately" in line 101 primarily to imply that
   (A) a medical practice in London can be especially demanding
   (B) Doyle had a naturally indolent and unambitious character
   (C) the popular demand for Doyle's writing had begun to grow at this time
   (D) Doyle's literary career was more significant than his medical practice
   (E) Doyle was strongly tempted at this time to abandon writing as a career

8. It can be inferred from the passage that the public finally became interested in Doyle's Sherlock Holmes stories as a result of
   (A) Doyle's persistence in publishing and publicizing them
   (B) their continued appearance in *The Strand* magazine
   (C) the public's growing interest in detective stories
   (D) the success of Doyle's other works
   (E) the first publication of a Holmes story in the United States

9. According to the passage, Doyle's reluctance to write further Holmes stories after 1891 was due primarily to
   (A) his belief that he was not fairly compensated for them
   (B) his lack of interest in Holmes as a character
   (C) his desire to be considered a serious author
   (D) his personal distaste for detective stories
   (E) the significant income provided by his other literary efforts

10. Which of the following titles best summarizes the content of the passage?
    (A) Arthur Conan Doyle and the Creation of the Modern Detective Story
    (B) A Detective's Reluctant Chronicler: The Birth of Sherlock Holmes
    (C) Physician and Author: How Arthur Conan Doyle Balanced Two Callings
    (D) The Many Strands in the Character of Sherlock Holmes
    (E) Joseph Bell: The Real-Life Inspiration for Sherlock Holmes

Questions 11–15 are based on the following passage.

In this passage, a historian describes how some of the world's earliest civilizations emerged along the banks of major rivers in the Middle East.

Line As the climate in the Middle East changed beginning around 7000 B.C.E., conditions emerged that were conducive to a more complex and advanced form of civilization in both Egypt and Mesopotamia. The process began when the swampy valleys of the Nile in Egypt and of the Tigris and Euphrates rivers in Mesopotamia became drier, producing riverine lands that were both habitable and fertile, and attracting settlers armed with the newly developed techniques of agriculture. This migration was further encouraged by the gradual transformation of the once-hospitable grasslands of these regions into deserts. Human population became increasingly concentrated into pockets of settlement scattered along the banks of the great rivers.

These rivers profoundly shaped the way of life along their banks. In Mesopotamia, the management of water in conditions of unpredictable drought, flood, and storm became the central economic and social challenge. Villagers began early to build simple earthworks, dikes, canals, and ditches to control the waters and reduce the opposing dangers of drought during the dry season (usually the spring) and flooding at harvest time.

Such efforts required a degree of cooperation that had not previously existed among large numbers of people. The individual village, containing only a dozen or so houses and families, was economically vulnerable; but when several villages, probably under the direction of a council of elders, learned to share their human resources in the building of a coordinated network of water-control systems, the safety, stability, and prosperity of all improved. In this new cooperation, the seeds of the great Mesopotamian civilizations were being sown.

Technological and mathematical invention, too, were stimulated by life along the rivers. Such devices as the noria (a primitive waterwheel) and the Archimedean screw (a device for raising water from the low riverbanks to the high ground where it was needed), two forerunners of many more varied and complex machines, were first developed here for use in irrigation systems.

Similarly, the earliest methods of measurement and computation and the first developments in geometry were stimulated by the need to keep track of land holdings and boundaries in fields that were periodically inundated.

The rivers served as high roads of the earliest commerce. Traders used boats made of bundles of rushes to transport grains, fruits, nuts, fibers, and textiles from one village to another, transforming the rivers into the central spines of nascent commercial kingdoms. Trade expanded surprisingly widely; we have evidence suggesting that, even before the establishment of the first Egyptian dynasty, goods were being exchanged between villagers in Egypt and others as far away as Iran.

Similar developments were occurring at much the same time along the great river valleys in other parts of the world—for example, along the Indus in India and the Hwang Ho in China. The history of early civilization has been shaped to a remarkable degree by the relationship of humans and rivers.

11. The primary purpose of the passage is to explain
    (A) how primitive technologies were first developed in the ancient Middle East
    (B) how climatic changes led to the founding of the earliest recorded cities
    (C) the influence of river life on the growth of early civilizations
    (D) some of the recent findings of researchers into early human history
    (E) the similarities and differences among several ancient societies

12. According to the passage, the unpredictability of water supplies in Mesopotamia had which of the following social effects?
    I. It led to warfare over water rights among rival villages.
    II. It encouraged cooperation in the creation of water-management systems.
    III. It drove farmers to settle in fertile grasslands far from the uncontrollable rivers.

    (A) I only
    (B) II only
    (C) III only
    (D) II and III only
    (E) Neither I, II, nor III

13. According to the passage, the earliest trade routes in the ancient Middle East
    (A) were those between various centrally-ruled commercial kingdoms
    (B) were those that linked villages in Egypt with others in Iran
    (C) were created to ease the transfer of technological and mathematical knowledge among villages
    (D) served to link the inhabitants of small villages with the dynastic kings who ruled them
    (E) connected villages that were scattered along the banks of the same river

14. It can be inferred from the passage that the emergence of complex civilizations in the Middle East was dependent upon the previous development of
    (A) basic techniques of agriculture
    (B) symbolic systems for writing and mathematical computation
    (C) tools for constructing houses quickly and easily
    (D) a system of centralized government
    (E) a method of storing and transferring wealth

15. The author refers to emerging civilizations in India and China primarily in order to emphasize the
    (A) importance of water transportation in the growth of early trade
    (B) relatively advanced position enjoyed by the Middle East in comparison to other regions
    (C) rapidity with which social systems developed in the Middle East spread to other places
    (D) crucial role played by rivers in the development of human cultures around the world
    (E) significant differences in social systems among various groups of early humans

EXERCISE 5

15 Questions

Time—15 Minutes

Directions: Each passage below is followed by questions based on its content. Answer the questions on the basis of what is *stated* or *implied* in the passage and in any introductory material that may be provided.

Questions 1–4 are based on the following passage.

The following passage is an excerpt from an article in a popular science magazine about the biological phenomenon known as regeneration.

Urodeles, a class of vertebrates that includes newts and salamanders, have the enviable ability to regenerate arms, legs, tails, heart muscle, jaws, spinal cords, and other organs. Planaria, simple worms, can be sliced and diced in hundreds of pieces, with each piece giving rise to a completely new animal.

However, while both urodeles and planaria have the capacity to regenerate, they use different means of accomplishing this feat.

In effect, urodeles turn back the biological clock. First the animal heals the wound at the site of the missing limb. Then various specialized cells at the site, such as bone, skin, and blood cells, lose their identity and revert to cells as unspecialized as those in the embryonic limb bud. This process is called dedifferentiation, and the resulting blastema, a mass of unspecialized cells, proliferates rapidly to form a limb bud. Ultimately, when the new limb takes shape, the cells take on the specialized roles they had previously cast off.

In contrast, planaria regenerate using cells called neoblasts. Scattered within the planarian body, these neoblasts remain in an unspecialized, stem-cell state, which enables them at need to differentiate into any cell type. Whenever planaria are cut, the neoblasts migrate to the site and form a blastema by themselves. It is interesting to note that this mechanism is similar to that following reproductive fission in these animals, and that species incapable of this form of asexual reproduction have poorly developed regenerative capacities.

1. The primary purpose of the passage is to
   (A) describe the roles of blastema in regenerating urodeles and planaria
   (B) describe how urodeles use the process of dedifferentiation to regenerate
   (C) contrast the mechanisms by which urodeles and planaria accomplish regeneration
   (D) show how methods of cellular regeneration have evolved in different animal species
   (E) explain the link between reproductive fission and regeneration in simple worms

2. All of the following are true of dedifferentiation in regenerating urodeles EXCEPT
   (A) the cells recover their specialized roles after the limb bud takes shape
   (B) it involves a regression by cells to an earlier stage of development
   (C) specialized cells migrate to the site of the blastema and proliferate rapidly
   (D) the healing of the wound at the site of the injury is the first step of the process
   (E) dedifferentiation is characterized by a loss, and then recovery, of cellular identity

3. The author says that urodeles "turn back the biological clock" (lines 13–14) because they can
   (A) revert the cells in a severed part to a nearly embryonic state
   (B) regrow body parts from existing cells
   (C) produce a new limb bud from formerly differentiated cells
   (D) create a blastema from unspecified cells
   (E) develop specified cells from a blastema

4. In the final sentence of the passage, the author implies that
   (A) those planaria which reproduce by splitting themselves in two are more likely to regenerate using the same mechanism
   (B) planaria which reproduce sexually use the process of dedifferentiation to regenerate entirely new animals
   (C) asexual reproduction is related to regeneration in planaria, but not in urodeles
   (D) the genetic makeup of planaria created through regeneration would be the same as in those created through reproductive fission
   (E) reproductive fission and regeneration in certain planaria differ solely in the quantity of new planaria produced

Questions 5–15 are based on the following passage.

The following passage was written in 1901 by Jacob Riis, a writer and photographer who was one of the very few people to document the slums of New York at the turn of the century. As many as 300,000 people per square mile were crowded into the tenement apartment buildings of New York's Lower East Side. Riis is remembered today not only as a pioneer photo-journalist but also as a compassionate and effective social reformer.

Line Leaving the elevated railroad where it dives under the Brooklyn Bridge at Franklin Square, scarce a dozen steps will take us where we wish to go. With its crush and roar echoing yet in our ears, we have turned the corner from prosperity to poverty. We stand upon the domain of the tenement.

In the shadow of the great stone abutments, the old knickerbocker houses linger like ghosts of a departed day. Down the winding slope of Cherry Street—proud and fashionable Cherry Hill that was—their broad steps, sloping roofs, and dormer windows are easily made out; all the more easily for the contrast with the ugly barracks that elbow them right and left. These never had other design than to shelter, at as little outlay as possible, the greatest crowds out of which rent could be wrung. They were the bad afterthought of a heedless day.

The years have brought to the old houses unhonored age, a querulous second childhood that is out of tune with the time, their tenants, the neighbors, and cries out against them and against you in fretful protest in every step on their rotten floors or squeaky stairs. Good cause have they for their fretting. This one, with its shabby front and poorly patched roof—what flowing firesides, what happy children may it once have owned? Heavy feet, too often with unsteady step, for the saloon is next door—where is it not next door in these slums?—have worn away the brownstone steps since; the broken columns at the door have rotted away at the base. Of the handsome cornice barely a trace is left. Dirt and desolation reign in the wide hallway, and danger lurks on the stairs. Rough pine boards fence off the roomy fireplaces; where coal is bought by the pail at the rate of twelve dollars a ton, these have no place.

The arched gateway leads no longer to a shady bower on the banks of the rushing stream, inviting daydreams with its gentle repose, but to a dark and nameless alley, shut in by high brick walls, cheerless as the lives of those they shelter. The wolf knocks loudly at the gate in the troubled dreams that come to this alley, echoes of the day's cares. A horde of dirty children play about the dripping hydrant, the only thing in the alley that thinks enough of its chance to make the most of it: it is the best it can do. These are the children of the tenements, the growing generation of the slums; this their home. From the great highway overhead, along which throbs the life-tide of two great cities, one might drop a pebble into half a dozen such alleys.

5. This passage serves primarily to
   (A) argue for the demolition of tenement buildings and restoration of the old houses
   (B) decry the lifestyle and habits of the Cherry Street tenement dwellers
   (C) describe how previous generations enjoyed their prosperous life on Cherry Street
   (D) contrast present and past conditions of life on Cherry Street
   (E) give a detailed accounting of the structural demise of the old knickerbocker houses

6. In line 20, the word "outlay" most nearly means
   (A) expense
   (B) inconvenience
   (C) need
   (D) danger
   (E) distance

7. The passage implies that the landlords of the Cherry Street "barracks" (line 17)
   (A) moved out themselves when the poor began to arrive on the Lower East Side
   (B) were unable to maintain their properties because rental income was so low
   (C) were discouraged from providing proper services by their tenants' destructive habits
   (D) maximized their profit by renting to many people and providing few services
   (E) planned to take over and demolish the older houses eventually

8. The author ascribes human feelings to the old houses in lines 24–35 ("The years have brought . . . what happy children may it once have owned?") primarily in order to
   (A) contrast the graceful houses with the poor tenement dwellers
   (B) emphasize how time and poverty have ravaged the houses
   (C) suggest that inanimate objects are capable of feelings and sensations
   (D) elicit sympathy from readers who may care more for houses than people
   (E) imply a value judgment about the current residents of the houses

9. The word "querulous" in line 25 most nearly means
   (A) queer
   (B) lonesome
   (C) petulant
   (D) surprising
   (E) senile

10. The author mentions the price of coal in lines 45–46 in order to explain the
   (A) inadequate heat enjoyed by tenement dwellers
   (B) high profits enjoyed by tenement landlords
   (C) low wages paid to the working poor
   (D) use of wooden boards as fuel
   (E) disuse of the fireplaces in the old houses

11. The "wolf" referred to in line 53 primarily suggests the
   (A) uncivilized qualities of tenement children
   (B) anxieties of life among the poor
   (C) formerly rural character of Cherry Hill
   (D) physical dangers of tenement life
   (E) noise and confusion that reigns in a slum neighborhood

12. The author implies that the present residents of the Cherry Street houses
   (A) are too unrefined to appreciate the architectural beauty of their houses
   (B) are too poor to properly maintain the old houses
   (C) would be better off in the more recently erected barracks nearby
   (D) are responsible for most of the physical damage to the houses
   (E) could easily escape the poverty of their surroundings if they so wished

13. In lines 56–60, the author's description of the children at play suggests that he views them with
   (A) disdain
   (B) revulsion
   (C) pity
   (D) admiration
   (E) fear

14. By saying "one might drop a pebble into half a dozen such alleys" (lines 64–69), the author emphasizes the
    (A) insignificance of the tenement residents' lives
    (B) anonymity of tenement housing
    (C) distance between the highway overhead and alleys below
    (D) density of the tenement communities
    (E) ephemeral nature of the tenement neighborhoods

15. The tone of the passage can best be described as one of
    (A) dispassionate criticism
    (B) moral indignation
    (C) sarcastic disapproval
    (D) wistful nostalgia
    (E) playful irony

Answer Key

Exercise 1	Exercise 2	Exercise 3	Exercise 4	Exercise 5
1. E	1. E	1. A	1. C	1. C
2. C	2. B	2. D	2. D	2. C
3. A	3. C	3. A	3. B	3. C
4. C	4. A	4. E	4. D	4. A
5. B	5. D	5. D	5. A	5. D
6. C	6. D	6. E	6. D	6. A
7. B	7. C	7. A	7. D	7. D
8. B	8. C	8. E	8. B	8. B
9. D	9. A	9. A	9. C	9. C
10. D	10. E	10. A	10. B	10. E
11. D	11. B	11. C	11. C	11. B
12. C	12. E	12. B	12. B	12. B
13. A	13. D	13. D	13. E	13. C
14. B	14. E	14. B	14. A	14. D
15. B	15. E	15. E	15. D	15. B

Explanatory Answers

EXERCISE 1

1. **The correct answer is (E).** All of the information and the many circumstantial details in the passage help to build up a picture of the lives of slaves on a particular plantation. The larger issues referred to in the other answer choices are only present by implication; the passage doesn't explicitly address them.
2. **The correct answer is (C).** Refer to the second paragraph of the passage. As long as the slave children were unable to work in the field, they were given almost nothing.
3. **The correct answer is (A).** A privation is something necessary that is lacking or taken away. It's related to the word *deprive*.
4. **The correct answer is (C).** The last sentence of the third paragraph explains this point.
5. **The correct answer is (B).** Choices (A), (C), (D), and (E) are all substantiated in the sixth and seventh paragraphs of the passage. "The fear of God," however, is not mentioned in connection with Mr. Severe.
6. **The correct answer is (C).** When Mr. Severe died, the slaves he had mistreated understandably viewed his death as a fortunate event. The word providence refers to the hand of God in human affairs; merciful means kind or generous. To Douglass and the other slaves, Mr. Severe's death was an act of kindness by God.

7. **The correct answer is (B).** The sentence in the third paragraph beginning "They find less difficulty . . . " makes this clear.

8. **The correct answer is (B).** This account of life on a particular plantation tells us nothing about how widespread or prevalent slavery was in the United States, which is what the *extent of slavery* would refer to.

9. **The correct answer is (D).** Choices (A) and (C) are too narrow; choices (B) and (E) are too broad. Choice (D) is good because it brings out the *practical* slant of the passage, which after all focuses on the industrial use of granular matter and the role played by science as a facilitator.

10. **The correct answer is (D).** Review the first two sentences of the third paragraph. The percolation theory deals with how small and large objects interrelate when a mass of granular material is shaken, as in a can of nuts.

11. **The correct answer is (D).** See the first sentence of the fourth paragraph. The engineer says that both theories can be right, "depending on the material."

12. **The correct answer is (C).** A conundrum is a puzzle, riddle, or mystery. An enigma is a close synonym.

13. **The correct answer is (A).** As the fourth paragraph makes clear, the problem pharmaceutical firms face in dealing with granular materials is based mainly on the fact that different-sized grains are present in a single product. Clearly, it would help matters if all the grains could be made the same size.

14. **The correct answer is (B).** The fifth paragraph explains that, unlike sand, the pressure in a liquid "increases in direct proportion to the liquid's height." In other words, the higher (or deeper) the mass of liquid, the greater the pressure at the bottom. Therefore, as the water trickled through (getting shallower, of course) the pressure would decrease.

15. **The correct answer is (B).** Notice the way the granular scientists' "low-cost, low-tech" experiments are contrasted with the complicated and expensive studies that particle physicists must somehow fund.

EXERCISE 2

1. **The correct answer is (E).** The first sentence of the second paragraph makes this point clearly.

2. **The correct answer is (B).** In the fourth paragraph, the passage explains that Wegener used the existence of similar plants and animals on widely separated continents as evidence that all the Earth's land masses were formerly connected in the supercontinent of Pangaea. For this evidence to be valid, it would have to mean that many plants and animals existed prior to the breakup of Pangaea that paragraph two tells us began late in the Paleozoic era.

3. **The correct answer is (C).** The first paragraph tells us that Wegener's hypothesis was accepted some fifty years after it was first proposed in 1912; thus, in the early 1960s. This answers question III. Question I is not answered; the passage only says (end of paragraph four) that Wegener himself had no answer for this question. Question II is not answered; in fact, paragraph five refers to evidence from the 1960s that seemed to undermine, rather than support, Wegener's hypothesis.

4. **The correct answer is (A).** Review the first sentence of the sixth paragraph. The "perhaps most significant" reason for many scientists' discomfort with Wegener's hypothesis was that it seemed to challenge their deep-seated belief in uniformitarianism.

5. **The correct answer is (D).** You'll find this stated in the last sentence of the fifth paragraph.

6. **The correct answer is (D).** As used in this passage, the word dramatic refers to changes on a vast scale—changes in the shape and appearance of the very continents.

7. **The correct answer is (C).** The author wants to remind his readers of the negative side of life in Victorian times, to counteract the romantic nostalgia he feels is prevalent when people think of that era. However, he is not harshly condemnatory or bitter in his criticism of "the good old days," merely seeking a more balanced perspective. Hence, choice (C) is correct.

8. **The correct answer is (C).** Most of the points the author makes have to do with the physical conditions of life a century ago and the scientific and technological breakthroughs that have changed and improved life.

9. **The correct answer is (A).** A "haze," of course, alters and distorts our image of whatever we see through it. "Nostalgia" means, literally, homesickness (it's related to the Greek word for home); we use it to refer to the longing and sadness we often feel when remembering the past.

10. **The correct answer is (E).** The examples mentioned in the last sentence of the third paragraph are chosen to illustrate the way "many of us" feel about life at the turn of the century.

11. **The correct answer is (B).** Idyllic means calm, peaceful, paradisal; think of how life was supposed to be in the Garden of Eden.

12. **The correct answer is (E).** All of the other points are made in various places in the passage, but the author nowhere speaks about "closeness to nature" as a Victorian trait.

13. **The correct answer is (D).** The author refers to $2,000 to $4,000 as "a very considerable sum" in Victorian times. In this particular context, the word is being used to describe a large expense.

14. **The correct answer is (E).** Clearly, the author disagrees with those who assume that the Victorian era was a generally better or happier time.

15. **The correct answer is (E).** Refer to the second sentence of the third paragraph and the last sentence of the entire passage. The author does agree that technology has made modern life fast-paced and a bit overwhelming, but he doesn't suggest that life without technology was better or more "fulfilling."

EXERCISE 3

1. **The correct answer is (A).** Notice that the first paragraph says that Morrison "bristles" at how her work is sometimes described and that the second and third paragraphs quote her own comments. Clearly, the passage is mainly concerned with presenting Morrison's own viewpoint about her writing.
2. **The correct answer is (D).** See the first sentence of the second paragraph, which makes clear the underlying point being made by the author in citing the use of the supernatural in Morrison's writing.
3. **The correct answer is (A).** The first sentence of the entire passage suggests this answer. The author seems to be saying that those who want to "deracialize" Morrison are trying to pay her the compliment of calling her work "universal"—though the author of the passage considers this a mistake.
4. **The correct answer is (E).** In the first paragraph, the author suggests that a writer should not "have to choose" between universal and particular identities. The implication is that a great writer can be both rooted in a particular culture and universal in appeal.
5. **The correct answer is (D).** All of the other answer choices imply an upper-class status for the narrator of Passage 1. However, her husband sent her onto a lifeboat not because of her class status, but because she was a woman. At that time, this would have been done no matter what class she and her husband belonged to.
6. **The correct answer is (E).** Refer to the quotation in the first paragraph. The steward believed that the ship had stopped without hitting the iceberg at all.
7. **The correct answer is (A).** As the context makes clear, the author is using the word "self-possessed" to mean calm and under emotional control.
8. **The correct answer is (E).** The narrator's husband never expresses the expectation that he will follow her on a later boat; he merely says (end of paragraph 4), "We will be all right," which sounds like an attempt to reassure his wife without making any promises.
9. **The correct answer is (A).** The small size of the shared cabin is emphasized by the fact that the narrator had to leave the room in order to make it possible for the others to dress.
10. **The correct answer is (A).** We can make this inference based on the fact that the seaman warns the narrator (in paragraph 4) that he is in danger of drowning.
11. **The correct answer is (C).** In the context, we can see that the narrator is "sorry" because he doesn't have his own lifebelt. In other words, he regrets leaving his cabin without it.
12. **The correct answer is (B).** The fact that the first-class passenger not only gives the narrator one of his lifebelts, but also pauses to help him put it on suggests a degree of generosity that is surprising under the desperate circumstances.

13. **The correct answer is (D).** The last sentence of the next-to-last paragraph establishes that it was necessary for the officers to fire warning shots before the men would obey their orders to leave the lifeboats.

14. **The correct answer is (B).** See the first two sentences of the last paragraph. The fact that the narrator, a young man, was openly crying is obviously relevant to the woman's behavior.

15. **The correct answer is (E).** Both narrators witnessed the sinking of the ship from a lifeboat just a short distance away.

EXERCISE 4

1. **The correct answer is (C).** The first two paragraphs show that Doyle pursued both writing and medicine simultaneously, apparently eager to succeed in both fields; he abandoned medicine only much later, after his writing had attained great popularity.

2. **The correct answer is (D).** In this context, the word deduction is used to refer to the practice of drawing logical conclusions from evidence—reasoning.

3. **The correct answer is (B).** Refer to the first sentence of the third paragraph, which explains what made Holmes "a different kind of detective" from his fictional predecessors.

4. **The correct answer is (D).** The word compelling is being used here to describe the effect of a character like Sherlock Holmes on readers; he compels the reader's interest because of his remarkable personal qualities.

5. **The correct answer is (A).** Although Doyle was writing historical novels at the same time as his mystery stories, neither of the Holmes tales mentioned here is described as "based on historical events."

6. **The correct answer is (D).** Refer to the seventh paragraph, "Doyle's other small literary successes had enabled him to move to London."

7. **The correct answer is (D).** If the author considers it "fortunate" that Doyle was able to concentrate on his writing rather than on practicing medicine, clearly Doyle's literary career must have been more important or worthwhile in the author's eyes than his medical work.

8. **The correct answer is (B).** The second sentence of the last paragraph makes this point.

9. **The correct answer is (C).** According to the last paragraph, Doyle "considered the Holmes stories insignificant compared to his 'serious' historical novels."

10. **The correct answer is (B).** Choices (C) and (E) are too narrow, while choices (A) and (D) are too broad. The passage concentrates quite specifically on the origin and early history of the Holmes character, which makes choice (B) the best choice.

11. **The correct answer is (C).** The last sentence of the passage neatly summarizes its main theme.

12. **The correct answer is (B).** The third paragraph of the passage describes how the need for water-management systems encouraged cooperation among large groups of Mesopotamian villagers. Statement I is not supported by the passage, and Statement III is contradicted by the last sentence of the first paragraph.

13. **The correct answer is (E).** See the first sentence of the fifth paragraph.

14. **The correct answer is (A).** In the first paragraph, we're told that the development of great civilizations in the Middle East began when the river valleys attracted "settlers armed with the newly developed techniques of agriculture."

15. **The correct answer is (D).** The last paragraph (where India and China are mentioned), is used to make the point that life along river valleys has played a crucial role in the development of civilization in many parts of the world.

EXERCISE 5

1. **The correct answer is (C).** The last sentence of the first paragraph sets forth this central theme. The paragraphs that follow give the relevant details.

2. **The correct answer is (C).** As paragraph two explains, the specialized cells "lose their identity and revert" to being unspecialized cells, forming a blastema. *Only after this* do they proliferate; so it's wrong to say that the "specialized cells . . . proliferate rapidly," as does choice (C).

3. **The correct answer is (C).** Urodeles "turn back the clock" because the specialized cells revert to the embryonic state of a limb bud. Choice (A) is wrong because it is not the cells "in a severed part" that revert but rather the cells near the site where the severed part formerly existed.

4. **The correct answer is (A).** The sentence says that those species of planaria that engage in "reproductive fission" (splitting) are the ones that are more likely to regenerate themselves in the same way.

5. **The correct answer is (D).** Throughout the passage, the details given serve to contrast the former prosperity and comfort of the Cherry Street neighborhood with its current poverty and squalor.

6. **The correct answer is (A).** The ugly barracks nearby were built at as little outlay as possible—in other words, cheaply. The *outlay* being referred to is a financial one.

7. **The correct answer is (D).** Refer to the next-to-last sentence of the second paragraph, which makes this point explicitly.

8. **The correct answer is (B).** The use of *personification* here (describing the houses as if they had personalities and feelings) is intended to heighten the pathos in the author's description of the decay the neighborhood has endured.

9. **The correct answer is (C).** The word *querulous* means anxious and complaining. The phrase "in fitful protest" later in the same sentence offers an image that describes the quality well.

10. **The correct answer is (E).** The author implies that the fireplaces are boarded up because coal is too costly for the poor tenants.

11. **The correct answer is (B).** Since the "wolf" is associated with "the troubled dreams that come to this alley, echoes of the day's cares," we can see that the author is using this image to suggest the anxiety and worry suffered by the poor.

12. **The correct answer is (B).** The third paragraph suggests this point, with its references to the "poorly patched roof" and the "broken columns at the door."

13. **The correct answer is (C).** The description of the children playing in the alley in the last paragraph suggests the author's feeling of sadness over their unfortunate circumstances.

14. **The correct answer is (D).** The fact that "half a dozen such alleys" can be found in such close proximity suggests that these poverty-stricken neighborhoods are closely packed together.

15. **The correct answer is (B).** The author is clearly dismayed and concerned over the fact that neighborhoods that were once pleasant and inviting have become dangerous and gloomy places to live.

Chapter 7

Multiple-Choice Math

Get the Scoop On . . .

- Proven strategies for tackling multiple-choice math problems
- How rounding off and guesstimating can save you time and help you avoid errors
- How to work backwards to untangle challenging questions
- How to find answers in the diagrams provided by the test-makers
- How and when to use your calculator—and when *not* to

THE TEST CAPSULE

What's the Big Idea?

Multiple-choice math questions are designed to test your knowledge of the basic facts and skills taught in most ninth- and tenth-grade math programs. You'll be given a varied mixture of problem types, including some word problems, problems that involve reading and interpreting graphs and charts, geometry problems with and without diagrams, and a few straightforward arithmetic and algebra problems. For each question, five answer choices are provided—you just have to pick the right one.

How Many?

Your SAT will probably have a total of thirty-five multiple-choice math problems. They'll fill one 30-minute section consisting of twenty-five multiple-choice problems and a 15-minute section with ten multiple-choice problems.

How Much Do They Count?

Multiple-choice problems are thirty-five out of sixty total math questions. They count as 58 percent of your overall math score.

How Much Time Should They Take?

Plan to answer multiple-choice math problems at a rate of almost one per minute. The test-makers give you slightly more time than this, so if you do finish one question each minute, you'll have a little extra time to check your work.

What's the Best Strategy?

When in doubt, try something. The problem itself will often suggest a procedure you've often used in math class. If so, use it, even if you can't see how it will lead to the answer you want. Quite often, this sort of "tinkering with the numbers" will quickly lead you toward the solution.

What's the Worst Pitfall?

Getting bogged down in lengthy or complex calculations. Most SAT math questions are deliberately designed to make complicated calculations unnecessary: the test-makers are more interested in seeing whether or not you understand the basic structure of the problem than if you can correctly complete a series of computations. If you find yourself starting a complicated set of calculations, stop—you're probably overlooking a simple shortcut.

THE OFFICIAL DESCRIPTION

What They Are

Multiple-choice math problems are designed to test your skill at "mathematical reasoning," which is your ability to use knowledge of specific math facts, formulas, techniques, and methods to solve problems. Basic information about the procedures of math is needed, but the questions focus more on the underlying concepts than on the procedures themselves.

Where They Are

In the typical SAT, you'll have three Math sections. Two will be 30 minutes long; one will be 15 minutes long. One of the 30-minute sections and the 15-minute section will consist entirely of multiple-choice problems. Reminder: the test-makers claim the right to change the format at any time! However, the typical format we just described is what you're most likely to encounter.

What They Measure

To score high, it's important to be very comfortable with the basic operations of arithmetic—not only addition, subtraction, multiplication, and division, but also procedures such as working with fractions and decimals or figuring out averages, and the like. You'll also need to be skilled at the basic operations of algebra, including solving equations, using negative numbers and square roots, and factoring. Finally, many of the basic principles of geometry are tested, including such concepts as the properties of triangles, circles, and quadrilaterals and determining the areas and volumes of simple figures.

What They Cover

The math areas tested on the SAT, including the multiple-choice items, are those studied by virtually every high school student: arithmetic, basic algebra, and plane and coordinate geometry. Many advanced and specialized math topics are *not* covered on the SAT, including trigonometry and calculus. See Appendix B, "The Insider's SAT Math Review," for a detailed review of the math concepts most frequently tested on the exam.

The Directions

In this section, solve each problem using any available space on the page for scratchwork. Then decide which is the best of the choices given and circle the corresponding letter.

Notes:

1. The use of a calculator is permitted. All numbers used are real numbers.
2. Figures that accompany problems in this test are intended to provide information useful in solving the problems. They are drawn as accurately as possible EXCEPT when it is stated in a specific problem that the figure is not drawn to scale. All figures lie in a plane unless otherwise indicated.

THE INSIDER'S REPORT: STRATEGIES THAT REALLY WORK

Focus on What's Actually Being Asked

Read the question carefully and make sure you know the answer being sought.

Most math problems will include a series of interrelated facts. The kinds of facts will vary depending on the kind of question.

In a word problem, these facts might include the speed of a train, the distance between two cities, and the time when the train leaves the station.

In a geometry problem, the facts might include the degree measures of two angles in a triangle, the length of one side of the triangle, and the diameter of a circle in which the triangle is inscribed.

In a graph-reading problem, the facts might include an entire series of numbers as depicted in the graph—monthly inches of rainfall in a particular county over a one-year period, for example.

One key to tackling any of these kinds of problems is to make sure you know which fact is being asked about and what form the answer should take. If you read hastily, you may *assume* a particular question when, in fact, the test-makers want to focus on a different question. Rather than ask about when the train will arrive at City B, they may ask when the train will reach the one-third point of the trip. Rather than ask about the area of either the triangle or the circle, they may ask instead about the area of the odd-shaped, shaded region that falls between them. And rather than asking about the amount of rainfall in any particular month, they may ask about the *difference* between two of the months—a number that doesn't appear directly on the graph itself.

When in Doubt, Try Something

FYI

Which of the following may be true? *has a very different meaning from* Which of the following must be true? *And both, of course, are very different from "Which of the following may not be true?" Don't skim—read every word carefully.*

Occasionally, you'll find yourself staring at a problem without knowing how to begin solving it. If you're at a loss—try something. Often the numbers stated in the problem will suggest a starting point by reminding you of operations and procedures you often used in math class.

If fractions are involved, for example, try reducing them to the lowest terms or multiplying them out to change them into whole numbers. Or change them into decimals or percentages if they lend themselves easily to that process (for example, $\frac{1}{10} = 10\%$).

If a geometry diagram appears, work from what you know (such as the degree measures of certain angles) to fill in other information you don't know—the complementary angle alongside the angle that's marked, for example, or the angle on the other side of the transversal that must be equal to the angle you know.

If you're given a problem involving probability or permutations (varying combinations of things), just start listing all the possibilities.

Quite often, seemingly random experimenting like this will lead you quickly toward the right answer. Why? It's because of the peculiar way that SAT math problems are designed. The test-makers want to test you on a wide array of math topics in a short period of time. That means they want to ask you lots of questions that you can do quickly—in just about a minute each. Therefore, the questions are written so that the numbers themselves are generally obvious. What's tricky is the underlying connection among the numbers. As soon as you see that connection, the math is usually simple.

As a result, SAT math tends to reward students who are willing to mess around with the numbers in the problem until an insight into the solution emerges. Once that *Aha!* moment happens, the answer is usually close at hand.

Round Off and "Guesstimate" Freely

FYI

Remember, when tackling math problems, you have about 1 minute per question. Don't get too lost in experimenting with the numbers. If no solution emerges after about 20 seconds, move on to the next item.

It's not always necessary to work with exact numbers in solving the math problems in the SAT. Sometimes the fastest and even the most accurate way to an answer is to guesstimate. Here's an example, using a real math problem from a past SAT exam.

> A total of 60 advertisements were sold for a school yearbook. If 20% of the first 20 sold were in color, 40% of the next 30 sold were in color, and 80% of the last 10 sold were in color, what percent of the 60 advertisements were in color?
>
> (A) 30%
>
> (B) $33\frac{1}{3}\%$
>
> (C) 40%
>
> (D) $46\frac{2}{3}\%$
>
> (E) 60%

Obviously, you can solve this problem precisely with a few calculations. If you're adept with percentages, you may be able to work it out in your head rather quickly; if you're not, but you have plenty of time, you can handle it slowly and carefully and come up with the exact answer after a minute or so.

However, if you're short on time and don't have the facility with numbers to figure it quickly in your head, here's a simple way to *see* the answer using approximations only. Look back at the facts in the problem. Of the first 20 ads, 20% were in color; of the next 30%, 40% were in color. Obviously, the overall average for these two groups will be between 20% and 40%. Now, the size of the two groups isn't the same, so we can't just average 20% and 40% to come up with the overall average—but we can see that the overall average for the first 50 ads will be fairly *close* to 30%, and a little higher (since there are more ads in the 40% group than in the 20% group).

That just leaves the last 10 ads, of which 80% were in color. All you need to understand about this are two things. First, since the percentage for this group is 80%, which is higher than 30%, it will raise the overall average somewhat. Second, this is a small group (just 10 ads) so it won't affect the overall average very much.

Without doing any calculations, we can guesstimate that the correct answer will be a percentage somewhat higher than 30%—but not too much higher. This immediately eliminates choices (A) and (E), and makes choices (B) and (D) look a little low and a little high, respectively.

It so happens that the correct answer, if you work it out in detail, is choice (C) 40%—pretty much what we figured, based on sheer guesstimating.

Rounding off and guesstimating isn't necessary on most SAT items; in many cases, the numbers used are so few and so simple that you might as well work with them directly. The chances are that you'll encounter several problems on every exam that will be made easier and quicker by guesstimating.

If Stymied, Plug in an Answer and Work Backward

FYI

Be guided in your guesstimating by the answer choices. If the answers are all close together—

(A) 270
(B) 272
(C) 275
(D) 278
(E) 282

you need a fairly precise answer. If they are far apart

(A) 110
(B) 272
(C) 348
(D) 512
(E) 721

feel free to work with approximate numbers. You'll probably come up with a result that's close enough to pick the right answer.

On some questions, a quick route to the answer will jump out at you within a few seconds. In other cases, experimenting in some obvious way with the numbers will quickly direct you toward a solution. If neither of these works, try grabbing an answer from the five multiple-choice options and plugging it into the question. This will often lead you to the right answer quickly.

Here's an example, based on a question from an actual SAT exam.

> A ball is dropped from 192 inches above level ground. After the third bounce it rises to a height of 24 inches. If the height to which the ball rises after each bounce is always the same fraction of the height reached on its previous bounce, what is this fraction?
>
> (A) $\frac{1}{8}$
>
> (B) $\frac{1}{4}$
>
> (C) $\frac{1}{3}$
>
> (D) $\frac{1}{2}$
>
> (E) $\frac{2}{3}$

It helps if you can picture what's happening. Think of a handball or a tennis ball, repeatedly bouncing, but each time rising less high until at last it settles on the ground, motionless. The problem suggests that, on each bounce, the ball will rise to a height that is some particular fraction of the previous bounce. The question is, what is that fraction—is it $\frac{1}{8}$, $\frac{1}{4}$, or what?

The fastest way to a solution is to plug in an answer. Try choice (C), and see what happens. If the ball bounces up one third as high as it started, then after the first bounce it will rise up one third as high as 192 inches. If you're fast with numbers—or use your calculator—you'll know that this is 64 inches. A precise number isn't essential; if you can tell it's around 60, you're close enough.

FYI

When plugging in a number, start with choice (C). The answer choices are normally in size order, choice (C) will be the middle-size choice. If it is wrong, you can usually tell whether the correct answer is probably larger or smaller—so you've already narrowed the possibilities to just two remaining answers.

After the second bounce, it'll rise one third as high, which is $21\frac{1}{3}$ inches (or, if you're guesstimating, around 20). *Stop!* The problem says that the ball rises to 24 inches after the *third* bounce. Obviously, if the ball rises less than that after *two* bounces, it'll be way too low after three! So choice (C) cannot be the answer.

We can see that the ball must be bouncing higher than one third of the way; the correct answer must be a larger fraction, meaning either choice (D) or choice (E). If you're pressed for time, choose one and move on (you have a 50 percent chance of being right). If you have time, plug in either and see whether or not it works. If you do, you'll see that choice (D) is correct.

Would it be possible to develop a formula to answer this question? Probably—some physicist has done it, I'll bet. But it would be unrealistic to try to devise a formula for the exam. Remember the unique advantage of a test like the SAT—*All the correct answers have been provided.* When it's not obvious which one is correct, pick one and try it. Even if the one you pick first is wrong, this method will usually let you hone in on the best choice fairly quickly.

THE INSIDER'S REPORT: THE BEST TIPS

Word Problems—Build an Equation that Will Yield the Answer You Want

For some students, word problems pose the toughest math challenge. You know the kind—they deal with planes traveling at a certain speed, pipes filling vats with liquid at a particular rate, and workers painting walls at so many square feet per hour.

Curiously enough, in most word problems, the math itself is not difficult. You may have a couple of fractions to multiply or divide, or a simple equation to solve, but the computations will be easy. What's tricky is setting up the math in the first place—in other words, turning the words into numbers and symbols. Here are some pointers that will help.

Let the Unknown Quantity Equal What You Want to Solve For

If the question asks "What fraction of the entire job will be completed after three hours?" begin writing your equation with $J =$, where J represents that fraction of the job. Conversely, if the question asks,

"How many hours will it take to do $\frac{3}{7}$ of the entire job?" then begin your equation with *H,* which should equal the hours of work needed. This way, once you've solved the equation, you automatically have your answer, with no further conversions needed.

FYI

*When creating an equation for a word problem, use obvious letter symbols (*T *for Ted's age,* H *for hours worked,* P *for price, etc.) rather than textbook letters like* x, y, *or* z. *They're easier to remember and less likely to cause you confusion.*

Break the Problem Down into Phrases and Translate Each into a Numerical Expression

Word problems can be intimidating because of their length and complexity. Your strategy—divide and conquer. Break the problem down into its component parts, and give each an appropriate number or symbol. Then devise an equation or formula that describes the relationship among these parts, and go ahead with the math.

Here's an example, using one typical kind of word problem—an age problem.

> Paul is eight years older than Sarah. Four years ago, Sarah was half the age Paul is now. How old is Sarah now?

First, notice that what you're looking for is Sarah's age now. So try to set up your equation making *S* (Sarah's age now) the unknown for which you will solve. The only other letter we'll need is *P*, which stands for Paul's age now.

Now create a couple of simple equations that state in symbols and numbers what the sentences in the problem say.

Paul is eight years older than Sarah becomes $P - 8 = S$.

Four years ago, Sarah was half the age Paul is now becomes $S - 4 = \frac{P}{2}$.
To get rid of the fraction (usually a good idea), multiply this equation through by 2. $2S - 8 = P$.

Now you can solve for *S* by substituting the expression $2S - 8$ for *P* in the first equation.

$$\begin{aligned}(2S - 8) - 8 &= S\\ 2S - 16 &= S\\ -16 &= -S\\ S &= 16\end{aligned}$$

So Sarah's age today is 16 (Paul is 24).

Check out Table 7.1. It gives you some of the most common translations of words and phrases into mathematical operations. Learn the list—it'll work as a kind of foreign phrasebook for turning English into numbers on the exam.

Table 7.1
Words and Phrases with Mathematical Translations

Equals	is, amounts to, is the same as
Addition	and, with, along with, added to, in addition to, increased by, more than, greater than, larger than
Subtraction	less than, fewer than, without, take away, difference, decreased by, reduced by, smaller than
Multiplication	times, each, per, by, of, product
Division	divided by, part of, fraction, piece, portion

Convert All Quantities into Units that Are Easier to Work With

Don't feel locked into the numbers presented in the problem. If you can see that a different number that you can easily get to will be simpler to work with, go for it by changing the units of measurement.

In particular, when you can, look for opportunities to convert working units into the units in which the answer is wanted. So, for example, if you see that the answers are all stated in terms of square feet, while one of the numbers in the problem is in square yards, change it to square feet before beginning your work. (One square yard equals nine square feet.)

FYI

Basic geometry facts and formulas are provided for you in the "Reference Information" at the start of every SAT math section. If you go blank, this makes a handy survival tool. But every time you refer to it costs you precious seconds. You should know the information in this chart backwards and forwards, so that looking it up on the day of the test is rarely or never necessary.

Geometry Problems: Mine the Diagram for Clues to the Answer

Most geometry problems on the SAT are accompanied by diagrams. They are there for a reason. You can usually leap from what you know—the facts you are given—to what you need to know simply by using the parts of the diagram as "stepping stones." Here's an example from a real SAT question.

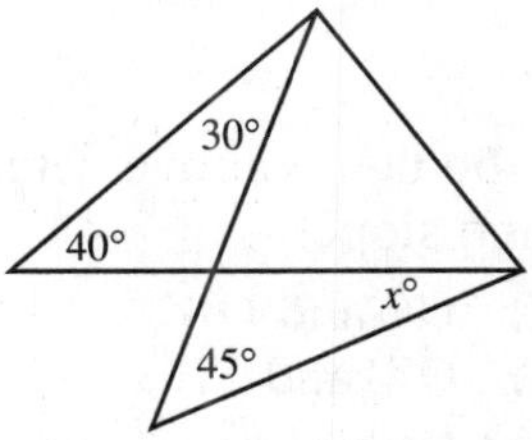

In the figure above, what is the value of x?

(A) 65
(B) 45
(C) 40
(D) 30
(E) 25

The diagram gives you three explicit facts: the degree measures of the angles that are marked as 30°, 40°, and 45°. However, a host of implicit facts are also contained there. If you recall some basic facts about geometric figures, they'll fall into your lap one by one. Quickly, as you'll see, they'll lead you to the answer.

First, you should remember that the number of degrees in the three (interior) angles of a triangle will always sum to 180°. This allows us to calculate the size of the third, unmarked angle in the upper-right triangle; it must measure 110°.

Next, you should recall that, when two straight lines intersect (cross), the opposite angles formed are equal. (This is easy to remember—the angles in such a figure *look* equal.) Based on this, we can see that the top angle in the bottom triangle must also measure 110°, like its twin.

From this fact, we can now figure out the size of the angle in question. Since, 110° + 45° = 155°, there are just 25° left for the third angle of the triangle; so the right answer is choice (E).

Solving a geometry problem like this one is easy. Just fill in the blank parts of the diagram using what you can deduce from the information you're given. (Use your pencil to mark the new facts right in the question booklet.) Once you get to the fact being asked about, you're home free.

In some geometry questions, studying the diagram can make "math" totally unnecessary.

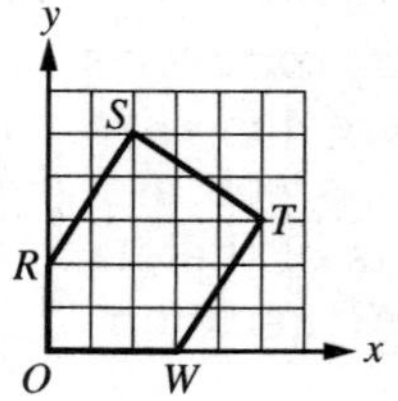

In the figure above, which two sides of polygon *ORSTW* have the same slope?

(A) *OR* and *OW*
(B) *OW* and *ST*
(C) *RS* and *ST*
(D) *RS* and *WT*
(E) *ST* and *WT*

When you studied coordinate geometry in school, you learned that the slope of a line is often expressed as a fraction. You also learned a formula for calculating the slope of a line from its endpoints. It's possible you may need to use that formula for one question on the SAT. (If you've forgotten it, don't worry; you can refresh your memory of it in Appendix B, "The Insider's SAT Math Review.")

However, the formula is totally unnecessary for this problem—and so are any numbers whatsoever. You can tell which two sides have the same slope just by looking at the diagram and deciding which two sides of the polygon go in the same direction. It's easy—the only possibility is choice (D), sides *RS* and *WT*, which are obviously parallel to one another.

As long as you have even a vague idea as to what the word *slope* means, you can scarcely get this question wrong. The diagram does all the work for you.

If No Diagram Is Given, Sketch One

Sometimes, a question without a diagram simply cries out for one. That's what your pencil is for—and that's also why the test-makers kindly leave a generous margin of blank space on most pages of the exam. Draw your own diagram and read the answer right off it.

Here's a real-SAT example.

> Five distinct points lie in a plane such that 3 of the points are on line l and 3 of the points are on a different line, *m*. What is the total number of lines that can be drawn so that each line passes through exactly 2 of these 5 points?
>
> (A) Two
> (B) Four
> (C) Five
> (D) Six
> (E) Ten

Can you picture this in your mind's eye? Me neither. Grab your pencil and start sketching. The only tricky thing to notice is the discussion of the number of points involved. You're told that three points line on one line and three points line on another line—and that the total number of points is five. 3 + 3 = 6, not 5—obviously something funny is going on here. What's the solution?

The answer is that one of the points must line on *both* lines, as shown below.

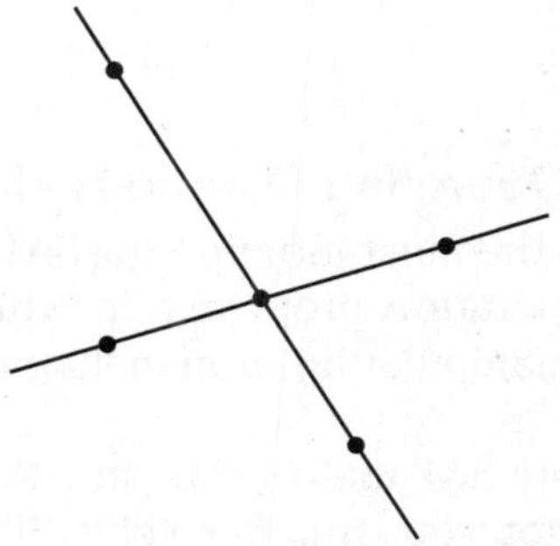

Now, how did we know how to draw these lines—the angle at which they cross, for example—and where to place the other four points? We didn't know; we just took a guess. Notice that the question strongly implies that it doesn't matter exactly how these details are drawn—there is one and only one answer, no matter what the sketch looks like.

If several answers were possible, the question would have to say something like, "Which of the following is a possible number of lines . . . ?" or "What is the greatest possible number of lines . . . ?" But it doesn't say that. It just says, "What is the number . . . ?" So you can tell that there's only one possible answer.

Now that we have our basic drawing, we just have to figure out how many lines can be drawn that pass through two of the five points. Don't agonize over it—just start drawing. In a flash, you'll have your answer. (The lines in question are the dotted lines in the figure below.)

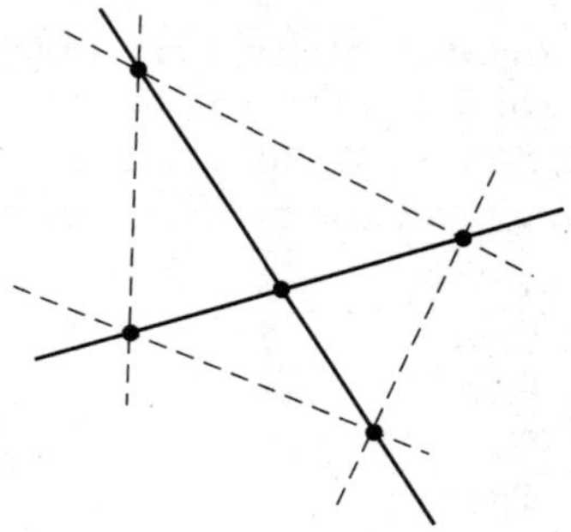

I can't think of any other way to fit in more lines here—can you? So the answer is choice (B), four. Don't get confused and pick choice (D), six. The original two lines don't count—because they pass through three dots each, not two.

This question is considered hard by SAT standards. But that's true only because many students allow the wording to confuse them and don't think to make a picture. Once you do, the answer almost jumps off the page.

Weird Operation Questions—Just Plug in Numbers

Perhaps the most intimidating SAT math problems of all are what we call weird operation problems, in which the test-makers create some new way of manipulating or mangling numbers and ask you to imitate it.

Like many SAT math problems, these are really tests of your reasoning ability, not your number skills. If you calmly and methodically plug in the simple numbers they give you, you'll usually find these problems laughably easy. Here's a real example.

Let $\left\langle \begin{matrix} & b & \\ a & & c \\ & d & \end{matrix} \right\rangle$ be defined for all numbers a, b, c, and d by $\left\langle \begin{matrix} & b & \\ a & & c \\ & d & \end{matrix} \right\rangle = ac - bd$. If $x = \left\langle \begin{matrix} & 4 & \\ 5 & & 2 \\ & 1 & \end{matrix} \right\rangle$, what is the value of $\left\langle \begin{matrix} & 10 & \\ x & & 2 \\ & 1 & \end{matrix} \right\rangle$?

(A) 1
(B) 2
(C) 18
(D) 38
(E) 178

This looks weird, all right. Arranging letters or numbers in a diamond and then treating this as a math computation? You never learned this in tenth grade!

Nonetheless, don't get nervous. The test-makers tell you precisely what to do, though in slightly cryptic style. When they define the diamond-shaped figure as $ac - bd$, what they are saying is that, whenever you see four numbers in a diamond like this, you should plug them into the mathematical expression shown in the order given. The question itself then requires you to perform this simple task twice.

First, let's figure out the value of x. If x is the diamond labeled as x, then $a - 5$, $b - 4$, $c - 2$, and $d -1$. Now we plug those numbers into the simple math computation.

$x = (5 \times 2) - (4 \times 1)$
$x = 10 - 4$
$x = 6$

There, that wasn't so bad, was it? Now the second step. Having figured out the value of x, we can plug it into our second diamond, where $a = 6$ (our old friend x that is), $b = 10$, $c = 2$, and $d = 1$. Again, plug in the numbers:

$(6 \times 2) - (10 \times 1)$
$12 - 10$
2

So the answer is choice (B), 2. Notice how ridiculously easy the math itself is. You could have done these calculations when you were seven years old! The only trick is understanding what the test-makers are doing, which is defining a new math operation, and then patiently plugging in the numbers.

With a little practice, you'll never get a "weird operation" problem wrong.

THE INSIDER'S REPORT: THE MOST IMPORTANT WARNINGS

Avoid Lengthy Calculations and Working with Big Numbers

We've already seen examples of how straightforward the mathematical computations on the SAT generally are. You can count on this. In fact, if you find yourself getting involved in long, complicated, or tricky calculations—especially ones using big numbers—stop work! You've probably overlooked a shortcut or trick that would make the calculations unnecessary.

Here's an example from a real SAT.

> The tip of a blade of an electric fan is 1.5 feet from the axis of rotation. If the fan spins at a full rate of 1,760 revolutions per minute, how many miles will a point at the tip of a blade travel in one hour? (1 mile = 5,280 feet)
>
> (A) 30π
> (B) 40π
> (C) 45π
> (D) 48π
> (E) 60π

If you're doubtful where to begin, glance at the answer choices. The presence of π should remind you that the blades of a fan travel in a circular path (since π gets involved only when circles are involved). The point we are following is going round and round, ticking off 1,760 circles every minute. Thus, the relevant geometric formula is the equation for the circumference of a circle: $c = 2\pi r$.

What is the radius of this circle? The axis of rotation is a fancy way of saying "the point the blade spins around"—or, in even simpler words, the middle of the fan. So the 1.5-foot measurement casually mentioned is the same as the radius of the circle. This makes it easy to figure the circumference: $c = 2\pi(1.5) = 3\pi$.

So every time the blade goes around once, it travels 3π feet. How many miles will it travel in an hour? Your instinct may be to grab your calculator and start working out the number of feet it will travel in an hour, then divide that by the number of feet in a mile (which the test-makers have kindly provided) . . . but stop! Remember our warning: don't get bogged down with big numbers! Instead, look for a shortcut.

Here's where it's hiding. The curious number 1,760 for the number of revolutions per minute wasn't chosen at random. (Curious numbers never are on the SAT.) It happens to be exactly one third the number of feet in a mile. (Try it out on your calculator. You'll confirm it's true.) Remember, the tip of the blade travels 3π feet for every revolution. Since $3 \times 1{,}760$ equals the number of feet in a mile, we can see that the blade tip will travel $\pi \times 1$ mile every minute

Now, just multiply this by 60 minutes to get the total distance traveled in an hour: 60π miles.

If you'd worked this out the long way—figuring out, to start with, that the tip traveled 316,800 feet per hour—you could have gotten the right answer. But it would have taken longer. And working the big numbers on your calculator raises other risks, which we'll discuss in a moment.

The lesson: Avoid long calculations, and especially shun working with big numbers. The test-makers usually don't want you to mess with them.

Use Your Calculator Sparingly

FYI

If you plan on using a calculator on the test, follow these tips: 1. Don't buy a special calculator—a simple machine that can add, subtract, multiply, and divide is all you need. 2. Practice beforehand with the exact calculator you plan to use the day of the exam. 3. Put in fresh batteries the day of the test—or use a solar-powered device that doesn't need batteries.

If you're used to working with a calculator, by all means bring your favorite to the test. You'll be happy you did if you blank out in the middle of the exam and forget what 8×7 equals.

But if you're smart, you'll be very selective in using the calculator. Most students should touch the calculator on only one question out of four—or less. Here are the reasons why.

- Math questions on the SAT are specifically designed *not* to require a calculator. As we've explained, the exam focuses on mathematical reasoning, not on your ability to perform computations.

- It's easy to hit the wrong key, hit the right key twice instead of once, or make other mistakes when using a calculator, especially when you are hurriedly working with big numbers. (Ever get a wrong number on the phone? Everyone has. It's even easier with the small, flimsy buttons on most calculators.)

- You may be lulled into a false sense of security because you rely on the accuracy of the machine. Therefore, you may overlook a math mistake you'd otherwise spot.

- If you do suspect a math error when using your calculator, it's impossible to retrace your steps, since there are no notes or figures to check. (Calculators that print on paper are forbidden on the SAT.)
- Don't get us wrong; a calculator can be a useful tool. But don't lean on it too heavily. If you find yourself working the calculator on all or even most questions, you're overdoing it. Put it aside, and grab it only when it's really necessary.
- Most important—start work on each question *without* the calculator in hand. The key is to decide what the question is asking, what information you have, and how to get from here to there. Only after you've figured these things out should you start calculating—if you must.

JUST THE FACTS

- On SAT multiple-choice math problems, guesstimate and look for shortcuts; most questions have them.
- Break word problems into simple phrases that you can translate into numbers or symbols.
- Mine geometry diagrams for answer clues—and sketch your own when necessary.
- On weird operation problems, just plug in numbers and work out the solutions carefully.
- Don't overuse your calculator—focus on concepts, not computations.

PRACTICE, PRACTICE, PRACTICE: MULTIPLE-CHOICE MATH EXERCISES

Instructions

The following exercises will give you a chance to practice the skills and strategies you've just learned for tackling multiple-choice math problems. As with all practice exercises, work under true testing conditions. Complete each exercise in a single sitting. Eliminate distractions (TV, music) and clear away notes and reference materials. Time yourself with a stopwatch or kitchen timer, or have someone else time you. If you run out of time before answering all the questions, stop and draw a line under the last question you finished. Then go ahead and tackle the remaining questions. When you are done, score yourself based only on the questions you finished in the allotted time.

Circle the letter of the correct response. In addition, any time your answer is a guess—that is, any time you enter a response about which you are not certain—circle the number of that question. After you've completed the exercises, count the number of circled items and the number of these items that you answered correctly. Then divide the number of correct answers by the number of circled items. The result is your Guessing Quotient (G.Q.). If your G.Q. is higher than .20, you will probably boost your overall score by guessing on the real SAT.

Understanding Your Scores

0–2 correct: A poor performance. Study this chapter again, as well as the "Insider's SAT Math Review" (Appendix B).

3–4 correct: A below-average score. Study this chapter again, as well as all portions of the "Insider's SAT Math Review" (Appendix B) that cover topics you find unfamiliar or difficult.

5–6 correct: An average score. You may want to study this chapter again. Also be sure you are managing your time wisely (as explained in Chapter 3) and avoiding errors due to haste or carelessness.

7–8 correct: An above-average score. Depending on your personal target score and your strength on other mathematical question types, you may or may not want to devote additional time to quantitative comparisons.

9–10 correct: An excellent score. You are probably ready to perform well on SAT multiple-choice math problems.

EXERCISE 1

10 Questions

Time—15 Minutes

Directions: In this section solve each problem, using any available space on the page for scratchwork. Then decide which is the best of the choices given and circle the corresponding letter.

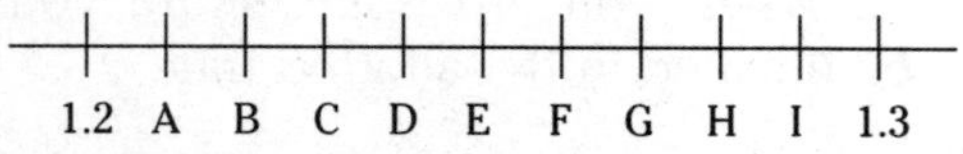

Note: All the points shown are equidistant.

1. On the number line shown, which point corresponds to the number 2.27?

   (A) I
   (B) H
   (C) G
   (D) F
   (E) Not a labeled point

2. If $m = 121 - 5k$ is divisible by 3, which of the following may be true?

   I. m is odd
   II. m is even
   III. m is divisible by 3

   (A) I only
   (B) II only
   (C) II and III only
   (D) I and II only
   (E) I, II, and III

3. The cost of 4 rolls, 6 muffins, and 3 loaves of bread is \$9.10. The cost of 2 rolls, 3 muffins, and a loaf of bread is \$3.90. What is the cost of a loaf of bread?

   (A) \$1.05
   (B) \$1.10
   (C) \$1.20
   (D) \$1.25
   (E) \$1.30

4. If $3x + 4y$ is an odd number, which of the following CANNOT be true?

   I. x is odd and y is odd
   II. x is even and y is even
   III. x is even and y is odd

   (A) I only
   (B) I and II only
   (C) II only
   (D) III only
   (E) II and III only

5. The ratio of Democrats to Republicans in a certain state legislature is 5:7. If the legislature has 156 members, all of whom are either Democrats or Republicans (but not both), what is the difference between the number of Republicans and the number of Democrats?

   (A) 14
   (B) 26
   (C) 35
   (D) 37
   (E) 46

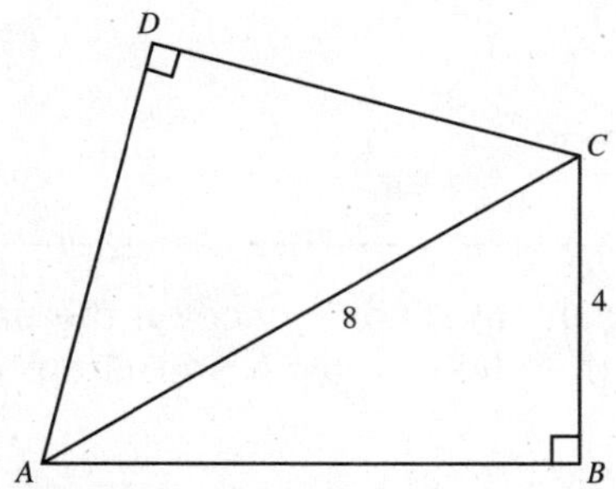

6. The area of the region shown above is

(A) $16 + 8\sqrt{3}$
(B) $8 + 8\sqrt{3}$
(C) $12 + 4\sqrt{3}$
(D) 16
(E) $8\sqrt{3}$

7. If $A < 2 - 4B$, which of the following is true?

(A) $\frac{2 - A}{4} > B$
(B) $\frac{2 - A}{4} < B$
(C) $B > 4A + 2$
(D) $B < 4A + 2$
(E) None of the above

8. A box contains five blocks numbered 1, 2, 3, 4, and 5. Johnnie picks a block and replaces it. Lisa then picks a block. What is the probability that the sum of the numbers they picked is even?

(A) $\frac{9}{25}$
(B) $\frac{2}{5}$
(C) $\frac{1}{2}$
(D) $\frac{13}{25}$
(E) $\frac{3}{5}$

9. If a fleet of m buses uses g gallons of gasoline every two days, how many gallons of gasoline will be used by 4 buses every 5 days?

(A) $\frac{10g}{m}$
(B) $10gm$
(C) $\frac{10m}{g}$
(D) $\frac{20g}{m}$
(E) $\frac{5g}{4m}$

10. If x and y are positive integers and $x + y = 10$, what is the value of $|x - y|$ when $x^2 + y^2$ is as small as possible?

(A) 8
(B) 6
(C) 4
(D) 2
(E) 0

EXERCISE 2

10 Questions

Time—15 Minutes

Directions: In this section solve each problem, using any available space on the page for scratchwork. Then decide which is the best of the choices given and circle the corresponding letter.

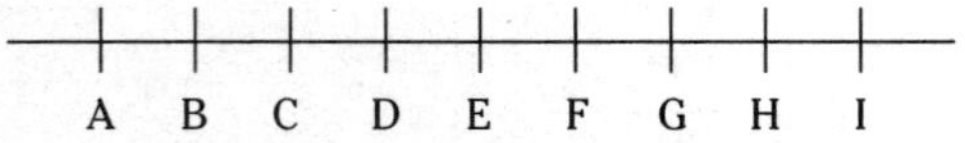

Note: All the points shown are equidistant.

1. On the number line shown, where is the number which is less than D and half as far from D as D is from G?

   (A) A
   (B) B
   (C) C
   (D) D
   (E) Not a labeled point

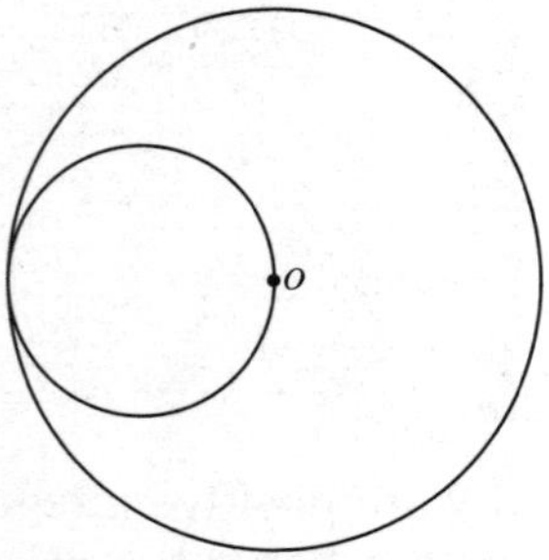

2. In the figure above, the larger circle shown has an area of 36π. What is the circumference of the smaller circle?

   (A) 2π
   (B) 4π
   (C) 6π
   (D) 8π
   (E) 12π

3. A faucet is dripping at a constant rate. If, at noon on Sunday, 3 ounces of water have dripped from the faucet into a holding tank and, at 5 p.m. on Sunday, a total of 7 ounces have dripped into the tank, how many ounces will have dripped into the tank by 2:00 a.m. on Monday?

   (A) 10
   (B) $\frac{51}{5}$
   (C) 12
   (D) $\frac{71}{5}$
   (E) $\frac{81}{5}$

4. If A and B are positive integers and $24AB$ is a perfect square, then which of the following CANNOT be possible?

   I. Both A and B are odd
   II. AB is a perfect square
   III. Both A and B are divisible by 6

   (A) I only
   (B) II only
   (C) III only
   (D) I and II only
   (E) I, II, and III

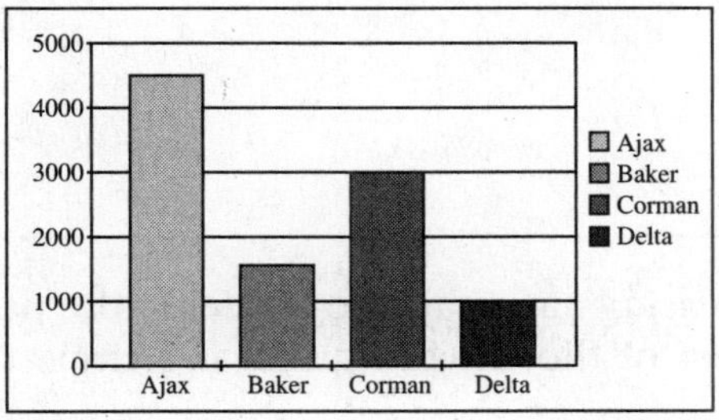

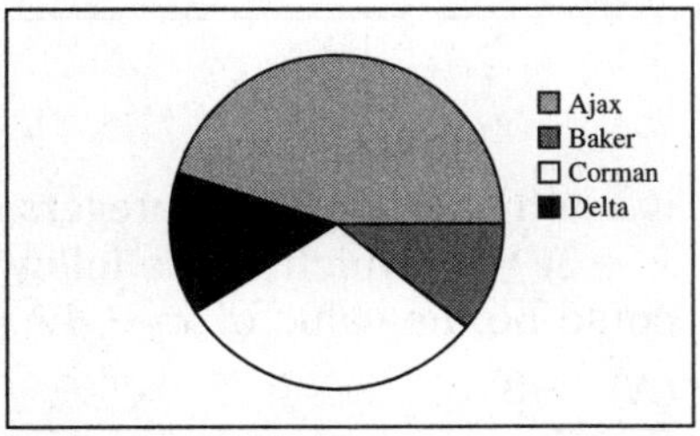

5. The two graphs in the figure above show the payments made by *XYZ* Corporation on contracts to four different suppliers last month. What is the degree measure of the angle marking the sector of the circle graph that represents payments to Corman?

(A) 36
(B) 60
(C) 100
(D) 108
(E) 120

6. If $r = -2$, then $r^4 + 2r^3 + 3r^2 + r =$

(A) -8
(B) -4
(C) 0
(D) 6
(E) 10

7. $[3(a^2b^3)^2]^3 =$

(A) $27a^{12}b^{18}$
(B) $729a^{12}b^{18}$
(C) $27a^7b^8$
(D) $3a^8b^{12}$
(E) $3a^{12}b^{18}$

$$\begin{array}{r} 7x \\ xy \\ \underline{xx} \\ 117 \end{array}$$

8. Shown above is a correct problem in addition, with x and y representing certain digits. What is the value of y?

(A) 1
(B) 2
(C) 3
(D) 4
(E) 5

9. How many liters of 50% antifreeze must be mixed with 80 liters of 20% antifreeze to get a mixture that is 40% antifreeze?

(A) 160
(B) 140
(C) 120
(D) 100
(E) 80

10. Horace averaged 70 on his first m exams. After taking n more exams, he had an overall average of 75 for the year. In terms of n and m, his average for his last n exams was

(A) $\frac{5m + 75}{n}$
(B) $\frac{5m}{n + 75}$
(C) $\frac{5n}{m + 75}$
(D) $\frac{70m + 75n}{m + n}$
(E) 80

EXERCISE 3

10 Questions

Time—15 Minutes

Directions: In this section solve each problem, using any available space on the page for scratchwork. Then decide which is the best of the choices given and circle the corresponding letter.

1. Which of the following numbers is evenly divisible by 3, 4, and 5, but not by 9?
   (A) 15,840
   (B) 20,085
   (C) 23,096
   (D) 53,700
   (E) 79,130

2. If $a = -1$ and $b = -2$, what is the value of $(2 - ab^2)^3$?
   (A) 343
   (B) 216
   (C) 125
   (D) 64
   (E) 27

3. Which of the following expressions is equivalent in value to $9y - \frac{6y^3}{2y^2}$?
   (A) $\frac{3y}{4}$
   (B) $\frac{3}{y}$
   (C) $3y$
   (D) $6y$
   (E) $-6y$

4. If x and y are positive integers, and $x - 2y = 5$, which of the following could be the value of $x^2 - 4y^2$?
   (A) -3
   (B) 0
   (C) 14
   (D) 45
   (E) 51

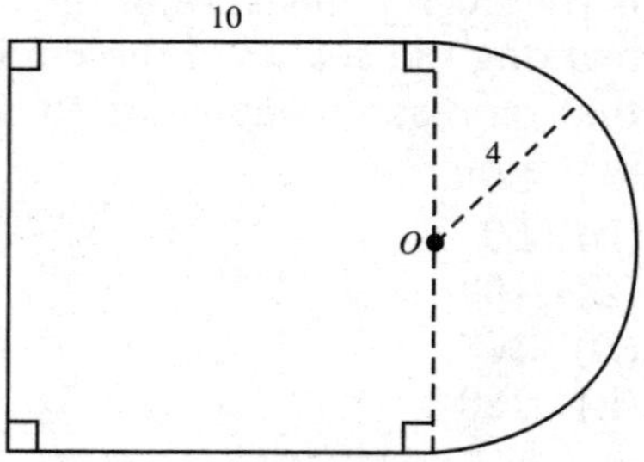

5. Find the area of the region shown in the figure above. *Note: The curved side is a semicircle.*
   (A) $20 + 4\pi$
   (B) $20 + 6\pi$
   (C) $40 + 6\pi$
   (D) $60 + 8\pi$
   (E) $80 + 8\pi$

6. If the result of squaring a number n is less than twice the number, then the value of n must be
   (A) negative
   (B) positive
   (C) between -1 and $+1$
   (D) greater than 1
   (E) between 0 and 2

Questions 7 and 8 are based on the following definition:

$$n\wedge = \frac{2n}{n-1}$$

7. If $n = p + 1$, what is the value of $n\wedge$?
   (A) 2
   (B) $\frac{2p}{p-1}$
   (C) $\frac{2p+1}{p-1}$
   (D) $2 + \frac{1}{p}$
   (E) $2 + \frac{2}{p}$

8. For which non-zero value of n is $n\wedge = n$?
   (A) 1
   (B) 2
   (C) 3
   (D) 4
   (E) 5

9. You roll a fair, six-sided die twice. What is the probability that the die will land with the same side facing up both times?
   (A) $\frac{1}{6}$
   (B) $\frac{1}{12}$
   (C) $\frac{2}{36}$
   (D) $\frac{1}{36}$
   (E) 0

10. The ratio of the arithmetic mean of two numbers to one of the numbers is 3:5. What is the ratio of the smaller number to the larger?
   (A) 1:5
   (B) 1:4
   (C) 1:3
   (D) 1:2
   (E) 2:3

EXERCISE 4

10 Questions

Time—15 Minutes

Directions: In this section solve each problem, using any available space on the page for scratchwork. Then decide which is the best of the choices given and circle the corresponding letter.

1. The advertised price of potatoes is 35¢ per pound. If a 3-pound bag actually weighs $3\frac{1}{4}$ pounds, what is the closest approximation in cents to the actual price per pound for that bag?
   (A) 36
   (B) 35
   (C) 34
   (D) 33
   (E) 32

2. If $\left(\frac{-2}{5}\right)^3$ is equal to N thousandths, what is N?
   (A) -100
   (B) -64
   (C) -32
   (D) 32
   (E) 64

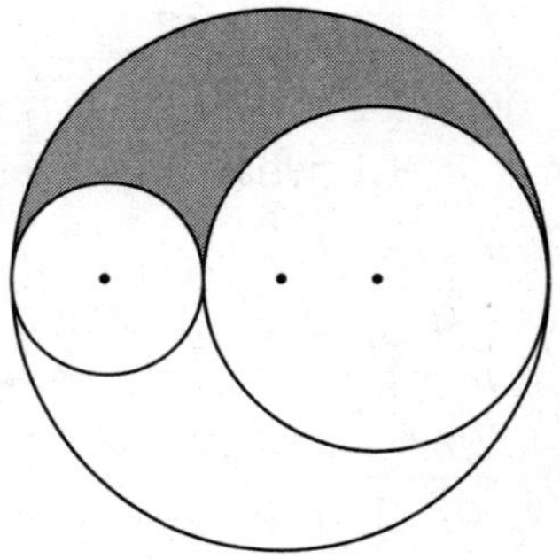

3. In the figure above, the centers of all three circles lie on the same line. The medium-sized circle has twice the radius of the smallest circle. The smallest circle has radius 1. What is the length of the boundary of the shaded region?
   (A) 12π
   (B) 6π
   (C) 12
   (D) 3π
   (E) 6

4. What is the perimeter of a rectangle that is twice as long as it is wide and has the same area as a circle of diameter 8?
(A) $8\sqrt{\pi}$
(B) $8\sqrt{2\pi}$
(C) 8π
(D) $12\sqrt{2\pi}$
(E) 12π

5. If the negative of the sum of two consecutive odd numbers is less than −35, which of the following may be one of the numbers?
(A) 18
(B) 16
(C) 15
(D) 13
(E) 11

6. How many gallons of milk that is 2% butterfat must be mixed with milk that is 3.5% butterfat to get 10 gallons that is 3% butterfat?
(A) 3
(B) $\frac{10}{3}$
(C) $\frac{7}{2}$
(D) $\frac{11}{3}$
(E) 4

7. If the arithmetic mean of x and y is m, and $z = 2m$, then the arithmetic mean of x, y, and z is
(A) m
(B) $\frac{4m}{3}$
(C) $\frac{4m}{3}$
(D) $\frac{3m}{4}$
(E) $\frac{3}{4m}$

8. Which of the following is a common factor of both $x^2 - 4x - 5$ and $x^2 - 6x - 7$?
(A) $x - 5$
(B) $x - 7$
(C) $x - 1$
(D) $x + 5$
(E) $x + 1$

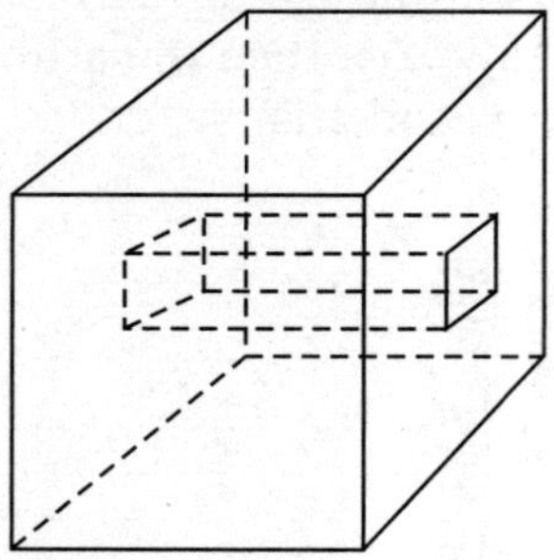

9. The figure above shows a cube 3 units on a side with a 1 × 1 square hole cut through it. How many square units is the total surface area of the resulting solid figure?
   (A) 66
   (B) 64
   (C) 60
   (D) 54
   (E) 52

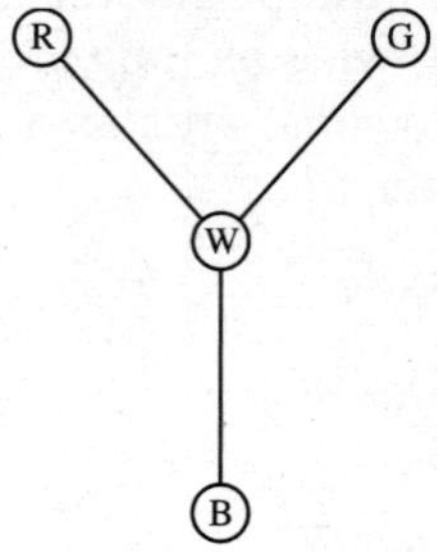

10. In a certain computer game, a light starts at the center (white) at time zero and moves once every second in the following pattern: from white to blue, back to white, then to green, back to white, then to red, in a clockwise direction. If the light continues to move in this way, what will be the color sequence at times 208–209?
    (A) White to green
    (B) White to blue
    (C) White to red
    (D) Red to white
    (E) Green to white

EXERCISE 5

10 Questions

Time—15 Minutes

Directions: In this section solve each problem, using any available space on the page for scratchwork. Then decide which is the best of the choices given and circle the corresponding letter.

1. For which n is the remainder largest when the number 817,380 is divided by n?

   (A) 4
   (B) 5
   (C) 6
   (D) 8
   (E) 9

2. The towns of Andover and Diggstown are 840 miles apart. On a certain map, this distance is represented by 14 inches. The towns of Lincoln and Charleston are 630 miles apart. On the same map, the distance between them in inches is

   (A) $9\frac{1}{2}$
   (B) 10
   (C) $10\frac{1}{2}$
   (D) 11
   (E) $11\frac{1}{2}$

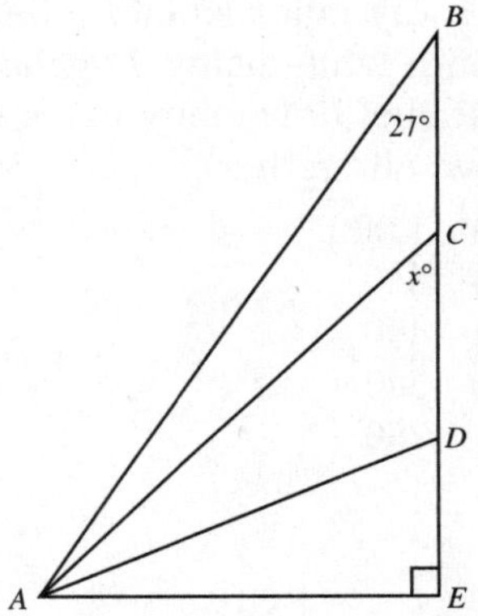

3. In the figure above, lines AC and AD trisect $\angle A$. What is the value of x?

   (A) 21
   (B) 27
   (C) 42
   (D) 48
   (E) 60

4. If the radius of a cylinder is tripled while its height is halved, its volume will be

   (A) halved
   (B) unchanged
   (C) doubled
   (D) increased by 350%
   (E) four times as large

5. Through how many degrees does the minute hand of a clock turn from 3:50 p.m. to 4:15 p.m. on the same day?
(A) 25
(B) 45
(C) 90
(D) 120
(E) 150

6. Harvey paid $400 for a used car that travels 28 miles per gallon on the highway and 20 miles per gallon in the city. If he drove twice as many highway miles as city miles last month while using 34 gallons of gasoline, how many miles did he drive altogether?
(A) 1,000
(B) 840
(C) 400
(D) 340
(E) 280

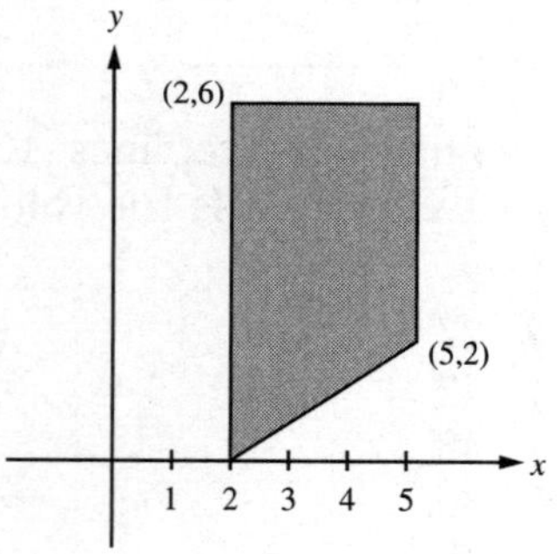

7. The area of the shaded region in the figure above is
(A) 15
(B) 16
(C) 17
(D) 18
(E) 20

8. What is the perimeter of a rectangle that is three times as long as it is wide and has the same area as a circle of circumference 6?
(A) $8\sqrt{3\pi}$
(B) $8\sqrt{\pi}$
(C) $4\sqrt{3\pi}$
(D) $\frac{8\sqrt{3}}{\sqrt{\pi}}$
(E) $\frac{8}{\sqrt{3\pi}}$

9. A plane is flying from City A to City B at *m* mph. Another plane flying from City B to City A travels 50 mph faster than the first plane. The cities are *R* miles apart. If both planes depart at the same time, in terms of *R* and *m*, how far are they from City A when they pass?
(A) $\frac{R}{m} + 50$
(B) $\frac{Rm}{2m} - 50$
(C) $\frac{rM}{2M + 50}$
(D) $\frac{R + 50}{m + 50}$
(E) $\frac{m + 50}{r}$

10. *P* percent of $20\sqrt{3}$ is 3. $P =$
(A) $\sqrt{3}$
(B) 3
(C) $5\sqrt{3}$
(D) $10\sqrt{3}$
(E) 20

EXERCISE 6

10 Questions

Time—15 Minutes

Directions: In this section solve each problem, using any available space on the page for scratchwork. Then decide which is the best of the choices given and circle the corresponding letter.

1. If a fleet of 7 taxicabs uses 180 gallons of gasoline every two days, how many gallons will be needed by 4 taxicabs for a 7-day week?

   (A) 420
   (B) 360
   (C) 300
   (D) 240
   (E) 180

2. Two rectangles have the same area. One is twice as long as the other. If the longer rectangle has length L and width W, what is the perimeter of the shorter rectangle?

   (A) $2L + 2W$
   (B) $2L + 4W$
   (C) $L + 4W$
   (D) $2L + W$
   (E) $4L + 2W$

3. If $4x + 2y = 13$ and $4y - x = 8$, what is the value of $x + 2y$?

   (A) 7
   (B) 5
   (C) 0
   (D) −3
   (E) −7

4. If z and w are positive integers and $z : = 2 : 3$, which of the following is a possible value of zw?

   I. 6
   II. 12
   III. 24

   (A) I only
   (B) I and II only
   (C) I and III only
   (D) II and III only
   (E) I, II, and III

Questions 5 and 6 refer to the following information:

An advertisement for a men's clothing store reads, "Men's shirts $22 apiece, 3 for $55. Receive a 10% discount on any sale of $100 or more."

5. What is the total cost of 8 shirts?

   (A) $176
   (B) $158.40
   (C) $154
   (D) $138.60
   (E) $136.80

6. What is the greatest number of shirts you can buy if you have \$100 to spend?
(A) 4
(B) 5
(C) 6
(D) 7
(E) 8

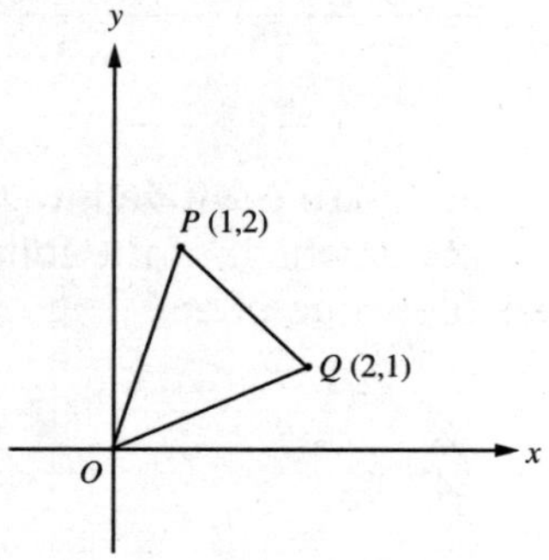

7. The perimeter of ΔOPQ in the figure above is
(A) $2\sqrt{5} + \sqrt{2}$
(B) $\sqrt{5} + 2\sqrt{2}$
(C) $\sqrt{5} + \sqrt{2}$
(D) 3
(E) $\sqrt{7}$

8. If $N = 3^P$ and $M = P - 1$, then in terms of M, $\frac{3}{N}=$
(A) $\frac{1}{3^M}$
(B) 3^M
(C) $\frac{9}{3^M}$
(D) 3^{2M}
(E) 3^{1-M}

9. When the units and tens digits of a certain two-digit number are reversed, the sum of the two numbers is 121 and the difference is 9. What is the tens digit of the original number?
(A) 1
(B) 3
(C) 4
(D) 6
(E) 7

10. If A and B are positive integers and $A^2 - B^2 = 36$, then $A =$
(A) 6
(B) 7
(C) 8
(D) 9
(E) 10

EXERCISE 7

10 Questions

Time—15 Minutes

Directions: In this section solve each problem, using any available space on the page for scratchwork. Then decide which is the best of the choices given and circle the corresponding letter.

1. If 6 drums of oil will heat 5 buildings for 3 days, how many days will 10 drums of oil last when heating 2 buildings?

    (A) 10
    (B) 12
    (C) 12.5
    (D) 14.5
    (E) 18

2. Among three circles, the area of the second circle is twice the area of the first circle, and the area of the third circle is 3 times the area of the second circle. If the area of the first circle is 6, what is the diameter of the largest circle?

    (A) 6
    (B) 12
    (C) 6π
    (D) 12π
    (E) 24

3. If $2x - y + 4z = 7$ and $-4x + 2y - 3z = 1$, what is the value of z?

    (A) 5
    (B) 3
    (C) 0
    (D) -3
    (E) It cannot be determined from the information provided.

4. If x and y are unequal positive integers and $xy = 36$, what is the smallest possible value of $x + y$?

    (A) 37
    (B) 20
    (C) 15
    (D) 13
    (E) 12

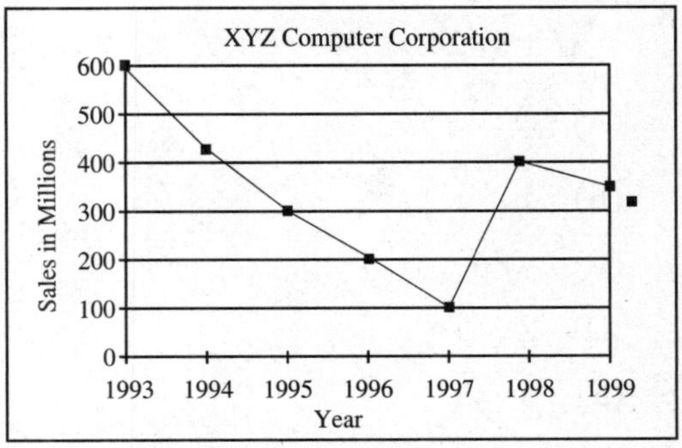

Questions 5 and 6 are based on the data in the graph above.

5. In which year was the percent drop in sales from the preceding year the greatest?

    (A) 1994
    (B) 1995
    (C) 1996
    (D) 1997
    (E) 1999

6. In which year were the annual sales the median value for the years shown?
   (A) 1994
   (B) 1995
   (C) 1996
   (D) 1997
   (E) 1999

$$\begin{array}{r} 25x \\ +\ 1y3 \\ \hline 362 \end{array}$$

7. In the correct addition problem shown above, x and y are digits. What is the value of y?
   (A) 0
   (B) 2
   (C) 4
   (D) 6
   (E) 8

8. $\sqrt{\dfrac{5}{\sqrt{25}}}$
   (A) $\dfrac{\sqrt{5}}{5}$
   (B) 1
   (C) $\sqrt{5}$
   (D) $2\sqrt{5}$
   (E) $5\sqrt{5}$

9. What is the largest possible value of x if $x^2 + 6x + 8 = 0$?
   (A) −6
   (B) −4
   (C) −2
   (D) 2
   (E) 4

10. If Rita pays $5 for monthly long-distance telephone service plus c cents per minute for each call, what is the average price in cents per minute for long-distance service in a month in which Rita makes n calls at an average length of 15 minutes?
   (A) $c + \dfrac{100}{3n}$
   (B) $c + 15n$
   (C) $15c + \dfrac{500}{n}$
   (D) $\dfrac{15c + nc}{n}$
   (E) $\dfrac{500 + nc}{15n}$

EXERCISE 8

10 Questions

Time—15 Minutes

Directions: In this section solve each problem, using any available space on the page for scratchwork. Then decide which is the best of the choices given and circle the corresponding letter.

1. If three men can paint 5 rooms in 9 days, how long will it take two men to paint 10 rooms?

(A) 27
(B) 25
(C) 22.5
(D) 20
(E) 16.5

2. Sarah has to put 76¢ worth of postage on a package. She has stamps in denominations of 1¢, 3¢, 5¢, 20¢, and 32¢. What is the minimum number of stamps she must use?

(A) 4
(B) 5
(C) 6
(D) 7
(E) 8

3. If four boxes of books each weighing at least 20 pounds have an average weight of 60 pounds, and if one box weighs 80 pounds, what is the maximum weight in pounds of the heaviest box?

(A) 140
(B) 120
(C) 110
(D) 100
(E) 90

4. If $x < y < -1$, which is of the following expressions has the greatest possible value?

(A) $\frac{x}{y}$
(B) $\frac{y}{x}$
(C) $\left(\frac{y}{x}\right)^2$
(D) 0
(E) $\left(\frac{x}{y}\right)^2$

5. The value of $\frac{x^2 - 16}{4x + 16}$ if $x = 4.04$ is

(A) 0.01
(B) 0.04
(C) 1.01
(D) 1.04
(E) 4.01

6. What is the area of a circle of diameter π?

(A) $\frac{1}{4}\pi^2$
(B) $\frac{1}{2}\pi^2$
(C) $\frac{1}{4}\pi^3$
(D) $\frac{1}{2}\pi^3$
(E) π^3

7. The altitude of a certain triangle is 20% longer than b, the length of its base. What is the area of the triangle in terms of b?

(A) $\frac{6b^2}{5}$
(B) $\frac{3b^2}{5}$
(C) $\frac{20b^2}{3}$
(D) $\frac{3b}{5}$
(E) $\frac{6b}{5}$

8. A jar contains 6 numbered blocks. Four of the blocks are numbered 0, and the other two are not. If two blocks are drawn at random from the jar, what is the probability that the product of the two numbers drawn is NOT zero?

(A) $\frac{1}{15}$
(B) $\frac{1}{12}$
(C) $\frac{2}{15}$
(D) $\frac{1}{6}$
(E) $\frac{1}{3}$

9. Four numbers, w, x, y, and z are arranged on a number line such that $w < x < y < z$, and the distance from w to y is 50% greater than the distance from x to z. If the distance from w to z is 6 units and the distance from w to x is 2 units, what is the distance in units from x to y?

(A) 6
(B) 4
(C) 2
(D) 1
(E) It cannot be determined from the information provided.

10. The ratio of Elaine's weekly salary to Carl's weekly salary is 3:2. If Elaine gets a 20 percent raise and Carl gets a $200 raise, the ratio of Elaine's salary to Carl's will drop to 6:5. Elaine's original weekly salary is

(A) $720
(B) $600
(C) $480
(D) $400
(E) $200

EXERCISE 9

10 Questions

Time—15 Minutes

Directions: In this section solve each problem, using any available space on the page for scratchwork. Then decide which is the best of the choices given and circle the corresponding letter.

1. The scale on a certain map is $\frac{2}{3}$ of an inch = 20 miles. If the distance between two cities on the map is 8 inches, the actual distance in miles is

(A) 120
(B) 180
(C) 200
(D) 240
(E) 360

2. If $2y - 6 = 16$, what is the value of $3 - y$?

(A) 8
(B) 6
(C) 0
(D) −6
(E) −8

3. Ms. Rodrigues deposited a certain amount in a checking account paying 2% per year interest, and she deposited $3,000 more than that amount in a savings account paying 3% interest. Her annual interest on the two accounts totaled $690. How much did she put into the savings account?

(A) $15,000
(B) $14,000
(C) $12,000
(D) $10,000
(E) $8,000

Questions 4–6 are based on the following definition:

$a \bigstar b = ab + 2b$ for all numbers a and b

4. $2 \bigstar 4 =$

(A) 8
(B) 12
(C) 16
(D) 18
(E) 20

5. For which value of a will $a \bigstar b = b$ for all b?

(A) −1
(B) 0
(C) 1
(D) 2
(E) There is no such value of a

6. If $x \bigstar y = y \bigstar x$, which of the following must be true?

(A) $x + y = 1$
(B) $y = 0$
(C) $x = y$
(D) $x = -2$
(E) $xy = 0$

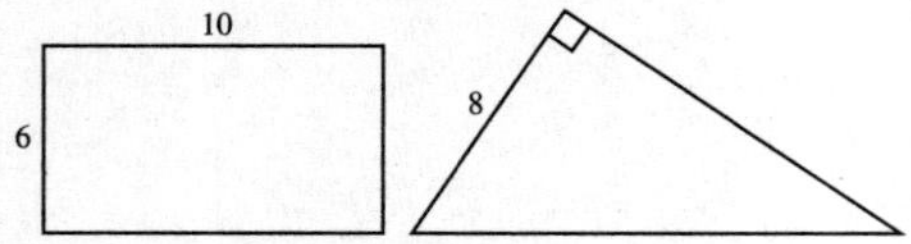

7. If the area of the rectangle in the figure above is equal to the area of the triangle, then the perimeter of the triangle is

(A) 42
(B) 40
(C) $8\sqrt{12}$
(D) $8 + \sqrt{15}$
(E) 17

8. The value of $\frac{x^2 - 3x}{3x - 9}$ if $x = 3.03$ is

(A) 303
(B) 101
(C) 3
(D) 1
(E) 1.01

9. When the tires of a taxicab are underinflated, the cab's odometer will read 10% over the true mileage driven. If the odometer of a cab whose tires are underinflated shows *m* miles, what is the actual distance driven?

(A) $\frac{10m}{11}$
(B) $1.1m$
(C) $\frac{10}{11m}$
(D) $0.9m$
(E) $\frac{11}{10m}$

10. If $2^3 = \sqrt{N}$, what is the value of N?

(A) 128
(B) 64
(C) 32
(D) 16
(E) 8

EXERCISE 10

10 Questions

Time—15 Minutes

Directions: In this section solve each problem, using any available space on the page for scratchwork. Then decide which is the best of the choices given and circle the corresponding letter.

1. If 12 is 5% of N, then $N =$
   (A) 3
   (B) 6
   (C) 24
   (D) 60
   (E) 240

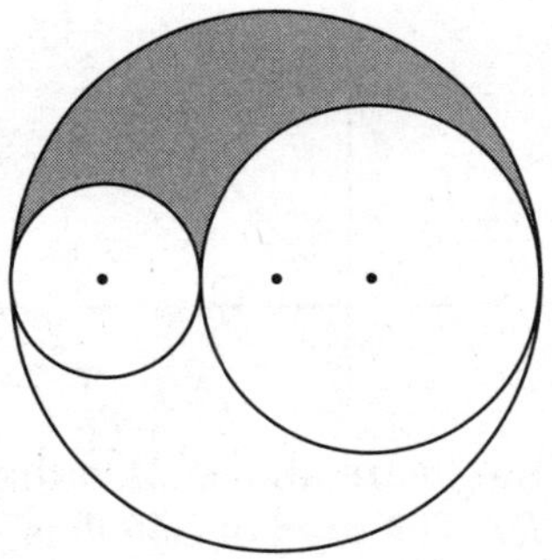

2. In the figure above, the centers of all three circles lie on the same line. The medium-sized circle has twice the radius of the smallest circle. The smallest circle has radius 2. What is the area of the shaded region?
   (A) 10π
   (B) 8π
   (C) 6π
   (D) 4π
   (E) 3π

3. If $y = 3 - x^2$, then $-3y =$
   (A) $-6 - x^2$
   (B) $-x^2$
   (C) $3x^2 - 6$
   (D) $3x^2 - 9$
   (E) $3x^2 - 3$

4. A certain quadrilateral has angles in the ratio 1:2:3 and a fourth angle that is 31° larger than the smallest angle. The difference in degree measure between the two middle-sized angles of the quadrilateral is
   (A) 16
   (B) 31
   (C) 47
   (D) 51
   (E) 63

5. Four boys own 150 baseball cards among them. If the first boy owns 28% of the cards, the second owns 24% of the cards, and the third owns 3 times as many cards as the fourth, the greatest number of cards owned by any one boy is
   (A) 64
   (B) 54
   (C) 42
   (D) 36
   (E) 28

6. If $(x - 2)(x + k) = x^2 + mx - 10$, then $mk =$

(A) 20
(B) 15
(C) 12
(D) −15
(E) −20

7. The figure above shows a square garden with a one-yard-wide concrete path around it. If the area of the path is 80 square yards, the length of one side of the garden in yards is

(A) 18
(B) 19
(C) 20
(D) 32
(E) 40

8. If a certain number is added to its square, and the units digit of the sum is zero, then which of the following may be true?

I. The number is odd.
II. The number is even.
III. The number is divisible by 3.

(A) I only
(B) II only
(C) III only
(D) I and II only
(E) I, II, and III

9. If 7 more than x is 1 less than twice x, which of the following numbers falls between $\frac{3}{x}$ and $\frac{4}{x}$?

(A) $\frac{1}{4}$
(B) $\frac{5}{16}$
(C) $\frac{7}{16}$
(D) $\frac{5}{8}$
(E) $\frac{3}{4}$

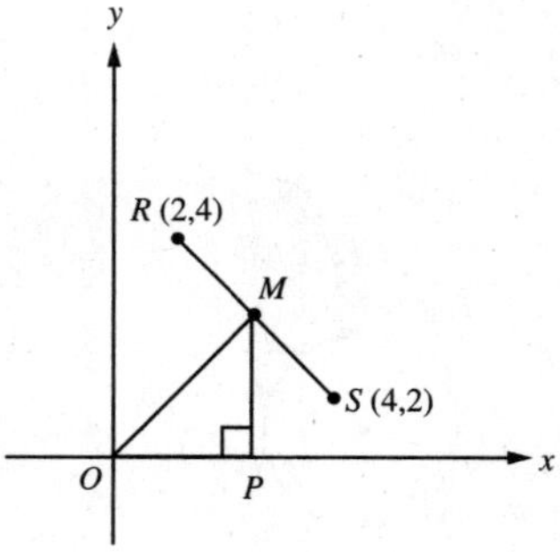

10. In the figure above, M is the midpoint of RS. The area of ΔMOP is

(A) 4.5
(B) 4
(C) 3.5
(D) 3
(E) $\sqrt{7}$

Answer Key

Exercise 1	Exercise 2	Exercise 3	Exercise 4	Exercise 5
1. C	1. E	1. D	1. E	1. D
2. D	2. C	2. D	2. B	2. C
3. E	3. D	3. D	3. B	3. D
4. E	4. D	4. D	4. D	4. D
5. B	5. D	5. E	5. C	5. E
6. A	6. E	6. E	6. B	6. D
7. A	7. A	7. E	7. C	7. A
8. D	8. C	8. C	8. C	8. C
9. A	9. A	9. A	9. B	9. C
10. E	10. B	10. A	10. C	10. C

Exercise 6	Exercise 7	Exercise 8	Exercise 9	Exercise 10
1. B	1. C	1. A	1. D	1. E
2. C	2. B	2. B	2. E	2. B
3. A	3. B	3. B	3. A	3. D
4. C	4. D	4. E	4. C	4. A
5. D	5. D	5. A	5. A	5. B
6. C	6. E	6. C	6. C	6. B
7. A	7. A	7. B	7. B	7. B
8. A	8. B	8. A	8. E	8. E
9. D	9. C	9. B	9. A	9. C
10. E	10. A	10. B	10. B	10. A

Explanatory Answers

EXERCISE 1

1. **The correct answer is (C).** Since the labeled end points are 2.2 and 2.3, the ten intervals between must each be one-tenth of the difference. Hence, the "tick marks" must represent hundredths. That is, $A = 2.21$, $B = 2.22$, and so on. Thus, we know that $G = 2.27$.

2. **The correct answer is (D).** The fact that a number is divisible by 3 does not make it odd. (Think of 6 or 12.) Therefore, $121 - 5k$ could be either odd or even. However, k cannot be divisible by 3, because 121 is not. Hence, only I or II is possible.

3. **The correct answer is (E).** Let r, m, and b be the prices in cents of rolls, muffins, and bread, respectively. This yields two equations:

   $$4r + 6m + 3b = 910$$

   and

   $$2r + 3m + b = 390$$

   If we multiply the second equation by -2 and add the two together, we have:

   $$\begin{array}{rr} \text{The first equation:} & 4r + 6m + 3b = 910 \\ -2 \text{ times the second equation:} & \underline{-4r - 6m - 2b = -780} \\ & b = 130 \end{array}$$

   Hence, the price of a loaf of bread is \$1.30, which is choice (E).

4. **The correct answer is (E).** $4y$ must be even, so for the sum of $3x$ and $4y$ to be odd, $3x$ must be odd. Since 3 is odd, $3x$ will be odd only if x is odd. Hence, x is odd and y can be anything. So II and III cannot be true.

5. **The correct answer is (B).** Let the number of Democrats be $5m$ and the number of Republicans be $7m$, so that D:R :: $5m{:}7m = 5{:}7$. The total is $5m + 7m = 12m$, which must be 156. Therefore, $12m = 156$, and $m = 13$. Of course, the difference is $7m - 5m = 2m = 2(13) = 26$. Hence, the answer is choice (B).

6. **The correct answer is (A).** Since $BC = 4$ and $AC = 8$, we know that ΔABC is a 30°-60°-90° right triangle. We know $AB = 4$, and taking one-half the product of the legs, the triangle has area $(4)(4) = 8$. Since ΔADC is an isosceles right triangle with hypotenuse 8, each leg must be $\frac{8}{\sqrt{2}}$. Again, taking one-half the product of the legs, the triangle has area $\frac{1}{2}\left(\frac{8}{\sqrt{2}}\right)\left(\frac{8}{\sqrt{2}}\right) = \frac{64}{4} = 16$. Adding the two areas, we have $16 + 8\sqrt{3}$.

7. **The correct answer is (A).** Add -2 to both sides.

$$\begin{array}{l} A \quad < \ 2 - 4B \\ \quad -2 = -2 \\ \hline A - 2 < -4B \end{array}$$

Divide by -4, remembering to reverse the inequality: $\frac{A-2}{-4} > B$; that is, $\frac{2-A}{4} > B$, which is choice (A).

8. **The correct answer is (D).** Since each person had 5 choices, there are 25 possible pairs of numbers. The only way the sum could be odd is if one person picked an odd number and the other picked an even number. Suppose that Johnnie chose the odd number and Lisa the even one. Johnnie had 3 possible even numbers to select from, and for each of these, Lisa had 2 possible choices, for a total of (3)(2) = 6 possibilities. However, you could have had Johnnie pick an even number and Lisa pick an odd one, and there are also 6 ways to do that. Out of 25 possibilities, 12 have an odd total, and 13 have an even total. The probability of an even total, then, is choice (D) $\frac{13}{25}$.

9. **The correct answer is (A).** Running m buses for 2 days is the same as running one bus for $2m$ days. If we use g gallons of gasoline, each bus uses $\frac{g}{2m}$ gallons each day. So if you multiply the number of gallons per day used by each bus by the number of buses and the number of days, you should get total gasoline usage. That is, $\frac{g}{2m} \times (4)(5) = \frac{10g}{m}$.

10. **The correct answer is (E).** If $x = 5$ and $y = 5$, $x^2 + y^2 = 50$. For any other choice, say 6 and 4, the sum is larger. Hence, $x^2 + y^2$ is at a minimum when $x = y$ and $|x - y|$ m= 0.

EXERCISE 2

1. **The correct answer is (E).** Any number less than D must lie to the left of D. The distance from D to G is 3 units. The point we want must be $1\frac{1}{2}$ units to the left of D, that is, halfway between B and C. Since this is not a labeled point, the correct choice is (E).

2. **The correct answer is (C).** The larger circle has area $A_L = \pi(r)^2 = 36p$. That means that $r^2 = 36$, and $r = 6$. The diameter of the smaller circle equals the radius of the larger one, so its radius is $\frac{1}{2}(6) = 3$. Its circumference must be $CS = 2\pi(3) = 6\pi$, choice (C).

3. **The correct answer is (D).** In 5 hours, 4 ounces (7 − 3) have dripped. Therefore, the drip rate is $\frac{4}{5}$ of an ounce per hour. From 5:00 p.m. on Sunday until 2:00 a.m. on Monday is 9 hours, causing the total to be:

$$7 + \frac{4}{5} \times 9 = 7 + \frac{36}{5} = \frac{71}{5}$$

4. **The correct answer is (D).** The prime factorization of 24 is $2^3 3$; if $24AB$ is a perfect square, then AB must have a factor of 2 and a factor of 3. This means, first of all, that both A and B cannot be odd. So I cannot be possible. II also cannot be possible, because if AB were a perfect square and $24AB$ were also a perfect square, then 24 would be a perfect square, which it is not. Of course, if, for example, A were 6 and B were 36, $24AB$ would be a perfect square with both A and B divisible by 6, so III is possible. Hence, the correct choice is (D).

5. **The correct answer is (D).** Totaling the payments made to all four suppliers, you have 4,500 + 1,500 + 3,000 + 1,000 = 10,000. Of this total, 3,000 was paid to Corman—that is, 30% of the total. Hence, the sector representing Corman must be 30% of 360° = 108°.

6. **The correct answer is (E).** Substituting: $(-2)^4 + 2(-2)^3 + 3(-2)^2 + (-2) = 16 - 16 + 12 - 2 = 10$.

7. **The correct answer is (A).** Working outward from the inner parentheses, $[3(a^2b^3)^2]^3 = [3a^4b^6]^3 = 27a^{12}b^{18}$.

8. **The correct answer is (C).** The only way that $7 + x + x$ in the left column can total 11 is if x is 2, since if there were a "carry" of 1, x would not be a whole number; and if you try for a "carry" of 2, x would be 1, and $x + y + x$ in the right column would be at most 11, with a carry of only 1. Since $x = 2$, the only way $2x + y$ could have a units digit of 7 is if $y = 3$. In other words, the original addition must have been 72 + 23 + 22.

9. **The correct answer is (A).** Let x be the unknown number of liters of 50% antifreeze. Now, the final mixture will have $(x + 80)$ liters, and the amount of antifreeze will be:

$$\begin{aligned} 0.50x + 0.20(80) &= 0.40(x + 80) \\ 0.5x + 16 &= 0.4x + 32 \\ 0.1x &= 16 \\ x &= 160 \end{aligned}$$

10. **The correct answer is (B).** Since Horace's average overall was 75, he had a total overall of $75(m + n) = 75m + 75n$ on $n + m$ exams. Since he averaged 70 on m exams, he had a total of $70m$ on the first m. That means that his total on the last n exams was $75m + 75n - 70m = 5m + 75n$, and his average was $(5m + 75n) \div n = + 75$.

EXERCISE 3

1. **The correct answer is (D).** The easiest thing to look for is divisibility by 5. Does the number end in 5 or 0? By inspection, we eliminate 23,096, which ends in 6. We want the number to be divisible by 4, which means it must be even, and its last two digits must form a number divisible by 4. That knocks out the one ending in 5 (which is odd), and also 79,130, because 30 is not divisible by 4. This leaves 15,840 and 53,700. The digits of 15,840 add up to 18, while those of 53,700 total 15. Both are divisible by 3, but 15,840 is also divisible by 9. Therefore, only Choice (D) 53,700 meets all the conditions.

2. **The correct answer is (D).** Substituting: $[2 - (-1)(-2)^2]^3 = [2 - (-4)]^3 = 6^3 = 216$.

3. **The correct answer is (D).** The fraction reduces to $3y$, and $9y - 3y = 6y$

4. **The correct answer is (D).** Since $x^2 - 4y^2 = (x - 2y)(x + 2y) = 5(x + 2y)$, $x^2 - 4y^2$ must be divisible by 5. Therefore, −3, 14, and 51 are not possible. If the result is to be zero, $x + 2y = 0$, which means $y = -2x$, so that both numbers cannot be positive. The expression must equal 45, which you get for $x = 7$ and $y = 1$.

5. **The correct answer is (E).** The dotted line divides the region into a rectangle and a semicircle. Since the radius of the circular arc is 4, the diameter is 8, and that is the width of the rectangle. The length is 10. Its area is 80. The area of the whole circle would be $\pi r^2 = \pi(4^2) = 16\pi$. The area of the semicircle is half of that, or 8π. Therefore, the total area is choice (E) $80 + 8p$.

6. **The correct answer is (E).** If $n^2 < 2n$, that means that $n^2 - 2n < 0$, or $n(n - 2) > 0$. Clearly, if n is any positive number less than 2, then n is positive and $(n - 2)$ is negative, making the result true.

7. **The correct answer is (E).** Substituting $(p + 1)$ for n, we have:

$$n^\wedge = \frac{2(p+1)}{(p+1)-1} = \frac{(2p+2)}{p} 2 + \frac{2}{p}$$

8. **The correct answer is (C).** It is easiest to try plugging in the values offered. You'll find that, for $n = 3$, $n^\wedge = \dfrac{2(3)}{3-1} = \dfrac{6}{2} = 3$.

9. **The correct answer is (A).** It really doesn't matter what number you roll on the first roll; the chance of matching it the next time is always $\frac{1}{6}$.

10. **The correct answer is (A).** Calling the numbers x and y, $\frac{x+y}{2}: x = \frac{3}{5}$. Cross-multiplying:

$$5x + 5y = 6x$$
$$5y = x$$

One number is five times as large as the other, so their ratio is 1:5.

EXERCISE 4

1. **The correct answer is (E).** At 35¢ per pound, the 3-pound bag will be marked $1.05 or 105¢. Dividing this by the weight of the bag, we have 105 ÷ 3.25. Hence, choice (E), 32 is the closest.

2. **The correct answer is (B).** Cubing, $\left(\frac{-2}{5}\right)^3 = \frac{-8}{125}$. To convert this fraction to thousandths, multiply both the numerator and the denominator by 8 to get $\frac{-64}{1000}$. Hence, $N = -64$.

3. **The correct answer is (B).** Since the smallest circle has a radius of 1, the medium circle has radius 2, and the diameter of the large circle must be 6, which makes its radius 3. The length of a semicircle is half that of a circle, that is, πr. So the length of the boundary of the shaded region is the sum of the lengths of the three semicircles:

   $$p + 2p + 3p = 6p.$$

4. **The correct answer is (D).** The area of a circle of diameter 8 is $\pi 4^2 = 16\pi$, since its radius is 4. Let the width of the rectangle be w. Its length is $2w$ and its area is $2w^2$, which must equal 16π. Thus:

   $$2w^2 = 16\pi$$
   $$w^2 = 8\pi \text{ and } w = \sqrt{8\pi} = 2\sqrt{2\pi}$$

   Therefore,

   $$L = 4\sqrt{2\pi}$$

   The perimeter is $2w + 2L = 8 + 4 = 12$.

5. **The correct answer is (C).** Calling the numbers x and $(x + 2)$, the negative of the sum is $-[x + (x + 2)]$, and this should be less than -35. That is, $-[2x + 2] < -35$. Solving the inequality:

   $$-2x - 2 < -35$$
   $$-2x < -33$$

   Dividing by -2 reverses the inequality:

   $$x > 16.5$$

   Looking at the choices, 18 and 16 are both even, and we need an odd number. $x = 15$ will work, because $(x + 2) = 17 > 16.5$.

6. **The correct answer is (B).** Let g be the number of gallons that is 2% butterfat. Then $10 - g$ will be the amount that is 3.5% butterfat. The total amount of butterfat is:

   $$0.02g + 0.035(10 - g) = 0.03(10)$$
   $$0.02g + 0.35 - 0.035g = 0.3$$

   Let's multiply by 1,000 to clear out the decimals:

   $$20g + 350 - 35g = 300$$
   $$-15g = -50; g = \frac{10}{3}$$

7. **The correct answer is (C).** The arithmetic mean of x and y is $\frac{x+y}{2} = m$, which means that $x + y = 2m$ and $x + y + z = 4m$. Dividing by 3 to get the arithmetic mean of x, y, and z, we get $= \frac{x+y+z}{3} = \frac{4m}{3}$.

8. **The correct answer is (C).** $x^2 - 4x - 5 = (x - 5)(x + 1)$, and $x^2 - 6x - 7 = (x - 7)(x + 1)$. The common factor is $x + 1$.

9. **The correct answer is (B).** Each side of the cube has an area of $3 \times 3 = 9$. Since there are 6 sides, the original cube had a surface area of 54 square units. Two 1×1 squares are missing, making the outside area 52. The hole has four 3×1 rectangular sides with a total area of 12, giving us a final total of 64.

10. **The correct answer is (C).** The sequence is:

0	1	2	3	4	5	6	7	8	9	10	11	12
W	B	W	G	W	R	W	B	W	G	W	R	W

Every time you reach a time divisible by 6, the sequence starts over with W and proceeds: WBWGWR. 204 is divisible by 6; hence, we must have the sequence:

204	205	206	207	208	209
W	B	W	G	W	R

Times 208 – 209 are W – R.

EXERCISE 5

1. **The correct answer is (D).** 817,380 is divisible by all the numbers in the list except 8. Hence, 8 must give the largest remainder because it is the only one that is not zero. To start, 7,380 is divisible by 5 because it ends in 0. It is divisible by 2 because it is even, and by 4 because 80 is divisible by 4. However, it is not divisible by 8 because 380 isn't. In addition, the sum of its digits is 27, which is divisible by 3 and by 9. Since it is divisible by both 2 and 3, it is also divisible by 6.

2. **The correct answer is (C).** The actual distance and the distance on the map must be in the same proportion. That is, $630{:}840 = x{:}14$, where x is the unknown distance. In fractions:

$$\frac{630}{840} = \frac{x}{14}; \frac{3}{14} = \frac{x}{14}$$

Cross-multiplying: $4x = 42$; $x = 10.5$.

3. **The correct answer is (D).** Looking first at ΔABE, we have a right triangle with one angle 90° and one 27°. Thus, $\angle A$ must be 63°. Hence, $\angle BAC$ is one-third of that, or 21°. So looking at ΔABC, $\angle BCA$ must be $180° - 21° - 27° = 132°$. Since x is the supplement to that angle, $x = 48$.

4. **The correct answer is (D).** The volume is $V = \pi rh^2$. Replacing r by $3r$ and h by $\frac{1}{2}h$, we have $V = \pi(3r)^2\left(\frac{1}{2}h\right) = \frac{9}{2}\pi r^2 h$. It is 4.5 times as large, which means it is 350% larger than it was.

5. **The correct answer is (E).** The clock hand has moved through 25 minutes, which is $\frac{25}{60} = \frac{5}{12}$ of the full circle. Thus, in degrees:

$$\frac{5}{12}(360) = 150$$

6. **The correct answer is (D).** Let x be the number of city miles Harvey drove, and let $2x$ be the number of highway miles. Miles divided by miles per gallon should give the number of gallons of gas used. Thus:

$$\frac{x}{20} + \frac{2x}{28} = 34$$

$$\frac{x}{20} + \frac{x}{14} = 34$$

Multiply the equation by the LCD 140 to get:

$$7x + 10x = 4{,}760$$

$$17x = 4{,}760;\ x = 280$$

Since Harvey drove a total of $3x$ miles, the correct choice is $3(280) = 840$.

7. **The correct answer is (A).** If we drop a perpendicular from the point (5,2) to the x-axis, it will hit the axis at (5,0), and we will have a rectangle that is 3 units wide and 6 units high (since it goes from the x-axis, where $y = 0$, to the height of (2,6), which is 6 units). The area of this rectangle is 18 square units. Subtracting the area of the missing triangle, which is $\frac{1}{2}(2)(3) = 3$, we see that the area of the shaded portion is 15.

8. **The correct answer is (C).** If the circle has a circumference of 6, its radius is given by $6 = 2\pi r$, so that $r = \frac{3}{\pi}$. The area of a circle of radius is $\frac{3}{\pi}$ is $\pi\left(\frac{3}{\pi}\right)^2 = \frac{9}{\pi}$. Let the width of the rectangle be w. Its length is $3w$, and its area is $3w^2$, which must equal $\frac{9}{\pi}$. Thus:

$$3w^2 = \frac{9}{\pi}$$

$$w^2 = \frac{3}{\pi}$$

and

$$w = \sqrt{\frac{3}{\pi}} = \frac{\sqrt{3}}{\sqrt{\pi}}$$

The perimeter is $2L + 2W = 6W + 2W = 8W = \frac{8\sqrt{3}}{\pi}$

9. **The correct answer is (C).** The planes pass at the time when the sum of the distances traveled by both is R. Call this time t. The first plane, going m miles per hour, has traveled mt miles. The second plane, going $(m + 50)$ miles per hour, has traveled $(m + 50)t$ miles. The two sum to R. Thus:

$$R = mt + mt + 50t$$
$$R = (2m + 50)t$$

Thus:

$$t = \frac{R}{2m + 50}$$

Hence, the planes' distance from City A is m times this time, or:

$$mt = \frac{Rm}{2m + 50}$$

10. **The correct answer is (C).** P percent means $\frac{P}{100}$. Hence, $\frac{P}{100} \times 20\sqrt{3} = 3$ must be solved for P. Thus, $\frac{P\sqrt{3}}{5} = 3$. Multiply by $\frac{5}{\sqrt{3}}$, and notice that $\frac{3}{\sqrt{3}} = \sqrt{3}$ gives $P = 5$.

EXERCISE 6

1. **The correct answer is (B).** Running 7 cabs for 2 days is the same as running one cab for 14 days. Running 4 cabs for 7 days is the same as running one cab for 28 days. Thus, you simply need twice as much gasoline! Another way to look at this is to say: We use 180 gallons of gasoline by running 7 cabs for 2 days. That means we use 180 gallons running one cab for 14 days. In other words, the cab uses $\frac{180}{14}$ gallons each day. So if you multiply the number of gallons per day used by each cab by the number of cabs and the number of days, you should get total usage. That is, $\frac{180}{14} \times (4)(7) = 360$.

2. **The correct answer is (C).** The perimeter of the longer rectangle is $2L + 2W$. The other rectangle has length $\frac{1}{2}L$ and width $2W$, to keep the area constant. Thus, the second rectangle has perimeter $2\left(\frac{1}{2}L\right) + 2(2W) = L + 4W$.

3. **The correct answer is (A).** We could solve the two equations simultaneously to find x and y. However, it is easier to proceed as follows. Reorder the terms in the second equation so as to start with the x term, thus:

$$-x + 4y = 8$$

Add to this the second equation:

$$\begin{array}{r} -x + 4y = 8 \\ 4x + 2y = 13 \\ \hline 3x + 6y = 21 \end{array}$$

Divide by 3:

$$x + 2y = 7$$

4. **The correct answer is (C).** Writing the proportion as a fractional equation, $\frac{z}{w} = \frac{2}{3}$, leads to $z = \frac{2w}{3}$, so that $zw = \frac{2w^2}{3}$. Trying to equate this expression to 6, 12, and 24, we find that $\frac{2w^2}{3} = 6$ gives $w^2 = 9$ and $w = 3$, and consequently $z = 2$. For $\frac{2w^2}{3} = 24$, $w = 6$, and $z = 4$. However, for $\frac{2w^2}{3} = 12$, $w^2 = 18$, and w is not an integer. Hence, the correct choice is (C)—I and III are possible.

5. **The correct answer is (D).** Eight shirts are 2 sets of 3 plus two singles, for \$110 plus \$44, or \$154. Then you get a \$15.40 discount, bringing the final cost to \$138.60.

6. **The correct answer is (C).** If you buy 5 shirts, you get 3 for \$55 plus 2 more for \$22 each, for a total of \$99. But if you buy 6 shirts (two sets of 3), you pay \$110 less a 10% discount of \$11, bringing your cost down to \$99. The extra shirt is free!

7. **The correct answer is (A).** The length of OQ and OP are the same: $\sqrt{2^2 + 1^2} = \sqrt{5}$. The length of PQ is $\sqrt{1^2 + 1^2} = \sqrt{2}$. The perimeter is $2\sqrt{5} + \sqrt{2}$.

8. **The correct answer is (A).** Since $P = M + 1$, $N = 3P = 3M^{+1} = 3(3M)$, and $\frac{3}{N} = \frac{3}{3(3^M)} = \frac{1}{3M}$.

9. **The correct answer is (D).** Calling the number $10t + u$, when we reverse the digits, we get $10u + t$. The sum is then $(10t + u) + (10u + t) = 11t + 11u = 121$. Dividing by 11, we have $t + u = 11$. Taking the difference, $(10t + u) - (10u + t) = 9t - 9u = 9$, and dividing by 9, $t - u = 1$. Adding:

$$\begin{aligned} t + u &= 11 \\ t - u &= 1 \\ 2t &= 12 \\ t &= 6 \end{aligned}$$

10. **The correct answer is (E).** Since $A^2 - B^2 = (A - B)(A + B)$, $(A - B)$ and $(A + B)$ must be factors of 36. The possibilities are:

$$\begin{array}{ll} A - B = 1 & A + B = 36 \\ A - B = 2 & A + B = 18 \\ A - B = 3 & A + B = 12 \\ A - B = 4 & A + B = 9 \\ A - B = 6 & A + B = 6 \end{array}$$

Only the second and fifth give integer solutions, and for the fifth case, $A = 6$ and $B = 0$, which is not positive. The only one that works is $A = 10$, $B = 8$, for which $A + B = 18$ and $A - B = 2$.

EXERCISE 7

1. **The correct answer is (C).** Letting x be the unknown number of days, we know that the ratio of "number of drums" to "number of building-days" must be constant; that is, $6{:}15 = 10{:}2x$. Written as a fractional equation, this means $\frac{6}{15} = \frac{10}{2x}$. That is, $\frac{2}{5} = \frac{5}{x}$. Cross-multiplying:

$$2x = 25$$
$$x = 12.5$$

2. **The correct answer is (B).** Since the area of the first circle is 6π, the second circle has area $2(6\pi) = 12\pi$, and the third circle has area $3(12\pi) = 36\pi$. Since $A = \pi r^2$, that makes the radius of the largest circle 6. The diameter is $2(6) = 12$.

3. **The correct answer is (B).** Doubling the first equation and adding it to the second gives:

$$\begin{array}{r} 4x - 2y + 8z = 14 \\ -4x + 2y - 3z = 1 \\ \hline 5z = 15 \\ z = 3 \end{array}$$

4. **The correct answer is (D).** The possible factors of 36 are (1,36), (2,18), (3,12), (4,9), and (6,6). The smallest possible sum is 12, but in that case, x and y are equal. So we must take 13, which we get for (4,9).

5. **The correct answer is (D).** The greatest drop in absolute numbers was from 1993 to 1994, when sales dropped 180 from 600 to 420. The percent drop was 30%. However, from 1996 to 1997, the drop was 200 to 100, a 50% decline.

6. **The correct answer is (E).** Reading from the graph, the sales figures were: 600, 420, 300, 200, 100, 400, and 350. The median of these seven numbers is 350 in 1999.

7. **The correct answer is (A).** In order that the units digit in the sum be 2, $x = 9$. Now, with a carry of 1, the tens digit in the sum must be given by $1 + 5 + y = 6$. Thus, $y = 0$.

8. **The correct answer is (B).** Since $\sqrt{25} = 5$, $\dfrac{5}{\sqrt{25}} = 1$ and $\sqrt{1} = 1$.

9. **The correct answer is (C).** Factoring:

$$\begin{aligned} x^2 + 6x + 8 = (x + 2)(x + 4) &= 0 \\ x + 2 &= 0 \\ \text{or} \quad x + 4 &= 0 \\ x &= -2 \\ \text{or} \quad x &= -4 \end{aligned}$$

The larger root is -2.

10. **The correct answer is (A).** The total cost for the month is $500 + 15nc$ for $15n$ minutes of calling. Thus, the average is $\dfrac{500 + 15nc}{15n} = c + (100)3n$.

EXERCISE 8

1. **The correct answer is (A).** Letting x be the unknown number of days, we know that the ratio of "number of man-days" to "number of rooms" must be constant; that is, $27{:}5 = 2x{:}10$. Written as a fractional equation, this is $\dfrac{27}{5} = \dfrac{2x}{10}$. Cross-multiplying: $270 = 10x$; $x = 27$. Another way to look at this is to say that it takes 27 man-days to paint 5 rooms. That is, it would take one man 27 days to paint 5 rooms, or $27 \div 5 = 5.4$ days per room. Therefore, to do 10 rooms, a man needs 54 days. Two men working together can do it in half the time, or 27 days.

2. **The correct answer is (B).** Sarah must use at least 5 stamps: $32 + 20 + 20 + 3 + 1$.

3. **The correct answer is (B).** If the boxes average 60 pounds, then the four must total 240. Since one weighs 80, the other three must total 160. The largest box could weigh 120, with the other two each weighing 20.

4. **The correct answer is (E).** Since $x < y < -1$, the ratios $\dfrac{x}{y}$ and $\dfrac{y}{x}$ are both positive, but $\dfrac{y}{x} < 1$, while $\dfrac{x}{y} > 1$. Therefore, $\left(\dfrac{x}{y}\right)^2 > \dfrac{x}{y}$, and must be the greatest.

5. **The correct answer is (A).** Factoring the numerator and denominator of the fraction, we see that we can divide out the common factor $(x + 4)$, thus: $\dfrac{x^2 - 16}{4x + 16} + \dfrac{(x - 4)(x + 4)}{4(x + 4)} = \dfrac{x - 4}{4}$. Substituting $x = 4.04$ yields $\dfrac{0.04}{4} = 0.01$.

6. **The correct answer is (C).** If the diameter is π, the radius is $\dfrac{1}{2}\pi$, and the area is $\pi r^2 = \pi\left(\dfrac{1}{2}\pi\right)^2 = \dfrac{1}{4}\pi^3$.

7. **The correct answer is (B).** If h is 20% longer than b, then $h = 1.2b = \frac{6b}{5}$. The area is $\frac{1}{2}bh = \frac{1}{2}(b)\left(\frac{6b}{5}\right) = \frac{3b^2}{5}$.

8. **The correct answer is (A).** Four out of six times, the first block drawn will be a zero. The remaining one third of the time, a non-zero number will be drawn, leaving one non-zero and four zero blocks. The chance of drawing a second non-zero block is $\frac{1}{5}$. Hence, the product will not be zero only $\frac{1}{5}$ of $\frac{1}{3}$ $= \frac{1}{5} \times \frac{1}{3} = \frac{1}{15} =$ of the time.

9. **The correct answer is (B).** The number line (not to scale) looks like this:

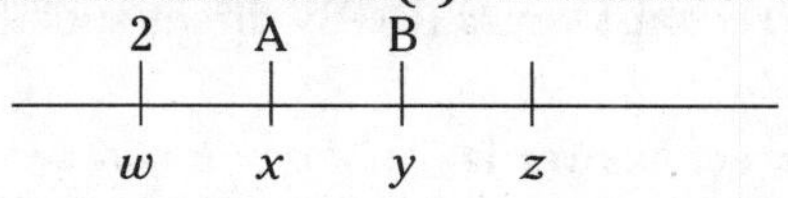

$2 + A + B = 6$, and we want to know A. This means that $A + B = 4$, or $B = 4 - A$. However, we know that $A + 2 = 1.5(A + B)$, because the distance from w to y is 50% greater than the distance from x to z. That is, $A + 2 = 1.5A + 1.5B$, or $1.5B + 0.5A = 2$. Substituting $B = 4 - A$:

$$1.5(4 - A) + 0.5A = 2$$
$$6 - 1.5A + 0.5A = 2$$
$$-A = -4$$
$$A = 4$$

10. **The correct answer is (B).** Let Elaine's salary be $3k$; Carl's will be $2k$. A 20% raise for Elaine will bring her salary to $(1.2)(3k) = 3.6k$, while a \$200 raise for Carl will bring his salary to $2k + 200$. Thus, $3.6k{:}(2k + 200) = 6{:}5$, or as a fraction, $\frac{3.6k}{2k + 2{,}000} = \frac{6}{5}$. Cross-multiplying:

$$18k = 12k + 1{,}200$$
$$6k = 1{,}200;\ k = 200$$

Since Elaine's salary is $3k$, the correct choice is (B) 600.

EXERCISE 9

1. **The correct answer is (D).** The ratio of distances should be the same. That is, $\frac{2}{3}{:}8 = 20{:}d$. So $\frac{2}{3} \div 8 = \frac{20}{d}, \frac{2}{24} = \frac{20}{d}$. Cross-multiplying: $2d = 480$; $d = 240$.

2. **The correct answer is (E).** We can solve $2y - 6 = 16$ by first adding 6 to both sides of the equation, giving $2y = 22$. Now dividing by $2{:}y = 11$. Hence, $3 - y = 3 - 11 = -8$.

3. **The correct answer is (A).** Let N be the amount in the checking account; $(x + 3{,}000)$ will be the amount in the saving account. The total interest earned is:

$$0.02N + 0.03(N + 3{,}000) = 690$$

Multiplying by 100:

$$\begin{aligned} 2N + 3(N + 3{,}000) &= 69{,}000 \\ 5N + 9{,}000 &= 69{,}000 \\ 5N &= 60{,}000 \\ N &= 12{,}000 \end{aligned}$$

Hence, the amount in the savings account is \$15,000.

4. **The correct answer is (C).** By direct substitution, $2 \bigstar 4 = (2)(4) + 2(4) = 16$.

5. **The correct answer is (A).** If $a \bigstar b = b$, we have $ab + 2b = b$. That is, $ab = b - 2b$, or $ab = -b$. This is true for any a if $b = 0$, but in order that it be true for all b, a must equal -1.

6. **The correct answer is (C).** If $x \bigstar y = y \bigstar x$, then $xy + 2y = xy + 2x$. Subtracting xy from both sides of the equation, $2y = 2x$, or $y = x$.

7. **The correct answer is (B).** The area of the rectangle is $6(10) = 60$. Using the legs of the right triangle as base and height with the unknown leg called h, we have $\frac{1}{2}(8)h = 60$; that is, $4h = 60$ and $h = 15$. Hence, the triangle is an 8-15-17 right triangle with perimeter 40.

8. **The correct answer is (E).** Factoring the numerator and denominator of the fraction, we see that we can divide out the common factor $(x - 3)$, thus: $\frac{x^2 - 3x}{3x - 9} = \frac{x(x - 3)}{3(x - 3)} = \frac{x}{3}$. Substituting $x = 3.03$ yields $\frac{3.03}{3} = 1.01$.

9. **The correct answer is (A).** If the true distance is T, then the odometer will show $m = T + 0.10T = 1.1T = \left(\frac{11}{10}\right)T$. That is, $T = \left(\frac{10}{11}\right)m$, which is the same as $\frac{10m}{11}$.

10. **The correct answer is (B).** $2^3 = 8$, and 8 is the square root of 64.

EXERCISE 10

1. **The correct answer is (E).** 12 is 5% of N means $0.05N = 12$. Dividing by 0.05, $N = 240$.

2. **The correct answer is (B).** Since the smallest circle has a radius of 2, the medium circle has a radius of 4, and the diameter of the large circle must be 12, which makes its radius 6. The area of a semicircle is half that of a circle, that is, $\frac{1}{2}\pi r^2$. The area of the shaded region is the area of the largest semicircle minus the areas of the two smaller ones; that is, $\frac{1}{2}\pi(36) - \frac{1}{2}\pi(16) - \frac{1}{2}\pi(4) = 8\pi$.

3. **The correct answer is (D).** Using the distributive law, $-3(3 - x^2) = -9 + 3x^2$, which is the same as $3x^2 - 9$.

4. **The correct answer is (A).** Calling the smallest angle x, the others are $2x$, $3x$, and $(x + 31)$. Since the angles in the quadrilateral must sum to 360, we get:

$$x + 2x + 3x + (x + 31) = 360$$
$$7x + 31 = 360$$
$$7x = 329$$
$$x = 47$$

That makes the four angles 47, 94, 141, and 78. The difference between the two in the middle is $94 - 78 = 16$.

5. **The correct answer is (B).** 28% of 150 = 0.28(150) = 42. 24% of 150 = 0.24(150) = 36. Thus, $150 - 42 - 36 = 72$ cards are divided between the other two boys in the ratio of 3:1. That is, one boy owns $\frac{1}{4}$ of the cards (18), and other owns 54.

6. **The correct answer is (B).** Using the FOIL Method, $(x - 2)(x + k) = x^2 + (k - 2)x - 2k$. Since $-2k = -10$, $k = 5$, and since $(k - 2) = m$, $m = 3$. Hence, $km = 15$.

7. **The correct answer is (B).** Calling the side x, then the entire area including the path is $(x + 2)^2$. The area of the garden is x^2. The difference is the area of the path. Thus:

$$(x + 2)^2 - x^2 = 80$$
$$x^2 + 4x + 4 - x^2 = 80$$
$$4x + 4 = 80$$
$$4x = 76; x = 19$$

8. **The correct answer is (E).** The number can certainly be odd and divisible by 3, because $9^2 + 9 = 90$. It can also be even, because $4^2 + 4 = 20$. Hence (E) is correct.

9. **The correct answer is (C).** The fact that 7 more than x is 1 less than twice x means that $7 + x = 2x - 1$; $8 = x$. If x is 8, then in this group, only $\frac{7}{16}$ lies between $\frac{3}{8} = \frac{6}{16}$ and $\frac{4}{8} = \frac{8}{16}$.

10. **The correct answer is (A).** The midpoint has coordinates that are the average of the end points; that is, (3,3). Hence, the triangle is an isosceles right triangle with legs of length 3 and area $\frac{1}{2}bh = (3)(3) = 4.5$.

Chapter 8

Quantitative Comparisons

Get the Scoop On . . .

- Proven strategies for scoring high on quantitative comparisons
- Shortcuts for saving time and minimizing complex calculations
- How the "plug-in" technique can help you decipher unknown quantities
- The most common traps set by the test-makers and how to avoid them

THE TEST CAPSULE

What's the Big Idea?

You'll be given two quantities—that is, numbers, formulas, or other statements that define a value. You have to decide how the quantities compare with one another: whether one quantity is greater than the other, the quantities are equal, or you've been given too little information to decide.

How Many?

Your SAT will probably have a total of fifteen quantitative comparisons. They'll appear together in one of the Math sections, where they'll be fifteen of the twenty-five total questions in the section.

How Much Do They Count?

Quantitative comparisons are fifteen out of sixty total math questions. They count as 25 percent of your overall math score.

How Much Time Should They Take?

You need to answer quantitative comparisons at a rate of 1 per minute. The usual batch of fifteen quantitative comparisons should take you 15 minutes.

What's the Best Strategy?

Don't sweat the details! Remember, these aren't conventional math problems: You aren't required to find the *exact* value of any quantity. All you need is enough information to determine which quantity is greater—and in most cases you can do that with approximate values or with *no definite values at all.*

What's the Worst Pitfall?

Making assumptions about information you haven't been given. Only a small handful of facts is provided for each QC item; you have to make the comparison based solely on these data. Be careful not to unconsciously assume additional facts or details that the test-makers haven't explicitly provided.

THE OFFICIAL DESCRIPTION

What They Are

Quantitative comparisons test your ability to recognize the relationships between pairs of mathematical quantities. You'll be given quantities in two columns, called Column A and Column B. Your job is to decide whether the quantity in Column A is greater, the quantity in Column B is greater, the two quantities are equal, or the information given is not enough to determine which quantity is greater.

Where They Are

In the typical SAT, you'll have three Math sections. Two will be 30 minutes long; one will be 15 minutes long. One of the 30-minute sections will include a batch of quantitative comparisons, which generally appear at the start of the section, before a batch of grid-in problems. Reminder: the test-makers claim the right to change the format at any time! However, the typical format we just described is what you're most likely to encounter.

What They Measure

Unlike the other math questions on the exam, quantitative comparisons don't require you to figure out the exact answer to any question. In fact, for many QC items, you'll have no calculations to do: you'll find that estimating, rounding, eliminating needless information, and other tricks which you'll learn in this chapter can allow you to choose the right answer without knowing the precise value of either quantity. Rather than your skill at calculating, QC items test your knowledge of mathematical concepts and your quickness, creativity, and accuracy at applying those concepts.

What They Cover

The math areas tested on the SAT, including the QC items, are those studied by virtually every high school student: arithmetic, basic algebra, and plane and coordinate geometry. Many advanced and specialized math topics are *not* covered on the SAT, including trigonometry and calculus. See Appendix B, "The Insider's SAT Math Review," for a detailed review of the math concepts most frequently tested on the exam.

The Directions

> **Directions:** Questions 1–15 each consist of two quantities in boxes, one in Column A and one in Column B. You are to compare the two quantities and write the correct answer next to the question number.
>
> A if the quantity in Column A is greater;
> B if the quantity in Column B is greater;
> C if the two quantities are equal;
> D if the relationship cannot be determined from the information given.
>
> AN E RESPONSE WILL NOT BE SCORED.
>
> Notes:
>
> In some questions, information is given about one or both of the quantities to be compared. In such cases, the given information is centered above the two columns and is not boxed.
>
> In a given question, a symbol that appears in both columns represents the same thing in Column A as it does in Column B.
>
> Letters such as x, n, and k stand for real numbers.

THE INSIDER'S REPORT: STRATEGIES THAT REALLY WORK

Make the Columns Look Alike

Start by doing whatever it takes to make the columns resemble one another. Only when the columns look alike—and therefore are comparable—can you easily tell which is greater. Here's a simple example:

Column A	Column B
Percent that a is of c	11

(Centered information: a is 30% of b; b is 40% of c)

First, let's be clear what you're looking at. This question starts with two lines of information that is centered between Column A and Column B. This information isn't part of either column but, instead, is provided to help you interpret the values given in the columns. Assume that this information is true and that it applies to whatever quantities appear in the columns underneath.

Now look at the two quantities that you're supposed to compare. Column A *describes* a quantity: the "percent that *a* is of *c*." Column B, by contrast, *states* a quantity, in the simplest possible form: it's the integer 11. Can you tell, at a glance, which is greater? Probably not. The reason is that the two quantities are named in terms so different that they're not readily comparable.

To compare them, you need to make them look alike. Since Column B is already stated in the simplest possible form, your plan should be to make Column A look like Column B—turn it into a simple number as well. To do that, you'll have to use your math skills. Since the shared information tells you that *a* is 30% of *b* and *b* is 40% of *c*, you can tell that *a* must be 30% of 40% of *c*. What is 30% of 40%? Multiply it out, using your calculator if you like:

$$.30 \times .40 = .12$$

You can tell from the information given that *a* is 12% of *c*. Now we have a quantity for Column A—12—which can easily be compared with the quantity in Column B. Since 12 is greater than 11, Column A is greater, and choice (A) is the answer for this question.

Here's another example:

FYI

When in doubt, try something! It may not be obvious what the test-makers want you to do with either quantity. If so, start messing around with the quantities, using whatever mathematical techniques strike you as natural or logical. Chances are good that some method you've used dozens of times in math class will yield the result the test-makers are looking for.

Column A	**Column B**
x and y are negative	
$(x + y)(x + y)$	$x^2 + y^2$

In this question, neither column contains a quantity that's easy to measure—especially since we don't know the value of either unknown, *x* or *y*. But don't despair! It may still be possible to figure out how the two quantities compare, if we can make them appear similar and therefore comparable.

Which column can more easily be made to resemble the other? In this case, you can probably see how Column A can be made to look something like Column B. Two quantities contained in parentheses, like those in Column A, are practically crying out to be multiplied together. And you can probably tell that, when you multiply them out, you'll end up with a quantity that includes x^2 and y^2, not unlike Column B. Here's what happens to the comparison when the multiplication in Column A is carried out:

Column A	Column B
$x^2 + 2xy = y^2$	$x^2 + y^2$

We've used a basic algebra process here: when you multiply two binomials, like those in Column A, you end up with a trinomial like the one we've now created. See Appendix B, "The Insider's SAT Math Review," if this procedure seems unfamiliar.

Now the two columns resemble one another, and we can compare them more easily. But, in this case, to determine which is greater, we need to use the second basic strategy for quantitative comparisons.

Eliminate Whatever the Columns Share

Remember, you're interested in figuring out the *difference* between the two quantities. That means that anything that the two quantities have in common—anything they share—is *irrelevant.*

Here's an analogy. Suppose you're trying to decide which of two used cars to buy. Also suppose that both cars are four-door models, about the same size, made in the same model year, with roughly the same amount of mileage on them. Since all of those factors are the *same*, they are all *irrelevant* to your choice—none of these will help you decide which car is better. Instead, you'll have to choose based on ways in which the two cars *differ*—price, for example, or appearance.

In the same way, when comparing two mathematical quantities on the SAT, you can eliminate as irrelevant anything both quantities share. Let's go back to the item we've been considering, with Column A transformed by having been multiplied out:

Column A	Column B
$x^2 + 2xy + y^2$	$x^2 + y^2$

At a glance, you can see that both columns now have two terms in common: x^2 and y^2. We don't know the numeric value of either of these terms, since we don't know the value of either x or y. Nonetheless, we can eliminate both x^2 and y^2 from the comparison, since they appear in both columns. The *difference* between the columns can't be contained in what they have in common!

Once we eliminate—remove—these two terms from both sides of the comparison, we can compare what remains:

FYI

Making the two columns resemble each other often requires you to simplify one or both quantities—for example, by reducing a fraction to lowest terms. It may also require you to translate one quantity so that both quantities are expressed in the same terms. For example, you might have to translate pounds into ounces, a fraction into a percentage, or minutes into hours.

Column A	Column B
$2xy$	0

Having eliminated x^2 and y^2 from Column A, all that's left ther is $2xy$. And having made the same elimination from Column B, all that's left there is nothing—zero! So to answer the question, we simply have to decide whether $2xy$ is greater, less than, or equal to zero.

FYI

In many QC items, it's impossible to determine the precise value of one or both quantities. This may tempt you to opt for answer (D), "the relationship cannot be determined." Not necessarily! Even imprecise or vague quantities can sometimes be compared. You know the Sears Tower is taller than your local post office, even if you don't know the actual height of either building.

By using the information given above the two quantities, you can determine this. If both unknowns are negative, then when the two are multiplied together, the result is positive. (A negative times a negative is always a positive—a basic algebra principle you need to remember.) So xy is positive, and $2xy$, of course, will also be positive—which means it is greater than zero. So the answer to this question is A: Column A is greater than Column B. The quickest way to determine this is to eliminate what both columns have in common and then compare what's left—which is easy.

Here's another example of the principle of eliminating what the columns share:

Column A	Column B
$35 \times 112 \times 76$	$78 \times 56 \times 2 \times 35$

Whatever you do, *don't* start multiplying. It's time-consuming and may lead to a careless mistake—especially if you start rushing. QC items are generally written to minimize calculations, and this question is no exception; you can answer it with no figuring whatever. Here's how.

First, notice that both "multiplication chains" have one factor in common—35. Eliminate it from both sides, either mentally or by physically crossing it out with your pencil. Now the comparison looks like this:

Column A	Column B
112×76	$78 \times 56 \times 2$

Now what? Do you have to start multiplying after all? Not if you're observant. The two columns now have something else in common. The term 112 in Column A is exactly the same in value as the two terms 56×2 in Column B! (You can probably "see" this even without calculating it.) So these values can be eliminated from the two columns as well. All that's left to compare now is:

Column A	Column B
76	78

Obviously, Column B is greater. Not a single multiplication is required.

One more example:

Column A	Column B
The number of prime numbers between 10 and 30	The number of prime numbers between 20 and 40

To answer this question, you need to figure out how many prime numbers there are between 10 and 30 and how many there are between 20 and 40—right? Not quite. Notice that there is an area of overlap between the range of numbers included in these two groups. Primes between 20 and 30 would fall into *both* categories. Therefore, they can be ignored! All you really need to consider is the primes between 10 and 20 (Column A) and the primes between 30 and 40 (Column B).

If you know the definition of a prime number—a number that can be evenly divided only by itself and 1—enumerating them isn't too hard. The primes between 10 and 20 are 11, 13, 17, and 19. Primes must be odd, of course, since all even numbers are divisible by two. The primes between 30 and 40 are 31 and 37. There are more primes between 10 and 20, so the answer to this item is choice (A). Notice the time we saved by, in effect, ignoring half of the question—the half that covered the overlap!

Plug in Values for X

Many quantitative comparisons include algebra-style unknowns: x, y, a, n, and so on. Often the QC item itself will naturally suggest some algebraic operation; we saw an example in the second problem above, where it seemed natural to multiply out the binomials so as to produce a quantity that would be easier to compare with its counterpart.

Once you've taken all the obvious steps, however—multiplying to remove parentheses, reducing and simplifying fractions, consolidating like terms, and so on—you will usually still have the mysterious unknown quantity to reckon with. When this happens, take a few seconds to try plugging in a couple of possible values for the unknown and see what happens. Often the correct answer will jump out at you as a result.

Here's an example:

Column A	**Column B**
$3r - 4 > 11$	
5	r

Of course, you need to understand the inequality sign here: it means, "is greater than," since it points toward the right side. If $3r - 4$ is greater than 11, what is a possible value of r? Could it be greater than the quantity you're supposed to compare it to, which is 5? Try plugging in an arbitrary value—6, for example—in place of r in the original inequality, and see whether it works:

$$3(6) - 4 > 11$$
$$18 - 4 > 11$$
$$14 > 11$$

FYI

On the real exam, you will have time to plug in possible values on most QC items. The math calculations are deliberately kept simple, because the test-makers are mainly concerned with whether you grasp the underlying arithmetic concepts. So unless you encounter an unusually complicated problem, don't hesitate to plug in numbers—on most QC items you can do the figuring in your head within a few seconds.

Yes, that's correct—14 is greater than 11; so r could equal 6. But to make sure choice (B) is the right answer, also try plugging in a value of r that is less than 5:

$$3(4) - 4 > 11$$
$$12 - 4 > 11$$
$$8 > 11 \text{ ? NO WAY}$$

Or try making r equal to 5 itself:

$$3(5) - 4 > 11$$
$$15 - 4 > 11$$
$$11 > 11 \text{ ? NOPE}$$

The value 11 is not greater than *itself*. So by plugging in three possible values for the unknown—one greater, one less than, and one equal to the quantity given in the "opposite" column—you can determine that the answer to this question is choice (B).

Note: We've printed out the steps in our calculations here just for clarity's sake, to make it easy for you to follow. But notice how easy the calculations are. Most likely, you won't have to write anything on the test paper at all.

Here's one more example of plugging in numbers:

Column A	**Column B**
$0 < m < 1$	
m^2	m^3

Again, we don't know the precise value of the unknown m. It doesn't matter. If you're not sure which of the two comparable quantities is greater, plug in a possible value and see what happens. In this case, we know that m is a positive fraction less than 1. Let's plug in the simplest possible value for m, $\frac{1}{2}$. That will make the calculations a breeze. If m is $\frac{1}{2}$, then $m^2 = \left(\frac{1}{2}\right)\left(\frac{1}{2}\right) = \frac{1}{4}$, and $m^3 = \left(\frac{1}{2}\right)\left(\frac{1}{2}\right)\left(\frac{1}{2}\right) = \frac{1}{8}$. Since $\frac{1}{4}$ is greater than $\frac{1}{8}$, Column A is greater.

But before filling in the answer space, stop and ask—will the answer be different if the value of m is different? In this case, no. If m is $\frac{1}{4}$, $\frac{3}{5}$, $\frac{11}{26}$, or any other positive fraction less than 1, the same relationship will exist—the value continues to go down as the fraction is multiplied repeatedly by itself. (That fact is what the question is designed to test.) But always ask that crucial question—will the answer be different if the value of the unknown is different when you plug in a number? That way, you won't be misled by an answer that just *happens* to be true with a particular value for x.

THE INSIDER'S REPORT: THE BEST TIPS

Memorize the Answer System

You should practice quantitative comparisons enough before the day of the test so that the weird multiple-choice answer system begins to feel like second nature. You shouldn't have to read the directions or spend any time during the section thinking about what choices (A), (B), (C), and (D) stand for. And be sure never to absent-mindedly fill in choice (E) for any QC item. That's an automatic wrong answer.

Look for Math Shortcuts

We've already seen that most quantitative comparisons require few calculations and simple ones. This is deliberate—the test-makers are eager to measure your understanding of the underlying concepts rather than your ability to handle the calculations. And keeping the math simple allows them to throw more questions at you in the same amount of time. So avoid lengthy or complicated figuring; if a question seems to require it, you've probably overlooked a built-in shortcut.

Here's an example:

Column A	**Column B**
The average (arithmetic mean) of 5 integers *m*, *n*, *o*, *p*, and *q* is 19.	
The average (arithmetic mean) of *m*, *n*, *o*, *p*, *q* and 17.5.	19

On the principle of "When in doubt, try something," your first instinct may be to start working with the definition of "average." As you know, an average is calculated by taking the sum of a set of numbers and dividing it by the number of numbers in the set. In this case, if five integers have an average of 19, it would be possible to calculate the sum of those integers by multiplying the average by the number of numbers ($19 \times 5 = 95$). Then you could go ahead and calculate the sum of the set of six integers shown in Column A, with the sixth integer 17.5 thrown in, and finally divide that new sum by 6 to come up with the new average.

But stop! None of this is necessary. Look at the quantities being compared. All you need to figure out is whether the new average is more or less than 19—the old average. Now, what makes the new average different from the old average? It's simply the new member of the set, the sixth integer 17.5 And will that new member raise or lower the overall average? Since 17.5 is below the old average, it will drag the average down—it will lower it. Therefore, *with no calculations at all*, you can see that the answer will be B; the old average, 19, is greater than the new average, *whatever it is*.

THE INSIDER'S REPORT: THE MOST IMPORTANT WARNINGS

Assume Nothing!

Quantitative comparisons are designed to test how quickly, creatively, and accurately you can think about a wide range of what might be called math situations. As you've seen, these situations can be drawn from every area of math: arithmetic, algebra, geometry, and word problems, enabling the test-makers to test your knowledge of techniques in all these areas. One key aspect of accuracy under these conditions is the ability to separate the *facts* you've been given from the *assumptions* you might make—which may or may not be correct.

FYI

You need to work QC items at the rate of one per minute. That's pretty fast, but it's doable, provided you don't get bogged down in lengthy calculations. If you find, after examining an item for fifteen seconds, that you can't see a way of tackling it, skip it for the moment—put an X next to the item in your question booklet and return to it at the end of the section.

Let's consider a few examples.

Column A	Column B
In 1990, the price of a certain item was \$50.00.	
The price of the same item in 1998	\$50.00

It's tempting to answer this question based on what you know about the real world. Because of the economic phenomenon known as inflation, prices of most things tend to go up over time (though this is not true of everything: computers, for example, have consistently fallen in price during the 1980s and 1990s). Therefore, it's extremely likely that the certain item which cost \$50.00 in 1990 cost more in 1998. The right answer, in that case, would be choice (A).

The logic is tempting—and wrong. You can't assume that inflation applies to this item because you haven't been told to assume it. We're not in the real world now but rather in SAT territory, where only the facts as stated in the question can be assumed to be true. The correct answer for this item is choice (D)—the relationship can't be determined.

FYI

The real meaning of answer choice (D) is slightly hidden by its wording ("the relationship cannot be determined"). Don't think of it as meaning, "I don't know what the answer is." Instead, think of it as meaning, "More than one answer could be true." If any two answers—(A) and (B), (A) and (C), or (B) and (C)—are both possible, then the correct answer for the item is (D).

Column A	Column B
Parking is legal on Pine Street only on even-numbered calendar days.	
Number of legal parking days in a calendar month	15

Obviously, the number of legal parking days in a calendar month will be somewhere around 15—since half the days are even-numbered days, and most months have around 30 days. But which month are we talking about? The question doesn't specify, so let's think it through. The month could be January or July, with 31 days, of which 15 are even-numbered (the 2nd, the 4th, the 6th, . . . the 30th); it could be June or September, with 30 days, of which the same 15 are even-numbered. The correct answer then would be (C): The number of legal parking days (Column A) would be equal to the number 15 (Column B). But the month could also be February, which has only 28 days (except in leap year), of which just 14 are even-numbered. In that case, the correct answer would be (B).

So there are two possible answers—(C) and (B)—and we don't know which is correct, because the question doesn't tell us. Sure, there are 11 chances out of 12 that the month is *not* February, but we can't make that assumption. Since choice (C) is correct under one possible assumption and choice (B) is correct under another, the correct answer is choice (D). It cannot be determined.

One more example of the danger of making assumptions:

Column A	**Column B**
On a certain day, 30% of the girls were absent and 50% of the boys were present in a history class.	
Number of girls present	Number of boys present

From the information given, you can tell that the percentage of girls present was greater than the percentage of boys present (70 versus 50). But notice what you are being asked to compare: not the percentage of girls and boys present, but the *number* present. We know nothing about this, because we don't know how many girls or boys were enrolled in the history class. You might, without much thought, assume that the number of girls and boys is approximately equal—but that's simply an assumption, with no special validity. The correct answer for this item is choice (D); it cannot be determined.

Strictly speaking, there are a few, a very few, facts you can safely assume on QC items:

- Everyday facts like the number of inches in a foot and the number of days in a week are fair game.
- The basic formulas from geometry (for calculating the area of a circle or a triangle) are not only assumed but provided as "Reference Information" at the start of each SAT Math section. You should know them by heart, however.
- And you can assume, as the test-makers state, that all unknowns like x stand for real numbers as opposed to imaginary numbers, a special kind of number used only in certain quite specialized and advanced math operations.

Other than these facts, however, you should avoid assuming anything—as you've seen, it's dangerous.

When There's No Unknown, Don't Guess Choice (D)

On QC items, as on every other kind of question, there may be times when you have to guess. Perhaps you will find yourself running out of time but with several questions left to answer, or perhaps a couple of items will call for math skills you just can't recall. General guessing strategy for quantitative comparisons should be much the same as for other question types: follow a hunch, if you have one; when you can, eliminate answers and guess from what remains.

However, there's one special rule about guessing that applies only to quantitative comparisons. On about one third of QC items, no unknown quantity is involved: there is no algebraic x or n, nor is there any geometric quantity (the degree measure of an angle or the length of a line segment, say) that is unknowable. Whenever this is true, the answer cannot be choice (D). Even if you can't figure out which quantity is greater, it is theoretically possible to figure it out—so choice (D) is an incorrect option.

Here's an example:

Column A	Column B
Price of a \$320 stereo after a discount of 15%	\$275

If you've run out of time, or forgotten how to multiply by a percentage, you may not be able to answer this question. Since \$320 × 85% = \$272, the answer is choice (B). However, the question itself does not contain any unknown quantity. Therefore, if you have to guess on a question like this, don't guess choice (D). Since there is no unknown, only choices (A), (B), and (C) are possible.

FYI

Be careful about assumptions when plugging in numbers for an unknown quantity. We're so accustomed to the counting numbers—1, 2, 3, and so on—that we easily forget that x may equal zero, a negative number, or a fraction. Any of these possibilities may change the outcome of the comparison. So when plugging in possible values, be sure to include one of each of these number types, unless they have been specifically ruled out.

JUST THE FACTS

- Quantitative Comparisons feature a challenging multiple-choice answer system, which you must understand and memorize.
- Do whatever you can to make the two quantities to be compared look as similar as possible.
- Simplify the comparison by eliminating what both quantities have in common.
- Use math shortcuts whenever you can.
- Never assume any information not explicitly stated in the question.

PRACTICE, PRACTICE, PRACTICE: QUANTITATIVE COMPARISON EXERCISES

Instructions

The following exercises will give you a chance to practice the skills and strategies you've just learned for tackling quantitative comparisons. As with all practice exercises, work under true testing conditions. Complete each exercise in a single sitting. Eliminate distractions (TV, music) and clear away notes and reference materials. Time yourself with a stopwatch or kitchen timer, or have someone else time you. If you run out of time before answering all the questions, stop and draw a line under the last question you finished. Then go ahead and tackle the remaining questions. When you are done, score yourself based only on the questions you finished in the allotted time.

Circle the letter of the correct response. In addition, any time your answer is a guess—that is, any time you enter a response about which you are not certain—circle the number of that question. After you've completed the exercises, count the number of circled items and the number of these items that you answered correctly. Then divide the number of correct answers by the number of circled items. The result is your Guessing Quotient (G.Q.). If your G.Q. is higher than .20, you will probably boost your overall score by guessing on the real SAT.

Understanding Your Scores

0–3 correct: A poor performance. Study this chapter again, as well as the Insider's SAT Math Review (Appendix B).

4–6 correct: A below-average score. Study this chapter again, as well as all portions of the Insider's SAT Math Review (Appendix B) that cover topics you find unfamiliar or difficult.

7–9 correct: An average score. You may want to study this chapter again. Also be sure you are managing your time wisely (as explained in Chapter 3) and avoiding errors due to haste or carelessness.

10–12 correct: An above-average score. Depending on your personal target score and your strength on other mathematical question types, you may or may not want to devote additional time to quantitative comparisons.

13–15 correct: An excellent score. You are probably ready to perform well on SAT quantitative comparison items.

EXERCISE 1

15 Questions

Time—15 Minutes

Directions: Compare the two quantities and write the correct answer next to the question number.

A if the quantity in Column A is greater;
B if the quantity in Column B is greater;
C if the two quantities are equal;
D if the relationship cannot be determined from the information given.

	Column A	Column B

The original price of a certain computer was $1,200.

	Column A	Column B
1.	The price of the computer after two 10% markdowns.	The price of the computer after a 20% markdown
2.	The remainder when 3,458,064 is divided by 4	The remainder when 5,559,063 is divided by 9
3.	x	$2x$

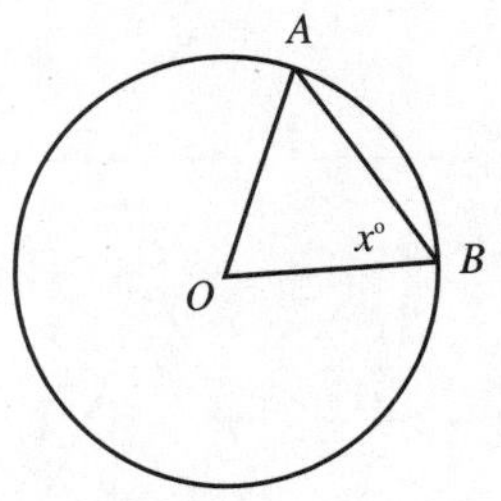

O is the center of the circle with diameter 10.
The perimeter of AOB = 16

	Column A	Column B
4.	x	60

	Column A	Column B

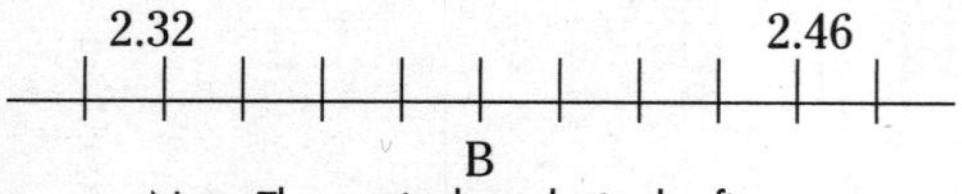

Note: The vertical marks in the figure above are equally spaced.

	Column A	Column B
5.	2.37	B

a, b, and c are positive, and $c < b$

	Column A	Column B
6.	The arithmetic mean (average) of a and b	The arithmetic mean (average) of b and c

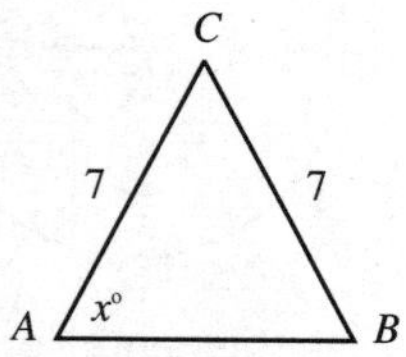

$x = 50$

	Column A	Column B
7.	AB	7

	Column A	Column B

a is chosen from the set $\{-1,-6,3\}$
b is chosen from the set $\{-4,4,5\}$

	Column A	Column B
8.	The greatest possible value of $\frac{a}{b}$	1.5

$0 < n < 1$

	Column A	Column B
9.	$3n^3$	3^3n

$10 - x > x$

	Column A	Column B
10.	x	5

	Column A	Column B
	$A \bigstar B = \dfrac{A}{A + B}$	
11.	$2 \star 4$	$(-2) \star 4$
	$y = \dfrac{1}{2}$	
12.	1.2	$y^0 + y^2$
	The number of miles from *A* to *B* by train is 42. The number of miles from *B* to *C* by train is 62.	
13.	The number of stations between *A* and *B*.	The number of stations between *B* and *C*.

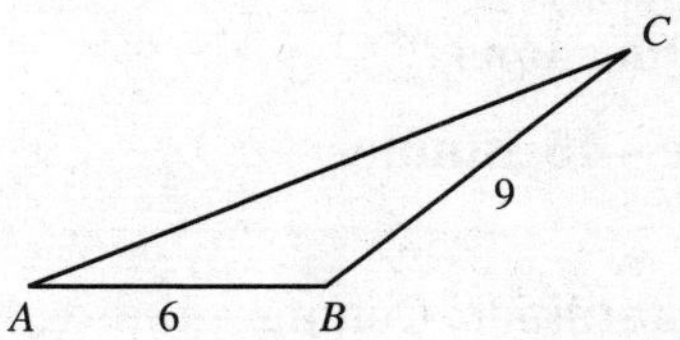

	Column A	Column B
14.	The area of ΔABC	27
	$x \neq -1$	
15.	$\dfrac{3x + 1}{x + 1}$	2

EXERCISE 2

15 Questions

Time—15 Minutes

Directions: Compare the two quantities and write the correct answer next to the question number.

A if the quantity in Column A is greater;
B if the quantity in Column B is greater;
C if the two quantities are equal;
D if the relationship cannot be determined from the information given.

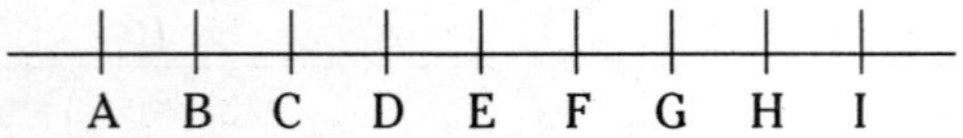

Note: The vertical marks in the figure above are equally spaced.

	Column A	Column B
1.	The ratio of AE to BD	The ratio of BH to CF
2.	A coat that cost \$200 wholesale sold at a 40% markup.	A coat listed at \$300 on sale for 10% off.
3.	x^3	x^2

Arnold's car used 22 gallons of gas last week.
Marla's car used 16 gallons of gas last week.

	Column A	Column B
4.	The number of miles Arnold drove last week.	The number of miles Marla drove last week.

Column A	Column B

Of 42 horses in a stable, $\frac{1}{3}$ are black, $\frac{1}{6}$ are white, and the rest are brown.

	Column A	Column B
5.	The number of brown horses	21

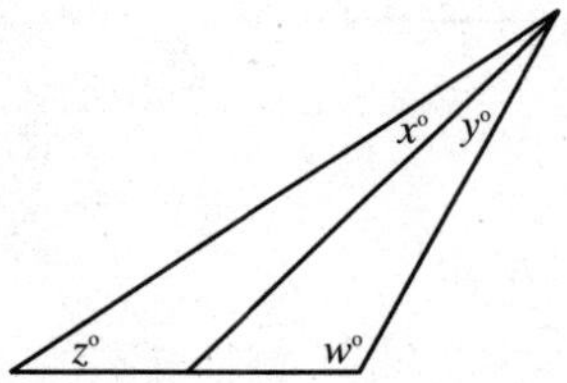

$x + z = 50$

	Column A	Column B
6.	$y + w$	130

Column A	Column B

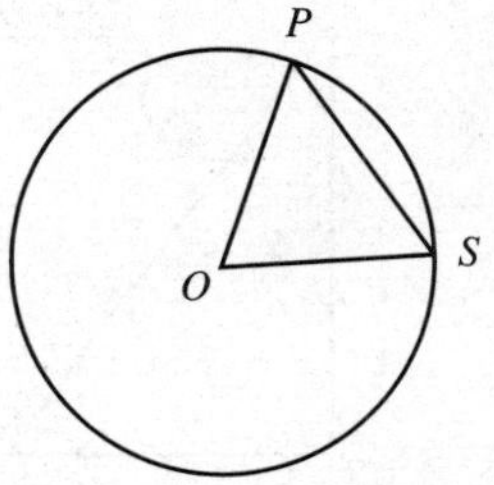

Arc *PS* in the diagram above has a degree measure of 62°. The diameter of the circle is 18.

	Column A	Column B
7.	The length of chord *PS*	9

Five more than twice a number n is 17.

	Column A	Column B
8.	3 less than n	2 less than $\frac{1}{2}n$

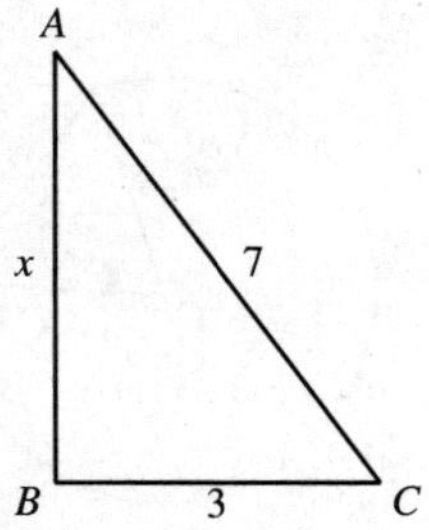

	Column A	Column B
9.	The area of ΔABC	9

$x + 6 > 7 > 2x$

	Column A	Column B
10.	3	x

$5r - 2s = 2$

	Column A	Column B
11.	$(-1)^{(10r - 4s)}$	$(-1)^{(15r - 6s)}$

	Column A	Column B
12.	$(x - 1)^2$	$x^2 - 1$

Point $P = (-1,2)$
Point $Q = (3,5)$
Point $R = (2,3)$

	Column A	Column B
13.	The slope of PQ	The slope of QR

$x \bigstar y = 2xy + x$

	Column A	Column B
14.	$(-3) \bigstar (-2)$	$(-2) \bigstar (-3)$

$x > 0$

	Column A	Column B
15.	$\frac{3x + 1}{x + 1}$	3

EXERCISE 3

15 Questions

Time—15 Minutes

Directions: Compare the two quantities and write the correct answer next to the question number.

A if the quantity in Column A is greater;
B if the quantity in Column B is greater;
C if the two quantities are equal;
D if the relationship cannot be determined from the information given.

	Column A	Column B
1.	The cost of 12 cans of peas at 34¢ per can	The cost of 12 cans of corn at 3 cans for $1.00
2.	The remainder when 6,037,854 is divided by 6	The remainder when 3,521,912 is divided by 8

$$x - 5 = 2$$

	Column A	Column B
3.	$x + 3$	11

$$xy^2 = 4$$
$$x = 9$$
$$y > 0$$

	Column A	Column B
4.	y	$\frac{2}{3}$

	Column A	Column B
	$n > 7$	
5.	$\frac{n}{6}$	$\frac{6}{n}$

	Column A	Column B
6.	The perimeter of a square with an area of 36 square feet	The circumference of a circle with a radius of of 6

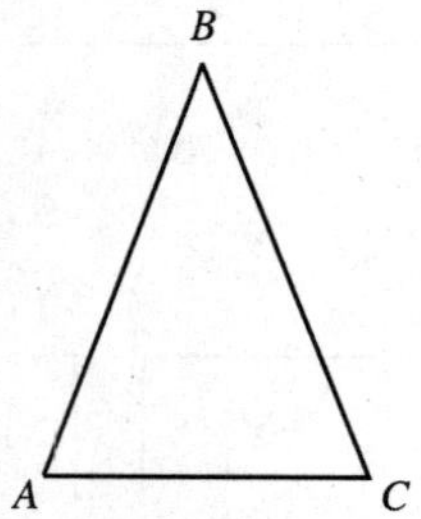

$AB = BC$

	Column A	Column B
7.	AC	AB

	Column A	Column B
	$a > b$	
8.	$(a - b)^2$	$a^2 - b^2$

Seven less than half a number k is 5

	Column A	Column B
9.	One third of k	8

$$s \star t = \frac{s}{s + t}$$

	Column A	Column B
10.	$2 \star 3$	$\frac{2}{3}$

Column A	Column B

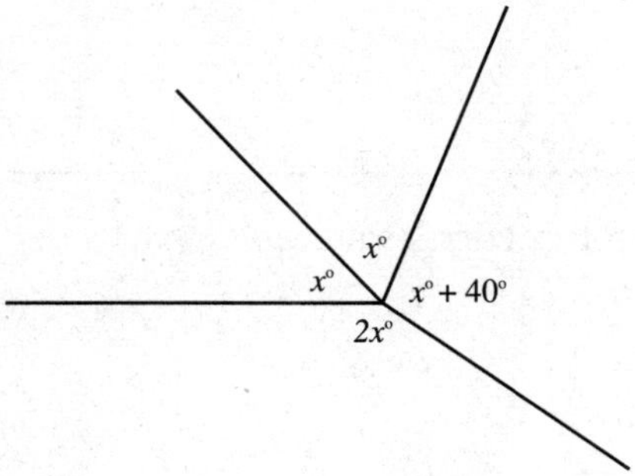

11. | x | 65 |
|---|---|

A circle of diameter d and a square of side s have the same area.

12. | s | d |
|---|---|

$t > 0$

13. | $\frac{t^2 + 5t}{t}$ | $t + 5$ |
|---|---|

Column A	Column B

$$x^2 + 2y^2 = 1$$
$$x = \frac{1}{2}$$

14. | $\lvert y \rvert$ | $\frac{1}{2}$ |
|---|---|

Marbles are drawn at random from a bag. A blue marble is drawn three times in a row.

15. | The number of blue marbles in the bag. | The number of red marbles in the bag. |
|---|---|

EXERCISE 4

15 Questions

Time—15 Minutes

Directions: Compare the two quantities and write the correct answer next to the question number.

A if the quantity in Column A is greater;
B if the quantity in Column B is greater;
C if the two quantities are equal;
D if the relationship cannot be determined from the information given.

	Column A	Column B
1.	$\frac{4}{7}$	$\frac{3}{5}$

$0 < n < 1$

	Column A	Column B
2.	$n \times n \times n$	$n + n + n$
3.	n^3	$1000n^2$

In a group of 18 students studying Spanish or German, 12 are studying Spanish and 4 are studying both languages.

	Column A	Column B
4.	The number taking Spanish, but not German.	The number taking German, but not Spanish.

Column A	Column B

$x > 2$

	Column A	Column B
5.	x^2	$2x$

	Column A	Column B
6.	The area of a circle with diameter 10.	The area of a square with diagonal 12.

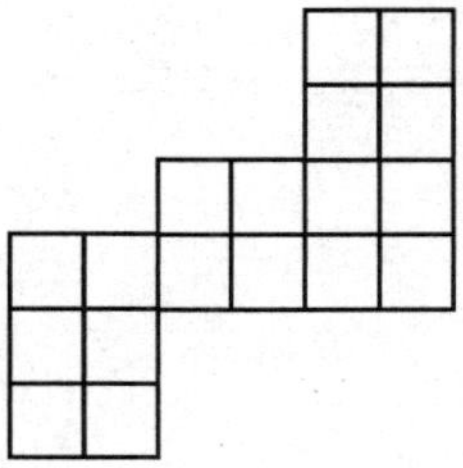

The area of the region shown is 72. All the small squares are the same size.

	Column A	Column B
7.	The perimeter of the region shown	50

Column A	Column B

$x = 2$

	Column A	Column B
8.	1.10	$x^0 + x^{-4}$

$xy = 21$
$x < 3$

	Column A	Column B
9.	7	y

$x < 0 < y$

	Column A	Column B
10.	$\frac{x}{y} - \frac{y}{x}$	$\frac{x}{y}$

	Column A	Column B
	p percent of 120 is less than 90	
11.	p	80
	$x \neq -2$	
12.	$\frac{x}{x+2}$	$1 + \frac{x}{2}$
	$x < -2$	
13.	x^2	$-2x$

	Column A	Column B
	$x^2 + 2y^2 = 2$ $y = \frac{1}{2}$	
14.	$\lvert x \rvert$	1
15.	The median of the set 1, 2, 2, 2, 2, 3, 4, 4, 4, 4, 4	4

EXERCISE 5

15 Questions

Time—15 Minutes

Directions: Compare the two quantities and write the correct answer next to the question number.

A if the quantity in Column A is greater;
B if the quantity in Column B is greater;
C if the two quantities are equal;
D if the relationship cannot be determined from the information given.

	Column A	Column B
1.	$\frac{-6}{11}$	$\frac{13}{-22}$

$x < 0$ and $y > 0$

	Column A	Column B
2.	$-4x^4y^3$	0

To mail an airmail letter costs 60¢ for the first half ounce and 15¢ for each additional half ounce or fraction thereof.

	Column A	Column B
3.	The cost of mailing an airmail letter letter weighing 2.1 ounces	$1.20

$y > 0$

	Column A	Column B
4.	$9y - \frac{6y^2}{2y^2}$	$6y$

Column A	Column B

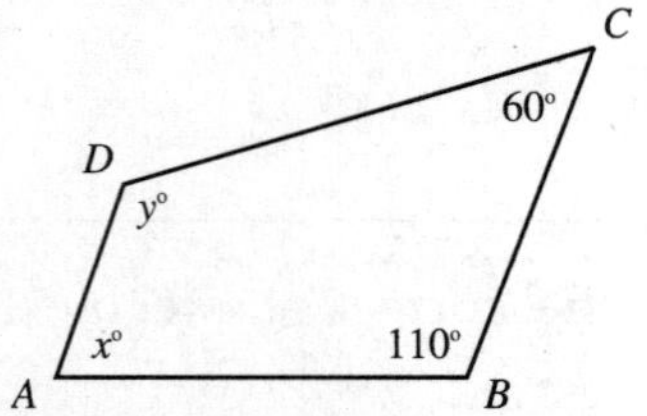

Note: Figure not drawn to scale

	Column A	Column B
5.	x	$180 - y$

	Column A	Column B
6.	The length of the hypotenuse of a right triangle with legs 6 and 8	The length of the longer leg of a right triangle with hypotenuse 11

Column A	Column B

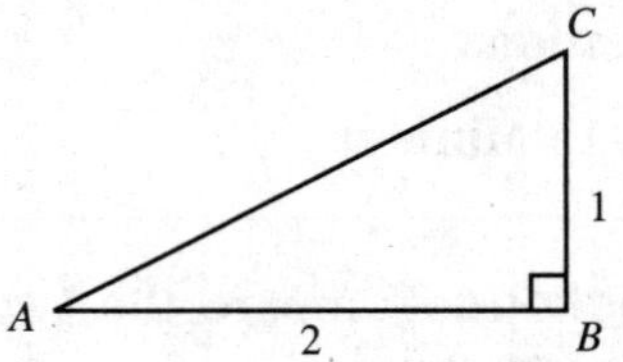

	Column A	Column B
7.	The perimeter of ΔABC	5

$$x^4 + 3y^2 = 0$$

	Column A	Column B
8.	$2x - 6y + 1$	1

$$x > 0$$

	Column A	Column B
9.	$x^2 + 3x$	$x + 3$

	Column A	Column B
	$x < y < 0$	
10.	$\frac{x}{y} \blacksquare \frac{y}{x}$	$\frac{x}{y}$

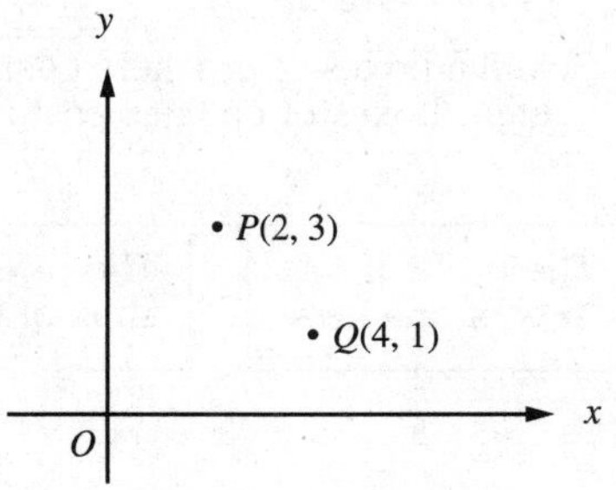

	Column A	Column B
11.	The distance from O to P	The distance from P to Q

	Column A	Column B
	$x^2 - x - 2 = 0$	
12.	x	-2

	Column A	Column B
13.	$\sqrt{13}$	$2\sqrt{3}$

	Column A	Column B
14.	The hypotenuse of a right triangle with legs of 3 and 5	6

$$x + 2y - 3z = 5$$
$$2x + 2y + 3z = 8$$

	Column A	Column B
15.	$9x + 12y$	39

EXERCISE 6

15 Questions

Time—15 Minutes

Directions: Compare the two quantities and write the correct answer next to the question number.

A if the quantity in Column A is greater;
B if the quantity in Column B is greater;
C if the two quantities are equal;
D if the relationship cannot be determined from the information given.

	Column A	Column B
1.	2.63	$\frac{29}{11}$
2.	$(2 + x)^2$	$(2x)^2$

Twelve boxes of crackers costs $4.80.
Eight boxes of cookies costs $4.00.

	Column A	Column B
3.	The price of one box of crackers	The price of one box of cookies

$5 - t = 3t$

	Column A	Column B
4.	$2t$	2

	Column A	Column B
	$m < n < 0$	
5.	$3m^2n^3$	0

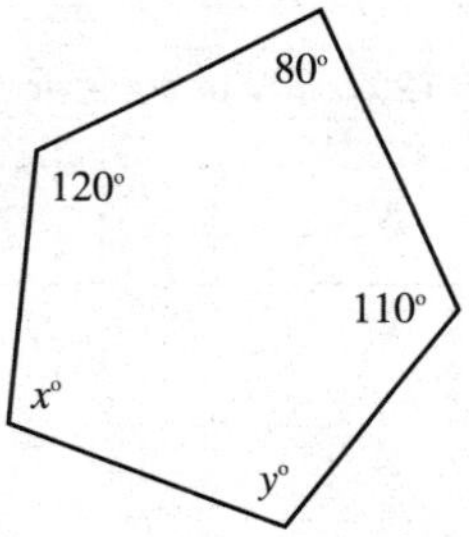

	Column A	Column B
6.	$x + y$	220

	Column A	Column B
	In a row of blocks, the only black block is the 7th block from the left end of the row and the 11th block from the right end of the row.	
7.	The number of blocks in the entire row	18

	Column A	Column B
	$S = \{1,2,2,2,3,5,6,7,8\}$	
8.	The mean minus the median of set S	The median minus the mode of set S

	Column A	Column B
	$x < -1$	
9.	$4x + x^2$	$4 + x$

	Column A	Column B
	$2n - 5 < 7$	
10.	n	6

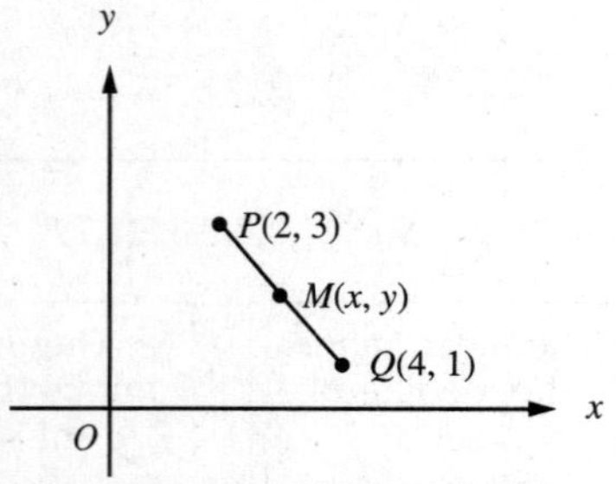

M is the midpoint of line segment *PQ*.

	Column A	Column B
11.	x	y

	Column A	Column B
	$4x - 2y = 2$	
12.	$(2x - y)^2$	1

	Column A	Column B
	$x = 2$	
13.	$\frac{x^2}{x^2 + 1}$	$\frac{x}{x + 1}$

	Column A	Column B
	12% of N is greater than 25.	
14.	N	200

	Column A	Column B
	The price of a hat and scarf together is \$38. The hat costs \$3 more than the scarf.	
15.	The price of the scarf	\$18

EXERCISE 7

15 Questions

Time—15 Minutes

Directions: Compare the two quantities and write the correct answer next to the question number.

A if the quantity in Column A is greater;
B if the quantity in Column B is greater;
C if the two quantities are equal;
D if the relationship cannot be determined from the information given.

	Column A	Column B
1.	$(234{,}906 - 457{,}219)(35)(-618)$	$(-2{,}356)(-89{,}021)(-3{,}125)$

	Column A	Column B
2.	$\frac{4}{5} \times M$	$\frac{2}{5} \times 2M$

$$3y - 6 = 2 - y$$

	Column A	Column B
3.	y^2	$2y$

$$x > y$$

	Column A	Column B
4.	x^2	y^2

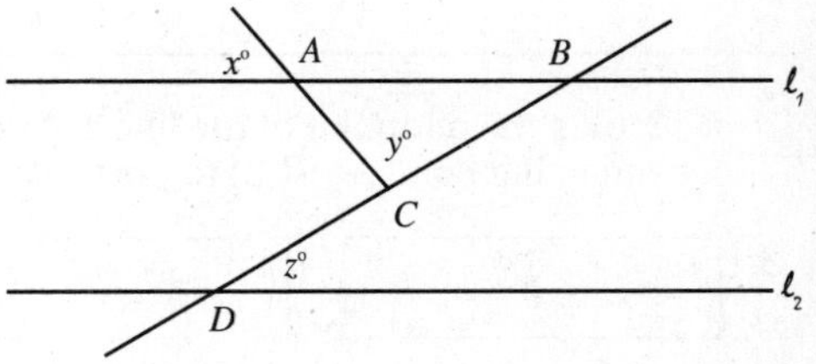

	Column A	Column B
5.	$x + y + z$	180

	Column A	Column B
	$r < s < t$ The average (arithmetic mean) of r, s, and t is 90.	
6.	The average of s and t	90

	Column A	Column B
	One side of a rectangle is the diameter of a circle. The opposite side of the rectangle is tangent to the circle.	
7.	The perimeter of the rectangle	The circumference of the circle

	Column A	Column B
	(2, 6) is the midpoint of the line segment connecting point $N(-1,3)$ to point $P(x, y)$.	
8.	y	$2x$

	Column A	Column B
	$x \neq \frac{1}{2}$	
9.	$\frac{x}{2x - 1}$	$\frac{1}{2} - x$

	Column A	Column B
	$3x + 9 > 6$	
10.	$x + 2$	1

	Column A	Column B
	The cost of 4 rolls, 6 muffins, and 3 loaves of bread is \$9.10. The cost of 2 rolls, 3 muffins, and a loaf of bread is \$3.90.	
11.	The cost of a roll	The cost of a muffin

	Column A	Column B
	$x \star y = x + 2y$	
12.	$2 \star n$	$n \star 2$

A marble is drawn at random from a box containing 4 red and 6 white marbles.

	Column A	Column B
13.	The probability that the marble is white	$\frac{2}{3}$

Three liters of a solution that is 10% salt is combined with five liters of a solution that is 20% salt.

	Column A	Column B
14.	The percentage of salt in the resulting mixture	15

	Column A	Column B
15.	$x^2 + 2x$	$(x + 1)^2$

EXERCISE 8

15 Questions

Time—15 Minutes

Directions: Compare the two quantities and write the correct answer next to the question number.

A if the quantity in Column A is greater;
B if the quantity in Column B is greater;
C if the two quantities are equal;
D if the relationship cannot be determined from the information given.

	Column A	Column B
1.	The price of $90 jacket after a markdown of 20%	The price of an $80 jacket after a markdown of 10%
2.	The greatest common divisor of 12 and 18	The number of proper divisors of 18

Apples sell for $2 a dozen. Pears sell for $3 a dozen.

	Column A	Column B
3.	The total cost of 18 apples and 24 pears	$9

$x > 0$

	Column A	Column B
4.	$\sqrt{x} + 2x$	$2\sqrt{x} + x$

Column A	Column B

$z + 3 = 5$

5. | $2z + 7$ | 10 |
|---|---|

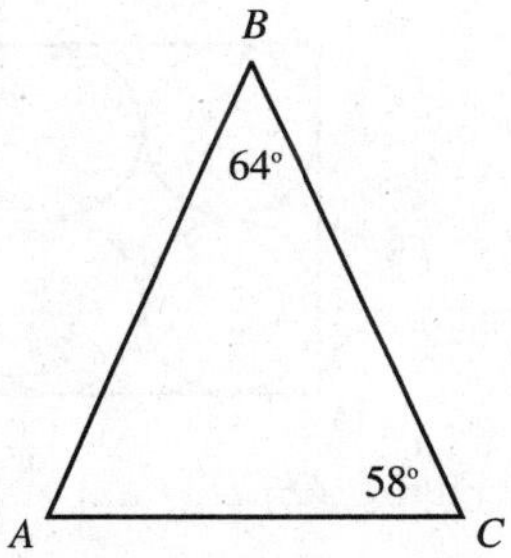

6. | AB | BC |
|---|---|

Column A	Column B

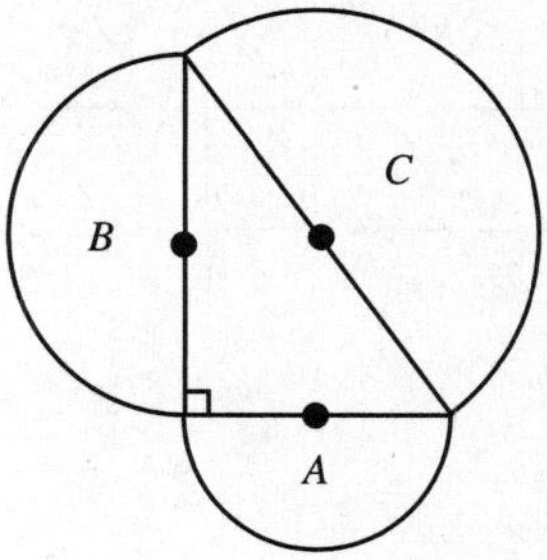

The sides of the triangle shown are the diameters of the semicircles.

7. | The area of semicircle C | The sum of the areas of semicircles A and B |
|---|---|

8. | The volume of a rectangular solid that is 6 feet long and has a square base of side 4 | The volume of a cylinder with a length of 7 feet and a diameter of 4 |
|---|---|

	Column A	Column B
	$\sqrt{5} \cdot \sqrt{x}$	
9.	$\sqrt{x}$	$2\sqrt{5}$

$$x = y + 3$$

$$y = 1 - z$$

	Column A	Column B
10.	x	z

The cost of 4 cookies, 6 doughnuts, and 3 boxes of doughnut holes is \$8.15. The cost of 2 cookies, 3 doughnuts, and 4 boxes of doughnut holes is \$7.20.

	Column A	Column B
11.	The cost of a box of doughnut holes	\$1.25

	Column A	Column B
	$m \star n = m^2 + 2n$	
12.	$2 \star 3$	10

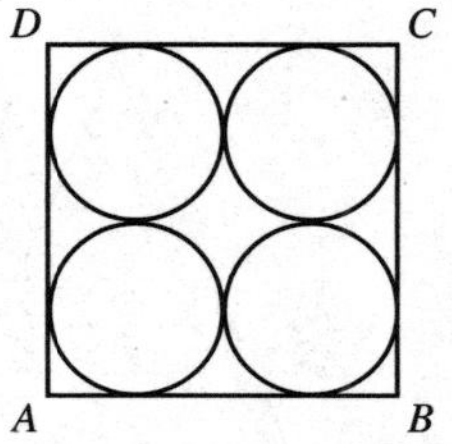

Figure *ABCD* is a 2×2 square.

	Column A	Column B
13.	The area inside the circles	The area inside the square but not inside the circles

	Column A	Column B
	$x > 0$	
14.	$x^2 + 4^2$	$(x + 4)^2$

	Column A	Column B
	n is a positive integer	
15.	The sum of the first n even integers divided by the sum of the first n odd integers	$\frac{n + 1}{n}$

EXERCISE 9

15 Questions

Time—15 Minutes

Directions: Compare the two quantities and write the correct answer next to the question number.

A if the quantity in Column A is greater;
B if the quantity in Column B is greater;
C if the two quantities are equal;
D if the relationship cannot be determined from the information given.

	Column A	Column B
1.	12% of 400	40% of 120

$$\frac{1.62}{x} = \frac{0.06}{0.003}$$

	Column A	Column B
2.	x	0.08

$$x - 5y = 12$$

	Column A	Column B
3.	$15y - 3x$	-35

A certain number *f* when multiplied by itself gives the same result as when it is added to itself.

	Column A	Column B
4.	n	1

	Column A	Column B

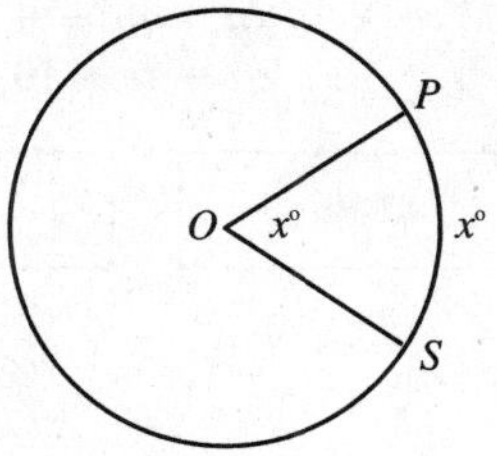

Arc $PS = 62°$

	Column A	Column B
5.	The length of chord PS	The radius of the circle

	Column A	Column B
6.	The number of 2 by 3 rectangles needed to cover a 12 by 12 square area	The number of 2 by 2 squares needed to cover a 6 by 16 rectangle area

a, b, and c are positive
$c < b$

	Column A	Column B
7.	The arithmetic mean (average) of a and b	The arithmetic mean (average) of a, b, and c

$b < 6$

	Column A	Column B
8.	The distance from $(3, b)$ to P (0, 2)	The distance from $(3, b)$ to Q (6, 10)

$x - 4 = -2$
$2 - y = 4$

	Column A	Column B
9.	x	y

	Column A	Column B
	$n = m - 2$ $m = s + 4$	
10.	n	s
	$\sqrt{6} \cdot \sqrt{3x} = \sqrt{30}$	
11.	x	2
	$x = 3$	
12.	$(-1)^{2x}$	$(-1)^{x+2}$

	Column A	Column B
	$2n - m = 6$ $2n + m = 10$	
13.	m	2
14.	$\frac{4 + 2x}{4}$	$2x$
	$xyz = 18$ $x < 0$	
15.	z	0

EXERCISE 10

15 Questions

Time—15 Minutes

Directions: Compare the two quantities and write the correct answer next to the question number.

A if the quantity in Column A is greater;
B if the quantity in Column B is greater;
C if the two quantities are equal;
D if the relationship cannot be determined from the information given.

	Column A	Column B
	The wholesale price of a compact disk player was $420.	
1.	$500	The price of the compact disk player after a 20% markup

	Column A	Column B
	$0 < x < 1$	
2.	$\sqrt{x}$	x^2

	Column A	Column B
	$A > B > 1$	
3.	A	AB

	Column A	Column B
4.	10% of $600	6% of $1,000

Column A	Column B

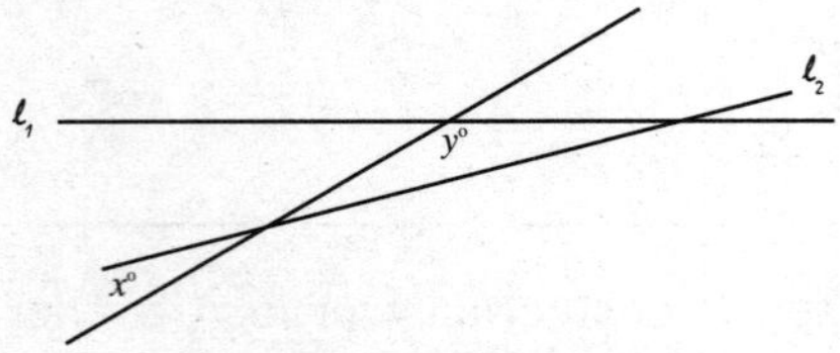

Note: Figure not drawn to scale.

	Column A	Column B
5.	x	$180 - y$

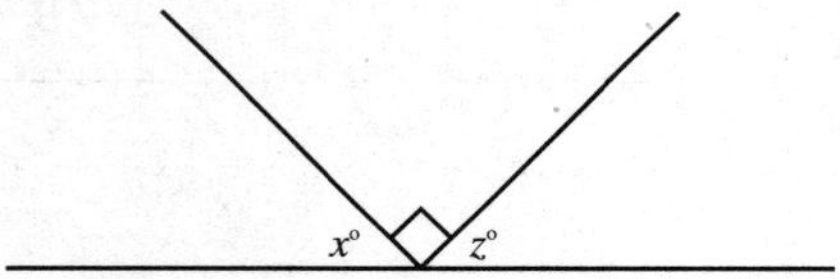

$x > z$

	Column A	Column B
6.	z	45

	Column A	Column B
7.	The perimeter of a rectangle with an area of 64 square inches	The perimeter of a rectangle with an area of 16 square inches

a is chosen from the set $\{-1, -3, 2\}$
b is chosen from the set $\{-4, 6, 8\}$

	Column A	Column B
8.	The largest possible value of $\frac{a}{b}$	1

$x < 0$

	Column A	Column B
9.	$\frac{2x}{x^2 + 2x}$	$\frac{2}{x + 2}$

	Column A	Column B
	$a > b$	
10.	$a^2 + b^2$	$2ab$

In ΔABC, $\angle B$ is 50° more than $\angle A$, and the degree measure of $\angle C$ is equal to three times the degree measure of $\angle A$.

	Column A	Column B
11.	The degree measure of $\angle B$	The degree measure of $\angle C$

$$\frac{y^2}{x} = 6$$
$$y = 3$$

	Column A	Column B
12.	x	2

	Column A	Column B
	$x < 0$	
13.	$x^2 + 81$	$(x + 9)^2$

	Column A	Column B
14.	$3^2 3^3$	$(3^2)^3$

	Column A	Column B
15.	$\sqrt{16} - \sqrt{9}$	$\sqrt{7} - \sqrt{6}$

Answer Key

Exercise 1	Exercise 2	Exercise 3	Exercise 4	Exercise 5
1. A	1. A	1. A	1. B	1. A
2. B	2. A	2. C	2. B	2. B
3. D	3. D	3. B	3. D	3. C
4. B	4. D	4. C	4. A	4. C
5. B	5. C	5. A	5. A	5. A
6. D	6. C	6. B	6. A	6. D
7. A	7. A	7. D	7. B	7. A
8. C	8. A	8. D	8. A	8. C
9. B	9. A	9. C	9. D	9. D
10. B	10. D	10. B	10. A	10. A
11. A	11. C	11. B	11. B	11. A
12. B	12. D	12. B	12. D	12. A
13. D	13. B	13. C	13. A	13. A
14. B	14. B	14. A	14. B	14. B
15. D	15. B	15. D	15. B	15. C

Exercise 6	Exercise 7	Exercise 8	Exercise 9	Exercise 10
1. A	1. A	1. C	1. C	1. B
2. D	2. C	2. A	2. A	2. A
3. B	3. C	3. C	3. B	3. B
4. A	4. D	4. D	4. D	4. C
5. B	5. C	5. A	5. A	5. B
6. A	6. A	6. C	6. C	6. B
7. B	7. B	7. C	7. D	7. D
8. C	8. B	8. A	8. B	8. B
9. D	9. D	9. C	9. A	9. C
10. B	10. A	10. D	10. A	10. A
11. A	11. D	11. C	11. B	11. B
12. C	12. D	12. C	12. A	12. B
13. A	13. B	13. A	13. C	13. A
14. A	14. A	14. B	14. D	14. B
15. B	15. B	15. C	15. D	15. A

Explanatory Answers

EXERCISE 1

1. **The correct answer is (A).** For Column A, marking down \$1,200 by 10% reduces the price by 10% of 1,200 = 120. The new price is 1,200 − 120 = 1,080. Marking this down 10% reduces the price by 10% of 1,080 = 108, so that the final price is 1,080 − 108 = 972. For Column B, a single 20% markdown reduces the price by 20% of 1,200 = 240 to a final price of 1,200 − 240 = 960, which is less than 972.

2. **The correct answer is (B).** Since 64 is divisible by 4, so is 3,458,064. Thus, the remainder is zero when dividing by 4. However, 5,559,063 is not divisible by 9, because its digits do not sum to a number divisible by 9. Hence, there is some remainder which must be greater than 0.

3. **The correct answer is (D).** This depends entirely upon what x is. If x is zero, the two are equal. If x is positive, $2x > x$, and if x is negative, $2x < x$.

4. **The correct answer is (B).** Since the diameter is 10, OA and OB, being radii, both have a length of 5. Since the perimeter is 16, we see that AB has a length of 6. Hence, $\angle O$ is the largest angle in the triangle. Since the other two angles are base angles of an isosceles triangle, they must be equal and have measure x. Hence, x must be less than 60, or the three angles would total more than 180°.

5. **The correct answer is (B).** The tick marks are at spacing 0.02, so B = 2.38 > 2.37.

6. **The correct answer is (D).** Since $c < b$, the arithmetic mean of b and c is less than b. But since we do not know the relative sizes of a and b, we cannot tell whether the arithmetic mean of a and b is greater than or less than b.

7. **The correct answer is (A).** Since $AC = BC = 7$, the triangle is isosceles. Hence, the base angles are both 50°, making the vertex angle 80°. Since the side opposite the larger angle is the longer side, $AB > 7$.

8. **The correct answer is (C).** To find the largest possible value of $\frac{a}{b}$, you certainly want a positive number, which you can get in two ways: A positive divided by a positive, or a negative divided by a negative. The largest fraction you can form using positive numbers from A and B is $\frac{3}{4}$. However, using the negative possibilities, we have $\frac{-6}{-4} = \frac{3}{2} = 1.5$. Hence, the two quantities are equal.

9. **The correct answer is (B).** Taking the difference, $3n^3 - 3^3n = 3n^3 - 27n = 3n(n^2 - 9)$. Since n is between 0 and 1, $n^2 < 9$ and $3n(n^2 - 9) < 0$. Thus, $3n^3 < 3^3n$.

10. **The correct answer is (B).** Adding x to both sides of the inequality, $10 > 2x$, and dividing by 2, $5 > x$.

11. **The correct answer is (A).** $2 \star 4 = \frac{2}{2+4} = \frac{2}{6} = \frac{1}{3}$. $(-2) \star 4 = \frac{-2}{-2+4} = \frac{-2}{2}$ $= -1$

12. **The correct answer is (B).** Substituting $y = \frac{1}{2}$ in Column B, we have $\left(\frac{1}{2}\right)^0 + \left(\frac{1}{2}\right)^2 = 1 + \frac{1}{4} = 1.25 > 1.2$.

13. **The correct answer is (D).** There is no information about the spacing of stations, so we cannot tell which quantity might be larger.

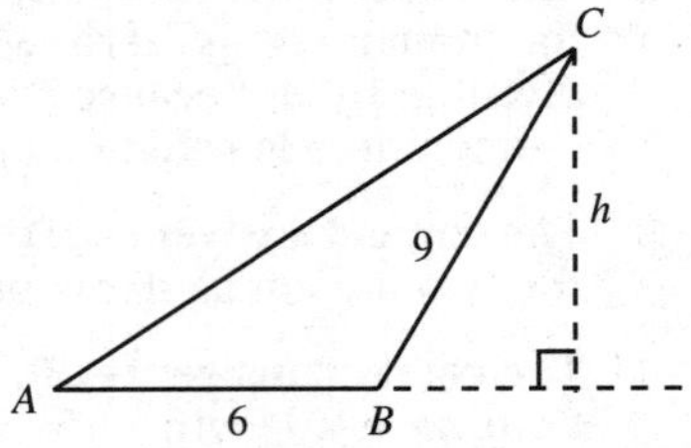

14. **The correct answer is (B).** Dropping the perpendicular from C down to the extension of AB (see the figure above), we see that the altitude of the triangle, h, is less than 9, and the area of ΔABC is thus less than $\frac{1}{2}(6)(9) = 27$.

15. **The correct answer is (D).** If $x = 0$, Column A is 1, which is less than 2; but if $x = 10$ (for example), Column A is $\frac{31}{11}$, which is greater than 2.

EXERCISE 2

1. **The correct answer is (A).** Counting spaces, we see that in Column A, we have $AE{:}BD = 5{:}2 = \frac{5}{2} = 2.5$, but in Column B, we have $BH{:}CF = 6{:}3 = \frac{6}{3} = 2$.

2. **The correct answer is (A).** 40% of 200 = 0.4(200) = 80, so with the markup, the value in Column A = 200 + 80 = 280. In Column B, subtracting 10% of 300 (30 from 300 leaves only 270.

3. **The correct answer is (D).** This depends entirely upon what x is. If x is 0 or 1, the two are equal. If $x > 1$, $x^3 > x^2$, with the reverse if x is between 0 and 1.

4. **The correct answer is (D).** Since you do not know how many miles per gallon the cars get, and they may not be the same, you cannot tell.

5. **The correct answer is (C).** $\frac{1}{3}$ of 42 is 14 and $\frac{1}{6}$ of 42 is 7. Thus, 21 horses are black or white, leaving 21 brown.

6. **The correct answer is (C).** $x + y$ is the measure of the top angle in the large triangle. Hence, $x + y + z + w = 180$. Since $x + z = 50$, $y + w = 130$.

7. **The correct answer is (A).** The triangle is isosceles, because all radii of a circle are equal in length. Therefore, the base angles are equal, and each is 59°. This implies that the chord is longer than the radius, which is 9.

8. **The correct answer is (A).** Five more than twice n is $2n + 5$. Thus, $2n + 5 = 17$, which we solve to get $n = 6$. Three less than 6 is 3, and 2 less than $\frac{1}{2}$ of 6 is 2 less than 3, or 1. Since $3 > 1$, the correct choice is (A).

9. **The correct answer is (A).** By the Pythagorean Theorem, $x = \sqrt{7^2 - 3^2} = \sqrt{40} = 2\sqrt{10}$. The area of the triangle is $A = \frac{1}{2}bh = \frac{1}{2}(3)2\sqrt{10} = 3\sqrt{10}$. Since $\sqrt{10} > 3$, the area is greater than 9.

10. **The correct answer is (D).** Since $x + 6 > 7$, we have $x > 1$. Since $7 > 2x$, we have $3.5 > x$. Therefore, x is a number between 1 and 3.5, and that is all we can say.

11. **The correct answer is (C).** Since $5r - 2s = 2$, $10r - 4s = 2(5r - 2s) = 4$; and $(-1)^4 = 1$. In Column B, $15r - 6s = 3(5r - 2s) = 6$; and $(-1)^6 = 1$.

12. **The correct answer is (D).** If $x = 1$ the two quantities are equal. However, when $x = 0$, the Column A quantity is positive, while the Column B quantity is negative and is thus smaller. If $x = 2$, however, the inequality goes the other way.

13. **The correct answer is (B)** $m_{PQ} = \dfrac{5-2}{3-(-1)} = \dfrac{3}{4}$

14. **The correct answer is (B)** $(-3) \star (-2) = 2(-3)(-2) + (-3) = 9$.

    $(-2) \star (-3) = 2(-2)(-3) + (-2) = 10$.

15. **The correct answer is (B).** Rewrite $\dfrac{3x+1}{x+1}$ as $\dfrac{3x+3-2}{x+1} = \dfrac{3(x+1)-2}{x+1} = 3 - \dfrac{2}{x+1}$. Since $x > 0$, $\dfrac{2}{x+1}$ is positive. Hence, $3 - \dfrac{2}{x+1}$ is less than 3.

EXERCISE 3

1. **The correct answer is (A).** Looking at Column B, we see that 3 for a dollar is $33\frac{1}{3}$¢ apiece, which is less than 34¢ apiece. It doesn't matter how many items you have; if the number of each is the same, the lower price per item gives the lower total.

2. **The correct answer is (C).** 6,037,854 is divisible by 6, and 3,521,912 is divisible by 8. Hence, both give remainder 0.

3. **The correct answer is (B).** We solve $x - 5 = 2$, getting $x = 7$. Column A is now $x + 3 = 10 < 11$.

4. **The correct answer is (C).** Since $x = 9$, the given equation is $9y^2 = 4$, or $y^2 = \frac{4}{9}$; $y = \pm\frac{2}{3}$. Since $y > 0$, it must be $y = \frac{2}{3}$.

5. **The correct answer is (A).** Since $n > 7$, $\frac{n}{6} > 1$, and $\frac{6}{n} < 1$.

6. **The correct answer is (B).** The square with area 36 has a side with a length of 6 and a perimeter of 24. A circle with radius 6 has a circumference $2\pi(6) = 12\pi$. Since $\pi > 3$, the circumference is greater than 36.

7. **The correct answer is (D).** Since the figure is not drawn to scale, there is no way to compare *AC* and *AB*.

8. **The correct answer is (D).** Try to set up the inequality:

   $$(a - b)^2 > a^2 - b^2$$

   Factoring:

   $$(a - b)(a - b) > (a - b)(a + b)$$

   Since $a > b$, $a - b$ is positive, and you divide both sides of the inequality without changing it, yielding:

   $$a - b > a + b$$

   This looks backward. That is, you would think that $a - b$ is less than $a + b$. But it doesn't have to be! Why? First, b could be zero, and the quantities would be equal. Second, if b is negative, the result is correct. Therefore, you need more information.

9. **The correct answer is (C).** The verbal description leads to the equation $\frac{1}{2}n - 7 = 5$, for which $n = 24$. One third of 24 is 8.

10. **The correct answer is (B).** $2 \star 3 = \frac{2}{2+3} = \frac{2}{5} < \frac{2}{3}$.

11. **The correct answer is (B).** The sum of the angles around a point must be 360°. Thus:

    $$\begin{aligned} x + x + (x + 40) + 2x &= 360 \\ 5x + 40 &= 360 \\ 5x &= 320 \\ x &= 64 \end{aligned}$$

12. **The correct answer is (B).** The radius of a circle is $\frac{1}{2}d$. Hence, the area of the circle is $\frac{1}{4}\pi d^2$. The area of the square is s^2. If the two are equal, $\frac{1}{4}\pi d^2 = s^2$. That is, $\pi d^2 = 4s^2$. Since $\pi < 4$, the two can be equal only if $d > s$. Geometrically, unless $d > s$, the entire circle can be fit inside the square and must have a smaller area.

13. **The correct answer is (C).** As long as $t \neq 0$, we can divide out the common factor of t in the numerator and denominator of $\frac{t^2 + 5t}{t}$ to get $t + 5$. Hence, the two are equal.

14. **The correct answer is (A).** If $x = \frac{1}{2}$, $x^2 + 2y^2 = \frac{1}{4} + 2y^2 = 1$ implies that $2y^2 = \frac{3}{4}$ and $y^2 = \frac{3}{8}$. Now $|y| = \sqrt{\frac{3}{8}} = \sqrt{0.375} \approx > 0.5$.

15. **The correct answer is (D).** Although it seems unlikely that there are fewer blue marbles in the bag, you cannot know for sure: three blue marbles in a row could certainly be drawn by sheer chance, even if red marbles outnumbered blue marbles.

EXERCISE 4

1. **The correct answer is (B).** The first fraction has a larger numerator, but it also has a larger denominator, so we rewrite both with the common denominator 35 by multiplying the top and bottom of $\frac{4}{7}$ by 5 and the top and bottom of $\frac{3}{5}$ by 7, to yield $\frac{20}{35}$ and $\frac{21}{35}$, respectively. Now it is easy to see that $\frac{3}{5}$ is the larger.

2. **The correct answer is (B).** In column A, we have n^3, and in Column B, we have $3n$. Since n is between 0 and 1, cubing n makes it smaller. So n^3 is less than n. Therefore, it is certainly less than $3n$.

3. **The correct answer is (D).** This depends upon what n is. If n is 0, the two are equal. If n is negative, n^3 is also negative, while $1000n^2$ is positive.

4. **The correct answer is (A).** Of the 12 students taking Spanish, 4 are taking German as well, leaving 8 taking only Spanish. Since 12 of the 18 are taking Spanish, just 6 are taking only German. Thus, the number in Column A is larger.

5. **The correct answer is (A).** Since $x > 2$, $xx > 2x$, that is, $x^2 > 2x$.

6. **The correct answer is (A).** A circle with diameter 10 has radius 5 and area $\pi 5^2 = 25\pi$. A square with diagonal 12 has a side $\frac{12}{\sqrt{2}}$ and area $\left(\frac{12}{\sqrt{2}}\right)^2 = 72$. Since $\pi > 3$, the area of the circle is greater than 75.

7. **The correct answer is (B).** There are 18 small squares with a total area of 72. Thus, each is 4 square units and has side of length 2. Counting the sides that make up the perimeter, there are 24, for a length of 48.

8. **The correct answer is (A).** If $x = 2$, $x^0 = 2^0 = 1$; and $x^{-4} = 2^{-4} = \frac{1}{2^4} = \frac{1}{16} = 0.0625$. Hence, $x + x^{-4} = 1.0625$, which is less than 1.10.

9. **The correct answer is (D).** If $x < 3$ and x is positive, then $xy = 21$ implies that $y > 7$. However, x could be negative, in which case so is y.

10. **The correct answer is (A).** $\dfrac{\frac{x}{y}}{\frac{y}{x}} = \dfrac{x}{y} \times \dfrac{x}{y} = \dfrac{x^2}{y^2} = \left(\dfrac{x}{y}\right)^2$. So the question is, which is larger, $\left(\dfrac{x}{y}\right)^2$ or $\dfrac{x}{y}$? But x and y have opposite signs, so the fraction $\dfrac{x}{y}$ is negative. The square of the fraction is positive and is, thus, larger than the fraction itself.

11. **The correct answer is (B).** p percent is $\dfrac{p}{100}$. Hence, p percent of 120 is less than 90 means $\dfrac{p}{100}(120) < 90$. That is $\dfrac{6p}{5} < 90$. Multiplying by 5, $6p < 450$, and dividing by 6, $p < 75$.

12. **The correct answer is (D).** If $x = 0$, Column A is 0 and Column B is 1. If $x = -3$, Column A is 3 and Column B is $-\dfrac{1}{2}$.

13. **The correct answer is (A).** If $x < -2$, then x is negative, so $x(x) > x(-2)$; that is, $x^2 > -2x$.

14. **The correct answer is (B).** If $y = \dfrac{1}{2}$, $x^2 + 2y^2 = x^2 + \dfrac{1}{2} = 1$ implies that $x^2 = \dfrac{1}{2}$, and $|x| = \sqrt{\dfrac{1}{2}} = \sqrt{0.5} \approx 7 < 1$.

15. **The correct answer is (B).** The median is the middle number. In this case, there are 11 numbers and the middle one is 3.

EXERCISE 5

1. **The correct answer is (A).** First of all, it does not matter where you put the minus sign—top, bottom, or opposite the fraction bar; if there is one minus sign, the fraction is negative. Remember, in comparing negative numbers, the one with the larger absolute value is the smaller number. So start by ignoring the signs, and compare the absolute values of the fractions. If the two fractions had a common denominator (or numerator) it would be easy. So multiply the top and bottom of $\dfrac{6}{11}$ by 2 to yield $\dfrac{12}{22}$ and it is easy to see that $\dfrac{13}{22}$ is the larger. Hence, $-\dfrac{6}{11}$ is the larger number.

2. **The correct answer is (B).** x^4 is positive because it has an even power. y^3 is positive because y is, and -4 is obviously negative. The product of two positives and a negative is negative. Thus, $-4x^4y^3 < 0$.

3. **The correct answer is (C).** The number of half ounces or part thereof in 2.1 is 5. The first one costs 60¢, and the other 4 cost 15¢ each, for a total of \$1.20.

4. **The correct answer is (C).** $\dfrac{6y^3}{2y^2} = 3y$, and $9y - 3y = 6y$.

5. **The correct answer is (A).** The four angles in the quadrilateral must total 360°. The two given angles total 170°. Hence, $x + y = 190$. Hence, $x = 190 - y$, which is certainly greater than $180 - y$.

6. **The correct answer is (D).** The triangle with legs of 6 and 8 has a hypotenuse of 10. The longer leg of a right triangle with a hypotenuse of 11 could be any number between $\frac{11}{\sqrt{2}}$ (for an isosceles right triangle) to almost 11. For example, the longer leg could be 10 if the other leg were $\sqrt{21}$.

7. **The correct answer is (A).** For the right triangle, the hypotenuse is $\sqrt{2^2 + 1^2} = \sqrt{5}$, which is greater than 2. Adding 3 for the other two legs gives a perimeter that is greater than 5.

8. **The correct answer is (C).** Since neither x^4 nor $3y^2$ can be negative, the only way their sum can be zero is if both x and y are zero. Therefore, $2x - 6y + 1 = +1$.

9. **The correct answer is (D).** Factoring $x^2 + 3x = x(x + 3)$. If $x > 1$, $x(x + 3) > (x + 3)$, but it is less if $x < 1$.

10. **The correct answer is (A).** $\dfrac{\frac{x}{y}}{\frac{y}{x}} = \frac{x}{y} \times \frac{x}{y} = \frac{x^2}{y^2} = \left(\frac{x}{y}\right)^2$. So the question is, which is larger, $\left(\frac{x}{y}\right)^2$ or $\frac{x}{y}$? Both x and y are negative, and x is smaller than y. Hence, in absolute value x is larger than y, and the fraction $\frac{x}{y} > 1$. Therefore, the square of the fraction is larger than the fraction itself.

11. **The correct answer is (A).** By the distance formula, $d_{OP} = \sqrt{(2-0)^2 + (3-0)^2} = \sqrt{13}$, and $d_{PQ} = \sqrt{(4-2)^2 + (1-3)^2} = \sqrt{8}$.

12. **The correct answer is (A).** We can factor the left-hand side to yield:

$$(x - 2)(x + 1) = 0$$

This gives two roots, $x = 2$ and $x = -1$, both of which are larger than -2.

13. **The correct answer is (A).** $2\sqrt{3} = \sqrt{12} < \sqrt{13}$.

14. **The correct answer is (B).** By the Pythagorean Theorem, $c^2 = \sqrt{3^2 + 5^2} = \sqrt{34} < 6$.

15. **The correct answer is (C).** Adding the two equations, we have $3x + 4y = 13$. Multiplying by 3, we have $9x + 12y = 39$.

EXERCISE 6

1. **The correct answer is (A).** $\frac{29}{11} = 2\frac{7}{11} = 2\frac{63}{99}$, but $2.63 = 2\frac{63}{100}$, which is less than $2\frac{63}{99}$.

2. **The correct answer is (D).** You really cannot tell. For example, if $x = 0$, in Column A you have 4, and in Column B you have 0. But if $x = -2$, Column A is 0, and Column B is 16.

3. **The correct answer is (B).** From the first line, each box of crackers costs $4.80 \div 12 = 0.40$ or 40¢. From the second line, each box of cookies costs $4.00 \div 8 = 0.50$ or 50¢.

4. **The correct answer is (A).** Solving the given equation, $5 = 4t$, $t = \frac{5}{4}$, and $2t = \frac{5}{2} = 2.5 > 2$.

5. **The correct answer is (B).** m^2 must be positive, since m is not zero. n^3 is negative, because n is. Hence, $3m^2n^3 < 0$.

6. **The correct answer is (A).** If you divide a pentagon into triangles, you should convince yourself that the sum of the angles it contains is 540°. Since the three given angles total 310°, the other two must total 230°.

7. **The correct answer is (B).** Since the black block is seven from the left, there are 6 blocks to its left. Similarly, there are 10 blocks to its right. Hence, there are 6 + 10 + 1 (the black one) = 17 blocks in all.

8. **The correct answer is (C).** The median (middle number) is 3, the mode is 2, and the mean is $(1 + 2 + 2 + 2 + 3 + 5 + 6 + 7 + 8) \div 9 = 4$. Thus, the mean minus the median is $4 - 3 = 1$. And the median minus the mode is $3 - 2 = 1$. Thus, the two quantities are equal.

9. **The correct answer is (D).** Factoring: $4x + x^2 = x(4 + x)$. The quantities are thus equal if $x = -4$, but not otherwise. For example, if $x = -2$, A < B, and if $x = -6$, B < A.

10. **The correct answer is (B).** Adding 5 to both sides of the inequality, $2n < 12$, and dividing by 2, $n < 6$.

11. **The correct answer is (A).** x is the average of 2 and 4, that is, $x = 3$. y is the average of 3 and 1, that is, $y = 2$.

12. **The correct answer is (C).** Dividing the given equation by 2, we get $2x - y = 1$, and thus, $(2x - y)^2 = 1$.

13. **The correct answer is (A).** If $x = 2$, $\frac{x^2}{x^2 + 1} = \frac{4}{5}$ and $\frac{x}{x + 1} = \frac{2}{3} < \frac{4}{5}$.

14. **The correct answer is (A).** 12% = 0.12. Hence, 12% of N is greater than 25 means $0.12N > 25$. That is, $N > \frac{25}{0.12} = 208.333 > 200$.

15. **The correct answer is (B).** Letting h be the price of the hat and s be the price of the scarf: $h + s = 38$, and $h = s + 3$

Substituting:

$$s + s + 3 = 38$$
$$2s = 35$$
$$s = 17.5 < 18$$

EXERCISE 7

1. **The correct answer is (A).** 457,219 is greater than 234,906, so the difference is a negative number. Now, you see that Column A is the product of two negative numbers and a positive number, which makes the result positive. Column B is the product of three negative numbers, and must be negative. Every positive number is greater than any negative number, and so Column A is greater than Column B.

2. **The correct answer is (C).** By the associative law, both quantities are $\frac{4M}{5}$.

3. **The correct answer is (C).** Solving the equation:

$$3y - 6 = 2 - y$$
$$4y = 8$$
$$y = 2$$

If $y = 2$, $y^2 = 2y = 4$. The quantities are the same.

4. **The correct answer is (D).** $x^2 > y^2$ if $x > y$ and both are positive. But either one or both variables could be negative, so you need more information.

5. **The correct answer is (C).** In ΔABC, the measure of $\angle A = x°$ by the property of vertical angles, and the measure of $\angle B = z°$ by the property of alternate interior angles. Hence, $x + y + z = 180$.

6. **The correct answer is (A).** The average of a group of numbers must increase if you take out the smallest number in the group. Thus, the average of s and t must be larger than 90.

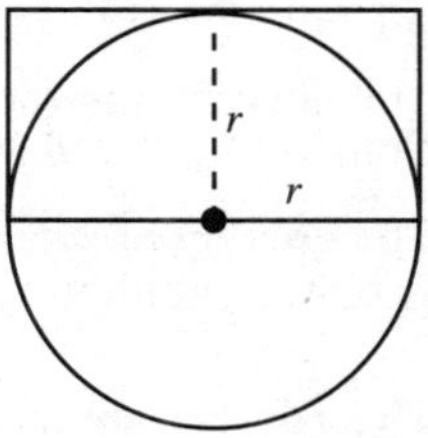

7. **The correct answer is (B).** From the description, the situation must be that shown in the figure above. Calling the radius r, we see that the perimeter of the rectangle is $2(2r) + 2(r) = 6r$. The circumference of the circle is $2\pi r$, but $\pi > 3$. Therefore, $2\pi > 6$, and the circumference of the circle is larger.

8. **The correct answer is (B).** We know that the average of x and -1 must be 2. That is, $2 = \frac{x + (-1)}{2}$, or $4 = x - 1$, $x = 5$. Similarly, we know that the average of y and 3 must be 6. Thus, $6 = \frac{y + 3}{2}$, or $12 = y + 3$, $y = 9$. Since $2x = 10$, $2x > y$.

9. **The correct answer is (D).** You cannot tell. For example, if $x = 0$, Column A is 0 and Column B is $\frac{1}{2}$. However, if $x = 1$, Column A is 1 and Column B is $-\frac{1}{2}$.

10. **The correct answer is (A).** Solving the inequality, $3x > 6 - 9$, $3x > -3$, and $x > -1$. Adding 2 to both sides now yields: $x + 2 > 1$.

11. **The correct answer is (D).** Using the obvious notation:

$$4r + 6m + 3b = 910$$
$$2r + 3m + b = 390$$

Multiplying the second equation by -2 and adding the two together, we have $b = 130$. Hence, we know the price of the bread, but that leaves us with two identical equations relating r and m, namely, $2r + 3m = 260$. We have no way of knowing whether r or b is larger.

12. **The correct answer is (D).** $2 \star n = 2 + 2n$, while $n \star 2 = n + 4$, and $2 + 2n > n + 4$ only when $n > 2$; the reverse is true when $n < 2$.

13. **The correct answer is (B).** The probability that the marble is white is given by the number of white marbles (6) divided by the total number of marbles (10); that is, $\frac{3}{5} < \frac{2}{3}$.

14. **The correct answer is (A).** 10% of 3 liters is 0.3, and 20% of 5 liters is 1. Hence, we have a total of 1.3 units of salt in 8 liters of solution. The fraction of salt, then, is $1.3 \div 8 = 0.1625 > 15\%$.

15. **The correct answer is (B).** Expanding the expression in Column B, $(x + 1)^2 = x^2 + 2x + 1$, which is greater than the expression in Column A by 1.

EXERCISE 8

1. **The correct answer is (C).** 20% of 90 is 18, and $90 - 18 = 72$ for the value in Column A. 10% of 80 is 8, and $80 - 8 = 72$ for the value in Column B.

2. **The correct answer is (A).** The greatest common denominator of 12 and 18 is 6. The number of proper divisors of 18 is 5: 1, 2, 3, 6, and 9.

3. **The correct answer is (C).** 18 apples is $1\frac{1}{2}$ or 1.5 dozen. At \$2 per dozen, that totals \$3.24 pears is 2 dozen. At \$3 per dozen, that totals \$6. The grand total is \$9.

4. **The correct answer is (D).** Try to set up the inequality:

$$\sqrt{x} + 2x > 2\sqrt{x} + x$$

Subtracting $\sqrt{x} + x$ from both sides yields

$$x > \sqrt{x}$$

This is true if $x > 1$, but false if $x < 1$. Therefore, you do not have enough information.

5. **The correct answer is (A).** Solving the equation, $z = 2$. Now $2z + 7 = 11 > 10$.

6. **The correct answer is (C).** Since the sum of the angles in any triangle is 180°, $\angle A$ must be 58°. Thus, the triangle is isosceles and $AB = BC$.

7. **The correct answer is (C).** Since the area of a circle is πr^2, the area of a semicircle is $\frac{1}{2}\pi r^2$. Since $r = \frac{1}{2}d$, we know the area of the semicircle is $\frac{\pi d^2}{8}$. Calling the sides of the triangles a, b, and c, we know that $a^2 + b^2 = c^2$, which we multiply by $\frac{\pi}{8}$ to see that the two are equal.

8. **The correct answer is (A).** The volume of the rectangular solid is:

$$V = (4)(4)(6) = 96$$

The radius of the cylinder is 2, so its volume is:

$$V_C = \pi(2)^2(7) = 28\pi$$

Using a value for π of around $\frac{22}{7}$, 28π = around 88. Therefore, the rectangular solid is larger.

9. **The correct answer is (C).** Since $10 = \sqrt{100}$ and $\sqrt{5} \cdot \sqrt{x} = \sqrt{5x}$, we know that $5x = 100$ and $x = 20$. But $20 = 4 \times 5$, so $\sqrt{20} = 2\sqrt{5}$. Hence, the two quantities are equal.

10. **The correct answer is (D).** Substituting from the second equation into the first gives us: $x = 1 - z + 3$, $x = 4 - z$. This tells us that $x + z = 4$. But, for example, x could be 3 and z could be 1, or the reverse, and both conditions would be satisfied.

11. **The correct answer is (C).** Using the obvious notation, we have:

$$4c + 6d + 3h = 815$$
$$2c + 3d + 4h = 720$$

Multiplying the second equation by -2 and adding yields:

$$-5h = -625$$
$$h = 125$$

12. **The correct answer is (C).** $2 \star 3 = 2^2 + 2(3) = 10$.

13. **The correct answer is (A).** Each of the circles has a diameter of 1 and a radius of $\frac{1}{2}$. Hence, the area of each circle is $\pi\left(\frac{1}{4}\right)$, and the combined area is $4\left(\frac{1}{4}\right)\pi = \pi$. The area of the square is $2^2 = 4$, so the area outside the circles is $4 - \pi$. Since π is about 3, we know that $\pi > 4 - \pi$.

14. **The correct answer is (B).** Expanding: $(x + 4)^2 = x^2 + 8x + 16$. Since x is positive, this is larger than $x^2 + 4^2$.

15. **The correct answer is (C).** Summing the even integers, we see:

    For 1 term: $2 = 2 = 1(2)$
    For 2 terms: $2 + 4 = 6 = 2(3)$
    For 3 terms: $2 + 4 + 6 = 12 = 3(4)$
    For 4 terms: $2 + 4 + 6 + 8 = 20 = 4(5)$
    In general, for n terms, the sum is $n(n + 1)$

    Summing the odd integers, we see:

    For 1 term: $1 = 1$
    For 2 terms: $1 + 3 = 4 = 2(2)$
    For 3 terms: $1 + 3 + 5 = 9 = 3(3)$
    For 4 terms: $1 + 3 + 5 + 7 = 16 = 4(4)$

    In general, for n terms, the sum is $n(n)$

    The ratio is $\frac{n(n + 1)}{n^2} = \frac{n + 1}{n}$, and the quantities are equal.

EXERCISE 9

1. **The correct answer is (C).** 12% of 400 = 0.12(400) = 48, and 40% of 120 = 0.40(120) = 48.

2. **The correct answer is (A).** $0.06 \div 0.003 = 20$. Therefore, we can rewrite the given equation as $20x = 1.62$, and $x = 1.62 \div 20 = 0.081$.

3. **The correct answer is (B).** We can see that $15y - 3x = -3(x - 5y)$; hence, it must equal $-3(12) = -36$, which is less than -35.

4. **The correct answer is (D).** The statement amounts to $n^2 = 2n$, which has two solutions: $n = 0$ and $n = 2$. The first is less than 1, and the second is greater than 1.

5. **The correct answer is (A).** Since all radii are equal, °*OPS* is isosceles, and the angles at *P* and *S* must be equal. Suppose each is x. Now $2x + 62 = 180$. Hence, $x = 59$. Therefore, *PS* is opposite the largest angle in the triangle, and must be the longest side. That is, *PS* is longer than a radius.

6. **The correct answer is (C).** A 12 by 12 square has an area of 144 square units. Each 2 by 3 rectangle covers 6 square units. Thus, you need $144 \div 6 = 24$ rectangles. A 6 by 16 rectangle is 96 square units. Each 2 by 2 square covers 4 square units. Thus, you need $96 \div 4 = 24$ squares.

7. **The correct answer is (D).** You really can't tell. Try some numbers. For example, if $a = 2$ and $b = 12$, their average is 7. If $c = 7$, then the three still average 7. However, if $c = 10$, the average becomes 8, and if $c = 4$, the average becomes 6.

8. **The correct answer is (B).** We see that (3, 6) is the midpoint of PQ. Therefore, in the x-direction, (3, b) will be equidistant from both P and Q. However, if $b < 6$, then b must be closer to 2 than to 10. Therefore, (3, b) is closer to (0, 2) than to (6, 10).

9. **The correct answer is (A).** Solving the first equation, $x = -2 + 4 = 2$. Solving the second equation, $-4 + 2 = y$, $y = -2$. Hence, $x > y$.

10. **The correct answer is (A).** Substituting from the second equation into the first gives $n = s + 4 - 2$; $n = s + 2$. Hence, $n > s$.

11. **The correct answer is (B).** Multiplying radicals gives $\sqrt{18x} = \sqrt{30}$. Hence, $18x = 30$, and $x = \frac{5}{3} < 2$.

12. **The correct answer is (A).** $(-1)^6 = 1$, but $(-1)^5 = -1$.

13. **The correct answer is (C).** Adding the two equations gives $4n = 16$, so $n = 4$. Knowing that $n = 4$, the second equation tells us that $8 + m = 10$, and $m = 2$.

14. **The correct answer is (D).** If x is 0, A is 1, and B is 0. However, if x is 1, A is $1\frac{1}{2}$ and B is 2, reversing the order.

15. **The correct answer is (D).** $xyz = 18$ means that the product of x, y, and z is positive. Since x is negative, then yz must be negative. That means either y or z is negative, but we do not know which, so we cannot tell the relationship between z and 0.

EXERCISE 10

1. **The correct answer is (B).** 20% of 420 = 0.20(420) = 84, so with the markup the amount in Column B is 420 + 84 = 504.

2. **The correct answer is (A).** For numbers between 0 and 1, $x^2 < x$, while $\sqrt{x} > x$. Thus, $\sqrt{x} > x^2$.

3. **The correct answer is (B).** If you multiply any positive number by a number larger than 1, the result is larger than the original number. Since $B > 1$, $AB > A$.

4. **The correct answer is (C).** 10% of 600 = 0.10(600) = 60, and 6% of 1000 = 0.06(1000) = 60.

5. **The correct answer is (B).** The corresponding angle to the one with measure $x°$ also has measure $x°$. Hence, if $x + y = 180$, then l_1 would be parallel to l_2. If $x + y > 180$, then the lines would intersect to the left. Hence, from the diagram, $x + y < 180$, which means that $x < 180 - y$.

6. **The correct answer is (B).** $x + z + 90 = 180$. Thus, $x + z = 90$. If x is larger than z, then $z < 45$.

7. **The correct answer is (D).** You can't tell! For Rectangle A, $LW = 64$. If it were a square, each side would be 8, and the perimeter would be 32, but the length could be any number greater than zero if W is picked to be $\frac{64}{L}$. Thus, you could make its perimeter (almost) as large as you wish! For example, it could be 64×1, with a perimeter of 130. For rectangle B, $LW = 16$. If it were a square, each side would be 4, and the perimeter would be 16 but, again, the length could be (nearly) any number greater than zero if W is picked to be $\frac{16}{L}$. For example, it could be 16×1, with a perimeter of 34, which is less than 130 but greater than 32.

8. **The correct answer is (B).** The largest possible value of $\frac{a}{b}$ using positive numbers in the numerator and denominator is $\frac{2}{6}$. Using negative options, the largest is $\frac{-3}{-4} = \frac{3}{4}$. In either case, it is smaller than 1.

9. **The correct answer is (C).** As long as $x \neq 0$, we can divide out the common factor x in the numerator and denominator of $\frac{2x}{x^2 + 2x}$ to get $\frac{2}{x + 2}$. The two quantities are equal.

10. **The correct answer is (A).** Take the difference. $a^2 + b^2 - 2ab = a^2 - 2ab + b^2 = (a - b)^2$, which must be positive unless $a = b$. But $a > b$. Hence, $a^2 + b^2 > 2ab$.

11. **The correct answer is (B).** The sum of the angles in the triangle must be 180. Letting the degree measure of $\angle A$ be x, we have $x + 50$ for B and $3x$ for C. Now:

$$x + (x + 50) + 3x = 180$$
$$5x + 50 = 180$$
$$x = 26$$

Hence, $\angle B = 76°$ and $\angle C = 78°$.

12. **The correct answer is (B).** For $y = 3$, the given relationship is $\frac{9}{x} = 6$, which means that $6x = 9$ and $x = 1.5 < 2$.

13. **The correct answer is (A).** Expanding: $(x + 9)^2 = x^2 + 18x + 81$. Since x is negative, this is less than $x^2 + 81$.

14. **The correct answer is (B).** $3^2 3^3 = 3^{2+3} = 3^5 = 243$, but $(3^2)^3 = 3^{2 \times 3} = 3^6 = 729$.

15. **The correct answer is (A).** $\sqrt{16} - \sqrt{9} = 4 - 3 = 1$, but $\sqrt{7}$ and $\sqrt{6}$ are both numbers between 2 and 3. Hence, their difference is less than 1.

Chapter 9

Math Grid-Ins

Get the Scoop On

- Proven strategies for solving math grid-in problems
- How to handle the special answer grid—and the easy-to-make mistakes that can cost you points
- Why you should be fearless about guessing on grid-ins
- The types of answers to avoid, because they can *never* be correct

THE TEST CAPSULE

What's the Big Idea?

Math grid-ins are similar to multiple-choice math problems, with one major difference: no answers are provided. Instead, you must come up with your own solution to the problem and enter it in a specially-designed answer grid.

How Many?

Your SAT will probably have a total of ten grid-ins. They'll appear together in one of the math sections, where they'll be ten of the twenty-five total questions in the section.

How Much Do They Count?

Grid-ins are ten out of sixty total math questions. They count as roughly 17 percent of your overall math score.

How Much Time Should They Take?

You need to answer grid-ins at a rate of about $1\frac{1}{2}$ minutes per item. The usual batch of ten grid-ins should take you 15 minutes.

What's the Best Strategy?

Be especially aggressive in guessing on this part of the test. Unlike the other question types, math grid-ins are scored with *no* guessing penalty. Therefore, you can't possibly lose points for any answer you give—and it's always possible to gain.

What's the Worst Pitfall?

Losing points needlessly by using the special answer grid incorrectly. Like the rest of your answer sheet, the grid will be read by a machine, which is too dumb to understand the answer you *meant* to put. Since there's no margin for error or ambiguity in the way you write your answers, it's crucial to master the technique of filling in the answer grid correctly through extensive practice before the day of the exam.

THE OFFICIAL DESCRIPTION

What They Are

Math grid-ins are officially known as student-produced response questions. Like multiple-choice math problems, SAT grid-ins are designed to test your skill at mathematical reasoning, which is your ability to use knowledge of specific math facts, formulas, techniques, and methods to solve problems. Basic information about the procedures of math is needed, but the questions focus more on the underlying concepts than on the procedures themselves. The major difference between the multiple-choice items and the math grid-ins is that you must generate your own answers for the grid-ins; no answer choices are provided by the test-makers.

Where They Are

In the typical SAT, you'll have three Math sections. Two will be 30 minutes long; one will be 15 minutes long. One of the 30-minute sections will include a batch of grid-in problems, usually following a set of fifteen quantitative comparisons. Reminder: The test-makers claim the right to change the format at any time! However, the typical format we just described is what you're most likely to encounter.

What They Measure

To score high on grid-ins, it's important to be very comfortable with the basic operations of arithmetic—not only addition, subtraction, multiplication, and division, but also such procedures as working with fractions and decimals, and figuring out averages. You'll also need to be skilled at the basic operations of algebra, including solving equations, using negative numbers and square roots, and factoring. Finally, many of the basic principles of geometry are tested, including such concepts as the properties of triangles, circles, and quadrilaterals and determining the areas and volumes of simple figures.

What They Cover

The math areas tested on the SAT, including the grid-in items, are those studied by virtually every high school student: arithmetic, basic algebra, and plane and coordinate geometry. Many advanced and specialized math topics are *not* covered on the SAT, including trigonometry and calculus. See Appendix B, "The Insider's SAT Math Review," for a detailed review of the math concepts most frequently tested on the exam.

Directions for Student-Produced Response Questions

Each of the remaining 10 questions requires you to solve the problem and enter your answer by marking the ovals in the special grid, as shown in the examples below.

Answer: $\frac{7}{12}$ or 7/12

Answer: 2.5

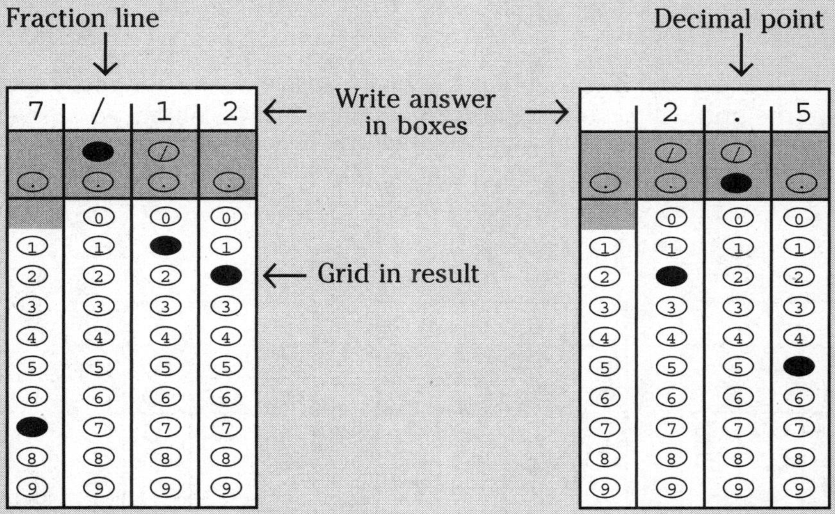

Answer: 201
Either position is correct.

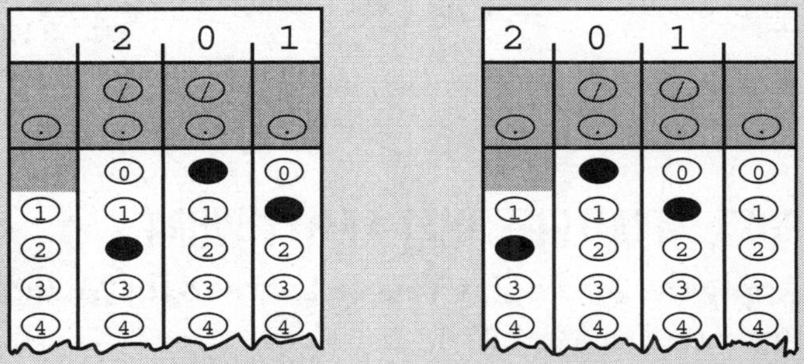

Note: You may start your answers in any column, space permitting. Columns not needed should be left blank.

- Mark no more than one oval in any column.
- Because the answer sheet will be machine-scored, you will receive credit only if the ovals are filled in correctly.
- Although not required, it is suggested that you write your answer in the boxes at the top of the columns to help you fill in the ovals accurately.

- Some problems may have more than one correct answer. In such cases, grid only one answer.
- No question has a negative answer.
- Mixed numbers such as $2\frac{1}{2}$ must be gridded as 2.5 or 5/2. If 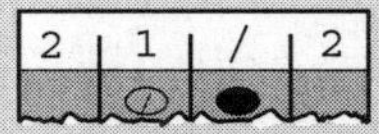

is gridded, it will be interpreted as $\frac{21}{2}$, not $2\frac{1}{2}$.
- **Decimal accuracy:** If you obtain a decimal answer, enter the most accurate value the grid will accommodate. For example, if you obtain an answer such as 0.6666 . . . , you should record the result as .666 or .667. Less accurate values such as .66 or .67 are not acceptable.

Acceptable ways to grid $\frac{2}{3} = .6666$

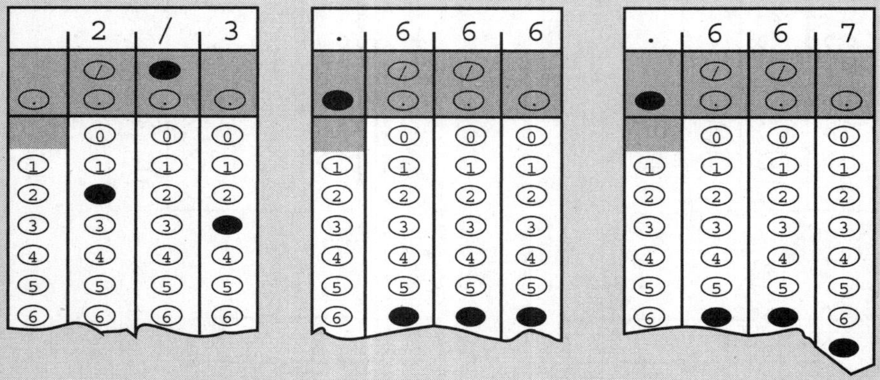

THE INSIDER'S REPORT: STRATEGIES THAT REALLY WORK

Apply the Strategies You've Learned for Multiple-Choice Math Problems to Math Grid-Ins

Grid-in items are the newest addition to the SAT. They were added to the exam in 1994 as part of an effort by the test-makers to respond to criticism concerning the limitations of multiple-choice questions.

Grid-in problems are much like multiple-choice math items, only without the answer choices: the kinds of math skills tested, and the types of calculations necessary, are almost the same for both question types. Therefore, the strategies and tips offered for multiple-choice problems in Chapter 7 generally apply to grid-ins (with a couple of exceptions we'll explain shortly).

To briefly recap:

- Focus on what the question really asks, not what you might hastily assume is being asked.

FYI

The scoring machine is programmed to accept any fraction with the right value as a correct answer, whether or not it has been reduced to lowest terms. ($\frac{6}{8}$ is considered as equally correct as $\frac{3}{4}$.) It will also accept any decimal number of equivalent value. (.75 is just as correct as $\frac{3}{4}$.) So don't spend time (as you might on a classroom exam) converting a fractional answer from one form to another; it's unnecessary and a possible source of errors.

- When in doubt, try something.
- Break word problems into phrases, which you can then translate into numbers and symbols.
- Use the geometry diagrams as sources of information, or sketch your own if none is provided.
- Finally, on "weird operation" questions, plug in the numbers and work out the math methodically.

All of these techniques, which work effectively on multiple-choice problems, will serve you well on grid-ins, too.

Be Somewhat Cautious in Guesstimating Values on Grid-Ins

Remember, on multiple-choice problems, we suggest that you be guided in guesstimating by the nature of the answer choices: If they are close to one another, you need a precise answer; if they are far apart, an approximation will do. Since no answer choices are provided on grid-ins, you don't have this clue to rely on. As a result, you'll have to calculate precise answers more often that you do on multiple-choice problems.

Nonetheless, guesstimating has its value on grid-ins, especially as a first step before whipping out your calculator. Here's why: If you eyeball the numbers on a particular grid-in problem and come up with a sense of the range where your answer should lie, it will help you avoid the obvious errors that a calculator can create. It's easy, for example, to hit the same button twice by mistake, punching in 8×166 when you mean to punch 8×16. But if you've guesstimated the answer first (a little less than 150), you'll immediately realize that an answer like 1,328 is too big.

Be Aggressive About Guessing

If your answer requires fewer than four spaces, you can start (and end) in any space on the grid. For example, if the correct answer choice is the single digit 6, you can put it in any of the four spaces available—all would be counted as correct by the scoring machine. The other spaces can simply be left blank.

Unlike every other SAT question type, grid-ins are scored without a guessing penalty. Your raw score on this part of the exam will equal the number of questions right, with no deduction either for wrong answer choices or for items left blank. Therefore, don't hesitate to fill in an answer choice for every question, even if you're very uncertain about its correctness. You can't possibly lose points, and you may gain some.

Master the Art of the Grid Through Plenty of Practice

As you've seen, the answer-gridding instructions provided on the exam are extremely detailed. They include 232 words of text, five examples, eight illustrations, and four captions. It would be crazy to spend time trying to read and absorb all this information on the day of the test. So don't try. Instead, be sure you know the instructions, and what you can and cannot do on the grid, extremely well *before* the exam. Then you won't have to even skim the instructions.

THE INSIDER'S REPORT: THE BEST TIPS

Start by Filling in the Answer Spaces at the Top of the Grid

Although these spaces aren't strictly necessary, because the test-scoring machine won't read what you write there, we recommend that you place your answer here before blackening the matching ovals below. There are two reasons why.

Don't grid in zeroes before a decimal point: The value 0.45 should be gridded in simply as .45. And don't grid in a decimal point or a final zero after an integral answer: the value 2 should be gridded that way, not as 2. or 2.0.

First, it will help you keep straight exactly what you want to enter in each column, whether it's a number, a decimal point, or the division sign (/). Second, it will help when you want to review and check your work later, since reading the handwritten numbers in the boxes is much easier than trying to decipher the blackened ovals below.

Use the Division Sign to Enter Fractions

Aside from the ten digits 0–9 and the decimal point (.), the "slash" or division sign (/) is the only symbol available for grid-in answers. If you come up with a fractional answer for a grid-in question, enter it using this sign. Thus, the fraction $\frac{2}{7}$ would be entered in three spaces on the grid like this: 2/7.

Make Decimal Values as Precise as the Grid Allows

As you know, many decimals have no precise values. Rather than ending after two, three, or four decimal places, these *irrational numbers* repeat endlessly. An example is the decimal value of $\frac{1}{3}$, which is an endlessly repeating .333.

If you find that a number like this is the correct answer for a grid-in item, you can handle it in several ways. You can, if appropriate, simply use the equivalent fraction as your answer (in this case, 1/3, gridded just like that). However, if you want to grid the decimal value, you must grid it in as completely and precisely as possible. In general, this means *filling all four places in the grid.* Using this example, the safest way to grid the decimal value of $\frac{1}{3}$ would be as .333. Any less precise answer would be marked wrong; so, for example, if you grid in .33 or .3, your answer will be considered incorrect.

Fill in *Any* Correct Answer

For some grid-ins, unlike other math problems on the SAT, a range of correct answers may be possible. Here's an example:

> If b is positive, and $4b - 8 < 5$, what is a possible value of b?

You'd solve this simple inequality as follows. Add 8 to both sides:

$$4b < 13$$

Then divide both sides by 4:

$$b < \frac{13}{4}$$

So the value of b is any positive number less than $\frac{13}{4}$ (a little more than 3).

Obviously, there are a myriad of possible values for b, including 3, 2.5, $\frac{2}{3}$, .82, and many, many others. On the SAT, the scoring machine will be programmed to consider *any* of these correct. So don't waste time pondering the issue or trying to narrow down the possibilities. Just grid in any possible answer and move on to the next item.

THE INSIDER'S REPORT: THE MOST IMPORTANT WARNINGS

Don't Lose Points Needlessly Through Careless Gridding

As you've already seen, one of the major challenges on grid-in questions is simply filling in your answers correctly. It's not brain surgery, but it's easy to make silly mistakes (and waste precious seconds) if you haven't practiced with the grid. Here are a few types of errors to watch out for.

- Don't forget to blacken the ovals representing the numbers or symbols of your answer. You'll get no credit for answers, however correct, that are filled in only in the spaces at the top.
- Be careful not to overlook any ovals that need blackening, and never blacken two ovals in the same column. (The fact that the columns are twelve rows high makes this easy to do; your eye has a long way to travel. So work deliberately.)
- Don't forget to blacken the appropriate oval when you want to insert a decimal point (.) or division sign (/), and give each symbol a space of its own in the grid.
- Forget any other marks or symbols, like the comma sometimes found in a four-digit number (5,280), the dollar sign ($), or the symbols sometimes used for feet and inches. These and all other symbols must be omitted.

Avoid Negative Answers and Other Answers that Are Impossible to Grid

The grid contains no minus sign, nor is there any other way to accommodate a value less than zero. So if your calculations suggest that the correct answer is a negative number, stop! Go back and reconsider your approach to the problem; something is wrong, since negative answers are impossible on SAT grid-ins.

Other answers that are impossible to grid are those that must contain symbols, like x or π, and those that include numbers (other than repeating decimals) that require more than four digits to express. If you come up with an answer like 10,634, your figuring has gone wrong, since this would require five spaces. Go back and reconsider the problem.

On the other hand, suppose you came up with the fraction $\frac{1}{100}$ as an answer. At first, it might appear to be an impossible answer, since this fraction, with the division sign, would require five spaces to grid. However, remember that this number can also be expressed as the decimal .01, which fits the grid nicely. If you come up with an answer that looks too big, but you think your math is correct, stop to consider whether there's an alternative way to express your answer before you junk it.

Never Try to Grid a Mixed Number

As you know, a mixed number combines a whole number with a fraction. For example, the time period of 90 minutes could also be expressed as the mixed number $1\frac{1}{2}$ hours. Unfortunately, the scoring machine that reads your answer grid can't cope with mixed numbers. If you were to write "1 1/2" in the grid, it would be read as the improper fraction "$\frac{11}{2}$," which of course is completely different in meaning. So if you come up with a mixed number as your answer to a question, you need to reframe it in one of two ways:

- You can turn the mixed number into an equivalent improper fraction: $1\frac{1}{2}$ becomes $\frac{3}{2}$.
- Or you can turn it into a decimal equivalent: $1\frac{1}{2}$ becomes 1.5.

Either way would be correct.

JUST THE FACTS

- Grid-in problems closely resemble multiple-choice problems, except that you must produce your own answers.
- Practice using the special answer grid—it's important to be familiar with its peculiarities.
- Always answer every grid-in item; there's never a guessing penalty for a wrong response.
- Be careful when gridding fractions and decimals, and never try to grid a mixed number or a negative.

PRACTICE, PRACTICE, PRACTICE: MATH GRID-IN EXERCISES

Instructions

The following exercises will give you a chance to practice the skills and strategies you've just learned for tackling math grid-ins. As with all practice exercises, work under true testing conditions. Complete each exercise in a single sitting. Eliminate distractions (TV, music) and clear away notes and reference materials. Time yourself with a stopwatch or kitchen timer, or have someone else time you. If you run out of time before answering all the questions, stop and draw a line under the last question you finished. Then go ahead and tackle the remaining questions. When you are done, score yourself based only on the questions you finished in the allotted time.

Enter your responses on the grid on the page facing the exercise.

Understanding Your Scores

0–2 correct: A poor performance. Study this chapter again, as well as the Insider's SAT Math Review (Appendix B).

3–4 correct: A below-average score. Study this chapter again, as well as all portions of the Insider's SAT Math review (Appendix B) that cover topics you find unfamiliar or difficult.

5–6 correct: An average score. You may want to study this chapter again. Also be sure you are managing your time wisely (as explained in Chapter 3) and avoiding errors due to haste or carelessness.

7–8 correct: An above-average score. Depending on your personal target score and your strength on other math question types, you may or may not want to devote additional time to grid-ins.

9–10 correct: An excellent score. You are probably ready to perform well on math grid-ins.

EXERCISE 1

10 Questions

Time—15 Minutes

Directions: Each question in this exercise requires you to solve the problem and enter your answer in the corresponding grid.

1. What is the value of $A = \dfrac{3 + B}{4 \cdot 3 - 3B}$ if $B = 3$?

2. Mario figures that, working every day, he can finish a certain task in 20 days. Angelo figures that he can finish the same task in 25 days. What fraction of the task can they get done by working on it together for 7 days?

3. Jasmine earns $\frac{3}{4}$ of what Sidney earns, and Sidney earns $\frac{2}{3}$ of what Paul earns. What fraction of Paul's salary does Jasmine earn?

4. At an art show, Eleanor sold six of her paintings for an average price of $70. At the next show, she sold four paintings for an average price of $100. What was the overall average price of the ten paintings Eleanor sold?

5. Mrs. Green and her three children went to a movie. The total cost of their admission tickets was $14. Mr. and Mrs. Arkwright and their five children went to the same movie, and they had to pay $25 for their tickets. What was the cost in dollars of one adult ticket plus one child's ticket for this movie?

6. If m is an integer, and $(x - 6)(x - m) = x^2 + rx + 18$, what is the value of $-r$?

7. In ΔABC, $\angle B$ is 20° more than three times the degree measure of $\angle A$, and the degree measure of $\angle C$ is equal to the sum of the other two angles. How many degrees are there in the smallest angle of ΔABC?

8. A triangle has sides with lengths of 9, 14, and h. If h is an integer, what is the difference between the maximum and minimum possible perimeters of the triangle?

9. In a coordinate grid, the midpoint between points (3, 4) and (2, −2) is point (x_M, y_M). What is the value of $x_M + y_M$?

10. How many different 3-digit license plate numbers can be formed if the only restriction on numbers used is that the first digit CANNOT be 0?

1.

2.

3.

4.

5.

6.

7.

8.

9.

10.

EXERCISE 2

10 Questions

Time—15 Minutes

Directions: Each question in this exercise requires you to solve the problem and enter your answer in the corresponding grid.

1. What positive integer below 10 represents the only value that B CANNOT have in the expression $\frac{3 + B}{4 \cdot 3 - 3B}$?

2. If the fraction $\frac{0.56}{1.26}$, when reduced to lowest terms, may be represented by $\frac{a}{b}$, where a and b are positive whole numbers, what is the value of b?

3. Pedro owns half as many compact disks as Andrea, and Marcia owns $\frac{3}{5}$ as many as Andrea. What fraction of the number of compact disks Marcia owns is the number Pedro owns?

4. Erica earned an average score of 76 on her first four French exams. What grade must Erica earn on the next exam to raise her average to 80?

5. Sally is 6 years older than Manuel. Three years ago, Sally was twice as old as Manuel. How old is Sally?

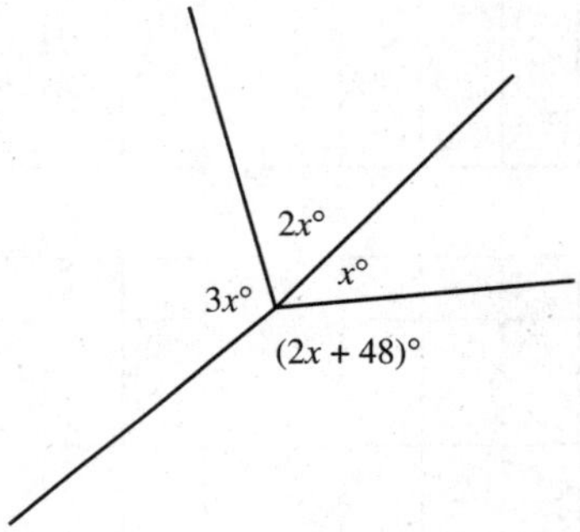

6. In the figure above, what is the value of x?

7. A rectangular garden is 20 yards long and 10 yards wide. If it costs 80¢ per square yard to seed the lawn and \$7.00 per running yard to put up a hedge around the garden, what is the total cost in dollars of seeding the garden and putting up a hedge around it? (Disregard the \$ sign when gridding your answer.)

8. A group of 85 people visited a casino. While they were there, 34 played blackjack, 71 played poker, and 9 did not play either game. How many played both blackjack and poker?

9. What is the largest possible value of the product of two consecutive integers for which the square of the smaller integer minus 8 times the larger integer equals 25?

10. Angela drives her car 8 miles per hour faster than Kim drives her car. If Angela drives 648 miles in the same time it takes Kim to drive 552 miles, what is the speed, in miles per hour, that Kim drives?

1.

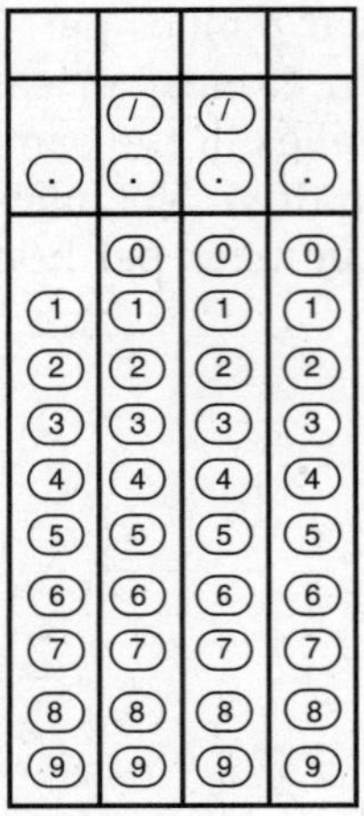

2.

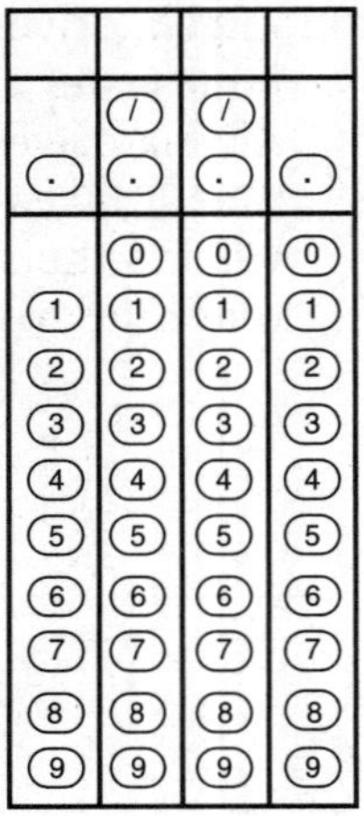

3.

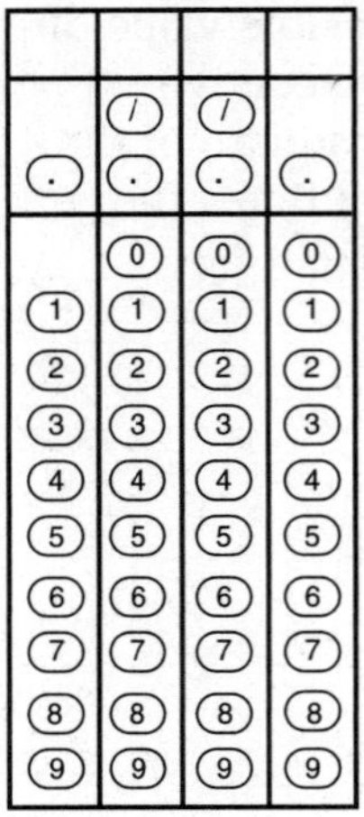

4.

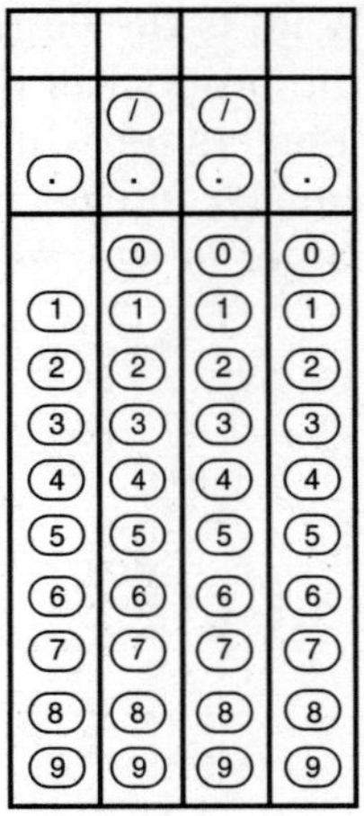

5.

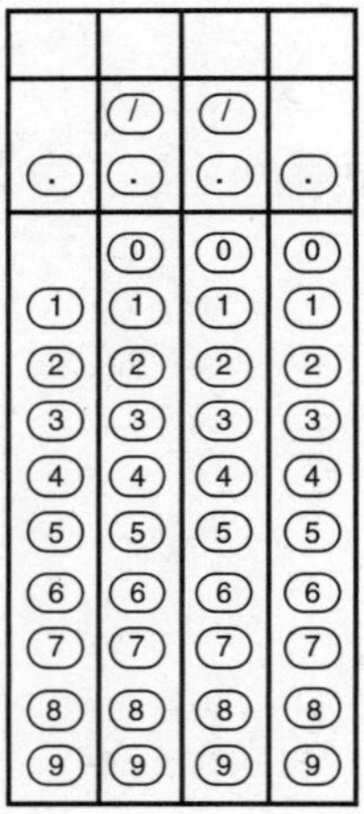

6.

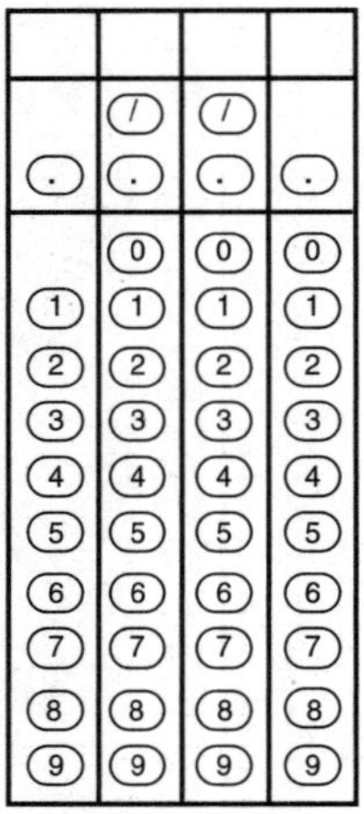

7.

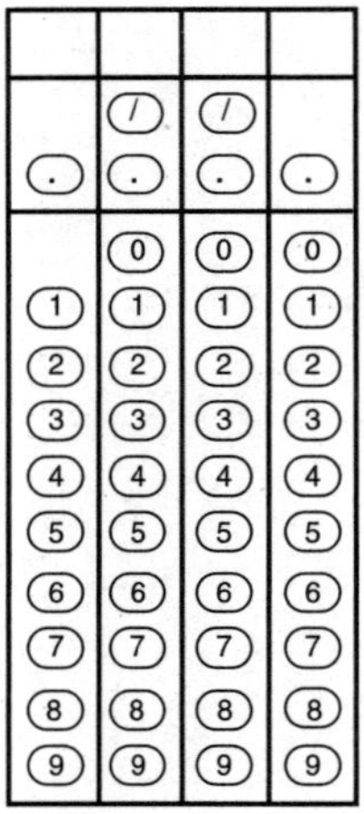

8.

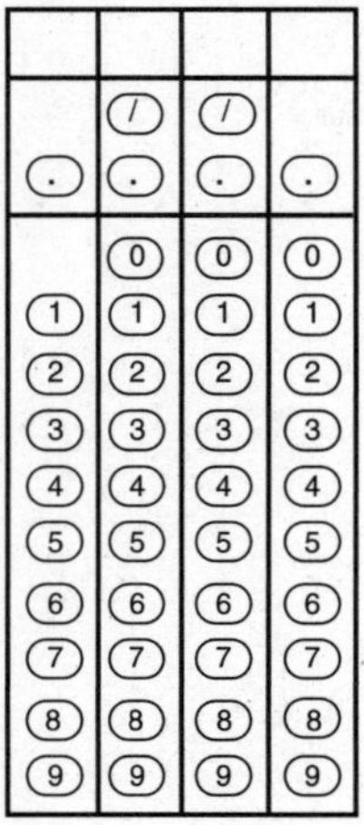

9.

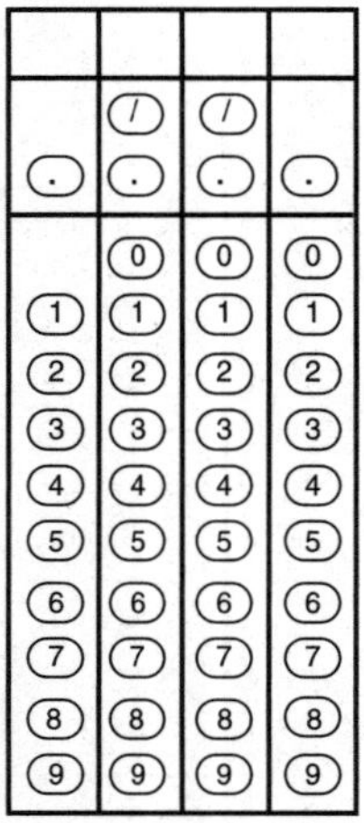

10.

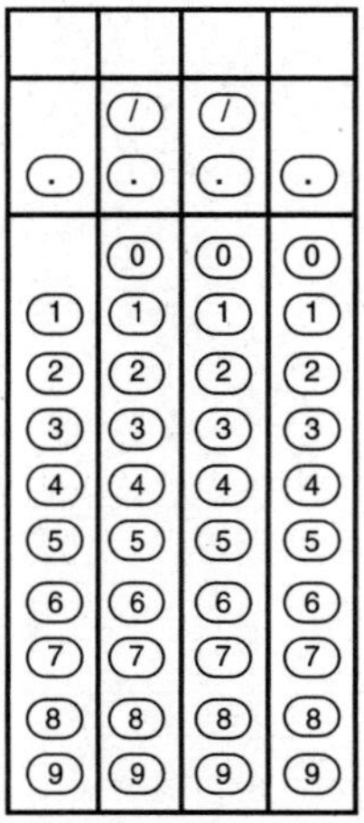

EXERCISE 3

10 Questions

Time—15 Minutes

Directions: Each question in this exercise requires you to solve the problem and enter your answer in the corresponding grid.

1. If m is divisible by 5, what is the largest number that must be evenly divisible into $5m + 25$?

2. What is the value of $N = -A - (-B)$ when $A = -6$ and $B = -5$?

3. Albert earned an average of \$435 per week for the first six weeks of the year. He earned \$700 in the sixth week alone. What were Albert's average earnings for the first five weeks of the year? (Disregard the \$ sign when gridding your answer.)

4. It took Andrew $1\frac{1}{2}$ hours to drive from Aurora to Zalesville at an average speed of 52 miles per hour. How fast did he have to drive back in order to reach home in 80 minutes?

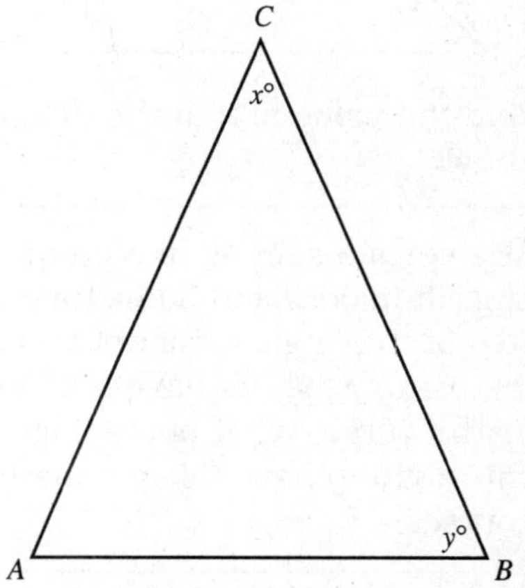

5. If in ΔABC above, side AC = side BC and $x \geq 64$, what is the greatest possible value for y?

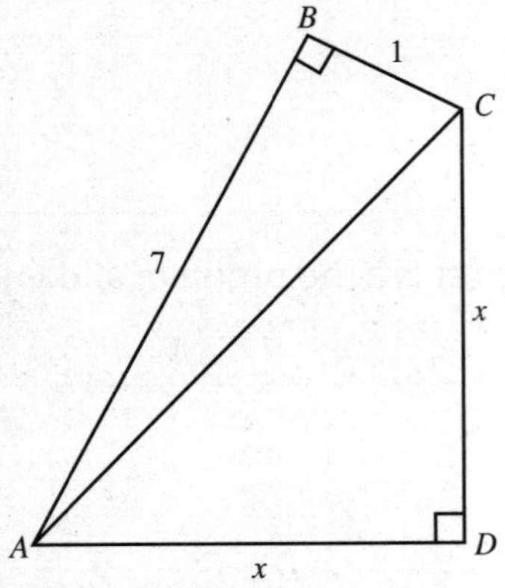

6. Find the value of x in the diagram above.

7. At a certain school, in a group of 20 English majors and 30 history majors, 50% of the English majors and 20% of the history majors have not taken a math course. What percentage of the entire group have taken a math course?

8. Three consecutive odd integers are written in increasing order. If the sum of the first and second integers and twice the third integer is 46, what is the second integer?

9. One positive number is 5 more than another. Their product is 23 more than their sum. What is their sum?

10. If $x \star y = x^y + y^x$, and the value of $2 \star P$ is greater than 17 but less than 32, what is one possible value of P?

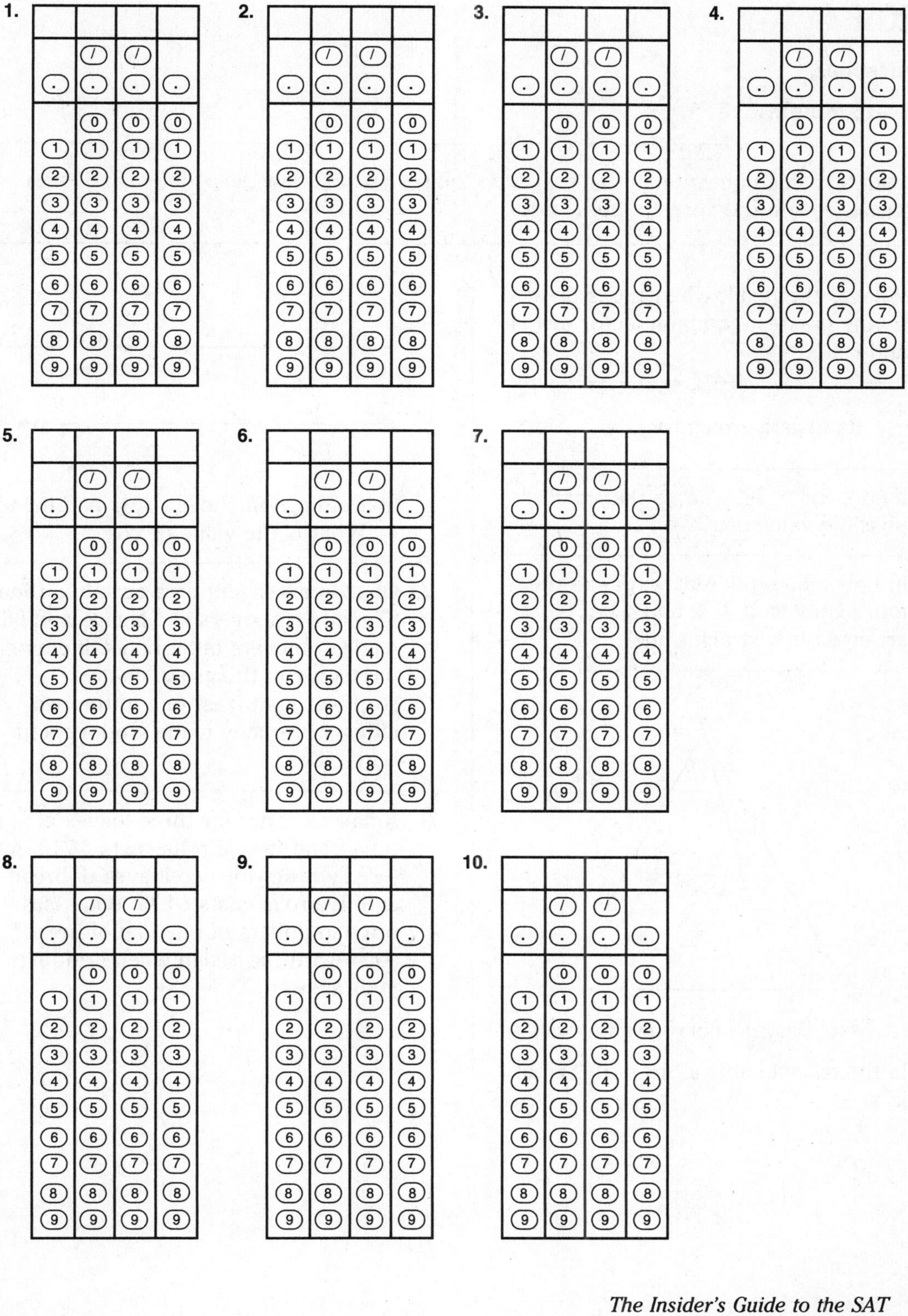
1.
2.
3.
4.
5.
6.
7.
8.
9.
10.

EXERCISE 4

10 Questions

Time—15 Minutes

Directions: Each question in this exercise requires you to solve the problem and enter your answer in the corresponding grid.

1. What is the result when 150 is divided by the greatest common factor of 144 and 600?

2. $\frac{4}{3}$ + its negative reciprocal = ?

3. If $(x - 3)^2 = 36$, what is the smallest possible value of x?

4. In how many different ways can the four symbols ©, J, #, and § be arranged in a straight line?

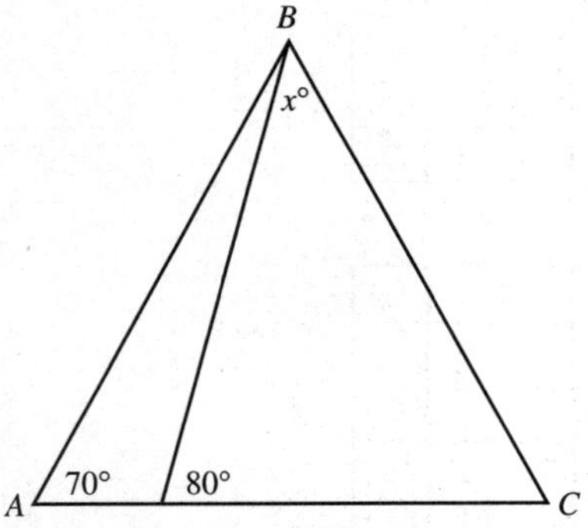

Note: Diagram not drawn to scale.

5. In the triangle above, $AB = BC$. What is x?

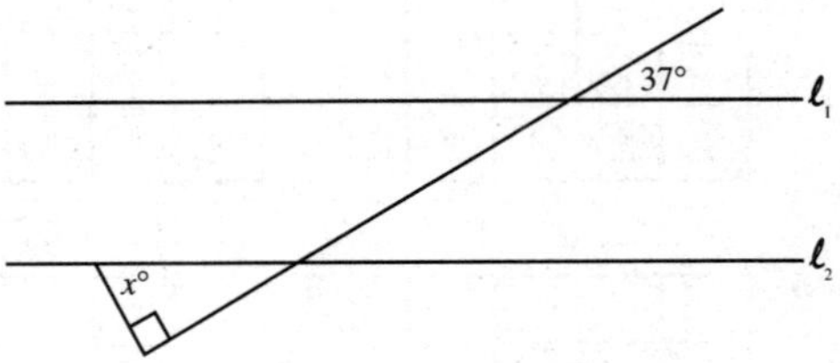

6. In the diagram shown, ℓ_1 is parallel to ℓ_2. What is the value of x?

7. Of 120 passengers on a certain airline, 87 made stopovers in Chicago and 96 made stopovers in St. Louis. If every passenger in the group made a stopover in at least one of the two cities, how many made stopovers in both cities?

8. A bakery order for three loaves of bread and twelve rolls costs \$8.10. A bakery order for two loaves of bread and five rolls costs \$4.35. What is the price in dollars of one loaf of bread? (Disregard the \$ sign when gridding your answer.)

9. The product of two numbers is 6. One of the two numbers is 5 less than the other. What is the absolute value of the sum of the two numbers?

10. If © *N* © = N^2 when *N* is odd and 2*N* + 1 when *N* is even, what is the value of © (© 5 ©) ©?

1.
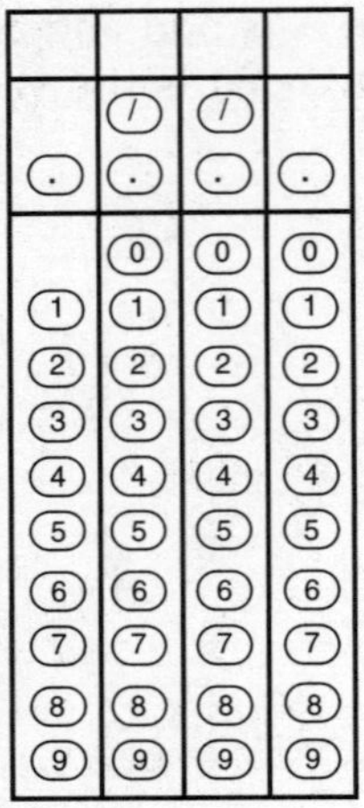

2.
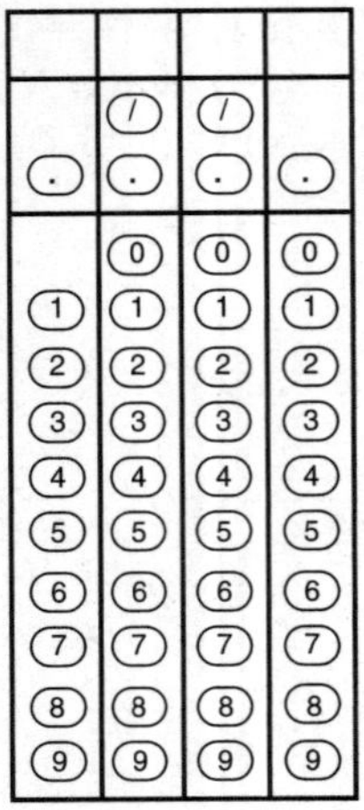

3.
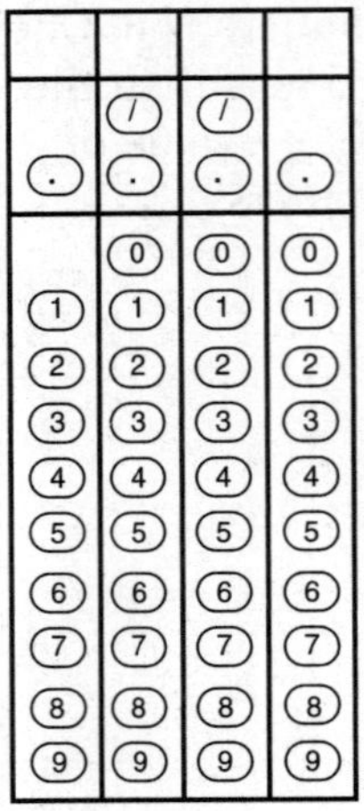

4.
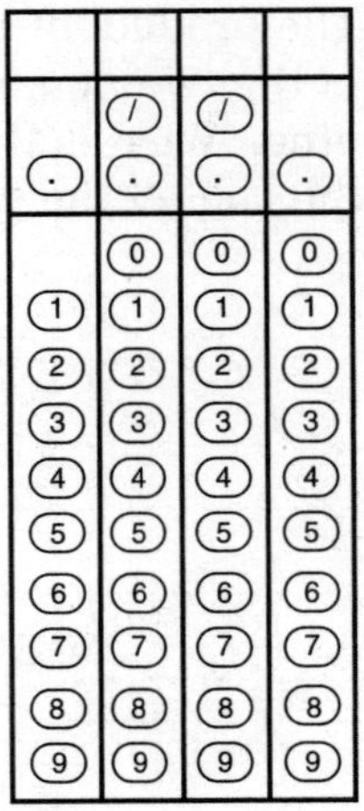

5.
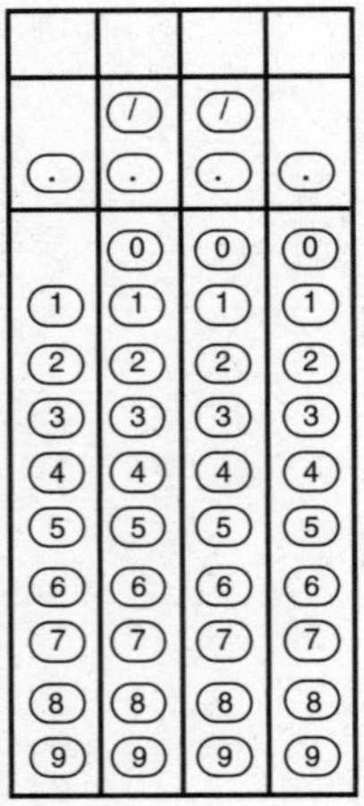

6.
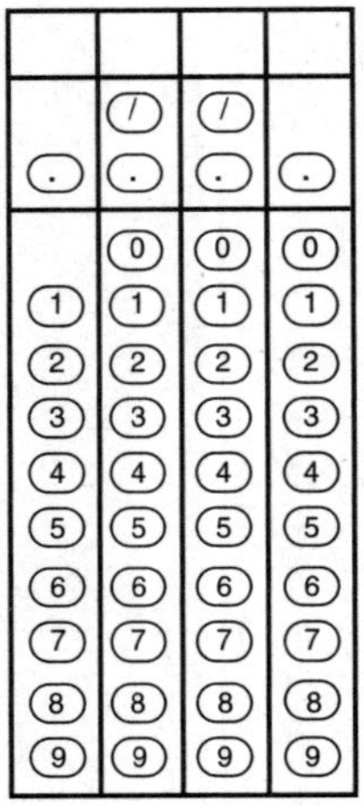

7.
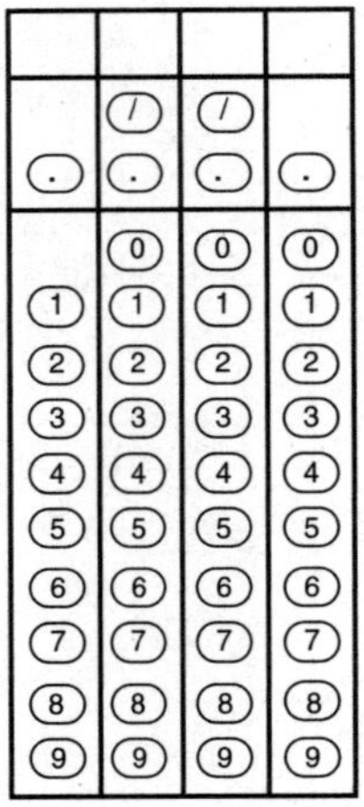

8.
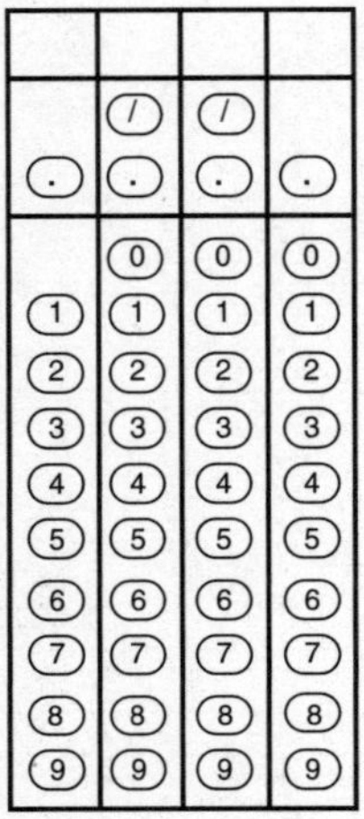

9.
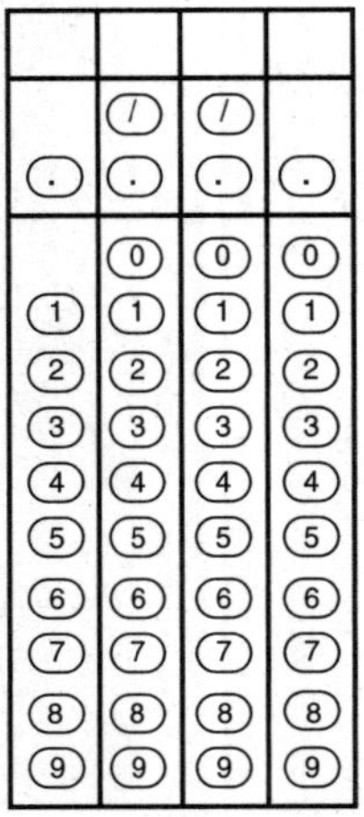

10.
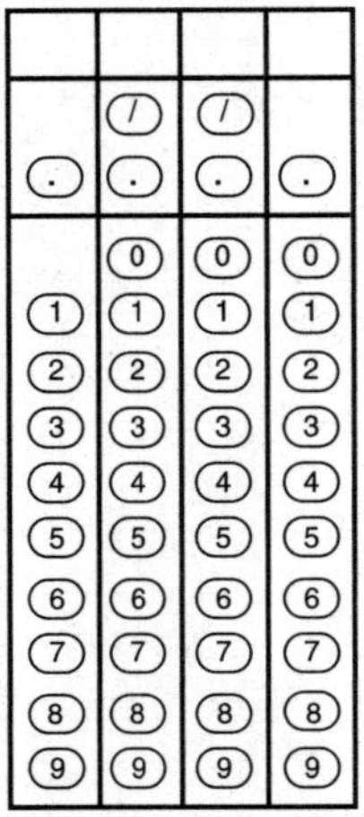

EXERCISE 5

10 Questions

Time—15 Minutes

Directions: Each question in this exercise requires you to solve the problem and enter your answer in the corresponding grid.

1. If $410{,}000 = 4.1 \times 10^n$, what is the value of n?

2. A water tank is exactly one-quarter full. At noon, a valve is opened, allowing water to pour into the tank at the rate of 90 gallons an hour. Half an hour later, the tank is exactly one-third full. How many gallons of water does the tank hold when it is completely full?

3. The expression $m \star n$ is defined as the product of all integers from m through n. For example, $5 \star 8 = (5)(6)(7)(8)$. What is the value of $\frac{4 \star 9}{2 \star 10}$?

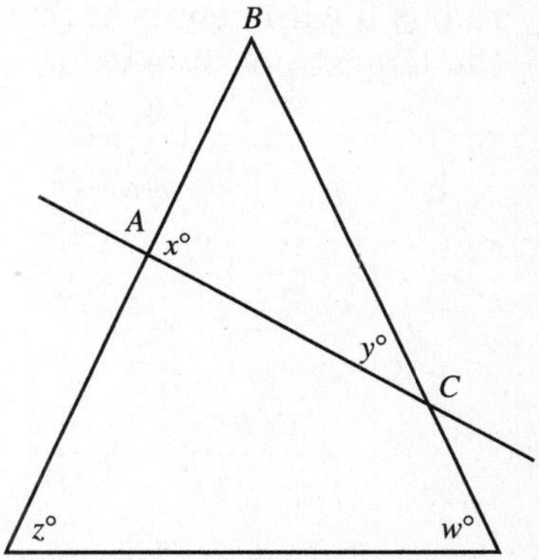

4. In the figure above, $(x + y)$ is an integer greater than 110. What is the smallest possible value of $(w + z)$?

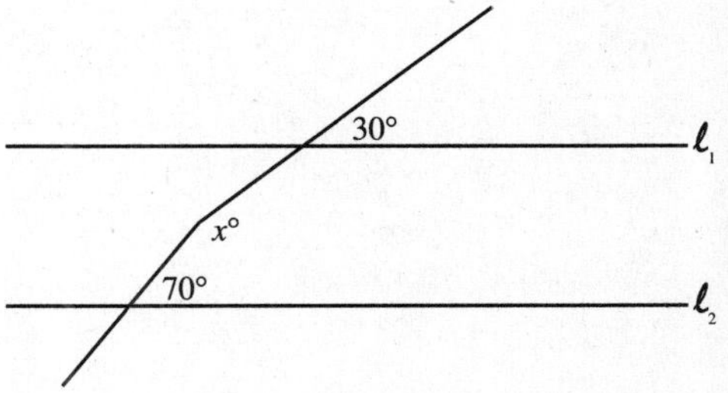

5. In the figure above, ℓ_1 is parallel to ℓ_2. What is the value of x?

6. The ratio of Alice's weekly salary to Joan's weekly salary last year was 5:4. This year, Alice got a 20% weekly raise, and Joan got a \$100 weekly raise. As a result, they now have the same salary. What was Joan's original weekly salary?

7. What is the slope of the line passing through points (6,4) and (3,−1)?

8. The point (t, −1) lies on a circle of radius 5 with center at (4,2). What is the largest possible value of t?

9. If four students are lined up randomly for a photograph, what is the chance that they will be lined up in order of height from shortest to tallest?

10. Mary drives her car 6 miles per hour faster than Joe. If Mary drives 336 miles in the same time it takes Joe to drive 294 miles, what is the speed that Mary drives in miles per hour?

1.
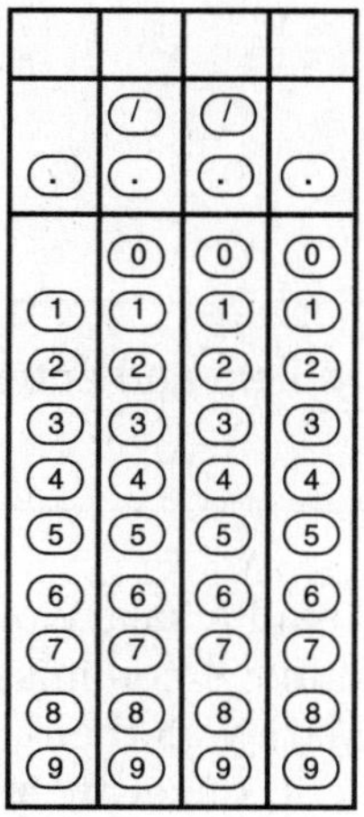

2.
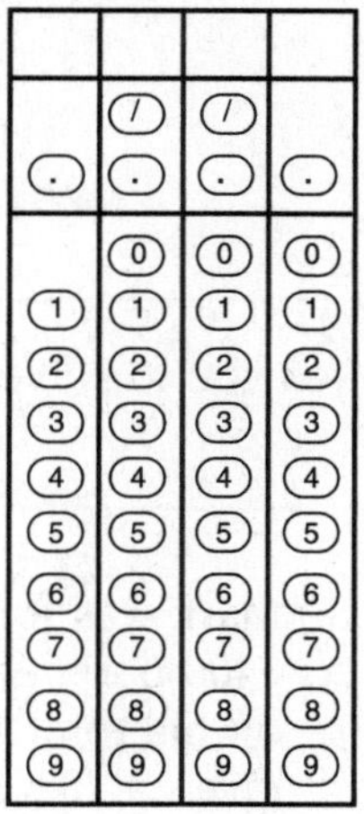

3.
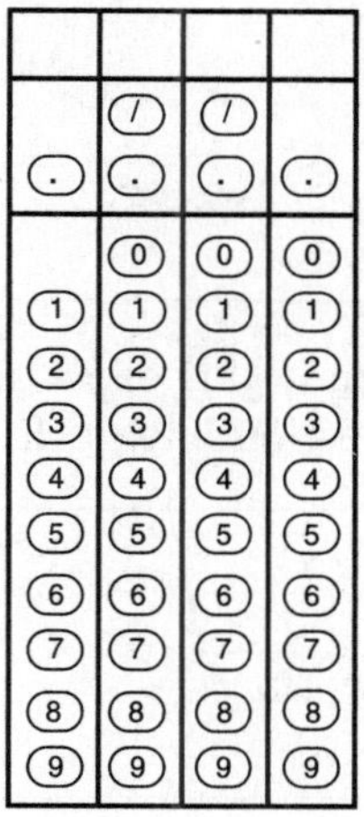

4.
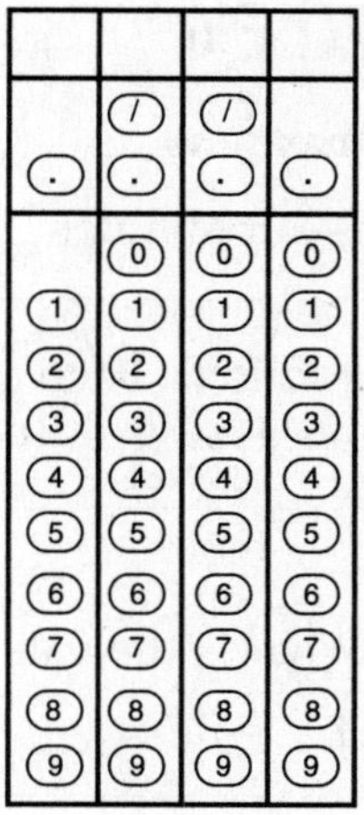

5.
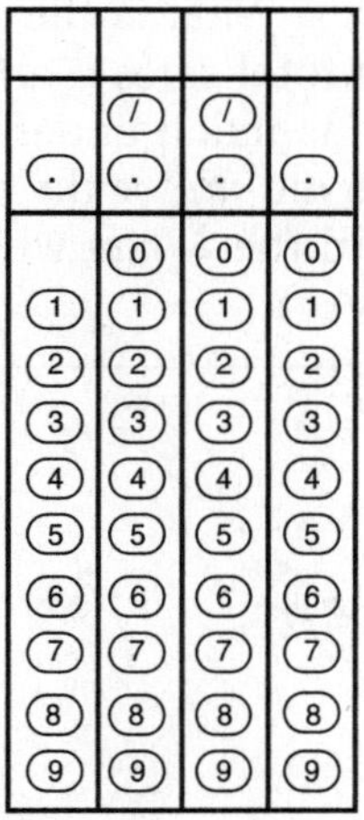

6.
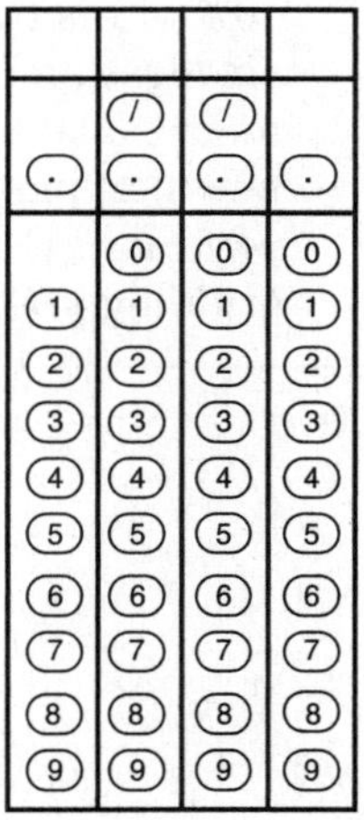

7.
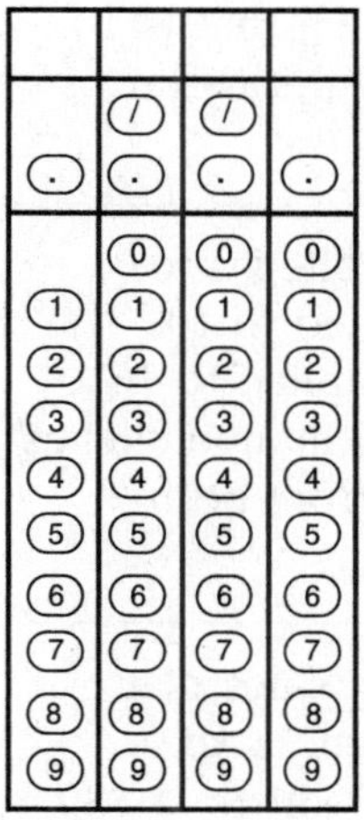

8.
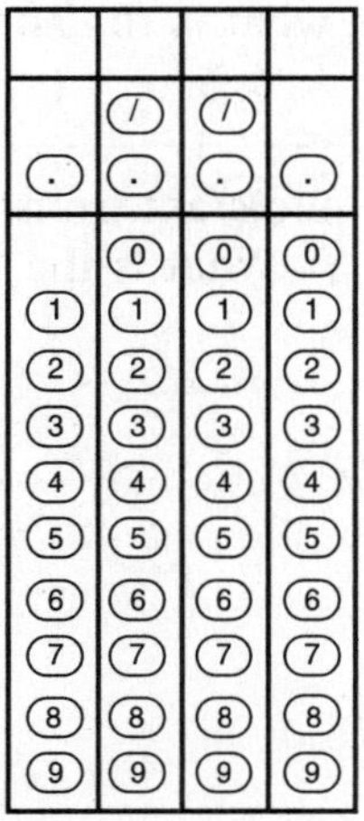

9.
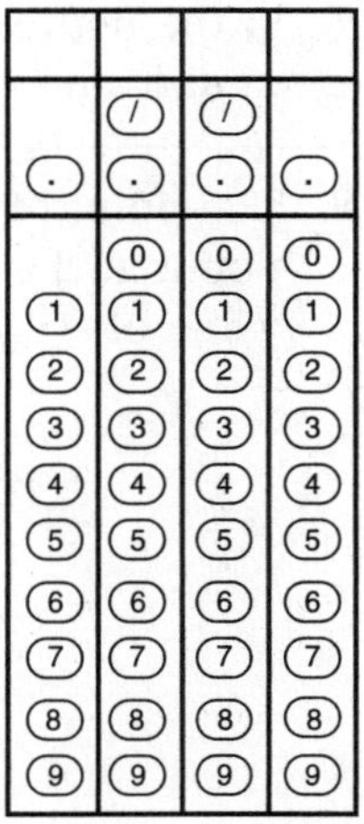

10.
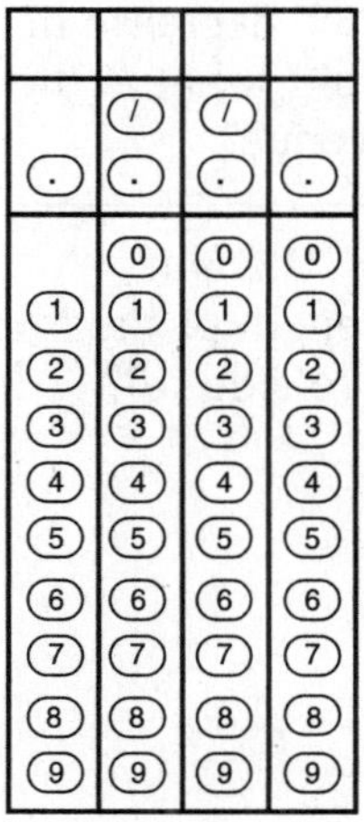

EXERCISE 6

10 Questions

Time—15 Minutes

Directions: Each question in this exercise requires you to solve the problem and enter your answer in the corresponding grid.

1. What is the value of $t = \dfrac{z - 1}{2z + 3}$ if $z = 3$?

2. A rectangle has one side that is 6 units long and a diagonal that is 10 units long. What is the perimeter of the rectangle?

3. Helena applied to 12 colleges for admission. Sergei applied to 10. Between them, they applied to 16 different colleges. How many colleges received applications from both Helena and Sergei?

4. The total revenue from sales of x items at price p per item is xp. A clothing store sold 100 shirts at \$30 per shirt. If increasing the price per shirt by 10% causes a 5% decrease in the number of shirts sold, what is the percent increase in revenue?

5. In ΔABC, $AC = 16$, $BC = 12$, and $AB = 20$. What is the length of the altitude from vertex C to side AB?

6. Mark was formerly paid a salary of \$400 per week plus an 8% commission on his total sales. Mark was then given a 20% salary cut, offset by an increase in his commission rate to 10% of his total sales. What is the smallest amount of total sales Mark must make to earn as much under the new pay plan as he did under the old pay plan? (Disregard the \$ sign when gridding your answer.)

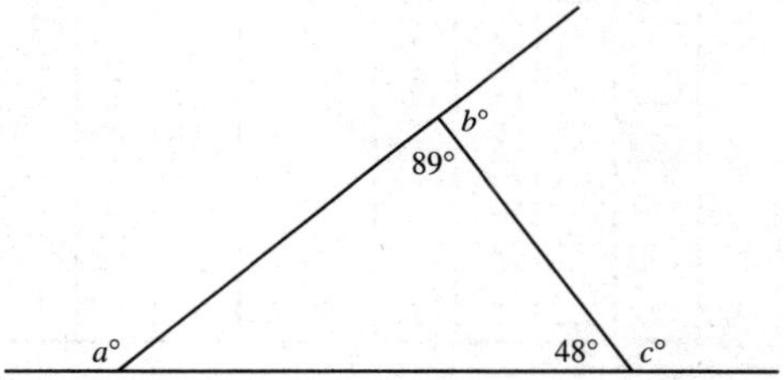

7. In the figure above, what is the sum of a, b, and c?

8. The point $(4,t)$ is equidistant from points $(1,1)$ and $(5,3)$. What is the value of t?

9. A bag contains three balls, one red, one white, and one blue. A ball is drawn at random and replaced in the bag, and another ball is drawn at random. What is the probability that the two colors drawn are NOT the same?

10. The product of two numbers is 30. One number is 7 more than the other. What is the largest possible value of the sum of the two numbers?

1.

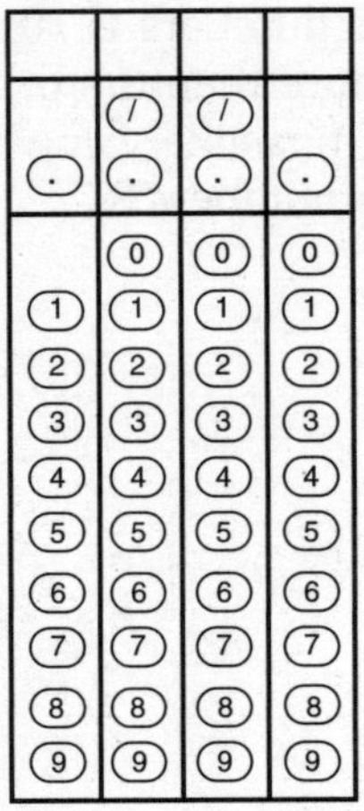

2.

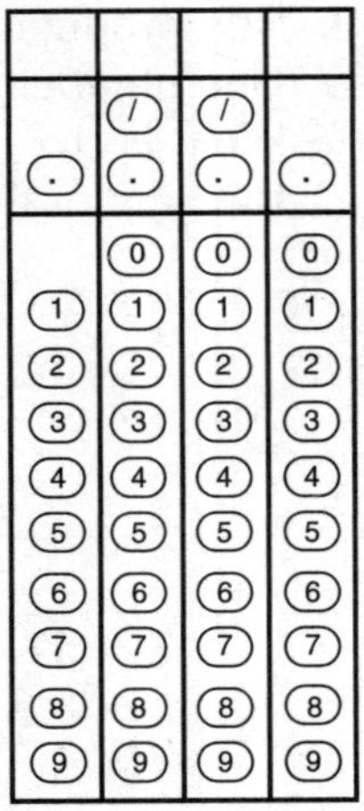

3.

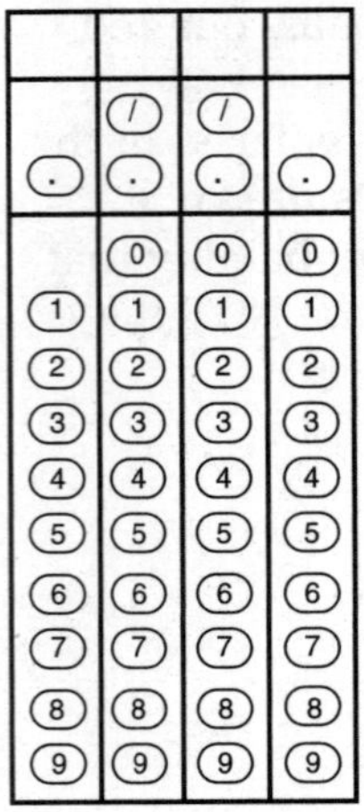

4.

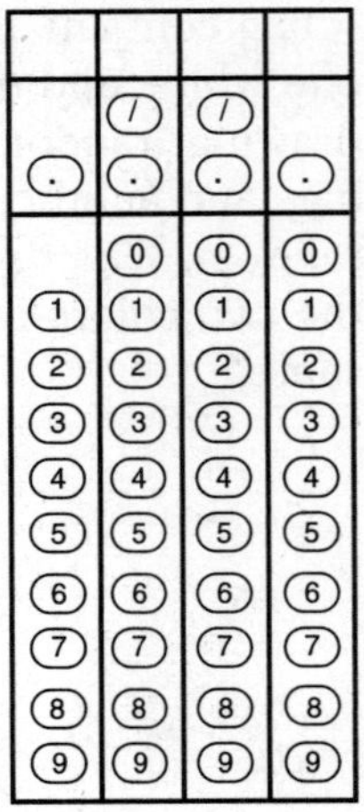

5.

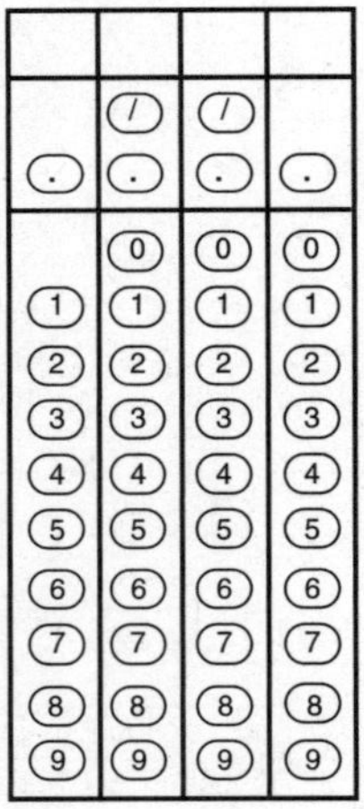

6.

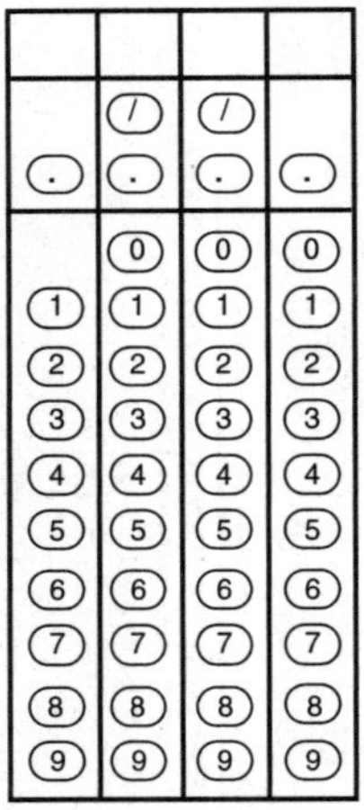

7.

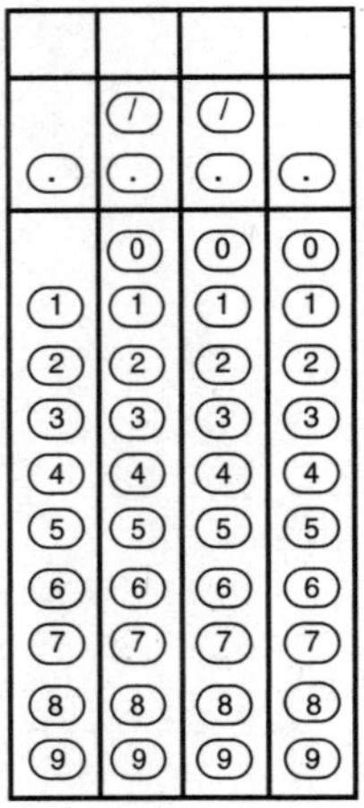

8.

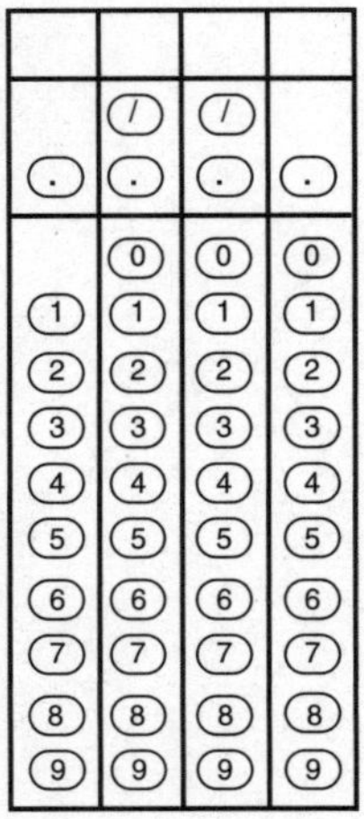

9.

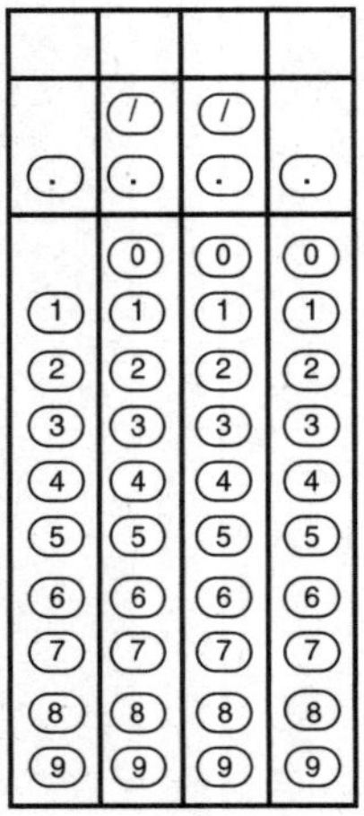

10.

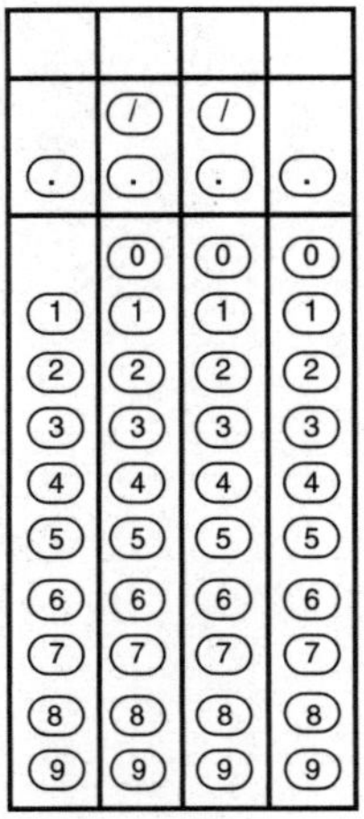

Answer Key

Exercise 1

1.
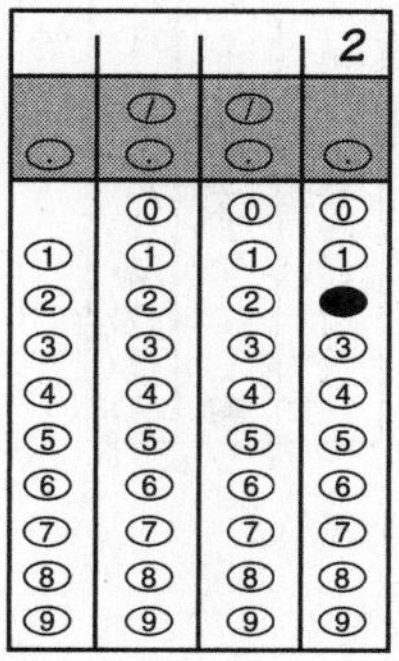

2.
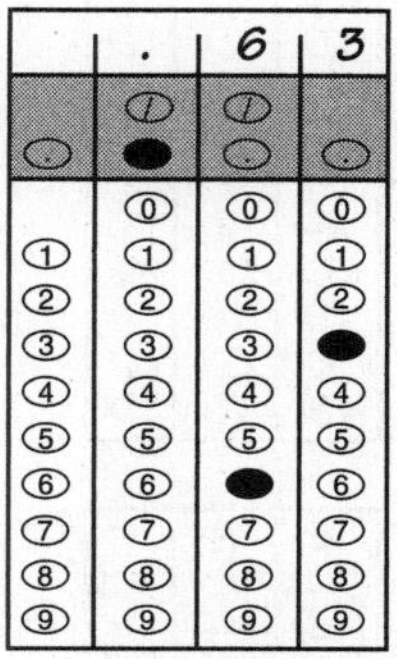

3.
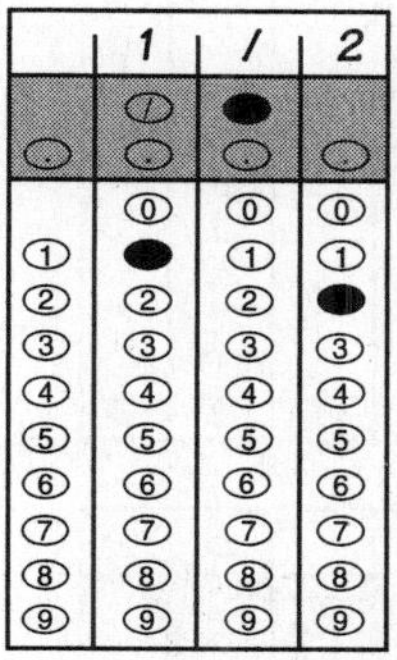

4.
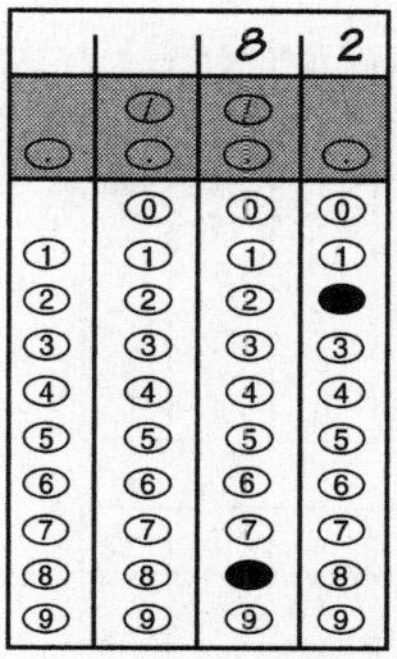

5.
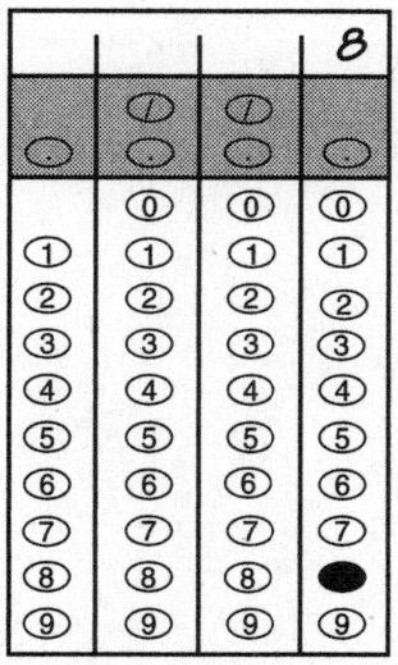

6.
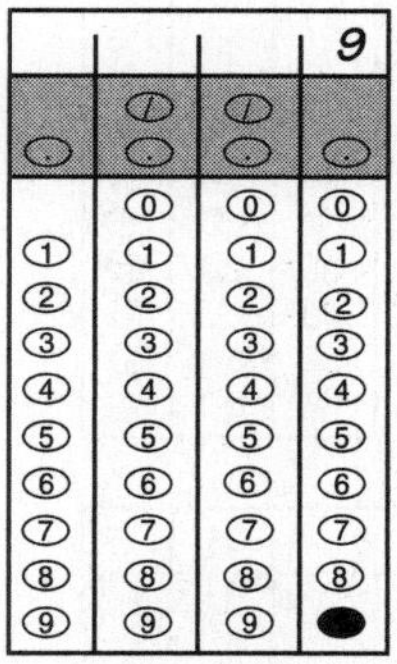

7.
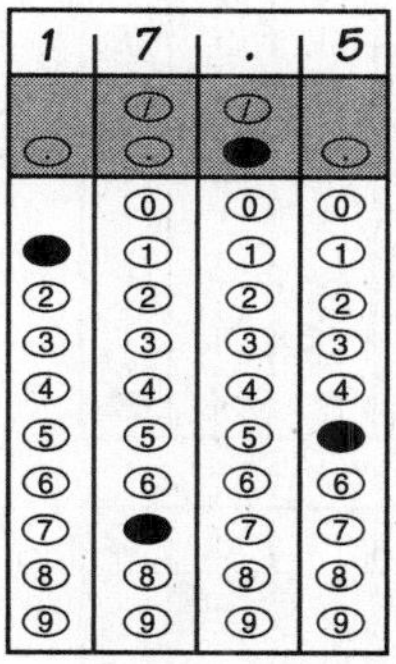

8.
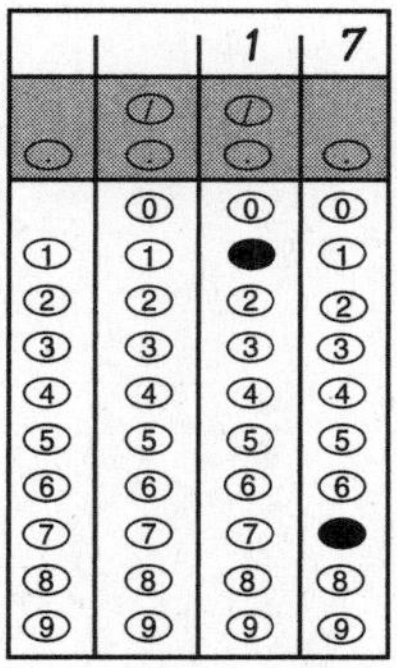

9.
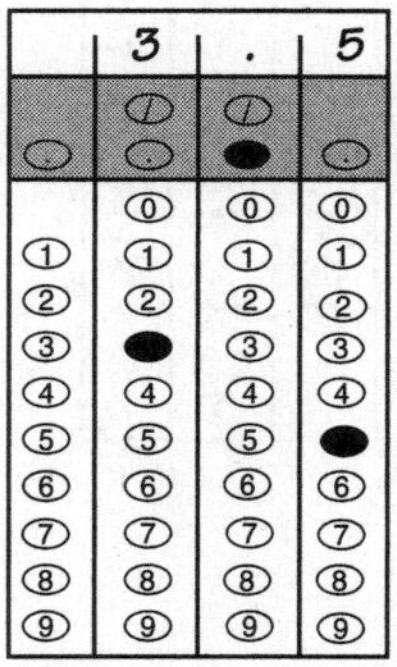

10.
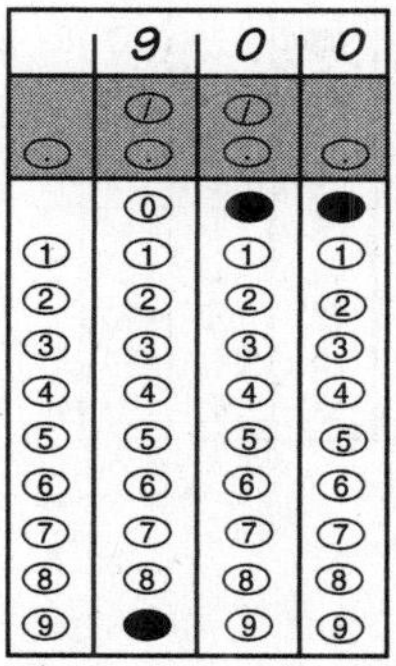

Exercise 2

1.

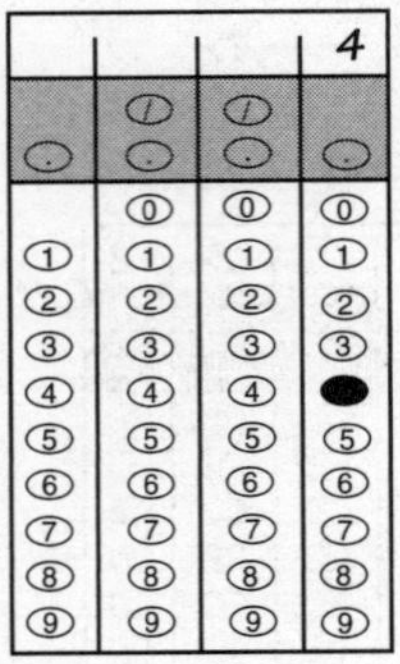

2.

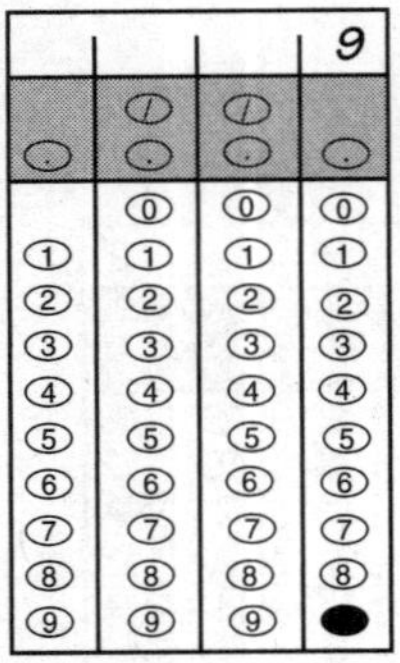

3.

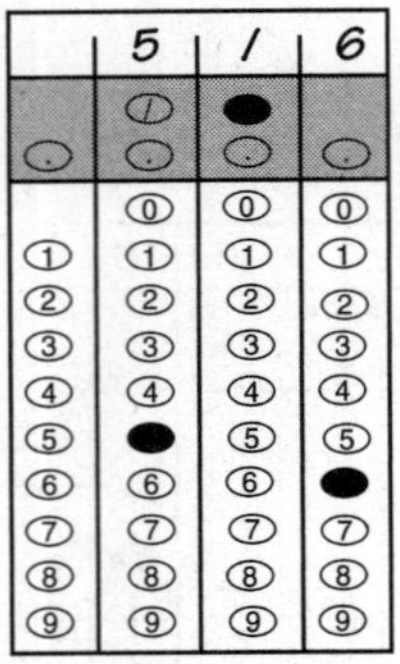

4.

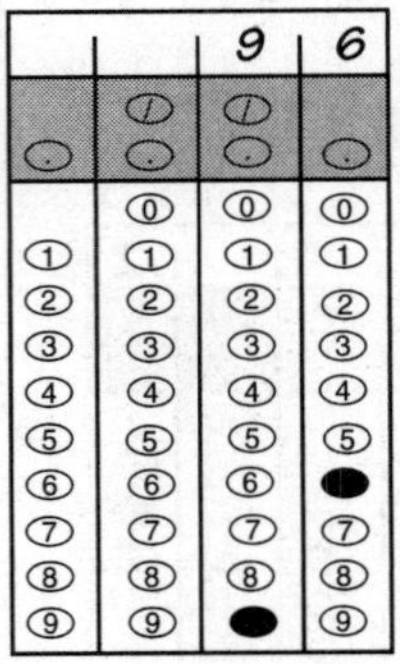

5.

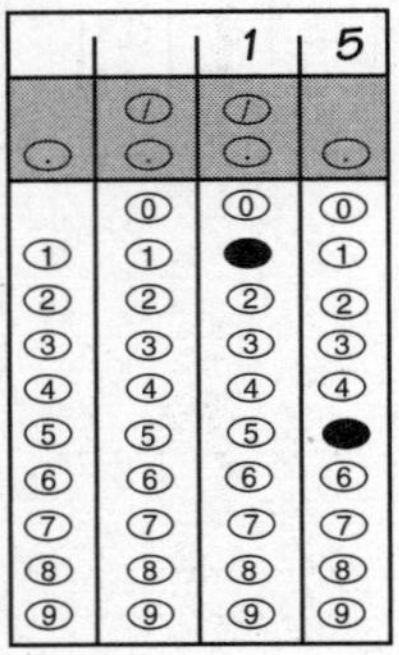

6.

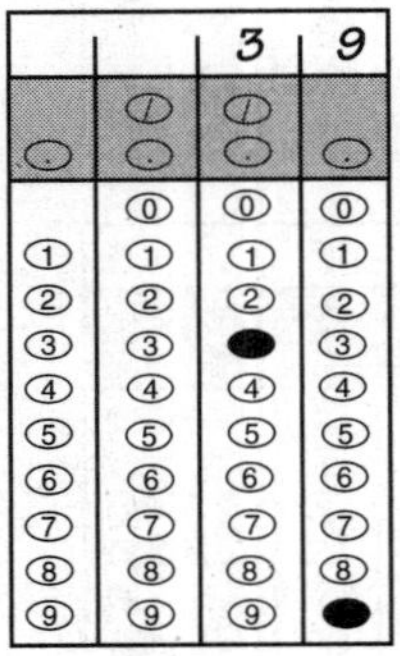

7.

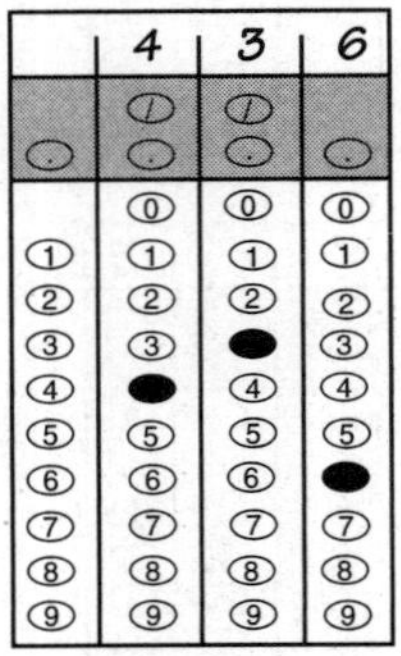

8.

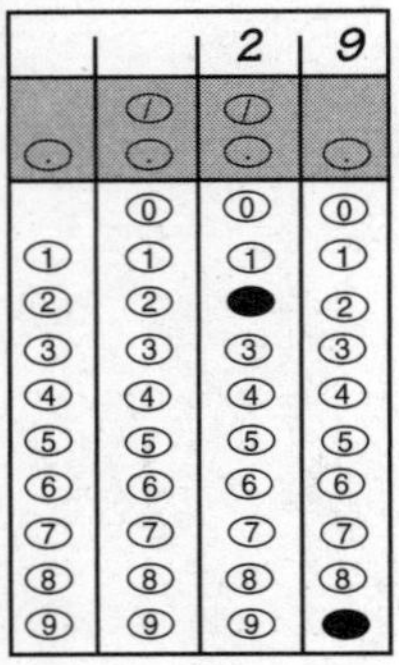

9.

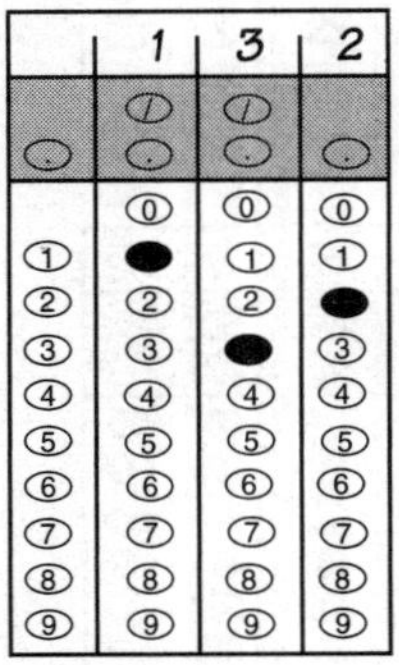

10.

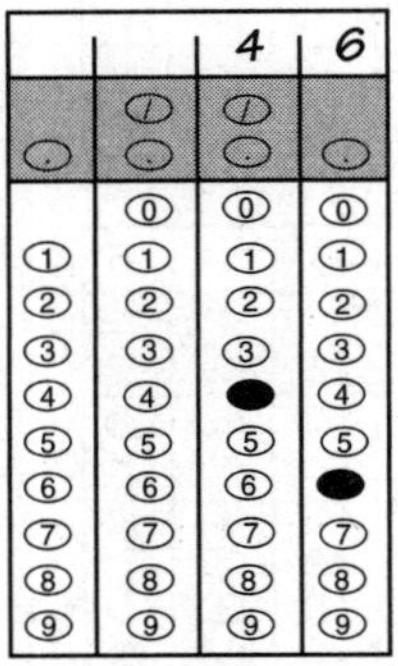

Exercise 3

1.
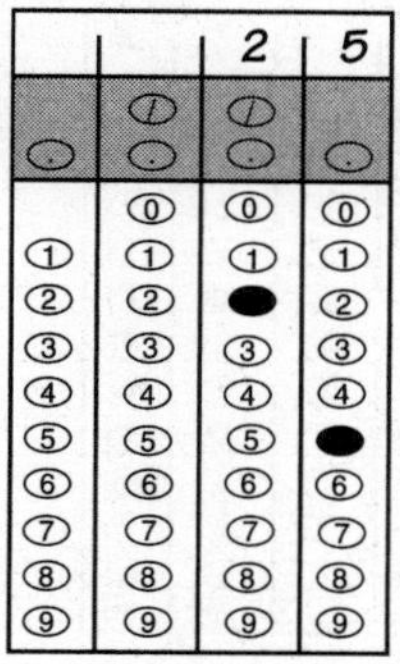

2.
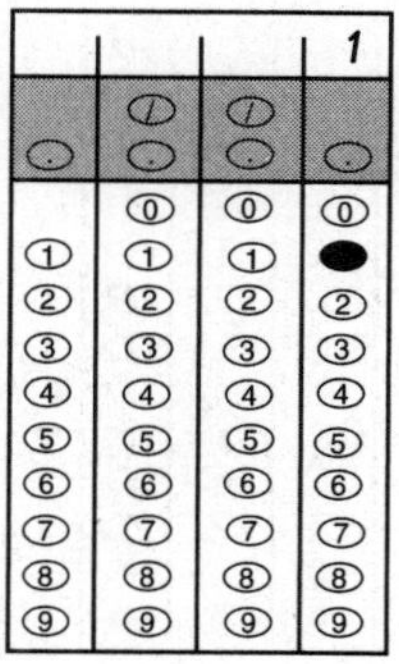

3.
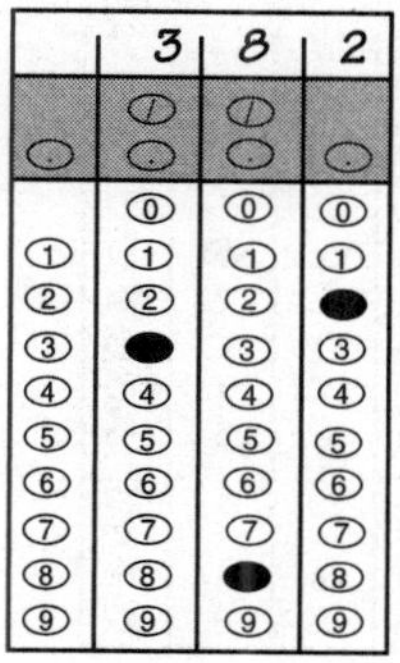

4.
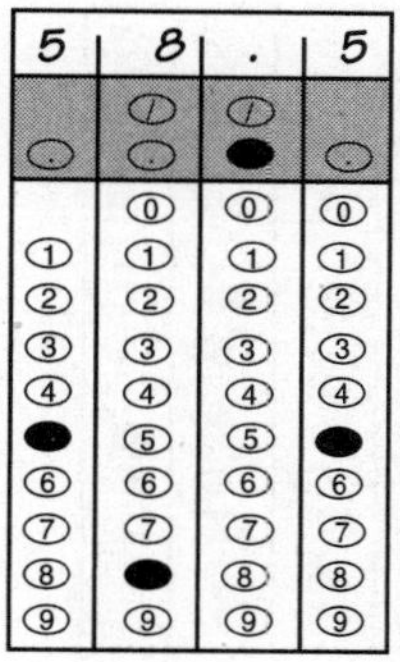

5.
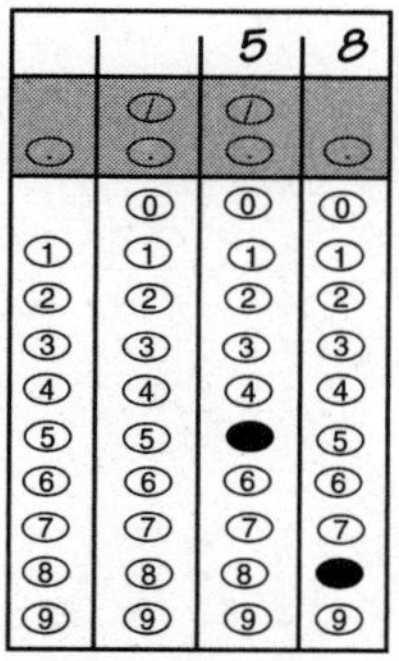

6.
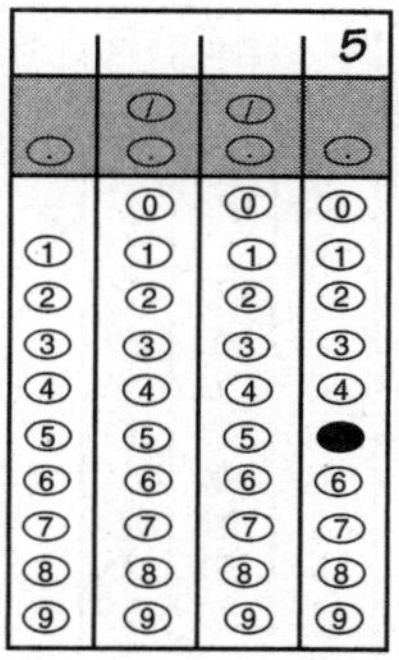

7.
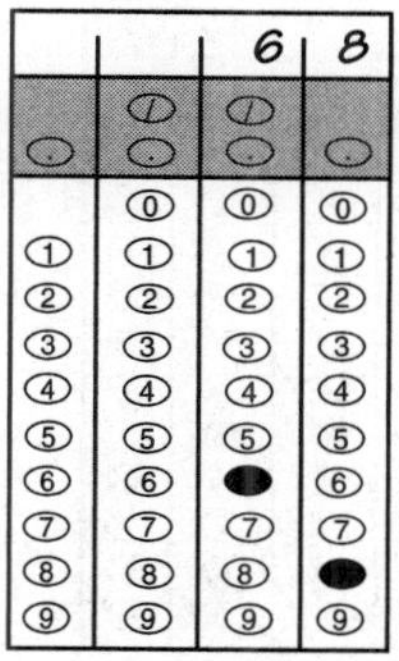

8.
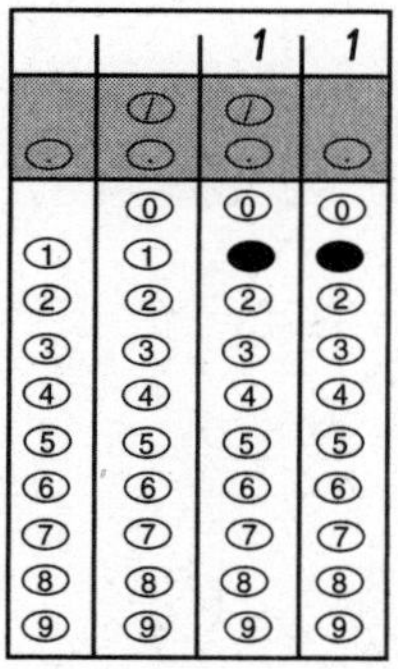

9.
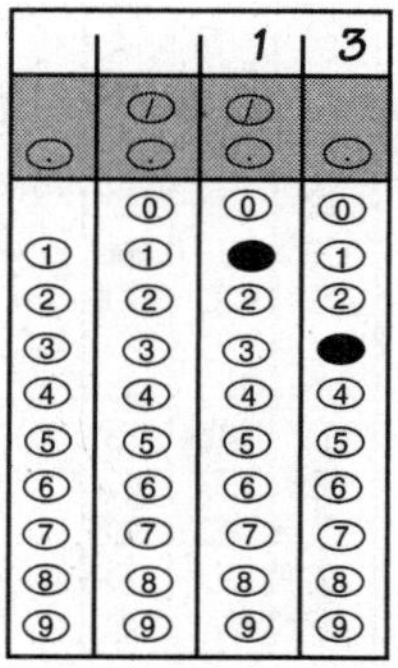

10.
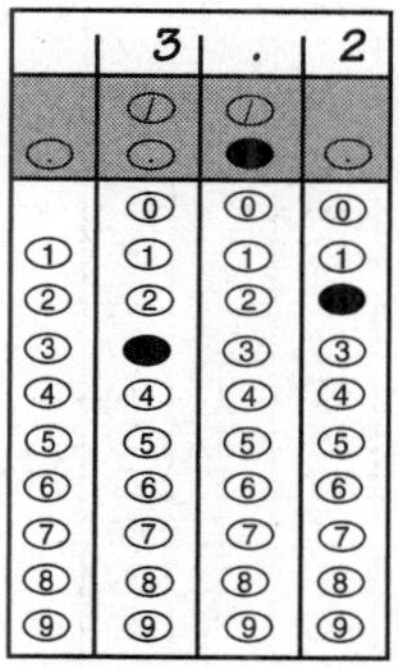

Exercise 4

1.
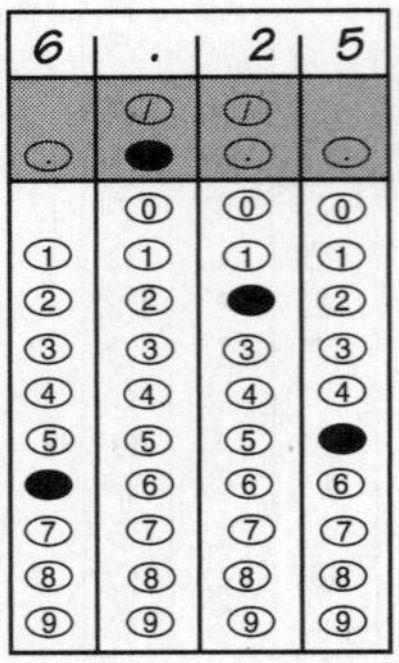

2.
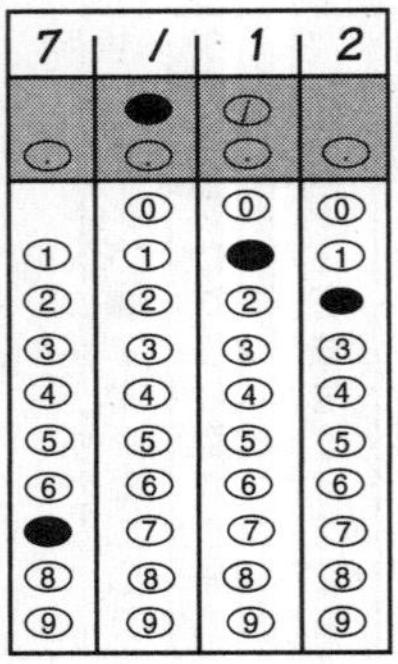

3.
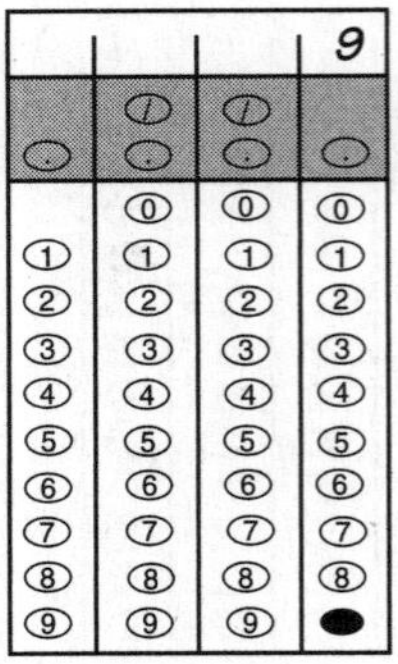

4.
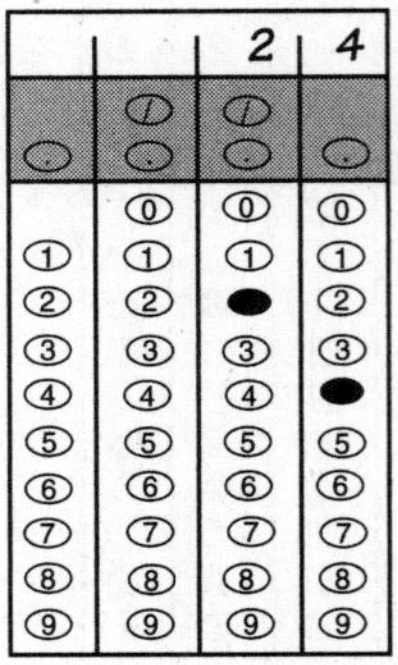

5.
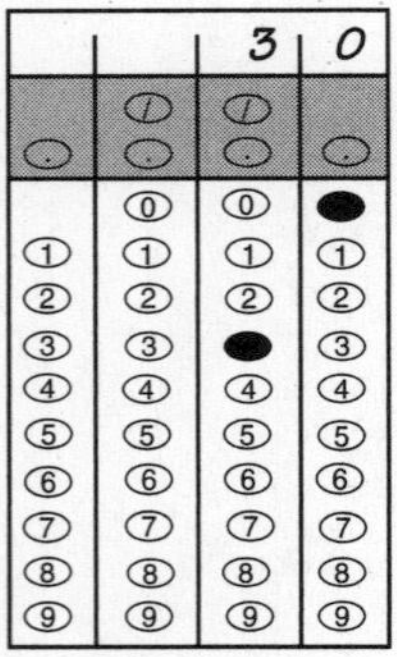

6.
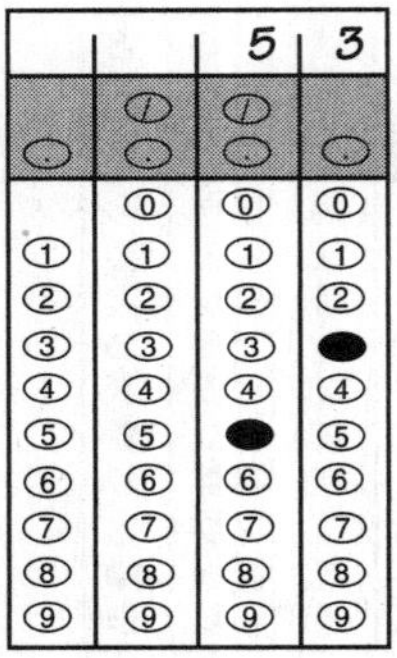

7.
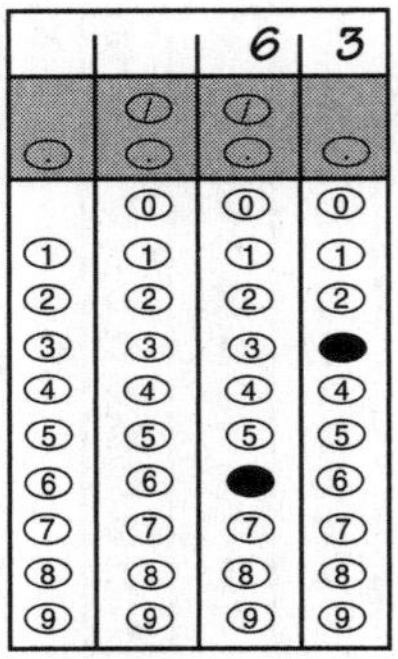

8.
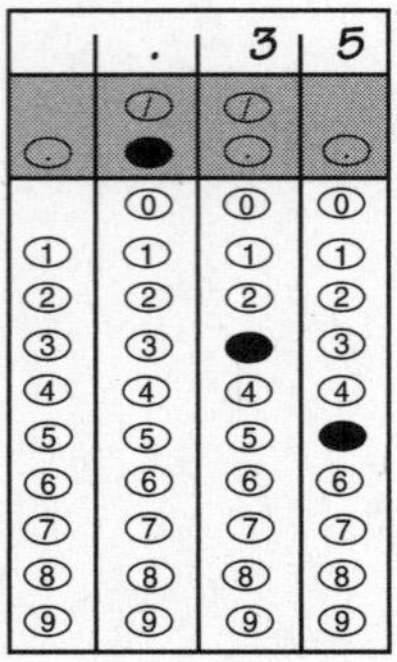

9.
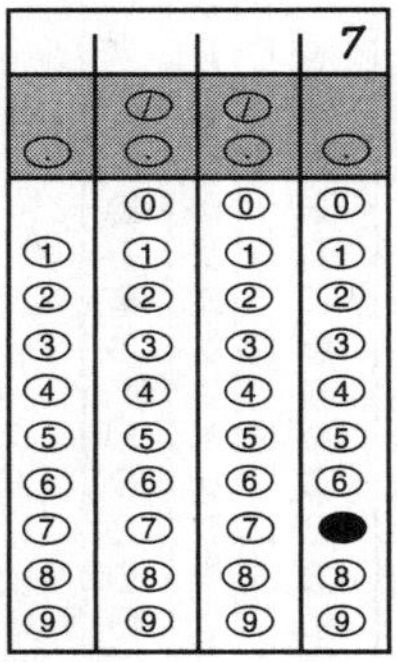

10.
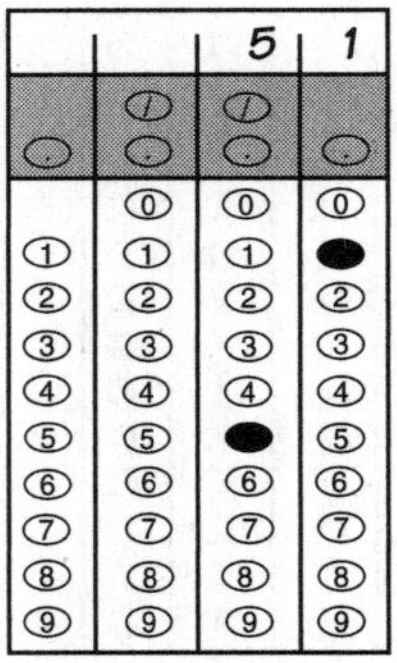

Exercise 5

1.
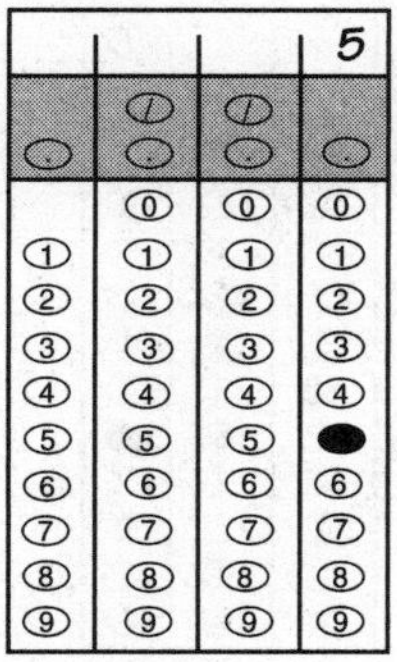

2.
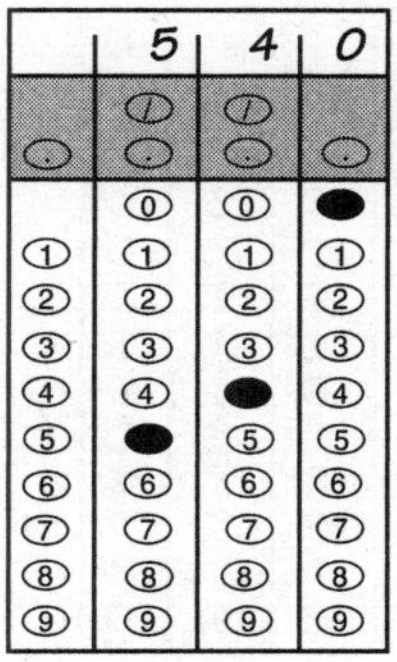

3.
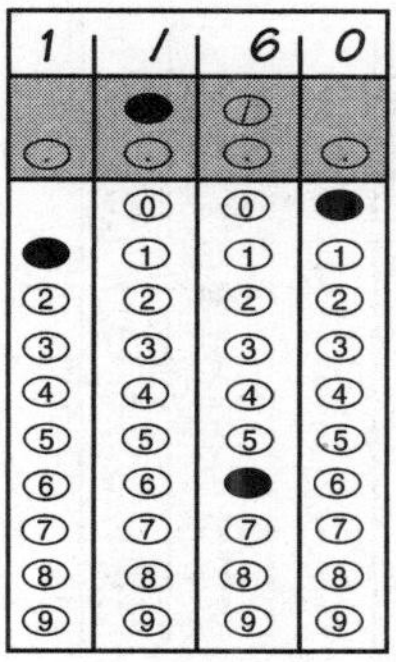

4.
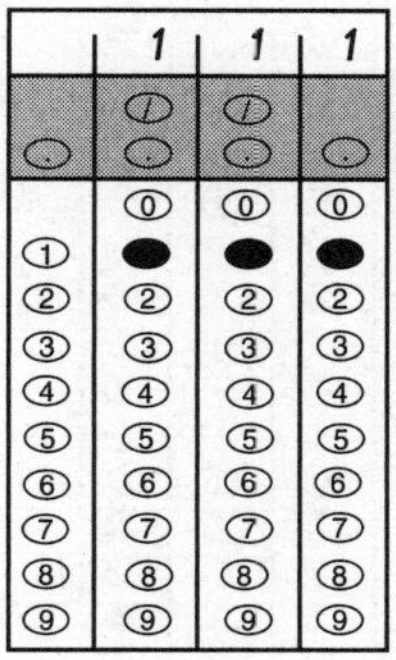

5.
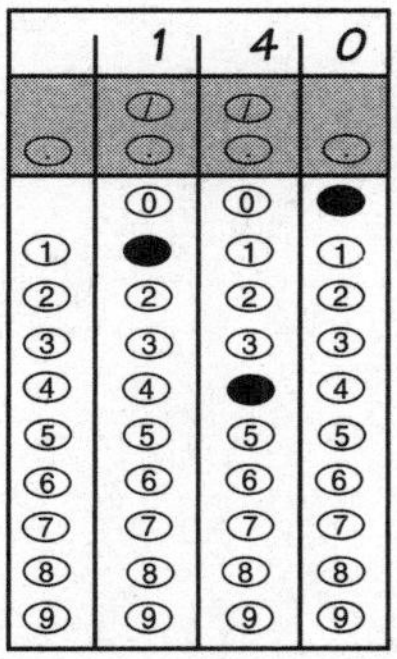

6.
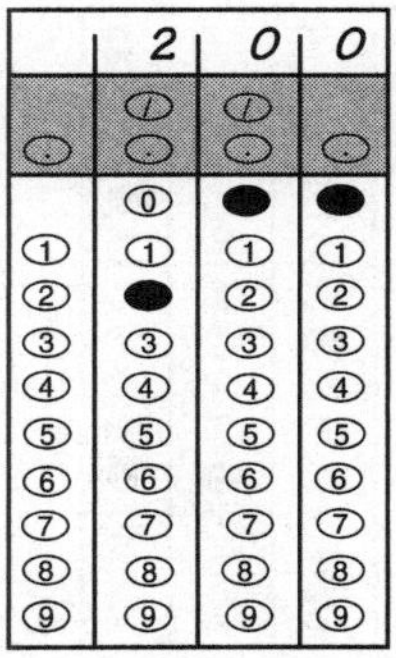

7.
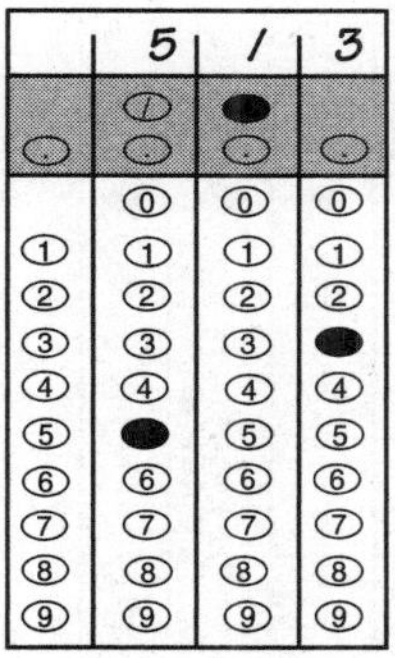

8.
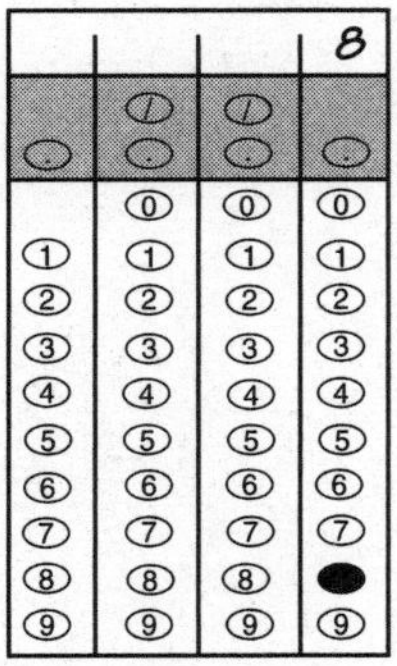

9.
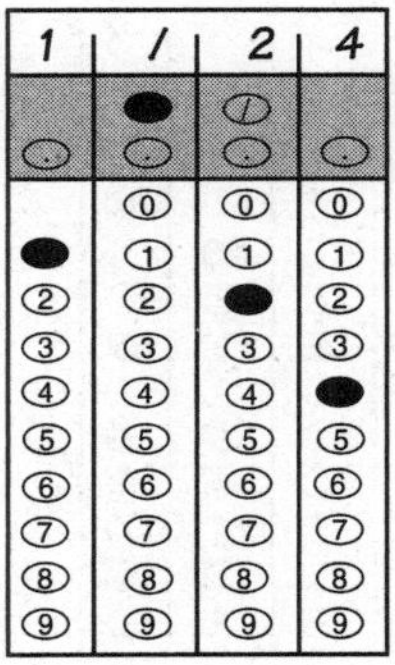

10.
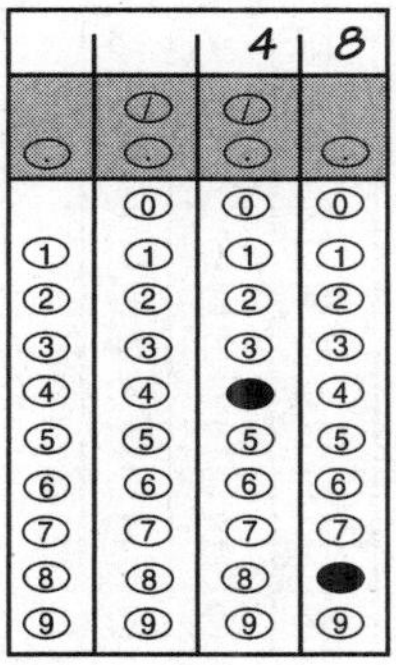

Exercise 6

1.
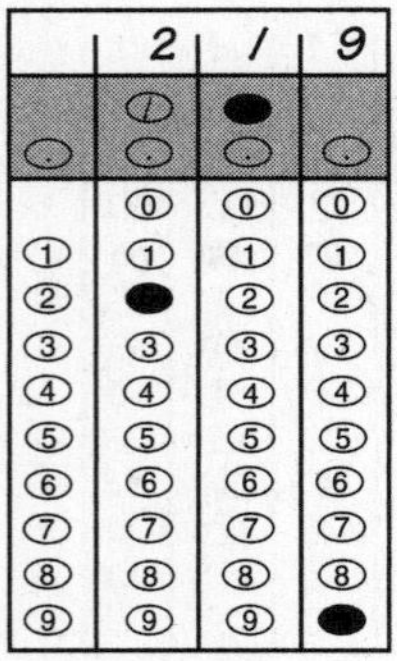

2.
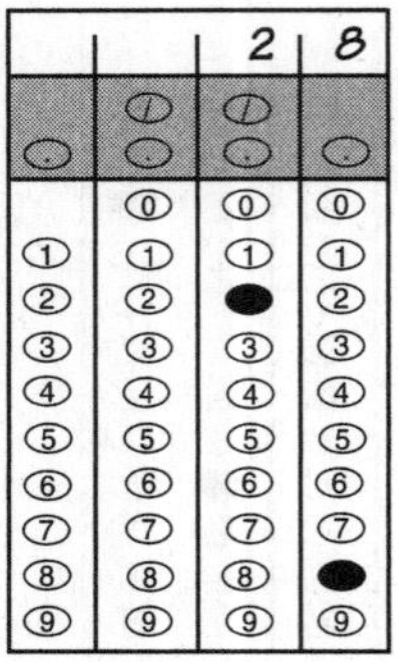

3.
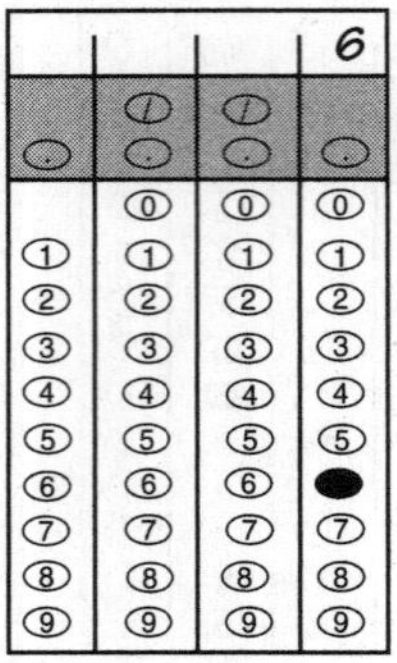

4.
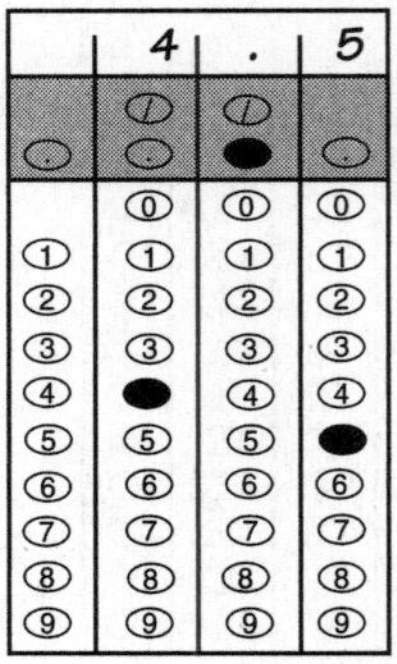

5.
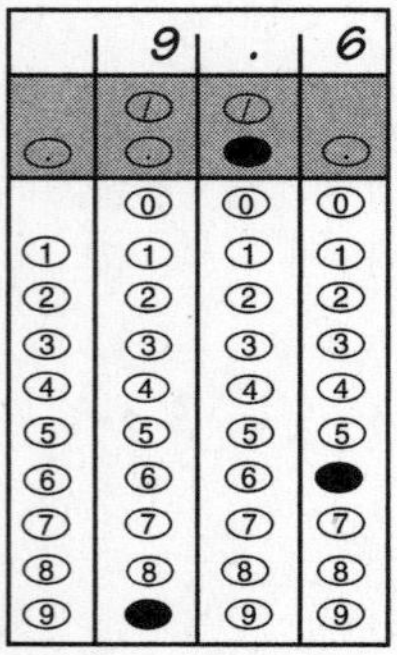

6.
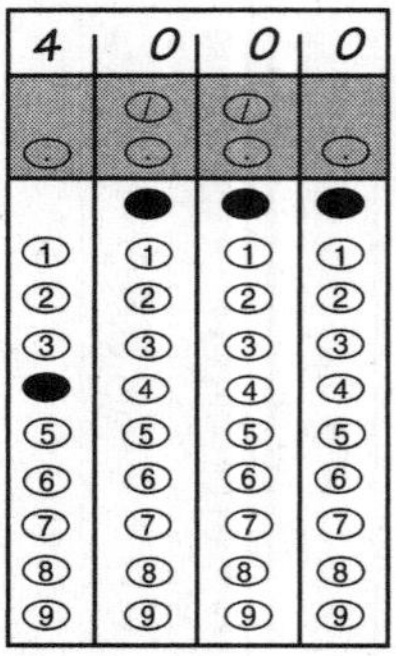

7.
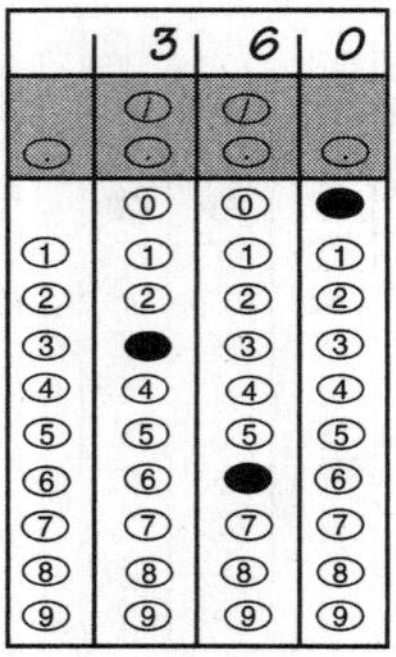

8.
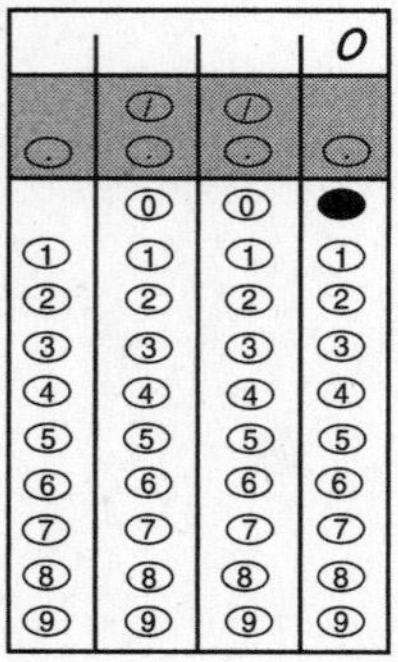

9.
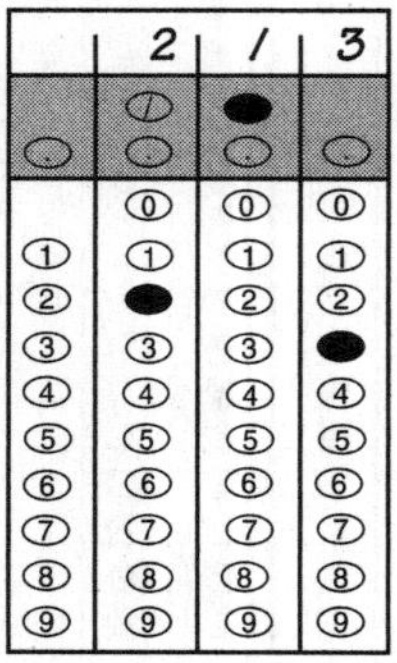

10.
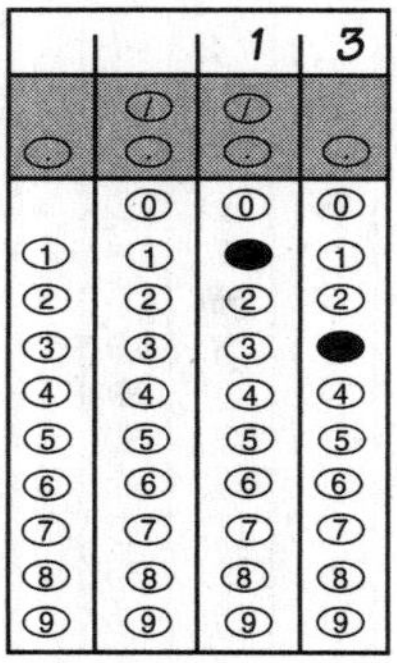

Explanatory Answers

EXERCISE 1

1. The fraction bar in a fraction acts as a grouping symbol like parentheses, meaning we should first calculate the numerator and denominator separately. That is, we should read this as $(3 + B) \div (4 \times 3 - 3 \times B)$. When $B = 3$, the numerator is $3 + 3 = 6$, and the denominator is $12 - 3 \times 3 = 12 - 9 = 3$. Therefore, the fraction is $\frac{6}{3} = 2$.

2. In 7 days, Mario would do $\frac{7}{20}$ of the entire task. In the same week, Angelo would do $\frac{7}{25}$ of the entire task. Therefore, together they do $\frac{7}{25} + \frac{7}{20}$. The lowest common denominator is 100. Thus, $\frac{7}{25} + \frac{7}{20} = \frac{28}{100} + \frac{35}{100} = 0.63$.

3. When working with fractions, *of* can usually be interpreted to mean *times*. So using J, S, and P to stand for the people's earnings respectively, we have:

   $$S = \frac{2}{3}P;\ J = \frac{3}{4}S$$

   Thus:

   $$J = \left(\frac{3}{4}\right)\left(\frac{2}{3}\right)P = \frac{1}{2}P$$

   Hence, Jasmine's earnings are one-half Paul's.

4. Since the prices of the first six paintings average \$70, the total received for the 6 was \$420. In the same way, the next 4 paintings must have brought in \$400 in order to average \$100 apiece. Therefore, we have a total of 10 paintings selling for \$420 + \$400 = \$820, and the average is $\frac{\$820}{10} = \$82$.

5. Expressing all amounts in dollars, let x = cost of an adult ticket, and let y = cost of a child's ticket. For the Greens:

   $$x + 3y = 14$$

   For the Arkwrights:

   $$2x + 5y = 25$$

   Solve the first equation for x, because that is the simpler one to isolate:

   $$x = 14 - 3y$$

Substitute into the second equation:

$$2(14 - 3y) + 5y = 25$$

This gives us one equation in one unknown that we can solve:

$$28 - 6y + 5y = 25$$
$$-y = -3; y = 3$$

Now that we know $y = 3$, we put this into $x = 14 - 3y$ to get:

$$x = 14 - 3(3) = 5$$

Thus, the adult tickets were \$5.00 each and the children's tickets were \$3.00 each; the cost of one of each totals \$8.00.

6. The product of the last two terms, $6m$, must be 18. Therefore, $m = 3$. If $m = 3$, then the sum of the outer and inner products becomes $-6x - 3x = -9x$, which equals rx. Hence, $r = -9$, and $-(-9) = 9$.
7. Calling the degree measure of $\angle A$ x, we have the following:

$$x = \text{number of degrees in } \angle A$$
$$3x + 20 = \text{number of degrees in } \angle B$$
$$x + (3x + 20) = 4x + 20 = \text{number of degrees in } \angle C$$

Summing, we have:

$$x + 3x + 20 + 4x + 20 = 180$$

Combining like terms:

$$8x + 40 = 180$$
$$8x = 140; x = 17.5$$

Clearly, $3x + 20$ and $4x + 20$ are larger than x, so the smallest angle is 17.5°.

8. In order to form a triangle, the sum of any two sides must exceed the third. Hence, $9 + 14 > x$. Therefore, x must be less than 23. The greatest integer less than 23 is 22. Hence, the maximum possible perimeter is $9 + 14 + 23 = 46$. Similarly, $x + 9 > 14$, which means that $x > 5$. The smallest integer greater than 5 is 6, and so the minimum possible perimeter is $9 + 14 + 6 = 29$. The difference between the two is $46 - 29 = 17$.
9. The average of the two x values is $\frac{(3 + 2)}{2} = \frac{5}{2}$. The average of the two y values is $\frac{(4 - 2)}{2} = 1$. Hence, $x_M + y_M = \frac{5}{2} + 1 = 3.5$.
10. We have 9 choices for the first digit, 10 choices for the second, and 10 choices for the third. Thus, the total is $9 \times 10 \times 10 = 900$.

EXERCISE 2

1. Since we cannot divide by zero, we cannot let $4 \times 3 - 3 \times B = 0$. But in order for this to be zero, $4 \times 3 = 3 \times B$. By the commutative law, $B = 4$. Thus, the only value that B cannot have is 4.

2. Rewriting both the numerator and denominator as their fractional equivalents, $0.56 = \frac{56}{100} = \frac{14}{25}$, and $1.26 = 1 + \frac{26}{100} = 1\frac{13}{50} = \frac{63}{50}$. We now accomplish the division by inverting and multiplying by the denominator. Thus: $\left(\frac{14}{25}\right)\left(\frac{50}{63}\right) = \frac{4}{9}$, and $b = 9$.

3. Using P, A, and M to stand for the number of CDs each owns respectively, we have:

$$P = \frac{1}{2}A;\ M = \frac{3}{5}A$$

Thus:

$$\frac{P}{M} = \frac{\frac{1}{2}A}{\frac{3}{5}A} = \frac{1}{2} \cdot \frac{5}{3} = \frac{5}{6}$$

Thus, Pedro has as many CDs as Marcia.

4. If Erica's average is 76 on four exams, she must have a total of $(4)(76) = 304$. In order to average 80 on five exams, her total must be $(5)(80) = 400$. Therefore, she must score $400 - 304 = 96$ on her last exam.

5. If S is Sally's age and M is Manuel's, $S = M + 6$. Three years ago, Sally was $S - 3$, and Manuel was $M - 3$. So, from the second sentence:

$$S - 3 = 2(M - 3), \text{ or } S - 3 = 2M - 6$$

That is:

$$S = 2M - 3$$

Now, substituting $S = M + 6$, $M + 6 = 2M - 3$; solving, we have $M = 9$; which means Sally is $9 + 6 = 15$.

6. Since the sum of the angles around a point must be 360°, we have $x + 2x + 3x + (2x + 48) = 360$. Removing parentheses and combining like terms:

$$8x + 48 = 360;\ 8x = 312;\ x = 39$$

7. The area of the garden is $(20)(10) = 200$ square yards. At 80¢ per square yard, the cost of seeding is $(200)(0.80) = \$16$. The perimeter of the garden is $2(20) + 2(10) = 60$ running yards. At \$7 per yard, the cost of the hedge is $7(60) = \$420$. The total cost is $420 + 16 = 436$.

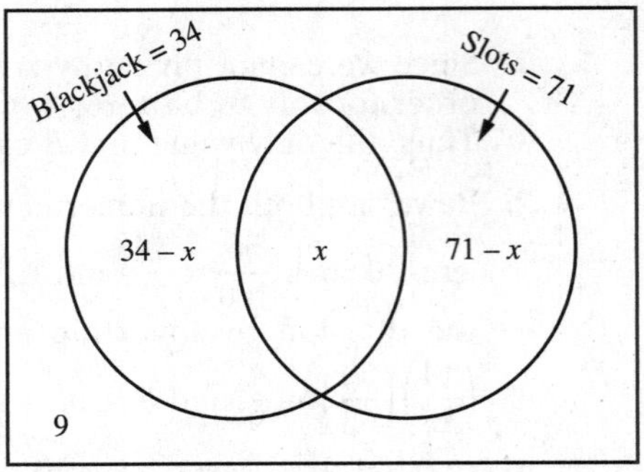

8. Since 9 played neither game, a total of 76 played at least one game. We display this information on a Venn diagram as shown above. Here we see that:

$$(34 - x) + x + (71 - x) = 76$$
$$105 - x = 76$$
$$x = 29$$

9. Let the first number be x. The second is $x + 1$. Now,

$$x^2 - 8(x + 1) = 25$$
$$x^2 - 8x - 8 = 25$$
$$x^2 - 8x - 33 = 0$$

This factors as:

$$(x + 3)(x - 11) = 0$$
$$x + 3 = 0 \text{ or}$$
$$x - 11 = 0$$

Hence, $x = -3$ and $x + 1 = -2$, with product 6, or $x = 11$ and $x + 1 = 12$, with product 132. Clearly, 132 is the larger possibility.

10. Let k = Kim's driving speed; then, $k + 8$ = Angela's driving speed. In some time t, $kt = 552$ and $(k + 8)t = 648$. Thus:

$$kt + 8t = 648$$
$$kt = 552\text{, subtracting}$$
$$8t = 96$$

and $t = 12$ hours. If Kim drives 552 miles in 12 hours, she drives $552 \div 12 = 46$ mph.

EXERCISE 3

1. Since m is divisible by 5, $5m$ can be divided by 25. Therefore, the sum $5m + 25$ can be divided by 25.

2. If $B = -5$, then $-B = +5$, and if $A = -6$, then $-A = 6$. Thus, $-A - (-B) = 6 - 5 = 1$.

3. To average \$435, Albert must have earned a total of (6)(435) = \$2610 for six weeks. Subtracting the \$700 he earned in the sixth week, he must have earned a total of \$1910 for the first 5 weeks, for an average of 1910 ÷ 5 = \$382.

4. The distance from Aurora to Zalesville must be given by $d = rt = (52)(1.5) = 78$ miles. Since 80 minutes is 1 hour and 20 minutes or $1\frac{1}{3} = \frac{4}{3}$ hours, we must solve $78 = \frac{4}{3}r$. Multiplying by 3, we have $234 = 4r$, and dividing by 4, $r = 58.5$ mph.

5. Since the sides AC and BC are of equal length, the two base angles, $\angle A$ and $\angle B$, must be equal. The three angles must total 180°. Hence, $x + 2y = 180$, which means that $y = \frac{180 - x}{2} = 90 - \frac{1}{2}$. The greatest possible value for y is achieved when x is as small as possible; that is, at $x = 64$, for which $y = 58$.

6. Using the Pythagorean Theorem in ΔABC and letting c represent the length of AC, $c^2 = 1^2 + 7^2 = 50$. Thus, $c = \sqrt{50}$. In ΔACD, the theorem tells us that $x^2 + x^2 = c^2 = 50$. Hence, $2x^2 = 50$, $x^2 = 25$, and $x = 5$.

7. Start with English. Since 50% = 0.50, 50% of 20 = (0.50)(20) = 10. For History, 20% = 0.20, 20% of 30 = (0.20)(30) = 6. Hence, a total of 16 out of 50 people in the group have not taken math, which means that 34 have. As a fraction, 34 out of 50 is $\frac{34}{50} = 0.68 = 68\%$.

8. Calling the smallest number x, the second is $x + 2$, and the third is $x + 4$. Therefore:

$$\begin{aligned} x + (x + 2) + 2(x + 4) &= 46 \\ x + x + 2 + 2x + 8 &= 46 \\ 4x + 10 &= 46 \\ 4x &= 36 \\ x &= 9 \end{aligned}$$

Hence, the middle number is $9 + 2 = 11$.

9. Letting the smaller number be x, the larger is $(x + 5)$. Hence:

$$x(x + 5) = x + (x + 5) + 23$$
$$x^2 + 5x = 2x + 28$$
$$x^2 + 3x - 28 = 0$$

This factors as

$$(x + 7)(x - 4) = 0$$
$$x + 7 = 0 \text{ or}$$
$$x - 4 = 0$$

Hence, $x = -7$ and $x + 5 = -2$, with sum -9, or $x = 4$ and $x + 5 = 9$, with sum 13. Since SAT grid-ins may not have a negative answer, we must choose the positive value, 13.

10. The best way to do this is by trial and error. $2 - P = 2^P + P^2$.

For $P = 1$, we have $2^1 + 1^2 = 5$
For $P = 2$, we have $2^2 + 2^2 = 8$
For $P = 3$, we have $2^3 + 3^2 = 17$
For $P = 4$, we have $2^4 + 4^2 = 32$

Any value of P between 3 and 4 will do. For example, $P = 3.5$.

EXERCISE 4

1. The greatest common factor of 144 and 600 is 24. $150 \div 24 = 6.25$.
2. The negative reciprocal of $\frac{4}{3}$ is $-\frac{3}{4}$. Adding the two means subtracting $\frac{3}{4}$ from $\frac{4}{3}$. $\frac{4}{3} - \frac{3}{4} = \frac{7}{12}$.
3. $(x - 3)^2 = 36$ implies $x - 3 = \pm 6$. For the choice $+6$, we have $x - 3 = 6$, $x = 9$, and $x^2 = 81$. For the choice -6, we have $x - 3 = -6$, $x = -3$ and $x^2 = 9$. Of course, 9 is the smaller.
4. There are $4! = 4 \times 3 \times 2 \times 1 = 24$ ways of arranging 4 distinguishable objects in a straight line.
5. Since the larger triangle is isosceles, the base angles are equal. Thus, $\angle A = \angle C = 70°$. This implies that $x + 70 + 80 = 180$, and $x = 30$.

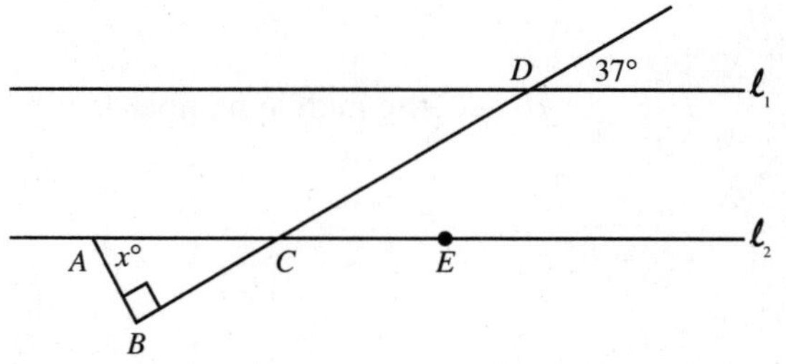

6. Labeling the diagram as shown above, we see that $\angle DCE = 37°$, which makes $\angle ACB = 37°$. Since ΔABC is a right triangle, x is the complement of 37°, or 53°.

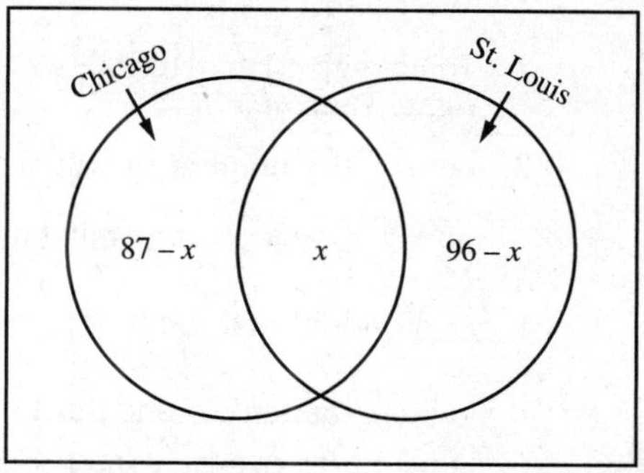

7. Displaying the information in a Venn diagram (see above), we find:

$$(87 - x) + x + (96 - x) = 120$$
$$87 - x + x + 96 - x = 120$$
$$-x = -63$$
$$x = 63$$

8. Using b and r for the unknown prices and expressing all prices in cents, we have:

$$3b + 12r = 810$$
$$2b + 5r = 435$$

Dividing the first equation by 3:

$$b + 4r = 270; b = 270 - 4r$$

Substituting into the other equation:

$$2(270 - 4r) + 5r = 435$$
$$540 - 8r + 5r = 435$$
$$-3r = -105$$
$$r = 35¢$$
$$= \$.35$$

9. Let the first number be x. The second is $x - 5$. The fact that the product is 6 means that:

$$x(x - 5) = 6$$
$$x^2 - 5x - 6 = 0$$

This factors as:

$$(x - 6)(x + 1) = 0$$
$$x - 6 = 0 \text{ or}$$
$$x + 1 = 0$$

Hence, $x = 6$ and $x - 5 = 1$, with sum 7, or $x = -1$ and $x - 5 = -6$, with sum -7. Either way, the absolute value of the sum is 7.

10. Start with the inner parentheses, © 5 © = 25. Now, © 25 © = 2(25) + 1 = 51.

EXERCISE 5

1. To change 4.1 to 410,000, we must move the decimal place 5 spaces to the right. Thus, $n = 5$.

2. Let t = the number of gallons the tank holds when full. Then, at noon the tank contains $\frac{1}{4}t$, or $\frac{t}{4}$, gallons of water, and half an hour later it contains $\frac{90}{2}$ = 45 additional gallons $\left(\frac{t}{4} + 45\right)$. You know that with the 45 additional gallons the tank is one-third full $\left(\frac{t}{3}\right)$, so set up the equation, multiply both sides by 12 (to clear the fractions), and solve for t:

$$\frac{t}{x} + 45 = \frac{t}{3}$$
$$3t + 540 = 4t$$
$$540 = t$$

3. $4 \star 9 = (4)(5)(6)(7)(8)(9)$, and $2 \star 10 = (2)(3)(4)(5)(6)(7)(8)(9)(10)$. Therefore, $\frac{4 \star 9}{2 \star 10} = \frac{(4)(5)(6)(7)(8)(9)}{(2)(3)(4)(5)(6)(7)(8)(9)(10)}$

4. We know that the sum of the angles in any triangle is 180°. Letting the measure of $\angle ABC$ be m, we have in the upper triangle $x + y = 180 - m$. Similarly, looking at the larger triangle, we know that $w + z = 180 - m$. Therefore, $x + y = w + z$. Since $(x + y)$ is an integer greater than 110, it is at least 111, and so is $(w + z)$.

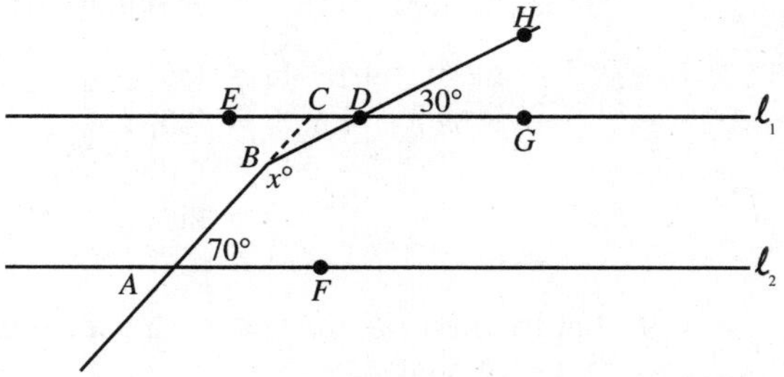

5. Extend the line AB as shown in the figure above. Look at the angles in ΔBCD. As alternate interior angles, $\angle BCE = \angle BAF = 70°$, so its supplement in the triangle, $\angle C = 110°$. As vertical angles, $\angle CDB = \angle HDG = 30°$. Therefore, in the triangle, $\angle D = 30°$. Since the three angles in the triangle must sum to 180°, $\angle B = 40°$. x is the supplement to 40°, that is, 140°.

6. Let Joan's original salary = $4x$; then Alice's original salary = $5x$. Alice got a 20% raise, making her new salary $(1.2)(5x) = 6x$. Joan got a \$100 raise, making her new salary $4x + 100$. Thus:

$$6x = 4x + 100$$
$$2x = 100$$
$$x = 50$$

Hence, Joan's original salary = $4x = 4(50) =$ \$200.

7. $m = \frac{4-(-1)}{6-3} = \frac{5}{3}$

8. Since every point on the circle must be 5 units from the center, we know that $(t, -1)$ must be 5 units from (4, 2). Using the distance formula:

$$\sqrt{(4-t)^2 + (2-(-1))^2} = 5$$

$$\sqrt{(16 - 8t + t^2) + 9} = 5$$

$$\sqrt{t^2 - 8t + 25} = 5$$

Squaring both sides, we have:

$$t^2 - 8t + 25 = 25$$

We subtract 25 from both sides to yield:

$$t^2 - 8t = 0$$

which factors as $t(t-8) = 0$, with two possibilities, $t = 0$ or $t = 8$. The larger one is 8.

9. There are 4 distinguishable people, who can be arranged in $4! = 4 \times 3 \times 2 \times 1 = 24$ ways. In only one of these ways will they be in the correct order. Therefore, the chance is $\frac{1}{24}$.

10. Let m = Mary's driving speed; then $m - 6$ = Joe's driving speed. In some time t, $mt = 336$ and $(m-6)t = 294$. Thus:

$$\begin{aligned} mt \quad &= 336 \\ mt - 6t &= 294, \text{ subtracting} \\ \hline 6t &= 42 \end{aligned}$$

and $t = 7$ hours. If Mary drives 336 miles in 7 hours, she drives $336 \div 7 = 48$ mph.

EXERCISE 6

1. Substituting $z = 3$, we have $\frac{3-1}{2(3)+3} = \frac{2}{9}$

2. Notice that the diagonal of a rectangle divides the rectangle into two identical right triangles; hence, the other side can be found by the Pythagorean Theorem. We recognize that side 6 and diagonal 10 implies that we have a 6-8-10 right triangle, so the unknown side is 8. The perimeter is, therefore, $2(6) + 2(8) = 28$.

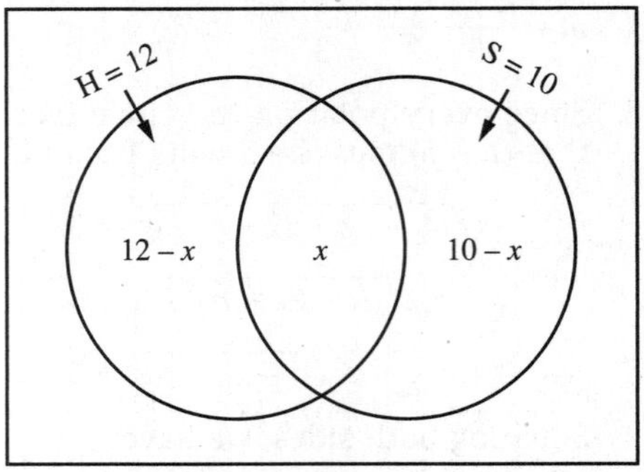

3. We let H be the set of colleges to which Helena applied, and S be those to which Sergei applied. Letting x be the number that are common to both sets, the diagram above displays the data. The central region is that common to both groups, and we can see that the total is $(12 - x) + x + (10 - x) = 16$. Removing parentheses and combining like terms, we have $22 - x = 16$; $x = 6$.

4. The total revenue was 100(30) = \$3000. A 10% price increase raises the price per shirt to \$33. A 5% decrease in sales reduces the number of sales to 95. The total revenue becomes (95)(33) = \$3135, which is an increase of 135 over 3000. 135 ÷ 3000 = 0.045 = 4.5%.

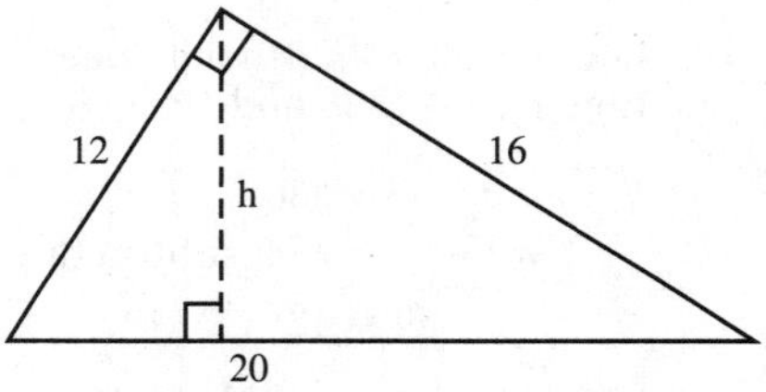

5. Since the sides are 12-16-20, the triangle is a disguised 3-4-5 right triangle, with AB being the hypotenuse. Drawing the triangle as shown, we see that, by using the two legs as base and height, the area of the triangle must be $A = \frac{1}{2}(12)(16) = 96$. By using the hypotenuse and the unknown altitude, the area must be $A = \frac{1}{2}(20)(h) = 10h$. Therefore, $10h = 96$ and $h = 9.6$.

6. Let N be the amount of sales. At \$400 plus 8% of sales, Mark would earn $400 + 0.08N$. A 20% cut in pay brings \$400 down to \$320, so with 10% commission he would earn $320 + 0.10N$. Equating the two, we have:

$$400 + 0.08N = 320 + 0.10N$$
$$80 = 0.02N$$
$$N = \frac{80}{0.02} = 4000$$

7. The angle not given in the triangle is 43°. The three angles are the supplements of the angles in the triangle. They are 132°, 91°, and 137°, which sum to 360°.

8. Since the distances from the two given points are the same, we use the distance formula twice and equate the results, thus:

$$\sqrt{(4-1)^2 + (t-1)^2} = \sqrt{(5-4)^2 + (3-t)^2}$$

$$\sqrt{9 + (t^2 - 2t + 1)} = \sqrt{1 + (9 - 6t + t^2)}$$

$$\sqrt{10 - 2t + t^2} = \sqrt{10 - 6t + t^2}$$

Squaring both sides:

$$10 - 2t + t^2 = 10 - 6t + t^2$$

Subtracting $t^2 + 10$ leaves:

$$-2t = -6t$$
$$4t = 0$$
$$t = 0$$

9. There are 9 equally likely combinations {RR, RW, RB, WW, WR, WB, BB, BR, BW}; in six the colors do not match. Hence, the probability is $\frac{6}{9} = \frac{2}{3}$.

10. Let the first number be x. The second is $x + 7$. The fact that the product is 30 means that:

$$x(x + 7) = 30$$
$$x^2 + 7x - 30 = 0$$

This factors as:

$$(x - 3)(x + 10) = 0$$
$$x - 3 = 0 \text{ or}$$
$$x + 10 = 0$$

Hence, $x = 3$ and $x + 7 = 10$, with sum 13, or $x = -10$ and $x + 7 = -3$, with sum -13. Clearly, 13 is the larger sum.

Part III

The Insider's SAT

Chapter 10

The Insider's SAT Sample Test

INSTRUCTIONS

The following *Insider's* SAT Sample Test will give you a chance to practice the skills and strategies you've just learned throughout this book. As with all practice exercises, work under true testing conditions. Complete the entire test in a single sitting. Eliminate distractions (TV, music) and clear away notes and reference materials.

Time each section of the test separately with a stopwatch or kitchen timer, or have someone else time you. If you run out of time before answering all the questions, stop and draw a line under the last question you finished. Then go on to the next test section. When you are done, score yourself based only on the questions you finished in the allotted time. Later, for practice purposes, you should answer the questions you were unable to complete in time.

Enter your responses on the answer sheet provided on pages 337–338. The answer key, explanatory answers, and information about interpreting your test results appear at the end of the test, beginning on page 376.

The Insider's SAT Sample Test Answer Sheet

Section 1

1. A B C D	7. A B C D	13. A B C D	19. A B C D	25. A B C D
2. A B C D	8. A B C D	14. A B C D	20. A B C D	26. A B C D
3. A B C D	9. A B C D	15. A B C D	21. A B C D	27. A B C D
4. A B C D	10. A B C D	16. A B C D	22. A B C D	28. A B C D
5. A B C D	11. A B C D	17. A B C D	23. A B C D	29. A B C D
6. A B C D	12. A B C D	18. A B C D	24. A B C D	30. A B C D

Section 2

1. A B C D	3. A B C D	5. A B C D	7. A B C D	9. A B C D
2. A B C D	4. A B C D	6. A B C D	8. A B C D	10. A B C D

Section 3

1. A B C D	8. A B C D	15. A B C D	22. A B C D	29. A B C D
2. A B C D	9. A B C D	16. A B C D	23. A B C D	30. A B C D
3. A B C D	10. A B C D	17. A B C D	24. A B C D	31. A B C D
4. A B C D	11. A B C D	18. A B C D	25. A B C D	32. A B C D
5. A B C D	12. A B C D	19. A B C D	26. A B C D	33. A B C D
6. A B C D	13. A B C D	20. A B C D	27. A B C D	34. A B C D
7. A B C D	14. A B C D	21. A B C D	28. A B C D	35. A B C D

Section 4

1. A B C D	6. A B C D	11. A B C D	16. A B C D	21. A B C D
2. A B C D	7. A B C D	12. A B C D	17. A B C D	22. A B C D
3. A B C D	8. A B C D	13. A B C D	18. A B C D	23. A B C D
4. A B C D	9. A B C D	14. A B C D	19. A B C D	24. A B C D
5. A B C D	10. A B C D	15. A B C D	20. A B C D	25. A B C D

Section 5

1. A B C D	4. A B C D	7. A B C D	10. A B C D	12. A B C D
2. A B C D	5. A B C D	8. A B C D	11. A B C D	13. A B C D
3. A B C D	6. A B C D	9. A B C D		

Section 6

1. A B C D	4. A B C D	7. A B C D	10. A B C D	13. A B C D
2. A B C D	5. A B C D	8. A B C D	11. A B C D	14. A B C D
3. A B C D	6. A B C D	9. A B C D	12. A B C D	15. A B C D

16.

17.

18.

19.

20.

21.

22.

23.

24.

25.

SECTION 1

30 Questions

Time—30 Minutes

Directions: For each question in this section, select the best answer from among the choices given and fill in the corresponding oval on the answer sheet.

Each sentence below has one or two blanks, each blank indicating that something has been omitted. Beneath the sentence are five words or sets of words labeled (A) through (E). Choose the word or set of words that, when inserted in the sentence, *best* fits the meaning of the sentence as a whole.

Example:

Medieval kingdoms did not become constitutional republics overnight; on the contrary, the change was _______.

(A) unpopular
(B) unexpected
(C) advantageous
(D) sufficient
(E) gradual

(A) (B) (C) (D) ●

1. The conditions were _______ for a day of ice skating; a thaw was forecast with eighty percent certainty for early that morning.
   (A) perfect
   (B) unfavorable
   (C) ideal
   (D) uncertain
   (E) suitable

2. The man's _______ was evident to any visitor in his home, for it was decorated as a kind of shrine _______ every aspect of his life, from his kindergarten graduation to his partnership at a well-known law firm.
   (A) egotism..celebrating
   (B) humility..recording
   (C) wealth..illustrating
   (D) eccentricity..honoring
   (E) prominence..encapsulating

GO ON TO THE NEXT PAGE

3. Fearing discovery, the dissenters held the meeting _______; those in attendance were warned not to _______ the meeting time, place, or the subjects of discussion.
   (A) secretly..forget
   (B) surreptitiously..suppress
   (C) quickly..reveal
   (D) clandestinely..disclose
   (E) covertly..deny

4. Although thousands of people die every year as a result of rabies, the disease is _______ in the United States thanks to the fact that dogs and other pets which are potential sources of the disease are _______.
   (A) unusual..quarantined
   (B) severe..widespread
   (C) rare..inoculated
   (D) atypical..uncommon
   (E) benign..vaccinated

5. The article presented the commander's courage as _______; it _______ his actions on the battlefield and even implied that others should follow in his footsteps.
   (A) rash..denigrated
   (B) exemplary..glorified
   (C) spurious..praised
   (D) noteworthy..analyzed
   (E) questionable..revered

6. Scientists who have been working for years to _______ the ongoing AIDS epidemic were _______ last year when a new regime of drugs was introduced that seems to lessen some of the worst symptoms.
   (A) end..successful
   (B) eliminate..surprised
   (C) overcome..cheerful
   (D) control..thwarted
   (E) combat..encouraged

7. The city police _______ the riots relatively quickly, but the sometimes brutal tactics they seemed to aim particularly at members of certain ethnic groups gave them a reputation for _______ that lingers today.
   (A) investigated..bigotry
   (B) prevented..malevolence
   (C) pacified..tolerance
   (D) denounced..mediocrity
   (E) quelled..racism

8. The fennec uses its huge six-inch-long ears to _______ its prey by lurking and listening quietly for its whereabouts; they are also an aid to desert survival, as they help _______ the otherwise unbearable heat.
   (A) locate..dissipate
   (B) obtain..intensify
   (C) trap..radiate
   (D) scare..dispel
   (E) capture..reduce

9. The _______ between how much the candidate had spent on her campaign and the reported donations she had received was _______, leading election officials to launch an investigation into how the campaign had been funded.
   (A) disparity..modest
   (B) discrepancy..considerable
   (C) similarity..obvious
   (D) gap..trivial
   (E) difference..uncertain

Directions: Each question below consists of a related pair or words or phrases, followed by five pairs of words or phrases labeled (A) through (E). Select the pair that *best* expresses a relationship similar to that expressed in the original pair.

Example:

CRUMB : BREAD : :

(A) ounce : unit
(B) splinter : wood
(C) water : bucket
(D) twine : rope
(E) cream : butter

Ⓐ ● Ⓒ Ⓓ Ⓔ

10. CENSUS : POPULATION : :

(A) index : information
(B) catalog : salesperson
(C) collection : specimens
(D) inventory : merchandise
(E) score : competition

11. WOOL : SHEEP : :

(A) down : duck
(B) cotton : field
(C) linen : cloth
(D) tusk : boar
(E) leather : shoe

12. SONG : DIRGE : :

(A) dance : march
(B) literature : novel
(C) music : ditty
(D) poem : elegy
(E) painting : portrait

13. PROSCENIUM : CURTAIN : :

(A) fence : gate
(B) house : facade
(C) movie : screen
(D) doorway : lintel
(E) window : shade

14. MOTORCADE : CAR : :

(A) flotilla : ship
(B) train : caboose
(C) parade : bandleader
(D) caravan : merchandise
(E) panorama : vista

15. MONEY : IMPECUNIOUS : :

(A) cruelty : ruthless
(B) bias : disinterested
(C) content : amorphous
(D) luxury : opulent
(E) energy : indefatigable

GO ON TO THE NEXT PAGE

Directions: Each passage below is followed by questions based on its content. Answer the questions on the basis of what is *stated* or *implied* in the passage and in any introductory material that may be provided.

Questions 16–23 are based on the following passage.

The following passage is from a speech by a disabled university professor to his colleagues.

I enjoyed the use of my legs for 44 years until a simple misstep on a hiking trail rendered them useless, paralyzed. Now, years after the initial shock, I can reflect more calmly on my fate, and what surprises me is that my own reactions to becoming disabled have been easier to live with and adapt to than able-bodied society's responses.

My responses are what I think of as "pure": grief, rage, self-pity, depression, pride, anger. Yet society's responses to me and to my disabled peers are less direct, akin to the averted gaze with which most people look not at us, but somewhere to the left of us. In nine encounters out of ten, an able-bodied person will be responding not to me, the reality of who I am and what I am, but to his own supreme discomfort with "the handicapped." In a culture which glorifies the body beautiful, a disabled person is overturning an American ideal. We are also a constant reminder of a terrible possibility: "This could happen to me."

One way that normal society manages its own discomfort with the abnormal is to classify us. First there was the word "cripple" a bald statement of the truth of our situation, yet one suggestive of deviance. Then came the less loaded terms, which are still, however, euphemisms: "handicapped" and "disabled." Today, as if the normal cannot get over their own guilt at being normal, we have the optimistic terms "differently abled" or "physically challenged"—labels so vague as to describe anyone and no one.

While I take the middle road and call myself "disabled," other peers call themselves "cripples," co-opting a word with pejorative associations by injecting it with a certain pride and bravado. Writer Nancy Mairs, who suffers from multiple sclerosis, says, "People—crippled or not—wince at the word *cripple* . . . Perhaps I want them to wince. I want them to see me as a tough customer." Mairs is brave, for if there is one thing I have discovered since I became bound to the wheelchair, it is that nothing can make an able-bodied person flee faster than being confronted by a disabled person's rage, fear, or sexuality—in short, our selves. One learns very quickly that the burden is upon the disabled to make the able-bodied comfortable. I often catch myself putting able-bodied visitors at ease with a cheery demeanor and jocular references to my condition, even—especially—on days when I feel wretched.

If being a cheery disabled person is one way to ease society's discomfort, being the object of their charity does double duty: it sets a firm wall between us and them and allows the able-bodied to congratulate themselves. Charity is a noble human endeavor, and I know that those who watch the parade of disabled children on a March of Dimes telethon may seem to be deeply concerned about those children. However, a child who thinks of himself as an object of charity is *a priori* "dependent." Only a considerable amount of resolve can save that child from being defined forever as dependent, which leads me to conclude that we can either choose to be accomplices to our own objectification or to carve out our own identities.

In the disabled circles in which I now move, I see how easily we choose the former. At a meeting of disabled activists, many will still give more serious attention to an able-bodied participant than to each other. Yet others there brandish their disability like a sword, carving an identity in bold, broad strokes. To me, this approach speaks more of limits than possibilities, of symbol rather than "self." I prefer to claim a self by simply enduring, thrusting myself into the averted gaze of the able-bodied, telling them who I am now, who I have always been.

16. The author's attitude toward the typical behavior of able-bodied society toward the disabled can best be described as
    (A) bitterly resentful
    (B) sarcastic and condescending
    (C) tolerant and bemused
    (D) forthrightly critical
    (E) angry and vindictive

17. The author's reference to "an American ideal" (line 23) implies a criticism of the tendency of Americans to
    (A) judge other people primarily on the basis of their appearance
    (B) feel uncomfortable around people with physical disabilities
    (C) regard physical disabilities as reflecting some moral failing
    (D) place undue importance on bodily perfection
    (E) value physical sensations over mental processes

18. In line 42, the world "pejorative" most nearly means
    (A) insulting
    (B) frightening
    (C) belligerent
    (D) misanthropic
    (E) grandiose

19. The author implies that the terms generally used to describe the disabled have moved over time along a continuum from
    (A) negative to neutral
    (B) specific to vague
    (C) truthful to dishonest
    (D) colorful to bland
    (E) succinct to verbose

20. In line 49, the author describes Nancy Mairs as "brave" because she
    (A) willingly courts rejection by her uncompromising honesty
    (B) faces the difficulties of her disability with cheerful fortitude
    (C) understands that the burden of maintaining relationships with the able-bodied rests mainly with the disabled
    (D) accepts the need to compete with others on terms set by the able-bodied
    (E) refuses the assistance of others in managing her physical and psychological needs

21. The author's description of a March of Dimes telethon (lines 70–78) implies that such activities
    (A) provide inadequate financial support to disabled people who are in need of aid
    (B) tend to reduce all those who participate to the level of children
    (C) may benefit the disabled generally, but only at the expense of the children who are paraded on the air
    (D) distort the intended charitable purpose by turning it into a form of televised entertainment
    (E) are designed primarily to provide psychological comfort to the able-bodied

GO ON TO THE NEXT PAGE

22. The author implies that the tendency of many disabled people to give more serious attention to an able-bodied person (lines 84–86) suggests all of the following EXCEPT:
    (A) They submit to their objectification by able-bodied society.
    (B) They see themselves as being of a lower social status than the able-bodied.
    (C) They have become overly dependent upon the assistance of the able-bodied.
    (D) They share some of the blame for the ways able-bodied society views them.
    (E) They fail to fully accept their own identities.

23. The author's comments concerning those who "brandish their disability like a sword" (lines 87–88) suggest that they
    (A) have chosen a belligerent stance rather than an accommodating one
    (B) see their own struggles as symbolic of the plight of all disabled people
    (C) continue to define themselves in terms of their disabilities
    (D) are taking an approach that is brave but foolhardy
    (E) have failed to gain serious attention from their disabled peers

Questions 24–30 are based on the following passage.

A dramatic episode in the American Civil War was the encounter in 1862 between two of the first ironclad battleships. The following excerpt tells how it came to pass.

From the opening days of the Civil War, one of the Union's strategies in its efforts to defeat the rebelling southern states was to blockade their ports. Compared to the Union, relatively little was manufactured in the Confederacy—either consumer goods or, more important, war material—and it was believed that a blockade could strangle the South into submission. But the Confederacy had 3,500 miles of coastline and, at the start of the war, the Union had only 36 ships to patrol them.

Even so, the Confederate government knew that the Union could and would construct additional warships and that in time all its ports could be sealed. To counter this, the Confederacy decided to take a radical step—to construct an ironclad vessel that would be impervious to Union gunfire. In doing so, the South was taking a gamble because, though the British and French navies had already launched experimental armor-plated warships, none had yet been tested in battle.

Lacking time as well as true ship-building capabilities, rather than construct an entirely new ship, in July, 1861, the Confederacy began placing armor-plating on the hull of an abandoned U.S. Navy frigate, the steam-powered *U.S.S. Merrimack*. Rechristened the *C.S.S. Virginia*, the ship carried ten guns and an iron ram designed to stave in the wooden hulls of Union warships.

Until then, Union Secretary of the Navy Gideon Welles had considered ironclads too radical an idea, and preferred to concentrate on building standard wooden warships. But when news of the Virginia reached Washington, the fear it engendered forced him to rethink his decision. In October, 1861, the Union began construction of its own ironclad—the *U.S.S. Monitor* which would revolutionize naval warfare.

Designed by John Ericson, a Swede who had already made substantial contributions to marine engineering, the *Monitor* looked like no other ship afloat. With a wooden hull covered with iron plating, the ship had a flat deck with perpendicular sides that went below the waterline and protected the propeller and other important machinery. Even more innovative, the ship had a round, revolving turret which carried two large guns. Begun three months after work started on the conversion of the *Virginia*, the *Monitor* was nevertheless launched in January, 1862, two weeks before the Confederacy launched its ironclad.

On March 8th, now completely fitted, the *Virginia* left the port of Norfolk, Virginia, on what was expected to be a test run. However, steaming into Hampton Roads, Virginia, the Confederate ship found no fewer than five Union ships at the mouth of the James River—the *St. Lawrence*, *Congress*, *Cumberland*, *Minnesota*, and *Roanoke*. The first three of these were already-obsolete sailing ships, but the others were new steam frigates, the pride of the Union navy.

Attacking the *Cumberland* first, the *Virginia* sent several shells into her side before ramming her hull and sinking her. Turning next to the *Congress*, the southern ironclad sent broadsides into her until fires started by the shots reached her powder magazine and she blew up. At last, after driving the *Minnesota* aground, the *Virginia* steamed off, planning to finish off the other ships the next day. In just a few hours, she had sunk two ships, disabled a third, and killed 240 Union sailors, including the captain of the *Congress*—more naval casualties than on any other day of the war. Although she had lost two of her crew, her ram, and two of her guns, and sustained other damage, none of the nearly 100 shots that hit her had pierced her armor.

Monitor, however, was already en route from the Brooklyn Navy Yard, and the next morning, March 9th, the two ironclads met each other for the first—and only—time. For nearly four hours the ships pounded at each other, but despite some damage done on both sides, neither ship could penetrate the armor-plating of its enemy. When a shot from the *Virginia* hit the *Monitor's* pilot house, wounding her captain and forcing her to withdraw temporarily, the Confederate ship steamed back to Norfolk.

Although both sides claimed victory, the battle was actually a draw. Its immediate significance was that, by forcing the withdrawal of the *Virginia*, it strengthened the Union blockade, enabling the North to continue its ultimately successful stranglehold on the South. Even more important, it was a turning point in the history of naval warfare. Although neither ship ever fought again, the brief engagement of the *Monitor* and *Virginia* made every navy in the world obsolete, and, in time, spelled the end of wooden fighting ships forever.

24. The passage implies that the South was vulnerable to a naval blockade because of its

(A) limited manufacturing capabilities
(B) relatively short coastline
(C) weak and ineffectual navy
(D) lack of access to natural resources
(E) paucity of skilled naval officers

25. All of the following were unusual design features of the *Monitor* EXCEPT its

(A) armor plating
(B) perpendicular sides
(C) revolving gun turret
(D) flat deck
(E) wooden hull

GO ON TO THE NEXT PAGE

26. It can be inferred from the passage that, by comparison with the design of the *Monitor*, that of the *Virginia* was more
    (A) offensively oriented
    (B) radical
    (C) costly
    (D) versatile
    (E) traditional

27. It can be inferred from the passage that, although construction on the *Monitor* began three months after that of the *Virginia*, the *Monitor* was completed first because
    (A) the Union had more money to spend on building its ship
    (B) the *Monitor* was less complicated to construct
    (C) the Union had greater manufacturing abilities and resources
    (D) the Confederacy did not feel compelled to hurry in completing its ship
    (E) the Confederacy was not concerned about the Union building an ironclad

28. It can be inferred from the passage that the *Virginia* was able to sink or disable the *St. Lawrence*, *Congress*, and *Cumberland* for which the following reasons?
    (A) It carried more guns
    (B) Its armor plating was virtually impervious to gunfire
    (C) Its steam-powered engines made it highly maneuverable
    (D) Its armor plating made it fireproof
    (E) It was capable of greater speed than the Union warships

29. In line 93, "sustained" most nearly means
    (A) survived
    (B) inflicted
    (C) suffered
    (D) risked
    (E) produced

30. The author suggests that the most important long-term result of the battle between the *Virginia* and the *Monitor* was that it
    (A) enabled the Union to maintain its blockade of southern ports
    (B) demonstrated that ironclad ships represented the future of naval warfare
    (C) saved the Union navy from destruction by the *Virginia*
    (D) demonstrated the superior technological prowess of the North
    (E) effectively ended the naval career of the captain of the *Monitor*

STOP End of section 1. If you have any time left, go over your work in this section only. Do not work in any other section of the test.

SECTION 2

10 Questions

Time—15 Minutes

Directions: In this section solve each problem, using any available space on the page for scratchwork. Then decide which is the best of the choices given and fill in the corresponding oval on the answer sheet.

Notes:

1. The use of a calculator is permitted. All numbers used are real numbers.
2. Figures that accompany problems in this test are intended to provide information useful in solving the problems. They are drawn as accurately as possible EXCEPT when it is stated in a specific problem that the figure is not drawn to scale. All figures lie in a plane unless otherwise indicated.

Reference Information

Circle:

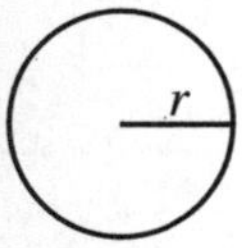

$C = 2\pi r$
$A = \pi r^2$

Rectangle:

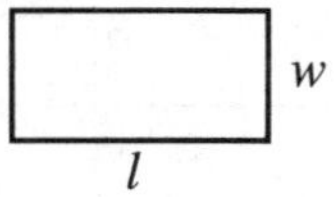

$A = lw$

Triangle:

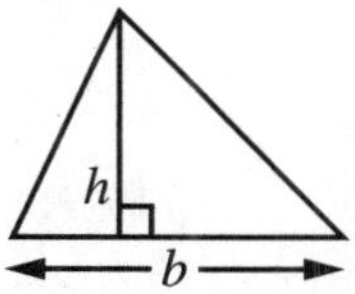

$A = \frac{1}{2}bh$

Rectangle Solid:

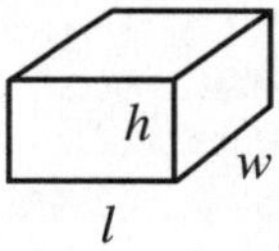

$V = lwh$

Cylinder:

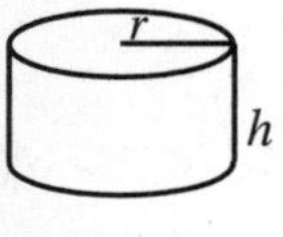

$V = \pi r^2 h$

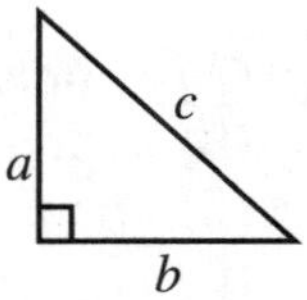

$a^2+b^2 = c^2$

Special Right Triangles

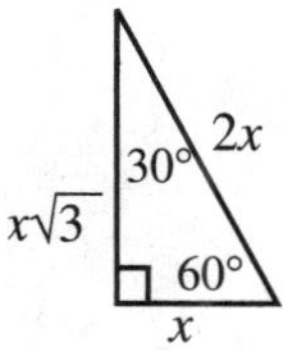

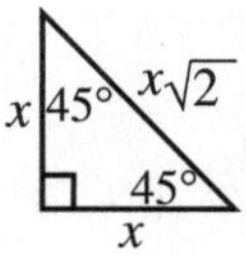

The number of degrees of an arc in a circle is 360.
The measure in degrees of a straight angle is 180.
The sum of the measures in degrees of the angles of a triangle is 180.

GO ON TO THE NEXT PAGE

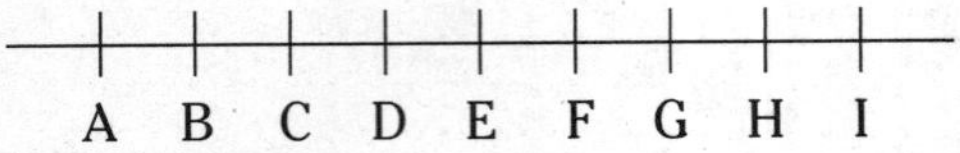

Note: All the vertical marks are equidistant.

1. On the number line shown, if all the labeled points are equidistant, which point represents the number which is greater than E and one third as far from E as G is from A?

   (A) F
   (B) G
   (C) H
   (D) I
   (E) Not a labeled point

---

2. In ΔABC $\angle B$ is 30° more than twice $\angle A$, and the measure of $\angle C$ is equal to the sum of the other two angles. What is the degree measure of the smallest angle?

   (A) 10
   (B) 15
   (C) 20
   (D) 25
   (E) 30

---

3. If $14 = 3x - 1$ and $B = 6x + 4$, what is the value of B?

   (A) 12
   (B) 14
   (C) 24
   (D) 30
   (E) 34

---

4. For what value of x is $12 - x \geq 3x + 8$?

   (A) $x \geq 1$
   (B) $x \geq 0$
   (C) $x \leq 0$
   (D) $x \leq 2$
   (E) $x \leq 1$

5. What is the length of a rectangular solid of height 6 that is twice as long as it is wide, if its volume is the same as that of a cube with total surface area 864 square inches?

   (A) 12
   (B) 14
   (C) 24
   (D) 30
   (E) 36

---

6. If $\frac{2x}{3} + 2 = a$, and $y = 2x + 6$, what is the value of y in terms of a?

   (A) $2a - 3$
   (B) $\frac{3}{a}$
   (C) $3 + a$
   (D) $3a$
   (E) $\frac{a}{3}$

---

7. If $a¶b = \frac{a}{a + b}$ and $x \neq 0$, which of the following must be true?

   I. $x¶y = y¶x$
   II. $x¶0 = 1$
   III. $x¶(1 - x) = x$

   (A) I only
   (B) I and II only
   (C) II and III only
   (D) I, II, and III
   (E) Neither I, II, nor III

8. In how many ways can 3 men and 3 women be seated in 6 theater seats if a woman must be seated in the first seat and men and women must be seated in alternate seats?

(A) 36
(B) 24
(C) 12
(D) 9
(E) 6

9. What is the perimeter of a triangle with vertices at (−2, 6), (3, 6), and (3, −6)?

(A) 60
(B) 50
(C) 40
(D) 30
(E) 24

10. The point (t, −1) lies on a circle of radius 5 with center at (4, 2). Which of the following is a possible positive value of t?

(A) 4
(B) 5
(C) 6
(D) 7
(E) 8

STOP End of Section 2. If you have any time left, go over your work in this section only. Do not work in any other section of the test.

SECTION 3

35 Questions

Time—30 Minutes

Directions: For each question in this section, select the best answer from among the choices given and fill in the corresponding oval on the answer sheet.

Each sentence below has one or two blanks, each blank indicating that something has been omitted. Beneath the sentence are five words or sets of words labeled (A) through (E). Choose the word or set of words that, when inserted in the sentence, *best* fits the meaning of the sentence as a whole.

Example:

Medieval kingdoms did not become constitutional republics overnight; on the contrary, the change was ________.

(A) unpopular
(B) unexpected
(C) advantageous
(D) sufficient
(E) gradual

(A) (B) (C) (D) ●

1. The magazine profile was a surprise to many because it explored the ________, wild side of a woman usually characterized in the media as demure and innocent.

(A) presumptuous
(B) tenacious
(C) scholarly
(D) provocative
(E) creative

2. The ________ terrain added ________ element to the trip; along with the beauty of nature came an ever-present sense of peril which gave the rafters a kind of permanent adrenaline rush.

(A) florid. .a relaxing
(B) treacherous. .an exciting
(C) verdant. .a hazardous
(D) formidable. .an enticing
(E) perilous. .enchanting

3. The ________ an aspiring dancer must exhibit is ________: she must be willing to focus her attention on her art to the exclusion of all else, including friends, outside interests, and hobbies.
   (A) diligence..variable
   (B) dedication..commendable
   (C) ambivalence..intimidating
   (D) devotion..uncompromising
   (E) fidelity..destructive

4. The ________ of the cloisters, with their shady, cool, enclosed gardens, made them the perfect place to meditate.
   (A) temperance
   (B) turbulence
   (C) dampness
   (D) tranquillity
   (E) domesticity

5. The couple was ________ to learn of their son's impending marriage, although their joy was ________ the knowledge that the couple would be unable to have children.
   (A) euphoric..alleviated by
   (B) jubilant..accentuated by
   (C) flabbergasted..based upon
   (D) forlorn..contaminated by
   (E) elated..dampened by

6. When hiking the desolate mountains of eastern Russia, a ________ method of communication is vital to survival, for without one even minor injuries may become ________.
   (A) modern..irksome
   (B) universal..hazardous
   (C) speedy..painful
   (D) reliable..life-threatening
   (E) rapid..enjoyable

7. Shirley Temple was the ________ of ________ child: at four, she sang and danced with an ability far beyond her years, and she starred in movies at an age when most children are just learning to read.
   (A) embodiment..a capricious
   (B) example..a typical
   (C) epitome..a precocious
   (D) stereotype..a lovable
   (E) model..an astute

8. Because the organization had been founded on the premise that it would devote its resources to ________ pursuits, its supporters felt profoundly ________ to learn that its president had been siphoning off funds for his personal use.
   (A) agricultural..distressed
   (B) humanitarian..empathetic
   (C) commercial..dismayed
   (D) philanthropic..betrayed
   (E) political..exploited

GO ON TO THE NEXT PAGE

9. Like the eight-track tape, it appears that the phonograph record is well on its way to ________ thanks to the ________ of the compact disk.
   (A) oblivion. .high cost
   (B) antiquity. .notoriety
   (C) resurgence. .quality
   (D) obsolescence. .superiority
   (E) popularity. .fame

10. With electricity erratic or ________ in most of Ho Chi Minh City, the neon signs, streetlights, and motorbike headlights filling one downtown area make it ________, a welcome escape from the darkness which covers the rest of the city at nightfall.
   (A) nonexistent. .an oasis
   (B) disliked. .a refuge
   (C) expensive. .an anomaly
   (D) unavailable. .an intrusion
   (E) disregarded. .a disturbance

Directions: Each question below consists of a related pair or words or phrases, followed by five pairs of words or phrases labeled (A) through (E). Select the pair that *best* expresses a relationship similar to that expressed in the original pair.

Example:

CRUMB : BREAD : :

(A) ounce : unit
(B) splinter : wood
(C) water : bucket
(D) twine : rope
(E) cream : butter

Ⓐ ● Ⓒ Ⓓ Ⓔ

11. PLUCK : FEATHERS : :
   (A) clip : hedge
   (B) catch : fish
   (C) skin : cat
   (D) shear : wool
   (E) fly : bird

12. KNOWLEDGE : IGNORANCE : :
   (A) money : poverty
   (B) education : learning
   (C) religion : superstition
   (D) understanding : skepticism
   (E) logic : clarity

13. STEER : CATTLE : :
   (A) rose : weed
   (B) bird : mammal
   (C) cow : food
   (D) rat : vermin
   (E) steed : horse

14. APPLAUD : APPRECIATION : :
(A) jeer : contempt
(B) hiss : failure
(C) clap : popularity
(D) boo : incompetence
(E) cheer : reaction

15. TREE : PALM : :
(A) creature : fish
(B) fruit : mango
(C) flower : bud
(D) river : lagoon
(E) bird : wing

16. MOISTURE : SPONGE : :
(A) pail : mop
(B) water : parasite
(C) lint : brush
(D) wound : bandage
(E) shock : spring

17. COPYRIGHT : BOOK : :
(A) statute : crime
(B) litigation : lawsuit
(C) patent : invention
(D) lease : property
(E) ownership : individual

18. PERIMETER : POLYGON : :
(A) dimension : figure
(B) boundary : surface
(C) circumference : circle
(D) length : rectangle
(E) area : square

19. CAMERA : IMAGE : :
(A) printing press : newspaper
(B) computer : calculation
(C) typewriter : word
(D) tape recorder : sound
(E) television : film

20. DIVERT : STREAM : :
(A) reroute : traffic
(B) cancel : activity
(C) dam : lake
(D) extinguish : fire
(E) refine : plan

21. SHYSTER : LAW : :
(A) huckster : religion
(B) professor : education
(C) financier : business
(D) mountebank : deception
(E) quack : medicine

22. BALLAST : STABILIZE : :
(A) anchor : drift
(B) cargo : transport
(C) insulation : heat
(D) concrete : harden
(E) fuel : power

23. DISSEMBLE : HONESTY : :
(A) impugn : integrity
(B) diverge : accuracy
(C) wobble : verticality
(D) garble : correctness
(E) wander : direction

GO ON TO THE NEXT PAGE

Directions: The passage below is followed by questions based on its content. Answer the questions on the basis of what is *stated* or *implied* in the passage and in any introductory material that may be provided.

Questions 24–35 are based on the following passage.

Bioluminescence is the process whereby some living things produce light. The following passage discusses the forms and uses of bioluminescence in various organisms.

If you've ever cupped your hand around a blinking firefly or noticed an eerie glow in the ocean at night, you are familiar with the phenomenon of bioluminescence. The ability of certain plants and animals to emit light has long been a source of fascination to humans. Why do certain species of mushrooms glow? Why are mid-water squids designed with ornate light-emitting organs underneath their eyes and ink glands? Why do certain particles and biological detritus floating in the depths of the ocean sparkle after a physical disturbance? Are these light displays simply an example of nature in its most flamboyant mode—a case of "if you've got it, flaunt it"—or do they serve any practical purposes?

As it turns out, the manifestations of bioluminescence are as diverse as they are elegant. Yet virtually all of the known or proposed ways in which bioluminescence functions may be classed under three major rubrics: assisting predation, helping escape from predators, and communicating.

Many examples of the first two uses can be observed in the ocean's mid-waters, a zone that extends from about 100 meters deep to a few kilometers below the surface. Almost all of the animals that inhabit the murky depths where sunlight barely penetrates are capable of producing light in one way or another. Certain animals, when feeding, are attracted to a spot of light as a possible food source. Hence, other animals use their own luminescence to attract them. Just in front of the angler fish's mouth is a dangling luminescent ball suspended from a structure attached to its head. What unwitting marine creatures see as food is really a bait to lure them into the angler fish's gaping maw.

The uses of luminescence to elude prey are just as sophisticated and various. Some creatures take advantage of the scant sunlight in their realm by using bioluminescence as a form of camouflage. The glow generated by photophores, light-producing organs, on the undersides of some fishes and squids acts to hide them through a phenomenon known as countershading: the weak downward lighting created by the photophores effectively erases the animals' shadows when viewed from below against the (relatively) lighted waters above.

Some marine animals use bioluminescence more actively in their own defense, turning their predators into prey. For instance, there is the so-called "burglar alarm effect," in which an animal coats an advancing predator with sticky glowing tissue that makes the would-be attacker vulnerable to visually-cued hunters—like bank robbers marked by exploding dye packets hidden in stolen currency.

Bioluminescence is used not only in such interspecific feeding frays between predators and prey, but also as an intraspecific communication facilitator. The fireflies that seem to blink on and off randomly in the summer woods are actually male and female members signaling each other during courtship. Certain fish use their luminescence as a kind of Morse code in which the female responds to the flashing of a male fish with own flash exactly two seconds later, which the male recognizes by its timing.

Bioluminescence clearly functions to help certain species ensure their survival, whether it helps them to trick predators or to mate and produce offspring. Yet, when we look at the larger evolutionary picture, bioluminescence as such is generally considered a "nonessential" characteristic. After all, closely related species and even strains of the same species may have both luminous and nonluminous members, and the nonluminous ones appear just as viable and vigorous as their glowing counterparts. For instance, while many of the small marine organisms known as dinoflagellates are luminous, many are not.

Yet, on closer inspection, we find that the nonluminous dinoflagellates may benefit from the diversionary flashing tactics of the luminous ones. When the sea is disturbed and light flashes create phosphorescence, the species which flash may provide enough light to serve the entire population.

Thus, selection pressure for the development or maintenance of luminescence in additional species is not great if light generated by a part of the population serves the entire community.

There are instances in which bioluminescence seems truly purposeless. What does one make of a creature, such as a newly discovered species of a tomopterid worm, that emits light for no apparent purpose? This agile swimmer with a multitude of paired legs spews a bright yellow bioluminescent fluid from each of its leg pores. While other types of spewers use this strategy to create a visual distraction, this worm's display remains enigmatic, particularly since the light produced is yellow, while most mid-water animals have eyes that are sensitive only to blue-green. Perhaps some animal species are simply exploiting their capacity for flamboyance, in the same way that some humans bring a distinctively colorful flair to whatever they do.

24. The passage focuses on all of the following aspects of bioluminescence EXCEPT
    (A) its role in interactions between predators and prey
    (B) its many functions in various animal species
    (C) its role in the evolution of various animal species
    (D) whether bioluminescence is a purely functional feature
    (E) how bioluminescent species may serve nonluminous ones

25. In line 24, the word "rubrics" most nearly means
    (A) conditions
    (B) categories
    (C) examples
    (D) components
    (E) stages

26. From the author's description of the angler fish in lines 39–42, we can infer that this fish
    (A) is attracted to light as a possible food source
    (B) uses its light-producing organ to deter predators
    (C) dwells primarily in the ocean's midwaters
    (D) uses countershading to elude predators below
    (E) uses light to communicate with other angler fish

GO ON TO THE NEXT PAGE

27. The angler fish's use of bioluminescence in predation is most nearly analogous to
    (A) a deer hunter's use of a flashlight to find his way in a dark and overgrown forest
    (B) an exterminator's use of insecticide to poison the insects that have infested a home
    (C) a duck hunter's use of a reed-shielded blind as a hiding place from which to shoot at ducks
    (D) a trout fisherman's use of a lure designed to resemble an insect that trout love to eat
    (E) a police detective's use of a bright lamp to blind and so intimidate a suspect during questioning

28. Each of the following statements about the use of bioluminescence in countershading is true EXCEPT
    (A) The light given off by photophores underneath certain fish and squid makes the animals appear to blend in with the sunlit waters above them.
    (B) Bioluminescence allows the parts of an animal normally in shadow to appear lighter.
    (C) Countershading is one of several ways in which bioluminescence is used to avoid predation.
    (D) Countershading is used most effectively in regions of relatively weak sunlight.
    (E) Bioluminescent animals use countershading as a way to elude predators that lurk in the sunlit waters above them.

29. The reference to bank robbers in line 69 serves mainly to
    (A) distinguish between two phenomena that appear similar but are fundamentally different
    (B) suggest a practical application for recent discoveries from natural science
    (C) point out the weaknesses in one proposed solution to a scientific conundrum
    (D) explain how scientists developed a theory concerning the underlying purpose of a natural phenomenon
    (E) clarify a phenomenon of the animal world by comparing it to human behavior

30. It can be inferred from the passage that bioluminescence is used for communication primarily
    (A) between animals of different species
    (B) when other means of communication are unavailable
    (C) between members of the same species
    (D) as a means of warning about approaching dangers
    (E) between predators and their prey

31. The author mentions the behavior of bioluminescent and nonluminous dionoflagellates (lines 99–109) primarily in order to illustrate
    (A) why bioluminescence is generally considered an unnecessary function in dinoflagellates
    (B) why the ocean waters sometimes sparkle when there is a physical disturbance
    (C) one of the functions of bioluminescence in the ocean's midwaters
    (D) why more species have not evolved with bioluminescence
    (E) how nonluminous animals may benefit from proximity to luminous ones

32. The passage implies that, if bioluminescence were NOT a nonessential characteristic, which of the following would be true?
    (A) Luminous species would be seen to thrive more successfully than closely related nonluminous ones.
    (B) Nonluminous species would enjoy a reproductive advantage by comparison to luminous ones.
    (C) Nonluminous species would benefit from the light-producing capabilities of luminous ones.
    (D) Luminous species would gradually die out and be replaced by closely related nonluminous ones.
    (E) Luminous and nonluminous species would not be observed living in close proximity to one another.

33. The phrase "selection pressure" in line 110 refers to
    (A) the potential extinction of an animal species due to the depletion of essential resources
    (B) environmental factors that favor development of a particular biological characteristic
    (C) competition among predators for a finite population of prey
    (D) selective winnowing of an animal population based on the attractiveness of specific individuals
    (E) changes in population density that affect the survival chances of a particular species

34. By comparison with the other species mentioned in the passage, the phenomenon of bioluminescence in the tomopterid worm discussed in lines 120–129 might best be described as
    (A) extreme
    (B) archetypal
    (C) exceptional
    (D) similar
    (E) prototypical

35. The author's comments about the tomopterid worm would be most seriously called into question by the discovery of which of the following?
    (A) A predator of the tomopterid worm that is sensitive to yellow light
    (B) Another species of tomopterid worm that produces bioluminescent blue-green fluid
    (C) Another species of tomopterid worm that does not exhibit bioluminescence
    (D) A prey of the tomopterid worm that does not exhibit bioluminescence
    (E) Other species of midwater animals that produce bioluminescent yellow fluids

STOP End of section 3. If you have any time left, go over your work in this section only. Do not work in any other section of the test.

SECTION 4

25 Questions

Time—30 Minutes

Directions: In this section solve each problem, using any available space on the page for scratchwork. Then decide which is the best of the choices given and fill in the corresponding oval on the answer sheet.

Notes:

1. The use of a calculator is permitted. All numbers used are real numbers.
2. Figures that accompany problems in this test are intended to provide information useful in solving the problems. They are drawn as accurately as possible EXCEPT when it is stated in a specific problem that the figure is not drawn to scale. All figures lie in a plane unless otherwise indicated.

Reference Information

Circle:

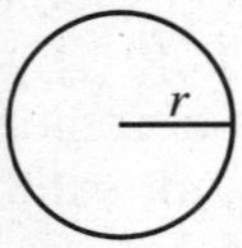

$C = 2\pi r$

$A = \pi r^2$

Rectangle:

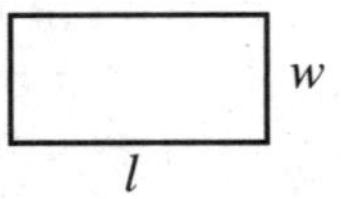

$A = lw$

Triangle:

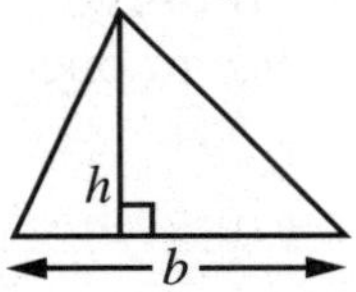

$A = \frac{1}{2}bh$

Rectangle Solid:

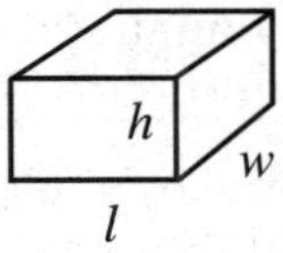

$V = lwh$

Cylinder:

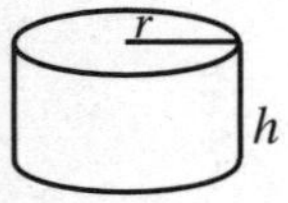

$V = \pi r^2 h$

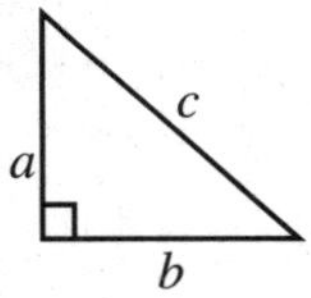

$a^2+b^2 = c^2$

Special Right Triangles

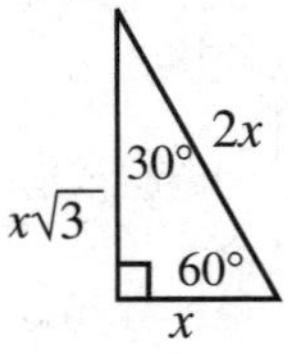

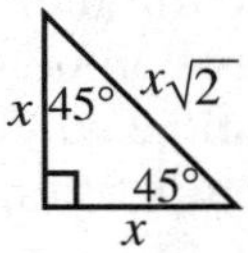

The number of degrees of an arc in a circle is 360.

The measure in degrees of a straight angle is 180.

The sum of the measures in degrees of the angles of a triangle is 180.

1. On a number line, A has coordinate -2 and B has coordinate 3. C is as far from B as A is from B. Which of the following is a possible coordinate of C?

(A) -5
(B) -3
(C) 5
(D) 7
(E) 8

---

2. If $(x - 5)^2 = (x + 5)^2$, then $x =$

(A) -10
(B) -5
(C) 0
(D) 5
(E) 10

---

3. Which of the following numbers is evenly divisible by 3 and 5, but not by 4 or 9?

(A) 16,840
(B) 20,085
(C) 23,094
(D) 56,790
(E) 79,260

---

4. When 3 times a certain number k is subtracted from 14, the result is 2 more than k. Which of the following equations expresses the value of k?

(A) $3k - 14 = k + 2$
(B) $3k + 14 = 2 - k$
(C) $14 - 3k = k + 2$
(D) $14 - 3k = 2k$
(E) $(k + 3) - 14 = (k + 2)$

---

5. A man buys \$12 worth of groceries. He presents \$2.50 worth of coupons which are deducted from the price of the groceries, and then receives a 10% senior citizen reduction on the balance. How much change will the man receive, if he pays with a \$20 bill?

(A) \$11.70
(B) \$11.45
(C) \$9.55
(D) \$8.55
(E) \$8.00

---

6. If x is one of the numbers from the set {1,3,5} and y is one of the numbers from the set {2,3,6}, how many different values are there for the number $|x - y|$?

(A) 5
(B) 6
(C) 7
(D) 8
(E) 9

---

7. 20% of what number is equal to $\frac{2}{3}$ of 90?

(A) 30
(B) 60
(C) 120
(D) 150
(E) 300

GO ON TO THE NEXT PAGE

8. 150 people were surveyed to determine their favorite soft drinks. The results of the survey in order from most to least popular are shown in the table below.

Brand	Number
A	55
B	43
C	x
D	y
E	12

If each brand was selected by a different number of individuals, what is the maximum possible value of x?

(A) 40
(B) 32
(C) 27
(D) 22
(E) 18

9. If $2(y - 3) = 4 + 3y$, then $y = ?$

(A) -10
(B) -7
(C) 2
(D) 7
(E) 10

10. In a group of 20 singers and 40 dancers, 20% of the singers are under 25 years old, and 40% of the entire group are under 25 years old. What percent of the dancers are under 25 years old?

(A) 20%
(B) 40%
(C) 50%
(D) 60%
(E) 80%

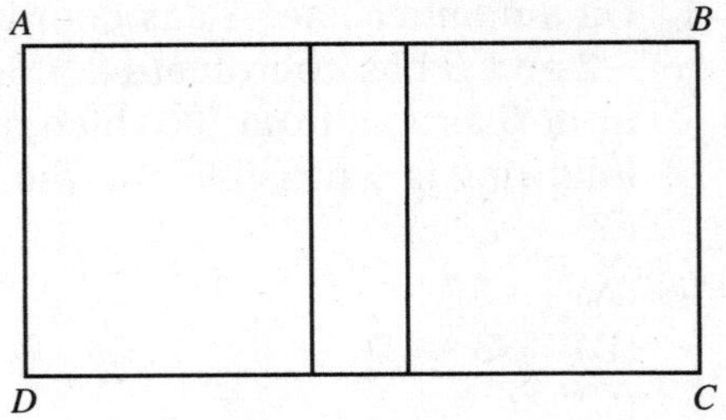

11. In rectangle *ABCD* above, the vertical lines divide the region into two squares and a center rectangle. If the area of each square is 25 and the area of the center rectangle is 15, what is the perimeter of *ABCD*?

(A) 20
(B) 26
(C) 30
(D) 36
(E) 50

12. The area of a rectangle is 60 and its perimeter is 32. What is the length of its shorter side?

(A) 3
(B) 6
(C) 10
(D) 12
(E) 15

13. A taxicab charges \$3.00 for the first one-fifth of a mile traveled and 30¢ for each additional one-fifth of a mile or part thereof. There is also a charge of 20¢ for every 30 seconds of time spent waiting in traffic but not moving. Angela took a cab from her hotel to the airport. She spent 4 minutes waiting in traffic, and the entire cab bill was \$22. Which of the following could have been the distance to the airport in miles?

(A) 8.4
(B) 9.2
(C) 10.9
(D) 11.5
(E) 11.7

14. Three consecutive odd integers are written in increasing order. If the sum of the first and second integers and twice the third integer is 46, what is the second integer?

(A) 17
(B) 15
(C) 13
(D) 11
(E) 9

15. If $\star x \star = \dfrac{x + \sqrt{x}}{2}$ which of the following is an even number?

(A) $\star 1 \star$
(B) $\star 4 \star$
(C) $\star 9 \star$
(D) $\star 25 \star$
(E) $\star 36 \star$

16. If p is an integer, and $(x - 3)(x + p) = x^2 + x - m$, what is the value of $m - p$?

(A) 8
(B) 4
(C) 0
(D) −4
(E) −8

17. Marla earns d dollars per hour plus tips working in a restaurant. On Monday she worked m hours and on Wednesday she worked w hours. If she received t dollars in tips and gave one-fifth of her tips to the busboy, in terms of d, m, w, and t, the amount she kept was

(A) $\dfrac{d + m + w + t}{5}$

(B) $\dfrac{d(m + w) + t}{5}$

(C) $d(m + w) = \dfrac{t}{5}$

(D) $d(m + w) = \dfrac{4t}{5}$

(E) $4\dfrac{d(m + w) + t}{5}$

18. Points $(-1, -1)$, $(3, 11)$, and $(1, t)$ lie on the same line. What is the value of t?

(A) 8
(B) 5
(C) 2
(D) −5
(E) −8

GO ON TO THE NEXT PAGE

19. If a and b are whole numbers and $3a = 2b$, which of the following statements must be true?

I. a is divisible by 2
II. b is divisible by 2
III. b is divisible by 3

(A) I only
(B) II only
(C) III only
(D) I and II only
(E) I and III only

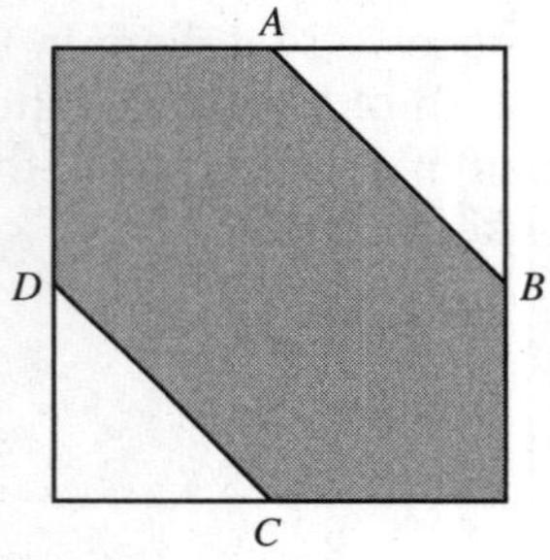

20. The figure above is a square of area 4. If the points A, B, C, D are the midpoints of the four sides, what is the perimeter of the shaded region?

(A) $2 + \sqrt{2}$
(B) 4
(C) $4 + \sqrt{2}$
(D) $4 + 2\sqrt{2}$
(E) $4 + 4\sqrt{2}$

21. If $\frac{x}{y} + \frac{2}{z}$ and $\frac{y}{x} + z$, what is the value of z?

(A) 3
(B) 2
(C) $\frac{3}{2}$
(D) $\frac{2}{3}$
(E) It cannot be determined from the information given.

22. A rectangle is inscribed in a circle of radius 2. The diagonals of the rectangle are diameters of the circle that cross at an angle of 60°. What is the area of the rectangle?

(A) $4\sqrt{3}$
(B) $2 + 2\sqrt{3}$
(C) $2 + 2\sqrt{2}$
(D) 4
(E) $2\sqrt{3}$

23. If x and y are positive integers, and $y^2 = x^2 + 7$, then $y =$

(A) 4
(B) 3
(C) 2
(D) 1
(E) It cannot be determined from the information given.

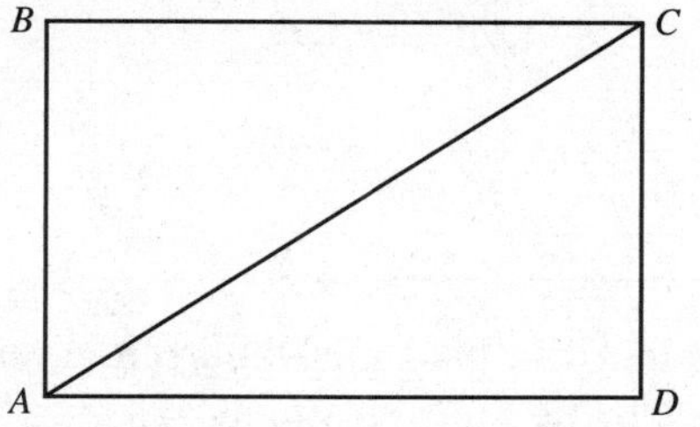

24. In a certain computer game illustrated above, a red square moves around rectangle *ABCD* in a counterclockwise direction, changing position once every second. At the same time, a green dot moves around ΔABC in a clockwise direction, changing position once every second. The values (R,G) represent the position of the red square and the green dot, respectively. If at time zero, their position is (A,A), which pair describes their position at time 415 seconds?

(A) (A,A)
(B) (A,B)
(C) (B,C)
(D) (C,B)
(E) (B,B)

25. A box contains five blocks numbered 1, 2, 3, 4, 5. Gloria picks a block and replaces it. Debbie then picks a block. What is the probability that the product of the numbers they picked is odd?

(A) $\frac{4}{5}$

(B) $\frac{16}{25}$

(C) $\frac{3}{5}$

(D) $\frac{9}{25}$

(E) $\frac{6}{25}$

STOP End of section 4. If you have any time left, go over your work in this section only. Do not work in any other section of the test.

SECTION 5

13 Questions

Time—15 Minutes

Directions: For each question in this section, select the best answer from among the choices given and fill in the corresponding oval on the answer sheet.

The two passages below are followed by questions based on their content and on the relationship between the two passages. Answer the questions on the basis of what is *stated* or *implied* in the passages and in any introductory material that may be provided.

Questions 1–13 are based on the following passages.

Sherwood Anderson (1876–1941) was one of the most original and influential early twentieth-century American writers. His first novel, the partly autobiographical Windy McPherson's Son, *was published in 1916 to moderate critical acclaim, but it was his second novel,* Winesburg, Ohio, *which brought Anderson international recognition. Passage 1 is a review of* Windy McPherson's Son *in which the reviewer critiques the "crudity" of Anderson's writing. Passage 2 is an excerpt from Anderson's own essay, "An Apology for Crudity," in which he explains his theory of literary style.*

Passage 1

Windy McPherson's Son has a certain raw vitality, but its crudity jars. One longs for less matter, with more art. Not a single person in this book seems real to me, and the reason is just the opposite from the common one. Most characters in works of fiction are unreal because their outlines are faint, vague, confused; the author has never realized them himself. Here each person is stressed with such force, the color laid on with such daubing profusion, that each man and woman is to me a caricature. They represent the *reductio ad absurdum* of certain traits and tendencies.

Nor is there any architectural skill displayed. As in so many "life" novels of the twentieth century, there is a plentiful supply of incidents without any plot. The hero is a little newsboy when we see him first, and he is well on in years, with a recrudescent paunch, when we see him last—yet the story progresses in time, but not in art. The last third of the book is picaresque. The hero takes to the road, and passes through a series of indiscriminate adventures, which might have taken twenty or twenty thousand pages, instead of the hundred arbitrarily allotted by the author.

Yet although I cannot admire this book as an achievement, I think its failure contains the seeds of success. It is more promising than many of the novels which surpass it in dignity. The conglomeration of incident and the exaggeration of human characteristics display an abundant vitality and a high aim. The author has done his level best to write the great American novel, to represent unsparingly what he believes to be the truth. Some day his decided natural gifts will ripen; he will not only see things in their proportion, he will be able to draw them according to scale; and he will read many pages of this work with a smile.

Passage 2

If you are in doubt as to the crudity of thought in America, try an experiment. Come out of your offices, where you sit writing and thinking, and try living with us. Get on a train at Pittsburgh and go west to the mountains of Colorado. Stop for a time in our towns and cities. Stay for a week in some Iowa corn-shipping town and for another week in one of the Chicago clubs.

As you loiter about, read our newspapers and listen to our conversations, remembering, if you will, that as you see us in the towns and cities, so we are. We are not subtle enough to conceal ourselves, and he who runs with open eyes through the Mississippi Valley may read the story of the Mississippi Valley.

To me it seems that as writers we shall have to throw ourselves with greater daring into the life here. We shall have to begin to write out of the people and not for the people. We shall have to find within ourselves a little of that courage. To continue along the road we are traveling is unthinkable. To draw ourselves apart, to live in little groups and console ourselves with the thought that we are achieving intellectuality, is to get nowhere. By such a road we can only hope to go on producing a literature that has nothing to do with life in these United States.

The road is rough and the times are pitiless. Who, knowing our America and understanding the life in our towns and cities, can close his eyes to the fact that life here is for the most part an ugly affair? As a people we have given ourselves to industrialism, and industrialism is not lovely. If anyone can find beauty in an American factory town, I wish he would show me the way. For myself, I cannot find it.

I do not know how far a writer may go on the road of subjective writing. The matter, I admit, puzzles me. There is something approaching insanity in the very idea of sinking yourself too deeply into modern American industrial life.

But it is my contention that there is no other road. If one would avoid neat, slick writing, he must at least attempt to be brother to his brothers and live as the people of his time live. He must share with them the crude expression of their lives. To our grandchildren the privilege of attempting to produce a school of American writing that has delicacy and color may come as a matter of course. One hopes that will be true, but it is not true now. And that is why, with so many of the younger Americans, I put my faith in the modern literary adventurers. We shall, I am sure, have much crude, blundering American writing before the gift of beauty and subtlety in prose shall honestly belong to us.

1. The author of Passage 1 implies that the most common failing of fiction writers is a tendency to
   (A) write so-called "life" novels with plots that are arbitrary and meaningless
   (B) write books with characters that are poorly developed
   (C) people their books with cartoonish, caricature-like figures
   (D) overexaggerate the humorous aspects of their characters
   (E) strive for variety at the expense of simplicity of structure

GO ON TO THE NEXT PAGE

2. When the author of Passage 1 says the last third of the book is "picaresque," he means that this portion of the book
   (A) consists of disconnected episodes involving a wandering protagonist
   (B) is merely picturesque as opposed to insightful or meaningful
   (C) is largely lacking in any narrative interest
   (D) emphasizes an interior view of the hero's psychology
   (E) draws heavily upon the author's own life story

3. The author of Passage 1 regards *Windy McPherson's Son* as fundamentally
   (A) worthwhile in its aims, but hopelessly flawed as a work of literary craftsmanship
   (B) plotless and confusing, yet stylistically passionate and arresting
   (C) similar to other "life" novels of the twentieth century
   (D) full of vital and promising writing, though crude in plot and character
   (E) lacking in interesting incidents, characters, and conflict

4. As used in line 41, the word "unsparingly" most nearly means
   (A) with abundant detail
   (B) in self-revelatory fashion
   (C) in vivid language
   (D) with complete accuracy
   (E) in elegant style

5. The tone of the final paragraph of Passage 1 most nearly resembles that of
   (A) a naturalist describing a unique biological specimen
   (B) a teacher admonishing a wayward student
   (C) a seasoned adult observing the vagaries of a callow youth
   (D) an impresario announcing his discovery of an unsuspected genius
   (E) a parent rebuking a lively but unruly child

6. The author of Passage 1 implies that the author of *Windy McPherson's Son* will someday
   (A) recognize the book's flaws
   (B) repudiate the book as an unworthy effort
   (C) revise the book to improve it
   (D) feel proud of the accomplishment it represents
   (E) write a true masterpiece

7. The author's primary purpose in Passage 2 is to
   (A) apologize for the crudity of expression in the author's own writing
   (B) analyze the relationship between intellectualism and anti-intellectualism in America
   (C) explain the link between industrialism and American literary expression
   (D) castigate academics and intellectuals for shying away from the challenges of real life
   (E) exhort writers to experience and depict American life in all its crudity

8. When the author of Passage 2 invites the reader to "try living with us" (lines 4–5), the word "us" refers mainly to
   (A) the author and his family
   (B) the community of American writers
   (C) the characters who people the author's writings
   (D) average American citizens
   (E) the author and his literary circle

9. As used in line 15, the word "subtle" most nearly means
   (A) deceptive
   (B) self-aware
   (C) refined
   (D) courageous
   (E) honest

10. With which of the following statements would the author of Passage 2 be most likely to agree?
   (A) Because rural America is not as crude as industrial America, beautiful writing is more characteristic of rural than industrial America.
   (B) If a way of life is particularly crude or ugly, then the literature depicting it should be crude and ugly as well.
   (C) Novelists must not attempt to write fiction unless they have participated personally in the experiences they are writing about.
   (D) Just as real life does not follow a pre-ordained story, the events in a novel should not follow a pre-ordained plot.
   (E) The writer who submerges himself too deeply into the lives of others in a quest for experience risks madness.

GO ON TO THE NEXT PAGE

11. In the sentence beginning "To our grandchildren . . ." (lines 57–60), the author of Passage 2 implies that crudity in writing is
    (A) a necessary counterpart to the crudity of life in an industrial society
    (B) a regrettable necessity that he hopes will be less apparent in the literature of future generations
    (C) less characteristic of the work of writers who are wealthy and privileged than of writers from working-class backgrounds
    (D) a vital element of literary art that deserves a revered place in any generation
    (E) more characteristic of young, adventurous writers than of older, more experienced writers

12. Which of the following pairs of words best summarizes how the authors of Passages 1 and 2, respectively, would view the characters in *Windy McPherson's Son*?
    (A) aimless; determined
    (B) confusing; clearly drawn
    (C) exaggerated; realistic
    (D) unintellectual; world-weary
    (E) ne'er-do well; intrepid

13. The authors of both passages would most likely agree that
    (A) crudity of literary expression is a natural expression of the American character
    (B) industrialism is largely responsible for the crudity of American expression
    (C) crudity of expression tends to give way in time to more subtle and delicate writing
    (D) intellectuals are too removed from the realities of American life to depict it honestly in their writing
    (E) it is only through exaggeration that a writer can depict the essence of a character's personality

STOP End of section 5. If you have any time left, go over your work in this section only. Do not work in any other section of the test.

SECTION 6

25 Questions

Time—30 Minutes

Directions: This section contains two types of questions. You have 30 minutes to complete both types. You may use any available space for scratchwork.

Notes:

1. The use of a calculator is permitted. All numbers used are real numbers.
2. Figures that accompany problems in this test are intended to provide information useful in solving the problems. They are drawn as accurately as possible EXCEPT when it is stated in a specific problem that the figure is not drawn to scale. All figures lie in a plane unless otherwise indicated.

Directions for Quantitative Comparison Questions

Questions 1–15 each consist of two quantities in boxes, one in Column A and one in Column B. You are to compare the two quantities and on the answer sheet fill in oval A if the quantity in Column A is greater; B if the quantity in Column B is greater; C if the two quantities are equal; D if the relationship cannot be determined from the information given.

E RESPONSES WILL NOT BE SCORED.

Notes:

1. In some questions, information is given about one or both of the quantities to be compared. In such cases, the given information is centered above the two columns and is not boxed.
2. In a given question, a symbol that appears in both columns represents the same thing in Column A as it does in Column B.
3. Letters such as *x*, *n*, and *k* stand for real numbers.

Examples

	Column A	**Column B**
E1	5^2	20

Answer: ⬤ Ⓑ Ⓒ Ⓓ Ⓔ

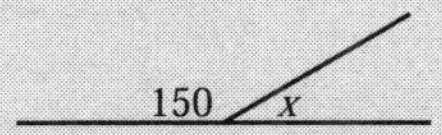

	Column A	**Column B**
E2	x	30

Answer: Ⓐ Ⓑ ⬤ Ⓓ Ⓔ

r and *s* are integers

	Column A	**Column B**
E3	$r + 1$	$s - 1$

Answer: Ⓐ Ⓑ Ⓒ ⬤ Ⓔ

	Column A	**Column B**
1.	The cost of 12 cans of peas at 34¢ apiece.	The cost of 12 cans of corn at 3 for a $1.00

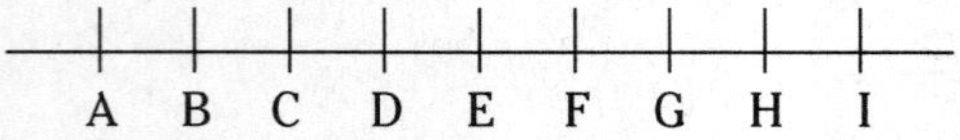

Note: All the vertical marks are equidistant.

	Column A	**Column B**
2.	The ratio of AE to BD	The ratio of BH to CF

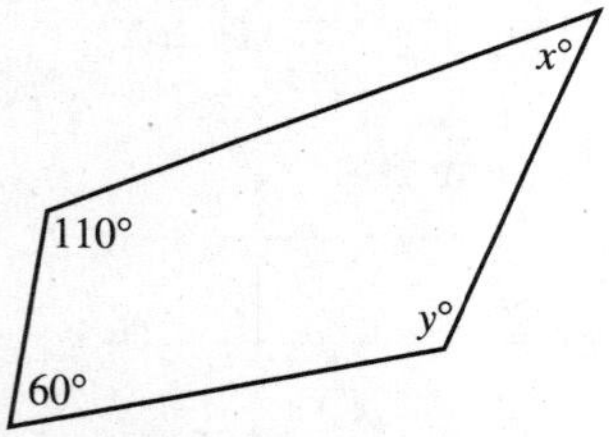

Note: Figure not drawn to scale.

	Column A	**Column B**
3.	x	$180 - y$

$2 - x = 4$ and $y - 4 = -2$

	Column A	**Column B**
4.	x	y

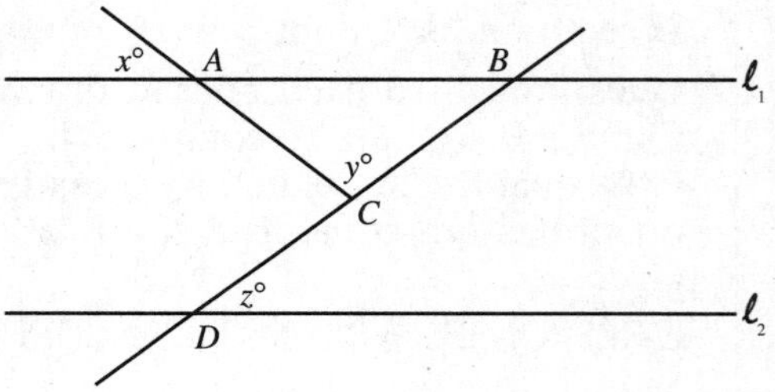

$\ell_1 \parallel \ell_2$

	Column A	**Column B**
5.	$x + y + z$	180

$3y - 6 = 2 - y$

	Column A	**Column B**
6.	y^2	$2y$

Column A	Column B

$x > 0$

7.

Column A	Column B
$\sqrt{x} + 2x$	$2\sqrt{x + x}$

One side of a rectangle is the diameter of a circle. The opposite side is tangent to the circle.

8.

Column A	Column B
The perimeter of the rectangle	The circumference of the circle

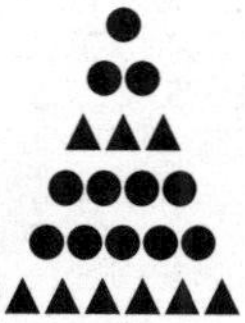

The pattern shown above continues for three more rows.

9.

Column A	Column B
The total number of ●s minus the total number of ▲s.	9

Column A	Column B

$x > 1$

10.

Column A	Column B
$x^2 + 3x$	$x + 3$

11.

Column A	Column B
The average speed in miles per hour needed to travel 240 miles in 4 hours.	The average speed in miles per hour needed to travel 20 miles in 20 minutes.

$$A \diamond B = \frac{A}{A + B}$$

12.

Column A	Column B
$-(2 \diamond 4)$	$(-2) \diamond 4$

GO ON TO THE NEXT PAGE

Column A		Column B
	$0 < x < y$	
13.	$\dfrac{\frac{x}{y}}{\frac{y}{x}}$	$\dfrac{x}{y}$

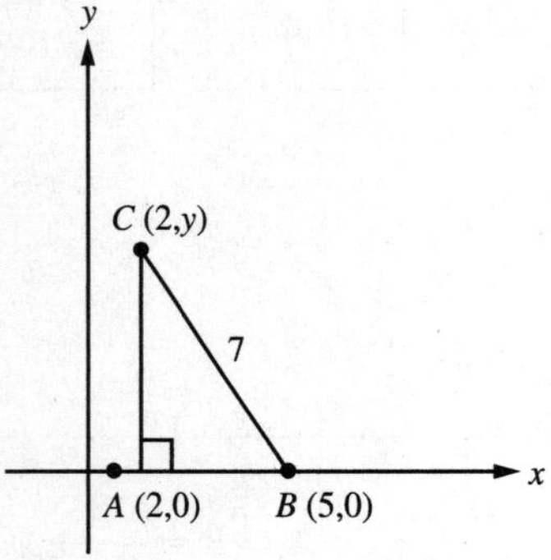

Column A		Column B
14.	The area of ΔABC	9

Column A		Column B
	$a > b$	
15.	$(a - b)^2$	$a^2 - b^2$

Directions for Student-Produced Response Questions

Each of the remaining 10 questions requires you to solve the problem and enter your answer by marking the ovals in the special grid, as shown in the examples below.

Answer: $\frac{7}{12}$ or 7/12

Answer: 2.5

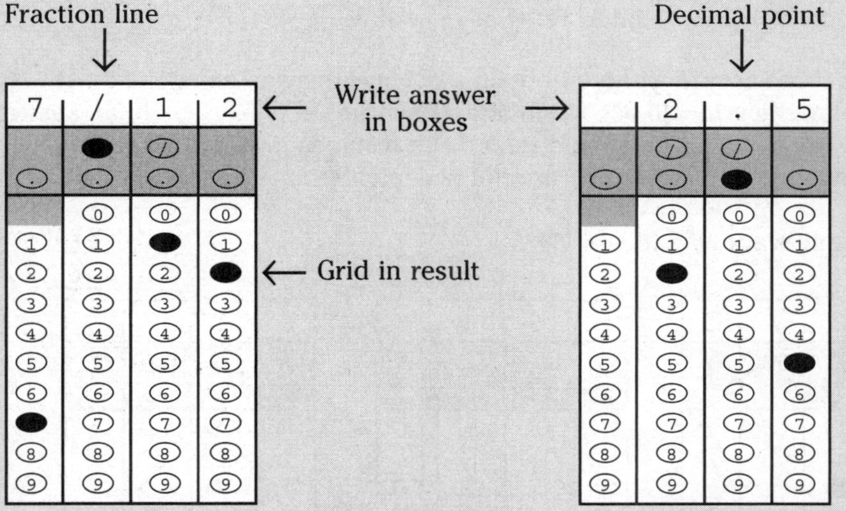

Answer: 201
Either position is correct.

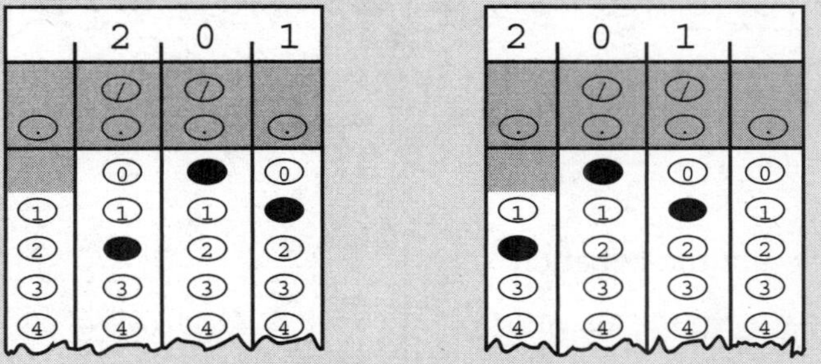

Note: You may start your answers in any column, space permitting. Columns not needed should be left blank.

- Mark no more than one oval in any column.
- Because the answer sheet will be machine-scored, you will receive credit only if the ovals are filled in correctly.
- Although not required, it is suggested that you write your answer in the boxes at the top of the columns to help you fill in the ovals accurately.

- Some problems may have more than one correct answer. In such cases, grid only one answer.
- No question has a negative answer.
- Mixed numbers such as $2\frac{1}{2}$ must be gridded as 2.5 or 5/2. If 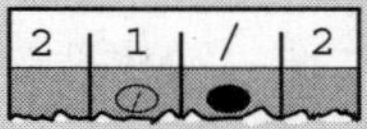

is gridded, it will be interpreted as $\frac{21}{2}$, not $2\frac{1}{2}$.
- **Decimal accuracy:** If you obtain a decimal answer, enter the most accurate value the grid will accommodate. For example, if you obtain an answer such as 0.6666 . . . , you should record the result as .666 or .667. Less accurate values such as .66 or .67 are not acceptable.

Acceptable ways to grid $\frac{2}{3} = .6666$

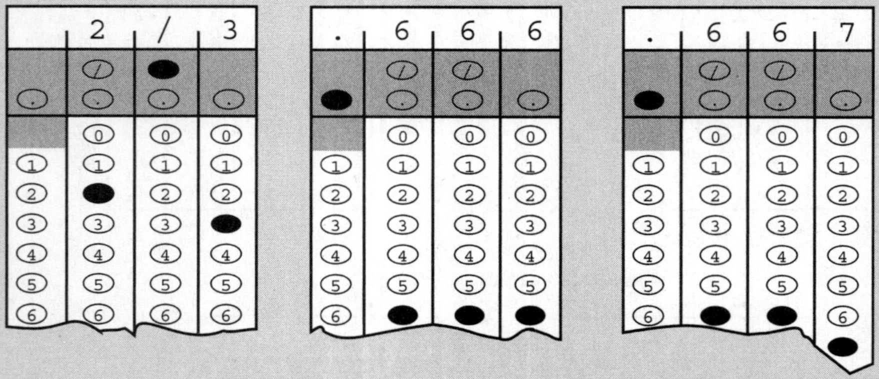

16. If $x = 8$ and $N = 4$ in the equation $N = \frac{x^2 + 24}{y}$, what is the value of y?

17. Jessica averaged 76 on her first three physics exams. What is the least she must average on her last two exams in order to have an overall average of 80 for the five exams?

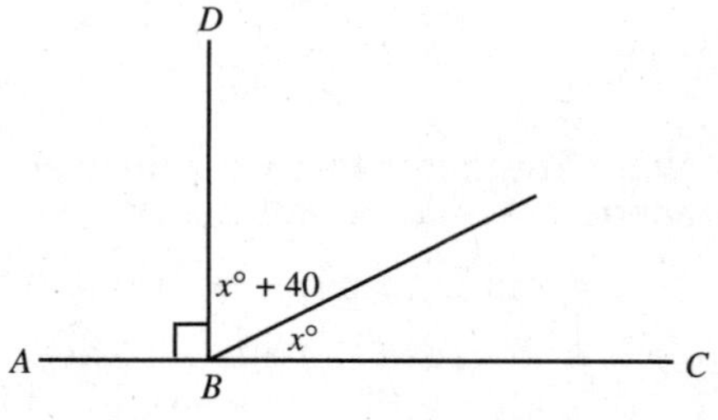

18. Find the value of x in the diagram above.

19. A survey of 150 individuals found that 43% listen to radio news reports, 45% listen to TV news reports, and 36% read a daily newspaper. What is the maximum possible number that do all three?

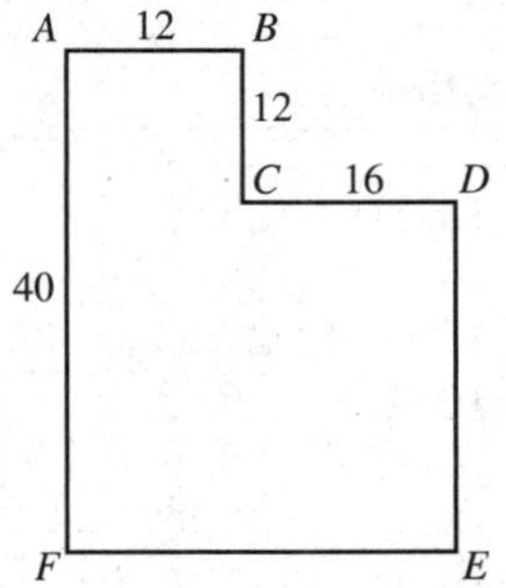

20. If sod comes in 4×4 foot squares costing \$3.50 per square, how much will it cost to sod the lawn shown above? (Distances in feet.) *Note:* All angles that appear to be right angles are right angles.

21. If in a certain baseball season, Felipe's ratio of hits to total times at bat was 2:7, and he had 365 times at bat without a hit, how many total times at bats did he have?

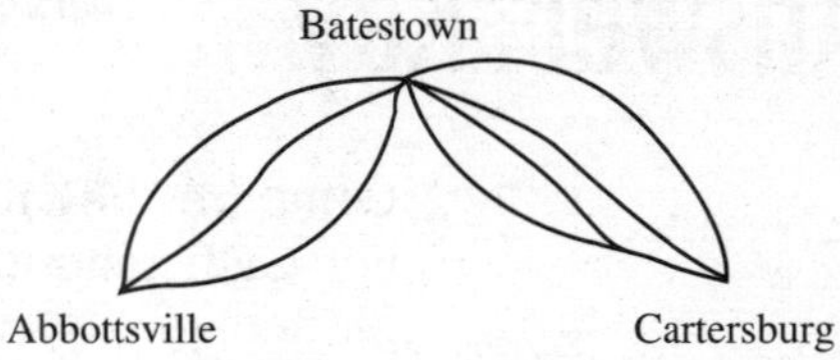

22. The diagram shown is a road map from Abbottsville to Cartersburg. How many different routes can a motorist follow to drive from Abbottsville to Cartersburg if she passes through Batestown exactly once?

23. Paula and Dennis both went to the bakery. Paula bought 3 rolls and 5 muffins for a total cost of \$3.55. Dennis bought 6 rolls and 2 muffins for a total cost of \$3.10. What is the price of one roll in cents?

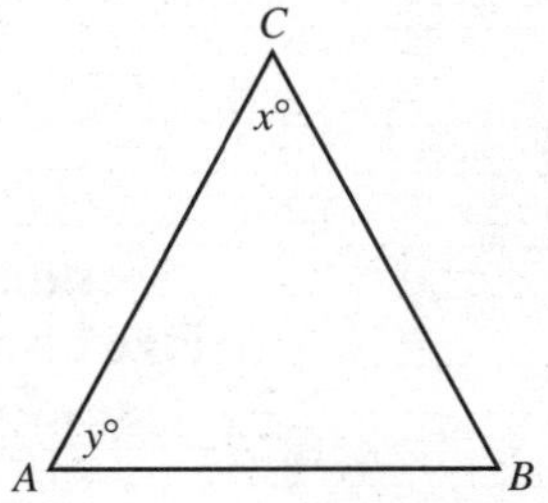

24. If in ΔABC, as shown, $AC = BC$ and $x \leq 50$, what is the smallest possible value of y?

25. If $3 < \frac{1}{x} < 4$, what is one possible value of x?

STOP End of section 6. If you have any time left, go over your work in this section only. Do not work in any other section of the test.

Answer Key

Compare the answers below with the answers on your answer sheets. For each section, fill in the number of correct answers and the number of incorrect answers (if indicated) in the spaces provided.

Verbal

Section 1			Section 3			Section 5	
1. B	11. A	21. E	1. D	13. D	25. B	1. B	8. D
2. A	12. D	22. C	2. B	14. A	26. C	2. A	9. A
3. D	13. E	23. C	3. D	15. B	27. D	3. D	10. B
4. C	14. A	24. A	4. D	16. C	28. E	4. A	11. B
5. B	15. B	25. E	5. E	17. C	29. E	5. B	12. C
6. E	16. D	26. E	6. D	18. C	30. C	6. A	13. C
7. E	17. D	27. C	7. C	19. D	31. E	7. E	
8. A	18. A	28. B	8. D	20. A	32. A		
9. B	19. B	29. C	9. D	21. E	33. B		
10. D	20. A	30. B	10. A	22. E	34. C		
			11. D	23. C	35. A		
			12. A	24. C			

Mathematical

Section 2 Five-Choice Questions		Section 4 Five-Choice Questions		Section 6 Four-Choice Questions		Student-Produced Response Questions
1. B	6. D	1. E	14. D	1. A	8. B	16. 22
2. C	7. C	2. C	15. C	2. A	9. C	17. 87.5
3. E	8. A	3. B	16. A	3. A	10. A	18. 25
4. E	9. D	4. C	17. D	4. B	11. C	19. 12
5. C	10. E	5. B	18. B	5. C	12. A	20. 203
		6. A	19. E	6. C	13. B	21. 511
		7. E	20. D	7. D	14. A	22. 12
		8. C	21. B		15. D	23. 35
		9. A	22. A			24. 65
		10. C	23. A			25. Any decimal greater than .25 and less than .333
		11. D	24. E			
		12. B	25. D			
		13. E				

Scoring Guide

COMPUTING YOUR VERBAL SCALED SCORE

Step 1. Count the number of correct answers you chose for the questions in Sections 1, 3, and 5. Write the total here: ________

Step 2. Count the number of incorrect answers you chose for the questions in Sections 1, 3, and 5. (Do not count questions you omitted.) Write the total here: ________

Step 3. Divide the total from Step 2 by 4. (The result may include a fraction.) Write the result here: ________

Step 4. Subtract the result from Step 3 from the total in Step 1. Write the result here: ________

Step 5. Round off the result from Step 4 to the nearest whole number. Round a number ending in $\frac{1}{2}$ *down*; for example, $48\frac{1}{2}$ rounds to 48. Write the result here: ________ This is your Verbal Raw Score.

Step 6. Look up your Verbal Raw Score on the Score Conversion Table (page 379). Find the corresponding Verbal Scaled Score and write it here: ________

COMPUTING YOUR MATHEMATICAL SCALED SCORE

Step 1. Count the number of correct answers you chose for the questions in Sections 2, 4, and 6. Write the total here: ________

Step 2. Count the number of incorrect answers you chose for the questions in Sections 2 and 4. (Do not count questions you omitted.) Write the total here: ________

Step 3. Count the number of incorrect answers you chose for questions 1–15 in Section 6. (Do not count questions you omitted.) Write the total here: ________

Step 4. Divide the total from Step 2 by 4. (The result may include a fraction.) Write the result here: ________

Step 5. Divide the total from Step 3 by 3. (The result may include a fraction.) Write the result here: ________

Step 6. Add the totals from Steps 4 and 5. Write the result here: ________

Step 7. Subtract the result from Step 6 from the total in Step 1. Write the result here: __________

Step 8. Round off the result from Step 4 to the nearest whole number. Round a number ending in $\frac{1}{2}$ *down*; for example, $38\frac{1}{2}$ rounds to 38. Write the result here: __________ This is your Mathematical Raw Score.

Step 9. Look up your Mathematical Raw Score on the Score Conversion Table (page 379). Find the corresponding Mathematical Scaled Score and write it here: __________

Score Conversion Table

Insider's SAT Sample Test

Raw Score	Verbal Scaled Score	Mathematical Scaled Score
78	800	
77	790	
76	780	
75	770	
74	760	
73	750	
72	740	
71	730	
70	720	
69	710	
68	700	
67	690	
66	680	
65	670	
64	660	
63	650	
62	650	
61	640	
60	630	800
59	630	780
58	620	770
57	610	760
56	610	750
55	600	740
54	590	730
53	590	710
52	580	700
51	570	690
50	570	680
49	560	670
48	560	660
47	550	650
46	550	640
45	540	640
44	540	630
43	530	620
42	530	610
41	520	600

Raw Score	Verbal Scaled Score	Mathematical Scaled Score
40	520	590
39	510	580
38	510	580
37	500	570
36	500	570
35	490	560
34	490	550
33	480	540
32	480	540
31	470	530
30	470	530
29	460	520
28	460	510
27	450	500
26	450	500
25	440	490
24	440	490
23	430	480
22	430	480
21	420	470
20	420	460
19	370	420
18	370	420
17	360	410
16	350	400
15	340	390
9	330	390
8	320	380
7	310	370
6	300	360
5	280	350
4	270	330
3	260	310
2	250	300
1	230	250
0 or less	200	200

Explanatory Answers

SECTION 1

1. **The correct answer is (B).** If a "thaw" is predicted, then clearly the weather conditions are "unfavorable" for ice skating.
2. **The correct answer is (A).** A man who decorates his home as "a kind of shrine" to his own life is certainly showing an extreme form of "egotism."
3. **The correct answer is (D).** We're looking for word choices here which would fit the cause-and-effect structure of the sentence. If the dissenters were afraid of being discovered, then it would make sense for them to hold the meeting "clandestinely" and warn one another not to "disclose" information about it.
4. **The correct answer is (C).** The word "Although" is a clue that the two halves of the sentence will contrast with one another. The first half speaks about how widespread rabies is; the second half makes the point that it is, in fact, "rare" in the United States, and explains why.
5. **The correct answer is (B).** As suggested by the semicolon (;) in the middle of the sentence, the two halves of the sentence make the same point in different ways. If the article implied that others should imitate the commander, then "exemplary" is a logical adjective to describe how it portrayed his behavior.
6. **The correct answer is (E).** "Encouraged" is the logical adjective to describe how AIDS researchers would feel in reaction to good news about possible treatment of the disease. In choice (C), "cheerful" seems an odd word; it describes a passing mood rather than a response to outside events.
7. **The correct answer is (E).** The use of "brutal tactics" by the police against particular ethnic groups would logically produce a reputation for "racism."
8. **The correct answer is (A).** Cause-and-effect relationships are at work in both halves of this sentence. If the fennec uses its ears by "listening quietly" for its prey, then clearly the ears are helping it to "locate" the prey. Similarly, if the ears help the fennec with "desert survival," then it would be logical to conclude that they help "dissipate" the heat.
9. **The correct answer is (B).** An investigation would likely be based on some kind of "discrepancy" between donations and money spent, since that might suggest some kind of deception by the candidate or her organization.
10. **The correct answer is (D).** Just as a census is a methodical count of a nation's population, so an inventory is a methodical count of the merchandise held in a store or warehouse.
11. **The correct answer is (A).** Wool is a substance that is removed from the outside of a sheep and used in making clothing; similarly, down in a substance removed from the outside of a duck and also used in making clothing.

12. **The correct answer is (D).** A dirge is a particular kind of song—one written to express sorrow over some sad event, such as a death. An elegey is a particular kind of poem—one written to commemorate a person who has died.

13. **The correct answer is (E).** In a theater, the proscenium is the front of the stage; when the curtain falls, the proscenium is "closed" and the stage is concealed. In much the same way, when the shade on a window is closed, what's beyond the window is concealed.

14. **The correct answer is (A).** A motorcade is a kind of parade in which many cars participate; a flotilla is a grand assemblage and parade of ships.

15. **The correct answer is (B).** To be impecunious is to be lacking in money; to be disinterested (as, for example, an honest judge should be) is to be lacking in bias.

16. **The correct answer is (D).** This summarizes the general tone of the passage. The author finds much to criticize about how able-bodied people behave toward him and other disabled people, but he is not bitter, sarcastic, or vindictive (as some of the wrong answers state). Instead, he analyzes his own reactions and the motives of others in an objective way, frankly revealing his own shortcomings even as he finds fault with society at large.

17. **The correct answer is (D).** See the next to last sentence of the second paragraph, which refers to "the body beautiful" as "an American ideal."

18. **The correct answer is (A).** A *pejorative* word is one with negative or insulting connotations—like *cripple,* the author's own example.

19. **The correct answer is (B).** Refer to the third paragraph of the passage, where the author says that the language in which disabilities are described has ended in "labels so vague as to describe anyone and no one."

20. **The correct answer is (A).** In the sentence in which he calls Mairs "brave," the author explains why he says this: because he knows that her forthright behavior is likely to make able-bodied people want to *flee.*

21. **The correct answer is (E).** The March of Dimes telethon is mentioned in the last paragraph to illustrate the author's point that offering charity to the disabled "allows the able-bodied to congratulate themselves." Choice (E) paraphrases this idea.

22. **The correct answer is (C).** All of these ideas are implied in the last paragraph of the passage except choice (C).

23. **The correct answer is (C).** In the last paragraph, the author says that these sword-brandishing people have chosen an approach that "speaks more of limits (i.e., physical limits) than possibilities." Hence, the notion that are "defining themselves in terms of their disabilities."

24. **The correct answer is (A).** This point is made in the second sentence of the passage.

25. **The correct answer is (E).** The last sentence of the third paragraph makes it obvious that wooden hulls were the rule, not the exception, among ships of the period.

26. **The correct answer is (E).** The *Virginia* was created simply by armor plating a traditional wooden boat, whereas the *Monitor* had an entirely new design that "looked like no other ship afloat."

27. **The correct answer is (C).** As the third paragraph suggests, the South by comparison with the North had fewer facilities for shipbuilding.

28. **The correct answer is (B).** See the last sentence of the seventh paragraph: "none of the nearly 100 shots that hit her had pierced her armor."

29. **The correct answer is (C).** To "sustain" damage, as the word is used in this sentence, means to receive or suffer it.

30. **The correct answer is (B).** Choice (B) restates the idea found in the last sentence of the passage.

SECTION 2

1. **The correct answer is (B).** The distance from A to G is 6 units, one-third of which is 2. Thus, the point we want is 2 units to the right of E, that is, point G.

2. **The correct answer is (C).** Calling the measure of $\angle A$ in degrees x, we have the following:

$$x = \text{number of degrees in } \angle A$$
$$2x + 30 = \text{number of degrees in } \angle B$$
$$x + (2x + 30) = 3x + 30 = \text{number of degrees in } \angle C$$

Summing, we have $x + 2x + 30 + 3x + 30 = 180$. Combining like terms:

$$6x + 60 = 180$$
$$6x = 120; x = 20$$

Clearly, $2x + 30$ and $3x + 30$ are larger than x, so the smallest angle is 20°.

3. **The correct answer is (E).** From the first equation, $3x - 1 = 14$. Adding 1 to both sides:

$$3x = 15$$

Dividing both sides by 3:

$$\frac{3x}{x} = \frac{15}{3}$$
$$x = 5$$

Of course, the question asked for B, not x. So, we substitute $x = 5$ into $B = 6x + 4$ and get $B = 6(5) + 4 = 34$, which is choice (E).

4. **The correct answer is (E).** We solve this just like an equation. Start by adding the like quantity $(x - 8)$ to both sides in order to group the x terms on one side and the constants on the other; thus:

$$\begin{array}{r} 12 - x \geq 3x + 8 \\ x - 8 = x - 8 \\ \hline 4 \geq 4x \end{array}$$

Now divide by 4, which does not change the sense of the inequality, yielding:

$$1 \geq x$$

which is the same as choice (E), $x \leq 1$.

5. **The correct answer is (C).** Let x = the width. Now, $2x$ = length. The volume of the rectangular solid is $V = 6(x)(2x) = 12x^2$. Since the cube has six faces, its total surface area is 6 times the area of one face. In symbols, $6s^2 = 864$. Dividing by 6, $s^2 = 144$; $s = 12$. Hence, the volume of the cube is $12^3 = 1728$. Since the two solids have the same volume:

$$12x^2 = 1728; x^2 = 144; x = 12$$

The length, which is twice the width, is thus 24.

6. **The correct answer is (D).** We want to solve $\frac{2x}{3} + 2 = a$ for x. Multiply by 3 to clear the fractions. You should now have:

$$2x + 6 = 3a$$

Now add -6 to both sides of the equation:

$$\begin{array}{r} 2x + 6 = 3a \\ -6 = -6 \\ \hline 2x = 3a - 6 \end{array}$$

Divide by 2:

$$\frac{2x}{2} = \frac{3a - 6}{2}; x = \frac{3a - 6}{2}$$

Substituting:

$$y = 2\left(\frac{3a - 6}{2}\right) + 6$$
$$y = 3a - 6 + 6$$

Therefore, $y = 3a$, which is choice (D).

7. **The correct answer is (C).** For I: $x¶y = \frac{x}{x + y}$, but $y¶x = \frac{y}{x + y}$. The two are not equal unless $x = y$. For II: $x¶0 = \frac{x}{x + 0}$, which is true. For III: $x¶(1 - x) = \frac{x}{x + (1 - x)} = \frac{x}{1} = x$ which is true. Hence, choice (C): only II and III are true.

8. **The correct answer is (A).** The 3 women can be arranged in 3! = 6 ways (that is, $3 \times 2 \times 1$). However, for each of these ways, the 3 men can be also arranged in 3! = 6 ways. Hence, there are really $6 \times 6 = 36$ ways altogether.

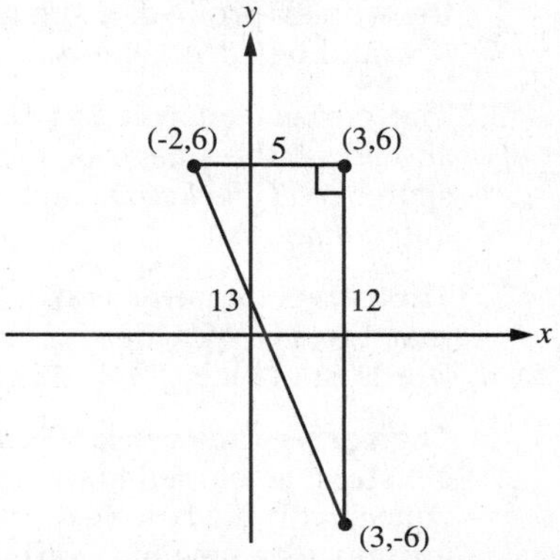

9. **The correct answer is (D).** Sketching the points on the *xy*-plane (as in the figure above), we see that they form a right triangle with one leg 5 and the other 12. Hence, the hypotenuse is 13, and the sum of the three sides is 5 + 12 + 13 = 30.

10. **The correct answer is (E).** Since every point on the circle must be 5 units from the center, we know that $(t, -1)$ must be 5 units from (4, 2). Using the distance formula,

$$\sqrt{(t-4)^2 + (2-(-1))^2} = 5$$

$$\sqrt{(t^2 - 8t + 16) + 9} = 5$$

$$\sqrt{t^2 - 8t + 25} = 5$$

Squaring both sides, we have:

$$t^2 - 8t + 25 = 25$$

We subtract 25 from both sides to yield:

$$t^2 - 8t = 0$$

which factors as:

$$t(t-8) = 0$$

with two possibilities, $t = 0$ or $t = 8$. The positive solution is 8.

SECTION 3

1. **The correct answer is (D).** The word *surprise* makes it clear that the contents of the magazine profile must contrast with the expected image of the women profiled. If she is normally viewed as *demure and innocent,* then it would be surprising to learn about her *provocative* side.

2. **The correct answer is (B).** The words to be inserted in the two blanks should fit the image of the landscape created in the second half of the sentence. *Treacherous* and *exciting* fit the ideas of a *sense of peril* and *an adrenaline rush.*

3. **The correct answer is (D).** The second half of the sentence makes it clear that the life of a dancer must be highly dedicated and disciplined. The words in choice (D) fit this picture.

4. **The correct answer is (D).** Tranquillity nicely summarizes the image of the cloisters developed in the rest of the sentence. The other answers could all conceivably be true (except choice (B), which is contradictory), but each introduces a new idea with no apparent justification in the sentence.

5. **The correct answer is (E).** Start with the second blank. Knowing that the newlyweds can never have children would most likely dampen or subdue the joy of their parents; so the second blank should be filled with a word meaning something like that. Now, the word *although* in the middle of the sentence tells us that the first half of the sentence should contrast with the second. Thus, the first blank should be filled with a word that implies unsubdued or very great joy.

6. **The correct answer is (D).** Since the sentence refers to "survival" as the issue, a strong word like *life-threatening* is necessary for the second blank.

7. **The correct answer is (C).** The words we insert in the first half of the sentence should be consistent with the picture of Shirley Temple found in the second half of the sentence. *Precocious* is the most appropriate adjective choice we are offered.

8. **The correct answer is (D).** If the president of an organization has been stealing its money, it makes sense that the supporters of the organization would feel betrayed. This sense of betrayal would be heightened if the organization were intended to be a philanthropic one.

9. **The correct answer is (D).** Clearly, the sentence is discussing the effects of competition from the compact disk on another music technology; the phonograph record. If those effects are powerful, as the sentence implies, it must be because the new technology has a particular advantage on its side: hence, *superiority* makes sense in the second blank.

10. **The correct answer is (A).** *Oasis* makes sense for the second blank, since the area is described as a *welcome escape.* Then, we're told that most of the city is dark at night, so it's logical that the first blank should say that electricity is *nonexistent* in many areas.

11. **The correct answer is (D).** Just as one would pluck feathers from a bird in order to use them (in a pillow, for example), one would shear wool from a sheep in order to use that (to make cloth).

12. **The correct answer is (A).** Ignorance is defined as the lack of knowledge; poverty is defined as the lack of money.

13. **The correct answer is (D).** A steer is a specific kind of animal in the category of animals called cattle. (Cows, bulls, and oxen would be others in the same category.) Similarly, a rat is a specific kind of animal in the category called vermin. (Mice would be another example.)

14. **The correct answer is (A).** A person might applaud in order to express a feeling of appreciation for another person; in the same way, one might jeer to express a feeling of contempt for another.

15. **The correct answer is (B).** A palm is a kind of tree—specifically, a kind associated with and usually found in a tropical climate. Similarly, a mango is a kind of fruit, and specifically a fruit associated with the tropics.

16. **The correct answer is (C).** A sponge would be used to pick up and remove moisture (from a spilled drink, for example). A brush would be used to pick up and remove lint (from a sweater or jacket, for instance).

17. **The correct answer is (C).** Copyright is a form of legal protection that prevents others from copying the creative work that goes into producing a book. Similarly, a patent is a form of legal protection that prevents others from copying the creative work of an inventor who develops a new device of some kind.

18. **The correct answer is (C).** The perimeter of a polygon is a measurement of the distance around it, just as the circumference of a circle is a measurement of the distance around it.

19. **The correct answer is (D).** A camera captures and records an image; a tape recorder does the same with a sound.

20. **The correct answer is (A).** To divert a stream is to turn it away from its usual path and make it flow somewhere else. To reroute traffic is to do the same thing with a flow of automobiles or other vehicles.

21. **The correct answer is (E).** A shyster is someone crooked or incompetent who swindles people while practicing law. Similarly, a quack is a crooked or incompetent doctor.

22. **The correct answer is (E).** The purpose of ballast (usually in a ship) is to weigh it down and therefore stabilize it—that is, to prevent it from rocking violently on the sea. The purpose of fuel (in an engine or motor) is to power it.

23. **The correct answer is (C).** To dissemble is to "play fast and loose with the truth"—not exactly to lie, but to depart from complete honesty. The wobble is to depart from perfect verticality (that is, straightness), the way a loose fence post fails to stand completely straight.

24. **The correct answer is (C).** Each of the other answer choices is discussed in one or more paragraphs of the passage.

25. **The correct answer is (B).** As used in this passage, the word *rubrics* refers to categories or types of bioluminescence.

26. **The correct answer is (C).** The first sentence of the third paragraph of the passage, which is where the angler fish is discussed, makes it clear that the paragraph is entirely devoted to examples of bioluminescence found in the midwaters of the ocean.

27. **The correct answer is (D).** Just as the angler fish uses a fake piece of food as bait to capture a hungry prey, so does the trout fisherman when he lures a trout with a tasty looking fake insect.

28. **The correct answer is (E).** Countershading is described in the fourth paragraph, where it is stated that this effect protects fish from predators *below* them, not above.

29. **The correct answer is (E).** The author mentions the "exploding dye packets" that help mark a bank robber in order to clarify how some animals coat predators with glowing tissue to mark them and make them vulnerable.

30. **The correct answer is (C).** The first sentence of the sixth paragraph explains that bioluminescence is used for communication between animals of the same, not different, species.

31. **The correct answer is (E).** This point is made in the first sentence of the eighth paragraph.

32. **The correct answer is (A).** The seventh paragraph says that bioluminescence is considered nonessential because nonluminous species seem to thrive as well as luminous ones. For this, we can conclude, that, if bioluminescence were essential, the opposite would be true—luminous species would do better than nonluminous ones.

33. **The correct answer is (B).** In the eighth paragraph, *selection pressure* is discussed specifically as an environmental force that helps promote the development or maintenance of luminescence among animal species. Choice (B) paraphrases this concept.

34. **The correct answer is (C).** The tomopterid worm is the only example in the passage of a kind of bioluminescence that seems to have no purpose at all; thus, it is exceptional.

35. **The correct answer is (A).** This discovery would suggest that the tomopterid worm's bioluminescence is, in fact, useful, since it would mean that the yellow fluid it spews could help to distract dangerous predators.

SECTION 4

1. **The correct answer is (E).** The distance from A to B is the distance from -2 to $+3$, or 5 units. Since C is 5 units from B, C is either 5 units greater than 3 or 5 units less. That is, either -2 or 8.

2. **The correct answer is (C).** By just checking the choices, you see that substituting $x = 0$ gives $5^2 = (-5)^2$, which is correct. So (C) is correct. To solve algebraically, expand both sides to yield:

$$x^2 - 10x + 25 = x^2 + 10x + 25$$
$$-10x = 10x$$
$$0 = 20x$$
$$x = 0$$

3. **The correct answer is (B).** The easiest thing to look for is divisibility by 5. Does the number end in 5 or 0? By inspection, we eliminate 23,094, which ends in 4. We want the number not to be divisible by 4, which means its last two digits must not form a number divisible by 4. That knocks out 16,840 and 79,260. This leaves 20,085 and 56,790. The digits of 20,085 add up to 15, while those of 56,790 total 27. Both are divisible by 3, but 56,790 is also divisible by 9. Therefore, only (B) 20,085 meets all the conditions.

4. **The correct answer is (C).** 3 times k subtracted from 14 means $14 - 3k$. 2 more than k means $k + 2$. Thus, $14 - 3k = k + 2$.

5. **The correct answer is (B).** From the $12.00 total bill, subtract the $2.50 worth of coupons, leaving a bill of $9.50. 10% of $9.50 is 95¢ or $0.95, which we subtract from $9.50, leaving only $8.55 to be paid. The change from a $20 bill is $20.00 − 8.55 = $11.45, which is choice (B).

6. **The correct answer is (A).** There are nine possible ways to form the difference $x - y$, but they do not all give different values, especially when you take the absolute values, so that numbers with the same magnitude but different signs give the same value. We can list the possibilities in a little table of $|x - y|$:

y/x	1	3	5
2	1	1	3
3	2	0	2
6	5	3	1

Now you can see that there are only 5 possible numbers: 0, 1, 2, 3, and 5.

7. **The correct answer is (E).** Calling the unknown N, $\frac{2}{3}$ of 90 means $\frac{2}{3} \times 90 = 60$. So we want 20% or $\frac{1}{5}$ of N to equal 60. That is, $\frac{1}{5}N = 60$, or $N = 300$, which is choice (E).

8. **The correct answer is (C).** Since the numbers in the table must total 150, we have $55 + 43 + x + y + 12 = 150$. That is, $x + y = 40$. Since y must be a whole number greater than 12, y must be at least 13. Therefore, x can be at most 27.

9. **The correct answer is (A).** Using the distributive law on the left-hand side gives us:

$$2y - 6 = 4 + 3y$$

To solve, we add $-2y - 4$ to both sides, thus:

$$\begin{array}{r} 2y - 6 = 4 + 3y \\ -2y - 4 = -2y - 4 \\ \hline -10 = y \end{array}$$

10. **The correct answer is (C).** Of the whole group of 60, 40% are under 25. 40% of 60 is (0.4)(60) = 24. For the singers, 20% of 20 = (0.2)(20) = 4 are under 25. Hence, the remaining "25 or unders" must be dancers. That is, 20 dancers, or one-half of all the dancers, fall into this category. Since one-half is 50%, the correct choice is (C).

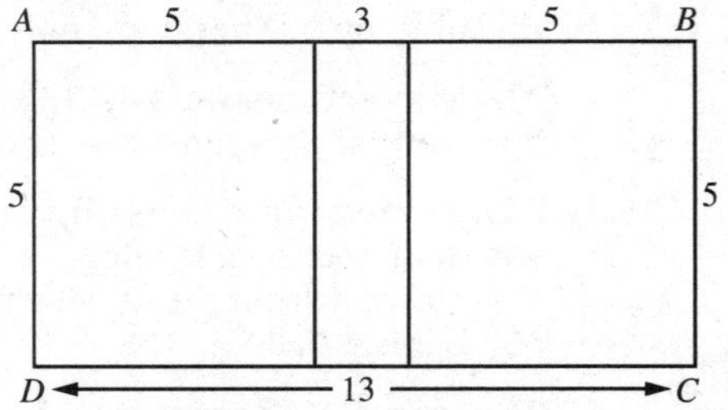

11. **The correct answer is (D).** If each square has an area of 25, each has a side of 5. Since that is also the side of the small central rectangle, which has area 15, the short side of the small rectangle must be 3 (see the figure above). Hence, the dimensions of the whole rectangle *ABCD* are 5×13. The perimeter is $2(5) + 2(13) = 36$.

12. **The correct answer is (B).** Calling the dimensions L and W, we have $LW = 60$ and $2L + 2W = 32$. Dividing by 2, $L + W = 16$. Therefore, $L = 16 - W$, which we substitute in $LW = 60$, giving us:

$$(16 - W)W = 60$$
$$16W - W^2 = 60$$

Grouping everything on the right-hand side, we have:

$$0 = W^2 - 16W + 60$$

Factoring:

$$0 = (W - 10)(W - 6)$$

yields:

$$W = 10 \text{ or } W = 6$$

Of course, if $W = 6$, then $L = 10$, and if $W = 10$, then $L = 6$. So the dimensions are 6×10 and the shorter side is 6.

13. **The correct answer is (E).** From the total bill of \$22, subtract the cost of waiting in traffic, which was 4 minutes, or 8 times 30 seconds. That cost 8 times 20¢, or \$1.60. Thus, the bill for mileage was \$22 − \$1.60 = \$20.40. \$3.00 for the first one-fifth mile leaves \$17.40 unaccounted for. Dividing by 30¢ per one-fifth mile we have $(17.4) \div (0.3) = 58$ fifths of a mile, or 11.6 miles. Adding back the first fifth, we have 11.8 miles. Of course, 11.7 costs the same as 11.8, so choice (E) is correct.

14. **The correct answer is (D).** Calling the smallest number x, the second is $(x + 2)$, and the third is $(x + 4)$. Therefore:

$$\begin{aligned} x + (x + 2) + 2(x + 4) &= 46 \\ x + x + 2 + 2x + 8 &= 46 \\ 4x + 10 &= 46 \\ 4x &= 36 \\ x &= 9 \end{aligned}$$

Hence the middle number is $9 + 2 = 11$.

15. **The correct answer is (C).** Try each of the choices: (A) $\star 1 \star = \frac{1 + \sqrt{1}}{2} = \frac{2}{2} = 1$. Similarly, (B) $\star 4 \star = 3$; (C) $\star 9 \star = 6$;)D) $\star 25 \star = 15$; (C) $\star 36 \star = 21$. Only choice (C) 6 is even.

16. **The correct answer is (A).** Using the FOIL method for multiplying the binomials, we see that the middle term should be $-3x + px = x$, which means that $-3 + p = 1$, or $p = 4$. The constant term is $-3p = -m$. That is, $m = 3p$, $m = 12$. Hence, $m - p = 12 - 4 = 8$.

17. **The correct answer is (D).** The total hourly wages Marla took in was the total number of hours, $m + w$, times the pay per hour; thus, $d(m + w)$. In addition, she kept $\frac{4}{5}$ of her tips, or $\frac{4}{5} \times t = \frac{4t}{5}$, which we add to the hourly wages to end up with $d(m + w) + \frac{4t}{5}$.

18. **The correct answer is (B).** Since the slope of a line is the same for any two points on the line, and $m = \frac{y_1 - y_2}{x_1 - x_2}$, using $(-1,-1)$ and $(3,11)$, we must have $m = \frac{11 - (-1)}{3 - (-1)} = \frac{12}{4} = 3$. Now, using the pair $(-1,-1)$ and $(1,t)$, $3 = \frac{t - (-1)}{1 - (-1)} = \frac{t + 1}{2}$. Multiplying by 2, $6 = t + 1$, and $t = 5$.

19. **The correct answer is (E).** If $3a$ equals $2b$, then $3a$ must be divisible by 2, which means a must be divisible by 2, since 3 is not. Similarly, $2b$ must be divisible by 3, which means b must be divisible by 3, since 2 is not. Thus, the correct choice is (E) both I and III must be true. Notice that II need not be true, since $b = 3$, $a = 2$ is a perfectly satisfactory solution.

20. **The correct answer is (D).** Knowing that the area is 4, we know that each side is of length 2. Therefore, half of each side is 1, and the unshaded triangles are each isosceles right triangles with legs of length 1 and a hypotenuse of length $\sqrt{2}$. Hence, the shaded region has 4 sides of length 1 and two of length $\sqrt{2}$, for a total of $4 + 2\sqrt{2}$.

21. **The correct answer is (B).** From the second equation, we have $\frac{y}{x} = -z$, so that $\frac{x}{y} = -\frac{1}{z}$, which we can substitute into the first equation. This gives us $-\frac{1}{z} + \frac{2}{z} = \frac{1}{2}$, that is, $\frac{1}{z} = \frac{1}{2}$ or $z = 2$, which is choice (B). Of course, this can also be solved by trying the various choices to see which one satisfies both equations.

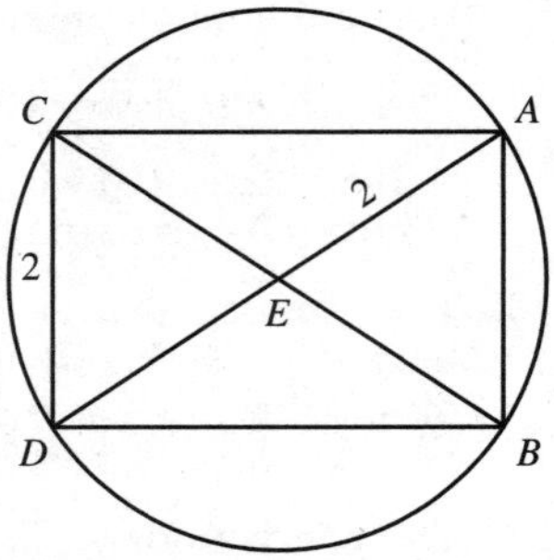

22. **The correct answer is (A).** If the diagonals of the rectangle meet at an angle of 60° (see the figure above), then ΔECD and ΔAEB are both equilateral triangles with side equal to the radius, 2. Hence, the length of CD is 2, which is the width of the rectangle. Further, since $\angle ECD$ is 60°, $\angle CBD$ is 30°, making ΔBCD a 30°-60°-90° triangle with shorter leg 2. That makes the longer leg $BD = 2\sqrt{3}$, which is the length of the rectangle. So its area $A = LW = 2(2\sqrt{3}) = 4\sqrt{3}$, which is choice (A).

23. **The correct answer is (A).** If we rewrite the equation as $y^2 - x^2 = 7$ and factor, we have $(y - x)(y + x) = 7$. Thus, 7 must be the product of the two whole numbers, $(y - x)$ and $(y + x)$. But 7 is a prime number which can only be factored as 7 times 1. Hence,

$$y + x = 7$$

and

$$y - x = 1$$

Adding the two equations gives us

$$2y = 8$$
$$y = 4$$

Of course, $x = 3$, but you weren't asked that.

24. **The correct answer is (E).** The square is moving A-D-C-B-A-D-C-B- . . . Thus, every time the number of seconds is divisible by 4, the red square is back at A. Hence, you can find its location by looking at the remainder when the time is divided by 4. 415 ÷ 4 leaves a remainder of 3, so the square has gone three steps beyond A and is at B. Similarly, the dot's location is given by the remainder when 415 is divided by 3. The remainder is 1, so the dot has reached one location beyond A, but it is moving A-B-C-A-B-C- . . . Hence, it too has reached B.

25. **The correct answer is (D).** Since each person had 5 choices, there are 25 possible picks. The only way the product could be odd is if both picked odd numbers. There are 3 ways for Gloria to pick an odd number and 3 ways for Debbie to pick an odd number, giving (3)(3) = 9 ways in all. Hence, out of 25 possibilities, 9 are odd. The probability is $\frac{9}{25}$.

SECTION 5

1. **The correct answer is (B).** See the fourth sentence of the passage, with its statement that "most characters in works of fiction are unreal because their outlines are faint, vague, confused."

2. **The correct answer is (A).** The last sentence of the second paragraph—the sentence *after* the one in which the word "picaresque" is used—defines what the author means by that term.

3. **The correct answer is (D).** This choice nicely summarizes the strengths and weaknesses that the author of Passage 1 sees in the novel.

4. **The correct answer is (A).** In this context, the author is using "unsparingly" to describe the "abundant vitality," "conglomeration of incident," and "exaggeration of human characteristics" he finds in Anderson's writing. He doesn't mean by "unsparingly" "with complete accuracy," since he thinks Anderson's novel is exaggerated and overdrawn.

5. **The correct answer is (B).** In expressing the hope that one day Anderson will see the flaws of his own early work and do better, the author of Passage 1 seems to be assuming that his own judgment and expertise is more mature that Anderson's—much like a teacher admonishing a pupil.

6. **The correct answer is (A).** The last phrase of Passage 1 contains this implication.

7. **The correct answer is (E).** This point is made throughout the passage, but see the first two sentences of the second paragraph for one of the balder statements.

8. **The correct answer is (D).** The examples cited in the first half of the first paragraph (Pittsburgh, Colorado, etc.) make it clear that the author is talking about ordinary people throughout America.

9. **The correct answer is (A).** By associating being "subtle" with "conceal ourselves," the author shows that he is using the word to mean "deceptive."

10. **The correct answer is (B).** Throughout Passage 2, the author defends the "crudity" of his writing by referring to the crudity and ugliness of life in modern America. His implication is that, if art is to be faithful to the realities of life, it must replicate crudity and ugliness if it finds them.

11. **The correct answer is (B).** In the sentence cited, the author suggests that "our grandchildren" may be able to write with "delicacy and color," an option not open to writers of today.

12. **The correct answer is (C).** The author of Passage 1 says that the characters in the novel are "caricatures," whose features exaggerate those of people in real life. The author of Passage 2 defends those characters by saying that they shows what American life is really like.

13. **The correct answer is (C).** As we saw in the answer to question 11, Anderson expresses the hope that his grandchildren would write with greater delicacy than he could, whereas, in Passage 1, the author says that he thinks Anderson himself will one day develop greater "proportion" and overcome the flaws of exaggeration he thinks the young Anderson is guilty of. So both writers seem to believe that it is a natural tendency for crude and exaggerated writing to give way, in time, to a more subtle and delicate style.

SECTION 6

1. **The correct answer is (A).** Looking at Column B, we see that 3 for a dollar is $33\frac{1}{3}$¢ apiece, which is less than 34¢ apiece. It doesn't matter how many items you have—when the number of items in each group is the same, the group with the lower price per item has the lower total.

2. **The correct answer is (A).** Counting spaces, we see that in Column A, we have AE:BD $= 5{:}2 = \frac{5}{2} = 2.5$, but in Column B, we have BH:CF $= 6{:}3 = \frac{6}{3} = 2$.

3. **The correct answer is (A).** The four angles in the quadrilateral must total 360°. The two given angles total 170°. Hence, $x + y = 190$. Thus, $x = 190 - y$, which is certainly greater than $180 - y$.

4. **The correct answer is (B).** Solving the first equation for x, we have $x = -2$. Solving the second equation for y gives us $y = 2$. Clearly, $2 > -2$.

5. **The correct answer is (C).** In ΔABC, the measure of $\angle A = x°$ by the property of vertical angles, and the measure of $\angle B = z°$ by the property of alternate interior angles. Hence, $x + y + z = 180$.

6. **The correct answer is (C).** Solving the equation:

$$3y - 6 = 2 - y$$
$$4y = 8$$
$$y = 2$$

For $y = 2$, $y^2 = 2y = 4$. The quantities are the same.

7. **The correct answer is (D).** Try to set up the inequality:

$$\sqrt{x} + 2x > 2\sqrt{x} + x$$

Subtracting $\sqrt{x} + x$ from both sides yields:

$$x > \sqrt{x}$$

This is true if $x > 1$, but false if $x < 1$. Therefore, you do not have enough information.

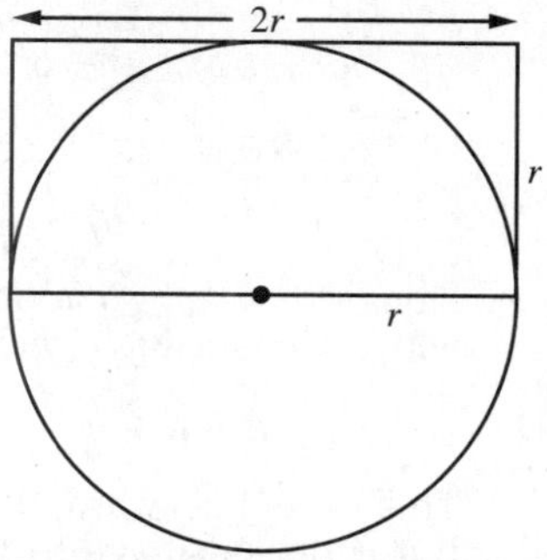

8. **The correct answer is (B).** From the description, the situation must be that shown in the figure above. Calling the radius r, we see that the perimeter of the rectangle is $2(2r) + 2(r) = 6r$. The circumference of the circle is $2pr$, but $p > 3$. Therefore, $2p > 6$, and the circumference of the circle is larger.

9. **The correct answer is (C).** Counting the circles, we see they are $(1 + 2)$ for the first two rows, then $(4 + 5)$ for the next two, so the two unshown are $(7 + 8)$, for a total of $3 + 9 + 15 = 27$. Counting the triangles, we see 3, then 6, so the unshown row must be 9 for a total of $3 + 6 + 9 = 18$. $27 - 18 = 9$, so Columns A and B are equal.

10. **The correct answer is (A).** Since $x > 1$, we know that $(x + 3)$ is a positive number. Hence, $x(x + 3) > 1(x + 3)$. The quantity in Column A is $x^2 + 3x = x(x + 3)$. The quantity in Column B is $(x + 3) = 1(x + 3)$. Hence (A) is the correct choice.

11. **The correct answer is (C).** We know that $d = rt$. Therefore, $r = \frac{d}{t}$. To go 240 miles in 4 hours, $r = 240 \div 4 = 60$ mph. To go 20 miles in 20 minutes, we need to go a mile a minute, or 60 mph. Thus, the two quantities are equal (C).

12. **The correct answer is (A).** $-(2 \diamond 4) = -\frac{2}{2 + 4} = -\frac{2}{6} = -\frac{1}{3}$. $(-2) \diamond 4 = \frac{-2}{-2 + 4} = -\frac{2}{2} = -1$. Since $\frac{-1}{3} > -1$, the correct choice is (A).

13. **The correct answer is (B).** $\frac{\frac{x}{y}}{\frac{y}{x}} = \left(\frac{x}{y}\right)\left(\frac{x}{y}\right) = \frac{x^2}{y^2} = \left(\frac{x}{y}\right)^2$. Since x and y are both positive numbers, and $y > x$, the number $\frac{x}{y} < 1$, and when you square it, it gets smaller. Therefore, quantity (B) is larger.

14. **The correct answer is (A).** From the diagram, we see that one leg of the triangle is 3 and the other is y, and the hypotenuse is 7. By the Pythagorean Theorem, $y^2 + 3^2 = 7^2$, that is, $y^2 = 40$, and $y = \sqrt{40} = 2\sqrt{10}$. The area of the triangle is $\left(\frac{1}{2}\right)(3)(2\sqrt{10}) = 3\sqrt{10}$. Since $\sqrt{10} > 3$, $3\sqrt{10} > 9$. Thus, (A) is larger.

15. **The correct answer is (D).** Try to set up the inequality:

$$(a - b)^2 > a^2 - b^2$$

Factoring:

$$(a - b)(a - b) > (a - b)(a + b)$$

Since $a > b$, $a - b$ is positive, and you divide both sides of the inequality without changing it, yielding:

$$a - b > a + b$$

This looks backward; that is, you would think that $a - b$ is less than $a + b$. But it doesn't have to be! Why? First, b could be zero and the quantities would be equal. Second, if b is negative the result is correct. Therefore, you need more information.

16. **The correct answer is 16.** Substituting into $N = \frac{x^2 + 24}{y}$, we have $4 = \frac{64 + 24}{y} = \frac{88}{y}$. Hence, $4y = 88$, and $y = 22$.

17. **The correct answer is 87.5.** To have an average of 75 on 3 exams, Jessica must have a total of 225. To average 80 on 5 exams, her total must reach 400. Therefore, she must score a total of at least 175 on her last two exams for an average of $175 \div 2 = 87.5$.

18. **The correct answer is 25.** Since $\angle ABD$ is a right angle, so is $\angle DBC$. Thus:

$$x + (x + 40) = 90$$

Removing parentheses:

$$x + x + 40 = 90$$
$$2x = 50$$
$$x = 25$$

19. **The correct answer is 12.** If the three sets were totally disjoint, that is, had no overlap, the sum of the percentages would be 100%. The extent of various kinds of overlap will show up as an excess over 100%. If we total 43 + 45 + 36, we find that we have accounted for 124% of the voters. Everyone common to all three will be included in this total three times. Therefore, if the number common to all three is greater than 8%, we would not be able to reach 100%. Hence, the maximum is 8%, which is reached only if everyone is in either one category or all three, and no one falls into two out of three categories. Since 8% of 150 is 12, that is the correct answer.

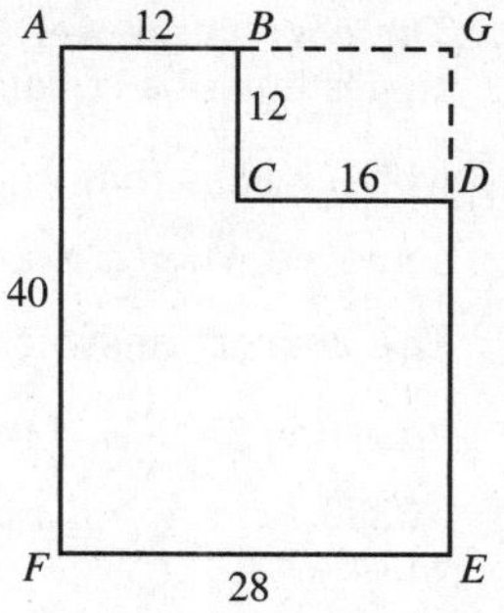

20. **The correct answer is 203.** Completing the rectangle as shown in the figure above, we see that the large rectangle *AGEF* is $40 \times 28 = 1120$ square feet. The smaller rectangle *BGDC* is $12 \times 16 = 192$ square feet. Hence, the area that must be sodded is $1120 - 192 = 928$ square feet. Each 4×4 piece of sod is 16 square feet. Therefore, we need $928 \div 16 = 58$ squares of sod at \$3.50 each. $(58)(3.50) = \$203$.

21. **The correct answer is 511.** Let the number of hits be $2k$; then, the total times at bat is $7k$, leaving $5k$ as the number of times at bats without a hit. Hence, $5k = 365$, which means $k = 73$ and $7k = 511$, which is what was asked for.

22. **The correct answer is 12.** You have 3 choices for a road from Abbottsville to Batestown and 4 roads from Batestown to Cartersburg. Hence, by the multiplication principle, the total number is $3 \times 4 = 12$.

23. **The correct answer is 35.** Let us express all amounts in cents. Let r = cost of a roll; let m = cost of a muffin. Paula paid $3r + 5m = 355$. Dennis paid $6r + 2m = 310$. We multiply the first equation by -2 and add the two equations:

$$\begin{array}{rr} -2 \text{ times the first equation is:} & -6r - 10m = -710 \\ \text{the second equation is:} & \underline{6r + \ \ 2m = \ \ \ 310} \\ \text{adding:} & -8m = -400 \end{array}$$

Dividing by -8, $m = 50$. We now substitute this into either of the two equations. Let's use the second:

$$\begin{aligned} 6r + (2)(50) &= 310 \\ 6r &= 210 \\ r &= 35 \end{aligned}$$

Thus, rolls are 35¢.

24. **The correct answer is 65.** Since the sides are of equal length, the two base angles must be equal. The three angles must total 180°. Hence, $x + 2y = 180$, which means that $y = \frac{180 - x}{2} = 90 - \frac{1}{2}x$. The smallest possible value for y is achieved when x is as large as possible. That is, at $x = 50$, for which $y = 65$.

25. **The correct answer is: Any decimal greater than .25 and less than .333.** Inverting $3 < \frac{1}{x} < 4$ the values gives $\frac{1}{3} > x > \frac{1}{4}$. That is, x is between 0.25 and 0.3333 . . . . Any decimal in that interval, such as 0.28, 0.3, 0.32, and so on, will do.

Part IV

Making It Official

Chapter 11

Scheduling and Taking the Test

Get the Scoop On . . .

- Choosing the test date and location that's best for you
- Saving time and money when you register for the exam
- Obtaining any special test accommodations you may need to do your best
- Which ETS and College Board services are worth buying—and which ones to skip
- How to ensure you'll feel good and perform well the day of the exam

DECIDING WHEN TO TAKE THE SAT

The SAT is usually administered six times a year: in early October, early November, early December, late January, early April, early May, and early June. So to begin with, you have a lot of flexibility in picking your test date. But when you start factoring in college application deadlines and other considerations, your options begin to narrow rapidly. Here are some of the main points to consider in choosing a test date.

- **Check the application deadlines for your college(s) of choice.** Most schools set a single date by which they want to receive all the supporting data they need—not only test scores but items such as high school transcripts, your application essay, and teacher recommendations. Determine which college you are applying to sets the *earliest* deadline, and count back six weeks from that date. (This allows a little extra time for your score report to be received; ETS aims to send reports out within three weeks of the test, but four to five weeks is more common.) The date you count back to should be your *latest* date for taking the SAT.

- **Allow yourself the option of retaking the SAT.** Suppose that, working backwards from your earliest college deadline, you determine that you must take the SAT no later than early November of your senior year. Don't simply apply for that test date. Instead, if you can, we recommend that you take the exam at least one test administration earlier, and preferably two. That means applying for an early October test or, better still, a test in May or June of your junior year in high school.

  Why the hurry? In the event your SAT scores don't hit the targets you've set, you'll want to have the opportunity to take the exam at least once more before your application deadline hits.

Most students find that their test scores rise the second time they take the SAT, and if you prepare in a focused and disciplined way before your second exam, you'll have the opportunity to achieve a significant score increase. (For more information about whether and how to plan on retaking the exam, see Chapter 12.) But this will be impossible if you schedule your exam during the final pre-deadline window.

- **Don't forget to schedule your SAT II Subject Tests.** Check with your college(s) of choice as to which SAT II exams they require or recommend. Then pencil those into your test-taking calendar as well. You can take up to three Subject Tests on any given testing day; you *cannot* take the SAT I on the same day. The most popular Subject Tests are generally given on the same days as the SAT I, except for the April date, when no Subject Tests are given.

  As you may know, it's considered best to take an SAT II Subject Test as soon as possible after you complete the relevant high school course. You may have begun taking Subject Tests as far back as tenth or even ninth grade. However, you probably have one or two more to schedule during your last year and a half of high school, and this can complicate your SAT planning further.

REGISTERING FOR THE EXAM

ETS supplies high schools with plentiful stacks of SAT bulletins and registration forms, so the easiest way to get the forms you need is to stop by the guidance office and ask for them. If for some reason you can't do this, call ETS at 1-609-771-7600 and have them send you the materials.

When you register by mail, you'll fill in a fairly lengthy (four-page) computerized form which requires you to blacken in ovals using a #2 pencil. Surprise—it's the same technology used on the SAT answer sheets, so you might as well get used to it. Take your time filling out the form; it's easier than a tax return, but not much. Be especially careful when looking up and transferring the code numbers for the test center where you want to take the exam and the code numbers for the colleges you're listing to receive your test scores. Mistakes are easy to make.

If you have access to the Internet and the use of a Visa, MasterCard, or American Express Card (to pay the fees), you can also register on line. Log in at http://www.collegeboard.org.

Either way, you'll need to register well in advance of your chosen test date. Regular registration deadlines are about four weeks prior to the exam. You can register late for an extra fee (currently $15), but this only gives you a few more days. So don't put off registration.

Once you've registered, you can use the phone to do things like register for subsequent tests, request a change in your test center, or add colleges to your score report list. The number for ETS customer service is 1-609-771-7600. Again, expect a fee for each service you request.

THE INSIDER'S REPORT: KNOW YOUR OPTIONS

Choosing the Best Location

Most high schools administer the SAT exams, but not every school serves as a test center on every test date. Study the listing of test centers in the SAT bulletin carefully. Your first choice of center, if it's available on the day you want to test, is probably your home high school; your second choice may be another nearby school.

However, there are times when a different location may serve you better. Ask your guidance counselor, or, better still, classmates who've taken the SAT at your school, about the quality of the facilities on test days. (Remember, you'll probably be taking the exam on Saturday, a day when you're usually *not* in the building.) Are the testing rooms noisy? Are they adequately heated or cooled? Are the rooms too crowded, or poorly lit? If you hear a lot of complaints about a particular test center, it may be worthwhile to select a different one, even if it's slightly further from home.

You may also want to consider a test center other than your home high school if you like the idea of taking the exam *away* from your classmates. Some students find it distracting to run into hordes of gossiping, nervous friends the morning of the test. If this might apply to you, taking the test in the near anonymity of a neutral site may be better.

If you do pick a center away from home, make sure you know exactly how to get there and how long it will take. You don't want to arrive late or experience a long, anxiety-producing drive in search of the right street address on the morning of your exam. If necessary, make a preliminary visit the week before, just to be sure you can get there with a minimum of fuss.

Taking the Test for Free

Taking the SAT isn't cheap. Currently, the minimum fee to register for the SAT I exam is $23.00. And if you sign up for the Question-and-Answer Service (which we recommend, as explained later in this chapter), request a few additional college score reports beyond the four you get free, and throw in one or two other services, the cost can easily climb to $70 or more.

If your family finances make SAT fees a problem, visit your high school counselor and ask for information about getting the fees waived. She should have a booklet explaining the process; if not, she can call the state's College Board Regional Office for information. You'll need to get a fee-waiver card from your counselor, which must be enclosed with your registration form when you send it in. So be sure to check in with your counselor at least a week before the registration deadline, so there'll be plenty of time to get the necessary paperwork completed.

Untimed Testing

If you have a learning disability or any physical or psychological condition that would make it impossible or unfair for you to have to complete the SAT exam under the same time limits as other students, you may be able to take the test with special extended timing.

To explore this option, start by visiting your school guidance counselor. She should have a copy of the booklet *SAT Services for Students with Disabilities*. If not, you can request one from:

> SAT Services for Students with Disabilities
> P.O. Box 6226
> Princeton, New Jersey 08541-6226

You'll be given a special Student Eligibility Form requiring evidence of your disability, which you'll need to enclose with your regular registration form. Plan early so you'll have enough time to get all the necessary paperwork done.

Other Accommodations

Some students need other accommodations when they take the test. For example, a student in a wheelchair or a student whose sight or hearing is impaired may need special seating arrangements, the use of a large-print test booklet, or a sign-language interpreter for the proctor's spoken instructions.

If you fall into a category like these, speak to your high school counselor. You'll need a letter from her describing the accommodation needed, explaining the reason for it, confirming that a similar accommodation is provided for you when you take classroom tests, and verifying that no extra testing time is needed. You'll enclose this letter with your regular test registration form.

Sunday Testing

If you can't take the SAT on Saturday because of your religion, you can apply for a Sunday administration. Choose a Saturday test date that is one day before the Sunday when you're available for the exam, and fill out your registration form as if you were registering for that Saturday's test. However, you should fill in code 01-000 as your first choice in the test center portion of the form. Then have your rabbi or minister write a letter explaining your religious restriction on letterhead, and enclose this with your mail-in registration form. You'll be notified as to the closest test center where Sunday testing is available.

Score Reporting

When you register for the SAT, you'll be allowed to pick four colleges or universities to receive reports of your scores. Even if you're not yet completely sure which schools you'll be applying to, take advantage of this opportunity to name four of your most likely choices. Additional reports will cost you money (currently $6.50 per school).

You can add to the list of colleges that will receive your scores in several ways.

- Space for up to four additional reports is provided on the test registration form. The $6.50 fee will be charged for each college listed here, of course.
- You can fill out and mail an Additional Report Request Form that you'll receive with your test admission packet. (Your school guidance counselor should have copies, too.)
- You can request additional reports on line at the College Board Web site (http://www.collegeboard.org).
- You can request additional reports by phone using a credit card. Dial 1-800-SAT SCORE.

See Chapter 12 for more information about your score reports.

Selecting Other Services

At the time you register for the SAT, you'll have the opportunity to select other ETS or College Board services. Here's a rundown of your options, with our explanation and recommendation concerning each one.

Student Search Service. If you opt for this service, your name and personal profile, based on the information you provide in the Student Descriptive Questionnaire that is part of your registration form, will be given to interested colleges. As a result, they may add you to their mailing lists to receive brochures and ads about their schools. Our recommendation: sign up. There's no fee, and you may find it fun and interesting to hear from colleges.

Question-and-Answer Service or Student Answer Service. Depending on the date of your exam, one or the other of these services will be available. They allow you to get detailed information about how you did on the SAT, which can be very useful if you retake the exam. (See Chapter 12 for more details.) Our recommendation: sign up. There is a fee (currently either \$5 or \$10), but it's well worth it.

SAT II Score Choice. This service allows you to put scores on SAT II Subject Tests on hold, not to be released to colleges until you decide to release them. It puts you in control over which Subject Test scores your colleges will see—a worthwhile option. Note: This service applies only to SAT II Subject Tests, not to the SAT I. Our recommendation: sign up. There's no fee.

WHEN TEST TIME COMES

The big weekend is here. You're about to face one of the important challenges of your young life, comparable to pitching in the county championship ball game or taking the leading role in the school musical. If you've used this book (and other resources) effectively, you can be confident that you're well prepared for the SAT exam. Here are some last-minute reminders and suggestions that will help you handle the stress of "game time" gracefully.

The Night Before

- Don't cram. Last-minute study isn't likely to make much difference in your skills or knowledge, but it can elevate your levels of anxiety and fatigue needlessly.
- Put out everything you'll want to bring with you to the test center. This includes: your official admission ticket; a photo ID (or other ID with a physical description of you); two #2 pencils with erasers; a calculator; and a small snack, like a granola bar or a piece of fruit.
- If the weather is cool, lay out a sweater or two—dressing in layers will let you adjust to conditions in the test room. If you're traveling to an unfamiliar test site, put out the map or directions you'll be following.
- Set your clock, and if possible have a backup system in place to wake you if the clock fails. (The best such system is called Mom or Dad.) You need to arrive at the test center by 8:15, so plan accordingly.

- Get to sleep early. Remember that the SAT—3½ to 4 hours long—is a physical as well as a mental challenge.

The Morning of the Test

- Wake up early and have your usual breakfast. If you normally skip breakfast, consider having something light this day—cereal or fruit. You'll be needing more energy than usual.
- Leave plenty of time for travel, so you can arrive early and relaxed, not late and frazzled.
- Don't listen to the predictions and advice of the students around you.

If you've prepared with the help of this book, you know exactly what to expect—probably better than your fellow test takers. Last-minute speculation can only fuel needless worry.

During the Test

Here's a relaxation routine to use during the test breaks: Close your eyes. Sit back. Begin taking deep, slow, cleansing breaths, filling your lungs completely. Then deliberately tense and release the muscles in each part of your body, one region at a time, from feet and legs to torso, arms, and head. When done, take a final deep breath and open your eyes, ready to return to work. See Appendix C "The Insider's Stress-Buster's Guide," for more tips on handling stress before and during your exam.

- Make sure your accommodations are appropriate and comfortable. You should have a comfortable chair, an adequate writing surface, plenty of light, and a space that is reasonably quiet, well-heated or cooled, and pollution free. If you're left-handed, you should have a left-handed desk. You should be able to easily see and hear the proctor as he reads the test instructions. If any of these conditions is lacking, raise your hand and ask for help.
- Use your basic test-taking skills: Preview each section before you begin working on it; save the hardest questions for last; keep track of the time; guess when in doubt; and mark your answer sheet neatly and accurately.
- If you find that you've mismarked your answer sheet, raise your hand and get the proctor's attention. Explain the problem and ask for a few minutes after the test with your answer sheet only to make corrections. This request will probably be granted.
- You'll have at least two short breaks during the test. Use these to eat your snack and to relax. A 3-minute relaxation routine (see sidebar) will help you feel refreshed before you tackle the next test section.

After the Test

- If you encountered any problems with the test or the testing procedures—a mistake by the proctor, incorrect timing, a disruptive environment, or a misprinted test booklet—make detailed notes about it immediately after the test. A letter of complaint should be faxed to ETS at 1-609-520-1092 no later than Wednesday of the following week.

- If you're convinced that you bombed on the exam, consider canceling your scores. See Chapter 12 for details on how this works and how to decide whether this option is right for you.
- If you think you encountered an erroneous or flawed test question, consider mounting an official challenge to the item. Chapter 12 tells how.
- Now go celebrate. You've earned it.

JUST THE FACTS

- Pick a testing date based on your college application deadlines, but leave yourself a chance to retake the test if needed.
- Find a test center that's comfortable and close to home.
- Be sure to request any test-taking accommodations you need and deserve.
- Some—not all—of the products and services offered by ETS and the College Board are worthwhile investments.
- Manage your energy the weekend of the exam to minimize anxiety and maximize performance.

Chapter 12

Understanding Your Scores

Get the Scoop On . . .

- What your score report really means
- How colleges interpret your SAT scores
- How and when to consider canceling your scores
- What to do if you think your score is wrong or the test was flawed
- How to decide whether to retake the SAT

You've taken the SAT . . . congratulations! Getting this far hasn't been easy. We hope you found that your study-and-practice program prepared you well for the challenge of the exam, and that you're feeling reasonably confident about how you did.

While you await your scores, don't agonize over the test, and don't assume that the way you feel is any indication of your real performance. Students who think they did poorly often get surprisingly high scores. (This happens more often than the reverse.) Here's why: when you took the exam, you spent more time puzzling over the hardest questions—the ones you may have gotten wrong—than over the easy ones, which you whizzed through. So when you think about the test later, your main memory is of struggling to figure out the toughest problems. That selective recall isn't necessarily an accurate gauge of how you did overall.

Even after you receive your scores, however, your "SAT work" may not be done. It's time now to analyze your scores and what they mean, which may be a little more complicated than you realize. And you may have some important decisions to make—especially about whether to try taking the exam again. In this chapter, we'll explain what you need to know to win this phase of the great SAT game.

YOUR SAT SCORE REPORT

Getting Your Scores

Despite ETS's use of computers to score their exams, it has always taken quite a while for students to receive their score reports in the mail.

Three weeks is what ETS predicts, but students say that four to five weeks is more common, and even longer delays aren't unusual. The wait can be nerve-racking.

ETS now offers a score-by-phone service to alleviate the waiting game. It allows you to get your SAT scores about two weeks after the date of your test. There's an extra charge (currently $8) for this service. To take advantage of the score-by-phone option, call 1-800-SAT-SCORE after 8:00 a.m. eastern time at least thirteen days after your test date.

Understanding Your Score Report

FYI

If you're worried that your SAT score may not arrive in time, you can request rush score reports to colleges starting three weeks after your test. ETS says the rush reports will go out within two working days. Use the ETS phone number 1-800-SAT SCORE to request this service. It's pricey—currently $20 plus $6.50 for each college requested.

The printed score report you'll eventually get in the mail offers more information than you can get by phone. However, even savvy test-takers don't always find it clear. Here's a point-by-point description and explanation of what your score report will tell you.

- **Your Verbal and Mathematical Scores.** These are your three-digit scaled scores, computed as we explained in Chapter 3. Each score ranges between 200 (low) and 800 (high). Average or mean scores vary from year to year and even from test to test, but both verbal and math scores now have averages close to 500 (having been "recalibrated" in 1995 for just that purpose—like resetting a watch).

- **Your Score Ranges.** These are windows approximately 60-points deep—30 points on either side of your scaled score—that ETS provides because of the imprecision of SAT scores. Here's what we mean. If you scored, say, 590 on the math part of the SAT, does that imply that your "true" math ability equals *exactly* 590 (whatever that would mean)? Obviously not; 590 is just ETS's best guesstimate as to how good you are at math, based on one morning's performance on one batch of questions. To reflect this imprecision, your score report will include a math score range of about 560-620, indicating (statistically) that it is ETS's opinion that your "true" math ability *probably* falls somewhere in that range.

- **Your Percentile Scores.** You'll also receive two sets of percentile scores, both math and verbal. One set compares your performance to that of a large, current group of high school seniors from throughout the country who've said they plan to go on to college; the other set compares you to students only from your own state. The percentile score indicates what percentage of these students scored *lower* than you on the test. So if you have a verbal percentile score of 70 (for instance), it means that 70 percent of students did less well than you. Obviously, the higher your percentile scores, the better.

FYI

Students are often surprised to learn what the SAT is supposed to show. The "psychometricians" (test experts) at ETS are frankly modest in their claims. They tell colleges that SAT scores—in combination with high school grades—are supposed to help predict the performance of students in first-year college classes. That's all. So don't take your SAT scores too seriously. The test-makers themselves don't!

- **Your Scores by Question Type.** If you are at all dissatisfied with your overall scores, this section of the score report may be vitally important to you. It shows how you did on each question type. The two test areas are handled a little differently. The verbal area is broken down by question format—critical reasoning, analogies, and sentence completions. However, the math area is broken down not by question format (quantitative comparisons, etc.) but into two general subject areas—arithmetic and algebraic reasoning, and geometric reasoning.

  For each question type, you'll be told how many questions you got right, how many you got wrong, how many you omitted, your raw score (which factors in the "guessing penalty"—see Chapter 3), and your percentile score for that question type. This table can be a useful guide if you decide to retake the test—it'll help you locate the test areas where you need the most extra work and where you have the best chances of improving your scores next time.

- **Your Scores on Other SAT Tests.** Your score report will also list your scores on past SAT I and SAT II tests—up to six of each. It's handy to have all these numbers in one place.

- **College Profile Data.** You'll also receive a printout with some information about the colleges to which you arranged to have your test scores sent. It includes some blindingly obvious facts that you surely already know (Is the school a college or a university? Is it in the city or the country?), as well as some useful facts that you have probably already uncovered elsewhere (for example, the range of SAT scores earned by most of the school's entering freshmen).

  This printout is a testimony to the fact that the SAT program is sponsored by the College Board, an organization of colleges and universities who naturally would like to help their members with marketing to prospective students. ("Marketing" means getting you to apply for admission. Like any business, colleges like getting more customers—in their case, students.) ETS's Student Search Service, which puts your name on the direct-mail list of colleges, is part of the same effort. If you checked the box to participate in that service when you registered for the exam, you'll probably be receiving a lot of mail from colleges over the next several months. It won't hurt, and you may even learn a useful thing or two.

Taking a Closer Look at Your Test

Thanks to Truth-in-Testing laws, ETS now offers—for a fee—two services that let you examine the SAT test you took more closely. These services are invaluable for the student who wants to consider retaking the exam.

The more extensive of the two programs is the Question-and-Answer Service. It's available only for selected test administrations, depending on the date when you take the exam. If you apply for this service, you'll receive a copy of the actual test questions from the SAT you took, an answer key, scoring instructions, and a printout of your own answers. Equating sections (see Chapter 3) aren't included. You can request this service at the time you register or up to five months after taking the exam. It's a good investment for reasons we'll explain later in this chapter.

There are some test administrations from which ETS is not legally required to release the questions publicly. Therefore, ETS keeps them secret so they can be used again on future tests, thereby saving the work and expense of writing a fresh exam (hey, everybody wants to economize these days). For these tests, the Question-and-Answer Service isn't available.

Instead, ETS offers the Student Answer Service. They won't give you a copy of the test questions, but you will get a printout of your item-by-item performance and an indication as to the general subject area of each question (analogy, geometry). It's much less valuable than the Question-and-Answer Service, but if it's all you can get, request it.

HOW COLLEGES INTERPRET SAT SCORES

ETS advises colleges not to use cutoff scores—rigid SAT requirements below which applications are automatically rejected. Most colleges deny using them, but admissions officers report that a significant percentage of schools do use cutoff scores, either explicitly or implicitly.

The colleges to which you ask ETS to send your scores will receive reports containing all the information from your own score report. The college reports also include your personal profile (high school grade point average, possible college major, etc.) based on a questionnaire you filled out for ETS at the time you registered.

What do colleges look for in reading your score report? Naturally, it varies from school to school. However, here are some general observations that apply to most colleges.

- Colleges look to SAT scores to amplify their picture of you. In combination with your high school grades, SAT scores are supposed to help admissions officers measure your academic abilities and achievements. Did you pursue a challenging high school program and earn grades that were good but not great? Or were your classroom grades hampered by difficult personal circumstances—loss of a parent, for instance, or the need to work throughout high school? In cases like these, good SAT scores could help confirm that you are brighter than your grades alone suggest.

- Colleges want to see a reasonable balance between math and verbal scores. A total score of 1200 on the SAT is a good one—but it's better to earn 600 on each test area rather than (say) 780 on math and just 420 on verbal. The balanced student is likely to be considered more promising than the unbalanced one, who, in this example, might be a math whiz who's weak in communication skills.
- Colleges generally focus on your *best* SAT scores. If you take the exam twice or more, most colleges will evaluate you on the basis of your highest score. A sizable minority—up to 40 percent—will even combine your highest verbal and math scores if those occurred on different days. Just a few insist on considering only your most recent scores—even if those were lower than some earlier scores. The admissions office will generally tell you their policy.
- Colleges evaluate you against this year's pool of applicants. Your college application—not only your test scores but all your credentials—will never be considered in a vacuum. You are always being measured against the hundreds or thousands of other students who've applied to a particular college. As the size and quality of this applicant pool rises and falls from one year to the next, a particular set of credentials may look better or worse by comparison.

  Luck and fashion play a huge role in this process. For reasons that are often hard to fathom, some colleges get popular at particular times; everybody and her brother decides to apply to University X, and the happy admissions officers there get a chance, for a time, to skim off the very best students. (As I write, for example, a popular TV series set on a New York campus has driven applications to New York colleges through the roof.) An applicant who might have waltzed through the door two years earlier may not make the cut now. And the opposite happens when a college falls out of vogue. Bear this in mind if you're tempted to apply to this year's fashionable school: although the education probably hasn't improved, getting in has gotten a lot harder.

THE INSIDER'S REPORT: KNOW YOUR OPTIONS

Now you know how colleges look at your SAT scores. What can you do about it all? Are there ways of managing the post-test part of the SAT process to make it work better for you?

Absolutely yes. Let's look at some of the options you have *after* your exam to minimize the damage from a bad day in the testing arena and to maximize your chances of getting your best possible scores.

Canceling Your Scores

FYI

Many schools now fill half or more of their entering class from the ranks of those who apply early and promise to attend if accepted. If you're in love with a certain school, consider applying early: you'll compete in a somewhat smaller candidate pool and have a better chance of getting in with the exact same credentials.

Occasionally, a student knows on the day of the test that he has truly bombed. Most often, the problem is physical: people do get ill, sometimes unexpectedly, and the stress of a three-hour-plus exam can worsen the early symptoms of a flu bug or stomach virus. Once in a great while, a student simply freezes up and is psychologically or emotionally unable to finish the test. And sometimes an ill-prepared student realizes, in despair, that he really should have studied and practiced before sitting down on test day. (If you've read the previous chapters in the book you're holding, you're not a candidate for this problem.)

If any of these calamities befalls you, there is an option—score cancellation. ETS will wipe clear your score slate for a particular day at your request; your test won't be graded, and neither you nor any school will know how well (or poorly) you did. However, these caveats:

- You must request score cancellation almost immediately. You can ask the test proctor for a cancellation form and fill it out on the spot, or you can cancel by notifying ETS via mail or fax by the Wednesday following your exam. (Fax your request to ETS at 1-609-771-7681.)
- The request is irrevocable. Once you cancel your scores, they can never be reinstated. And you can't cancel just your verbal or just your math score: the whole day's testing must be wiped out.
- No score will be reported to anyone, but your college score reports after subsequent test days will note that you did take the exam previously and chose to cancel your scores. Most colleges don't care about this, but—who knows?—it could raise a question in the mind of an admissions officer if your application is borderline.
- You won't receive any refund of your testing fee.

FYI

If you merely feel you may have done poorly on the exam, you should probably go ahead and allow the test to be graded. Then take advantage of the Question-and-Answer Service to examine what you did right and what you did wrong. This will help you a lot in preparing to do better next time—and it's an option that's not available if you cancel your scores.

Obviously, canceling your scores is a fairly serious step. Probably most significantly, it will put you in a position where you must retake the exam a few months later, by which time college application deadlines may be looming. The sense of pressure you feel on this subsequent test date may be even greater than before. Therefore, you should cancel your scores only if you really must—illness being the most likely culprit.

If Your Scores Are Delayed

On rare occasions, a student's SAT scores are delayed. A simple glitch in mail delivery may be to blame. We suggest that, if you haven't received your scores by six weeks after the test date, you take advantage of the score-by-phone service (described above) to make sure your scores have been recorded. If they have, call the admissions offices of the colleges to which you are applying, and ask whether they've received your score report. If they have, the problem on your end is with the mail. Send a fax to ETS at 1-609-771-7681 to request a duplicate of your score report.

If neither you nor your colleges have received a report by six weeks after the test date, ask your high school guidance counselor whether other students are experiencing delays. Once in a while, computer or other problems at ETS cause general delays for all students who took a particular test. It's rare but frustrating, and there's not much you can do except sit tight.

Finally, if it appears that the score delay involves you alone (or only a handful of other students), it's possible that ETS may be investigating an apparent testing irregularity or a test security problem.

A *testing irregularity* means a problem with the way the test was administered. It could be due to a proctor's error (test-takers were given too much or too little time to work), an ETS error (faulty test booklets were printed), or circumstances beyond anyone's control (a test center is disrupted by fire or flood).

A *test security problem* means, quite specifically, a suspicion that students had access to the test beforehand; used books, computers, or other forbidden aids during the exam; took the test under false names; passed answers to one another, or otherwise cheated.

If you fall under suspicion of cheating, you'll be in for an unpleasant experience, whether or not you are guilty. Although ETS makes an effort at "due process," the adjudication of such cases is basically an internal process controlled by the test-makers.

This doesn't mean, however, that you are helpless, much less that you should meekly accept a guilty verdict if you are really innocent. Here is some advice as to what to do if you find yourself accused of misconduct on the SAT.

- Insist on understanding the accusation and the process. When an investigation is started, you should receive a copy of the ETS booklet *Why and How Educational Testing Service Questions Test Scores.* Read it thoroughly. Then make sure that the test-makers inform you as to exactly what misconduct is supposed to have occurred, so that you can marshal evidence in your defense.
- Enlist the help and advice of your parents and a college counselor, teacher, or other trusted advisor. This is an important problem that can seriously affect your college prospects, and the bureaucracy at ETS can be intimidating. Don't try to handle it alone.

- Communicate with ETS clearly and in writing. Use registered mail and keep copies of all your communications with the test-makers. Make sure that you admit nothing that is not completely true.

- As soon as you can, make detailed notes of everything you remember about your test-preparation and test-taking experience. In particular, if you remember anything odd that happened on the day of the exam, jot it down. (A mistake by a proctor, for example, may innocently explain some discrepancy ETS thinks is sinister.) Be sure to be as complete and accurate as possible. The sooner you make these notes, the clearer and more convincing your memory of events is likely to be.

- Provide the test-makers with any facts that could help exonerate you. If you know why you're suspected of wrongdoing, you may be able to resolve the dispute by responding with information. For example, if you're suspected of cheating because you left the test room several times during the exam, you may want to ask your doctor to provide a letter confirming that you were suffering from a stomach complaint on the day of the test (if that was the case).

  Sometimes, ETS will investigate a test-taker solely because of a dramatic score increase—200 points or more over a previous test. If you're in this category, be prepared to explain (and document, if possible) how you prepared for your second test. Describe your use of coaching, tutoring, books, software, and any other test-prep tools, and estimate the number of hours you devoted to study before the exam. A convincing account of your significant test-prep effort can go a long way toward showing that your score increase was produced not by trickery but by good, old-fashioned hard work.

- Consider enlisting legal help. In America, of course, final recourse in disputes between groups and individuals is to the law. Most problems with ETS don't require the help of a lawyer, but you may want to consider this option if you've been unjustly accused, if the test-makers refuse to resolve the dispute quickly and fairly, and if the cost is not a major problem for you and your family.

- If the dispute is not resolved within a reasonable time (say, four to six weeks), insist on your right to retake the exam as soon as possible, at no charge to you. ETS is supposed to provide this service to give an innocent test-taker the chance to demonstrate his abilities again without penalty and free from any cloud of suspicion.

If You Think Your Scores Are Wrong

On rare occasions, a student who requests the Question-and-Answer Service or the Student Answer Service (as we recommend you do) becomes convinced, upon review of her test, that one or more of her test scores is inaccurate. Here's what to do if this happens to you.

FYI

Test-question challenges have been much more effective in regard to math questions than to verbal ones—not because the verbal questions are better, but because it's far easier to demonstrate actual errors on math questions.

- **Requesting hand scoring.** Sometimes, a student finds a discrepancy between the answer choices she is supposed to have made and the choices she remembers making. It's rare, but it happens. The machine that reads your answer grid could malfunction, for example, reading a choice (C) as a choice (D) or as no choice at all. If you strongly believe that the printout of your answer choices doesn't reflect your actual work on the day of the test, this may have happened to you.

  Your best option in this case is to request hand scoring of your answer sheet. You can do this up to five months after taking the exam, using the order form you received with your score report. (As you probably guessed, there's a fee for this service—currently $25.) You'll get a new score report within three to five weeks. If it's found that your test *was* misgraded, ETS will send a notification letter to all of your colleges—and they'll refund your hand-scoring fee.

- **Challenging a test question or procedure.** A more complicated problem arises if you become convinced that you were harmed either by some unfair procedure on the day of the test or by an inaccurate and flawed test question. There's a system for appealing such problems, but be prepared for a fairly lengthy process.

If you feel burned by a test procedure or question, write down all the details you can remember as soon as possible. Then send a registered letter to the test-makers at this address:

Assessment Division
Educational Testing Service
P.O. Box 6656
Princeton, New Jersey 08541-6656

FYI

ETS confirms that most students who take the SAT a second time enjoy at least a modest score increase, due to sheer familiarity with the exam.

Include your name, address, birth date, sex, social security number, and test registration number; mention the name of the test you took and the date you took it; and provide the name, number, and address of the test center you used. In your letter, explain what happened and why you think it was unfair.

ETS will investigate and respond. In most cases, they will defend their procedure or test question (and often they are right to do so). If you aren't satisfied, there are several further levels of appeal you can request, culminating in a formal review by an independent panel. It's up to you to decide how significant your complaint is, how strongly you feel about it, and how much time and effort you want to invest in the process.

ETS is obviously not perfect. Over the years since Truth-in-Testing laws made challenges to test questions a genuine option, they have been forced to admit errors in over a dozen test questions, increasing the scores of hundreds of thousands of students.

So don't hesitate to challenge the test-makers if you're convinced it's appropriate. The only way powerful institutions like ETS can be kept responsive to human concerns is if individuals hold them accountable for their actions, right and wrong.

FairTest, the nonprofit organization dedicated to fair and open testing, may be able to help you with information and referrals if you have a complaint or dispute about the SAT. Contact them at:

FairTest
342 Broadway
Cambridge, Massachusetts 02139-1802
Phone: 617-864-4810
Fax: 617-497-2224
E-mail: fairtest@aol.com

The Decision to Retest

FYI

Colleges differ in their policies about which SAT scores they look at when a student has been tested more than once. Before you decide whether or not to retake the SAT, call your top three college choices and check their policies. Make sure you'll get the full benefit of any score increase you may obtain.

Should you retake the SAT if you're not satisfied with your scores? In many cases, the answer is yes. Here are some of the factors to consider in making this decision.

- How do the scores you've already received match the credentials wanted by the college(s) of your choice? We spoke about your need to establish target SAT scores based on the admission requirements of the schools you want to attend, as well as the other credentials you bring to the table—such as your high school grades. If the test scores you've already earned fall outside the range in which most freshmen at your ideal school score—or if they are at the lower end of that range—you should strongly consider retaking the test.
- How often have you already been tested? If you've taken the SAT twice or more previously—and especially if you prepared beforehand—you may have already tapped most of your potential for improvement. However, if you've been tested just once before—and especially if your preparation in the past was superficial—there's every reason to believe your score can go up, perhaps a lot.
- Can you identify test areas with potential for improvement? You're an especially strong candidate to retake the exam if your score report reveals specific areas of weakness. For example, if you performed well on all the verbal areas except analogies, where you got most of the items wrong, a targeted practice program focusing

on analogies can boost your overall score significantly. Similarly, if a particular math area gave you trouble the first time around, work with a review book, teacher, or tutor to master that topic, and the chances are good that your math score will rise when you retake the test.

- Do you have time to invest in preparing for another test? Look realistically at your plans for school and other activities. Before you schedule another exam, make sure you can block out hours during the prior weeks for study and practice. If you take the second test cold, without any real preparation or warm-up, you may wind up spinning your wheels, earning scores no higher than your first scores.

A final tip about retaking the exam: don't forget to review *every* test area, at least briefly, before your second or later SAT. Although you may need to focus the bulk of your study on algebra (for example), it's important to keep your verbal skills and your knowledge of other math areas sharp, too. You don't want to gain points on one end while losing them on the other.

JUST THE FACTS

- Study your score report carefully, and make sure you understand what each number means.
- Evaluate your performance as colleges will—against the credentials of their pool of applicants.
- If you think you completely bombed on the exam, consider canceling your scores.
- If you think your SAT was unfair for any reason, you have ways to complain and be heard.
- Consider retaking the exam if your scores fall below the targets you need to achieve.
- If you do retake the test, focus your preparation on areas where you need the most improvement.

Chapter 13

The Insider's Tip Sheet

Get the Scoop On . . .

- The most important test-taking strategies to review just before taking the SAT

It's the night before you'll be taking the SAT—or maybe the very morning of the exam. You've been studying, practicing, and preparing for days, weeks, even months, and you're about as ready to take the test as you'll ever be.

Trouble is, the strategies, techniques, and methods you've learned from this book feel as if they're lodged in dozens of separate compartments scattered throughout your overloaded brain. A few weeks may have passed since you last tried your hand at a particular question type; you've probably become a little fuzzy about exactly how to tackle it. But you don't have time now—hours before the test—to review hundreds of pages covering strategies for six separate question types. If you try, you may just intensify that gnawing sense of anxiety in the pit of your stomach—and maybe even develop a full-blown case of panic.

That's where this chapter comes in. It's a concise recap of the most important tips, strategies, warnings, and techniques from the entire book, organized for easy study during the final day before your exam. You may want to tear these pages out of the book and carry them with you in the car, bus, or train that takes you to the test center for a true last-minute review. It's even better to read them the night before—that way, if any one or two ideas don't ring a bell, you can look them up in the relevant chapters and refresh your memory.

OVERALL STRATEGIES FOR THE SAT

- Spend a few seconds previewing each test section before you begin work on it. Check how many pages and questions there are so you can budget your time accordingly.
- Work at a steady pace. You don't need to rush madly through the test sections, but you shouldn't dawdle, either. Remember, every question is worth the same amount, so rather than getting bogged

down in an especially challenging question, move on to the next one—it may be more to your liking.

- Mark up the margins of the test booklet freely—to perform computations, outline reading passages, cross out answers as you eliminate them, and so on.
- Don't be afraid to guess. Use what you know to eliminate any answer that is clearly wrong, then pick the best answer from among those that remain. Chances are you'll gain points by following this method.
- Scale the difficulty ladder. Questions in a group will gradually become more difficult; expect to spend more time on the last few questions in a batch, and be prepared to guess, if necessary, on the toughest items.
- Your test will include one section made up of unscored questions for equating purposes. This section will not be labeled as an equating section, so all sections should be taken seriously. But if a test section is made up of "weird" questions of a type you've never seen before, don't fret about it—it is almost certainly an experimental section and will not affect your score.
- Fill in the answer sheet carefully. Make sure you don't skip any spaces unintentionally, and don't mark two answers for the same question. Erase all stray pencil marks.

VERBAL STRATEGIES

On All Verbal Questions

- Read every answer choice. In the verbal sections, there are degrees of right and wrong; the first answer may be partially correct, while the second answer is a little better, and the third answer is better still. Don't jump to select the first answer that appears tempting.

Analogies

- Build a bridge to define the relationship between the two words in the stem pair, and narrow the definition as needed to eliminate potential answer choices.
- Use the analogy relationship to help you guess the meanings of words you're not sure about.
- Don't be afraid to draw analogies between concrete, physical relationships and abstract ideas.

Sentence Completions

- Focus on how the ideas in the two parts of the sentence are related to one another—this usually offers a crucial clue to the meaning of the missing word(s).

- Try to anticipate a possible answer before you look at the answer choices.

- Avoid answers that are inconsistent with the rest of the sentence or that introduce new ideas.

- When necessary, eliminate answers where one word or the other doesn't work and guess from among the answer choices that remain.

Critical Reading

- Use the three-stage method (previewing, reading, reviewing) to get the most out of each reading passage.

- Focus on the big ideas in each passage, not the small details.

- Look for the connections among the ideas in each passage.

- Use your pencil as you read to mark the main ideas and the connections among them. These notes will make it easier and faster to find the answers to the questions that follow.

- Review the passage as often as necessary to locate the answer for a specific question.

- Don't pick an answer just because it sounds familiar, seems to be true, or reflects information that actually appears in the passage—the answer must also accurately respond to the question being asked.

MATH STRATEGIES

On All Math Items

- As soon as you've found the right answer, mark it and move on—there are no "degrees of rightness" to be considered.

- Use your pencil to mark up diagrams with additional information as you find it, or to sketch simple drawings when no diagram is provided. This can often help you "see" the answers to questions, with little or no figuring needed.

Multiple-Choice Math

- The questions are designed to focus primarily on the underlying relationships among the numbers presented, not your ability to perform calculations—therefore, if you find yourself spending too much time doing figuring, you've probably overlooked a simple shortcut.
- Feel free to round off and guesstimate, using approximate values.
- Don't over-use your calculator. Most questions can and should be answered using a few simple computations.
- When in doubt about how to get started on a problem, try something—anything! This will often lead you toward a solution.

Quantitative Comparisons

- Remember, you usually *don't* have to calculate exact values for the two columns—you only need to be able to tell which column is greater, for which approximate values will often suffice.
- Work on one or both columns to make them look as much alike as possible.
- Eliminate whatever the two columns have in common.
- When stymied, try plugging in possible values for x or any other unknown—but remember to try zero, a fraction, and a negative number unless specifically ruled out.
- When there *is* no unknown quantity, don't pick choice (D) ("It cannot be determined").

Math Grid-Ins

- Fill in the grid carefully. Remember to blacken the ovals for the numbers or symbols of your answer, and check to make sure you've marked the right spaces.
- Grid in the most precise answer value possible. If your solution is $\frac{1}{3}$, grid it that way or as .333. Any less precise answer, such as .33, will be scored as incorrect.
- Don't try to grid an answer that doesn't fit, such as a mixed number; instead, restate $2\frac{1}{2}$ as 2.5.
- Negative answers are impossible for math grid-ins. If you come up with a negative solution, start over!

Part V

Appendices

Appendix A

The Insider's SAT Word List

VOCABULARY: DOES IT MATTER?

In a word: Yes.

Vocabulary *as such* is not tested on the SAT. Until a few years ago, the exam included antonym questions, which required you to pick a word whose meaning was the opposite of some other word. Those questions have been eliminated. So the most direct and obvious form of a vocabulary question on the SAT is no more.

That leaves *indirect* and *hidden* vocabulary questions—of which there are plenty.

1. **Reading comprehension passages now include vocabulary-in-context questions.** These focus on particular words in the passage and ask you to determine their meaning *in the passage*. Sometimes the words chosen are obviously "hard" words (*latent, replete,* and *eminent,* to name three real examples). More often, they are seemingly "easy" words that are tricky because they have so *many* possible meanings (*camp, idea,* and *hard*, for example). In both cases, the broader, more varied, and more accurate your vocabulary knowledge, the better your chances are of answering these questions quickly and correctly.
2. **Analogy questions obviously depend to a large extent on vocabulary.** It's difficult—though not impossible, as we discuss in Chapter Five—to decipher the analogy relationships unless you understand the words that are involved. One typical group of thirteen analogy items includes the words *proficiency, embellish, carping, reclusive, tactile, criterion, intransigent,* and *strenuous,* among others. (How many of these can you define?) You don't have to throw up your hands in despair if an analogy item contains a word or two you don't know; there's more than one way to skin that cat. But the process will be a lot easier and faster if you know most of the words used, or at least have a nodding acquaintance with them.
3. **The better your vocabulary knowledge, the easier you'll find it to understand both the critical reading passages and the sentence completion items** (which are, in effect, mini-reading passages, each one sentence long). Even an occasional math item is made a little more complicated by the use of a challenging vocabulary word.

Therefore, vocabulary knowledge makes a clear and significant difference in your performance on the SAT. Fortunately, the kinds of words that regularly appear on the SAT, as with so much else on the exam, fall into definite patterns.

The SAT is basically a test of "book learning." It's written and edited by bookish people for the benefit of the other bookish people who run colleges and universities. It's designed to test your ability to handle the kinds of academic tasks college students usually have to master: reading textbooks, finding information in reference books, deciphering scholarly journals, studying research abstracts, writing impressive-sounding term papers, etc.

The hard words on the SAT are hard words of a particular sort: scholastic words that deal, broadly speaking, with the manipulation and communication of *ideas*—words like *ambiguous, amplify, arbitrary,* and *arcane.* The better you master this sort of vocabulary, the better you'll do on the exam.

Fortunately, you don't need to find these words on your own. We've done the spadework for you. By examining actual SAT exams from the last several years, we've been able to list the words most commonly used in reading passages, analogies, and sentence completions, including both the question stems and the answer choices. This list became the basis of the Insider's SAT Word List. It includes about 500 primary words that are most likely to appear in one form or another on your SAT exam. It also includes hundreds of related words—words that are either variants of the primary words (*ambiguity* as a variant of *ambiguous*, for example) or that share a common word root (like *ample, amplify,* and *amplitude*).

If you make yourself acquainted with all the words in the Insider's SAT Word List, you will absolutely learn a number of new words that will appear on your SAT. You'll earn extra points as a result.

THE SIX BEST INSIDER'S VOCABULARY-BUILDING TIPS FOR THE SAT

Study Vocabulary Daily

There are some topics you can easily cram. Vocabulary isn't one of them. In general, words don't stay in mind until the fourth or fifth time you learn them. Try to begin your vocabulary study several weeks before the exam. Take 15 or 20 minutes a day to learn new words. Periodically review all the words you've previously studied; quiz yourself, or have a friend quiz you. This simple regimen can enable you to learn several hundred new words before you take the SAT.

Learn a Few Words at a Time

Don't try to gobble dozens of words in one sitting. They're likely to blur into an indistinguishable mass. Instead, pick a reasonable quantity—say, 10 to 15 words—and study them in some depth. Learn the definition of each word; examine the sample sentence provided in the word list; learn the related words; and try writing a couple of sentences of your own that include the word. Refer to your own dictionary for further information if you like.

Learn Words in Families

Language is a living thing. Words are used by humans, innately creative beings who constantly twist, reshape, invent, and recombine words. (Think of the jargon of your favorite sport or hobby, or the new language currently blossoming in cyberspace, for some examples.) As a result, most words belong to families, in which related ideas are expressed through related words. This makes it possible to learn several words each time you learn one.

In the Insider's SAT Word List, we've provided some of the family linkages to help you. For example, you'll find the adjective *anachronistic* in the word list. It means "out of the proper time," as illustrated by the sample sentence: *The reference, in Shakespeare's* Julius Caesar, *to "the clock striking twelve" is anachronistic, since there were no striking timepieces in ancient Rome.*

When you meet this word, you should also get to know its close kinfolk. The noun *anachronism* means something that is out of its proper time. The clock in *Julius Caesar,* for example, is an anachronism; in another way, so are the knickers worn by modern baseball players, which reflect a style in men's fashions that went out of date generations ago. When you learn the adjective, learn the noun (and/or verb) that goes with it at the same time.

Become a Word Root Tracer

The two words we just discussed—*anachronistic* and *anachronism*—are like brother and sister. Slightly more distant relatives can be located and learned through the Word Origin feature you'll find near many of the words in the list. The origin for *anachronistic* connects this word to its source from another language: The Greek word *chronos* = time. Ultimately, this is the root from which the English word *anachronistic* grows.

As you explore the Word Origins, you'll find that many words—especially bookish SAT words—come from roots in Latin and Greek. There are complicated (and interesting) historical reasons for this, but the nub is that, for several centuries, learned people in England and America knew ancient Latin and Greek and deliberately imported words from those languages into English.

They rarely imported just one word from a given root. Thus, many word roots can enable you to learn several English words at once. The Word Origin for *anachronistic* tells you that *chronos* is also the source of the English words *chronic, chronicle, chronograph, chronology, synchronize.* All have to do with the concept of time:

chronic = lasting a long time
chronicle = a record of events over a period of time
chronograph = a clock or watch
chronology = a timeline
synchronize = to make two things happen at the same time

Learning the word root *chronos* can help you in several ways. It will make it easier to learn all the words in the *chronos* family, as opposed to trying to learn them one at a time. It will help you to remember the meanings of *chronos* words if they turn up on the exam, and it may even help you to guess the meaning of an entirely new *chronos* word when you encounter it.

Use the Words You Learn

Make a deliberate effort to include the new words you're learning in your daily speech and writing. It will impress people (teachers, bosses, friends and enemies) and it will help solidify your memory of the words and their meanings. Maybe you've heard this tip about meeting new people: if you use a new acquaintance's name several times, you're unlikely to forget it. The same is true with new words: use them, and you won't lose them.

Create Your Own Word List

Get into the habit of reading a little every day with your dictionary nearby. When you encounter a new word in a newspaper, magazine, or book, look it up. Then jot down the new word, its definition, and the sentence in which you encountered it in a notebook set aside for this purpose. Review your vocabulary notebook periodically—say, once a week. This is a great way to supplement our Insider's SAT Word List, because it's personally tailored. Your notebook will reflect the kinds of things you read and the words you find most difficult. The fact that you've taken the time and made the effort to write down the words and their meanings will help to fix them in your memory. Chances are good that you'll encounter a few words from your vocabulary notebook on the exam.

THE WORD LIST

Word Origin

Latin brevis = *short. Also found in English* brevity.

abbreviate (verb) to make briefer, to shorten. *Because time was running out, the speaker had to abbreviate his remarks.* **abbreviation** (noun).

abrasive (adjective) irritating, grinding, rough. *The manager's rude, abrasive way of criticizing the workers was bad for morale.* **abrasion** (noun).

abridge (verb) to shorten, to reduce. *The Bill of Rights is designed to prevent Congress from abridging the rights of Americans.* **abridgment** (noun).

absolve (verb) to free from guilt, to exonerate. *The criminal jury absolved O. J. Simpson of the murder of his ex-wife and her friend.* **absolution** (noun).

abstain (verb) to refrain, to hold back. *After his heart attack, he was warned by the doctor to abstain from smoking, drinking, and over-eating.* **abstinence** (noun), **abstemious** (adjective).

accentuate (verb) to emphasize, to stress. *The overcast skies and chill winds accentuated our gloomy mood.*

Word Origin

Latin acer = *sharp. Also found in English* acerbity, acrid, exacerbate.

acrimonious (adjective) biting, harsh, caustic. *The election campaign became acrimonious, as the candidates traded insults and accusations.* **acrimony** (noun).

adaptable (adjective) able to be changed to be suitable for a new purpose. *Some scientists say that the mammals outlived the dinosaurs because they were more adaptable to a changing climate.* **adapt** (verb), **adaptation** (noun).

adulation (noun) extreme admiration. *Few young actors have received greater adulation than did Marlon Brando after his performance in* A Streetcar Named Desire. **adulate** (verb), **adulatory** (adjective).

adversary (noun) an enemy or opponent. *When the former Soviet Union became an American ally, the United States lost its last major adversary.*

adversity (noun) misfortune. *It's easy to be patient and generous when things are going well; a person's true character is revealed under adversity.* **adverse** (adjective).

aesthetic (adjective) relating to art or beauty. *Mapplethorpe's photos may be attacked on moral grounds, but no one questions their aesthetic value—they are beautiful.* **aestheticism** (noun).

affected (adjective) false, artificial. *At one time, Japanese women were taught to speak in an affected high-pitched voice, which was thought girlishly attractive.* **affect** (verb), **affectation** (noun).

aggressive (adjective) forceful, energetic, and attacking. *A football player needs a more aggressive style of play than a soccer player.* **aggression** (noun).

alacrity (noun) promptness, speed. *Thrilled with the job offer, he accepted with alacrity—"Before they can change their minds!" he thought.*

allege (verb) to state without proof. *Some have alleged that Foster was murdered, but all the evidence points to suicide.* **allegation** (noun).

Word Origin

Latin levis = *light. Also found in English* levitate, levity.

alleviate (verb) to make lighter or more bearable. *Although no cure for AIDS has been found, doctors are able to alleviate the sufferings of those with the disease.* **alleviation** (noun).

ambiguous (adjective) having two or more possible meanings. *The phrase, "Let's table that discussion" is ambiguous; some think it means, "Let's discuss it now," while others think it means, "Let's save it for later."* **ambiguity** (noun).

ambivalent (adjective) having two or more contradictory feelings or attitudes; uncertain. *She was ambivalent toward her impending marriage; at times she was eager to go ahead, while at other times she wanted to call it off.* **ambivalence** (noun).

Word Origin

Latin amare = *love. Also found in English* amicable, amity, amorous.

amiable (adjective) likable, agreeable, friendly. *He was an amiable lab partner, always smiling, on time, and ready to work.* **amiability** (verb).

amicable (adjective) friendly, peaceable. *Although they agreed to divorce, their settlement was amicable and they remained friends afterward.*

amplify (verb) to enlarge, expand, or increase. *Uncertain as to whether they understood, the students asked the teacher to amplify his explanation.* **amplification** (noun).

Word Origin

Greek chronos = *time. Also found in English* chronic, chronicle, chronograph, chronology, synchronize.

anachronistic (adjective) out of the proper time. *The reference, in Shakespeare's* Julius Caesar, *to "the clock striking twelve" is anachronistic, since there were no striking timepieces in ancient Rome.* **anachronism** (noun).

anarchy (noun) absence of law or order. *For several months after the Nazi government was destroyed, there was no effective government in parts of Germany, and anarchy ruled.* **anarchic** (adjective).

anomaly (noun) something different or irregular. *The tiny planet Pluto, orbiting next to the giants Jupiter, Saturn, and Neptune, has long appeared to be an anomaly.* **anomalous** (adjective).

antagonism (noun) hostility, conflict, opposition. *As more and more reporters investigated the Watergate scandal, antagonism between Nixon and the press increased.* **antagonistic** (adjective), **antagonize** (verb).

antiseptic (adjective) fighting infection; extremely clean. *A wound should be washed with an antiseptic solution. The all-white offices were bare and almost antiseptic in their starkness.*

apathy (noun) lack of interest, concern, or emotion. *American voters are showing increasing apathy over politics; fewer than half voted in the last election.* **apathetic** (adjective).

arable (adjective) able to be cultivated for growing crops. *Rocky New England has relatively little arable farmland.*

arbiter (noun) someone able to settle dispute; a judge or referee. *The public is the ultimate arbiter of commercial value: It decides what sells and what doesn't.*

Word Origin

Latin arbiter = *judge. Also found in English* arbitrage, arbitrary, arbitrate.

arbitrary (adjective) based on random or merely personal preference. *Both computers cost the same and had the same features, so in the end I made an arbitrary decision about which to buy.*

arcane (adjective) little-known, mysterious, obscure. *Eliot's "Waste Land" is filled with arcane lore, including quotations in Latin, Greek, French, German, and Sanskrit.* **arcana** (noun, plural).

ardor (noun) a strong feeling of passion, energy, or zeal. *The young revolutionary proclaimed his convictions with an ardor that excited the crowd.* **ardent** (adjective).

arid (adjective) very dry; boring and meaningless. *The arid climate of Arizona makes farming difficult. Some find the law a fascinating topic, but for me it is an arid discipline.* **aridity** (noun).

ascetic (adjective) practicing strict self-discipline for moral or spiritual reasons. *The so-called Desert Fathers were hermits who lived an ascetic life of fasting, study, and prayer.* **asceticism** (verb).

assiduous (verb) working with care, attention, and diligence. *Although Karen is not a naturally gifted math student, by assiduous study she managed to earn an A in trigonometry.* **assiduity** (noun).

astute (adjective) observant, intelligent, and shrewd. *Safire's years of experience in Washington and his personal acquaintance with many political insiders make him an astute commentator on politics.*

atypical (adjective) not typical; unusual. *In* The Razor's Edge, *Bill Murray, best known as a comic actor, gave an atypical dramatic performance.*

audacious (adjective) bold, daring, adventurous. *Her plan to cross the Atlantic single-handed in a twelve-foot sailboat was audacious, if not reckless.* **audacity** (noun).

Word Origin

Latin audire = *to hear. Also found in English audition, auditorium, auditory.*

audible (adjective) able to be heard. *Although she whispered, her voice was picked up by the microphone, and her words were audible throughout the theater.* **audibility** (noun).

auspicious (adjective) promising good fortune; propitious. *The news that a team of British climbers had reached the summit of Everest seemed an auspicious sign for the reign of newly crowned Queen Elizabeth II.*

authoritarian (adjective) favoring or demanding blind obedience to leaders. *Despite Americans' belief in democracy, the American government has supported authoritarian regimes in other countries.* **authoritarianism** (noun)

belated (adjective) delayed past the proper time. *She called her mother on January 5th to offer her a belated "Happy New Year."*

belie (verb) to present a false or contradictory appearance. *Lena Horne's youthful appearance belies her long, distinguished career in show business.*

Word Origin

Latin bene = *well. Also found in English* benediction, benefactor, beneficent, beneficial, benefit, benign.

benevolent (adjective) wishing or doing good. *In old age, Carnegie used his wealth for benevolent purposes, donating large sums to found libraries and schools.* **benevolence** (noun).

berate (verb) to scold or criticize harshly. *The judge angrily berated the two lawyers for their unprofessional behavior.*

bereft (adjective) lacking or deprived of something. *Bereft of parental love, orphans sometimes grow up insecure.*

bombastic (adjective) inflated or pompous in style. *Old-fashioned bombastic political speeches don't work on television, which demands a more intimate style of communication.* **bombast** (noun).

bourgeois (adjective) middle-class or reflecting middle-class values. *The Dadaists of the 1920s produced art deliberately designed to offend bourgeois art collectors, with their taste for respectable, refined, uncontroversial pictures.* **bourgeois** (noun).

buttress (noun) something that supports or strengthens. *The endorsement of the American Medical Association is a powerful buttress for the claims made about this new medicine.* **buttress** (verb).

camaraderie (noun) a spirit of friendship. *Spending long days and nights together on the road, the members of a traveling theater group develop a strong sense of camaraderie.*

candor (noun) openness, honesty, frankness. *In his memoir about the Vietnam War, former defense secretary McNamara describes his mistakes with remarkable candor.* **candid** (adjective).

capricious (adjective) unpredictable, willful, whimsical. *The pop star Madonna has changed her image so many times that each new transformation now appears capricious rather than purposeful.* **caprice** (noun).

Word Origin

Latin vorare = *to eat. Also found in English* devour, omnivorous, voracious.

carnivorous (adjective) meat-eating. *The long, dagger-like teeth of the Tyrannosaurus make it obvious that this was a carnivorous dinosaur.* **carnivore** (noun).

carping (adjective) unfairly or excessively critical; querulous. *New York is famous for its demanding critics, but none is harder to please than the carping John Simon, said to have single-handedly destroyed many acting careers.* **carp** (verb).

catalytic (adjective) bringing about, causing, or producing some result. *The conditions for revolution existed in America by 1765; the disputes about taxation that arose later were the catalytic events that sparked the rebellion.* **catalyze** (verb).

Word Origin

Greek kaustikos = *burning. Also found in English* holocaust.

caustic (adjective) burning, corrosive. *No one was safe when the satirist H. L. Mencken unleashed his caustic wit.*

censure (noun) blame, condemnation. *The news that Senator Packwood had harassed several women brought censure from many feminists.* **censure** (verb).

chaos (noun) disorder, confusion, chance. *The first few moments after the explosion were pure chaos: no one was sure what had happened, and the area was filled with people running and yelling.* **chaotic** (adjective).

Word Origin

Latin circus = *circle. Also found in English* circumference, circumnavigate, circumscribe, circumspect, circumvent.

circuitous (adjective) winding or indirect. *We drove to the cottage by a circuitous route so we could see as much of the surrounding countryside as possible.*

circumlocution (noun) speaking in a roundabout way; wordiness. *Legal documents often contain circumlocutions which make them difficult to understand.*

circumscribe (verb) to define by a limit or boundary. *Originally, the role of the executive branch of government was clearly circumscribed, but that role has greatly expanded over time.* **circumscription** (noun).

circumvent (verb) to get around. *When Jerry was caught speeding, he tried to circumvent the law by offering the police officer a bribe.*

clandestine (adjective) secret, surreptitious. *As a member of the underground, Balas took part in clandestine meetings to discuss ways of sabotaging the Nazi forces.*

cloying (adjective) overly sweet or sentimental. *The deathbed scenes in the novels of Dickens are famously cloying: as Oscar Wilde said, "One would need a heart of stone to read the death of Little Nell without laughing."*

cogent (adjective) forceful and convincing. *The committee members were won over to the project by the cogent arguments of the chairman.* **cogency** (noun).

cognizant (adjective) aware, mindful. *Cognizant of the fact that it was getting late, the master of ceremonies cut short the last speech.* **cognizance** (noun).

Word Origin

Latin cognoscere *= to know. Also found in English* cognition, cognitive, incognito, recognize.

cohesive (adjective) sticking together, unified. *An effective military unit must be a cohesive team, all its members working together for a common goal.* **cohere** (verb), **cohesion** (noun).

collaborate (verb) to work together. *To create a truly successful movie, the director, writers, actors, and many others must collaborate closely.* **collaboration** (noun), **collaborative** (adjective).

colloquial (adjective) informal in language; conversational. *Some expressions from Shakespeare, such as the use of thou and thee, sound formal today but were colloquial English in Shakespeare's time.*

competent (adjective) having the skill and knowledge needed for a particular task; capable. *Any competent lawyer can draw up a will.* **competence** (noun).

complacent (adjective) smug, self-satisfied. *During the 1970s, American auto makers became complacent, believing that they would continue to be successful with little effort.* **complacency** (noun).

composure (noun) calm, self-assurance. *The president managed to keep his composure during his speech even when the TelePrompTer broke down, leaving him without a script.* **composed** (adjective).

conciliatory (adjective) seeking agreement, compromise, or reconciliation. *As a conciliatory gesture, the union leaders agreed to postpone a strike and to continue negotiations with management.* **conciliate** (verb), **conciliation** (noun).

Word Origin

Latin caedere = *to cut. Also found in English decide,* excise, incision, precise.

Word Origin

Latin dolere = *to feel pain. Also found in English dolorous, indolent.*

concise (adjective) expressed briefly and simply; succinct. *Less than a page long, the Bill of Rights is a concise statement of the freedoms enjoyed by all Americans.* **concision** (noun).

condescending (adjective) having an attitude of superiority toward another; patronizing. *"What a cute little car!" she remarked in a condescending style. "I suppose it's the nicest one someone like you could afford!"* **condescension** (noun).

condolence (noun) pity for someone else's sorrow or loss; sympathy. *After the sudden death of Princess Diana, thousands of messages of condolence were sent to her family.* **condole** (verb).

confidant (noun) someone entrusted with another's secrets. *No one knew about Janee's engagement except Sarah, her confidant.* **confide** (verb), **confidential** (adjective).

conformity (noun) agreement with or adherence to custom or rule. *In my high school, conformity was the rule: everyone dressed the same, talked the same, and listened to the same music.* **conform** (verb), **conformist** (adjective).

consensus (noun) general agreement among a group. Among *Quakers, voting traditionally is not used; instead, discussion continues until the entire group forms a consensus.*

consolation (noun) relief or comfort in sorrow or suffering. *Although we miss our dog very much, it is a consolation to know that she died quickly, without suffering.* **console** (verb).

consternation (noun) shock, amazement, dismay. *When a voice in the back of the church shouted out, "I know why they should not be married!" the entire gathering was thrown into consternation.*

consummate (verb) to complete, finish, or perfect. *The deal was consummated with a handshake and the payment of the agreed-upon fee.* **consummate** (adjective), **consummation** (noun).

contaminate (verb) to make impure. *Chemicals dumped in a nearby forest had seeped into the soil and contaminated the local water supply.* **contamination** (noun).

Word Origin

Latin tempus = *time. Also found in English* temporal, temporary, temporize.

contemporary (adjective) modern, current; from the same time. *I prefer old-fashioned furniture rather than contemporary styles. The composer Vivaldi was roughly contemporary with Bach.* **contemporary** (noun).

contrite (adjective) sorry for past misdeeds. *The public is often willing to forgive celebrities who are involved in some scandal, as long as they appear contrite.* **contrition** (noun).

conundrum (noun) a riddle, puzzle, or problem. *The question of why an all-powerful, all-loving God allows evil to exist is a conundrum many philosophers have pondered.*

convergence (noun) the act of coming together in unity or similarity. *A remarkable example of evolutionary convergence can be seen in the shark and the dolphin, two sea creatures that developed from different origins to become very similar in form.* **converge** (verb).

Word Origin

Latin volvere = *to roll. Also found in English devolve,* involve, revolution, revolve, voluble.

convoluted (adjective) twisting, complicated, intricate. *Tax law has become so convoluted that it's easy for people to accidentally violate it.* **convolute** (verb), **convolution** (noun).

corroborating (adjective) supporting with evidence; confirming. *A passerby who had witnessed the crime gave corroborating testimony about the presence of the accused person.* **corroborate** (verb), **corroboration** (noun).

corrosive (adjective) eating away, gnawing, or destroying. *Years of poverty and hard work had a corrosive effect on her beauty.* **corrode** (verb), **corrosion** (noun).

credulity (noun) willingness to believe, even with little evidence. *Con artists fool people by taking advantage of their credulity.* **credulous** (adjective).

criterion (noun) a standard of measurement or judgment. (The plural is criteria.) *In choosing a design for the new taxicabs, reliability will be our main criterion.*

Word Origin

Greek krinein = *to choose. Also found in English* criticize, critique.

critique (noun) a critical evaluation. *The editor gave a detailed critique of the manuscript, explaining its strengths and its weaknesses.* **critique** (verb).

culpable (adjective) deserving blame, guilty. *Although he committed the crime, because he was mentally ill he should not be considered culpable for his actions.* **culpability** (noun).

cumulative (adjective) made up of successive additions. *Smallpox was eliminated only through the cumulative efforts of several generations of doctors and scientists.* **accumulation** (noun), **accumulate** (verb).

curtail (verb) to shorten. *Because of the military emergence, all soldiers on leave were ordered to curtail their absences and return to duty.*

debased (adjective) lowered in quality, character, or esteem. *The quality of TV journalism has been debased by the many new tabloid-style talk shows.* **debase** (verb).

debunk (verb) to expose as false or worthless. *Magician James Randi loves to debunk psychics, mediums, clairvoyants, and others who claim supernatural powers.*

decorous (adjective) having good taste; proper, appropriate. *The once reserved and decorous style of the British monarchy began to change when the chic, flamboyant young Diana Spencer joined the family.* **decorum** (noun).

decry (verb) to criticize or condemn. *Cigarette ads aimed at youngsters have led many to decry the marketing tactics of the tobacco industry.*

Word Origin

Latin ducere = *to lead. Also found in English ductile,* induce, produce, reduce.

deduction (noun) a logical conclusion, especially a specific conclusion based on general principles. *Based on what is known about the effects of greenhouse gases on atmospheric temperature, scientists have made several deductions about the likelihood of global warming.* **deduce** (verb).

delegate (verb) to give authority or responsibility. *The president delegated the vice-president to represent the administration at the peace talks.* **delegate** (noun).

Word Origin

Latin delere = *to destroy. Also found in English* delete.

deleterious (adjective) harmful. *About thirty years ago, scientists proved that working with asbestos could be deleterious to one's health, producing cancer and other diseases.*

delineate (verb) to outline or describe. *Naturalists had long suspected the fact of evolution, but Darwin was the first to delineate a process—natural selection—through which evolution could occur.*

demagogue (noun) a leader who plays dishonestly on the prejudices and emotions of his followers. *Senator Joseph McCarthy was a demagogue who used the paranoia of the anti-Communist 1950s as a way of seizing fame and power in Washington.* **demagoguery** (noun).

demure (adjective) modest or shy. *The demure heroines of Victorian fiction have given way to today's stronger, more opinionated, and more independent female characters.*

denigrate (verb) to criticize or belittle. *The firm's new president tried to explain his plans for improving the company without seeming to denigrate the work of his predecessor.* **denigration** (noun).

depose (verb) to remove from office, especially from a throne. *Iran was formerly ruled by a monarch called the Shah, who was deposed in 1976.*

derelict (adjective) neglecting one's duty. *The train crash was blamed on a switchman who was derelict, having fallen asleep while on duty.* **dereliction** (noun).

derivative (adjective) taken from a particular source. *When a person first writes poetry, her poems are apt to be derivative of whatever poetry she most enjoys reading.* **derivation** (noun), **derive** (verb).

desolate (adjective) empty, lifeless, and deserted; hopeless, gloomy. *Robinson Crusoe was shipwrecked and had to learn to survive alone on a desolate island. The murder of her husband left Mary Lincoln desolate.* **desolation** (noun).

destitute (adjective) very poor. *Years of rule by a dictator who stole the wealth of the country had left the people of the Philippines destitute.* **destitution** (noun).

deter (verb) to discourage from acting. *The best way to deter crime is to insure that criminals will receive swift and certain punishment.* **deterrence** (noun), **deterrent** (adjective).

detractor (noun) someone who belittles or disparages. *Neil Diamond has many detractors who consider his music boring, inane, and sentimental.* **detract** (verb).

deviate (verb) to depart from a standard or norm. *Having agreed upon a spending budget for the company, we mustn't deviate from it; if we do, we may run out of money soon.* **deviation** (noun).

devious (adjective) tricky, deceptive. *Milken's devious financial tactics were designed to enrich his firm while confusing or misleading government regulators.*

didactic (adjective) intended to teach, instructive. *The children's TV show "Sesame Street" is designed to be both entertaining and didactic.*

diffident (adjective) hesitant, reserved, shy. *Someone with a diffident personality should pursue a career that involves little public contact.* **diffidence** (noun).

diffuse (verb) to spread out, to scatter. *The red dye quickly became diffused through the water, turning it a very pale pink.* **diffusion** (noun).

digress (verb) to wander from the main path or the main topic. *My high school biology teacher loved to digress from science into personal anecdotes about his college adventures.* **digression** (noun), **digressive** (adjective).

dilatory (adjective) delaying, procrastinating. *The lawyer used various dilatory tactics, hoping that his opponent would get tired of waiting for a trial and drop the case.*

diligent (adjective) working hard and steadily. *Through diligent efforts, the townspeople were able to clear away the debris from the flood in a matter of days.* **diligence** (noun).

diminutive (adjective) unusually small, tiny. *Children are fond of Shetland ponies because their diminutive size makes them easy to ride.* **diminution** (noun).

discern (verb) to detect, notice, or observe. *I could discern the shape of a whale off the starboard bow, but it was too far away to determine its size or species.* **discernment** (noun).

disclose (verb) to make known; to reveal. *Election laws require candidates to disclose the names of those who contribute money to their campaigns.* **disclosure** (noun).

discomfit (verb) to frustrate, thwart, or embarrass. *Discomfited by the interviewer's unexpected question, Peter could only stammer in reply.* **discomfiture** (noun).

disconcert (verb) to confuse or embarrass. *When the hallway bells began to ring halfway through her lecture, the speaker was disconcerted and didn't know what to do.*

Word Origin

Latin credere = *to believe. Also found in English* credential, credible, credit, credo, credulous, incredible.

discredit (verb) to cause disbelief in the accuracy of some statement or the reliability of a person. *Although many people still believe in UFOs, among scientists the reports of "alien encounters" have been thoroughly discredited.*

discreet (adjective) showing good judgment in speech and behavior. *Be discreet when discussing confidential business matters—don't talk among strangers on the elevator, for example.* **discretion** (noun).

discrepancy (noun) a difference or variance between two or more things. *The discrepancies between the two witnesses' stories show that one of them must be lying.* **discrepant** (adjective).

disdain (noun) contempt, scorn. *Millionaire Leona Helmsley was disliked by many people because she treated "little people" with such disdain.* **disdain** (verb), **disdainful** (adjective).

disingenuous (adjective) pretending to be candid, simple, and frank. *When Texas billionaire H. Ross Perot ran for president, many considered his "jest plain folks" style disingenuous.*

disparage (verb) to speak disrespectfully about, to belittle. *Many political ads today both praise their own candidate and disparage his or her opponent.* **disparagement** (noun), **disparaging** (adjective).

disparity (noun) difference in quality or kind. *There is often a disparity between the kind of high-quality television people say they want and the low-brow programs they actually watch.* **disparate** (adjective).

disregard (verb) to ignore, to neglect. If you don't write a will, when you die, your survivors may disregard your wishes about how your property should be handled. **disregard** (noun).

disruptive (adjective) causing disorder, interrupting. *When the senator spoke at our college, angry demonstrators picketed, heckled, and engaged in other disruptive activities.* **disrupt** (verb), **disruption** (noun).

dissemble (verb) to pretend, to simulate. *When the police questioned her about the crime, she dissembled innocence.*

Word Origin

Latin sonare = *to sound. Also found in English* consonance, sonar, sonic, sonorous."

dissipate (verb) to spread out or scatter. *The windows and doors were opened, allowing the smoke that had filled the room to dissipate.* **dissipation** (noun).

dissonance (noun) lack of music harmony; lack of agreement between ideas. *Most modern music is characterized by dissonance, which many listeners find hard to enjoy. There is a noticeable dissonance between two common beliefs of most conservatives: their faith in unfettered free markets and their preference for traditional social values.* **dissonant** (adjective).

diverge (verb) to move in different directions. Frost's poem *"The Road Less Traveled" tells of the choice he made when "Two roads diverged in a yellow wood."* **divergence** (noun), **divergent** (adjective).

diversion (noun) a distraction or pastime. *During the two hours he spent in the doctor's waiting room, his hand-held computer game was a welcome diversion.* **divert** (verb).

divination (noun) the art of predicting the future. *In ancient Greece, people wanting to know their fate would visit the priests at Delphi, supposedly skilled at divination.* **divine** (verb).

divisive (adjective) causing disagreement or disunity. *Throughout history, race has been the most divisive issue in American society.*

divulge (verb) to reveal. *The people who count the votes for the Oscar awards are under strict orders not to divulge the names of the winners.*

dogmatic (adjective) holding firmly to a particular set of beliefs with little or no basis. *Believers in Marxist doctrine tend to be dogmatic, ignoring evidence that contradicts their beliefs.* **dogmatism** (noun).

dominant (adjective) greatest in importance or power. *Turner's "Frontier Thesis" suggests that the existence of the frontier had a dominant influence on American culture.* **dominate** (verb), **domination** (noun).

dubious (adjective) doubtful, uncertain. *Despite the chairman's attempts to convince the committee members that his plan would succeed, most of them remained dubious.* **dubiety** (noun).

Word Origin

Latin durare = *to last. Also found in English* durance, duration, endure.

durable (adjective) long-lasting. *Denim is a popular material for work clothes because it is strong and durable.*

duress (noun) compulsion or restraint. *Fearing that the police might beat him, he confessed to the crime, not willingly but under duress.*

eclectic (adjective) drawn from many sources; varied, heterogeneous. *The Mellon family art collection is an eclectic one, including works ranging from ancient Greek sculptures to modern paintings.* **eclecticism** (noun).

efficacious (adjective) able to produce a desired effect. *Though thousands of people today are taking herbal supplements to treat depression, researchers have not yet proved them efficacious.* **efficacy** (noun).

effrontery (noun) shameless boldness. *The sports world was shocked when a pro basketball player had the effrontery to choke his head coach during a practice session.*

effusive (adjective) pouring forth one's emotions very freely. *Having won the Oscar for Best Actress, Sally Field gave an effusive acceptance speech in which she marveled, "You like me! You really like me!"* **effusion** (noun).

Word Origin

Latin grex = *herd. Also found in English* aggregate, congregate, gregarious.

egoism (noun) excessive concern with oneself; conceit. *Robert's egoism was so great that all he could talk about was the importance—and the brilliance—of his own opinions.* **egoistic** (adjective).

egregious (adjective) obvious, conspicuous, flagrant. *It's hard to imagine how the editor could allow such an egregious error to appear.*

elated (adjective) excited and happy; exultant. *When the Green Bay Packers' last, desperate pass was dropped, the elated fans of the Denver Broncos began to celebrate.* **elate** (verb), **elation** (noun).

elliptical (adjective) very terse or concise in writing or speech; difficult to understand. *Rather than speak plainly, she hinted at her meaning through a series of nods, gestures, and elliptical half-sentences.*

elusive (adjective) hard to capture, grasp, or understand. *Though everyone thinks they know what "justice" is, when you try to define the concept precisely, it proves to be quite elusive.*

Word Origin

Latin ludere = *to play. Also found in English* delude, illusion, interlude, ludicrous.

embezzle (verb) to steal money property that has been entrusted to your care. *The church treasurer was found to have embezzled thousands of dollars by writing phony checks on the church bank account.* **embezzlement** (noun).

emend (verb) to correct. *Before the letter is mailed, please emend the two spelling errors.* **emendation** (noun).

emigrate (verb) to leave one place or country to settle elsewhere. *Millions of Irish emigrated to the New World in the wake of the great Irish famines of the 1840s.* **emigrant** (noun), **emigration** (noun).

eminent (adjective) noteworthy, famous. *Vaclav Havel was an eminent author before being elected president of the Czech Republic.* **eminence** (noun).

emissary (noun) someone who represents another. *In an effort to avoid a military showdown, Carter was sent as an emissary to Korea to negotiate a settlement.*

emollient (noun) something that softens or soothes. *She used a hand cream as an emollient on her dry, work-roughened hands.* **emollient** (adjective).

empathy (noun) imaginative sharing of the feelings, thoughts, or experiences of another. *It's easy for a parent to have empathy for the sorrow of another parent whose child has died.* **empathetic** (adjective).

empirical (adjective) based on experience or personal observation. *Although many people believe in ESP, scientists have found no empirical evidence of its existence.* **empiricism** (noun).

emulate (verb) to imitate or copy. *The British band Oasis admitted their desire to emulate their idols, the Beatles.* **emulation** (noun).

encroach (verb) to go beyond acceptable limits; to trespass. *By quietly seizing more and more authority, Robert Moses continually encroached on the powers of other government leaders.* **encroachment** (noun).

enervate (verb) to reduce the energy or strength of someone or something. *The stress of the operation left her feeling enervated for about two weeks.*

engender (verb) to produce, to cause. *Countless disagreements over the proper use of national forests have engendered feelings of hostility between ranchers and environmentalists.*

enhance (verb) to improve in value or quality. *New kitchen appliances will enhance your house and increase the amount of money you'll make when you sell it.* **enhancement** (noun).

enmity (noun) hatred, hostility, ill will. *Long-standing enmity, like that between the Protestants and Catholics in Northern Ireland, is difficult to overcome.*

enthrall (verb) to enchant or charm. *When the Swedish singer Jenny Lind toured America in the nineteenth century, audiences were enthralled by her beauty and talent.*

ephemeral (adjective) quickly disappearing; transient. *Stardom in pop music is ephemeral; most of the top acts of ten years ago are forgotten today.*

Word Origin

Latin anima = *mind, spirit. Also found in English* animate, magnanimous, pusillanimous, unanimous."

equanimity (noun) calmness of mind, especially under stress. *Roosevelt had the gift of facing the great crises of his presidency—the Depression, the Second World War—with equanimity and even humor.*

eradicate (verb) to destroy completely. *American society has failed to eradicate racism, although some of its worst effects have been reduced.*

espouse (verb) to take up as a cause; to adopt. *No politician in American today will openly espouse racism, although some behave and speak in racially prejudiced ways.*

euphoric (adjective) a feeling of extreme happiness and well-being; elation. *One often feels euphoric during the earliest days of a new love affair.* **euphoria** (noun).

evanescent (adjective) vanishing like a vapor; fragile and transient. *As she walked by, the evanescent fragrance of her perfume reached me for just an instant.*

exacerbate (verb) to make worse or more severe. *The roads in our town already have too much traffic; building a new shopping mall will exacerbate the problem.*

Word Origin

Latin asper = *rough. Also found in English* asperity.

exasperate (verb) to irritate or annoy. *Because she was trying to study, Sharon was exasperated by the yelling of her neighbors' children.*

exculpate (verb) to free from blame or guilt. *When someone else confessed to the crime, the previous suspect was exculpated.* **exculpation** (noun), **exculpatory** (adjective).

exemplary (adjective) worthy to serve as a model. *The Baldrige Award is given to a company with exemplary standards of excellence in products and service.* **exemplar** (noun), **exemplify** (verb).

exonerate (verb) to free from blame. *Although Jewell was suspected at first of being involved in the bombing, later evidence exonerated him.* **exoneration** (noun), **exonerative** (adjective).

expansive (adjective) broad and large; speaking openly and freely. *The LBJ Ranch is located on an expansive tract of land in Texas. Over dinner, she became expansive in describing her dreams for the future.*

expedite (verb) to carry out promptly. *As the flood waters rose, the governor ordered state agencies to expedite their rescue efforts.*

expertise (noun) skill, mastery. *The software company was eager to hire new graduates with programming expertise.*

expiate (verb) to atone for. *The president's apology to the survivors of the notorious Tuskegee experiments was his attempt to expiate the nation's guilt over their mistreatment.* **expiation** (noun).

Word Origin

Latin proprius = *own. Also found in English* appropriate, property, proprietary, proprietor.

expropriate (verb) to seize ownership of. *When the Communists came to power in China, they expropriated most businesses and turned them over to government-appointed managers.* **expropriation** (noun).

extant (adjective) currently in existence. *Of the seven ancient "Wonders of the World," only the pyramids of Egypt are still extant.*

extenuate (verb) to make less serious. *Karen's guilt is extenuated by the fact that she was only twelve when she committed the theft.* **extenuating** (adjective), **extenuation** (noun).

extol (verb) to greatly praise. *At the party convention, speaker after speaker rose to extol their candidate for the presidency.*

extricate (verb) to free from a difficult or complicated situation. *Much of the humor in the TV show* I Love Lucy *comes in watching Lucy try to extricate herself from the problems she creates by fibbing or trickery.* **extricable** (adjective).

extrinsic (adjective) not an innate part or aspect of something; external. *The high price of old baseball cards is due to extrinsic factors, such as the nostalgia felt by baseball fans for the stars of their youth, rather than the inherent beauty or value of the cards themselves.*

exuberant (adjective) wildly joyous and enthusiastic. *As the final seconds of the game ticked away, the fans of the winning team began an exuberant celebration.* **exuberance** (noun).

Word Origin

Latin facere = *to do. Also found in English* facility, factor, facsimile, faculty.

facile (adjective) easy; shallow or superficial. *The one-minute political commercial favors a candidate with facile opinions rather than serious, thoughtful solutions.* **facilitate** (verb), **facility** (noun).

fallacy (noun) an error in fact or logic. *It's a fallacy to think that "natural" means "healthful"; after all, the deadly poison arsenic is completely natural.* **fallacious** (adjective).

felicitous (adjective) pleasing, fortunate, apt. *The sudden blossoming of the dogwood trees on the morning of Matt's wedding seemed a felicitous sign of good luck.* **felicity** (noun).

feral (adjective) wild. *The garbage dump was inhabited by a pack of feral dogs, which had escaped from their owners and become completely wild.*

fervent (adjective) full of intense feeling; ardent, zealous. *In the days just after his religious conversion, his piety was at its most fervent.* **fervid** (adjective), **fervor** (noun).

flagrant (adjective) obviously wrong; offensive. *Nixon was forced to resign the presidency after a series of flagrant crimes against the U.S. Constitution.* **flagrancy** (noun).

flamboyant (adjective) very colorful, showy, or elaborate. *At Mardi Gras, partygoers compete to show off the most wild and flamboyant outfits.*

florid (adjective) flowery, fancy; reddish. *The grand ballroom was decorated in a florid style. Years of heavy drinking had given him a florid complexion.*

foppish (adjective) describing a man who is foolishly vain about his dress or appearance. *The foppish character of the 1890s wore bright-colored spats and a top hat; in the 1980s, he wore fancy suspenders and a shirt with a contrasting collar.* **fop** (noun).

formidable (adjective) awesome, impressive, or frightening. *According to his plaque in the Baseball Hall of Fame, pitcher Tom Seaver turned the New York Mets "from lovable losers into formidable foes."*

fortuitous (adjective) lucky, fortunate. *Although the mayor claimed credit for the falling crime rate, it was really caused by several fortuitous trends.*

fractious (adjective) troublesome, unruly. *Members of the British Parliament are often fractious, shouting insults and sarcastic questions during debates.*

Word Origin

Latin frater = *brother. Also found in English* fraternal, fraternity, fratricide."

fragility (noun) the quality of being easy to break; delicacy, weakness. *Because of their fragility, few stained glass windows from the early Middle Ages have survived.* **fragile** (adjective).

fraternize (verb) to associate with on friendly terms. *Although baseball players aren't supposed to fraternize with their opponents, players from opposing teams often chat before games.* **fraternization** (noun).

frenetic (adjective) chaotic, frantic. *The floor of the stock exchange, filled with traders shouting and gesturing, is a scene of frenetic activity.*

frivolity (noun) lack of seriousness; levity. *The frivolity of the Mardi Gras carnival is in contrast to the seriousness of the religious season of Lent which follows.* **frivolous** (adjective).

frugal (adjective) spending little. *With our last few dollars, we bought a frugal dinner: a loaf of bread and a piece of cheese.* **frugality** (noun).

fugitive (noun) someone trying to escape. *When two prisoners broke out of the local jail, police were warned to keep an eye out for the fugitives.* **fugitive** (adjective).

gargantuan (adjective) huge, colossal. *The building of the Great Wall of China was one of the most gargantuan projects ever undertaken.*

genial (adjective) friendly, gracious. *A good host welcomes all visitors in a warm and genial fashion.*

grandiose (adjective) overly large, pretentious, or showy. *Among Hitler's grandiose plans for Berlin was a gigantic building with a dome several times larger than any ever built.* **grandiosity** (noun).

gratuitous (adjective) given freely or without cause. *Since her opinion was not requested, her harsh criticism of his singing seemed a gratuitous insult.*

gregarious (adjective) enjoying the company of others; sociable. *Marty is naturally gregarious, a popular member of several clubs and a sought-after lunch companion.*

guileless (adjective) without cunning; innocent. *Deborah's guileless personality and complete honesty make it hard for her to survive in the harsh world of politics.*

gullible (adjective) easily fooled. *When the sweepstakes entry form arrived bearing the message, "You may be a winner!" my gullible neighbor tried to claim a prize.* **gullibility** (noun).

hackneyed (adjective) without originality, trite. *When someone invented the phrase, "No pain, no gain," it was clever, but now it is so commonly heard that it seems hackneyed.*

haughty (adjective) overly proud. *The fashion model strode down the runway, her hips thrust forward and a haughty expression, like a sneer, on her face.* **haughtiness** (noun).

hedonist (noun) someone who lives mainly to pursue pleasure. *Having inherited great wealth, he chose to live the life of a hedonist, traveling the world in luxury.* **hedonism** (noun), **hedonistic** (adjective).

heinous (adjective) very evil, hateful. *The massacre by Pol Pot of over a million Cambodians is one of the twentieth century's most heinous crimes.*

hierarchy (noun) a ranking of people, things, or ideas from highest to lowest. *A cabinet secretary ranks just below the president and vice president in the hierarchy of the executive branch.* **hierarchical** (adjective).

hypocrisy (noun) a false pretense of virtue. *When the sexual misconduct of the television preacher was exposed, his followers were shocked at his hypocrisy.* **hypocritical** (adjective).

iconoclast (noun) someone who attacks traditional beliefs or institutions. *Comedian Dennis Miller enjoys his reputation as an iconoclast, though people in power often resent his satirical jabs.* **iconoclasm** (noun), **iconoclastic** (adjective).

idiosyncratic (adjective) peculiar to an individual; eccentric. *Cyndi Lauper sings pop music in an idiosyncratic style, mingling high-pitched whoops and squeals with throaty gurgles.* **idiosyncrasy** (noun).

idolatry (noun) the worship of a person, thing, or institution as a god. *In Communist China, Chairman Mao was the subject of idolatry; his picture was displayed everywhere, and millions of Chinese memorized his sayings.* **idolatrous** (adjective).

impartial (adjective) fair, equal, unbiased. *If a judge is not impartial, then all of her rulings are questionable.* **impartiality** (noun).

impeccable (adjective) flawless. *The crooks printed impeccable copies of the Super Bowl tickets, making it impossible to distinguish them from the real things.*

impetuous (adjective) acting hastily or impulsively. *Ben's resignation was an impetuous act; he did it without thinking, and he soon regretted it.* **impetuosity** (noun).

impinge (verb) to encroach upon, touch, or affect. *You have a right to do whatever you want, so long as your actions don't impinge on the rights of others.*

implicit (adjective) understood without being openly expressed; implied. *Although most clubs had no rules excluding blacks and Jews, many had an implicit understanding that no blacks or Jews would be allowed to join.*

impute (verb) to credit or give responsibility to; to attribute. *Although Sarah's comments embarrassed me, I don't impute any ill will to her; I think she didn't realize what she was saying.* **imputation** (noun).

Word Origin

Latin articulus = *joint, division. Also found in English* arthritis, articulate.

inarticulate (adjective) unable to speak or express oneself clearly and understandably. *A skilled athlete may be an inarticulate public speaker, as demonstrated by many post-game interviews.*

incisive (adjective) expressed clearly and directly. *Franklin settled the debate with a few incisive remarks that summed up the issue perfectly.*

incompatible (adjective) unable to exist together; conflicting. *Many people hold seemingly incompatible beliefs: for example, supporting the death penalty while believing in the sacredness of human life.* **incompatibility** (noun).

inconsequential (adjective) of little importance. *When the stereo was delivered, it was a different shade of gray than I expected, but the difference was inconsequential.*

incontrovertible (adjective) impossible to question. *The fact that Sheila's fingerprints were the only ones on the murder weapon made her guilt seem incontrovertible.*

incorrigible (adjective) impossible to manage or reform. *Lou is an incorrigible trickster, constantly playing practical jokes no matter how much his friends complain.*

incremental (adjective) increasing gradually by small amounts. *Although the initial cost of the Medicare program was small, the incremental expenses have grown to be very large.* **increment** (noun).

incriminate (adjective) to give evidence of guilt. *The fifth amendment to the Constitution says that no one is required to reveal information that would incriminate him in a crime.* **incriminating** (adjective).

incumbent (noun) someone who occupies an office or position. *It is often difficult for a challenger to win a seat in Congress from the incumbent.* **incumbency** (noun), **incumbent** (adjective).

indeterminate (adjective) not definitely known. *The college plans to enroll an indeterminate number of students; the size of the class will depend on the number of applicants and how many accept offers of admission.* **determine** (verb).

indifferent (adjective) unconcerned, apathetic. *The mayor's small proposed budget for education suggests that he is indifferent to the needs of our schools.* **indifference** (noun).

indistinct (adjective) unclear, uncertain. *We could see boats on the water, but in the thick morning fog their shapes were indistinct.*

indomitable (adjective) unable to be conquered or controlled. *The world admired the indomitable spirit of Nelson Mandela; he remained courageous despite years of imprisonment.*

induce (verb) to cause. *The doctor prescribed a medicine which is supposed to induce a lowering of the blood pressure.* **induction** (noun).

ineffable (adjective) difficult to describe or express. *He gazed in silence at the sunrise over the Taj Mahal, his eyes reflecting an ineffable sense of wonder.*

inevitable (adjective) unable to be avoided. *Once the Japanese attacked Pearl Harbor, American involvement in World War Two was inevitable.* **inevitability** (noun).

inexorable (adjective) unable to be deterred; relentless. *It's difficult to imagine how the mythic character of Oedipus could have avoided his evil destiny; his fate appears inexorable.*

ingenious (adjective) showing cleverness and originality. *The Post-It note is an ingenious solution to a common problem—how to mark papers without spoiling them.* **ingenuity** (noun).

inherent (adjective) naturally part of something. *Compromise is inherent in democracy, since everyone cannot get his way.* **inhere** (verb), **inherence** (noun).

innate (adjective) inborn, native. *Not everyone who takes piano lessons becomes a fine musician, which shows that music requires innate talent as well as training.*

innocuous (adjective) harmless, inoffensive. *I was surprised that Andrea took offense at such an innocuous joke.*

inoculate (verb) to prevent a disease by infusing with a disease-causing organism. *Pasteur found he could prevent rabies by inoculating patients with the virus that causes the disease.* **inoculation** (noun).

insipid (adjective) flavorless, uninteresting. *Most TV shows are so insipid that you can watch them while reading without missing a thing.* **insipidity** (noun).

insolence (noun) an attitude or behavior that is bold and disrespectful. *Some feel that news reporters who shout questions at the president are behaving with insolence.* **insolent** (adjective).

insular (adjective) narrow or isolated in attitude or viewpoint. *New Yorkers are famous for their insular attitudes; they seem to think that nothing important has ever happened outside of their city.* **insularity** (noun).

insurgency (noun) uprising, rebellion. *The angry townspeople had begun an insurgency bordering on downright revolution; they were collecting arms, holding secret meetings, and refusing to pay certain taxes.* **insurgent** (adjective).

integrity (noun) honesty, uprightness; soundness, completeness. *"Honest Abe" Lincoln is considered a model of political integrity. Inspectors examined the building's support beams and foundation and found no reason to doubt its structural integrity.*

Word Origin

Latin loqui = *to speak. Also found in English* colloquial, colloquy, eloquent, grandiloquent, locution, loquacious.

interlocutor (noun) someone taking part in a dialogue or conversation. *Annoyed by the constant questions from someone in the crowd, the speaker challenged his interlocutor to offer a better plan.* **interlocutory** (adjective).

interlude (noun) an interrupting period or performance. *The two most dramatic scenes in King Lear are separated, strangely, by a comic interlude starring the king's jester.*

interminable (adjective) endless or seemingly endless. *Addressing the United Nations, Castro announced, "We will be brief"—then delivered an interminable 4-hour speech.*

intransigent (adjective) unwilling to compromise. *Despite the mediator's attempts to suggest a fair solution, the two parties were intransigent, forcing a showdown.* **intransigence** (noun).

Word Origin

Latin trepidus = *alarmed. Also found in English* trepidation.

intrepid (adjective) fearless and resolute. *Only an intrepid adventurer is willing to undertake the long and dangerous trip by sled to the South Pole.* **intrepidity** (noun).

intrusive (adjective) forcing a way in without being welcome. *The legal requirement of a search warrant is supposed to protect Americans from intrusive searches by the police.* **intrude** (verb), **intrusion** (noun).

intuitive (adjective) known directly, without apparent thought or effort. *An experienced chess player sometimes has an intuitive sense of the best move to make, even if she can't explain it.* **intuit** (verb), **intuition** (noun).

inundate (verb) to flood; to overwhelm. *As soon as playoff tickets went on sale, eager fans inundated the box office with orders.*

Word Origin

Latin varius = *various. Also found in English* prevaricate, variable, variance, variegated, vary.

invariable (adjective) unchanging, constant. *When writing a book, it was her invariable habit to rise at 6 and work at her desk from 7 to 12.* **invariability** (noun).

inversion (noun) a turning backwards, inside-out, or upside-down; a reversal. *Latin poetry often features inversion of word order; for example, the first line of Vergil's* Aeneid: *"Arms and the man I sing."* **invert** (verb), **inverted** (adjective).

inveterate (adjective) persistent, habitual. *It's very difficult for an inveterate gambler to give up the pastime.* **inveteracy** (noun).

invigorate (verb) to give energy to, to stimulate. *As her car climbed the mountain road, Lucinda felt invigorated by the clear air and the cool breezes.*

invincible (adjective) impossible to conquer or overcome. *For three years at the height of his career, boxer Mike Tyson seemed invincible.*

inviolable (adjective) impossible to attack or trespass upon. *In the president's remote hideaway at Camp David, guarded by the Secret Service, his privacy is, for once, inviolable.*

irrational (adjective) unreasonable. *Charles knew that his fear of insects was irrational, but he was unable to overcome it.* **irrationality** (noun).

irresolute (adjective) uncertain how to act, indecisive. *When McGovern first said he supported his vice president candidate "one thousand percent," then dropped him from the ticket, it made McGovern appear irresolute.* **irresolution** (noun).

jeopardize (verb) to put in danger. *Terrorist attacks jeopardize the fragile peace in the Middle East.* **jeopardy** (noun).

juxtapose (verb) to put side by side. *It was strange to see the old-time actor Charlton Heston and rock icon Bob Dylan juxtaposed at the awards ceremony.* **juxtaposition** (noun).

languid (adjective) without energy; slow, sluggish, listless. *The hot, humid weather of late August can make anyone feel languid.* **languish** (verb), **languor** (noun).

latent (adjective) not currently obvious or active; hidden. *Although he had committed only a single act of violence, the psychiatrist who examined him said he had probably always had a latent tendency toward violence.* **latency** (noun).

Word Origin

Latin laus = *praise. Also found in English* applaud, laud, laudable, plaudit.

laudatory (adjective) giving praise. *The ads for the movie are filled with laudatory comments from critics.*

lenient (adjective) mild, soothing, or forgiving. *The judge was known for his lenient disposition; he rarely imposed long jail sentences on criminals.* **leniency** (noun).

lethargic (adjective) lacking energy; sluggish. *Visitors to the zoo are surprised that the lions appear so lethargic, but in the wild lions sleep up to 18 hours a day.* **lethargy** (noun).

liability (noun) an obligation or debt; a weakness or drawback. *The insurance company had a liability of millions of dollars after the town was destroyed by a tornado. Slowness afoot is a serious liability in an aspiring basketball player.* **liable** (adjective).

lithe (adjective) flexible and graceful. *The ballet dancer was almost as lithe as a cat.*

longevity (noun) length of life; durability. *The reduction in early deaths from infectious diseases is responsible for most of the increase in human longevity over the past two centuries.*

lucid (adjective) clear and understandable. *Hawking's* A Short History of the Universe *is a lucid explanation of modern scientific theories about the origin of the universe.* **lucidity** (noun).

lurid (adjective) shocking, gruesome. *While the serial killer was on the loose, the newspapers were filled with lurid stories about his crimes.*

malediction (noun) curse. *In the fairy tale "Sleeping Beauty," the princess is trapped in a death-like sleep because of the malediction uttered by an angry witch.*

Word Origin

Latin malus = *bad. Also found in English* malefactor, malevolence, malice, malicious.

malevolence (noun) hatred, ill will. *Critics say that Iago, the villain in Shakespeare's* Othello, *seems to exhibit malevolence with no real cause.* **malevolent** (noun).

malinger (verb) to pretend illness to avoid work. *During the labor dispute, hundreds of employees malingered, forcing the company to slow production and costing it millions in profits.*

malleable (adjective) able to be changed, shaped, or formed by outside pressures. *Gold is a very useful metal because it is so malleable. A child's personality is malleable and deeply influenced by the things her parents say and do.* **malleability** (noun).

Word Origin

Latin mandare = *entrust, order. Also found in English* command, demand, remand.

mandate (noun) order, command. *The new policy on gays in the military went into effect as soon as the president issued his mandate about it.* **mandate** (verb), **mandatory** (adjective).

maturation (noun) the process of becoming fully grown or developed. *Free markets in the former Communist nations are likely to operate smoothly only after a long period of maturation.* **mature** (adjective and verb), **maturity** (noun).

mediate (verb) to reconcile differences between two parties. *During the baseball strike, both the players and the club owners were willing to have the president mediate the dispute.* **mediation** (noun).

Word Origin

Latin medius = *middle. Also found in English* intermediate, media, medium.

mediocrity (noun) the state of being middling or poor in quality. *The New York Mets, who'd finished in ninth place in 1968, won the world's championship in 1969, going from horrible to great in a single year and skipping mediocrity.* **mediocre** (adjective).

mercurial (adjective) changing quickly and unpredictably. *The mercurial personality of Robin Williams, with his many voices and styles, made him perfect for the role of the ever-changing genie in* Aladdin.

meticulous (adjective) very careful with details. *Repairing watches calls for a craftsperson who is patient and meticulous.*

mimicry (noun) imitation, aping. *The continued popularity of Elvis Presley has given rise to a class of entertainers who make a living through mimicry of "The King."* **mimic** (noun and verb).

misconception (noun) a mistaken idea. *Columbus sailed west under the misconception that he would reach the shores of Asia that way.* **misconceive** (verb).

mitigate (verb) to make less severe; to relieve. *Wallace certainly committed the assault, but the verbal abuse he'd received helps to explain his behavior and somewhat mitigates his guilt.* **mitigation** (noun).

Word Origin

Latin modus = *measure. Also found in English* immoderate, moderate, modest, modify, modulate.

modicum (noun) a small amount. *The plan for your new business is well designed; with a modicum of luck, you should be successful.*

mollify (verb) to soothe or calm; to appease. *Carla tried to mollify the angry customer by promising him a full refund.*

morose (adjective) gloomy, sullen. *After Chuck's girlfriend dumped him, he lay around the house for a couple of days, feeling morose.*

mundane (adjective) everyday, ordinary, commonplace. *Moviegoers in the 1930s liked the glamorous films of Fred Astaire because they provided an escape from the mundane problems of life during the Great Depression.*

munificent (adjective) very generous; lavish. *Ted Turner's billion-dollar donation to the United Nations is probably the most munificent act of charity in history.* **munificence** (noun).

Word Origin

Latin mutare = *to change. Also found in English* immutable, mutant, mutation.

mutable (adjective) likely to change. *A politician's reputation can be highly mutable, as seen in the case of Harry Truman—mocked during his lifetime, revered afterward.*

narcissistic (adjective) showing excessive love for oneself; egoistic. *Andre's room, decorated with photos of himself and the sports trophies he has won, suggests a narcissistic personality.* **narcissism** (noun).

nocturnal (adjective) of the night; active at night. *Travelers on the Underground Railroad escaped from slavery to the North by a series of nocturnal flights. The eyes of nocturnal animals must be sensitive in dim light.*

nonchalant (adjective) appearing to be unconcerned. *Unlike the other players on the football team, who pumped their fists when their names were announced, John ran on the field with a nonchalant wave.* **nonchalance** (noun).

nondescript (adjective) without distinctive qualities; drab. *The bank robber's clothes were nondescript; none of the witnesses could remember their color or style.*

notorious (adjective) famous, especially for evil actions or qualities. *Warner Brothers produced a series of movies about notorious gangsters such as John Dillinger and Al Capone.* **notoriety** (noun).

Word Origin

Latin novus = *new. Also found in English* innovate, novelty, renovate."

novice (noun) beginner, tyro. *Lifting your head before you finish your swing is a typical mistake committed by the novice at golf.*

nuance (noun) a subtle difference or quality. *At first glance, Monet's paintings of water lilies all look much alike, but the more you study them, the more you appreciate the nuances of color and shading that distinguish them.*

nurture (verb) to nourish or help to grow. *The money given by the National Endowment for the Arts helps nurture local arts organizations throughout the country.* **nurture** (noun).

Word Origin

Latin durus = *hard. Also found in English* durable, endure."

obdurate (adjective) unwilling to change; stubborn, inflexible. *Despite the many pleas he received, the governor was obdurate in his refusal to grant clemency to the convicted murderer.*

objective (adjective) dealing with observable facts rather than opinions or interpretations. *When a legal case involves a shocking crime, it may be hard for a judge to remain objective in her rulings.*

oblivious (adjective) unaware, unconscious. *Karen practiced her oboe with complete concentration, oblivious to the noise and activity around her.* **oblivion** (noun), **obliviousness** (noun).

obscure (adjective) little known; hard to understand. *Mendel was an obscure monk until decades after his death, when his scientific work was finally discovered. Most people find the writings of James Joyce obscure; hence the popularity of books that explain his books.* **obscure** (verb), **obscurity** (noun).

obsessive (adjective) haunted or preoccupied by an idea or feeling. *His concern with cleanliness became so obsessive that he washed his hands twenty times every day.* **obsess** (verb), **obsession** (noun).

obsolete (adjective) no longer current; old-fashioned. *W. H. Auden said that his ideal landscape would include water wheels, wooden grain mills, and other forms of obsolete machinery.* **obsolescence** (noun).

obstinate (adjective) stubborn, unyielding. *Despite years of effort, the problem of drug abuse remains obstinate.* **obstinacy** (noun).

obtrusive (adjective) overly prominent. *Philip should sing more softly; his bass is so obtrusive that the other singers can barely be heard.* **obtrude** (verb), **obtrusion** (noun).

ominous (adjective) foretelling evil. *Ominous black clouds gathered on the horizon, for a violent storm was fast approaching.* **omen** (noun).

onerous (adjective) heavy, burdensome. *The hero Hercules was ordered to clean the Augean Stables, one of several onerous tasks known as "the labors of Hercules."* **onus** (noun).

opportunistic (adjective) eagerly seizing chances as they arise. *When Princess Diana died suddenly, opportunistic publishers quickly released books about her life and death.* **opportunism** (noun).

opulent (adjective) rich, lavish. *The mansion of newspaper tycoon Hearst is famous for its opulent decor.* **opulence** (noun).

ornate (adjective) highly decorated, elaborate. *Baroque architecture is often highly ornate, featuring surfaces covered with carving, sinuous curves, and painted scenes.*

ostentatious (adjective) overly showy, pretentious. *To show off his wealth, the millionaire threw an ostentatious party featuring a full orchestra, a famous singer, and tens of thousands of dollars worth of food.*

ostracize (verb) to exclude from a group. *In Biblical times, those who suffered from the disease of leprosy were ostracized and forced to live alone.* **ostracism** (noun).

pallid (adjective) pale; dull. *Working all day in the coal mine had given him a pallid complexion. The new musical offers only pallid entertainment: the music is lifeless, the acting dull, the story absurd.*

parched (adjective) very dry; thirsty. *After two months without rain, the crops were shriveled and parched by the sun.* **parch** (verb).

pariah (noun) outcast. *Accused of robbery, he became a pariah; his neighbors stopped talking to him, and people he'd considered friends no longer called.*

partisan (adjective) reflecting strong allegiance to a particular party or cause. *The vote on the president's budget was strictly partisan: every member of the president's party voted yes, and all others voted no.* **partisan** (noun).

Word Origin

Greek pathos = *suffering. Also found in English* apathy, empathy, pathetic, pathos, sympathy.

pathology (noun) disease or the study of disease; extreme abnormality. *Some people believe that high rates of crime, are symptoms of an underlying social pathology.* **pathological** (adjective).

pellucid (adjective) very clear; transparent; easy to understand. *The water in the mountain stream was cold and pellucid. Thanks to the professor's pellucid explanation, I finally understand relativity theory.*

penitent (adjective) feeling sorry for past crimes or sins. *Having grown penitent, he wrote a long letter of apology, asking forgiveness.*

penurious (adjective) extremely frugal; stingy. *Haunted by memories of poverty, he lived in penurious fashion, driving a twelve-year-old car and wearing only the cheapest clothes.* **penury** (noun).

perfunctory (adjective) unenthusiastic, routine, or mechanical. *When the play opened, the actors sparkled, but by the thousandth night their performance had become perfunctory.*

permeate (verb) to spread through or penetrate. *Little by little, the smell of gas from the broken pipe permeated the house.*

perceptive (adjective) quick to notice, observant. *With his perceptive intelligence, Holmes was the first to notice the importance of this clue.* **perceptible** (adjective), **perception** (noun).

Word Origin

Latin fides = *faith. Also found in English* confide, confidence, fidelity, infidel.

perfidious (adjective) disloyal, treacherous. *Although he was one of the most talented generals of the American Revolution, Benedict Arnold is remembered today as a perfidious betrayer of his country.* **perfidy** (noun).

persevere (adjective) to continue despite difficulties. *Although several of her teammates dropped out of the marathon, Laura persevered.* **perseverance** (noun).

perspicacity (noun) keenness of observation or understanding. *Journalist Murray Kempton was famous for the perspicacity of his comments on social and political issues.* **perspicacious** (adjective).

peruse (verb) to examine or study. *Mary-Jo perused the contract carefully before she signed it.* **perusal** (noun).

pervasive (adjective) spreading throughout. *As news of the disaster reached the town, a pervasive sense of gloom could be felt everywhere.* **pervade** (verb).

phlegmatic (adjective) sluggish and unemotional in temperament. *It was surprising to see Tom, who is normally so phlegmatic, acting excited.*

placate (verb) to soothe or appease. *The waiter tried to placate the angry customer with the offer of a free dessert.* **placatory** (adjective).

plastic (adjective) able to be molded or reshaped. *Because it is highly plastic, clay is an easy material for beginning sculptors to use.*

plausible (adjective) apparently believable. *The idea that a widespread conspiracy to kill President Kennedy has been kept secret for over thirty years hardly seems plausible.* **plausibility** (noun).

polarize (adjective) to separate into opposing groups or forces. *For years, the abortion debate polarized the American people, with many people voicing extreme views and few trying to find a middle ground.* **polarization** (noun).

portend (verb) to indicate a future event; to forebode. *According to folklore, a red sky at dawn portends a day of stormy weather.*

potentate (noun) a powerful ruler. *Before the Russian Revolution, the Tsar was one of the last hereditary potentates of Europe.*

pragmatism (noun) a belief in approaching problems through practical rather than theoretical means. *Roosevelt's approach toward the Great Depression was based on pragmatism: "Try something," he said; "If it doesn't work, try something else."* **pragmatic** (adjective).

Word Origin

Latin ambulare = *to walk. Also found in English* ambulatory, circumambulate, perambulate.

preamble (noun) an introductory statement. *The preamble to the Constitution begins with the famous words, "We the people of the United States of America . . ."*

precocious (adjective) mature at an unusually early age. *Picasso was so precocious as an artist that, at nine, he is said to have painted far better pictures than his teacher.* **precocity** (noun).

predatory (adjective) living by killing and eating other animals; exploiting others for personal gain. *The tiger is the largest predatory animal native to Asia. Microsoft has been accused of predatory business practices that prevent other software companies from competing with them.* **predation** (noun), **predator** (noun).

predilection (noun) a liking or preference. *To relax from his presidential duties, Kennedy had a predilection for spy novels featuring James Bond.*

Word Origin

Latin dominare = *to rule. Also found in English* dominate, domineer, dominion, indomitable.

predominant (adjective) greatest in numbers or influence. *Although hundreds of religions are practiced in India, the predominant faith is Hinduism.* **predominance** (noun), **predominate** (verb).

prepossessing (adjective) attractive. *Smart, lovely, and talented, she has all the prepossessing qualities that mark a potential movie star.*

presumptuous (adjective) going beyond the limits of courtesy or appropriateness. *The senator winced when the presumptuous young staffer addressed him as "Chuck."* **presume** (verb), **presumption** (noun).

pretentious (adjective) claiming excessive value or importance. *For an ordinary shoe salesman to call himself a "Personal Foot Apparel Consultant" seems awfully pretentious.* **pretension** (noun).

procrastinate (verb) to put off, to delay. *If you habitually procrastinate, try this technique: never touch a piece of paper without either filing it, responding to it, or throwing it out.* **procrastination** (noun).

profane (adjective) impure, unholy. *It seems inappropriate to have such profane activities as roller blading and disco dancing in a church.* **profane** (verb), **profanity** (noun).

proficient (adjective) skillful, adept. *A proficient artist, Louise quickly and accurately sketched the scene.* **proficiency** (noun).

proliferate (verb) to increase or multiply. *Over the past fifteen years, high-tech companies have proliferated in northern California, Massachusetts, and other regions.* **proliferation** (noun).

prolific (adjective) producing many offspring or creations. *With over three hundred books to his credit, Isaac Asimov was one of the most prolific writers of all time.*

prominence (noun) the quality of standing out; fame. *Kennedy's victory in the West Virginia primary gave him a position of prominence among the Democratic candidates for president.* **prominent** (adjective).

promulgate (verb) to make public, to declare. *Lincoln signed the proclamation that freed the slaves in 1862, but he waited several months to promulgate it.*

propagate (verb) to cause to grow; to foster. *John Smithson's will left his fortune for the founding of an institution to propagate knowledge, without saying whether that meant a university, a library, or a museum.* **propagation** (noun).

propriety (noun) appropriateness. *Some people had doubts about the propriety of Clinton's discussing his underwear on MTV.*

prosaic (adjective) everyday, ordinary, dull. *"Paul's Case" tells the story of a boy who longs to escape from the prosaic life of a clerk into a world of wealth, glamour, and beauty.*

Word Origin

Latin vocare = *to call. Also found in English* evoke, invoke, revoke, vocal, vocation.

protagonist (noun) the main character in a story or play; the main supporter of an idea. *Leopold Bloom is the protagonist of James Joyce's great novel Ulysses.*

provocative (adjective) likely to stimulate emotions, ideas, or controversy. *The demonstrators began chanting obscenities, a provocative act that they hoped would cause the police to lose control.* **provoke** (verb), **provocation** (noun).

proximity (noun) closeness, nearness. *Neighborhood residents were angry over the proximity of the sewage plant to the local school.* **proximate** (adjective).

prudent (adjective) wise, cautious, and practical. *A prudent investor will avoid putting all of her money into any single investment.* **prudence** (noun), **prudential** (adjective).

Word Origin

Latin proximus = *near, next. Also found in English* approximate.

pugnacious (adjective) combative, bellicose, truculent; ready to fight. *Ty Cobb, the pugnacious outfielder for the Detroit Tigers, got into more than his fair share of brawls, both on and off the field.* **pugnacity** (noun).

punctilious (adjective) very concerned about proper forms of behavior and manners. *A punctilious dresser like James would rather skip the party altogether than wear the wrong color tie.* **punctilio** (noun).

pundit (noun) someone who offers opinions in an authoritative style. *The Sunday afternoon talk shows are filled with pundits, each with his or her own theory about this week's political news.*

Word Origin

Latin pungere = *to jab, to prick. Also found in English* pugilist, punctuate, puncture, pungent.

punitive (adjective) inflicting punishment. *The jury awarded the plaintiff one million dollars in punitive damages, hoping to teach the defendant a lesson.*

purify (verb) to make pure, clean, or perfect. *The new plant is supposed to purify the drinking water provided to everyone in the nearby towns.* **purification** (noun).

quell (verb) to quiet, to suppress. *It took a huge number of police to quell the rioting.*

querulous (adjective) complaining, whining. *The nursing home attendant needed a lot of patience to care for the three querulous, unpleasant residents on his floor.*

rancorous (adjective) expressing bitter hostility. *Many Americans are dis- gusted by recent political campaigns, which seem more rancorous than ever before.* **rancor** (noun).

rationale (noun) an underlying reason or explanation. *At first, it seemed strange that several camera companies would freely share their newest technology; but their rationale was that offering one new style of film would benefit them all.*

raze (verb) to completely destroy; demolish. *The old Coliseum building will soon be razed to make room for a new hotel.*

reciprocate (verb) to make a return for something. *If you'll baby-sit for my kids tonight, I'll reciprocate by taking care of yours tomorrow.* **reciprocity** (noun).

reclusive (adjective) withdrawn from society. *During the last years of her life, actress Greta Garbo led a reclusive existence, rarely appearing in public.* **recluse** (noun).

reconcile (verb) to make consistent or harmonious. *Roosevelt's greatness as a leader can be seen in his ability to reconcile the demands and values of the varied groups that supported him.* **reconciliation** (noun).

recriminate (verb) to accuse, often in response to an accusation. *Divorce proceedings sometimes become bitter, as the two parties recriminate each other over the causes of the breakup.* **recrimination** (noun), **recriminatory** (adjective).

recuperate (verb) to regain health after an illness. *Although she left the hospital two days after her operation, it took her a few weeks to fully recuperate.* **recuperation** (noun), **recuperative** (adjective).

redoubtable (adjective) inspiring respect, awe, or fear. *Johnson's knowledge, experience, and personal clout made him a redoubtable political opponent.*

refurbish (verb) to fix up; renovate. *It took three days' work by a team of carpenters, painters, and decorators to completely refurbish the apartment.*

refute (adjective) to prove false. *The company invited reporters to visit their plant in an effort to refute the charges of unsafe working conditions.* **refutation** (noun).

relevance (noun) connection to the matter at hand; pertinence. *Testimony in a criminal trial may be admitted only if it has clear relevance to the question of guilt or innocence.* **relevant** (adjective).

remedial (adjective) serving to remedy, cure, or correct some condition. *Affirmative action can be justified as a remedial step to help minority members overcome the effects of past discrimination.* **remediation** (noun), **remedy** (verb).

remorse (noun) a painful sense of guilt over wrongdoing. *In Poe's story "The Tell-Tale Heart," a murderer is driven insane by remorse over his crime.* **remorseful** (adjective).

remuneration (noun) pay. *In a civil lawsuit, the attorney often receives part of the financial settlement as his or her remuneration.* **remunerate** (verb), **remunerative** (adjective).

renovate (verb) to renew by repairing or rebuilding. *The television program "This Old House" shows how skilled craftspeople renovate houses.* **renovation** (noun).

renunciation (noun) the act of rejecting or refusing something. *King Edward VII's renunciation of the British throne was caused by his desire to marry an American divorcee, something he couldn't do as king.* **renounce** (verb).

replete (adjective) filled abundantly. *Graham's book is replete with wonderful stories about the famous people she has known.*

reprehensible (adjective) deserving criticism or censure. *Although Pete Rose's misdeeds were reprehensible, not all fans agree that he deserves to be excluded from the Baseball Hall of Fame.* **reprehend** (verb), **reprehension** (noun).

repudiate (verb) to reject, to renounce. *After it became known that Duke had been a leader of the Ku Klux Klan, most Republican leaders repudiated him.* **repudiation** (noun).

Word Origin

Latin putare = *to reckon. Also found in English* compute, dispute, impute, putative.

reputable (adjective) having a good reputation; respected. *Find a reputable auto mechanic by asking your friends for recommendations based on their own experiences.* **reputation** (noun), **repute** (noun).

resilient (adjective) able to recover from difficulty. *A pro athlete must be resilient, able to lose a game one day and come back the next with confidence and enthusiasm.* **resilience** (adjective).

resplendent (adjective) glowing, shining. *In late December, midtown New York is resplendent with holiday lights and decorations.* **resplendence** (noun).

responsive (adjective) reacting quickly and appropriately. *The new director of the Internal Revenue Service has promised to make the agency more responsive to public complaints.* **respond** (verb), **response** (noun).

restitution (noun) return of something to its original owner; repayment. *Some Native American leaders are demanding that the U.S. government make restitution for the lands taken from them by white settlers.*

revere (verb) to admire deeply, to honor. *Millions of people around the world revered Mother Teresa for her saintly generosity.* **reverence** (noun), **reverent** (adjective).

rhapsodize (verb) to praise in a wildly emotional way. *That critic is such a huge fan of Toni Morrison that she will surely rhapsodize over the writer's next novel.* **rhapsodic** (adjective).

sagacious (adjective) discerning, wise. *Only a leader as sagacious as Nelson Mandela could have united South Africa so successfully and peacefully.* **sagacity** (noun).

salvage (verb) to save from wreck or ruin. *After the earthquake destroyed her home, she was able to salvage only a few of her belongings.* **salvage** (noun), **salvageable** (adjective).

Word Origin

Latin sanctus = *holy. Also found in English* sanctify, sanction, sanctity, sanctuary.

sanctimonious (adjective) showing false or excessive piety. *The sanctimonious prayers of the TV preacher were interspersed with requests that the viewers send him money.* **sanctimony** (noun).

scapegoat (noun) someone who bears the blame for others' acts; someone hated for no apparent reason. *Although Buckner's error was only one reason the Red Sox lost, many fans made him the scapegoat, booing him mercilessly.*

scrupulous (adjective) acting with extreme care; painstaking. *Disney theme parks are famous for their scrupulous attention to small details.* **scruple** (noun).

scrutinize (verb) to study closely. *The lawyer scrutinized the contract, searching for any sentence that could pose a risk for her client.* **scrutiny** (noun).

secrete (verb) to emit; to hide. *Glands in the mouth secrete saliva, a liquid that helps in digestion. The jewel thieves secreted the necklace in a tin box buried underground.*

Word Origin

Latin sedere = *to sit. Also found in English* sedate, sedative, sediment.

sedentary (adjective) requiring much sitting. *When Officer Samson was given a desk job, she had trouble getting used to sedentary work after years on the street.*

sequential (adjective) arranged in an order or series. *The courses for the chemistry major are sequential; you must take them in the order, since each course builds on the previous ones.* **sequence** (noun).

serendipity (noun) the ability to make lucky accidental discoveries. *Great inventions sometimes come about through deliberate research and hard work, sometimes through pure serendipity.* **serendipitous** (adjective).

servile (adjective) like a slave or servant; submissive. *The tycoon demanded that his underlings behave in a servile manner, agreeing quickly with everything he said.* **servility** (noun).

Word Origin

Latin simulare = *to resemble. Also found in English* semblance, similarity, simulacrum, simultaneous, verisimiltude.

simulated (adjective) imitating something else; artificial. *High-quality simulated gems must be examined under a magnifying glass to be distinguished from real ones.* **simulate** (verb), **simulation** (noun).

solace (verb) to comfort or console. *There was little the rabbi could say to solace the husband after his wife's death.* **solace** (noun).

spontaneous (adjective) happening without plan or outside cause. *When the news of Kennedy's assassination broke, people everywhere gathered in a spontaneous effort to share their shock and grief.* **spontaneity** (noun).

spurious (adjective) false, fake. *The so-called Piltdown Man, supposed to be the fossil of a primitive human, turned out to be spurious, although who created the hoax is still uncertain.*

squander (verb) to use up carelessly, to waste. *Those who had made donations to the charity were outraged to learn that its director had squandered millions on fancy dinners and first-class travel.*

staid (adjective) sedate, serious, and grave. *This college is no "party school"; the students all work hard, and the campus has a reputation for being staid.*

stagnate (verb) to become stale through lack of movement or change. *Having had no contact with the outside world for generations, Japan's culture gradually stagnated.* **stagnant** (adjective), **stagnation** (noun).

stimulus (noun) something that excites a response or provokes an action. *The arrival of merchants and missionaries from the West provided a stimulus for change in Japanese society.* **stimulate** (verb).

stoic (adjective) showing little feeling, even in response to pain or sorrow. *A soldier must respond to the death of his comrades in stoic fashion, since the fighting will not stop for his grief.* **stoicism** (noun).

strenuous (adjective) requiring energy and strength. *Hiking in the foothills of the Rockies is fairly easy, but climbing the higher peaks can be strenuous.*

submissive (adjective) accepting the will of others; humble, compliant. *At the end of Ibsen's play* A Doll's House, *Nora leaves her husband and abandons the role of submissive housewife.*

substantiated (adjective) verified or supported by evidence. *The charge that Nixon had helped to cover up crimes was substantiated by his comments about it on a series of audio tapes.* **substantiate** (verb), **substantiation** (noun).

sully (verb) to soil, stain, or defile. *Nixon's misdeeds as president did much to sully the reputation of the American government.*

superficial (adjective) on the surface only; without depth or substance. *Her wound was superficial and required only a light bandage. His superficial attractiveness hides the fact that his personality is lifeless and his mind is dull.* **superficiality** (noun).

superfluous (adjective) more than is needed, excessive. *Once you've won the debate, don't keep talking; superfluous arguments will only bore and annoy the audience.*

suppress (verb) to put down or restrain. *As soon as the unrest began, thousands of helmeted police were sent into the streets to suppress the riots.* **suppression** (noun).

surfeit (noun) an excess. *Most American families have a surfeit of food and drink on Thanksgiving Day.* **surfeit** (verb).

surreptitious (adjective) done in secret. *Because Iraq has avoided weapons inspections, many believe it has a surreptitious weapons development program.*

surrogate (noun) a substitute. *When the congressman died in office, his wife was named to serve the rest of his term as a surrogate.* **surrogate** (adjective).

sustain (verb) to keep up, to continue; to support. *Because of fatigue, he was unable to sustain the effort needed to finish the marathon.*

tactile (adjective) relating to the sense of touch. *The thick brush strokes and gobs of color give the paintings of Van Gogh a strongly tactile quality.* **tactility** (noun).

talisman (noun) an object supposed to have magical effects or qualities. *Superstitious people sometimes carry a rabbit's foot, a lucky coin, or some other talisman.*

Word Origin

Latin tangere = *to touch. Also found in English* contact, contiguous, tangent, tangible.

tangential (adjective) touching lightly; only slightly connected or related. *Having enrolled in a class on African-American history, the students found the teacher's stories about his travels in South America only of tangential interest.* **tangent** (noun).

tedium (noun) boredom. *For most people, watching the Weather Channel for 24 hours would be sheer tedium.* **tedious** (adjective).

temerity (noun) boldness, rashness, excessive daring. *Only someone who didn't understand the danger would have the temerity to try to climb Everest without a guide.* **temerarious** (adjective).

temperance (noun) moderation or restraint in feelings and behavior. *Most professional athletes practice temperance in their personal habits; too much eating or drinking, they know, can harm their performance.* **temperate** (adjective).

Word Origin

Latin tenere = *to hold. Also found in English* retain, tenable, tenant, tenet, tenure.

tenacious (adjective) clinging, sticky, or persistent. *Tenacious in pursuit of her goal, she applied for the grant unsuccessfully four times before it was finally approved.* **tenacity** (noun).

tentative (adjective) subject to change; uncertain. *A firm schedule has not been established, but the Super Bowl in 2002 has been given the tentative date of January 20.*

terminate (verb) to end, to close. *The Olympic Games terminate with a grand ceremony attended by athletes from every participating country.* **terminal** (noun), **termination** (noun).

terrestrial (adjective) of the Earth. *The movie* Close Encounters *tells the story of the first contact between beings from outer space and terrestrial humans.*

therapeutic (adjective) curing or helping to cure. *Hot-water spas were popular in the nineteenth century among the sickly, who believed that soaking in the water had therapeutic effects.* **therapy** (noun).

timorous (adjective) fearful, timid. *The cowardly lion approached the throne of the wizard with a timorous look on his face.*

toady (noun) someone who flatters a superior in hopes of gaining favor; a sycophant. *"I can't stand a toady!" declared the movie mogul. "Give me someone who'll tell me the truth—even if it costs him his job!"* **toady** (verb).

tolerant (adjective) accepting, enduring. *San Franciscans have a tolerant attitude about lifestyles: "Live and let live" seems to be their motto.* **tolerate** (verb), **toleration** (noun).

toxin (noun) poison. *DDT is a powerful toxin once used to kill insects but now banned in the U.S. because of the risk it poses to human life.* **toxic** (adjective).

tranquillity (noun) freedom from disturbance or turmoil; calm. *She moved from New York City to rural Vermont seeking the tranquillity of country life.* **tranquil** (adjective).

transient (adjective) passing quickly. *Long-term visitors to this hotel pay at a different rate than transient guests who stay for just a day or two.* **transience** (noun).

transgress (verb) to go past limits; to violate. *If Iraq has developed biological weapons, then it has transgressed the United Nation's rules against weapons of mass destruction.* **transgression** (noun).

transitory (adjective) quickly passing. *Public moods tend to be transitory; people may be anxious and angry one month, but relatively content and optimistic the next.* **transition** (noun).

translucent (adjective) letting some light pass through. *Blocks of translucent glass let daylight into the room while maintaining privacy.*

transmute (verb) to change in form or substance. *In the middle ages, the alchemists tried to discover ways to transmute metals such as iron into gold.* **transmutation** (noun).

treacherous (adjective) untrustworthy or disloyal; dangerous or unreliable. *Nazi Germany proved to be a treacherous ally, first signing a peace pact with the Soviet Union, then invading. Be careful crossing the rope bridge; parts are badly frayed and treacherous.* **treachery** (noun).

tremulous (adjective) trembling or shaking; timid or fearful. *Never having spoken in public before, he began his speech in a tremulous, hesitant voice.*

trite (adjective) boring because of over-familiarity; hackneyed. *Her letters were filled with trite expressions, like "All's well that ends well," and "So far so good."*

truculent (adjective) aggressive, hostile, belligerent. *Hitler's truculent behavior in demanding more territory for Germany made it clear that war was inevitable.* **truculence** (noun).

truncate (verb) to cut off. *The manuscript of the play appeared truncated; the last page ended in the middle of a scene, halfway through the first act.*

Word Origin

Latin turba = *confusion. Also found in English disturb, perturb, turbid.*

turbulent (adjective) agitated or disturbed. *The night before the championship match, Martina was unable to sleep, her mind turbulent with fears and hopes.* **turbulence** (noun).

unheralded (adjective) little known, unexpected. *In a year of big-budget, much-hyped mega-movies, this unheralded foreign film has surprised everyone with its popularity.*

unpalatable (adjective) distasteful, unpleasant. *Although I agree with the candidate on many issues, I can't vote for her, because I find her position on capital punishment unpalatable.*

unparalleled (adjective) with no equal; unique. *Tiger Woods's victory in the Masters golf tournament by a full twelve strokes was an unparalleled accomplishment.*

unstinting (adjective) giving freely and generously. *Eleanor Roosevelt was much admired for her unstinting efforts on behalf of the poor.*

untenable (adjective) impossible to defend. *The theory that this painting is a genuine Van Gogh became untenable when the artist who actually painted it came forth.*

untimely (adjective) out of the natural or proper time. *The untimely death of a youthful Princess Diana seemed far more tragic than Mother Teresa's death of old age.*

unyielding (adjective) firm, resolute, obdurate. *Despite criticism, Cuomo was unyielding in his opposition to capital punishment; he vetoed several death penalty bills as governor.*

usurper (noun) someone who takes a place or possession without the right to do so. *Kennedy's most devoted followers tended to regard later presidents as usurpers, holding the office they felt he or his brothers should have held.* **usurp** (verb), **usurpation** (noun).

utilitarian (adjective) purely of practical benefit. *The design of the Model T car was simple and utilitarian, lacking the luxuries found in later models.*

utopia (noun) an imaginary, perfect society. *Those who founded the Oneida community dreamed that it could be a kind of utopia—a prosperous state with complete freedom and harmony.* **utopian** (adjective).

validate (verb) to officially approve or confirm. *The election of the president is validated when the members of the Electoral College meet to confirm the choice of the voters.* **valid** (adjective), **validity** (noun).

variegated (adjective) spotted with different colors. *The brilliant, variegated appearance of butterflies makes them popular among collectors.* **variegation** (noun).

venerate (verb) to admire or honor. *In Communist China, Chairman Mao Zedong was venerated as an almost god-like figure.* **venerable** (adjective), **veneration** (noun).

verdant (adjective) green with plant life. *Southern England is famous for its verdant countryside filled with gardens and small farms.* **verdancy** (noun).

vestige (noun) a trace or remainder. *Today's tiny Sherwood Forest is the last vestige of a woodland that once covered most of England.* **vestigial** (adjective).

vex (verb) to irritate, annoy, or trouble. *Unproven for generations, Fermat's last theorem was one of the most famous, and most vexing, of all mathematical puzzles.* **vexation** (noun).

vicarious (adjective) experienced through someone else's actions by way of the imagination. *Great literature broadens our minds by giving us vicarious participation in the lives of other people.*

vindicate (verb) to confirm, justify, or defend. *Lincoln's Gettysburg Address was intended to vindicate the objectives of the Union in the Civil War.*

Word Origin

virtus = *strength. Also found in English* virtue.

virtuoso (noun) someone very skilled, especially in an art. *Vladimir Horowitz was one of the great piano virtuosos of the twentieth century.* **virtuosity** (noun).

vivacious (adjective) lively, sprightly. *The role of Maria in "The Sound of Music" is usually played by a charming, vivacious young actress.* **vivacity** (noun).

volatile (adjective) quickly changing; fleeting, transitory; prone to violence. *Public opinion is notoriously volatile; a politician who is very popular one month may be voted out of office the next.* **volatility** (noun).

whimsical (adjective) based on a capricious, carefree, or sudden impulse or idea; fanciful, playful. *Dave Barry's* Book of Bad Songs *is filled with the kind of goofy jokes that are typical of his whimsical sense of humor.* **whim** (noun).

zealous (adjective) filled with eagerness, fervor, or passion. *A crowd of the candidate's most zealous supporters greeted her at the airport with banners, signs, and a marching band.* **zeal** (noun), **zealot** (noun), **zealotry** (noun).

Appendix B

The Insider's SAT Math Review

Perhaps more than any other school subject, math creates a gulf between classes of students. Generally speaking, there are students who think of themselves as "good at math," who do well in all the usual math subjects and often take advanced classes in their junior and senior years of high school. Then there are the others, more numerous, who are a little afraid of math. They take only those math classes they are required to take, and breathe a sigh of relief when they pass.

Here's the good news. The test-makers know that the SAT will be taken by hundreds of thousands of students in both classes. *They've deliberately designed the exam to be fair to both.* As a result, many of the math topics that high school students find most intimidating—such as trigonometry and calculus—do not appear on the test. Since many students are never exposed to these subjects, the test-makers wouldn't consider it fair to test them. Instead, they restrict their questions to topics that virtually all high school students study in the ninth and tenth grades.

This doesn't mean that all of the SAT math questions are easy. But it does mean that it's highly unlikely that you'll be tested on any topic you never learned in high school.

In the Insider's SAT Math Review, we've selected the fifty math topics most frequently tested on the exam. For each, we've created a mini-lesson reviewing the basic facts, formulas, and concepts you need to know. We've also provided an example or two of how these concepts might be turned into test questions.

You'll probably find that you are comfortable with many of the topics included in the "Nifty Fifty" that follows. If so, great. Make a note of the other topics—the ones you find confusing, tricky, or difficult. Perhaps you never quite mastered those concepts when they were presented in class, or you've forgotten the details in the intervening months. In your study between now and the day of the SAT, concentrate on reviewing and practicing these topics. You can boost your SAT math score significantly by mastering as many of your personal "math demons" as possible.

ARITHMETIC

Topic 1. Numbers and the Number Line

Real numbers can be represented as points on a line. Usually, we think about a horizontal line, with one point chosen to represent zero. All the positive numbers are to the right of zero, and all the negative numbers are to the left. The numbers get larger as you go from left to right.

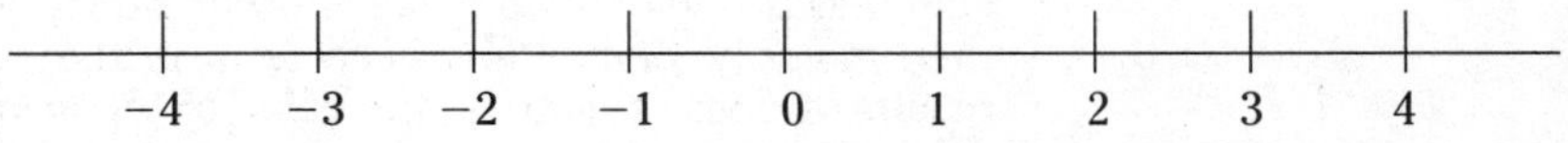

The farther you get from zero, the larger the *absolute value* of a number is. So, numbers far to the left are negative numbers with large absolute values.

Example 1

On the number line shown below, where is the number that is less than E and half as far from E as E is from H?

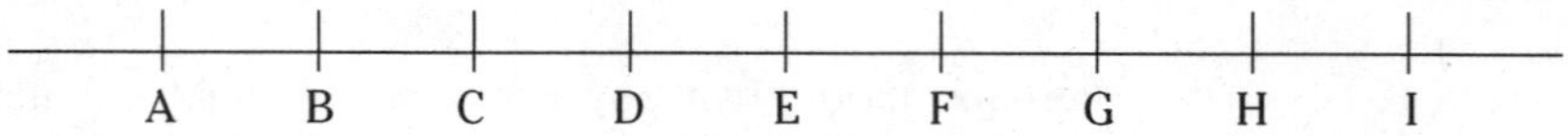

Solution

First, any number less than E must lie to the left of E. (Get it? Left = Less!) The distance from E to H is 3 units. Thus, the point we want must be 1 units to the left of E. Hence, it is halfway between C and D.

FYI

When a number line is shown on the exam, you can safely assume that the line is drawn to scale (unless otherwise indicated) and that numbers between the markings are at appropriate locations. However, be sure to check the scale, because the "tick marks" do not *have to be at unit intervals!*

Example 2

On the number line shown below, which point corresponds to the number 1.26?

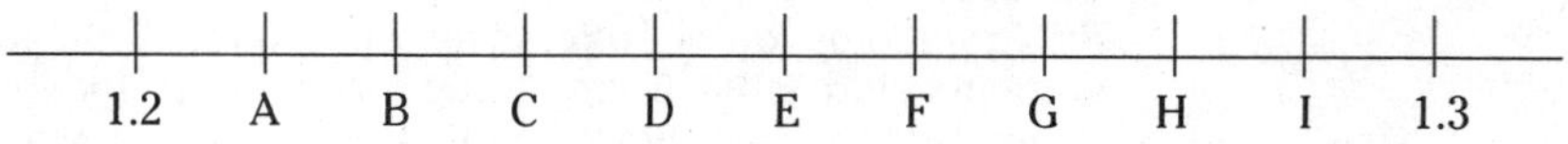

Solution

Since the labeled end points are 1.2 and 1.3, the ten intervals between must each represent one-tenth of the difference. Hence the "tick marks" must represent hundredths. That is, A = 1.21, B = 1.22, and so on. Thus, we know that F = 1.26.

Topic 2. Laws of Arithmetic and Order of Operations

In carrying out arithmetic or algebraic operations, you should follow the famous mnemonic (memory) device Please My Dear Aunt Sally. The operations of Parentheses, Multiplication, Division, Addition, and Subtraction should be carried out *in that order.*

If we want to indicate a change in order, we place the operation in parentheses creating one number. In other words, calculate the number within parentheses first. Thus, $5 + 3 \times 4 = 5 + 12 = 17$, because we multiply before adding. If we instead want the number $5 + 3$ to be multiplied by 4, we must write $(5 + 3) \times 4 = 8 \times 4 = 32$.

The basic laws of arithmetic were defined for whole numbers, but they carry over to all numbers. You should be very familiar with all of them from past experience. They are:

- **The commutative law.** This says that it doesn't matter in which order you add or multiply two numbers. That is, $a + b = b + a$, and $ab = ba$.
- **The associative law** (also called *the Regrouping law*). This law says that it doesn't matter how you group the numbers when you add or multiply more than two. That is, $a + (b + c) = (a + b) + c$, and $a(bc) = (ab)c$. Notice that enclosing the numbers in parentheses indicates that the operation within the parentheses should be done first.
- **The distributive law** for multiplication over addition. This law can be stated as $a(b + c) = ab + ac$. In other words, you can either add first and then multiply, or multiply each term in the sum by a and then add the results. It doesn't matter—the value of the answer will be the same.
- **The properties of zero and one.** Zero times any number is zero. Zero added to any number leaves the number unchanged. One times any

number leaves the number unchanged. Finally, it is very important to know that if the product of several numbers is zero, at least one of the numbers must be zero.

- **The additive inverse** (or opposite). For every number n there is a number $-n$ such that $n + (-n) = 0$.
- **The multiplicative inverse.** For every number n except 0, there exists a number $\frac{1}{n}$, such that $\left(\frac{1}{n}\right)(n) = 1$. Division by n is the same as multiplication by $\frac{1}{n}$. And *division by zero is never allowed.*

Example

What is the value of $\frac{3 + 4 \cdot 3}{6 \cdot 3 - 3A}$ if $A = 3$? What value may A NOT have?

Solution

The fraction bar in a fraction acts as a "grouping symbol" like parentheses, meaning we should calculate the numerator and denominator separately. Therefore, we should read this as $(3 + 4 \times 3)$, $(6 \times 3 - 3 \times A)$. The numerator is $3 + 12 = 15$. When $A = 3$, the denominator is $18 - 3 \times 3 = 18 - 9 = 9$.

Therefore, the fraction is $\frac{15}{9} = \frac{5}{3}$. Since we cannot divide by zero, we cannot let $6 \times 3 - 3 \times A = 0$. But in order for this to be zero, $6 \times 3 = 3 \times A$. By the commutative law, $A = 6$. Thus, the only value that A cannot have is 6.

Topic 3. Divisibility Rules

FYI

If you want to know whether k *is a divisor of* n, *simply try to divide* k *into* n *and see if there is any remainder. If the remainder is zero, then* n *is divisible by* k.

A *factor* or *divisor* of a whole number is a number that divides evenly into the given number, that is, leaving no remainder. For example, the divisors of 28 are 1, 2, 4, 7, 14, and 28 itself. A *proper divisor* is any divisor except the number itself. Thus, the proper divisors of 28 are 1, 2, 4, 7, and 14.

There are several useful rules for testing for divisibility for certain small numbers. These are summarized in the following table.

Number	Divides into a number N if:
2	N is even, that is, it ends in 2, 4, 6, 8, or 0
3	the sum of the digits if N is divisible by 3
4	the last two digits form a number divisible by 4
5	the number ends in 5 or 0
6	the number is divisible by 2 and 3
8	the last three digits form a number divisible by 8
9	the sum of the digits of N is divisible by 9
10	the number ends in 0

For example, consider the number 7,890. It is divisible by all the numbers in the table except 4, 8, and 9. Do you see why? To start, 7,890 is divisible by 10 and 5 because it ends in 0. It is divisible by 2, because it is even—but not by 4, because 90 is not divisible by 4. Of course, it cannot be divisible by 8 unless it is already divisible by 4. In addition, the sum of its digits is 24, which is divisible by 3 but not 9. Finally, since it is divisible by both 2 and 3, it is also divisible by 6.

Example

Which numbers in the following list are divisible by 5 and 3, but NOT 4?

10,435
20,085
23,096
56,700
79,140

Solution

The easiest thing to look for is divisibility by 5. Just ask, does the number end in 5 or 0? By inspection, we eliminate 23,096, which ends in 6. Now, we don't want the number to be divisible by 4, so we knock out all the even numbers, leaving 10,435 and 20,085. The digits of 10,435 add up to 13, while those of 20,085 total 15. Therefore, only 20,085 is divisible by 3 and 5, but not by 4.

Topic 4. Divisibility in Addition, Subtraction, and Multiplication

If you add or subtract two numbers that are both divisible by some number k, then the new number formed will also be divisible by k. For example, 21 and 15 are both divisible by 3. If you take their sum, 36, or their difference, 6, either number is also divisible by 3.

If you multiply two numbers together, any number that divides either one will divide the product. That is: if j divides M and k divides N, then jk divides MN. If both have a common divisor, then the product is divisible by the square of that number. Thus, $21 \times 15 = 315$ is divisible by 7, because 7 divides 21, and by 5 because 5 divides 15. It is also divisible by $35 = 5 \times 7$ and by 9, because $9 = 3^2$ and 3 divides both 21 and 15.

Example 1

If k is divisible by 7, what is the largest number that must divide into $8k + 14$?

Solution

Since k is divisible by 7, and 8 is divisible by 2, $8k$ can be divided by 14. Therefore, the sum $8k + 14$ can be divided by 14.

Example 2

If a and b are whole numbers and $5a = 4b$ which of the following must be true?

I. a is divisible by 4
II. b is divisible by 4
III. b is divisible by 5

(A) I only
(B) II only
(C) III only
(D) I and II only
(E) I and III only

Solution

If $5a$ equals $4b$, then $5a$ must be divisible by 4, which means a must be divisible by 4, since 5 is not. Similarly, $4b$ must be divisible by 5, which means b must be divisible by 5, since 4 is not. Which means the correct choice is (E): Both I and III must be true. Notice that II need not be true; since $b = 5$, $a = 4$ is a perfectly satisfactory solution.

Topic 5. Even Numbers and Odd Numbers

Even numbers are those that are divisible by 2: 0,2,4,6, . . . Odd numbers are not divisible by 2: 1,3,5, . . . Certain simple results follow from these definitions, and they can be very useful. They are:

- If you add or subtract two even numbers, the result is even.
- If you add or subtract two odd numbers the result is even.
- Only when you *add or subtract* an *odd and an even* number is the result *odd.* (Thus, $4 + 8$ is even, as is $9 - 3$. But $4 + 5$ is odd.)
- If you multiply any whole number by an even number, the result is even.
- Only when you *multiply two odd numbers* will the result be *odd.* (Again, (4)(6) and (4)(7) are both even, but (5)(7) is odd.)

Example 1

If $3k + 2c$ is an even number, is k odd or even—or can't you tell?

Solution

$2c$ must be even (because of the even factor 2), so for the sum of $3k$ and $2c$ to be even, $3k$ must also be even. But 3 is odd, so k is even.

Example 2

If $121 - 5k$ is divisible by 3, can k be odd?

Solution

The fact that a number is divisible by 3 does not make it odd. (Think of 6 or 12.) Therefore, $121 - 5k$ could be either odd or even. It will be odd when k is even, and even when k is odd. (Do you see why?) Thus, k could be odd or even. For example, for $k = 2$, $121 - 5k = 111$, which is divisible by 3; and for $k = 5$, $121 - 5k = 96$, which is divisible by 3.

Topic 6. Least Common Multiples

Given two numbers M and N, any number that is divisible by both is called a *common multiple* of M and N. The *least common multiple* (LCM) of the two numbers is the *smallest* number that is divisible by both. For example, 9 and 12 both divide into 108, so 108 is a common multiple of 9 and 12, but the LCM is 36.

For small numbers, the easiest way to find the LCM is to mentally, or in writing, list the multiples of each until you find the first "common" multiple. For example, for 9 and 12 we have:

$9\ 18\ 27\ \underline{36}\ 45 \ldots$

$12\ 24\ \underline{36}\ 48\ 60 \ldots$

We see that the first number that appears in both lists is 36.

However, the traditional method, which is really the method that translates most readily into algebra, requires that you find the *prime factorization* of the numbers. You are expected to know that every whole number is either *prime* or *composite*. A prime is a whole number greater than 1 for which the only factors (divisors) are 1 and the number itself. Any number not a prime is a composite number.

All composite numbers can be factored into primes in an essentially unique way. To find an LCM, you must find the smallest number that contains all the prime factors of both numbers. Thus, 9 factors as (3)(3), and 12 factors as (2)(2)(3). The smallest number to use all the prime factors of both has to have factors (3)(3)(2)(2) = 36.

This definition also extends to sets of more than two numbers. Thus, the LCM of 12, 15, and 20, must contain all the prime factors of all three numbers: (2)(2)(3), (3)(5), (2)(2)(5). That is, (2)(2)(3)(5) = 60.

Example 1

Find the LCM for 36 and 30.

Solution

Using prime factorization, 36 = (2)(2)(3)(3); 30 = (2)(3)(5). Since the prime factorization of both numbers includes 2 and 3, we'll start with those. Then we need to multiply in one more 2 and one more 3 to have all the prime factors of 36 and one 5 to have all the prime factors of 30. Thus, the LCM = (2)(2)(3)(3)(5) = 180.

Example 2

If the LCM of $5k$ and 20 is 100, what is k?

Solution

Using prime factorization, 20 = (2)(2)(5) and 100 = (2)(2)(5)(5). Why are there two factors of 5 in the LCM? It must be that $5k$ has two factors of 5. That is, k must itself have a factor 5. Hence, $k = 5x$, for some x. In order to have only two 2's and two 5's in the LCM, x could only be 1, 2, or 4. That is, k = 5, 10, or 20.

Topic 7. Equality of Fractions

Two fractions $\frac{a}{b}$ and $\frac{c}{d}$ are defined to be equal if $ad = bc$. For example, $\frac{3}{4} = \frac{9}{12}$ because (3)(12) = (4)(9). This definition, using *cross-multiplication*, is very useful in solving algebraic equations involving fractions. However, for working with numbers, the important thing to remember is that multiplying the numerator and denominator of a fraction by the same number (other than zero) results in a fraction equal in value to the original fraction. Thus, by multiplying top and bottom by 3, we have $\frac{3}{4} = \frac{(3)(3)}{(3)(4)} = \frac{9}{12}$.

Similarly, dividing the numerator and denominator of a fraction by the same number (other than zero) results in a fraction equal in value to the original fraction. It is usual to divide through top and bottom by the greatest common factor of both numerator and denominator to "reduce the fraction to lowest terms." Thus, by dividing top and bottom by 5, we have $\frac{15}{25} = \frac{15 \div 5}{25 \div 5} = \frac{3}{5}$.

Example 1

If b and c are both positive integers (whole numbers) greater than 1, and $\frac{5}{c} = \frac{b}{3}$, what are b and c?

Solution
Using cross-multiplication, $bc = 15$. The only ways 15 can be the product of two positive integers is as (1)(15) or (3)(5). Since both b and c must be greater than 1, one must be 3 and the other 5. Trying both cases, it is easy to see that the only possibility is that $b = 3$ and $c = 5$, and both fractions are equal to 1.

Example 2
If the fraction $\frac{60}{N}$ has been reduced to lowest terms, which of the following numbers can be a factor of N: {25, 27, 49, 110, 213}?

Solution
If the fraction has been reduced to lowest terms, N cannot have as a factor any number whose prime factorization has any numbers in common with the prime factors of 60. But $60 = (2)(2)(3)(5)$. Thus, the answer must be 49, since in this set, only $49 = (7)(7)$ has a prime factorization lacking 2, 3, and 5. Check the others for yourself.

Topic 8. Comparing Fractions

For positive numbers: If two fractions have the same denominator, the one with the larger numerator is larger. If two fractions have the same numerator, the one with the *smaller* denominator is the larger one. For example, $\frac{5}{19}$ is smaller than $\frac{8}{19}$, but $\frac{8}{17}$ is larger than $\frac{8}{19}$.

Example 1
Which is larger, $\frac{6}{11}$ or $\frac{13}{22}$?

Solution
If the two fractions had a common denominator (or numerator), it would be easy. But it's easy to get there, since the denominator 11 is exactly half of the denominator 22. Just multiply the top and bottom of $\frac{6}{11}$ to yield $\frac{12}{22}$, and it is easy to see that $\frac{13}{22}$ is the larger.

Example 2
Which is larger, $\frac{4}{7}$ or $\frac{3}{5}$?

Solution
The first fraction has a larger numerator, but it also has a larger denominator, so we rewrite both with the common denominator 35 by multiplying the top and bottom of $\frac{4}{7}$ by 5 and the top and bottom of $\frac{3}{5}$ by 7 to yield $\frac{20}{35}$ and $\frac{21}{35}$ respectively. Now, it is easy to see that $\frac{3}{5}$ is the larger.

Example 3

If a must be chosen from the set {1,4,5} and b must be chosen from {3,6,7}, what is the largest possible value of $\frac{4}{2a - b}$?

Solution

To make the fraction as large as possible, we should make the denominator the smallest possible positive number it can be. We can't let $a = 1$, because that would make the denominator negative for any of the possible b's. However, choosing $a = 4$, we see that for $b = 7$, $2a - b = 1$, which is the smallest possible positive whole number. Therefore, the maximum value of the fraction is $\frac{4}{1} = 4$.

Topic 9. Multiplication and Division of Fractions

When multiplying two fractions, the result is the product of the numerators divided by the product of the denominators. In symbols, $\frac{a}{b} \cdot \frac{c}{d} = \frac{ac}{bd}$. Thus, $\frac{3}{7} \cdot \frac{2}{5} = \frac{6}{35}$. Don't forget that the resulting fraction can be reduced to lowest terms by canceling out like factors in numerator and denominator, such as $\frac{3}{5} \cdot \frac{10}{9} = \frac{2}{3}$.

Example 1

Joan earns $\frac{3}{4}$ of what Sally earns, and Sally earns $\frac{2}{3}$ of what Pedro earns. What fraction of Pedro's salary does Joan earn?

Using J, S, and P, to stand for the people's earnings respectively, we have

$$S = \frac{2}{3}P; J = \frac{3}{4}S$$

thus

$$J = \left(\frac{3}{4}\right)\left(\frac{2}{3}\right)P = \frac{1}{2}P$$

Hence, Joan's earnings are one-half of Pedro's.

When dividing fractions, simply invert the divisor and then multiply. Remember, the divisor is the one you are dividing by (usually the second one named) or the denominator in a "built-up" fraction. In symbols,

$$\frac{a}{b} \div \frac{c}{d} = \frac{a}{b} \cdot \frac{d}{c} = \frac{ad}{bc}$$

or

$$\frac{\frac{a}{b}}{\frac{c}{d}} = \frac{a}{b} \cdot \frac{d}{c} = \frac{ad}{bc}$$

For example:

$$\frac{3}{5} \div \frac{4}{11} = \frac{3}{5} \cdot \frac{11}{4} = \frac{33}{20}$$

Example 2

Patty has half as many pairs of jeans as Alfred has, and Marco has $\frac{3}{5}$ as many pairs of jeans as Alfred. What fraction of Marco's number of pairs does Patty have?

Solution

Using P, A, and M to stand for the number of jeans each person owns respectively, we have

$$P = \frac{1}{2}A; M = \frac{3}{5}A$$

thus

$$\frac{P}{M} = \frac{\frac{1}{2}A}{\frac{3}{5}A} = \frac{1}{2} \cdot \frac{5}{3} = \frac{5}{6}$$

Thus, Patty has $\frac{5}{6}$ as many pairs as Marco.

Topic 10. Addition and Subtraction of Fractions

To add (or subtract) fractions with the same denominator, simply add (or subtract) the numerators. For example, $\frac{5}{17} + \frac{3}{17} = \frac{8}{17}$ and $\frac{5}{17} - \frac{3}{17} = \frac{2}{17}$.

However, if the denominators are different, you must first rewrite the fractions so they will have the same denominator. Most books stress that you should use the *least common denominator* (LCD), which is the least common multiple (LCM) of the original denominators. This will keep the numbers smaller. However, any common denominator will do! For example, to add $\frac{5}{12} + \frac{3}{8}$, the LCM of 12 and 8 is 24. You should write $\frac{5}{12} = \frac{10}{24}$ and $\frac{3}{8} = \frac{9}{24}$, so that $\frac{5}{12} + \frac{3}{8} = \frac{10}{24} + \frac{9}{24} = \frac{19}{14}$.

However, if you are rushed, you can always find *a* common denominator by just taking the product of the two denominators, that is, $12 \times 8 = 96$. Thus,

$$\frac{5}{12} + \frac{3}{8} = \frac{5 \cdot 8}{12 \cdot 8} + \frac{3 \cdot 12}{8 \cdot 12} = \frac{40}{96} + \frac{36}{96} = \frac{76}{96}.$$

Now, you can divide numerator and denominator by 4 to reduce the fraction to its lowest terms, that is, $\frac{76}{96} = \frac{19}{24}$. Maybe not as efficient—but guaranteed to work!

Example

Mark figures that, working every day, he could finish a certain task in 30 days. Alfonso figures that he could finish the same task in 20 days. What fraction of the task could they get done by working on it together for a week?

Solution

In one week (7 days), Mark would do $\frac{7}{30}$ of the entire task. In the same week, Alfonso would do $\frac{7}{20}$ of the entire task. Therefore, together they do $\frac{7}{30} + \frac{7}{20}$.

Now, we have to add two fractions that have the same numerator. Can we add them directly by just summing the denominators? No! To add directly, it is the bottoms that must be the same! So, we must find a common denominator.

Find the LCD, which is 60. Thus, $\frac{7}{30} + \frac{7}{20} = \frac{14}{60} + \frac{21}{60} = \frac{35}{60}$, which reduces to $\frac{7}{12}$.

Topic 11. Fractions and Decimals

FYI

Any repeating decimal can be written as the repeating portion divided by an equal number of 9's. Thus,

$0.333333 = \frac{3}{9} = \frac{1}{3}$,

$0.279279279\ldots = \frac{279}{999} = \frac{31}{111}$,

$2.636363\ldots = 2 + \frac{63}{9} = 2\frac{7}{11} = \frac{29}{11}$.

Every fraction can be expressed as a decimal, which can be found by division. Those fractions for which the prime factorization of the denominator involves only 2's and 5's will have terminating decimal expansions. All others will have repeating decimal expansions. For example, $\frac{3}{20} = 0.15$, and $\frac{3}{11} = 0.272727\ldots$

To convert a decimal given to a fixed number of decimal places into a fraction, you must know what the decimal means. In general, the decimal represents a fraction with denominator 10, or 100, or 1000 . . . where the number of zeros is equal to the number of digits to the right of the decimal point. Thus, for example,

$$0.4 \text{ means } \frac{4}{10} = \frac{2}{5},$$

$$0.52 \text{ means } \frac{52}{100} = \frac{13}{25},$$

$$0.103 = \frac{103}{1000}.$$

Decimals of the form 2.15 are equivalent to mixed numbers. Thus, $2.15 = 2 + \frac{15}{100} = 2 + \frac{3}{20} = 2\frac{3}{20}$. For purposes of addition and subtraction, mixed numbers can be useful, but for purposes of multiplication or division, it is usually better to convert a mixed number to an *improper fraction* (one whose numerator is larger than its denominator). That is, $2\frac{3}{20} = \frac{43}{20}$.

How did we figure that? Formally, we realize that $2 = \frac{2}{1}$, and we add the two fractions $\frac{2}{1}$ and $\frac{3}{20}$ using the common denominator 20. More simply, we multiply the whole number part (2) by the common denominator (20), and add the numerator of the fraction (3) to get the numerator of the resulting improper fraction. That is, (2)(20) + 3 = 43.

Example

If $\frac{0.56}{1.26}$ reduced to lowest terms is $\frac{a}{b}$, where a and b are positive whole numbers, what is b?

Solution

Rewriting both numerator and denominator as their fractional equivalents, 0.56 $= \frac{56}{100} = \frac{14}{25}$, and $1.26 = 1 + \frac{26}{100} = 1\frac{13}{50} = \frac{63}{50}$. We now accomplish the division by inverting and multiplying by the denominator. Thus, $\left(\frac{14}{25}\right)\left(\frac{50}{63}\right) = \frac{4}{9}$ and $b = 9$.

Of course, you could also do this example by changing the numerator and denominator of the original fraction to whole numbers. That is, multiply top and bottom by 100 to move both decimal points two places to the right, thus: $\frac{0.56}{1.26} = \frac{56}{126}$. Now you can divide out the common factor of 14 in the numerator and the denominator to reduce the fraction to $\frac{4}{9}$.

Notice that by using long division or dividing on a calculator you will find that $\frac{0.56}{1.26} = 0.4444444\ldots$, which you might recognize as $\frac{4}{9}$.

Topic 12. Decimals and Percents

FYI

To convert a number given as a percent to decimal form, simply move the decimal point two places to the left. *To convert decimals to percent, reverse the process; that is, move the decimal point two places to the* right.

Remember, per*cent* means per *hundred.* (The word comes from the Latin *centum*, which means "hundred.") For example, 30% means 30 per hundred, or, as a fraction, $\frac{30}{100}$; as a decimal, 0.30.

Example

In a group of 30 doctors and 20 lawyers, 20% of the doctors and 40% of the lawyers wear contact lenses. What percent of the entire group wear contact lenses?

Solution

Start with the doctors. Since 20% = 0.20, 20% of 30 = (0.20)(30) = 6 doctors wear contacts. For the lawyers, 40% = 0.40, 40% of 20 = (0.40)(20) = 8 lawyers wear contacts. Hence, a total of 14 out of 50 people in the group wear contacts. The fraction of contact wearers is $\frac{14}{50} = 0.28 = 28\%$.

ALGEBRA

Topic 13. Addition and Subtraction of Signed Numbers

To add two numbers of the same sign, just add them and attach their common sign. So $7 + 9 = 16$, and $(-7) + (-9) = -16$. [Of course, you could drop the parentheses and instead of $(-7) + (-9)$ you could write $-7 - 9$, which means the same thing.]

When adding numbers of opposite signs, temporarily ignore the signs, subtract the smaller from the larger, and attach to the result the sign of the number with the larger absolute value. Thus, $9 + (-3) = 6$ but $(-9) + 3 = -6$. [Again, we could have written $9 + (-3) = 9 - 3 = 6$, and $(-9) + 3 = -9 + 3 = -6$.]

When subtracting, change the sign of the "second" number (the *subtrahend*) and then use the rules for addition. Thus, $7 - (-3) = 7 + 3 = 10$, and $-7 - 3 = -7 + (-3) = -10$.

Example:

What is the value of $A - (-B)$ when $A = -5$ and $B = -6$?

Solution

All the minus signs can be confusing. However, if you remember that "minus a minus is a plus," you can do this in two ways. The first is to realize that if $B = -6$, then $-B = +6$. Thus, $A - (-B) = A - 6 = -5 - 6 = -11$. Alternatively, you can work with the letters first: $A - (-B) = A + B = -5 + (-6) = -11$.

Topic 14. Multiplication and Division of Signed Numbers

FYI

If you have a string of multiplications and divisions to do, if the number of negative factors is even, *the result will be positive; if the number of negative factors is* odd, *the result will be negative.*

If you multiply two numbers with the same sign, the result is positive. If you multiply two numbers with opposite signs, the result is negative. Thus, $(-4)(-3) = +12$, and $(-4)(3) = -12$.

Furthermore, the exact same rule holds for division. For division, it doesn't matter which number is negative and which positive, thus $(-6) \div (2) = -3$ and $(6) \div (-2) = -3$, but $(-6) \div (-2) = +3$.

Example 1

If $A = (234{,}906 - 457{,}219)(35)(-618)$, and $B = (-2{,}356)(-89{,}021)(-3{,}125)$, which is larger, A or B?

Solution

Don't actually do the arithmetic. 457,219 is greater than 234,906, so the difference is a negative number. Now, you see that A is the product of two negative numbers and one positive number, which makes the result positive. B is the product of three negative numbers, and so must be negative. Every positive number is greater than any negative number, and so A is greater than B.

Example 2

If $\frac{AB}{MN}$ is a negative number, and N is negative, which of the following are possible?

I. A is positive, but B and M are negative.
II. A, B, and M are all negative.
III. A, B, and M are positive.

(A) I only
(B) II only
(C) I and II only
(D) I and III only
(E) II and III only

Solution

To determine the sign of the fraction, just think of A, B, M, N as four factors. Knowing that N is negative, the product of the other three must be positive in order that the result be negative. The only possibilities are that all three are positive, or one is positive and the other two are negative. This corresponds to cases I and III. Thus, the correct choice is (D).

Topic 15. Laws of Exponents

FYI

Commit to memory small powers of small numbers that come up in many questions. For example: The powers of 2: 2, 4, 8, 16, 32, . . .; The powers of 3 : 3, 9, 27, 81, . . . and so on.

In an expression of the form bn, b is called the *base* and n is called the *exponent* or *power*. We say, "b is raised to the power n." Notice, $b^1 = b$ and hence the power 1 is usually omitted.

If n is any positive integer, then bn is the product of n b's. For example, 4^3 is the product of three 4's, that is, $4^3 = 4 \times 4 \times 4 = 64$. Certain rules for operations with exponents are forced upon us by this definition. They are:

- $b^m \times b^n = b^{m+n}$. That is, when multiplying powers of the same base, keep the base and add the exponents.

  Thus, $3^2 \times 3^3 = 3^{2+3} = 3^5 = 243$.

- $(ab)^n = a^n b^n$, and $\left(\frac{a}{b}\right)^n = \frac{a^n}{b^n}$.

  That is, to raise a product or a quotient to a power, raise each factor to that power, whether that factor is in the numerator or denominator (top or bottom). Thus,

  $$(2x)^3 = 2^3x^3 = 8x^3$$

  and

  $$\left(\frac{2}{x}\right)^3 = \frac{2^3}{x^3} = \frac{8}{x^3}.$$

- $(b^m)^n = b^{nm}$. That is, to raise to a power, multiply exponents. Thus,

  $$(2^3)^2 = 2^6 = 64.$$

- $\frac{b^n}{b^m} = b^{n-m}$ if $n > m$, and $\frac{b^n}{b^m} = \frac{1}{b^{m-n}}$ if $n < m$.

That is, to divide powers with the same base, retain the base and subtract exponents. For example,

$$\frac{4^5}{4^2} = 4^3 = 64$$

and

$$\frac{4^2}{4^5} = \frac{1}{4^3} = \frac{1}{64}.$$

For various technical reasons, $x^0 = 1$ for all x except $x = 0$, in which case it is undefined.

Topic 16. Even Powers and Odd Powers

Even powers of real numbers cannot be negative. Thus, x^2 is positive, except for $x = 0$, when it is zero. Note that -3^2 means $-(3^2) = -9$. If you want the square of -3, which equals $+9$, you must write it $(-3)^2$.

Odd powers are either positive or negative, depending upon whether the base is positive or negative. Thus, $2^3 = 8$, but $(-2)^3 = -8$. Zero to any power is zero, except zero to the zero, which is undefined.

Example 1

If $x < 0$ and $y > 0$, what is the sign of $-4x^4y^3$?

Solution

x^4 is positive, because it has an even power. y^3 is positive because y is positive, and -4 is obviously negative. The product of two positives and a negative is negative. Thus, $-4x^4y^3$ is negative.

Example 2

If $x^4 + 3y^2 = 0$, what is the sign of $2x - 6y + 1$?

Solution

Since neither x^4 nor $3y^2$ can be negative, the only way their sum can be zero is if both x and y are zero. Therefore, $2x - 6y + 1 = +1$, which is positive.

FYI

Notice that the average of the set does not have to be a number in the set. It is important to realize that to find an average, you don't have to know the individual numbers—just the total.

Topic 17. Averages

The *average* or *arithmetic mean* of a collection of numbers is simply the sum of the numbers divided by the number of numbers in the collection. In symbols, $A = \frac{T}{n}$. So, for example, if your grades on four math exams are 92, 86, 67, and 91, your average in math is $(92 + 86 + 67 + 91) \div 4 = 326 \div 4 = 81.5$.

Example 1

Arnold picked six bags of apples. His average bag weighed 12 pounds. Frank picked four bags of apples. His average bag weighed 16 pounds. What was the overall average of the ten bags?

Solution

You can't just say the answer is 14, the average of 12 and 16, because we do not have the same number of bags in each group. We need to know the total weight of all ten bags. Since Arnold's 6 bags averaged 12 pounds, the total weight of the 6 bags was 72. ($12 = \frac{T}{6}$ means $T = (6)(12) = 72$). In the same way, Frank's 4 bags must have weighed 64 pounds in order to average 16 per bag. Therefore, we have a total of 10 bags weighing $72 + 64 = 136$, and the average is $\frac{136}{10} = 13.6$.

Example 2

Margaret earns an average of 88 on her first four calculus exams. To get an A for the course, she must have a 90 average. What grade must she earn on the next exam to bring her average to 90?

Solution

If her average is 88 on four exams, she must have a total of $(4)(88) = 352$. In order to average 90 on five exams, her total must be $(5)(90) = 450$. Therefore, she must score $450 - 352 = 98$ on her last exam. Study hard, Margaret!

There are two other quantities that are sometimes used in ways similar to averages. They are the *median*, which is the middle number when the numbers are arranged in order of size, and the *mode*, the most common number. Thus, for the set of nine integers {1,2,2,2,3,5,6,7,8} the median (middle number) is 3, the mode is 2 (since there are more 2's in the set than any other number), and the mean is

$$(1 + 2 + 2 + 2 + 3 + 5 + 6 + 7 + 8) \div 9 = 4.$$

Topic 18. Ratio and Proportion

FYI

When people analyze statistics, they sometimes speak as if the mean, median, and mode are interchangeable—but as you can see, they are not. Be careful to keep in mind the differences among these three terms.

The ratio of two quantities defines a fractional relationship between the quantities. This can be expressed as a fraction, in the form of $\frac{b}{a}$, or in the form $b : a$, (read "b is to a").

A proportion is a statement that two ratios are equal. To say, for example, that the ratio of passing to failing students in a class is 5 : 2 means that if we set up the fraction $\frac{P}{F}$ it should reduce to $\frac{5}{2}$. If we write this statement as $P : F :: 5 : 2$, we read it as "P is to F as 5 is to 2," and it means $\frac{P}{F} = \frac{5}{2}$.

Very frequently, a good way to handle ratios is to write the actual numbers as multiples of the same number.

Example

The ratio of passing to failing students in a certain class is 5 : 2. Which of the following could be the number of students in the class?

(A) 12
(B) 15
(C) 21
(D) 30
(E) 34

Solution

$P : F = 5 : 2$, we let $P = 5k$ and $F = 2k$. But the total number in the class must be $P + F = 5k + 2k = 7k$. Clearly, choice (C), 21, will work, since 21 is evenly divisible by 7; in this instance, $k = 3$. If you try the other possibilities, k will be a fraction for which neither $5k$ nor $2k$ will be a whole number. Of course, you can't have a fractional number of students (there's no such thing as "one-third of a student"), so the answer must be choice (C).

Topic 19. Solving Linear Equations

The keys to solving linear equations are two:

- If you add or subtract the same quantity from both sides of an equation, the equation is still true.
- If you multiply or divide both sides of an equation by any number *except zero*, the equation is still true.

The idea in solving most equations is to use these two properties in order to isolate the unknown quantity on one side of the equation, leaving only known quantities on the other side.

Example 1

If $A = 3x - 1$, and $A = \frac{1}{2}x + 4$, what is the numerical value of A?

Solution

Since things equal to the same thing are equal to each other, we can equate the two expressions in x that are both equal to A. That is,

$$3x - 1 = \frac{1}{2}x + 4$$

As a general rule, when an equation involves one or more fractional coefficients, it pays to multiply by a common denominator in order to clear (eliminate) the fractions. So, we multiply by 2 to get rid of the $\frac{1}{2}$. (Be careful when you multiply by 2: be sure to use the distributive law, and multiply every term on both sides by 2.) You should now have

$$6x - 2 = x + 8$$

Since we want to have x (the unknown) on one side of the equation and only known quantities on the other, we first add $-x + 2$ to both sides:

$$\begin{array}{r} 6x - 2 = \quad x + 8 \\ -\ \ x + 2 = -x + 2 \\ \hline 5x = 10 \end{array}$$

Now we can divide both sides by 5:

$$\frac{5x}{5} = \frac{10}{5};\ x = 2$$

Of course, the question asked for A, not x. So we substitute $x = 2$ into $A = 3x - 1$ and get $A = 3(2) - 1 = 5$.

Example 2

If $3x + 7 = b$, and $y = 2x + 5$, find an expression for y in terms of b.

Solution

How do we do this? We realize that if we knew what x was in terms of b, we could substitute that expression for x into $y = 2x - 5$ and have y in terms of b. In other words, we want to solve $3x + 7 = b$ for x. To do so, we start by adding -7 to both sides of the equation:

$$\begin{array}{rl} 3x + 7 &= b \\ -7 &= \;\; -7 \\ \hline 3x \qquad &= b - 7 \end{array}$$

Now divide by 3:

$$\frac{3x}{3} = \frac{(b-7)}{3}$$

$$x = \frac{(b-7)}{3}$$

Substituting:

$$y = 2\left(\frac{b-7}{3}\right) + 5$$

Combining fractions with common denominator 3:

$$y = \frac{2b - 14}{3} + \frac{15}{3} = \frac{2b + 1}{3}$$

Topic 20. Solving Linear Inequalities

To say that one number, M, is less than another number, N, is to say that $N - M$ is positive. That is, when you subtract a smaller number from a larger number, the result is positive. We say that M is less than N, and write $M < N$ (read as "M is less than N"), or $N > M$ ("N is greater than M").

Graphically, we think M lies to the left of N on the number line. This means, in particular, that any negative number is less than any positive number. It also implies that for negative numbers, the one with the larger absolute value is the smaller number.

The keys to solving *linear inequalities* (or *inequations*) are three:

1. If you add or subtract the same quantity from both sides of an inequation, the inequality remains in the same order.

   Thus, $14 > 7$ and $14 - 5 < 7 - 5$.

2. If you multiply or divide both sides of an inequation by the same positive number, the inequality remains in the same order. Thus, $3 < 8$ and $(6)(3) < (6)(8)$.
3. If you multiply or divide both sides of an equation by the same *negative* number, the inequality remains, but the order is *reversed*. Thus, $4 < 9$; but if you multiply by (-2), you get $-8 > -18$. Remember, for negative numbers, the one with the larger absolute value is the smaller number.

The idea in solving most inequalities is to use these three properties in order to isolate the unknown quantity on one side of the inequality leaving only known quantities on the other side. Notice that these rules hold whether you are working with $<$ and $>$ or $\leq$ ("is less than or equal to") and $\geq$ ("is greater than or equal to").

Example 1

For what values of x is $2x - 5 \leq 4x + 3$?

Solution

We solve this just like an equation. Start by adding the like quantity $(-2x - 3)$ to both sides in order to group the x terms on one side and the constants on the other; thus,

$$\begin{array}{rcl} 2x - 5 & \leq & 4x + 3 \\ -2x - 3 & = & -2x - 3 \\ \hline -8 & \leq & 2x \end{array}$$

Now divide by 2, which does not change the sense of the inequality, yielding

$$-4 \leq x$$

Hence, the inequality will be true for any number less than or equal to -4 and false for any number greater than -4. For example, for $x = 3$, $2x - 5 = 1$, $4x + 3 = 15$, and the inequality is *not* satisfied.

Example 2

If $A < 1 - 3B$, can you tell how large B is in terms of A? Can you tell how small B is?

Solution

We are really being asked to solve the inequality for B. To start, we add -1 to both sides, thus:

$$\begin{array}{rcl} A & < & 1 - 3B \\ -1 & = & -1 \\ \hline A - 1 & < & -3B \end{array}$$

Next divide by -3, remembering to reverse the inequality, thus:

$$\frac{A-1}{-3} > B; \frac{1-A}{3} > B$$

Notice that to change the denominator on the left-hand side from -3 to $+3$, we multiplied top and bottom by -1 and, of course, $(-1)(A - 1) = (1 - A)$. This tells us what B is less than, but tells us nothing about what B might be greater than. For example, if A were 7, then $B < -2$, but B could be -100 or -1000 or anything "more negative."

Topic 21. Solving Two Linear Equations in Two Unknowns

Many word problems lead to equations in two unknowns. Usually, one needs two equations to solve for both unknowns, although there are exceptions. There are two generally used methods to solve two equations in two unknowns. They are the method of *substitution* and the method of *elimination by addition and subtraction*.

We'll illustrate both methods via example. Here is one that uses the method of substitution.

Example 1

Mr. Green took his four children to the local craft fair. The total cost of their admission tickets was $14. Mr. and Mrs. Molina and their six children had to pay $23. What was the cost of an adult ticket to the craft fair, and what was the cost of a child's ticket?

Solution

Expressing all amounts in dollars, let x = cost of an adult ticket and let y = cost of a child's ticket.

For the Greens:

$$x + 4y = 14$$

For the Molinas:

$$2x + 6y = 23$$

The idea of the method of substitution is to solve one equation for one variable in terms of the other and then substitute that solution into the second equation. So we solve the first equation for x, because that is the simplest one to isolate:

$$x = 14 - 4y$$

and substitute into the second equation:

$$2(14 - 4y + 6y) = 23$$

This gives us one equation in one unknown that we can solve:

$$28 - 8y + 6y = 23$$
$$-2y = -5$$
$$y = 2.5$$

Now that we know $y = 2.5$, we substitute this into $x = 14 - 4y$ to get:

$$x = 14 - 4(2.5) = 4$$

Thus, the adult tickets were $4.00 each, and the children's tickets were $2.50 each.

Here is an example using the method of elimination.

Example 2

Paul and Denise both have after-school jobs. Two weeks ago, Paul worked 6 hours, Denise worked 3 hours, and they earned a total of $39. Last week, Paul worked 12 hours, Denise worked 5 hours, and they earned a total of $75. What is each one's hourly wage?

Solution

Again, let us express all amounts in dollars. Let x = Paul's hourly wage, and let y = Denise's hourly wage.

For the first week:

$$6x + 3y = 39$$

For the second week:

$$12x + 5y = 75$$

The idea of the method of elimination is that adding equal quantities to equal quantities gives a true result. So we want to add some multiple of one equation to the other one so that *if we add the two equations together,* one variable will be eliminated. In this case, it is not hard to see that if we multiply the first equation by -2, the coefficient of x will become -12. Now when we add the two equations, x will drop out.

$$\begin{array}{rr} -2 \text{ times the first equation is:} & -12x - 6y = -78 \\ \text{the second equation is:} & 12x + 5y = 75 \\ \hline \text{adding them:} & -y = -3 \end{array}$$

Thus, $y = 3$. We now substitute this into either of the two equations. Let's use the first:

$$6x + (3)(3) = 39; x = 5$$

Thus, Denise makes only \$3 per hour, while Paul gets \$5.

Topic 22. Word Problems in One or Two Unknowns

Word problems can be broken down into a number of categories. To do *consecutive integer* problems, you need to remember that consecutive integers differ by 1, so a string of such numbers can be represented as $n, n + 1, n + 2, \ldots$

Consecutive even integers differ by 2, so a string of such numbers can be represented as $n, n + 2, n + 4, \ldots$ Consecutive odd integers also differ by 2! So a string of such numbers can also be represented as $n, n + 2, n + 4, \ldots$

Rate-time-distance problems require you to know the formula $d = rt$. That is, distance equals rate times time.

Here are some examples of several types of word problems.

Example 1

Sibyl is 5 years older than Moira. Three years ago, Sibyl was twice as old as Moira. How old is Sibyl?

Solution

If you have trouble setting up the equations, try using numbers. Suppose that Moira is 11. If Sibyl is 5 years older than Moira, how old is Sibyl? She is 16. You got from 11 to 16 by *adding* 5. So, if S is Sibyl's age and M is Moira's age, $S = M + 5$. Three years ago, Sibyl was $S - 3$, and Moira was $M - 3$. So, from the second sentence, $S - 3 = 2(M - 3)$ or $S - 3 = 2M - 6$; or, adding 3 to both sides,

$$S = 2M - 3$$

Now, substituting $S = M + 5$,

$$\begin{aligned} M + 5 &= 2M - 3 \\ M &= 8 \end{aligned}$$

Which means Sybil is $8 + 5 = 13$.

Example 2

Three consecutive integers are written in increasing order. If the sum of the first and second and twice the third is 93, what is the second number?

Solution

Calling the smallest number x, the second is $x + 1$, and the third is $x + 2$. Therefore,

$$\begin{aligned} x + (x + 1) + 2(x + 2) &= 93 \\ x + x + 1 + 2x + 4 &= 93 \\ 4x + 5 &= 93 \\ 4x &= 88 \\ x &= 22 \end{aligned}$$

Hence the middle number is $22 + 1 = 23$.

Example 3

It took Andrew 15 minutes to drive downtown at 28 miles per hour to get a pizza. How fast did he have to drive back in order to be home in ten minutes?

Solution

15 minutes is $\frac{1}{4}$ of an hour. Hence, going 28 miles per hour, the distance to the Pizza Parlor can be computed using the formula $d = rt$; $d = (28)\left(\frac{1}{4}\right) = 7$ miles. Since ten minutes is $\frac{1}{6}$ of an hour, we have the equation $7 = r\left(\frac{1}{6}\right)$ and multiplying by 6, $r = 42$ mph.

Topic 23. Monomials and Polynomials

When we add a collection of expressions together, each expression is called a *term*. *Monomial* means one term. For example, we might say that $2x + 3y^2 + 7$ is the sum of three terms or three monomials. When we talk about a monomial, we generally mean a term that is just the product of constants and variables, possibly raised to various powers. Examples might be 7, $2x$, $-3y^2$, and $4x^2z^5$. The constant factor is called the *coefficient* of the variable factor. Thus, in $-3y^2$, -3 is the coefficient of y^2.

If we restrict our attention to monomials of the form Ax^n, the sums of such terms are called *polynomials* (in one variable). Expressions like $3x + 5$, $2x^2 - 5x + 8$, and $x^4 - 7x^5 - 11$, are all examples of polynomials. The highest power of the variable that appears is called the *degree* of the polynomial. The three examples just given are of degree 1, 2, and 5 respectively.

In evaluating monomials and polynomials for negative values of the variable, the greatest pitfall is keeping track of the minus signs. Always remember that in an expression like $-x^2$, the power 2 is applied to the x and the minus sign in front should be thought of as (-1) times the expression. If you want to have the power apply to $-x$ you must write $(-x)^2$.

Example

Find the value of $3x - x^3 - x^2$, when $x = -2$.

Solution

Substitute -2 every place you see an x, thus:

$$3(-2) - (-2)^3 - (-2)^2 = -6 - (-8) - (+4) = -6 + 8 - 4 = -2.$$

Topic 24. Combining Monomials

Monomials with identical variable factors can be added together by adding their coefficients. So $3x^2 + 4x^2 = 7x^2$. Of course, subtraction is handled the same way, thus:

$$3x^4 - 9x^4 = -6x^4$$

Monomials are multiplied by taking the product of their coefficients and taking the product of the variable part by adding exponents of factors with like bases. So $(3xy^2)(2xy^3) = 6x^2y^5$.

Monomial fractions can be reduced to lowest terms by dividing out common factors of the coefficients and then using the usual rules for subtraction of exponents in division. An example might be

$$\frac{6x^3y^5}{2x^4y^3} = \frac{3y^2}{x}$$

Example

Combine into a single monomial $\frac{8x^3}{4x^2} - 6x$.

Solution

The fraction reduces to $2x$, and $2x - 6x = -4x$.

Topic 25. Combining Polynomials and Monomials

Polynomials are added or subtracted by just combining like monomial terms in the appropriate manner. Thus,

$$(3x^2 - 3x - 4) + (2x^2 + 5x - 11)$$

is summed by removing the parentheses and combining like terms, to yield

$$5x^2 + 2x - 15$$

In subtraction, when you remove the parentheses with a minus sign in front, be careful to change the signs of *all* the terms within the parentheses. So:

$$\begin{aligned}(3x^2 - 3x - 4) - (2x^2 + 5x - 11) &= 3x^2 - 3x - 4 - 2x^2 - 5x + 11 \\ &= x^2 - 8x + 7\end{aligned}$$

(Did you notice that $3x^2 - 2x^2 = 1x^2$ but the "1" is not shown?)

To multiply a polynomial by a monomial, use the distributive law to multiply each term in the polynomial by the monomial factor. For example, $2x(2x^2 + 5x - 11) = 4x^3 + 10x^2 - 22x$.

When multiplying a polynomial by a polynomial, you are actually repeatedly applying the distributive law to form all possible products of the terms in the first polynomial with the terms in the second polynomial. The most common use of this is in multiplying two *binomials* (polynomials with two terms), such as $(x + 3)(x - 5)$. In this case, there are four terms in the result, $x \times x = x^2$; $x(-5) = -5x$; $3 \times x = 3x$; and, $3 \times (-5) = -15$; but the two middle terms are added together to give $-2x$. Thus, the product is $x^2 - 2x - 15$.

This process is usually remembered as the FOIL method. That is, form the products of First, Outer, Inner, Last, as shown below.

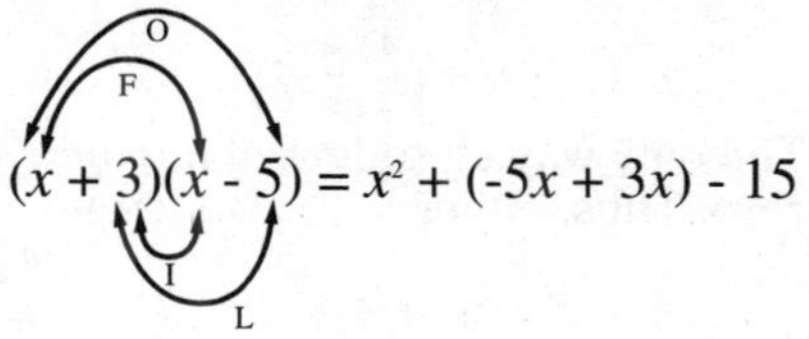

Example

If d is an integer, and $(x + 2)(x + d) = x^2 - kx - 10$, what is the value of $k + d$?

Solution

The product of the two last terms, $2d$, must be -10. Therefore, $d = -5$. If $d = -5$, then the sum of the outer and inner products becomes $-5x + 2x = -3x$, which equals $-kx$. Hence, $k = 3$, and $k + d = 3 + (-5) = -2$.

Topic 26. Factoring Monomials

Factoring a monomial simply involves reversing the distributive law. For example, if you are looking at $4x^2 + 12xy$, you should see that $4x$ is a factor of both terms. Hence, you could just as well write this as $4x(x + 3y)$. Multiplication using the distributive law will restore the original formulation.

Example

If $3x - 4y = -2$, what is the value of $9x - 12y$?

Solution

Although you seem to have one equation in two unknowns, you can still solve the problem, because you do not need to know the values of the individual variables. Just rewrite: $9x - 12y = 3(3x - 4y)$. Since $3x - 4y = -2$, $9x - 12y$ is 3 times -2, or -6.

Topic 27. Trinomial Factoring and Quadratic Equations

When you multiply two binomials $(x + r)(x + s)$ using the FOIL method, the result is a *trinomial* (a polynomial with three terms) of the form $x^2 + bx + c$, where b, the coefficient of x, is the sum of the constants r and s, and the constant term c is their product.

Trinomial factoring is the process of reversing this multiplication. For example, to find the binomial factors of $x^2 - 4x - 5$, we need to find two numbers whose product is -5 and whose sum is -4. Since the product is negative, one of the numbers must be negative and the other positive. The only possible factors of 5 are 1 and 5. In order for the sum to be -4, we must choose -5 and $+1$. Thus,

$$x^2 - 4x - 5 = (x - 5)(x + 1)$$

One major use of this skill is in solving *quadratic equations*. If you have an equation like

$$x^2 - 6x + 8 = 0$$

you can factor the trinomial. You need two numbers whose product is 8 and whose sum is -6. Since the product is positive, both numbers must have the same sign, and since the sum is negative, they must both be negative. It is not hard to see that -2 and -4 are the correct options. Thus, the equation becomes

$$(x - 2)(x - 4) = 0$$

The only way a product of numbers can be zero is for one of the numbers to be zero. Thus, either

$$x - 2 = 0 \text{ or } x - 4 = 0$$

Therefore,

$$x = 2 \text{ or } x = 4$$

It's common for this kind of problem to yield two possible solutions.

Example

The area of a rectangle is 28 and its perimeter is 22. What are its dimensions?

Solution

As you probably know, the area of a rectangle is calculated by multiplying the length by the width (see Topic 36). Calling the dimensions L and W, we have $LW = 28$, and $2L + 2W = 22$. Dividing by 2, $L + W = 11$. Therefore, $L = 11 - W$, which we substitute in $LW = 28$, giving

$$(11 - W)W = 28.$$
$$11W - W^2 = 28$$

Grouping everything on the right hand side, we have

$$0 = W^2 - 11W + 28.$$

Now, factoring

$$0 = (W - 7)(W - 4)$$

yields

$$W = 7 \text{ or } W = 4.$$

Of course, if $W = 4$, $L = 7$, and if $W = 7$, $L = 4$. So the dimensions of the rectangle are 4×7.

Topic 28. The Difference and the Sum of Two Squares

The difference of two squares $A^2 - B^2 = (A - B)(A + B)$. For example, $x^2 - 9$ can be thought of as

$$x^2 - 3^2 = (x - 3)(x + 3)$$

If your calculator were broken, you could still find $101^2 - 99^2$ as $(101 - 99)(101 + 99) = 2(200) = 400$. However, binomials such as $x^2 + 16$, which is the *sum* of two squares, cannot be factored.

Example 1

If x and y are positive integers, and $2x + y = 7$, which of the following is the value of $4x^2 - y^2$?

(A) 0
(B) 16
(C) 35

Solution

Since $4x^2 - y^2 = (2x - y)(2x + y) = 7(2x - y)$, $4x^2 - y^2$ must be divisible by 7. Therefore, 16 is not a possible value. If the result is to be zero, $2x - y = 0$, which means $y = 2x$, so that $2x + 2x = 4x = 7$, which is also impossible (remembering that x is an integer). Hence the result must be 35, which you get for $x = 3$ and $y = 1$.

Example 2

If x and y are positive integers, and $y^2 = x^2 + 11$, find the value of y.

Solution

If we rewrite the equation as $y^2 - x^2 = 11$ and factor, we have $(y - x)(y + x) = 11$. Thus, 11 must be the product of the two whole numbers $(y - x)$ and $(y + x)$. But 11 is a prime number which can only be factored as 11 times 1. Since $y + x$ must be larger than $y - x$, we know that

$$y + x = 11$$

and

$$y - x = 1$$

Adding the two equations gives us

$$2y = 12; y = 6.$$

(Of course, $x = 5$, but we weren't asked that.)

Topic 29. Operations with Radicals

The *square root* of a number N, written $\sqrt{N}$, is a number that when squared produces N. Thus, $\sqrt{4} = 2$, $\sqrt{9} = 3$, $\sqrt{16} = 4$, and so on. You should be aware that $\sqrt{0} = 0$ and $\sqrt{1} = 1$; Square roots of negative numbers are not real numbers.

The symbol $\sqrt{\ }$ is called a *radical,* and many people refer to $\sqrt{N}$ as "radical N". When we write $\sqrt{N}$, it is understood to be a positive number. So when you are faced with an algebraic equation like $x^2 = 4$, where you must allow for both positive and negative solutions, you must write $x = \pm\sqrt{4} = \pm 2$, where, as you know, $\pm$ is read "plus or minus."

All positive numbers have square roots, but most are *irrational numbers.* Only numbers that are *perfect squares* like 4, 9, 16, 25, 36, . . . have integer square roots.

If you assume that you are working with non-negative numbers, you can use certain properties of the square root to simplify radical expressions. The most important of these rules is $\sqrt{AB} = \sqrt{A} \cdot \sqrt{B}$.

This rule can be used to your advantage in either direction. Reading it from right to left, we may write $\sqrt{3} \cdot \sqrt{12} = \sqrt{36} = 6$. But you should also know how to use this rule to simplify radicals by extracting perfect squares from "under" the radical. Thus,

$$\sqrt{18} = \sqrt{9 \cdot 2} = \sqrt{9} \cdot \sqrt{2} = 3\sqrt{2}$$

The key to using this technique is to recognize the perfect squares in order to factor them out in a sensible manner. Thus, it would do you little good to factor 18 as 3×6 in the preceding example, since neither 3 nor 6 is a perfect square.

Example

If $\sqrt{5} \cdot \sqrt{x} = 10$, which is larger, $\sqrt{x}$ or $2\sqrt{5}$?

Solution

Since $10 = \sqrt{100}$ and $\sqrt{5} \cdot \sqrt{x} = \sqrt{5x}$, we know that $5x = 100$ and $x = 20$. But $20 = 4 \times 5$, so $\sqrt{20} = 2\sqrt{5}$. Hence the two quantities are equal.

GEOMETRY

Topic 30. Angles, Complements, and Supplements

When two *rays* originate from the same point, they form an *angle*. Angles are usually measured in *degrees* or *radians*. For our purposes, we shall use degree measure, as is customary on the SAT.

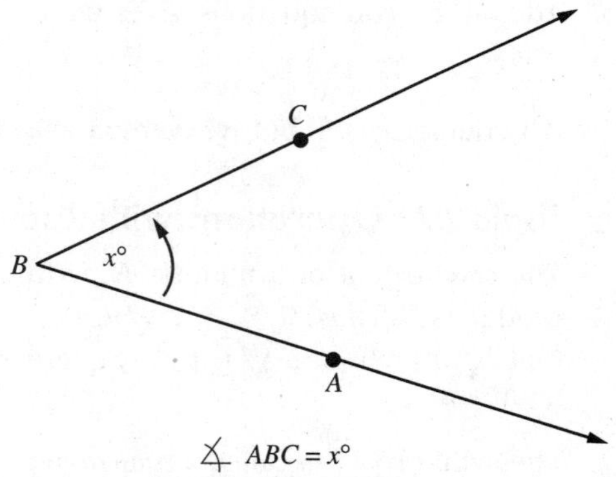

$\measuredangle\ ABC = x°$

It's useful to be familiar with the following terminology. The terminology itself is not tested on the exam, but the geometry problems will require you to rapidly use and manipulate all these concepts, so the more comfortable you are with them, the better.

The measure of a *straight angle* is 180°. Any two angles that sum to a straight angle are called *supplementary.* Thus, angles measuring 70° and 110° are supplementary. Two equal supplementary angles are 90° each, and a 90° angle is called a *right angle.*

Two angles that sum to a right angle are called *complementary.* Thus, angles measuring 30° and 60° are complementary. Angles less than 90° are called *acute,* and angles between 90° and 180° are called *obtuse.* The sum of all the angles around a given point must equal 360°.

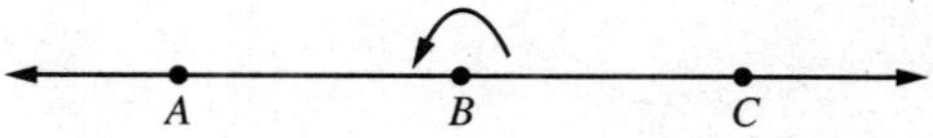

Straight Angle, $\measuredangle ABC = 180°$

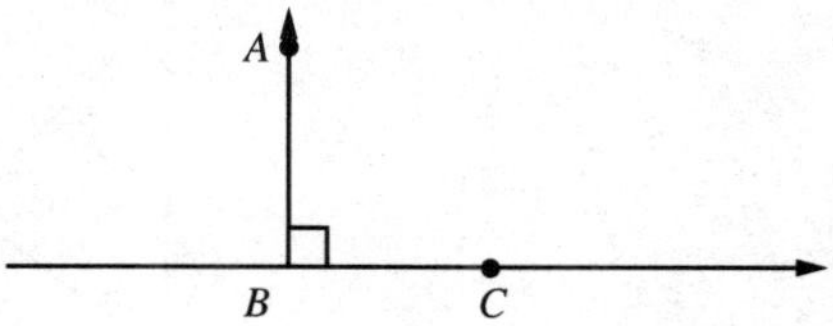

Right Angle, $\measuredangle ABC = 90°$

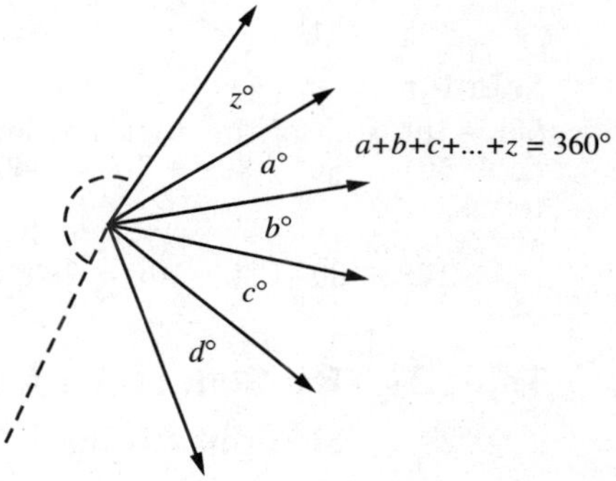

Example 1

Find the value of x in the figure below.

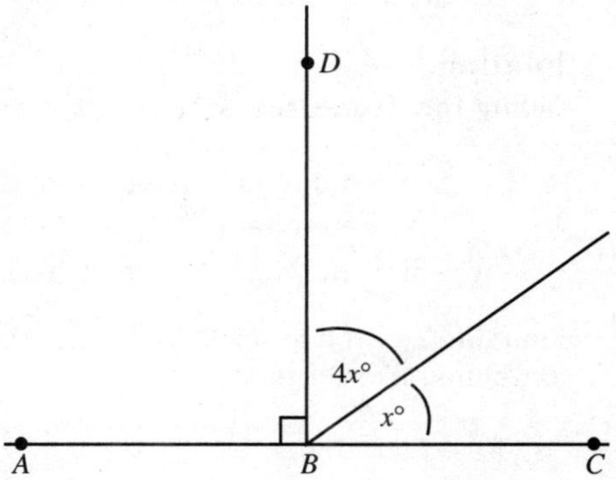

Solution

Since $\angle ABD$ is a right angle, so is $\angle DBC$. Thus, $x + 4x = 90$, $5x = 90$, and $x = 18$.

Example 2

Find the value of x in the figure below.

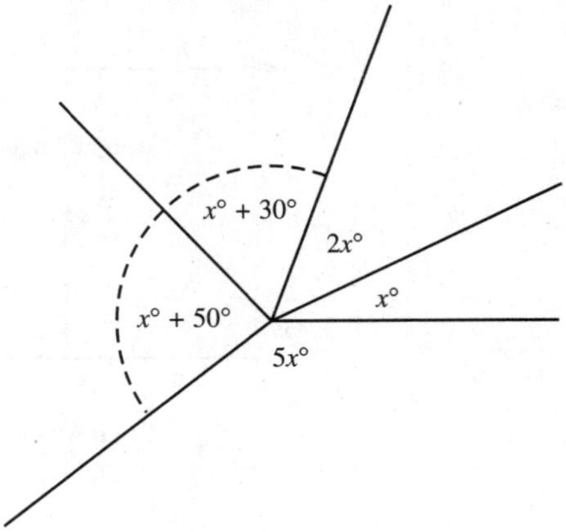

Solution

Since the sum of the angles around a point must be 360°, we have $x + 2x + (x + 50) + (x + 30) + 5x = 360$. Removing parentheses and combining like terms,

$$10x + 80 = 360;\ 10x = 280;\ x = 28.$$

Topic 31. The Sum of the Angles in Any Triangle is a Straight Angle

The measure of a straight angle is 180°. Regardless of the shape of a triangle, the sum of its angles is always 180°. In an *equilateral* triangle, all of whose sides are equal in length, all of the angles have the same degree measure, 60°.

Example

In triangle ABC, $\angle B$ is three times $\angle A$, and $\angle C$ is 30° more than $\angle A$. How many degrees are there in the largest angle?

Solution

Calling the degree measure of $\angle A$ x, we have the following:

$$\begin{aligned} x &= \text{number of degrees in } \angle A \\ 3x &= \text{number of degrees in } \angle B \\ x + 30 &= \text{number of degrees in } \angle C \end{aligned}$$

Summing, we have $x + 3x + (x + 30) = 180$. Removing parentheses and combining like terms:

$$\begin{aligned} 5x + 30 &= 180 \\ 5x &= 150 \\ x &= 30 \end{aligned}$$

Therefore, $x = 30$, $3x = 90$, and $x + 30 = 60$. We have here an example of the 30°-60°-90° right triangle (see Topic 39), and the largest angle is 90°.

Topic 32. Isosceles and Equilateral Triangles

A triangle with exactly two sides of equal length is called an *isosceles* triangle. If all three sides are equal, it is called an *equilateral* triangle. The angles opposite the equal sides in an isosceles triangle (as shown in the figure below) are equal in degree measure, and if two angles are equal then the triangle must be isosceles. If all three angles are equal, the triangle is equilateral.

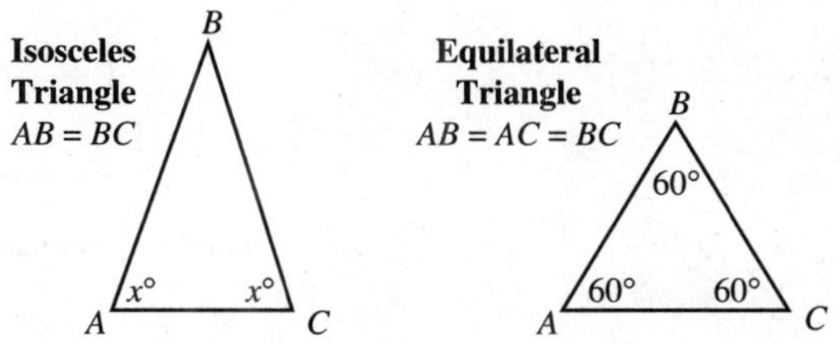

Example

If, in ΔABC as shown in the figure below, $AC = BC$ and $x \geq 70$, what is the greatest possible value for y?

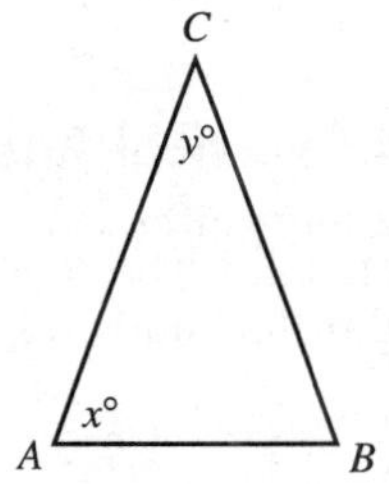

Solution

Since the sides are of equal length, the two base angles must be equal. The three angles, as always, must total 180°. Hence, $2x + y = 180$, which means that $y = 180 - 2x$. The greatest possible value for y is achieved when x is as small as possible. That is, at $x = 70$, for which $y = 40$.

Topic 33. Other Triangle Properties

In a triangle, the sum of the lengths of any two sides must exceed the length of the third. Thus, you cannot draw a triangle with sides of lengths 3, 6, 10, because $3 + 6 < 10$. In addition, in comparing any two sides of a triangle, the longer side will be opposite the larger angle.

Example 1

A triangle has sides 5, 12, x. If x is an integer, what is the maximum possible perimeter of the triangle?

Solution

Since the sum of the lengths of any two sides must exceed the length of the third, $x < 5 + 12 = 17$. The largest integer less than 17 is 16. Hence, the maximum perimeter is $5 + 12 + 16 = 33$. (Bonus question: Can you see why the minimum possible perimeter must be 25?)

Example 2

In the triangle shown in the figure below, $AB = BC$. Which is longer, AC or AB?

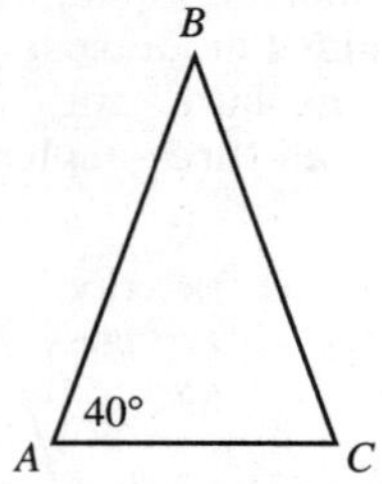

Note: Diagram not drawn to scale

Solution

Since the triangle is isosceles, the base angles are equal. Thus, $\angle A = \angle C = 40°$. This implies that $\angle B = 100°$ in order to reach the full 180° in the triangle. But that means that $AC > AB$, because it is the side opposite the larger angle.

Topic 34. Vertical Angles Are Equal

When two lines intersect, two pairs of *vertical angles* are formed (as shown in the figure below). The "facing" pairs are equal and, of course, each pair on one side of either line adds up to 180°.

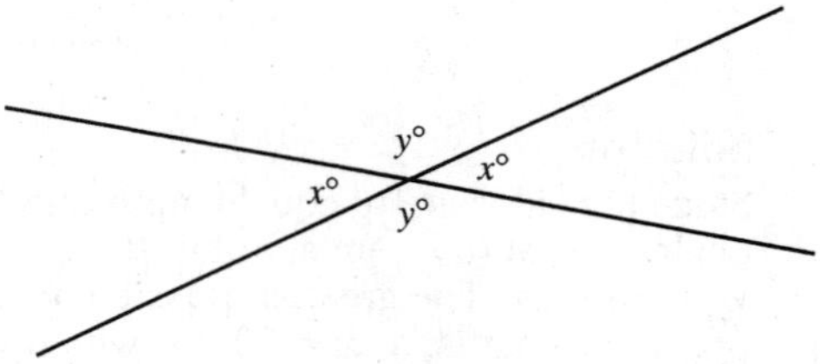

Note

$x + y = 180$. This fact can be used in a number of different ways. Try the following example.

Example

In the figure below, which is larger, $x + y$ or $c + d$?

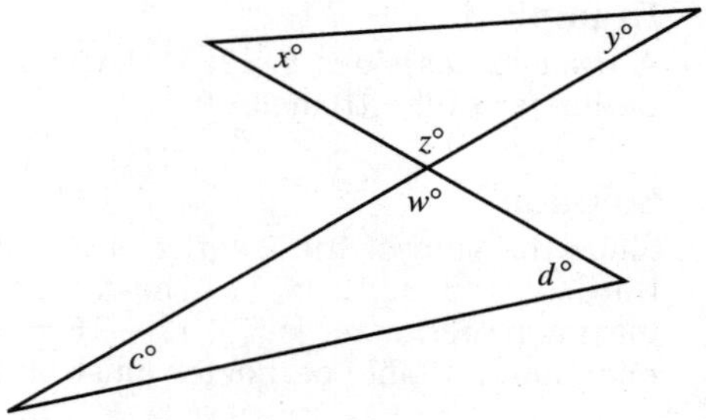

Solution
We know that the sum of the angles in any triangle is 180°. Therefore, looking at the upper triangle, we know that

$$x + y + z = 180$$

that is,

$$x + y = 180 - z$$

Similarly, looking at the lower triangle, we know that

$$c + d = 180 - w$$

But $w = z$ (vertical angles are equal). Therefore, $x + y = c + d$.

Topic 35. Parallel Lines and Transversals

Parallel lines are lines that run in the same direction. No matter how far they are extended, parallel lines will never meet. When two parallel lines are cut by a third line, called a *transversal*, several sets of equal angles are formed. In particular, the *corresponding angles*, labeled A in the figure below, and the *alternate interior angles* labeled B in the same figure, are equal.

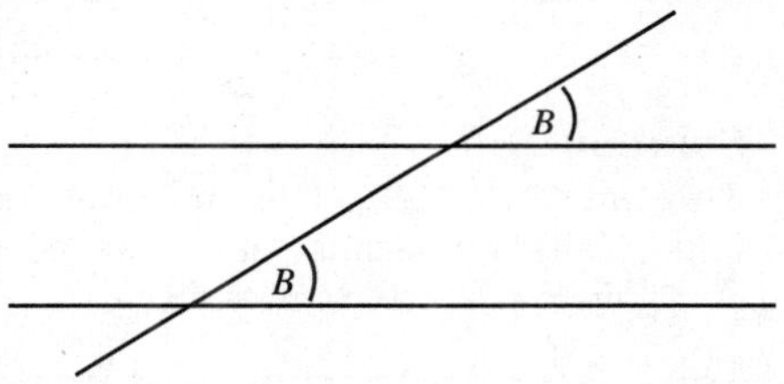

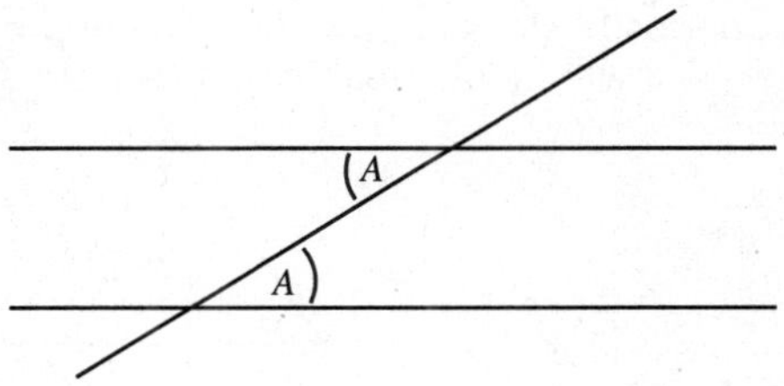

These facts are commonly combined with the properties of vertical angles and the number of degrees in a triangle in constructing problems.

Example 1
In the figure below, l_1 is parallel to l_2. Find the value of x.

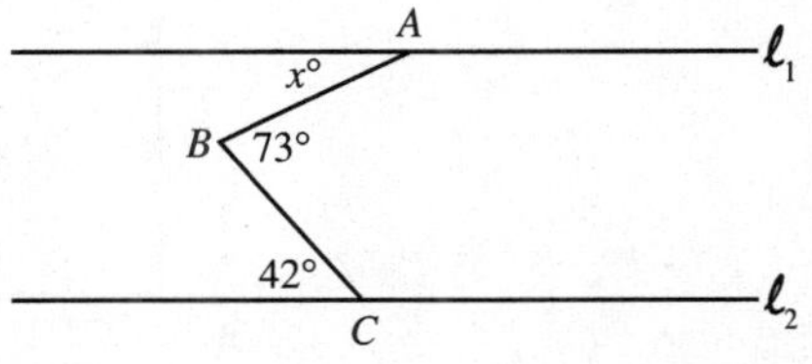

Solution

Extending the line AB until it intersects l_2 at D as shown below, we have a triangle, ΔBCD.

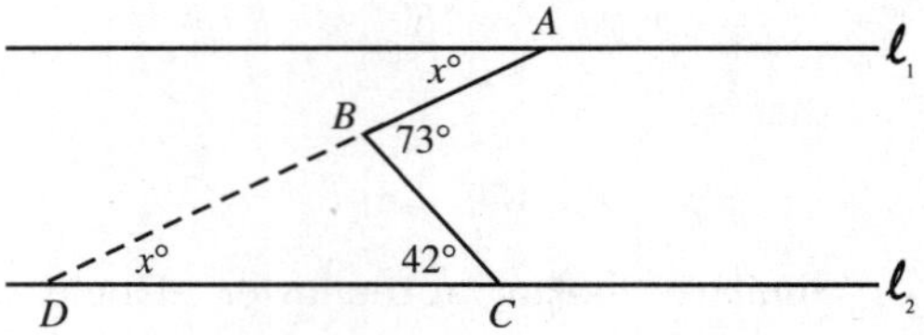

In the triangle, $\angle B$ is the supplement of 73°, that is, 107°. $\angle C$ is given as 42°, and $\angle D$ is $x°$ because it is the alternate interior angle to $\angle A$. Now, the sum $107 + 42 + x = 180$, so $x = 31$.

Example 2

In the figure below, l_1 is parallel to l_2. Find the value of x.

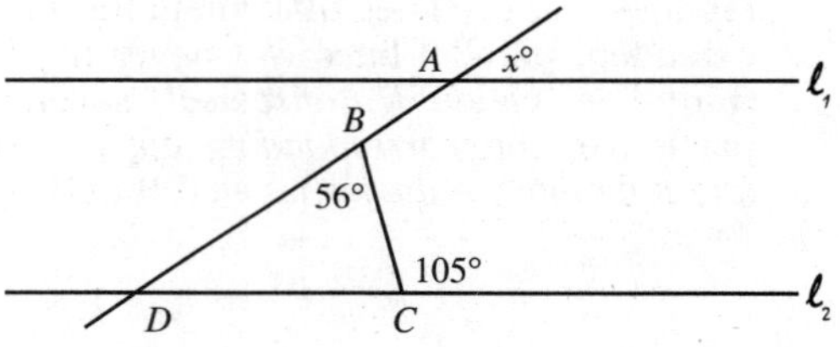

Solution

This time, in ΔBCD, $\angle C$ is the supplement of 105°, that is, 75°. $\angle B$ is given as 56°, and $\angle D$ is $x°$ because it is the corresponding angle to $\angle A$. Now, the sum $75 + 56 + x = 180$, so $x = 49$.

Topic 36. Rectangles and Parallelograms

A *parallelogram* is a *quadrilateral* (a four-sided figure) in which the pairs of opposite sides are parallel. The opposite angles will be equal, and the opposite sides will be of equal length (see the following figure).

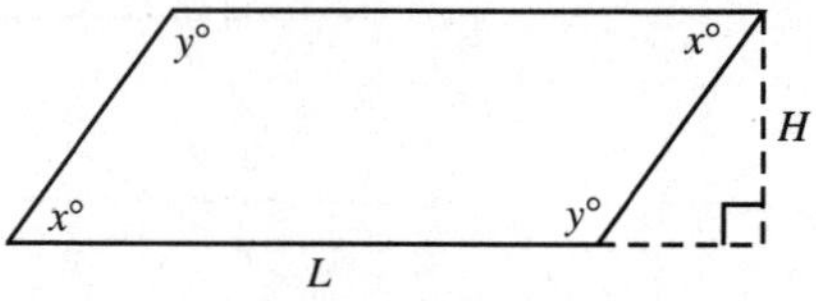

The area of a parallelogram is calculated by multiplying the length times the height. That is, $A = LH$, as labeled in the diagram.

If the angles in the parallelogram are right angles, then we have a *rectangle*. For a rectangle of length L, and width W, the area is $A = LW$, and the *perimeter* (the distance around the figure) is $P = 2L + 2W$ (see the figure below).

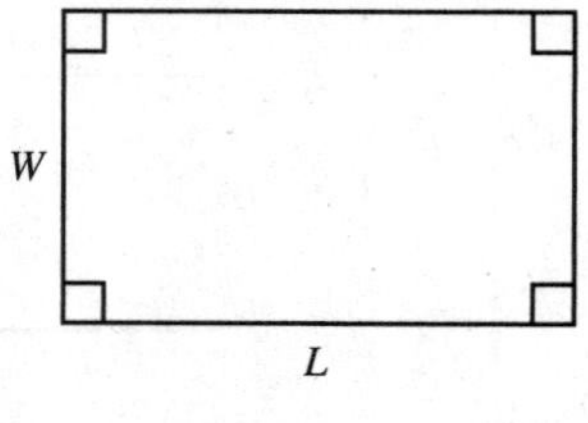

For example, to carpet a rectangular room that is 12 feet long and 9 feet wide requires (12)(9) = 144 square feet of carpeting. However, to put up a molding strip around the edge of the ceiling of the same room requires 2(12) + 2(9) = 42 running feet of molding.

Example 1

The total area of the figure below is 70 square inches. Find the total perimeter of the region *ABCDE*. (Note: You may assume that all the angles that appear to be right angles are right angles.)

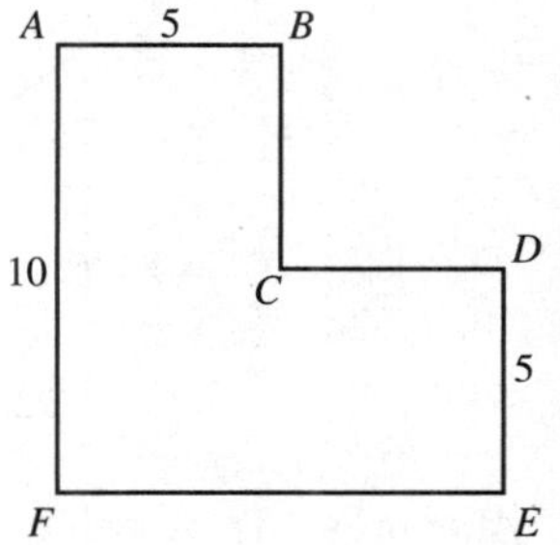

Solution

Inserting a vertical line as shown in the next figure, we see that the larger rectangle has an area of $5 \times 10 = 50$. Hence, the smaller rectangle must be 20. This tells us that the line segment *CD* must be of length 4, and *FE* must be $5 + 4 = 9$. Also $CG = DE = 5$, which means that $BC = 5$. We now find the perimeter by adding the lengths of the segments, starting at *A* and proceeding in a clockwise direction: $5 + 5 + 4 + 5 + 9 + 10 = 38$.

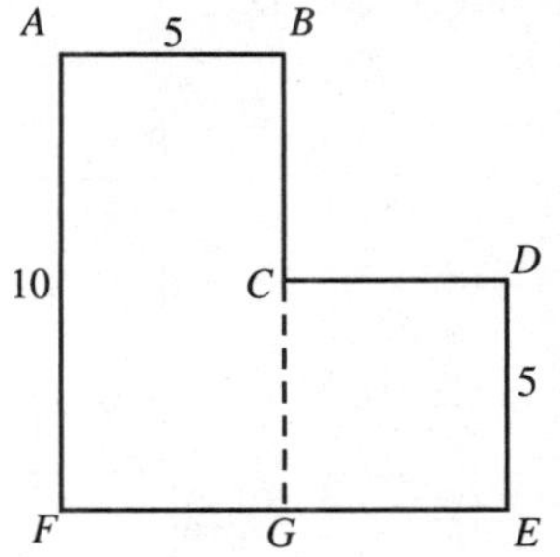

Example 2

Rectangle 1 has perimeter 36 and Rectangle 2 has perimeter 8. Which has a larger area?

Solution

We can't tell! For Rectangle 1, $2L + 2W = 36$, which means that $L + W = 18$. The area could be as large as $9 \times 9 = 81$, but it could be *virtually as small as you like.* After all, we could make it $(17.9) \times (0.1) = 1.79$.

Similarly, Rectangle 2 must have $L + W = 4$. The area could be $2 \times 2 = 4$, which is larger than 1.79, but smaller than 81. In fact, it too could be as small as you like.

Topic 37. The Pythagorean Theorem

FYI

You should remember some well-known Pythagorean Triples, *that is, sets of whole numbers such as 3-4-5 for which* $a^2 + b^2 = c^2$. *You'll encounter right triangles on the SAT with sides whose lengths correspond to these values. Other Pythagorean triples are: 5-12-13, 8-15-17, and 7-24-25. Also look for multiples of them, such as 6-8-10 or 15-20-25.*

A *right triangle* is a triangle that contains a right angle—an angle with a degree measure of 90 degrees. Right triangles figure prominently in western civilization (think of the corners found in street grids, houses, the shapes of books and windows, etc. etc.) and in SAT geometry problems. Many of these problems are based on the *Pythagorean Theorem.*

The Pythagorean Theorem states that the square on the *hypotenuse* (the longest side) of a right triangle is equal to the sum of the squares on the other two sides. In symbols, it is depicted below.

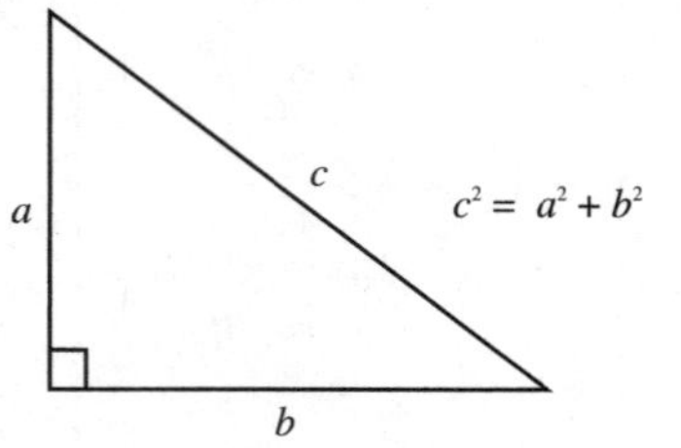

The Pythagorean Triples are integer solutions of the Pythagorean Theorem—that is, sets of integers that represent possible lengths of the three sides of a right triangle. However, there are other important cases that yield non-integer solutions. For example, the hypotenuse of a triangle with one leg of length 1 and the other of length 2 can be found by applying the Pythagorean Theorem: $c^2 = 1^2 + 2^2$, that is, $c^2 = 5$ and $c = \sqrt{5}$.

Example 1

In the following figure, $AB = 3$, $AD = 4$, and $BC = 12$. Find the perimeter of the quadrilateral $ABCD$.

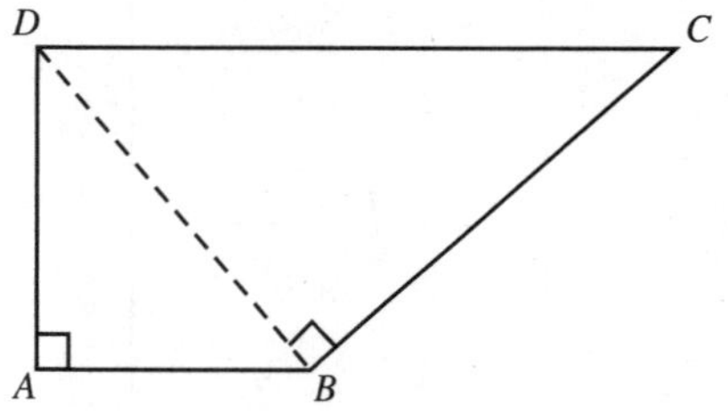

Solution

This example uses two well-known right triangles. We see that in ΔABD, one leg is 3 and one is 4, which makes the length of the hypotenuse, $BD = 5$. This tells us that ΔBDC is a 5-12-13 right triangle (another Pythagorean Triple). Thus, CD is 13, and the entire perimeter is $3 + 4 + 12 + 13 = 32$.

Example 2

A rectangle has one side 5 and area 60. What is the length of its diagonal?

Solution

Notice that the diagonal of a rectangle divides the rectangle into two identical right triangles. Hence, if you know the lengths of the sides of the rectangle, the length of its diagonal can be found by using the Pythagorean Theorem.

In this case, since the area, 60, is the product of the length and the width, and one side is 5, the other must be 12. These two sides with the diagonal form a 5-12-13 triangle. Thus, the diagonal is 13.

Topic 38. The Area of a Triangle

The area of a triangle is given by the formula

$$A = \frac{1}{2}bh$$

where b = length of the *base* of the triangle and h = the length of the *altitude*. The base is any side of the triangle (for convenience, often the side at the "bottom" of the triangle); the altitude is a line perpendicular to the base that goes through the opposite *vertex* (or point of the triangle). Although we tend to think of the altitude as being inside the triangle, it can actually lie outside the triangle (as seen in the following figure).

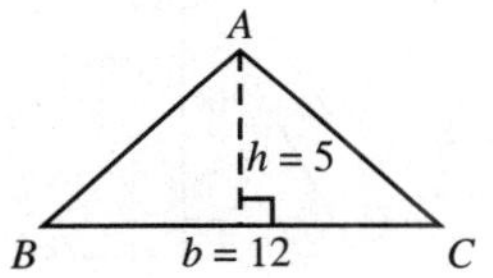

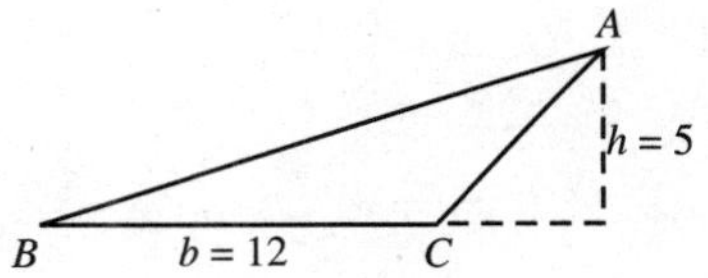

Both triangles shown have the same area: $A = \frac{1}{2}(12)(5) = 30$.

Example

In ΔABC, $AC = 6$, $BC = 8$, and $AB = 10$. Find the length of the altitude from vertex C to side AB.

Solution

Since the sides have lengths 6-8-10 (double the Pythagorean Triple 3-4-5), the triangle is a right triangle with AB being the hypotenuse. By using the two legs as base and height, the area of the triangle must be: $A = \frac{1}{2}(6)(8) = 24$. By using the hypotenuse and the unknown altitude (see the following figure), the area must be $A = \frac{1}{2}(10)(h) = 5h$. Therefore, $5h = 24$ and $h = 4.8$.

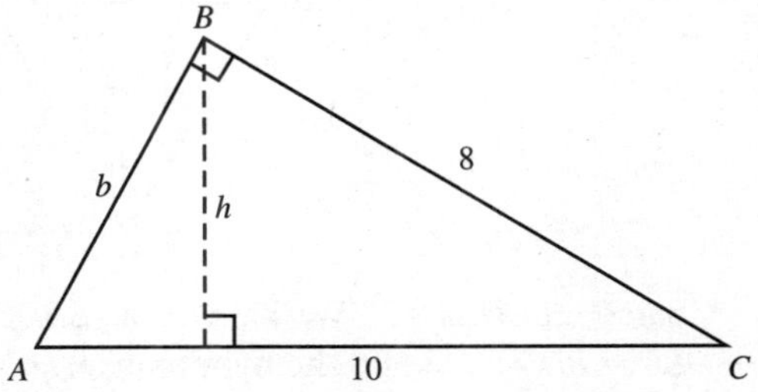

Topic 39. Other Special Triangles

FYI

Remember that, in a right triangle, you can use the two legs (the two sides other than the hypotenuse) as base and altitude. Thus, the area of a 3-4-5 right triangle is $A\frac{1}{2}(3)(4) = 6$ square units.

Besides the Pythagorean Triples (see Topic 37), there are two other special kinds of right triangles that you should be on the lookout for.

The first is the 45°-45°-90° triangle. This is an isosceles triangle, so its legs are of equal length, and the hypotenuse is $\sqrt{2}$ times as long as the leg (see the following figure).

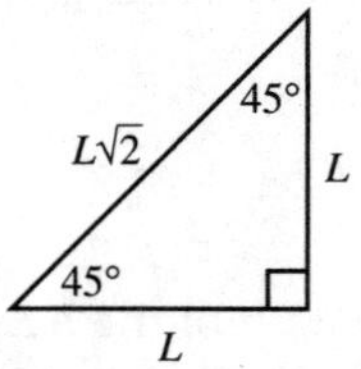

The second is the 30°-60°-90° triangle. This is half of an equilateral triangle. Hence, the shorter leg is half the hypotenuse and the longer leg (the one opposite the 60° angle) is $\sqrt{3}$ times the shorter leg (see below).

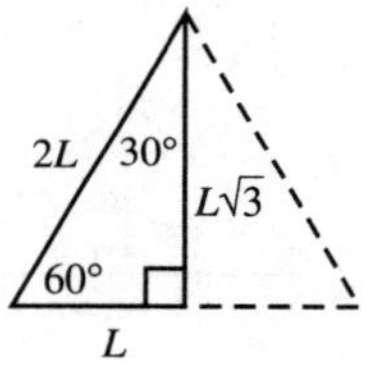

Example

Find the perimeter of the region shown in the following figure.

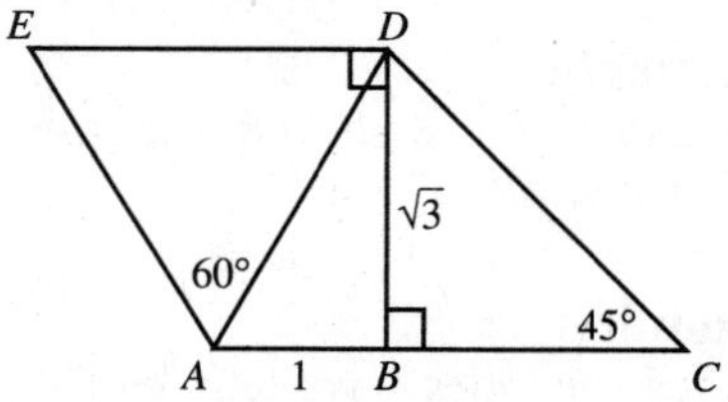

Solution

Since $BD = \sqrt{3}$ and $AB = 1$, we know that ABD is a 30°-60°-90° right triangle. Hence, we know three things: First, $AD = 2$ (twice the shorter leg); second, $\angle ADB$ is 30°; third, $\angle ADE$, which is the complement of $\angle ADB$, must be 60°. This makes ΔAED equilateral, so $AE = ED = 2$.

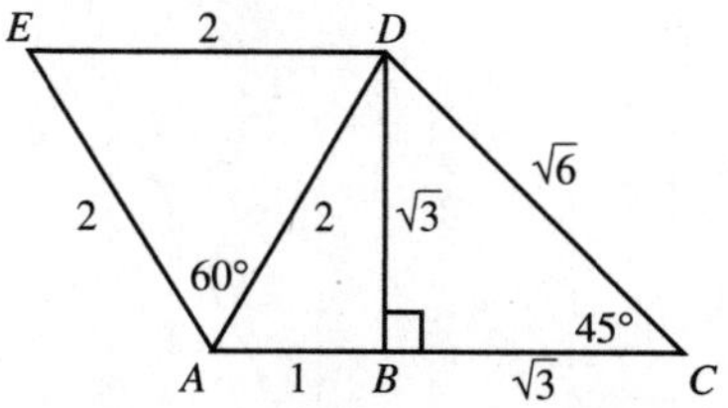

Since $\angle BCD$ is 45°, we know that ΔBDC is a 45°-45°-90° right triangle, so that $BC = BD = \sqrt{3}$ and the hypotenuse, $DC = (\sqrt{2})(\sqrt{3}) = \sqrt{6}$. Starting at A, and proceeding clockwise, we add the lengths we have just found to get the perimeter $2 + 2 + \sqrt{6} + \sqrt{3} + 1 = 5 + \sqrt{6} + \sqrt{3}$.

(This is an acceptable answer. Since $\sqrt{6}$ and $\sqrt{3}$ are irrational numbers, whose values cannot be precisely represented, they are conventionally expressed in this form, including on the SAT.)

Topic 40. Other Polygons

Any geometric figure with straight line segments as sides is called a *polygon*. To analyze any polygon (for example, to calculate its area), connect the vertices by line segments to divide it into triangles.

Example

Find the area of figure *ABCDE* below.

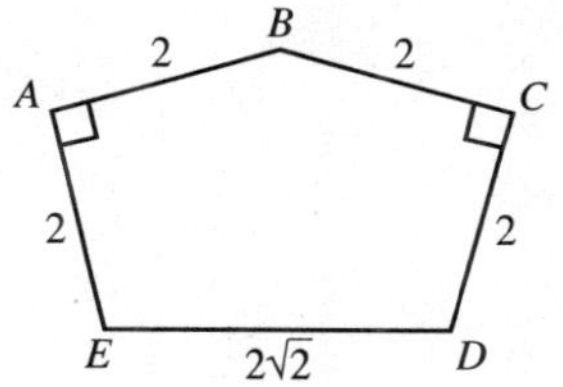

Solution

Drawing the line segments *BE* and *BD* divides the region into three triangles (see below).

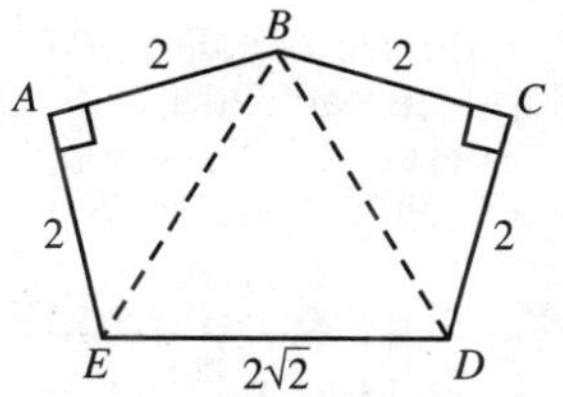

ΔABE and ΔBCD are both 45°-45°-90° right triangles, making $BE = BD = 2\sqrt{2}$. This makes the central triangle an equilateral triangle. The area of each of the two outer triangles is $\frac{1}{2}(2)(2) = 2$. So the two together have area 4.

The center triangle has base $2\sqrt{2}$. If you draw the altitude, you get a 30°-60°-90° right triangle with shorter leg $\sqrt{2}$, which makes the height $\sqrt{3}$ times that, or $\sqrt{6}$. This gives an area of $\frac{1}{2}(2\sqrt{2})(\sqrt{6}) = \sqrt{12} = 2\sqrt{3}$. Hence, the total area of the polygon is $4 + 2\sqrt{3}$.

Topic 41. Basic Properties of Circles

Any line cutting across a circle is called a *chord*. The longest possible chord is one that goes through the center of the circle; it's called the *diameter*. The *radius* is half the diameter, and all radii are equal in length. An *arc* is a segment of the circle. Its size may be measured in degrees. The degree measure of an arc is the measure of the *central angle* subtended by it, as shown in the following figure.

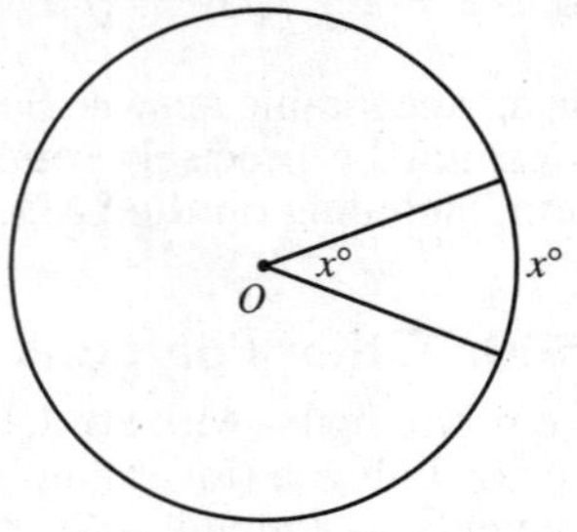

Example 1

If the arc *PS* in the following figure has a degree measure of 57°, is the chord *PS* longer or shorter than the radius?

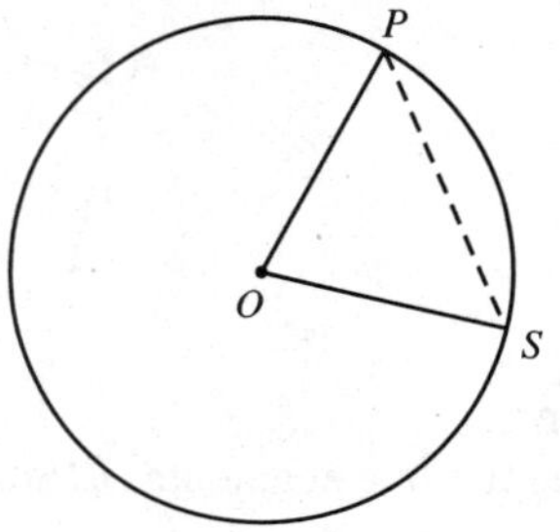

Solution

Since all radii are equal, ΔOPS is isosceles, and the angles at *P* and *S* must be equal. Suppose each has a degree measure of *x*. Now, $2x + 57 = 180$. Hence, $x = 61.5$. Therefore, *PS* is opposite the smallest angle in the triangle and must be the shortest side. That is, *PS* is shorter than a radius.

Topic 42. The Area and Circumference of a Circle

FYI

Don't confuse the two circle formulas. A good way to keep them straight is to remember the square *in* r^2. *It should remind you that area must be in square units, such as square inches.*

There are two formulas that you must know for working with circles.

- The circumference of a circle is calculated by the formula $C = 2\pi r$.
- The area of a circle is calculated by the formula $A = \pi r^2$.

In both formulas, π (the Greek letter pi) is a constant, a number whose value is approximately 3.1416 (or about $\frac{22}{7}$), while *r* is the radius.

Example 1

Find the circumference of the region shown in the figure below. (Note: the curved side shown is a *semicircle*, an arc representing half a complete circle.)

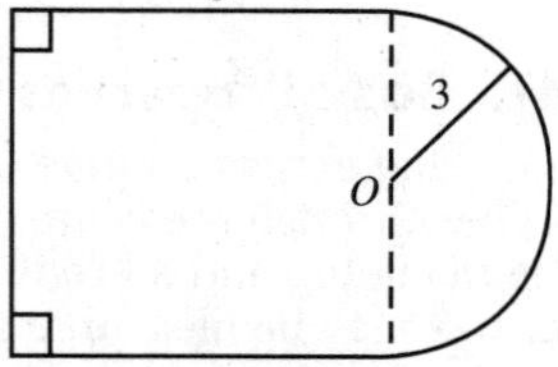

Solution

The dotted line divides the region into a rectangle and a semicircle. Since the radius of the circular arc is 3, the diameter is 6, and that is the width of the rectangle. The length is 8. Hence, the length of the three straight sides total $8 + 8 + 6 = 22$. The circumference of the whole circle would be $2\pi r = 2\pi(3) = 6\pi$. Therefore, the semicircular arc must be half that length or 3π, which added to the previous total gives a length of $22 + 3\pi$.

Example 2

If the larger circle shown below has radius 4, find the area of the shaded region.

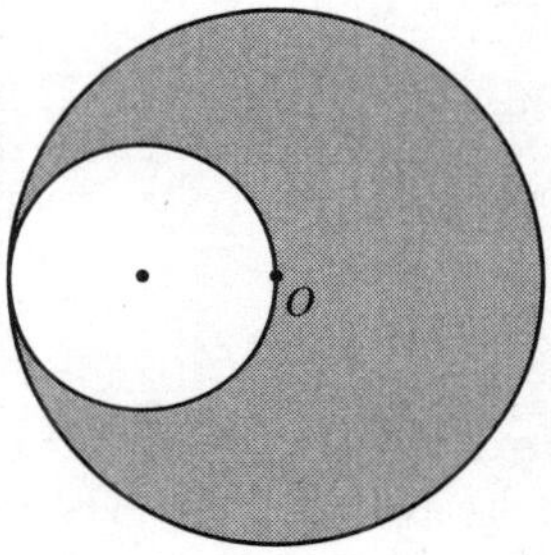

Solution

The larger circle has area $AL = \pi(4)^2 = 16\pi$. The diameter of the smaller circle equals the radius of the larger one, so its radius is $\frac{1}{2}(4) = 2$. Its area must be $AS = \pi(2)^2 = 4\pi$. The shaded area is the larger area minus the smaller area, or $16\pi - 4\pi = 12\pi$.

FYI

When an SAT problem asks you to find the area of a shaded region, you will usually be unable to calculate it directly. Don't worry—instead, think of the shaded region as being whatever is left over when one region is "cut out" or subtracted from a larger region. Use the formulas you know to find those two regions and perform the necessary subtraction.

Topic 43. Volumes

For solid figures with straight line edges and flat surfaces (known as *polyhedra*), it can sometimes be unclear as to whether the word *side* refers to one of the flat surfaces bounding the solid or one of the line segments bounding the surfaces. To avoid confusion, people usually refer to these as *faces* and *edges* respectively, and this is the usage followed on the SAT.

A solid also has a *surface area*, which is the sum of the areas of all its faces, and a *volume,* or capacity. Volumes are given in cubic units. You should be familiar with the following formulas for the volumes of regular figures:

- A *rectangular solid* is a polyhedron with rectangular faces at right angles to one another (see the figure below). Its volume is calculated by the formula $V = LWH$; that is, Volume = Length × Width × Height.

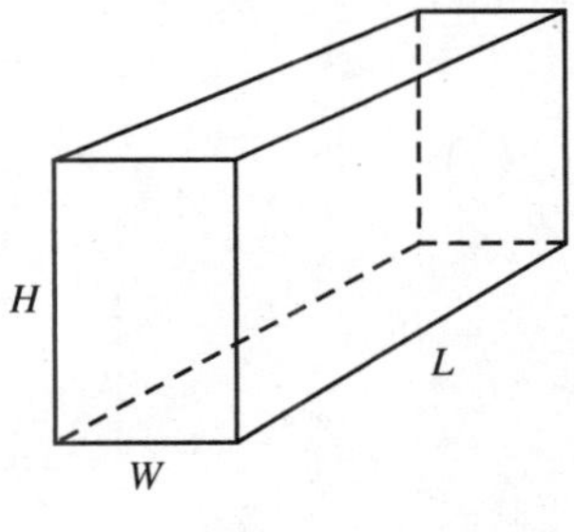

- A *cube* is a rectangular solid with all edges of equal length, *s*, that is $L = W = H = s$, like one of a pair of dice. Therefore, $V = s^3$; that is, Volume = side × side × side.
- A *right circular cylinder* is a figure with a circular base and a side perpendicular to that base, like a soda can (see the following figure). The volume is the area of the base times the height; that is, $V = \pi r^2 h$.

Example 1

Find the area of one face of a cube that has the same volume as a rectangular solid that is 18 inches long and has a base with one side 3 inches long and a diagonal 5 inches long.

Solution

To find the volume of the rectangular solid, we must first find the length of the third edge (see the following figure).

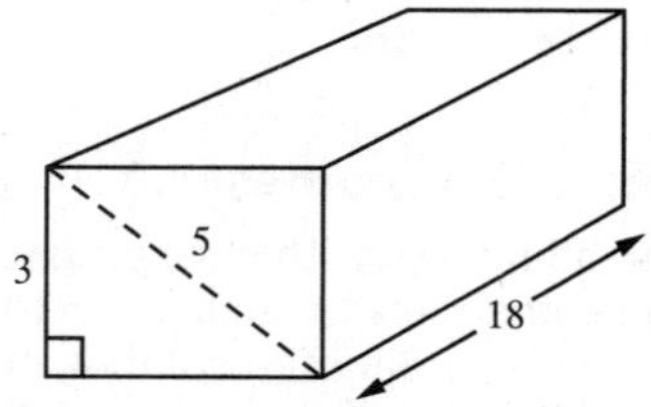

On that side, since the diagonal is 5 and one edge is 3, we must have a 3-4-5 triangle; so the other edge must be 4. Thus, the solid is 3 × 4 × 18, which means its volume is $VB = (3)(4)(18) = 216$. For the cube to have the same volume, we have $216 = s^3$. Thus, $s = 6$. The area of one side of the cube, being a square, is $6^2 = 36$.

Example 2

Arlene has a block of wood in the form of a rectangular solid 14 inches long, with a square base that is 6 inches on a side. A right circular cylinder is drilled out of the block as shown below. Find the volume of the wood remaining to the nearest cubic inch.

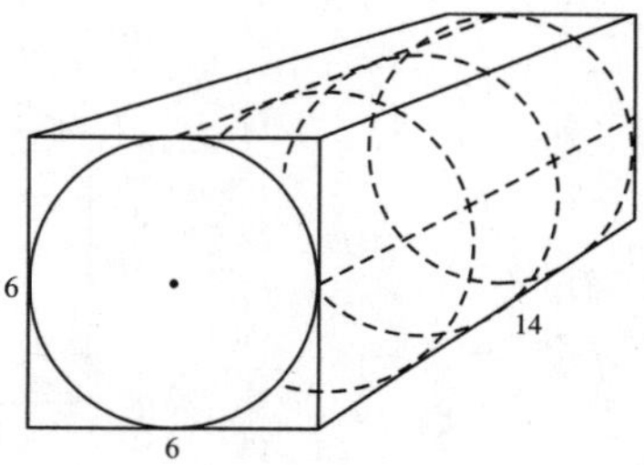

Solution

The original volume of the solid was

$$V_B = (6)(6)(14) = 504$$

Since the circle just goes from one side to the other of the square base, it must have a diameter of 6, which means its radius is 3. Hence the volume of the piece drilled out is:

$$V_H = \pi(3)^2(14) = 126\pi$$

Using an approximate value for π of $\frac{22}{7}$, 126π = about 396. Therefore, to the nearest cubic inch, the volume of the remaining wood is $504 - 396 = 108$ in.^{3}.

COORDINATE GEOMETRY

Topic 44. The Midpoint Formula

Given two points $P(x_1,y_1)$ and $Q(x_2,y_2)$, the midpoint, M, of the line segment PQ has coordinates:

$$x_M = \frac{x_1 + x_2}{2},\ y_M = \frac{y_1 + y_2}{2}$$

In words, this says that the coordinates of the midpoint are simply the averages of the coordinates of the end points. For example, the midpoint between (6,5) and (3,−1) is

$$x_M = \frac{6 + 3}{2} = \frac{9}{2},\ y_M = \frac{5 + (-1)}{2} = \frac{4}{2} = 2$$

Hence, the midpoint is $(\frac{9}{2},2) = (4.5,2)$.

Example 1

If (5,7) is the midpoint of the line segment connecting (−1,3) to $P(x,y)$, which is larger, x or y?

Solution

We know that the average of x and -1 must be 5. That is, $5 = \frac{x + -1}{2}$, or $10 = x - 1$. Therefore, $x = 11$. Similarly, we know that the average of y and 3 must be 7. Thus, $7 = \frac{y + 3}{2}$, or $14 = y + 3$, $y = 11$. Therefore, $x = y$. So x is larger.

Example 2

If $b > 5$, is $(2,b)$ closer to $P(-1,3)$ or $Q(5,7)$?

Solution

We see that (2,5) is the midpoint of PQ. Therefore, in the x-direction, $(2,b)$ will be equidistant from both P and Q. However, if $b > 5$, then b must be closer to 7 than to 3. Therefore, $(2,b)$ is closer to (5,7) than (−1,3).

Topic 45. The Distance Formula

Given two points $P(x_1,y_1)$ and $Q(x_2,y_2)$, the distance from P to Q is given by the formula:

$$d = (\sqrt{x_1 - x_2})^2 + (9y^1 - y^2)^2$$

In words, this says that the distance is the square root of the sum of the change in x squared plus the change in y squared, or $d = \sqrt{(\Delta x)^2 + (\Delta y)^2}$. For example, the distance from (6,2) to (3,−1) is $d = \sqrt{(6-3)^2 + (3-(-1))^2}$. Thus, $d = \sqrt{3^2 + 4^2} = \sqrt{9 + 16} = \sqrt{25} = 5$

Example 1

The point $(a,5)$ lies on a circle of radius 10 with center at (2,−3). What are the possible values of a?

Solution

Since every point on the circle must be 10 units from the center, we know that $(a,5)$ must be 10 units from (2,−3). Using the distance formula:

$$\sqrt{(a-2)^2 + (5-(-3))^2} = 10$$

$$\sqrt{(a^2 - 4a + 4) + 64} = 10$$

$$\sqrt{a^2 - 4a + 68} = 10$$

Squaring both sides, we have:

$$a^2 - 4a + 68 = 100$$

We subtract 100 from both sides to yield:

$$a^2 - 4a - 32 = 0$$

which factors as:

$$(a - 8)(a + 4) = 0$$

with two possible values for a:

$$a - 8 = 0 \text{ or } a + 4 = 0$$

$$a = 8 \text{ or } a = -4$$

Example 2

The point $(1,b)$ is equidistant from (−2,3) and (2,5). What are the possible values of b?

Solution

Since the distances from the two given points are the same, we use the distance formula twice and equate the results, thus:

$$\sqrt{18 - 6b + b^2} = \sqrt{26 - 10b + b^2}$$

Squaring both sides:

$$18 - 6b + b^2 = 26 - 10b + b^2$$

The b^2 terms subtract out, leaving:

$$-6b + 18 = -10b + 26$$

Adding $10b - 18$ to both sides of the equation gives us:

$$4b = 8 \text{ and } b = 2$$

Topic 46. The Slope of a Line

Given two points $P(x_1,y_1)$ and $Q(x_2,y_2)$, the *slope* of the line passing through P and Q is given by the formula:

$$m = \frac{y_1 - y_2}{x_1 - x_1 - x_2}$$

In words, this says that the slope is the change in y divided by the change in x, or $m = \frac{\Delta y}{\Delta x}$. For example, the slope of the line passing through (6,2) to (3,−2) is $m = \frac{2-(-2)}{6-3} = \frac{4}{3}$. Notice that it doesn't matter which you consider to be the first point and which the second, as long as you are consistent in plugging in the numbers into the top and bottom of the fraction.

Example

The point $(a,5)$ lies on a line of slope $\frac{1}{3}$ that passes through (2,−3). What is the value of a?

Solution

Since $m = \frac{y_1 - y_2}{x_1 - x_2}$, we must have $\frac{1}{3} = \frac{5-(-3)}{a-2}$.

$$\frac{1}{3} = \frac{8}{a-2}$$

Cross-multiplying:

$$a - 2 = 24;\ a = 26$$

COUNTING AND PROBABILITY

Topic 47. The Addition Principle for Counting

FYI

In logic, the word "or" means "either one or both"—that is, and/or.

If set A contains m objects, and set B contains n objects, and there are no objects common to the two sets, then the total number of objects in the two sets combined is $m + n$. But if there are k objects common to the two sets, then the total in the combined set is $m + n - k$. That is, you must take into account the double-counting of objects common to both groups. This kind of situation is usually handled most easily by displaying the given information in a *Venn diagram,* which depicts the sets as circles that may or may not overlap.

Example 1

Of a group of students at a fast-food restaurant, 12 ate hamburgers and 9 had fries. If 4 had both hamburgers and fries, how many had either hamburgers or fries?

Solution

If we let H be the set of those who had hamburgers and F be the set of those who had fries, then the diagram below displays the data.

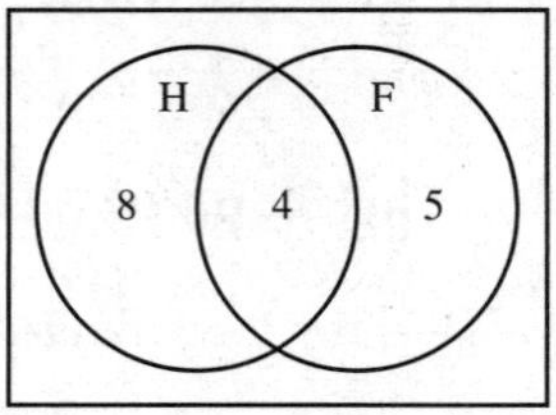

The shaded region holds those items that are common to both groups, and we can see that the total who had either burgers or fries is $8 + 4 + 5 = 17$.

Sometimes problems of this type can involve more than two sets.

Example 2

A survey of TV viewing habits including 50 individuals found 45 who watched news shows, 38 who watched mysteries, and 40 who watched sitcoms. If everyone surveyed watched at least one of these types of shows and 32 watched all three types, how many watched exactly two of the three?

Solution

We draw a Venn Diagram showing the given data (see figure below). Here N = News, M = Mystery, and S = Sitcoms. The number in each region is given, with the unknowns labeled, x, y, z, u, v, and w. However, we do not need to find all the unknowns, simply the sum $x + y + z$. Now,

$$x + u + y = 13$$
$$y + z + v = 6$$
$$x + z + w = 8$$

Adding all three equations,

$$2x + 2y + 2z + u + v + w = 27$$

But,

$$x + y + z + u + v + w = 18$$

Subtracting,

$$x + y + z = 9$$

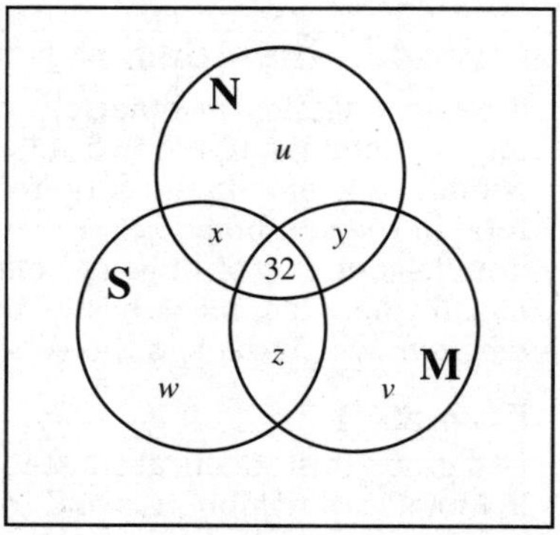

Topic 48. The Multiplication Principle for Counting

The *multiplication principle for counting* states that if an operation takes two steps and the first step can be performed in m ways, and if, for each of those ways, the second step can be performed in n ways, then the total number of ways of performing the operation is $T = mn$.

For example, suppose that a jar contains four balls numbered 1, 2, 3, and 4. If a ball is selected and the number is noted down, and then a second ball is selected without replacing the first, the number of two-digit numbers that can be formed is $(4)(3) = 12$. This process extends to more than two steps in the same way, by continuing to multiply the number of options at each step.

Example 1

A class contains 4 boys and 5 girls. In how many ways can a person choose a pair of one boy and one girl from this class?

Solution

You have 4 choices for a boy and 5 for a girl. By the multiplication principle, the total number of possible pairs is $4 \times 5 = 20$.

Example 2

From a club with 10 members, a slate of officers, including a president, vice-president, and secretary must be chosen. How many different possible slates are there if no one person can hold two offices?

Solution

By a natural extension of the principle to a three-step process, we see that we have 10 choices for president, for each of which we have 9 choices for vice-president (since one person has been eliminated, having been chosen as president); and for each such pair we have 8 choices for secretary (since two people have been eliminated, having been chosen as president and vice-president). Thus, the total number of possible slates is $10 \times 9 \times 8 = 720$.

Topic 49. The Number of Ways of Arranging *n* Objects in a Row

As a natural extension of the multiplication principle, it is not hard to show that the number of distinct arrangements of n distinguishable objects in a row is

$$n! = n(n - 1)(n - 2) \times 2 \times 1$$

(The expression $n!$ is called n factorial.)

For example, the number of ways of lining up the five starting players on the boys' basketball team for a team picture is $5! = 5 \times 4 \times 3 \times 2 \times 1 = 120$.

Example 1

If four textbooks—math, English, French, and Spanish—are arranged randomly on a shelf, what is the chance that they will be in alphabetical order from left to right?

Solution

There are 4 distinguishable objects which can be arranged in $4! = 4 \times 3 \times 2 \times 1 = 24$ ways. In only one of these ways will they be in alphabetical order. Therefore, the chance is $\frac{1}{24}$.

Example 2

In how many ways can four textbooks—math, English, French, and Spanish—be arranged on the shelf, if the Spanish and French textbooks must be next to each other?

Solution

If we "glue" the two books together, than we can think of the group as being only 3 books, which can be arranged in $3! = 3 \times 2 \times 1 = 6$ ways. However, for each of these ways, we could have set up the "glued" books in two sequences, either French/Spanish or Spanish/French. Hence, there are really $2 \times 6 = 12$ ways altogether.

Topic 50. Probability

To find the probability of a random event, divide the number of possible outcomes favorable to the event by the total number of possible outcomes. For example, if a bag contains 12 blue marbles and 9 red marbles, the probability of randomly selecting a blue marble is $\frac{\text{number of blue marbles}}{\text{total number of marbles}} = \frac{12}{21} = \frac{4}{7}$.

Example

If six girls line up in random order to have a group picture taken, what is the probability that the tallest girl will be at the left end and the shortest girl will be at the right end?

Solution

The 6 girls could line up in $6! = 120$ ways. If the tallest girl must be at the left and the shortest at the right, there are $4! = 24$ ways that the other girls can line up between them. Thus, there are 24 line-ups favorable to the event in question. Hence the probability is $\frac{24}{120} = \frac{1}{5}$.

Appendix C

The Insider's Stress-Buster's Guide

by Mary-Jo D. Weber
M.S. Psychiatric Nurse Practitioner

THE ROLE OF STRESS IN PEAK TEST PERFORMANCE

Let's face it—if you're like most people, you're not really looking forward to taking the SAT. In fact, the very thought of the test might make your stomach queasy and your neck and shoulders tight. You might become aware of your heart beating, and your hands might get clammy. You might even feel restless and be tempted to close this book right now and get a snack!

All of these physical responses to the stress of test-taking can work for you or against you. Conditioned by millions of years of evolution, your body has developed a complex natural reaction, sometimes called the fight or flight response, which comes into play whenever you feel physically or psychologically threatened. This reaction has a very real value in getting you ready to meet whatever challenge you face, whether it's a menacing stranger on a dark street, an auditorium full of people waiting to hear you deliver a speech, or a standardized exam.

The adrenaline and other hormones that are released when you are under stress can get you ready for peak performance. They arouse your senses to increased sensitivity, alert your brain cells to pay attention, sharpen your mental focus, increase the amounts of energizing oxygen delivered to all parts of your body, and raise the levels of glucose available to fuel your brain. These chemical processes account for the sense of excitement you feel when you're under stress. Some people—artists who thrill to public applause, for example, or world-class athletes—actually relish this state of physical and mental arousal, and even the average person finds it exhilarating, though perhaps scary, too.

The problem comes when these responses get out of control, freezing your thoughts and leaving you feeling uncomfortably tense or anxious. When that happens, you may develop "tunnel vision," a narrowing of perception that hampers your awareness of what's around you; you may even feel that your mind is "going blank," as if your brain is on overload and is starting to shut down.

Fortunately, you can manage your stress so that the natural stress response will sharpen your focus without limiting your perspective or closing off your options, making you more creative and imaginative and helping you to retrieve more of the useful information stored in your memory.

This appendix will give you specific, scientifically tested techniques to use in the weeks before the exam, while you are studying, and on the very day you take the SAT. If you practice these methods, you may find yourself almost looking forward to the opportunity to tackle the test—and beat it!

PREPARING FOR PEAK PERFORMANCE

Top athletes find that mental preparation is as important to their success in competition as practicing their specific athletic skills. The field of sports psychology has taught us a lot about how you can best prepare for your test. Practicing your academic skills is something like a basketball player working on his foul shot or a swimmer perfecting her stroke: it's essential, but it's not enough. The best performers don't stop there. They also use relaxation and visualization techniques to ensure that they'll be able to apply their skills and to respond effectively and creatively to the challenges that game day will bring their way.

Similar relaxation and visualization techniques can help keep you from freezing up and allow you to efficiently handle whatever comes your way in the test-taking situation. They can also help you experience the test as a positive challenge, not a looming source of terror. You will maintain a degree of comfort and be able to manage the unpleasant symptoms of anxiety without letting them overwhelm you.

Learning to Relax

First, you'll need to learn to relax whenever you decide you want to. Yes—for most people, it's a skill that must be learned. If you're like most people, you probably tend to keep going—with work, play, or just hanging around—until you're physically exhausted, and then you crash. It's not the most efficient way to harness the energy in your body and mind. Instead, if you learn to relax whenever you want to, you'll be able to control your stress responses so that you'll feel only the amount of anxiety you need to wake up your brain cells and perform your best.

The following exercise is a good way to start. If you're feeling any sense of tiredness or anxiety—after a couple of hours of studying, for example—this is a better way to refresh yourself than napping or taking a TV break. It takes only a few minutes and will leave you feeling energized and alert. You can either read through this suggested exercise and then try it, or, even better, get a friend with a pleasant voice to read it aloud to you while you try it. (Later, you can return the favor.) As you go through the exercise, feel free to alter it in any way that seems pertinent to your individual situation.

Relaxation Exercise

Start by sitting comfortably with both feet flat on the floor. Take some time to notice how the floor is supporting your feet. Allow the surface on which you are resting to support you completely. Take all the time you need to notice the comfort and security of this.

Next, turn your mind toward your breathing. Don't try to change it; just observe it. Observe how effortless your breathing is, realizing that, with every exhalation, the tension of the day is flowing out, and, with every inhalation, revitalizing oxygen is flowing in to nourish all parts of your body.

Turn your attention again to your feet. Notice that they are comfortably resting on the floor. Notice that feeling of comfort spreading up to your ankles, calves, and knees. Feel how securely the chair is supporting your thighs, your buttocks, your lower back, and your upper back.

Your hands may be in your lap or at your sides. Allow them to open, and as you continue to breathe comfortably and naturally, experience any tension flowing down from your shoulders to your arms and out your fingertips. You will notice that the more relaxed you can keep your hands, the more relaxed and alert you will be.

Notice whether your eyes are open or closed. Either way is fine. Take some time now to notice the muscles around your eyes, in your cheeks, and around your mouth. Notice whatever expression you naturally have on your face, whether it's frowning, neutral, or smiling. Don't feel you need to change it. Allow these muscles to soften. Close your eyes if you wish. Feel the heaviness of your jaw, and don't try to hold it up.

As you continue to notice the comfort in your body, pay attention to your neck and scalp. If you perceive any tension there, allow it to flow out with your next breath. Scan your body now, and if you notice any areas of discomfort or tension, notice that, as you breathe, any tension or discomfort flows out with each exhalation, while energy flows in with each inhalation.

Now, as you continue to enjoy the comfort of your body securely supported by the chair and energized by your breathing, imagine that you are in a special, favorite place. It may be the beach, or the mountains, or your room, or just inside yourself. Notice how comfortable and alert you are to all the things that make that place pleasurable for you. Notice the sights, sounds, smells, and feelings that make the place so nice.

Take your time enjoying your special place. When you are ready to return to the room in which you are sitting, gently reorient yourself, experiencing your calm alertness and renewed enthusiasm for all your endeavors.

Now that you're back from your special place, notice how revitalized you feel.

With practice, this process of relaxation will become easier and quicker, but you already have noticed that, from the very first attempt, you can recharge your batteries in a way that is even better than a nap because your alertness will be increased and your focus will be sharpened. Try using this method of relaxation whenever the pressure of studying is making you feel exhausted or tense. You'll find yourself learning more—and enjoying it more, too.

Visualizing Success

The next step is to add visualization of the test-taking situation and your desired successful outcome. It's a favorite preparation strategy of many successful athletes and entertainers; they find that visualizing themselves hitting the perfect tennis stroke or playing a difficult piano concerto with fluency and ease makes it much easier to actually perform that way.

It works for test-takers, too. Here's how to use it in preparing for the SAT.

Visualization Exercise

Repeat the relaxation exercise. This time, however, after you've imagined your special place and while you're alertly and attentively noting the sights, sounds, and feelings that you experience there, imagine that you are entering the room in which you'll take the SAT. Notice the rows of desks and chairs, the other students sitting and waiting for the exam to begin, and the proctor at the front of the room with a stack of sealed test booklets on the desk before her.

Take your seat, noting how comfortably your feet are supported by the floor, how your body is supported by the chair, and how your breathing is energizing your body and mind. The proctor walks up and down the rows of desks, handing out the SAT booklets and giving you instructions for the exam. When the proctor says, "Begin work," you tear open the seal on the booklet in front of you and turn to the first page of questions. You begin your work, knowing that you have prepared for this test and that you will correctly answer all the questions you need to in order to achieve your desired goal.

You experience just the right amount of anxiety you need to feel in order to achieve your peak performance. As you work, the questions appear familiar and interesting to you. You look forward to reading each question because you know you will find it to be an interesting challenge to the skills you've been learning and practicing. You work efficiently, and, when you come to the end of the test, you experience the sense of a job well done.

At this time, reorient yourself to the room.

You may also use this exercise before going to sleep, perhaps after a strenuous study session. If you do the exercise in bed, when it's completed, simply allow yourself to drift into a refreshing sleep.

During the weeks while you are studying for your exam, you can ensure peak performance by practicing relaxation and visualization every day. The best time for many people is at night, just before sleep. This will help your learning because your mind is working even while you sleep. Thus, if you practice visualizing test-taking success before you go to sleep, your brain will probably continue to process that information while you sleep, reinforcing the positive message.

Some people find it very effective to make an audiotape of the relaxation and visualization exercises, to be played while they fall asleep.

TECHNIQUES OF POWER STUDYING

If you're an athlete, a musician, or an actor, you know how important your physical condition is to your training. What you eat or drink before practice will influence how effective your training will be. The same is true of test preparation.

Physical Conditioning for Effective Study

Everyone knows his or her own best time of the day for studying. For some people, it's early in the morning, before class or work; for others, it's late at night. Whatever time you favor, make sure you're in peak condition before you hit the books. It should go without saying, but remember that if you drink alcohol or use mood-altering chemicals in the days preceding your exam, your performance will definitely be impaired. You're using this book, so you have an obvious interest in doing your best. Avoid these performance killers.

Nutrition is just as important for studying as it is for athletic training, because thinking and learning are physical functions of your body, carried out by the cells of your brain. It so happens that your brain cells work on glucose (sugar) only. That said, it would be incorrect to deduce that your diet while studying should consist of candy bars and sodas. But you do learn and think best when your brain has a steady stream of glucose.

The best way to ensure this is to eat high-protein and so-called "complex carbohydrate" foods before studying and about every three hours during studying. Fruit, lean meat and fish, vegetables, pasta with low-fat sauce, cereal, crackers, bread, and legumes (such as peas and beans) are the foods associated with high mental performance. These foods will keep your blood sugar steady at an optimal level.

Avoid greasy or fatty foods; the work of digesting them actually pulls oxygen-rich blood away from your brain and toward your digestive system. (So pizza, although you may love it, is really not the best study food. Wait until after the exam, and then treat yourself to a pie with your favorite toppings—as a reward for the high score you've earned.)

Rest is often neglected when people are studying very hard, but this is a mistake. Research has shown that people who are in a state of chronic sleep deprivation just don't think or perform very well. When hospitals shorten the working shifts of their medical residents, the doctors suffer fewer mental lapses and make better treatment decisions. The same applies to anyone working with his or her brain. The optimal amount of sleep varies from one person to another, but few people do well on less than 6 hours a night over any extended period of time, and most people thrive on 7 or 8 hours a night. Don't pull an all-nighter; get the sleep you need, and you'll find yourself learning more, and more easily, the next morning.

Reducing Stress When You Study

When you sit down to study, you can improve your memory and creativity by practicing the relaxation and visualization exercises earlier in this chapter. If you don't want to spend that much time, there is a brief technique that can be used just before studying or as needed during breaks in your study sessions. It takes only a few minutes. It works best if you have already experienced the longer exercise, and the more familiar you become with the long exercise, the better this short one will work.

The 3-Minute Relaxation Technique

Sit comfortably wherever you like, with your feet flat on the floor. Rest your hands on your lap or desk. Place the thumbs and index fingers of each hand together.

Close your eyes. Take a moment to notice your breathing. After a few seconds, turn your attention to the pressure of your thumbs on your index fingers. The pressure can be light or firm. Notice that pressure as you inhale and exhale several times; really notice how your fingers feel.

Then, as you exhale, release the pressure, relaxing your hands, feeling your tension and fatigue flowing out with your exhalation and melting down your arms and out your fingertips.

Continue to focus on your breathing for a few minutes. When you are ready, open your eyes and reorient yourself to your surroundings.

This quick exercise will allow you to capture a sense of calm alertness whenever you need it.

Music to Learn By

Many people enjoy listening to music while they are studying. There is nothing wrong with music as long as you like it and don't find it distracting, but there are some things to consider when you choose music for your study sessions.

Music can help you to concentrate by filtering out extraneous sounds or thoughts. For this purpose, it is helpful if the music is familiar, so listening to a selection of favorite CDs would help you to study more efficiently than listening to the radio (which will probably play both familiar and unfamiliar selections, as well as interjecting a stream of chatter and commercials that may well be distracting).

Music can also set a helpful mood while you're studying. It's a very personal choice, but in certain recent studies, when research subjects listened to classical music, particularly the works of Mozart, just before and during cognitive (mental) tasks, their performance on those tasks improved. You might want to experiment with different kinds of music to see which help you to concentrate best.

STRESS-BUSTING STRATEGIES FOR TEST DAY AND TEST DAY MINUS ONE

Hopefully you're not reading these suggestions for peak performance for the first time the day before your test. Ideally you'll have used the ideas we've presented for developing your personal test-preparation plan, and you will be following it, more or less closely, in the weeks leading up to the exam. In particular, repeatedly visualizing success in the weeks before the test will motivate you to study and to view the test as a challenge you can meet, not a disaster in the making.

The Night Before

On the day before the test, make sure you have your admission form, your identification, a pen and pencil, and your directions to the test site, all ready and available for the morning. Make sure you know how to get to the test center and how long it will take you to get there given the expected weather conditions and traffic patterns. If you control these "petty" details, they won't inject an unnecessary note of anxiety or uncertainty on the morning of the exam.

It's really helpful if you can do something pleasant and relaxing the night before the test. Make sure you go to bed early enough to get the amount of sleep you need to do your best. If you've made a tape of your relaxation and visualization exercises, have it playing as you drift off into a refreshing sleep.

However, if you're going to be worrying about that one last math rule or analogy technique while you're watching that movie—or if you're feeling that you haven't suffered enough yet to appease the testing gods so they'll allow you to get your highest score—here are some tips for last-minute studying.

Don't try to reread this book or do any kind of comprehensive review. At this point that will only increase your anxiety and convince you, incorrectly, that all the studying you have already done was inadequate and futile. Instead, decide how long you can study while still getting a good night's sleep. If you need 9 hours to feel rested, your score will be boosted more by getting the full 9 hours than by another few hours of studying.

Then pick a few topics you can comfortably cover in the amount of time you have left. Choose topics you are good at but feel can use a little more polishing, keeping in mind that you don't need a "perfect" score or to get every question correct.

Always remember, it is really all the previous study you've done that will determine your score; you're only reviewing the night before to appease the testing gods. When it's time to go to sleep, set your alarm clock to give you plenty of time to get ready, eat breakfast, and get to the testing site without rushing. Then practice your relaxation and visualization exercises, and have pleasant dreams of test-taking victory.

The Morning of the Exam

In the morning, eat something, even if you normally don't eat breakfast. Study after study has demonstrated that people perform better on tests when they have eaten about 30 to 60 minutes beforehand. The foods you should eat are the same as those recommended during studying—high protein, low fat, and complex carbohydrate. Bring a piece of fruit or a power bar to the test center to eat during the brief mid-exam break.

During the exam itself—especially during the short breaks provided between test sections—you might try using the 3-Minute Relaxation technique if you feel fatigued or stressed.

All these tips, if practiced along with the study outlined in this book, will ensure your optimal performance on the SAT. They'll also help you attain an even higher goal: to feel balanced and sane before and after the test.

Appendix D

College Admissions Calendar and Checklist*

11TH GRADE

This year the college search process begins in earnest. Exploration and testing should help you start developing a list of target schools by spring. Poor grades will not be as easily forgiven as those from previous years, and colleges will look for commitment and accomplishment outside of the classroom.

September

- ❑ Make sure that PSAT/NMSQT registration is handled by your guidance counselor staff (except in regions where ACT test is prevalent). Ascertain and save the date.
- ❑ Ask your guidance department about college fairs in your area and college admission-representative visits to the school. Attend fairs and sessions with reps at school.
- ❑ Familiarize yourself with guidance-office resources.

October

- ❑ Make sure PSAT/NMSQT date is on your calendar. Read the student bulletin and try the practice questions.
- ❑ Schedule a day trip to visit nearby colleges. Don't worry if these are places where you won't apply. The goal is to explore different types of schools. Aim for variety. Discuss which characteristics are attractive and which aren't.

December

- ❑ Questions about PSAT scores? Contact your guidance counselor. If necessary, discuss strategies for improving weak areas. Evaluate different SAT prep options, as needed.
- ❑ Take advantage of college students home for vacation. Ask them questions.
- ❑ Take an introductory look at financial-aid forms, just to see what you'll need by this time next year.

---

* Reprinted from Arco's *College Admissions/A Crash Course for Panicked Parents* (Sally Rubenstone & Sidonia Dalby) Macmillan USA.

January

- ❑ Evaluate academic progress so far. Are grades up to par? Are course levels on target? Do study habits need improvement?
- ❑ Begin thinking about worthwhile summer plans (job, study, camp, volunteer work, travel, etc.)
- ❑ Mark projected SAT I & II or ACT test dates on your calendar. Also mark registration deadlines.

February

- ❑ Look ahead to SAT or ACT registration deadlines for the tests you plan to take. Are you about to miss one? Mark appropriate dates on your calendar. (A few juniors have reason to take the SAT I in March. If you will do so, heed February registration deadline).
- ❑ Buy a general guidebook to U.S. colleges and universities.

March

- ❑ Consider and plan spring-vacation college visits.
- ❑ Begin listing target colleges in a notebook ("The College Bible").
- ❑ Begin calling, writing, or e-mailing target colleges to request publications.
- ❑ Set aside an area for college propaganda. Invest in folders for materials from front-runner schools.
- ❑ Look ahead to SAT or ACT registration deadlines for the tests you plan to take. Are you about to miss one? Mark appropriate test and registration dates on your calendar.
- ❑ Make sure you discuss plans to take Advanced Placement exams with teachers and/or guidance counselor as needed.

April

- ❑ Look ahead to SAT or ACT registration deadlines for the tests you plan to take. Are you about to miss one? Mark appropriate test and registration dates on your calendar.
- ❑ Decide on senior-year classes. Include at least one math course or lab science, as well as the most challenging courses possible. Recognize that colleges weigh senior classes and grades as heavily as the junior record.
- ❑ Update activities record.

May

- ❑ Look ahead to SAT or ACT registration deadlines for the tests you plan to take. Are you about to miss one? Mark the appropriate test and registration dates on your calendar.
- ❑ Assess the need for and affordability of special services such as standardized test-prep courses, independent college counselors, and private group-tour programs.
- ❑ Do you need to take the TOEFL (Test of English as a Foreign Language)? Select date and oversee registration.

June

- ❑ Look ahead to SAT or ACT registration deadlines for the tests you plan to take. Are you about to miss one? Mark the appropriate test and registration dates on your calendar.

Summer

- ❑ Make sure you have a job or constructive activities throughout most of the summer. Study, jobs, and volunteer work always rate high with admission officials.
- ❑ Consider and plan summer and fall college visits.
- ❑ Request publications from additional target colleges.
- ❑ Plan and execute supplemental submissions such as audition tapes and art slides/portfolio, if required and/or appropriate.
- ❑ Review and update target college list. Include pros and cons. Make tentative plans for fall visits.

12TH GRADE

This is the year when the college search can feel like a full-time job—with all of the toil, tedium, and triumphs that that implies.

September

- ❑ Discuss plans and goals for the months ahead; pros and cons of target schools.
- ❑ Look ahead to SAT or ACT registration for the tests you plan to take. Are you about to miss one? Mark the appropriate test and registration dates on your calendar.
- ❑ Ask your guidance counselor about college fairs in your area and college admission-representative visits to the school. Make certain that you attend fairs and sessions with reps at schools.
- ❑ Finalize fall college-visit plans. Include campus overnights, where possible. Visit!
- ❑ Request additional publications and applications from target colleges.

October

- ❑ Look ahead to SAT or ACT registration for the tests you plan to take. Are you about to miss one? Mark the appropriate test and registration dates on your calendar.
- ❑ Draw up a master schedule of application and financial-aid due dates, and then put them on your calendar.
- ❑ Begin considering essay topics and requesting teacher recommendations.
- ❑ Visit colleges. Include interviews on campus (or with local alumni representatives).

- ❑ Attend college fairs.
- ❑ For another look at college life, rent a movie like *Animal House* or *School Daze.*
- ❑ Look at "Early Decision" and "Early Action" options.

November

- ❑ Look ahead to SAT or ACT registration for the tests you plan to take. Are you about to miss one? Mark the appropriate test and registration dates on your calendar.
- ❑ Reduce target college "long list" to a "short list," where applications will be made.
- ❑ Plan a Thanksgiving break that includes college visits (to almost-empty campuses).
- ❑ What is the status of your applications? Get someone to proofread your applications and essay(s).

December

- ❑ Look ahead to SAT or ACT registration for the tests you plan to take. Are you about to miss one? Mark the appropriate test and registration dates on your calendar.
- ❑ Pick up financial-aid material from guidance office and attend planning workshops, if available.
- ❑ Make sure that teachers and guidance counselors are up to date with reference forms and that transcripts are being sent to all short-list colleges.

January

- ❑ Begin filling out financial-aid forms. Finish and mail these forms as soon as possible and *never LATE.*
- ❑ Complete all applications, including those with later deadlines. Don't forget to photocopy everything and save in accordion files.
- ❑ If SAT's are being taken this month, are "Rush" scores required? Ask target colleges, if you're not certain.

February

- ❑ Unless confirmations have been received, call colleges to check on completion of applications. Record the name of the person you spoke with. Track down missing records.

March

- ❑ WAIT!

April

- ❑ Keep in mind that "thin " letters aren't always rejections. Some schools send out enrollment forms later.
- ❑ Rejoice in acceptances; keep rejections in perspective.
- ❑ Plan "crunch-time" visits to campuses, as needed, to help prompt final decisions.
- ❑ Compare financial-aid decisions, where applicable. Contact financial-aid offices with questions.
- ❑ Make sure your return "Wait-List" cards, as needed. Contact admission offices to check on Wait-List status. Send updated records and other information, if available. Write an upbeat "Please take me, and this is why you should" letter.
- ❑ Is the verdict final? Have your parents send the required deposit. Don't dawdle and miss the May 1 deadline or colleges can give away your place. Also notify those schools you won't be attending, especially if an aid offer was made.

May

- ❑ Take AP exams, if appropriate.
- ❑ Stay abreast of housing choices, etc. When will forms be mailed? Should you be investigating living-situations options? When is a freshman orientation? (Some schools have spring and summer programs.) When is course registration?

June

- ❑ Write a thank-you note to anyone who may have been especially helpful. Guidance counselors are often unsung heroes. Don't forget teachers who wrote recommendations, admission counselors or secretaries, tour guides, or other students.
- ❑ Consider summer school if you want to accelerate or place out of requirements. ALWAYS check with colleges first to make sure credits will count. Get permission in writing when it's questionable.
- ❑ Make sure that a final high-school transcript is sent to the college you will attend. (Most schools should do this automatically.)

Appendix E

College Application Log

Use this log for every school you apply to in order to track the application process:

School Name: ______________________________

____

School Telephone Number: ______________________________

____

School Address: ______________________________

____

School Web site: ______________________________

____

Catalog/Application Request Date: ______________________________

____

Catalog/Application Receipt Date: ______________________________

____

Application Deadline: ______________________________

____

Application Fee: ______________________________

____

Rolling Admissions, Standard or Early: ____________________

____

Date Application Mailed: ____________________

____

Financial Aid Material Request Date: ____________________

____

Financial Aid Material Receipt Date: ____________________

____

Financial Aid Deadline: ____________________

____

Letter of Recommendation 1

Name: ____________________

____

Telephone Number: ____________________

____

Date Requested: ____________________

____

Verified Sent: ____________________

____

Date School Received: ____________________

____

Letter of Recommendation 2

Name: ______________________________

____

Telephone Number: ______________________________

____

Date Requested: ______________________________

____

Verified Sent: ______________________________

____

Date School Received: ______________________________

____

Letter of Recommendation 3

Name: ______________________________

____

Telephone Number: ______________________________

____

Date Requested: ______________________________

____

Verified Sent: ______________________________

____

Date School Received: ______________________________

____

ACT Scores Request Date: ______________________________

____

Date School Received ACT Scores: ______________________________

____

Personal Statement Due Date: ______________________________

____

Personal Statement Completion Date: ______________________________

____

Appendix F

State Student Financial Aid Offices*

Following are current addresses and phone numbers for each state's student financial aid office. (Puerto Rico and the Virgin Islands are also included.) Call the agency to find out about state financial aid programs, requirements for resident and nonresident students, and to obtain all application forms, deadline information, and the phone number of your state's Guaranty Agency (the entity responsible for student loans). Information on your state's Guaranty Agency can also be obtained from the Federal Student Aid Information Center at 800-433-3243.

Alabama
Commission on Higher Education
100 North Union Street
P.O. Box 302000
Montgomery, AL 36130–2000
334-242-1998

Alaska
Commission on Postsecondary Education
3030 Vintage Boulevard
Juneau, AK 99801-7109
907-465-2962

Arizona
Commission for Postsecondary Education
2020 North Central Avenue, Suite 275
Phoenix, AZ 85004-4503
602-229-2591

Arkansas
Department of Higher Education
114 East Capitol Street
Little Rock, AR 72201
501-371-2000

California
Student Aid Commission
P.O. Box 419026
Rancho Cordova, CA 95741-9026
916-526-7590

Colorado
Commission on Higher Education
1300 Broadway, Second Floor
Denver, CO 80203
303-866-2723

---

* Reprinted from Arco's *10 Minute Guide to Paying for Grad School* (Ellen Liichtenstein).

Connecticut
Department of Education
61 Woodland Street
Hartford, CT 06105-2326
860-947-1855

Delaware
Commission on Higher Education
820 North French Street
Wilmington, DE 19801
302-577-6765

District of Columbia
Office of Postsecondary Education
2100 Martin Luther King, Jr. Avenue SE, Suite 401
Washington, DC 20020
202-727-3688

Florida
Office of Student Financial Aid Assistance
1344 Florida Education Center
325 West Gaines Street
Tallahassee, FL 32399
888-827-2004

Georgia
Student Finance Authority
2082 East Exchange Place, Suite 100
Tucker, GA 30084
770-724-9030

Hawaii
Postsecondary Education Commission
2444 Dole Street. Room 209
Honolulu, HI 96822-2394
808-956-8207

Idaho
State Board of Education
P.O. Box 83720
Boise, ID 83720-0037
208-334-2270

Illinois
Student Assistance Commission
1755 Lake Cook Road
Deerfield, IL 60015
800-899-4722

Indiana
State Student Assistance Commission
150 West Market Street, Suite 500
Indianapolis, IN 46204
317-232-2350

Iowa
College Student Aid Commission
200 10th Street, 4th Floor
Des Moines, IA 50309-3609
515-281-3501

Kansas
Board of Regents
700 SW Harrison, Suite 1410
Topeka, KS 66603-3760
785-296-3517

Kentucky
Higher Education Assistance Authority
1050 U.S. 127 South
Frankfort, KY 40601-4323
800-928-8926

Louisiana
Office of Student Financial Assistance
P.O. Box 91202
Baton Rouge, LA 70821-9202
800-259-5626 ext. 1012

Maine
Finance Authority of Maine
P.O. Box 949
Augusta, ME 04332-0949
207-288-3734

Maryland
Maryland Higher Education Commission
Jeffrey Building
16 Francis Street
Annapolis, MD 21401-1781
410-974-5370

Massachusetts
Board of Higher Education
Office of Student Financial Assistance
330 Stuart Street, 3rd Floor
Boston, MA 02116
617-727-1205

Michigan
Michigan Higher Education Assistance Authority
Office of Scholarships and Grants
P.O. Box 30462
Lansing, MI 48909-7962
517-373-3394

Minnesota
Higher Education Services Office
1450 Energy Park Drive, Suite 350
St. Paul, MN 55108-5227
651-642-0567

Mississippi
Postsecondary Education Financial Assistance Board
3825 Ridgewood Road
Jackson, MS 39211-6453
601-982-6663

Missouri
Student Assistance Resource Services
3515 Amazonas Drive
Jefferson City, MO 65109-5717
573-751-3940

Montana
Office of Commissioner of Higher Education
Montana Guaranteed Student Loan Program
P.O. Box 203101
Helena, MT 59620-3101
800-537-7508

Nebraska
Coordinating Commission for Postsecondary Education
P.O. Box 95005
Lincoln, NE 68509-5005
402-471-2847

Nevada
Department of Education
700 East Fifth Street
Carson City, NV 89701-5096
402-687-9200

New Hampshire
Postsecondary Education Commission
Two Industrial Park Drive
Concord, NH 03301-8512
603-271-2555

New Jersey
Higher Education Student Assistance Authority
P.O. Box 340
Trenton, NJ 08625
609-588-3316

New Mexico
Commission on Higher Education
1608 Cerrillos Road
Santa Fe, NM 87501
800-279-9777

New York
Higher Education Services Corporation
One Commerce Plaza
Albany, NY 12255
888-697-4372

North Carolina
Education Assistance Authority
P.O. Box 13663
Research Triangle Park, NC 27709-3663
800-700-1775

North Dakota
Student Financial Assistance Program
600 East Boulevard Avenue, Dept. 215
Bismarck, ND 58505-0230
701-328-4114

Ohio
Board of Regents
P.O. Box 182452
Columbus, OH 43218-2452
888-833-1133

Oklahoma
State Regents for Higher Education
500 Education Boulevard
Oklahoma City, OK 73105-4503
405-858-4356

Oregon
State Scholarship Commission
1500 Valley River Drive
Eugene, OR 97401-2130
800-452-8807

Pennsylvania
Higher Education Assistance Authority
1200 North Seventh Street
Harrisburg, PA 17102-1444
800-692-7435

Puerto Rico
Council on Higher Education
Fernandez Juncos Station
P.O. Box 19900
San Juan, PR 00910-1900
787-724-7100

Rhode Island
Higher Education Assistance Authority
560 Jefferson Boulevard
Warwick, RI 02886
401-736-1170

South Carolina
Higher Education Tuition Grants Commission
1310 Lady Street, Suite 801
Columbia, SC 29211
803-734-1200

South Dakota
Department of Education and Cultural Affairs
Office of the Secretary
700 Governors Drive
Pierre, SD 57501-2291
605-773-3134

Tennessee
Student Assistance Corporation
404 James Robertson Parkway, Suite 1950
Nashville, TN 37243
615-741-1346

Texas
Texas Higher Education Coordinating Board
P.O. Box 12788, Capitol Station
Austin, TX 78711
800-242-3062

Utah
State Board of Regents
355 West North Temple
3 Triad Center, Suite 550
Salt Lake City, UT 84180-1205
801-321-7200

Vermont
Student Assistance Corporation
P.O. Box 2000
Winooski, VT 05404-2601
800-642-3177

Virginia
State Council of Higher Education
101 North 14th Street
Richmond, VA 23219-3684
804-786-1690

Virgin Islands
Joint Boards of Education
Charlotte Amelie
P.O. Box 11900
St. Thomas, VI 00801
340-774-4546

Washington
Higher Education Coordinating Board
917 Lakeridge Way
Olympia, WA 98501-3430
360-753-7850

West Virginia
State College and University Systems Central Office
1018 Lanawha Boulevard East, Suite 700
Charleston, WV 25301-2827
304-558-4016

Wisconsin
Higher Education Aids Board
P.O. Box 7885
Madison, WI 53707-7885
608-267-2944

Wyoming
Wyoming Community College Commission
2020 Carey Avenue, 8th Floor
Cheyenne, WY 82002
307-777-7763

Appendix G

Financial Aid Glossary*

Assistantships Financial aid provided for performing work (usually on a part-time basis). Types of assistantships include teaching, research, administrative, and residence. Assistantships are usually awarded according to merit.

Campus-Based Programs Federal aid programs administered by a school's financial aid administrator. For graduate study, these programs include Federal Work-Study (FWS) and Perkins Loans.

Consolidated Loan Program Federal loan consolidation program enabling students to combine different types of federal loans to simplify repayment after graduation. The lender pays off the existing loans; the borrower then repays the consolidation loan. Borrowers have from ten to thirty years to repay it.

Cooperative Education Work-study arrangements in which the student receives academic credit for work outside the school. Students work full- or part-time as salaried employees for participating companies.

Cost of Attendance (COA) Also called Student Budget. The total amount it will cost a student to go to school, usually expressed in a yearly figure. The COA covers tuition and fees; housing; food; and allowances for books, supplies, transportation, loan fees, dependent care, costs related to a disability, and miscellaneous expenses. For part-time students, the COA does not include room and board.

Default Borrower's failure to repay a loan according to the terms agreed upon. Default may also result from failure to submit requests for deferment or cancellation on time. Borrowers in default may be subject to garnishment of wages, credit difficulties, and other penalties.

Endowments As pertaining to financial aid, the portion of private donations to schools that is administered by the financial aid office in the form of loans, grants, scholarships, and other awards.

Expected Family Contribution (EFC) For graduate students, the amount you and your spouse are expected to contribute to your educational costs. This figure is subtracted from the Cost of Attendance to determine your financial need. Factors such as taxable and nontaxable income, assets (such as savings and checking accounts), and benefits (such as unemployment and social security) are all considered in this calculation. If you're married, your spouse's contribution is also calculated. No student contribution is calculated for eligibility of unsubsidized Stafford Loans.

Federal Work-Study (FWS) Federal subsidy program that provides jobs for students with financial need, allowing them to earn money to pay educational expenses. The program encourages community service work and work related to student's course of study.

Fellowship An outright stipend usually awarded on a merit basis.

Financial Aid Financial assistance from government, institutional, and private sources given to supplement the student's family contribution.

Financial Aid Package The total amount of financial aid a student receives. Federal and nonfederal aid, such as scholarships, loans, or work-study, are

---

* Reprinted from Arco's *10 Minute Guide to Paying for Grad School* (Ellen Liichtenstein).

combined to help the student. One of the major responsibilities of a school's financial aid administrator is to use available resources to give each student the best possible package.

Financial Aid PROFILE Form from the College Scholarship Service (CSS). This form has replaced the CSS Financial Aid Form. Many schools use this needs-analysis form along with the Free Application for Financial Aid.

Forbearance Regarding the repayment of loans, forbearance means that the lender has agreed to let the borrower defer payments for a period of time. During this period of time, interest accrues on the loan. The act of forbearance is solely at the discretion of the lender.

Free Application for Federal Student Aid (FAFSA) Needs-analysis form required for obtaining all federal aid as well as state aid. Many schools use it as their only financial aid application form.

Grant Outright award usually awarded to students in particular fields of study.

Institution A postsecondary educational institution. The terms "institution" and "school" are used interchangeably.

Internship Work-study arrangement allowing students to gain practical experience through off-campus work with participating companies. In some instances, stipends are paid to the student by the outside organization.

Merit-Based Aid Outright awards, such as fellowships, grants, and scholarships, that may or may not have a work-related component. Much merit-based aid is determined by GRE scores.

Need Analysis Process of analyzing the financial information on the student's financial aid application and calculating the amount the family (student) can contribute to his or her educational costs.

Need-Based Aid Aid awarded on the basis of financial need usually determined by the government need formula: Cost of Attendance (COA) minus expected family contribution equals Student's Financial Need.

Origination Fee Loan process fee charged to borrower by lender, usually calculated as a percentage of the loan amount. On federal loans, this fee is deducted from the loan amount before the borrower receives the loan.

Outright Award Financial aid that does not have to be repaid. Loans are not outright awards.

Perkins Loan Federal low-interest loan to students with exceptional financial need. Federal Perkins Loans are administered through a school's financial aid office; the school is the lender and the loan is made with government funds. Borrowers must repay this loan.

Professional Judgment Authority of the financial aid administrator to make individual adjustments in determining financial need. For graduate students, the administrator is allowed to adjust the components of the student's Cost of Attendance (budget) and adjust the data elements used to calculate the Expected Family Contribution (EFC). These adjustments must be made on a case-by-case basis, and the adjustment reasons must be documented in the student's file.

Promissory Note The binding legal document a borrower signs to get a student loan. It lists both borrowing and repayment terms. It includes information about the loan's interest rate and about deferment and cancellation provisions.

State Guaranty Agency The state agency responsible for administering student loans. Telephone numbers of state agencies can be found by calling the Federal Student Aid Information Center at 800-433-3243.

Statement of Educational Purpose/Certification Statement on Refunds and Default Statement that must be signed by the borrowers to receive federal student aid. It signifies that the borrower does not owe a refund on a federal grant, is not in default on a federal loan, and that the amount borrowed does not exceed the allowable limits. Borrowers also agree to use their student aid only for education-related purposes.

Student Aid Report (SAR) Document received from the FAFSA processor about four weeks after submitting the original FAFSA form. The SAR must be carefully read and verified to ensure accuracy of all data.

Subsidized Stafford Loan (formerly Guaranteed Student Loan—GSL) Federally subsidized low-interest loans available to students who demonstrate financial need. The federal government pays interest on the loan until the borrower begins repayment and during authorized periods of loan deferment. Students do not begin repayment until after graduation.

Targeted Aid Both outright awards and loans from government, institutional, and private sources earmarked for specific groups of students. These special aid programs often aid minorities and women.

Unmet Need Portion of the financial aid package that the student is eligible to receive but that the school is unable to fund.

Unsubsidized Stafford Loan Federal loan not awarded on the basis of need. Interest is charged on the loan from the time the loan is disbursed until it's paid in full. Payment of interest and principal can be deferred while student is in school.

Verification Procedure used by the school financial aid office for verifying accuracy of the financial aid data filled out on the FAFSA and other financial aid applications. Students may be asked to fill out additional forms or submit additional documentation, such as tax returns and earnings statements. Some schools verify 100 percent of all financial aid applications; others do not.

NOTES

NOTES

NOTES

NOTES

NOTES